Volcanic Degassing

Special Publication reviewing procedures

The Society makes every effort to ensure that the scientific and production quality of its books matches that of its journals. Since 1997, all book proposals have been refereed by specialist reviewers as well as by the Society's Books Editorial Committee. If the referees identify weaknesses in the proposal, these must be addressed before the proposal is accepted.

Once the book is accepted, the Society has a team of Book Editors (listed above) who ensure that the volume editors follow strict guidelines on refereeing and quality control. We insist that individual papers can only be accepted after satisfactory review by two independent referees. The questions on the review forms are similar to those for *Journal of the Geological Society*. The referees' forms and comments must be available to the Society's Book Editors on request.

Although many of the books result from meetings, the editors are expected to commission papers that were not presented at the meeting to ensure that the book provides a balanced coverage of the subject. Being accepted for presentation at the meeting does not guarantee inclusion in the book.

Geological Society Special Publications are included in the ISI Index of Scientific Book Contents, but they do not have an impact factor, the latter being applicable only to journals.

More information about submitting a proposal and producing a Special Publication can be found on the Society's web site: www.geolsoc.org.uk.

GEOLOGICAL SOCIETY SPECIAL PUBLICATION NO. 213

Volcanic Degassing

EDITED BY

C. OPPENHEIMER
Department of Geography, University of Cambridge

D.M. PYLE
Department of Earth Sciences, University of Cambridge

and

J. BARCLAY
School of Environmental Sciences, University of East Anglia

2003
Published by
The Geological Society
London

THE GEOLOGICAL SOCIETY

The Geological Society of London (GSL) was founded in 1807. It is the oldest national geological society in the world and the largest in Europe. It was incorporated under Royal Charter in 1825 and is Registered Charity 210161.

The Society is the UK national learned and professional society for geology with a worldwide Fellowship (FGS) of 9000. The Society has the power to confer Chartered status on suitably qualified Fellows, and about 2000 of the Fellowship carry the title (CGeol). Chartered Geologists may also obtain the equivalent European title, European Geologist (EurGeol). One fifth of the Society's fellowship resides outside the UK. To find out more about the Society, log on to www.geolsoc.org.uk.

The Geological Society Publishing House (Bath, UK) produces the Society's international journals and books, and acts as European distributor for selected publications of the American Association of Petroleum Geologists (AAPG), the American Geological Institute (AGI), the Indonesian Petroleum Association (IPA), the Geological Society of America (GSA), the Society for Sedimentary Geology (SEPM) and the Geologists' Association (GA). Joint marketing agreements ensure that GSL Fellows may purchase these societies' publications at a discount. The Society's online bookshop (accessible from www.geolsoc.org.uk) offers secure book purchasing with your credit or debit card.

To find out about joining the Society and benefiting from substantial discounts on publications of GSL and other societies worldwide, consult www.geolsoc.org.uk, or contact the Fellowship Department at: The Geological Society, Burlington House, Piccadilly, London W1J 0BG. Tel: +144 (0)20 7434 9944; Fax: +144 (0)20 7439 8975; E-mail: *enquiries@geolsoc.org.uk*.

For information about the Society's meetings, consult *Events* on *www.geolsoc.org.uk*. To find out more about the Society's Corporate Affiliates Scheme, write to *enquiries@geolsoc.org.uk*.

Published by The Geological Society from:
The Geological Society Publishing House
Unit 7, Brassmill Enterprise Centre
Brassmill Lane
Bath BA1 3JN, UK

(*Orders:* Tel: +144 (0)1225 445046
        Fax: +144 (0)1225 442836)
Online bookshop: http//bookshop.geolsoc.org.uk

British Library Cataloguing Publication Data
A catalogue record for this book is available from the British Library.

ISBN 1-86239-136-X

Typeset by Exe Valley Dataset Ltd, Exeter, UK
Printed by The Cromwell Press, Wiltshire, UK
Project management by Swales & Willis, Exeter, UK

Distributors
USA
  AAPG Bookstore
  PO Box 979
  Tulsa
  OK 74101-0979
  USA
Orders: Tel: +1 918 584-2555
        Fax: +1 918 560-2652
        E-mail: bookstore@aapg.org
India
  Affiliated East-West Press PVT Ltd
  G-1/16 Ansari Road, Daryaganj,
  New Delhi 110 002
  India
Orders: Tel: +91 11 327-9113
        Fax: +91 11 326-0538
        E-mail: affiliat@nda.vsnl.net.in
Japan
  Kanda Book Trading Company
  Cityhouse Tama 204
  Tsurumaki 1-3-10
  Tama-shi
  Tokyo 206-0034
  Japan
Orders: Tel: +81 (0)423 57-7650
        Fax: +81 (0)423 57-7651
        E-mail: geokanda@ma.kcom.ne.jp

Contents

OPPENHEIMER, C., PYLE, D. M. & BARCLAY, J. Introduction   1

Part I Magma degassing: models and experiments

SPARKS, R. S. J. Dynamics of magma degassing   5

SCAILLET, B. & PICHAVANT, M. Experimental constraints on volatile abundances in arc magmas and their implications for degassing processes   23

FREDA, C., BAKER, D. R., ROMANO, C. & SCARLATO, P. Water diffusion in natural potassic melts   53

VILLEMANT, B., BOUDON, G., NOUGRIGAT, S., POTEAUX, S. & MICHEL, A. Water and halogens in volcanic clasts: tracers of degassing processes during Plinian and dome-building eruptions   63

MORETTI, R., PAPALE, P. & OTTONELLO, G. A model for the saturation of C-O-H-S fluids in silicate melts   81

Part II Characterizing volcanic emissions

THORDARSON, T., SELF, S., MILLER, D. J., LARSEN, G. & VILMUNDARDÓTTIR, E. G. Sulphur release from flood lava eruptions in the Veidivötn, Grímsvötn and Katla volcanic systems, Iceland   103

OBENHOLZNER, J. H., SCHROETTNER, H., GOLOB, P. & DELGADO, H. Particles from the plume of Popocatépetl volcano, Mexico – the FESEM/EDS approach   123

MCGONIGLE, A. J. S. & OPPENHEIMER, C. Optical sensing of volcanic gas and aerosol emissions   149

GERLACH, T. M. Elevation effects in volcano applications of the COSPEC   169

CARN, S. A., KRUEGER, A. J., BLUTH, G. J. S., SCHAEFER, S. J., KROTKOV, N. A., WATSON, I. M. & DATTA, S. Volcanic eruption detection by the Total Ozone Mapping Spectrometer (TOMS) instruments: a 22-year record of sulphur dioxide and ash emissions   177

EDMONDS, M., OPPENHEIMER, C., PYLE, D. M. & HERD, R. A. Rainwater and ash leachate analysis as proxies for plume chemistry at Soufrière Hills volcano, Montserrat   203

Part III Field investigations of degassing volcanoes

YOUNG, S. R., VOIGHT, B. & DUFFELL, H.J. Magma extrusion dynamics revealed by high-frequency gas monitoring at Soufrière Hills volcano, Montserrat   219

WARDELL, L. J., KYLE, P. R. & CAMPBELL, A. R. Carbon dioxide emissions from fumarolic ice towers, Mount Erebus volcano, Antarctica — 231

VASELLI, O., TASSI, F., MINISSALE, A., MONTEGROSSI, G., DUARTE, E., FERNÁNDEZ, E., & BERGAMASCHI, F. Fumarole migration and fluid geochemistry at Poás volcano (Costa Rica) from 1998 to 2001 — 247

VARLEY, N. R. & TARAN, Y. Degassing processes of Popocatépetl and Volcán de Colima, Mexico — 263

BURTON, M., ALLARD, P., MURÈ, F. & OPPENHEIMER, C. FTIR remote sensing of fractional magma degassing at Mount Etna, Sicily — 281

Part IV Atmospheric, climatic and environmental impacts of volcanic emissions

STEVENSON, D. S., JOHNSON, C. E., COLLINS, W. J. & DERWENT, R. G. The tropospheric sulphur cycle and the role of volcanic SO_2 — 295

TEXTOR, C., SACHS, P.M., GRAF, H.-F. & HANSTEEN, T.H. The 12 900 years BP Laacher See eruption: estimation of volatile yields and simulation of their fate in the plume — 307

GRAINGER, R. G. & HIGHWOOD, E. J. Changes in stratospheric composition, chemistry, radiation and climate caused by volcanic eruptions — 329

HORROCKS, L. A., OPPENHEIMER, C., BURTON, M. R. & DUFFELL, H. J. Compositional variation in tropospheric volcanic gas plumes: evidence from ground-based remote sensing — 349

BLAKE, S. Correlations between eruption magnitude, SO_2 yield, and surface cooling — 371

DELMELLE, P. Environmental impacts of tropospheric volcanic gas plumes — 381

GRATTAN, J., DURAND, M. & TAYLOR, S. Illness and elevated human mortality in Europe coincident with the Laki Fissure eruption — 401

INDEX — 415

It is recommended that reference to all or part of this book should be made in one of the following ways:

OPPENHEIMER, C., PYLE, D.M. & BARCLAY, J. (eds) 2003. *Volcanic Degassing.* Geological Society, London, Special Publications, **213**.

MORETTI, R., PAPALE, P. & OTTONELLO, G. 2003. A model for the saturation of C-O-H-S fluids in silicate melts *In*: OPPENHEIMER, C., PYLE, D.M. & BARCLAY, J. (eds) 2003. *Volcanic Degassing.* Geological Society, London, Special Publications, **213**, 81–101.

Introduction

C. OPPENHEIMER[1], D. M. PYLE[2] & J. BARCLAY[3]

[1]*Department of Geography, University of Cambridge, Downing Place,
Cambridge, CB2 3EN, UK.
(e-mail: co200@cam.ac.uk)*
[2]*Department of Earth Sciences, University of Cambridge, Downing Street,
Cambridge CB2 3EQ, UK.*
[3]*School of Environmental Sciences, University of East Anglia,
Norwich NR4 7TJ, UK.*

Think of volcanoes, and you might picture an eruption column jetting from a summit crater, punching through the atmosphere with roiling coils of dark ash. Or perhaps you are of a more tranquil disposition and imagine a peaceful summit crater but brightly stained with orange and yellow minerals deposited from fumarolic clouds hissing through vents and fissures amidst the scree. It goes without saying that gases are behind both these manifestations, providing the violence needed to propel eruption plumes to altitudes of tens of kilometres, or leaking more slowly from unseen magma bodies to fuel hydrothermal systems (Fig. 1). The speciation and exsolution of these volatiles in magmas, the quantification of their emissions into the atmosphere, the application of such measurements for volcano monitoring purposes, and characterization of their impacts on the environment (in its broadest sense) are the subjects of this book.

'Next to nothing is known about the sources of the volatile components of magmas or how they are distributed and transported between the mantle and shallow levels of the crust.' This is how Williams and McBirney began the chapter on volcanic gases in their influential 1979 textbook, *Volcanology*. In the following two decades, diverse investigations spanning experimental phase petrology, isotope geochemistry, and thermodynamical and fluid dynamical modelling, have replaced this pessimistic view by a much more encouraging outlook on our understanding of the origins, storage and transport of volcanic volatiles. In particular, laboratory analytical work on natural and synthetic melts has gone a long way in establishing and quantifying the factors controlling the solubility of volatiles in magmas, and their speciation in both the melt and vapour phase.

Surveillance of gas compositions and their rate of release from volcanoes is a vital part of efforts to interpret volcanic activity, since the nature of degassing exerts a strong control on eruption style, and is closely associated with volcano seismicity and ground deformation. While the modelling frameworks for interpretation of geochemical measurements from different kinds of volcanoes remain poorly developed, observational capabilities are improving all the time, thanks largely to ground-based- and satellite remote sensing techniques. One of the enduring challenges of volcanology is to integrate multi-parameter monitoring data streams, and incorporate them in theoretically sound modelling environments to maximize their potential for predictive hazard assessment.

Thanks to the many (and still on-going) investigations of the 1991 Pinatubo eruption cloud, we have gained, in the past decade, a vastly improved understanding of the impacts of volcanoes on the atmosphere, climate and environment. We know that key factors determining the climate-forcing credentials of an eruption are the fluxes and emission altitudes and latitudes of sulphur gases (principally SO_2 and H_2S). Intense, explosive eruptions in the tropics, like Pinatubo 1991, Krakatau 1883, or Tambora 1815, provide the principal perturbation to stratospheric aerosol levels in the form of sulphate aerosol. These particulates form from oxidation of the sulphur gas species released in the eruption cloud, and evolve through complex dynamical and chemical pathways. Because of their small size and entrainment in the dry stratosphere, they remain aloft for comparatively long periods, enhancing their interaction with solar and terrestrial radiation. Sulphate aerosol influences the Earth's radiation budget by intercepting both short-wave and long-wave

From: OPPENHEIMER, C., PYLE, D.M. & BARCLAY, J. (eds) *Volcanic Degassing*. Geological Society, London, Special Publications, **213**, 1–3. 0305–8719/03/$15.00
© The Geological Society of London 2003.

Fig. 1. 'The burning Valley called Vulcan's Cave near Naples' or Solfatara (Campi Flegrei), from Bankes's New System of Geography (c.1800).

radiation, and by seeding or modifying clouds, which also scatter and absorb radiation. Numerous studies have investigated the spatially and temporally complex patterns of warming and cooling of the atmosphere and surface following large equatorial eruptions, and the chemistry by which volcanic sulphate veils result in stratospheric ozone loss.

Surprisingly, perhaps, we have a poorer understanding of the chemistry and atmospheric and radiative impacts of volcanic aerosol in the layer of the atmosphere we actually inhabit, the troposphere. This partly reflects the much greater heterogeneity of volcanological, meteorological and atmospheric factors, and the less intense scale of the eruptive or passive degassing pheno-mena, and hence greater influence of local topography, vegetation cover, etc. Nevertheless, some recent analyses suggest that up to forty per cent of the global tropospheric sulphate burden may be volcanogenic, much of it derived from open vent volcanoes, fumarole fields, and mildly erupting systems like Kīlauea. When they are deposited at the Earth's surface, volcanic sulphur and halogen compounds can result in profound environmental impacts. There is abundant evi-dence for the potential harm caused by eruptive releases of these gases and particles into the troposphere, affecting local to regional, to possibly hemispheric scales (in the case of an eruption like that of Laki in 1783–1784). Release of other volatile species, such as heavy metals, from volcanoes may also have a significant but hitherto poorly constrained, environmental impact.

This book explores these topics in detail. It provides a collection of papers by experts in various fields, and covers the key issues in the observation and modelling of volcanic degassing and its atmospheric and environmental consequences. We have divided the book into four sections, which lead broadly from magma, via the atmosphere, to the environment, as follows:

1. Petrological experiments and measurements concerning volatile abundance, diffusion, saturation, and degassing in magma; and fluid dynamical aspects of magma transport and degassing. We are just beginning to put together very diverse approaches to studying volcanic degassing. Combining experimental measurements to constrain the natural pro-cesses we can never hope to observe directly,

with surface measurements and observations of erupted products, and putting them into the melting pot of fluid dynamical and thermodynamical theory offers a powerful approach to building a quantitative framework for modelling volcanic degassing, that will pay dividends, especially in understanding magmatic evolution and eruption prediction. The individual chapters here provide strong clues to the way ahead.

2. Techniques to measure and characterize the composition and flux of volcanic emissions. These span petrological methods (based on studies of the iron and titanium content of erupted lavas and tephra), direct collection of airborne particulates, use of ash leachate and rainwater chemistry as a proxy for plume composition, portable remote sensing methods (vital for volcano observatories), and satellite observations. Accurate estimates of volatile fluxes and yields are invaluable not only for the volcano monitoring community, but also for understanding and modelling environmental impacts on different temporal and spatial scales.

3. Case studies of volcanic degassing. This part of the book takes us on a Cook's tour of degassing volcanoes from Antarctica to Italy, spanning lava domes, crater lakes, open-vents, diffuse degassing, and lava flows. In addition to representing a broad spectrum of volcanic behaviour, the individual studies cover a variety of direct sampling and remote sensing techniques aimed at characterizing the chemical and isotopic composition, and fluxes of volcanic gases and hot springs, and elucidating relationships between degassing and conduit dynamics and geometry, the relative proportions of diffuse and open-vent degassing, and the interactions between magmatic and hydrothermal fluids.

4. The atmospheric, climatic and environmental impacts of volcanic emissions. This section contains seven chapters. These begin with a quantification of the tropospheric budget of volcanic sulphur at the global scale, then consider the chemistry and radiative and climatic impact of major stratosphere-bound eruption clouds. Three chapters return to the local to regional scale impacts of tropospheric volcanic emissions on the atmosphere and terrestrial environment, including, in the final chapter, an examination of the human health consequences of the Laki 1783–1784 eruption.

There is still much to learn about the degassing process, and the diverse consequences of volcanic volatile emissions, but the papers in this volume are a testament to the significance of recent discoveries and developments. They also indicate clearly the tremendous opportunities for the next few years in combining research in experimental petrology, multi-phase flow modelling, volcano monitoring (especially gas and aerosol surveillance and integrated modelling of geophysical, geodetic and geochemical datasets), and atmospheric chemistry and transport, in order to improve understanding of the coupling of volcanism to the Earth system, and to advance efforts to mitigate the effects of volcanism on human society.

This volume developed from a two-day 'Flagship Meeting' of the Geological Society of London, *Origins, emissions and impacts of volcanic gases*, convened at Burlington House (London) in October 2001. The meeting was held in memory of Peter Francis, who died in 1999. Peter was one of the pioneers of volcanological remote sensing, and latterly held a keen interest in the application of spectroscopic techniques to field measurement of volcanic gases. He was known to many of the participants of the conference, and the diversity and quality of oral and poster presentations, and depth of discussion during and between sessions, served as a very fitting tribute to a remarkable person.

This book exists thanks to the contributions and cooperation of the many authors represented. But it has also been nurtured behind the scenes by the kind assistance and editorial support of the Geological Society Publishing staff (particularly Angharad Hills), and the goodwill and expertise of the many referees who rigorously reviewed all the submissions. We warmly thank all involved in the publication, as well as those who supported and participated in the October 2001 meeting held at Burlington House. In particular, we thank C. Hawkesworth for promoting the original meeting concept, H. Wilson, the Society's conference manager, for ensuring a smooth-running event, and the many participants who travelled from outside the UK to make it a truly international conference.

Dynamics of magma degassing

R. S. J. SPARKS

Department of Earth Sciences, Bristol University, Bristol BS8 1RJ, UK
(e-mail: Steve.Sparks@bristol.ac.uk)

Abstract: Gas exsolution and segregation are fundamental controls on eruption dynamics and magma genesis. Basaltic magma loses gas relatively easily because of its low viscosity. However, bubbles grown by decompression and diffusion during magma ascent are too small to segregate. Coalescence, however, can create bubbles big enough for gas to escape from the rising basalt magma. In evolved magmas, such as andesite and rhyolite, high viscosity prevents bubbles rising independently through the magma. The original gas content of magma erupted as lava is commonly the same as that erupted explosively, so that a gas separation mechanism is required. A permeable magma foam can form to allow gas escape once bubbles become interconnected. Magma permeabilities can be much higher than wall-rock permeabilities, and so vertical gas loss can be an important escape path, in addition to gas loss through the conduit walls. This inference is consistent with observations from the Soufrière Hills Volcano, Montserrat, where gas escapes directly from the dome, and particularly along shear zones (faults) related to the conduit wall. Dynamical models of magma ascent have been developed which incorporate gas escape. The magma ascent rate is sensitive to gas escape, as the volume proportion of gas affects density, magma compressibility and rheology, resulting in both horizontal and vertical pressure gradients in the magma column to allow gas escape. Slight changes in gas loss can make the difference between explosive and effusive eruption, and multiple steady-state flow states can exist. In certain circumstances, there can be abrupt jumps between effusive and explosive activity. Overpressures develop in the ascending magma, caused primarily by the rheological stiffening of magma as gas exsolves and crystals grow. A maximum overpressure develops in the upper parts of volcanic conduits. The overpressure is typically several MPa and increases as permeability decreases. Thus, the possibility of reaching conditions for explosions increases as permeability decreases, both due to overpressure increase and the retention of more gas. Models of magma ascent from an elastic magma chamber, combined with concepts of permeability and overpressure linked to degassing, provide an explanation for the periodic patterns of dome growth with short-lived explosive activity, as in the 1980–1986 activity of Mount St Helens. Degassing of magma in conduits can also cause strong convective circulation between deep magma reservoirs and the Earth's surface. Such circulation not only allows degassing to occur from deep reservoirs, but may also be a significant driving force for crystal differentiation.

Degassing of magma is one of the most fundamental processes of volcanism, affecting the dynamics of their eruptions and the evolution of magmas in the crust. Volcanic eruptions are sometimes explosive and at other times more passive – with separation of gas from magma and discharge of lava. Gas exsolution and gas separation can have profound effects on the physical properties of magmas. In particular, loss of water (usually the main volcanic gas) results in large increases in melt viscosity and causes crystallization due to undercooling of the melt. Magma density is also greatly affected by degassing, decreasing substantially if exsolving gas is retained and increasing if the gas escapes. These physical property changes have profound effects on eruptions, as they are the first-order controls on the flow along volcanic conduits, and therefore have a large influence on the geo-physical manifestations of volcanism. Thus, understanding of degassing is central to monitoring and forecasting of eruptions.

Degassing has profound effects on the phase equilibria of magmas, because rather small amounts of water dissolved in magmas can reduce their liquidus temperature by hundreds of degrees. Conversely, degassing of magma can cause spontaneous crystallization. While these effects have been known about for many decades (e.g. Tuttle & Bowen 1958; Cann 1970), it is only relatively recently that their significance for understanding volcanic processes has been widely appreciated. Crystallization due to degassing during magma ascent may prove to be as important as cooling in igneous petrogenesis. Additionally, volcanic conduits provide pathways for exchanges between deep magma reservoirs and the Earth's surface, so that gases

From: OPPENHEIMER, C., PYLE, D.M. & BARCLAY, J. (eds) *Volcanic Degassing.* Geological Society, London, Special Publications, 213, 5–22. 0305-8719/03/$15.00

and gas-rich magmas can rise and, in principle, degassed and oxidized magmas can return into deep chambers. The role of degassing and resulting convection exchanges along conduits has not been widely considered as a major mechanism for differentiation of magmas.

This contribution focuses on the role of volatiles in the dynamics of volcanic flows through conduits. Other aspects of gas bubble nucleation and growth, the effects of water on melt viscosity and the more geochemical aspects of volcanic degassing have been well covered in other recent publications (e.g. Dingwell 1998; Navon & Lyakhovsky 1998; Blower et al. 2001a, b; Wallace 2001;). In the last few years there have been significant advances in understanding the role of degassing in conduit flows. I draw attention in particular to modelling research, which shows that conduit flows are highly unstable due to strong non-linearities and feedback loops caused by degassing. Much of the complexity and unpredictability of volcanic eruptions is related to these effects. On the other hand, these same non-linearities related to degassing can result in periodic behaviours, so that there is some prospect of being able to forecast volcanic activity. I will also emphasize that the main geophysical signals monitored at volcanic eruptions are usually controlled by degassing processes and related side effects, such as rheological stiffening of ascending magma and development of high overpressures in volcanic conduits. I also discuss an idea that does not seem to have been widely considered in the evolution of magmas in chambers, namely that in a long-lived conduit system the degassed magma can drain back into the chamber. The liquidus of degassed magma increases markedly with rising pressure, so that this descending magma will either crystallize extensively during descent or will be supersaturated and therefore cause crystallization in the chamber. Finally, I raise the issue of gas contents in magmas, and suggest that in some volcanic systems – notably in arcs – gas contents may be higher than commonly thought. Very wet magmas may degas significantly when emplaced in shallow upper crustal magma chambers, and large amounts of exsolved gas can be present in the chamber prior to eruption.

Gas segregation dynamics

The basaltic case

The separation of exsolving gas from magma is strongly controlled by viscosity. The usual mantra is that basaltic magma has sufficiently low viscosity that gas bubbles can rise at speeds that are comparable with or much larger than the speed of rising magma. This assumption is, however, worth somewhat closer scrutiny. In basaltic eruptions the typical speeds of magma ascent along dykes are of order 1 m/s (Wilson & Head 1981; Sparks et al. 1997). The rise speed, u, of a spherical bubble of diameter d can be estimated from Stokes' law as follows:

$$u = d^2 \rho g / 18 \mu \qquad (1)$$

where ρ is the magma density, g is gravity and μ is the viscosity. For values of $\rho = 2700$ kg/m^3 and $g = 9.81$ m/s^2, a bubble has to exceed about 14 cm diameter for $\mu = 30$ Pa s and 4.5 cm for $\mu = 3$ Pa s to move significantly faster than the magma. Sparks (1978) modelled the diffusive growth of water bubbles in ascending basaltic magma, and found that bubbles would be in the range of 0.1 to 1 cm diameter for typical rates of magma ascent. This inference is consistent with the observation that most of the bubbles in basaltic scoria are in this size range. Bubbles of this size have speeds in the range 0.5 to 5 mm/s. Thus, the segregation process even in basalt magma is not simply a matter of growing gas bubbles rising faster than magma, even though this will be a viable mechanism in a static magma column or very slowly rising magma. Other mechanisms need to be invoked, such as bubble coalescence, recirculation of degassed magma within the conduit due to fire-fountaining, and convection processes within magma conduits and magma reservoirs.

What is commonly observed in many basaltic eruptions is that magma can erupt both explosively, typically in Strombolian style or Hawaiian fire-fountains, and as degassed lava. In many basaltic eruptions, the two kinds of activity can be observed simultaneously. Thus the fact that efficient gas segregation occurs is certain. Fire-fountaining is one well-established way of segregating gas. Here bubbly gas-rich magma expands into the atmosphere (Parfitt & Wilson 1995), the magma is torn apart, and degassed lumps either fall back to amalgamate into clastogenic lava flows (Swanson & Fabbi 1973) or are mixed back into the rising magma within the conduit. These mechanisms may at least partly explain how degassed lava can emerge slowly at the base of cinder cones, simultaneously with Strombolian or fountaining activity.

It is harder to explain the extrusion of large amounts of degassed lava in cases where the explosive activity is weak or even absent. Thus, ideas have emerged which invoke deeper level segregation processes. Pioneering research on degassing of ascending basaltic magma was carried out by Y. Slezin of the Institute of Volcanic Geology, Petropavlovsk, Kamchatka in the 1980s (summarized in Slezin 1995, 2003). Unfortunately, much of this work is in Russian or in rather poor translations, and is not widely known outside Russia. However, this research pioneered advances in understanding of basaltic eruptions, and showed for the first time that volcanic flows could be intrinsically unstable and could fluctuate between stable steady flow states. The key ingredients of Slezin's model are shown schematically in Figure 1, where two conceptual states of flow are envisaged. In the first state (Fig. 1a) the magma rises slowly and the bubbles have time to coalesce and to grow to a large enough diameter that they can rise at speeds much faster than the surrounding magma. Large bubbles sweep up and assimilate small bubbles, and so this is a potential runaway process. The gas pockets may become big enough to fill the vent (slugs), and so the gas escapes in bursts while the degassed magma quietly effuses. In the second state (Fig. 1b), the flow is so fast that the bubbles do not separate and have no time to coalesce during ascent. An intense explosive flow develops at the surface, with the bubbly magma fragmenting as it nears the surface.

Slezin developed a quantitative model of bubbly magmatic flow, which incorporated coalescence. His model involved larger bubbles rising and absorbing smaller bubbles. Conceptually, it is easy to imagine that bubble coalescence and efficient gas segregation will occur when the time-scale of bubble rise and interaction is fast compared with the ascent time of the magma. A typical result is shown schematically in Figure 2, where flow rate along a conduit is shown as a function of chamber pressure. These results are fundamental to understanding volcanic eruptions, and are not immediately intuitive. At first, it might be expected that there would be a smooth monotonic transition between the two end member regimes. However, the steady solutions to the flow equations delineate a sigmoidal shaped curve. The lower branch (A–B) in Figure 2 represents the slow ascent and well-degassed end member, and the upper branch (C–D) represents the explosive flow end member. The intermediate branch (between B and D), however, may not be stable. Further, for a wide range of conduit widths and magma viscosities it is possible to have two steady flows corresponding with the upper and lower branches. Close to conditions of points B and D, the system is

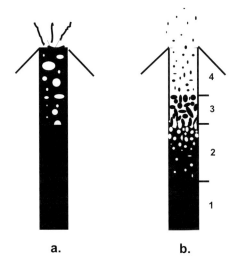

a.   **b.**

Fig. 1. Schematic of two regimes of basaltic eruptions. In (**a**) the magma rises so slowly that large bubbles of gas can form by coalescence. These bubbles are large enough to rise at speeds much greater than the magma rise speed, and thus gas escapes from the top of the magma column. In (**b**) the magma rises so fast that growing bubbles do not have time to coalesce and are too small to have speeds which are significantly different from the magma. The numbers refer to: 1, the region of magma without bubbles; 2, the region of bubbly magma; 3, the region of concentrated particle–gas dispersion; and 4, the region of an expanded dilute concentration gas and particle dispersion.

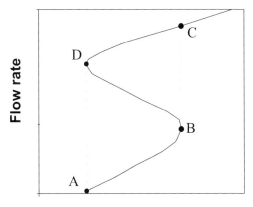

Magma chamber pressure

Fig. 2. A general schematic diagram of steady-state flow rate up a conduit against magma chamber pressure, to illustrate the abrupt changes in flow regime that can occur. The two stable branches (A–B and C–D) may correspond with different non-linear physical processes such as bubble coalescence and crystal growth.

intrinsically unstable and there can be jump-like changes of flow behaviour from predominantly effusive to explosive and vice versa. Points like B and D are known as cusps in catastrophe theory. Figure 3 shows some example calculations by Slezin (2003) for a magma with 4.6% water, which show conditions where jump-like behaviours can be anticipated. The parameter conduit resistance is defined as b^2/μ, with b being the conduit width or diameter and μ the magma viscosity. The steady-state curves are characteristically sigmoidal.

The shape of the curves from Slezin's models reflect the strong non-linearities in bubbly flows with strong feedback loops, and can be explained intuitively by a thought experiment. If the chamber pressure is varied, but conduit resistance is kept constant, then similar sigmoidal curves are calculated (Slezin 1995, 2003). So here we consider the horizontal axis to be magma chamber pressure – imagine that the system is on the branch A to B, with magma source pressure increasing. We shall not enquire into the cause of this increase, although there are a number of mechanisms that can lead to such an increase (e.g. chamber replenishment). As pressure increases, the flow rate increases, but the ascent speed is sufficiently slow that growth and coalescence result in large bubbles. For a given parcel of magma, the gas escapes well before the parcel nears the surface. The rising column is thus divided into gas-rich slugs and parcels of partially degassed magma, with the slugs travelling much faster than the magma. Additionally,

the overall density of the magma column is high, so that the pressure difference driving flow (the difference between the weight of the magma column and the chamber pressure) is small. At Point B there is no stable steady flow for a very tiny increase in driving pressure. The flow accelerates, there is less time for bubble segregation and coalescence, and the system inexorably moves to the high-flow condition where the gas does not segregate. Here the magma and gas expand together, and very high volumetric fractions of gas develop in the upper parts of the conduit. If the magma is broken apart at some threshold condition as it vesiculates, then the column is divided into a lower region of bubbly magma and an upper region of particles mixed with gas. The conduit system contains much more gas, and so the weight of the magma columns is much less. Thus, the pressure difference driving flow at C is much higher than at B, even though the chamber pressure has not changed. Differences in flow rates between B and C are typically factors of tens to thousands; in other words, the flow jumps from quiet effusion with occasional intermittent bursts of gas slugs, to sustained explosive discharge at very high rates. Similar logic holds at D, where a slight decrease of chamber pressure results in the system dropping to the lower branch with a feedback loop such that, as the flow slows, coalescence and segregation once again become dominant.

Cyclic behaviour is easily envisaged. During the high-discharge explosive phase, volume is

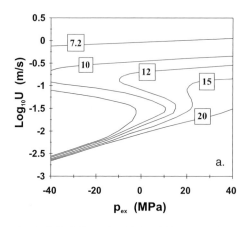 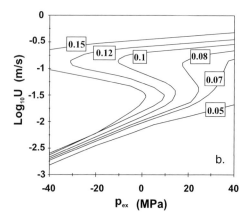

Fig. 3. Calculations after Slezin (1995, 2003) of the steady-state magma speed along a vertical conduit against the magma chamber excess pressure. The calculations are for a magma containing 4.6% water. On graph (**a**) the conduit resistance (see text) is fixed at 10^{-4} m^2/Pa, and curves are shown for different conduit lengths in km. On graph (**b**) the conduit length is fixed at 12 km, and curves are shown for different values of the conduit resistance (multiplied by 10^3).

removed rapidly from a magma chamber, reducing pressure faster than can be restored by recharge. The system then drops to the lower branch, and recharge is then sufficient to build the pressure up once again to the point that sustained explosive discharge can begin again. Periodic alternation of intense explosive discharges and quieter effusive activity have been observed, for example, in the recent eruptions at Etna (Burton et al. 2003).

Another mechanism of gas segregation was proposed by Vergniolle & Jaupart (1986, 1990), who showed that the architecture of the magma plumbing system could have an important effect. In experiments, they demonstrated that, in a chamber containing bubbly magma with a flat roof and narrow conduit outlet, gas bubbles would accumulate at the roof to form a foam. They further showed that this foam would periodically become unstable. Thus, the output of fluid from the conduit would be punctuated with pulses of gas-rich magma. They proposed that this was a plausible explanation of the remarkably regular 21-day fire-fountaining in episodes at Pu'u 'O'o on Kilauea, Hawaii. The concepts developed by Vergniolle and Jaupart can be generalized to a common observation on basaltic shield volcanoes. Eruptions from the summit or high-altitude vents commonly are explosive, with large amounts of gas separation, whereas flank and lower altitude eruptions are weakly explosive or just quiet lava effusions. Examples include: the activity of Etna in the last decades, with explosive activity and degassing largely at the summit crater and quiet effusion of degassed lava in flank vents (Burton et al., 2003); and the 1999 and 2000 eruptions of Mount Cameroon (Suh et al. 2003), where almost all the explosive degassing took place at near summit high-altitude vents and almost all the lava effused quietly from lower altitude flank vents. This behaviour might be explained by lateral flow of magma through dykes from a central conduit to flank vents, with progressive gas segregation to the roof of the dyke and down flow of degassed denser magma to erupt at lower altitude vents.

Another idea for gas segregation is convective circulation in the conduit (Kazahaya et al. 1994; Allard 1997; Stevenson & Blake 1998) with drain-back of degassed magma into the chamber (Dixon et al. 1991; Wallace & Anderson 1998). This idea was developed to explain volcanoes like Oshima (Japan), Stromboli (Italy), Etna (Italy), Villarricca (Chile) and Popocatépetl (Mexico), where substantial gas emissions are observed without any eruption of degassed lava. Degassing can continue for many months or years, or even indefinitely as at Stromboli. The quantities of gas

released can be orders of magnitude greater than the gas expected to be available in the narrow conduit (Wallace 2001). To explain these observations the idea is that gas-rich magma rises in the conduit and convectively exchanges with degassed magma. Thus, a large volume of magma from the chamber becomes available. The fluid dynamical analysis of Stevenson & Blake (1998) shows that the large gas fluxes are easily attained in narrow conduits.

In view of the development of these ideas of gas segregation processes, it is worthwhile to re-examine another commonly held axiom; namely that a common pattern of basaltic eruptions involves magma with progressively lower gas content with time. The pattern is well established in monogenetic volcanoes, where the early phase of an eruption typically is quite explosive, with sustained discharges and violent Strombolian activity constructing cinder cones. The eruptions then progressively calm down, with lava effusion becoming increasingly important with time and a declining magma effusion rate. Examples include the 1973 eruption of Heimaey (Self et al. 1974), the 1949–1956 eruption of Paricutín (Luhr & Simkin 1993) and the 1989–1990 eruption of Lonquimay, Chile (Moreno & Gardeweg 1989). One explanation of such sequences is that the source magma body is stratified with respect to dissolved gas content (Kennedy 1955) or (exsolved) bubble content. Alternatively, the sequence can be interpreted as a consequence of increasingly efficient shallow gas segregation processes with time as the magma ascent rate declines. Gas bubble coalescence, slugging and convective recycling of degassed magma back down the conduit are plausible contributions to these changes, which do not necessarily imply decreasing gas content with time in the deeply sourced magmas.

The silicic case

The problem with silicic magmas is that speeds of gas bubbles are negligible compared with the ascent speeds of magmas, so that segregation of gas from magma due to a significant speed contrast between bubble and melt is not plausible even if bubbles coalesce significantly. Thus, a different mechanism of gas escape is required. It has also been long recognized that silicic magma that erupts explosively typically has similar volatile contents to magma that erupts as degassed lava. There are now many documented examples of degassed silicic and intermediate lavas that must have started ascent with water contents of several per cent as constrained by melt inclusion studies and phenocryst assemblages (e.g. Hervig *et al.* 1989; Barclay *et al.* 1996; Martel *et al.* 1998; Devine *et al.* 1998; Blundy & Cashman 2001). This problem was resolved by Taylor *et al.* (1983) and Eichelberger *et al.* (1986), who postulated that silicic magmas must develop permeability as they vesiculate during ascent. The gas can then escape through the permeable magma foam. Whether the magma erupts explosively or as lava then depends on the competition between magma ascent and gas escape. Slow rates of ascent allow the gas to escape and lava extrusion, whereas gas is retained for fast rates of extrusion and explosive activity results.

Models of magma ascent with permeable foam degassing generate results very like those of Slezin (2003). Jaupart and Allegre (1991) considered models with a horizontal gas mass flux from the permeable magma with constant permeability and pressure difference dependent on the depth in the magma column. They found that for different magma flow rates multiple steady-state flows were possible, and concluded that in some circumstances the transitions from one eruptive state to another (i.e. between explosive and effusive eruption) were extremely sensitive to flow conditions. Woods and Koyaguchi (1994) presented somewhat similar calculations, assuming a hydrostatic pressure in the conduit wall rather than a lithostatic pressure, as in the calculations of Jaupart and Allegre (1991). They reached the same conclusions. Massol & Jaupart (1999) developed models of conduit flow that take account of variations of magma viscosity due to gas exsolution, compressibility effects of gas bubbles and development of gas overpressure due to bubble expansion. They demonstrated that large horizontal pressure gradients can develop across volcanic conduits as a consequence of larger bubble overpressures developing in faster rising magma at the centre of the conduit. If bubbles are interconnected, then gas can escape to the conduit walls.

These models assumed, following Eichelberger *et al.* (1986), that the gas is lost horizontally through the wall-rocks. Jaupart (1998) also suggested that gas was also lost along fracture networks developed in the magma and in the conduit walls, based on field observations at the Mule Creek vent complex (Stasiuk *et al.* 1996). Observations at the Soufrière Hills volcano, Montserrat, suggest that vertical permeable flow can be dominant. In this case, the gas plume emerges from the dome interior (Edmonds *et al.*, 2001), and in particular is focused on shear zones associated with lava lobe extrusion (Fig. 4). At Soufrière Hills, the lava dome is extruded in pulses along shear faults, in which a viscous plug is commonly first extruded followed by a lava dome lobe (Watts *et al.* 2002). The shear faults are rooted along the conduit wall, and much of the gas is observed to escape either along such a boundary or pervasively across the upper surface of the dome. Láscar, Chile, is another case where a high-permeability boundary between magma and a conduit has guided the gas escape vertically. Here, the vigorous gas fumaroles that feed the persistent gas plume are concentrically arranged at the margins of the vent and lava dome (Matthews *et al.* 1997). Such observations support the concept of lateral gas escape from permeable magma to the conduit walls (Massol & Jaupart 1999). If the wall-rocks have significantly lower permeability, then vertical gas escape through the magma or along the conduit walls may be much easier. Wall-rocks can also be self-sealed by precipitation from escaping gases, as seems to have been the case at Montserrat (Hammouya *et al.* 1998). Additional permeability can develop in lava domes and upper parts of the conduit as fracture networks develop (Stasiuk *et al.* 1996; Jaupart 1998; Sparks *et al.* 2000).

An important but incompletely understood issue is the development of bubble connectivity in magmas to allow gas to escape by permeable flow. Theoretical and experimental work suggests that magmas first become permeable at about 30% porosity, when bubbles start to interact and coalesce (Klug & Cashman 1996; Blower 2001). Permeability increases rapidly as bubble concentration rises, and permeabilities as high as 10^{-12} m^2 can develop in magma foams with high vesicularity (60–70%). However, the development of magma permeability is complex. If bubbles grow in a static melt then very high porosities can develop without the thin melt films between bubbles being disrupted (e.g. reticulites). On the other hand, shearing can bring bubbles into contact and promote connectivity (Whalley 1987). Thus, magma permeability may develop preferentially near to the conduit margins (Stasiuk *et al.* 1996). Microlite crystallization can also enhance permeability. Gas bubbles are confined to areas of residual melt that form a distributed phase between the crystals. In a highly crystalline and relatively low-porosity magma, the permeability can thus be high because the distributed residual melt has very high porosity and high connectivity. For example, measurements in Melnik & Sparks (2002) show that, despite low porosity (10–15%), samples of the Soufrière Hills dome have similar permeability to high-porosity pumice (60–70%). In this case, the residual melt component had very high porosity (70–90%).

Fig. 4. View of the Soufrière Hills andesite lava dome, Montserrat, on 21 December 1997, showing a plume of volcanic gas being transported by the wind to the west (right to left). The photograph was taken from the south.

Models incorporating vertical gas flow were developed by Melnik and Sparks (1999) in application to Montserrat. Their treatment developed the earlier models of Jaupart and Allegre (1991) and Woods and Koyaguchi (1994) by including the coupling between the magma permeability and porosity to calculate gas escape rates. The model of Melnik and Sparks focused on slow ascent rates to model dome extrusion, and did not consider flow rates high enough to result in explosive eruptions. The model also included the kinetics of crystallization due to gas exsolution. Thus, calculations for vertical gas escape in a situation where explosive magma fragmentation is permissible have yet to be done. It is, however, certain that similar dynamical regimes will be found. The alternation of Vulcanian explosions and lava dome extrusion in 1997 at the Soufrière Hills Volcano (Druitt *et al.* 2002) is what would be expected in an unstable system where the flow rates are high enough for transitions between eruption style to be sensitively poised.

Observations at the Soufrière Hills Volcano have provided further insights into degassing processes in viscous magma systems. One of the most remarkable features of the eruption has been the cyclic patterns of activity marked by regular patterns of seismicity, ground deform-

ation recorded by tiltmeter and eruptive behaviour (Fig. 5; Voight *et al.* 1999). The cyclic behaviour had typical periods ranging from a few hours to just over a day (Neuberg 2000). In some periods, the system locked on to a very regular period for up to a couple of weeks. Each cycle involved a swarm of shallow hybrid earthquakes with long-period components accompanying inflation of the ground localized around the dome. The inflation cycle would peak, and then a period of elevated activity would immediately follow, accompanying deflation. The nature of the elevated activity would vary. In many cases, there was an increase in rock-falls from the dome, and this was interpreted as evidence of enhanced dome extrusion rates (Voight *et al.* 1999). In some cases, strong ash-venting occurred

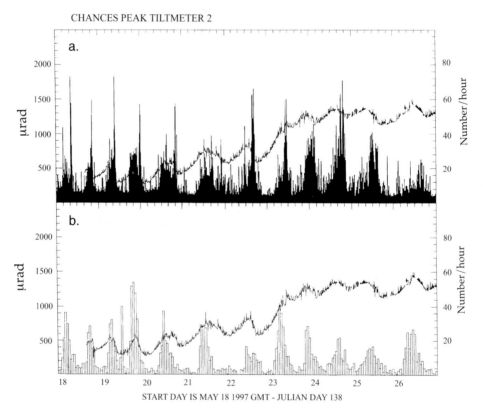

Fig. 5. The tilt pattern at Chances Peak in May 1997 (after Voight *et al.* 1999). The tiltmeter was approximately 400 m from the centre of the dome, with the tilt axis for data shown being approximately radial to the dome centre. The earthquake event frequency in events per hour (right hand vertical axis) at the Gage's seismometer is shown as histograms. The tilt variation in micro-radians (left-hand vertical axis) is shown as the continuous curves. The upper diagram (**a**) shows tilt data along the horizontal axis radial to the dome, and the lower diagram (**b**) shows tilt data along the horizontal axis tangential to the dome. All the instrument output displays the cyclic pattern of deformation and seismicity, with hybrid earthquakes occurring in the inflation periods and rock-fall signals occurring during the deflation periods. Marked episodes of degassing were observed at the peaks in the tilt cycle and during deflation (see Watson *et al.* 2000).

at the peak of the cycle and declined during deflation. Most spectacularly, Vulcanian explosions lasting a few minutes occurred at the peaks, followed by ash-venting for tens of minutes during the deflation. In early August 1997, 11 explosions occurred every 12 hours (Druitt *et al.* 2002). In September and October 1997, there were 75 explosions, with an average period of 9.5 hours between explosions. Watson *et al.* (2000) have also shown that the flux of SO_2 increases over the peak of cycles and, together with the vigorous ash-venting activity, implies that the cycles involve release of pressurized gas from within the dome and upper conduit. The tilt returns to almost the same position over a single cycle, indicating that the deformation is almost completely recovered. Release of pressurized gas provides the most compelling explanation of this recovery. Comparable cyclic patterns of explosive degassing were observed at Mount Pinatubo during lava dome extrusion prior to the paroxysmal phase of the eruption on 15 June 1991 (Denlinger & Hoblitt 1999)

The cyclic patterns at Montserrat can be interpreted as strong evidence for the pressurization of the rising magma (Sparks 1997). The cycles are interpreted as a build-up of a large overpressure in the upper parts of the conduit and the relief of that pressure at the peak of the cycle when some threshold overpressure is reached. In some cases, the relief of pressure involves a surge of lava extrusion. This might be a consequence of the overpressure reaching the yield strength of the non-Newtonian and highly crystalline andesite or some kind of stick-slip mechanism along the conduit wall (Denlinger & Hoblitt 1999). At other times, the pressure can be relieved by the escape of pressurized gases, as manifested in the ash-venting and elevated SO_2 fluxes. These observations thus illustrate a very potent way of degassing magma by vertical permeable flow. In the explosions the overpressure was sufficient to exceed the fracture strength of the magma, and degassing was accomplished in the most spectacular way.

The detailed mechanism of the pressurization and degassing cycles and the controls on their duration are not yet fully understood. As discussed further in the next section, large overpressures can be developed at shallow levels in ascending magma due to rheological stiffening (Sparks 1997; Massol & Jaupart 1999; Melnik & Sparks, 1999). There are a number of possible controls on the time-scales of the degassing cycles. Rheological properties may be important. Highly crystalline degassed magma is highly non-Newtonian. Uniaxial compression tests on samples of Montserrat andesite at eruption

temperatures and pressures comparable with those expected in the conduit system have been carried out (A. M. Lejeune, unpublished data) and one of these experiments was presented in Sparks *et al.* (2000). In a typical experiment, the sample had a strongly non-linear response to a constant load pressure (Fig. 6). The initial period involves slow viscous deformation. Deformation accelerates with a decrease in apparent viscosity and development of microcracks, with failure taking place after several hours. Thus, the threshold conditions reached at the peak of a cycle and the time-scale of a cycle may partly be governed by the non-linear response of the non-Newtonian magma to the pressurization. The pressurization itself could be controlled by a number of effects. First, the pressurization may relate to gas exsolution. Bubble formation is governed by diffusion of gas from supersaturated melt and expansion of gas due to pressure decrease during magma ascent. Gas supersaturation can also be coupled to crystal growth (Stix *et al.* 1997; Sparks 1997), which concentrates gas into the melt. Bubble growth and gas pressure are also coupled to magma viscosity, which resists growth. In the upper parts of conduits, viscosities are very high, and considerable gas overpressure can develop (Sparks 1978; Navon & Lyakhovsky 1998; Massol & Jaupart 1999). Finally, the magma pressure is itself a function of flow speed, magma compressibility and viscosity (Massol & Jaupart 1999; Melnik & Sparks 1999) and can regulate gas exsolution and gas pressure.

There remain many uncertainties and outstanding problems in understanding conduit degassing of silicic magmas. The interactions of gas exsolution, gas escape and crystallization in magma flows are complex, because all of these processes greatly affect key magma properties such as density, rheology and compressibility. For example, Massol and Jaupart (1999) demonstrated that large lateral variations of these properties can develop across conduits during magma flow. Most models are one-dimensional, assuming averaged properties across the conduit. Thus, fully realistic models have yet to be developed, and represent a considerable challenge to volcano physicists.

Coupled crystallization and degassing in ascending magma

Although the large depression of the liquidus of magmas due to small amounts of water has been understood for a long time (e.g. Tuttle & Bowen 1958), the implications for volcanology have only recently become well established (e.g. Sparks & Pinkerton 1978; Cashman 1992;

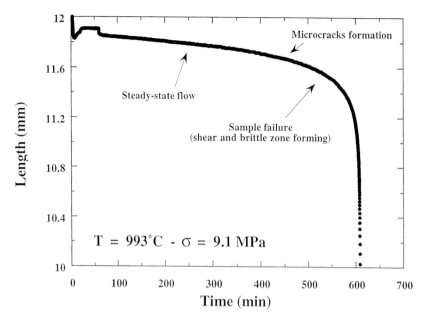

Fig. 6. Deformation curve of a sample of the Soufrière Hills andesite subjected to a uniaxial compression (9.1 MPa load pressure). The experiment has been performed at room pressure and at 993 °C on lava dome material erupted in January 1996. The plot shows the length of a cylindrical core of lava as a function of time (the initial sample length was 12 mm for a 4.8 mm diameter). Initially the sample deforms in a regular manner at a constant strain rate with a viscosity of about 10^{14} Pa s. After a few hours sample deformation accelerates and the apparent viscosity decreases substantially, with an estimated value of 10^{11} Pa s just before failure. The increasing strain rate results from a rising rate of formation of micro-cracks. Failure takes place along a shear surface, which develops from a zone of micro-fractures (after Sparks *et al.* 2000).

Geschwind & Rutherford 1995; Sparks 1997; Hammer *et al.* 1999; Blundy & Cashman 2001; Hammer & Rutherford 2002). The exsolution of water causes magmas to become strongly under-cooled, and this induces spontaneous crystalliz-ation. As an example, the porphyritic Soufrière Hills magma is thought to start in the magma chamber with a melt content of about 35%, 4–5% water dissolved in the rhyolitic melt phase and a temperature of 850 °C. By the time that it reaches the surface at slow flow rates, the magma has effectively solidified due to degassing with only a few per cent residual melt (Sparks *et al.* 2000). During ascent, the magma changes from a Newtonian fluid, with an estimated viscosity of about 7×10^6 Pa s, to a hot partially molten solid with a strength of around 1 MPa and a power law rheology, in which the apparent viscosity varies with increasing strain rate from 10^{14} to 10^{11} Pa s (Fig. 6; Voight *et al.* 1999; Sparks *et al.* 2000). These degassing-induced changes domin-ate flow behaviour.

The dynamical model of Melnik and Sparks (1999, 2002) explores the coupling of crystalliz-ation, gas exsolution, gas escape and magma flow

in lava dome eruptions, applying the results to the Soufrière Hills andesite. A key element of the model is the kinetics of crystallization. Their results show the same kind of sigmoidal relationship between magma extrusion rate and magma chamber pressure as Slezin's models (Fig. 7), but the reason for this structure is quite different. Here the upper branch represents the case where magma ascent rate is too rapid for crystallization to take place and so the viscosity remains relatively low, although the viscosity still increases as the magma ascends due to the effects of dissolved water on viscosity. The lower branch represents the case where the flow is slow and so there is plenty of time for crystallization. In this case, the magma can erupt as a solid. As before, the system can jump between these states of high and low flow rates close to the critical bends in the curves. In this case, however, the transition between fast and slow dome growth is expected to take place slowly, due to the viscous nature of the flows.

A key feature of magma ascent and degassing is that the rheological stiffening caused by degassing results in large overpressures being

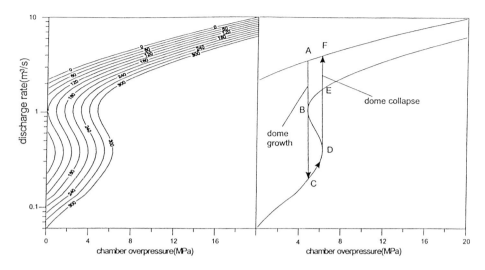

Fig. 7. The relationship between steady-state extrusion rate and magma chamber pressure. The curves were calculated by Melnik & Sparks (1999) for conduit conditions and magma properties appropriate to the degassing eruption of the Soufrière Hills andesite on Montserrat. The curves are characteristically sigmoidal as in Figures 2 and 3. However, here the upper, stable branch is for flows where the rate is too fast for crystallization to occur during magma ascent, and the lower branch is for flows where the flow rate is sufficiently slow that substantial microlite crystallization can occur. The behaviour is related to degassing as the microlite growth is triggered by gas exsolution. In (**a**) curves are shown for different dome heights in metres. In (**b**) the curves for 0 and 300 m from (a) are isolated, and a possible cause of cyclic activity is indicated. Starting at C on the 300 m dome height curve, the magma pressure increases and the discharge rate increases. At the cusp D, the steady-state flow rate must jump to E where the flow rate is much faster and the chamber pressure declines as magma is removed form the chamber. At B there is another cusp, and the steady-state conditions fall to C. If magma chamber pressure then increases, the cycle can be repeated. If at point D there was a dome collapse, then the jump could be to F on the 0 m dome height curve. After the collapse, further eruption may reduce the chamber pressure to A, and the flow rates once again fall back to C.

developed in the upper parts of the volcanic conduit (Sparks 1997; Voight *et al.* 1999; Melnik & Sparks 1999). Overpressure can be defined in two different ways. One definition is the difference between the pressure at some depth and the weight of the surrounding rocks (the lithostatic pressure). Another definition is the pressure difference between the local pressure at some depth and the weight of the overlying column of magma. Which of these overpressures is relevant depends on the circumstances. The second definition is relevant in considering magma ascent from depth and local overpressures that might exceed the strength of the magma and result in explosions. On the other hand, the first definition is relevant if one is interested in the deformation of the volcanic edifice and interpretation of ground deformation. There may not be much difference in the values of these overpressures, although they can be very different in certain circumstances at shallow levels.

In a system with constant viscosity and constant conduit cross-section, overpressure decreases linearly between the magma source region at depth and the surface. However, in a system with large vertical viscosity gradients the overpressure variation is highly non-linear and focused in the uppermost parts of the volcanic conduit where the high-viscosity degassed magma offers most of the frictional resistance to flow. Figure 8 shows the calculations of overpressure variation with height by Melnik and Sparks (1999) for eruption of Soufrière Hills andesite. The key result is that a large overpressure maximum up to several MPa can be predicted at depths of a few hundred metres. The value of the maximum depends on many parameters, and in Figure 8 the dependence on magma permeability is shown. The lower the magma permeability, the higher is the overpressure maximum. Even without crystallization, large overpressures can develop due to the strong decrease of viscosity at water contents below 1% (Massol & Jaupart 1999).

These ideas have been developed further by Barmin *et al.* (2002) to investigate the unsteady

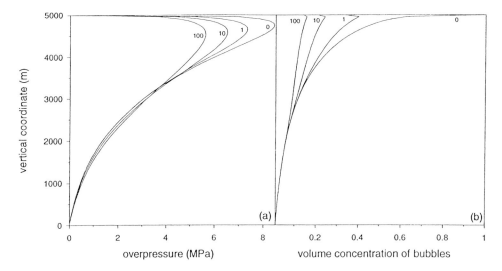

Fig. 8. Calculated profiles of overpressure (**a**) and porosity (**b**) along a conduit. Conditions for calculations are described in Melnik & Sparks (1999) and relate to conduit conditions and magma properties of the eruption of the Soufrière Hills andesite lava dome. Overpressure (the difference between the magma pressure and surrounding lithostatic pressure) reaches a maximum in the uppermost few hundred metres of a volcanic conduit. Curves are shown for values of the permeability coefficient k_o from values of 0 to 100. This parameter is the constant coefficient in a power law that relates permeability to porosity (see Melnik & Sparks 2002). Values of k_o are bounded in the range 1 to 10 for samples of the Soufrière Hills andesite (see Melnik & Sparks 2002 for details). Low values of k_o give unrealistically high porosities at the top of the conduit, and explosive conditions are likely to develop in practice. The calculations here assumed no crystallization in the conduit.

behaviour of lava extrusions with the incorporation of visco-elastic deformation of the magma chamber and conduit wall for the case of an open system chamber being replenished at a constant rate. In the model of Melnik & Sparks (1999), the chamber pressure was kept constant but, with a flexible elastic chamber, the pressure can vary. This model generates a much richer range of behaviours (Fig. 9), with both steady extrusion and highly pulsed periodic extrusion. Barmin *et al.* (2002) have been able to mimic the pulsatory character of the 1980–1986 dacite dome extrusion of Mount St Helens and the 1922–present dome growth of Santiaguito, Guatemala. Such models are moving towards a more complete total system description of eruptions, in which magma chamber dynamics, degassing, degassing-induced crystallization, rheological stiffening, conduit flow and dome growth are coupled together. However, as mentioned earlier, fully realistic models that incorporate two-dimensional effects remain a future goal.

Degassing in magma chamber evolution

It is usually assumed that the principal ways in which magmas differentiate is by heat loss (e.g.

Shaw 1985). This is a slow process because heat loss from magma chambers is by conduction, although hydrothermal circulation can greatly increase heat loss. The key point of this paradigm is that crystallization and differentiation are related to a time-dependent loss of heat, which is usually assumed to be sufficiently slow that large bodies of magma can develop and slowly differentiate in the crust. The role of degassing has been given far less attention, although the process is widely recognized and is occasionally mentioned in passing. Degassing, however, can result in large undercoolings and crystallization, and is therefore also able to explain crystallization and differentiation if crystals are separated from the melt. Gas exsolution in magma chambers can also have important dynamic effects: for example magma chamber pressure increases when gas exsolution occurs concurrently with crystallization (Tait *et al.* 1989) and gas exsolution may result in filter pressing of residual melts from crystal mushes (Sisson & Bacon 1999).

One mechanism of magma chamber differentiation that has not been given much attention is the role of convective circulation and drainback of degassed magma. This has been dis-

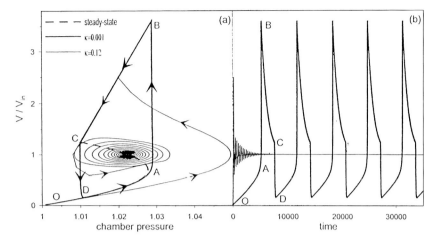

Fig. 9. Models of unsteady cyclic conduit flow and dome extrusion with degassing from an open-system magma chamber, after Barmin *et al.* (2002). In (**a**) the velocity, *v*, of magma ascent is plotted against magma chamber pressure, with the velocity being normalized by the velocity of input, v_{in}, of new magma into the chamber, and the magma chamber pressure being normalized by the lithostatic pressure at the top of the chamber. The dashed curve (O–D–A–C–B) shows steady-state solutions, and the two curves (thick and thin solid curves) show unsteady calculations for two values of the parameter, κ, which is a dimensionless number defined as $(\pi D^2 \gamma/4 V_{ch}\rho g)$ where *D* is the conduit diameter, γ is the rigidity of the conduit walls, V_{ch} is the magma chamber volume, ρ the density of the magma, and *g* is gravity. Large values of κ are for small chambers with relatively wide conduits and small values of κ are for large chambers with relatively narrow conduits. The equivalent time series for the discharge rate is shown in (**b**). For small κ (=0.001) the magma discharge is highly periodic, with short periods of very high discharge alternating with much longer periods of low discharge along the path A–B–C–D–A. For large κ (=0.12), initial rapid oscillations of discharge rate are damped and the system evolves to a steady-state output. In both cases the time-averaged output rate is equal to the input into the chamber (v/v_{in}=1). The calculations were carried out for magma properties similar to the dacite of Mount St Helens, and details can be found in Barmin *et al.* (2002).

cussed earlier in the context of explaining excess magma degassing in open conduits. However, another implication of the process is that degassed magma draining back into the chamber will develop strong undercooling not only because of degassing at the surface, but because the liquidus of dry degassed magma increases with increasing pressure. For example, a wet basalt with 2% water and a liquidus of 1050 °C has a liquidus of 1200–1250 °C in the chamber after a cycle of surface degassing and drain-back. Consequently, this process can drive substantial amounts of crystallization and differentiation in the chamber. Evidence for this process has been found at Kilauea on Hawaii, from studies of volatiles in lavas and melt inclusions (Dixon *et al.* 1991; Wallace & Anderson 1998). The importance of degassing may have been underestimated, and there is a case to be made that it can, in some circumstances, be the dominant mechanism of magma chamber crystallization.

An alternative view of intermediate to silicic magmatic systems is as follows. Magmas are generated, stored and evolved largely at deeper levels in the crust (Annen & Sparks 2002). The mechanisms of evolved melt generation involve simultaneous crystallization and partial melting as mantle-derived mafic magmas invade the deep crust. In these circumstances, some of the evolved melts may have very high water contents. Such water-rich magmas ascend to shallow depths, and degas during ascent. When they reach upper-crustal depths, they become increasingly viscous due to degassing and crystal growth. They may proceed directly to erupt at the surface, or stagnate to form shallow magma chambers where further degassing results in crystallization (Blundy & Cashman 2000). Wallace (2001) has recently reviewed evidence for large amounts of exsolved gas in many shallow magma chambers. The very detailed study of volatile inventories in the Bishop Tuff magma chamber (Wallace *et al.* 1999) provides strong evidence for the major role of an excess exsolved volatile phase. A major exsolved volatile phase in magmas can explain the otherwise puzzling excess degassing of SO_2 in many eruptions as suggested by several studies

(Gerlach *et al.* 1996; Scaillet *et al.* 1998; Keppler 1999). There are other important implications for magmas having higher volatile contents than has been supposed and, as a consequence, of undergoing coupled crystallization and degassing in chambers. Such notions will influence concepts about formation of ore deposits, leakages of deep volcanic gases in hydrothermal fields, and the dynamics of eruption. In particular, a chamber with large amounts of exsolved gas will be highly compressible, and this will make large differences to the evolution of magma chamber pressure (Huppert & Woods 2002).

Degassing also can have a major role in the dynamics of open-system magma chambers. Replenishment is widely accepted as a major factor in triggering volcanic eruptions (e.g. Sparks *et al.* 1977; Blake 1981, 1984). The presence of exsolved gas in the incoming magma may reverse the usual density relations in which mafic magma is denser than more evolved magma. The presence of exsolved gas can lead to immediate magma mixing (Phillips & Woods 2001), gradual mixing (Eichelberger 1980), catastrophic overturn and mixing (Huppert *et al.* 1982; Turner *et al.* 1982) or gradual transfer of gas without mixing, from more mafic magma emplaced at the base of the chamber to more silicic overlying magma (Wallace 2001).

Magma volatile contents and depth of degassing

In the discussions of magma degassing so far, not much has been said about the typical volatile contents of magmas and the depths at which gas exsolution and escape becomes important. An important issue is: at what depths do magmas become sufficiently permeable for gas to start to escape? Figure 10 shows calculations of the pressures and approximate depth equivalents at which magma reaches 30% porosity for different water contents. A porosity threshold of 30% has been chosen, as this is approximately the value above which significant bubble interaction and permeability development might be expected (Blower 2001). Here, 30% is simply used to illustrate that the depth at which gas escape becomes important will be a strong function of water content.

There are grounds for thinking that water contents of magmas may have been underestimated, particularly in arc magmas. Melt inclusion data and experimental studies on arc basalts, for example, indicate water contents in the range 2–6% (e.g. Sisson & Layne 1993; Moore & Carmichael 1998; Roggensack 2001). Inspection of Figure 10 indicates that significant degassing processes can start at depths of several

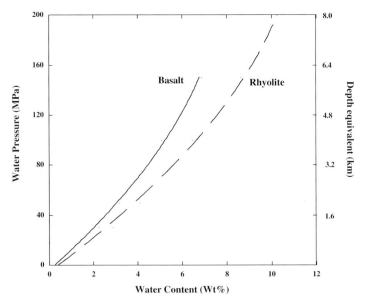

Fig. 10. Plots of water content of magma (melt) against pressure for magma with a vesicularity of 30 vol. %. Curves are shown for basalt and rhyolite with assumed solubility constants of 3 and 4.1×10^{-6} $Pa^{-1/2}$ respectively. Magma density and temperatures are assumed to be 2300 kg/m^3 and 800 °C for rhyolite and 2600 kg/m^3 for 1100 °C basalt. The approximate depth equivalents of the pressures are shown on the right-hand vertical axis, assuming a crustal density of 2500 kg/m^3.

kilometres in water-rich basalts, as also deduced by Roggensack (2001). For intermediate and silicic magmas, numerous studies of melt inclusions and experimental simulations (see Wallace 2001 for review) indicate water contents invariably in the 4–6% range. However, these water content estimates are lower limits, because they are determined by study of phenocrysts that trap melt inclusions and by comparison of phenocryst assemblages with experimental products. A critical problem is that magmas with water contents significantly in excess of 6% may not crystallize during ascent. Experimental studies (e.g. Holtz & Johannes 1994) indicate that very wet magmas (6–12% water) do not crystallize during ascent until the water pressure is sufficiently low, and this happens at pressures where only 6% or less remains dissolved in the melt. If the wet basalts typical of many arcs were to stall and differentiate in the deeper parts of the crust, then evolved intermediate and silicic melt with very high water contents could be generated. Inspection of Figure 10 indicates that these very wet magmas can become very bubble rich at depths of several kilometres, and connectivity can develop in the chamber.

Conclusions

Degassing has a profound effect on the dynamics of volcanic eruptions. Gas exsolution as magma ascends causes large changes in physical properties, such as density and viscosity, and phase equilibria, with spontaneous crystallization resulting from gas loss. The compressibility of bubble-rich magma also greatly complicates the dynamics of flows in conduits and degassing processes. The coupling of gas exsolution, gas separation processes, crystallization and compressibility effects lead to a very rich diversity of flow and eruptive phenomena. The processes of degassing and crystallization are kinetically controlled, and their coupling with flow, largely through their effects on density and viscosity, is highly non-linear. This makes volcanoes classically dynamical systems, in which strong feedback loops, strong unsteadiness, and strong and sometimes catastrophic jumps in flow regime, are intrinsic. The range of behaviours can be from steady discharge, to highly periodical patterns, to more chaotic and complex behaviours.

Volcanic systems can be inherently unpredictable, as a consequence of non-linear dynamics. Perhaps the most important concept, which emerges from this analysis of degassing dynamics, is the discovery that a completely determined volcanic system with all properties known precisely can have multiple stable states. It is not

possible to determine which state will actually occur, without knowing the full dynamical history of the system. This concept was pioneered by the research of Y. Slezin, and has subsequently been developed in more elaborate models of magma ascent and eruption dynamics (e.g. Jaupart & Allegre 1991; Massol & Jaupart 1999; Melnik & Sparks 1999; Barmin et al. 2002). Of course, none of the parameters that control eruptions are known precisely, and indeed, some critical parameters, such as chamber size, may be highly uncertain. These results indicate that prediction of volcanic eruptions can only be developed in a probabilistic way, in which uncertainties are taken into account. The notion that volcanic eruptions can be inherently unpredictable is not a comfortable truth, and will require some changes in thinking about the goals of volcanology.

On the other hand, these same dynamical models can provide an explanation of beautifully periodic behaviours and some basis for forecasting. Sudden changes of state in an eruption need no longer be surprises or perplexing phenomena. Also, the dynamical flow models provide the conceptual framework for interpreting geophysical, geochemical and phenomenological data monitored in eruptions. For example, models, such as those of Melnik and Sparks (1999), show how large overpressures develop in the uppermost parts of volcanic conduits, thereby explaining several geophysical features.

Another important concept is that degassing may be a major factor in the differentiation in magma. Although it has long been understood that magmas crystallize when they exsolve the major volcanic gas (water), the implications have perhaps been overlooked. The majority of petrological and geochemical studies implicitly interpret data in terms of the concept of a shallow, slowly cooling magma body, where heat loss is the driver for crystallization and fractionation. Of course, heat loss undoubtedly occurs, and there is no suggestion here that it is not going to be an important process in the evolution of igneous rocks. However, degassing is also likely to be important in at least two ways. First, water-rich magmas spontaneously crystallize if emplaced into a shallow magma chamber, and this is clearly an effective way of differentiation to generate evolved melts. Second, the only way to explain huge volumes of degassing with little eruption of magma is by very effective convective exchanges between the surface and deep chambers along conduits (Kazahaya et al. 1994; Stevenson & Blake 1998). An overlooked process is that sinking degassed magma must crystallize due to compression, and this can also be a driver for differentiation. Finally, magma volatile contents have evidently been underestimated, and some magma chambers may contain large amounts of exsolved gas (Wallace 2001). The presence of substantial gas in magma chambers will profoundly affect how magmas behave and erupt. I also draw attention to the possibility that water contents of magmas, particularly in arcs, may have been underestimated. Gas loss processes in water-rich magmas can initiate at depth in volcanic conduits and even in the magma chamber. Degassing is not necessarily a shallow process.

First of all I remember Pete Francis as an outstanding scientist and good friend, and I dedicate this paper to his memory. I thank all my many collaborators who have made contributions to understanding degassing. I first acknowledge the close collaboration with staff of the Montserrat Volcano Observatory during the eruption. The ideas and data from that eruption were a team effort, involving a large number of dedicated and outstanding people. I particularly recognize the pioneering research of Y. Slezin, and acknowledge the collaboration with O. Melnik over the last few years. Oleg's mathematical skills and physical insights have been pivotal in developing models of the interactions between degassing and rheological stiffening in controlling conduit flows and eruptive behaviour. P. Wallace is thanked for his comments. C. Jaupart, S. Blake, C. Connor and T. Gerlach are thanked for their helpful reviews. I acknowledge the support of a NERC fellowship.

References

ALLARD, P. 1997. Endogenous degassing and storage at Mount Etna. *Geophysical Research Letters*, **24**, 2219–2222.

ANNEN, C. & SPARKS, R.S.J. 2002. Effects of repetitive emplacement of basaltic intrusions on thermal evolution and melt generation in the crust. *Earth and Planetary Science Letters* **203**, 937–955.

BARCLAY, J., CARROLL, M. R., HOUGHTON, B. F. & WILSON, C. J. N. 1996. Pre-eruptive volatile content and degassing history of an evolving peralkaline volcano. *Journal of Volcanology and Geothermal Research*, **74**, 75–87.

BARMIN, A., MELNIK, O. & SPARKS, R. S. J. 2002. Periodic behaviour in lava dome eruptions. *Earth and Planetary Science Letters*, **199**, 173–184.

BLAKE, S. 1981. Volcanism and dynamics of open magma chambers. *Nature*, **289**, 783–785.

BLAKE, S. 1984. Volatile oversaturation during evolution of silicic magma chambers as a trigger for an eruption. *Journal of Geophysical Research*, **89**, 8937–8244.

BLOWER, J. D. 2001. A three-dimensional network model of permeability in vesicular material. *Computers and Geosciences*, **27**, 115–118.

BLOWER, J. D., KEATING, J. P., MADER, H. M. & PHILLIPS, J. C. 2001a. Inferring volcanic degassing processes from vesicle size distributions. *Geophysical Research Letters*, **28**, 347–350.

BLOWER, J. D., MADER, H. M. & WILSON, S. D. R. 2001b. Coupling of viscous and diffusive controls on bubble growth during explosive volcanic eruptions. *Earth and Planetary Science Letters*, **193**, 47–56.

BLUNDY, J. & CASHMAN, K. V. 2001. Ascent-driven crystallization of dacite magmas of Mount St Helens, 1980–1986. *Contributions to Mineralogy and Petrology*, **140**, 631–650.

BURTON, M., ALLARD, P., MURÈ, F. & OPPENHEIMER, C. 2003. FTIR remote sensing of fractional magma degassing at Mt. Etna, Sicily. *In:* OPPENHEIMER, C., PYLE, D. M. & BARCLAY, J. (eds) *Volcanic Degassing.* Geological Society, London, Special Publications **213**, 281–293.

CANN, J. R. 1970. Upward movement of granite magma. *Geological Magazine*, **107**, 335–340.

CASHMAN, K. V. 1992. Groundmass crystallization of Mount St Helens dacite, 1980–1986 – a tool for interpreting shallow magmatic processes. *Contributions to Mineralogy and Petrology*, **109**, 431–449.

DENLINGER, R. P. & HOBLITT, R. P. 1999. Cyclic behavior of silicic volcanoes. *Geology*, **27**, 459–462.

DEVINE, J. D., MURPHY, M. D., *ET AL.* 1998. Petrologic evidence for pressure–temperature conditions and recent reheating of andesite magma at Soufriere Hills Volcano, Montserrat, West Indies. *Geophysical Research Letters*, **25**, 3669–3672.

DINGWELL, D. B. 1998. Recent experimental progress in the physical description of silicic magma relevant to explosive volcanism. *In:* GILBERT, J. S. & SPARKS, R. S. J. *The Physics of Explosive Volcanic Eruptions.* Geological Society, London, Special Publications, **145**, 9–26.

DIXON, J. E., CLAGUE, J. E. & STOLPER, E. M. 1991. Degassing history of water, sulfur, and carbon in submarine lavas from Kilauea volcano, Hawaii. *Journal of Geology*, **99**, 371–394.

DRUITT, T. H. & YOUNG, S. R. *ET AL.* 2002. Episodes of cyclic vulcanian explosive activity with fountain collapse at Soufrière Hills volcano, Montserrat. *In:* DRUITT, T. H. AND KOKELAAR, B. P. (eds) *The Eruption of the Soufrière Hills Volcano, Montserrat, 1995 to 1999.* Geological Society, London, Memoirs **21**, 281–306.

EDMONDS, M., PYLE, D. & OPPENHEIMER, C. 2001. A model for degassing at the Soufrière Hills Volcano, Montserrat, West Indies, based on geochemical data. *Earth and Planetary Science Letters*, **186**, 159–173.

EICHELBERGER, J. C. 1980. Vesiculation of mafic magma during replenishment of silicic magma chambers. *Nature*, **288**, 446–450.

EICHELBERGER, J. C., CARRIGAN, C. R., WESTRICH, H. R. & PRICE, R. H. 1986. Non-explosive silicic volcanism. *Nature*, **323**, 598–602.

GESCHWIND, C. H. & RUTHERFORD, M. J. 1995. Crystallization of microlites during magma ascent: the fluid mechanics of the 1980–86 eruptions at Mount St Helens. *Bulletin of Volcanology*, **57**, 356–370.

GERLACH, T. M., WESTRICH, H. R. & SYMONDS, R. B. 1996. Pre-eruption vapor in magma of the climactic

Mount Pinatubo eruption: source of the giant stratospheric sulfur dioxide cloud. *In:* NEWHALL, C. G. & PUNONGBAYAN, R. S. (eds) *Fire and Mud: Eruptions and Lahars of Mount Pinatubo, Philippines.* University of Washington Press, Seattle, WA, 415–433.

HAMMER, J. E. & RUTHERFORD, M. J. 2002. An experimental study of the kinetics of decompression-induced crystallization in silicic melt. *Journal of Geophysical Research,* **107.**

HAMMER, J. E., CASHMAN, K. V., HOBLITT, R. P. & NEWMAN, S. 1999. Degassing and microlite crystallization during pre-climactic events of the 1991 eruption of Mt. Pinatubo, Philippines. *Bulletin of Volcanology,* **60,** 355–380.

HAMMOUYA, G., ALLARD, P., JEAN-BAPTISTE, P., PARELLO, F., SEMET, M. P. & YOUNG, S. R., 1998. Pre- and syn-eruptive geochemistry of volcanic gases from Soufrière Hills of Montserrat, West Indies. *Geophysical Research Letters,* **25,** 3685–3689.

HERVIG, R. L., DUNBAR, N. W., WESTRICH, H. R., & KYLE, P. R. 1989. Pre-eruptive water content of rhyolitic magmas as determined by ion microprobe analyses of melt inclusions in phenocrysts. *Journal of Volcanology and Geothermal Research,* **36,** 293–302.

HOLTZ, F. & JOHANNES, W. 1994. Maximum and minimum water contents of granitic melts – implications for chemical and physical properties of ascending magmas. *Lithos,* **32,** 149–159.

HUPPERT, H.E. & WOODS, A.W. 2003. The role of volatiles in magma chamber dynamics. *Nature,* **420,** 493–495.

HUPPERT, H., SPARKS, R. S. J. & TURNER, J. S. 1982. The effects of volatiles on mixing in calcalkaline magma systems. *Nature,* **297,** 554–557.

JAUPART, C. 1998. Gas loss from magmas through conduit walls. *In:* GILBERT, J. S. AND SPARKS, R. S. J. *The Physics of Explosive Volcanic Eruptions.* Geological Society, London, Special Publications, **145,** 73–90.

JAUPART, C. & ALLEGRE, C. 1991. Gas content, eruption rate and instabilities of eruption in silicic volcanoes. *Earth and Planetary Science Letters,* **102,** 413–429.

KAZAHAYA, K., SHINOHARA, H. & SAITO, G. 1994. Excessive degassing of Izu–Oshima volcano: magma convection in a conduit. *Bulletin of Volcanology,* **56,** 207–216.

KENNEDY, G. C. 1955. Some aspects of the role of water in rock melts. *Geological Society of America Special Paper,* **62,** 489–506.

KEPPLER, H. 1999. Experimental evidence for the source of excess sulfur in explosive volcanic eruptions. *Science,* **284,** 1652–1654.

KLUG, C. & CASHMAN, K. V. 1996. Permeability development in vesiculating magmas: implications for fragmentation. *Bulletin of Volcanology,* **58,** 87–100.

LUHR, J. F. & SIMKIN, T. 1993. *Paricutin: the Volcano Born in a Mexican Cornfield.* Geoscience Press/Smithsonian Institution Press, Washington D.C.

MARTEL, C., PICHAVANT, M., BOURDIER, J.-L., TRAINEAU, H., HOLTZ, F. & SCAILLET, B. 1998. Magma storage conditions and control of eruption regimes in silicic volcanoes: experimental evidence from Mont Pelée. *Earth and Planetary Science Letters,* **156,** 89–99.

MASSOL, H. & JAUPART, C. 1999. The generation of gas overpressure in volcanic eruptions. *Earth and Planetary Science Letters,* **166,** 57–70.

MATTHEWS, S. J., GARDEWEG, M. C. & SPARKS, R. S. J. 1997. The 1984 to 1996 cyclic activity of Lascar Volcano, Northern Chile; cycles of dome growth, dome subsidence, degassing and explosive eruption. *Bulletin of Volcanology,* **59,** 72–82.

MELNIK, O. & SPARKS, R. S. J. 1999. Nonlinear dynamics of lava extrusion. *Nature,* **402,** 37–41.

MELNIK, O. & SPARKS, R. S. J. 2002. Dynamics of magma ascent and lava extrusion at the Soufrière Hills Volcano, Montserrat. *In:* DRUITT, T. H. & KOKELAAR, B. P. (eds) *The Eruption of the Soufrière Hills Volcano, Montserrat, 1995 to 1999.* Geological Society, London, Memoir, **21,** 153–172.

MORENO, H. & GARDEWEG, M. C. 1989. La erupcion riciente en el complejo volcanica Lonquimay (Dicembre 1988–) Andes del Sur. *Revista Geologica de Chile,* **16,** 93–117.

MOORE, G. & CARMICHAEL, I. S. E. 1998. The hydrous phase equilibria (to 3 kbar) of an andesite and basaltic andesite from western Mexico: constraints on water content and conditions of phenocryst growth. *Contributions to Mineralogy and Petrology,* **130,** 304–319.

NAVON, O. & LYAKHOVSKY, V. 1998. Vesiculation processes in silicic magmas. *In:* GILBERT, J. S. AND SPARKS, R. S. J. *The Physics of Explosive Volcanic Eruptions.* Geological Society, London, Special Publications, **145,** 27–50.

NEUBERG, J. 2000. Characteristics and cause of shallow seismicity in andesite volcanoes. *Philosophical Transactions of the Royal Society, Series A,* **358,** 1533–1546.

PARFITT, E. A. & WILSON, L. 1995. Explosive volcanic eruptions – IX. The transition between Hawaiian-style lava fountaining and Strombolian explosive activity. *Geophysical Journal International,* **121,** 226–232.

PHILLIPS, J. C. & WOODS, A. W. 2001. Bubble plumes generated during recharge of basaltic reservoirs. *Earth and Planetary Science Letters,* **186,** 297–309.

ROGGENSACK, K. 2001. Unravelling the 1974 eruption of Fuego volcano (Guatemala) with small crystals and their melt inclusions. *Geology,* **29,** 911–914.

SCAILLET, B., CLEMENTE, B., EVANS, B. W. & PICHAVANT, M. 1998. Redox control of sulfur degassing in silicic magmas. *Journal of Geophysical Research,* **103,** 23 937–23 949.

SELF, S., SPARKS, R. S. J., BOOTH, B. & WALKER, G. P. L. 1974. The 1973 Heimaey Strombolian scoria deposit. *Geological Magazine,* **111,** 539–548.

SHAW, H. R. 1985. Links between magma-tectonic rate balances, plutonism and volcanism. *Journal of Geophysical Research,* **90,** 11 275–11 288.

SISSON, T. W. & BACON, C. R. 1999. Gas-driven filter pressing in magmas. *Geology,* **27,** 127–162.

SISSON, T. W. & LAYNE, G. D. 1993. H_2O in basalt and basaltic andesite glass inclusions from four subduction-related volcanoes. *Earth and Planetary Science Letters*, **117**, 619–635.

SLEZIN, Y. B. 1995. Principal regimes of volcanic eruptions. *Volcanology and Seismology*, **17**, 193–206.

SLEZIN, Y. B. 2003. The mechanism of volcanic eruption (steady state approach). *Journal of Volcanology and Geothermal Research*, **122**, 7–50.

SPARKS, R. S. J. 1978 The dynamics of bubble formation and growth in magmas: a review and analysis. *Journal of Volcanology and Geothermal Research*, **3**, 1–37.

SPARKS, R. S. J. 1997. Causes and consequences of pressurisation in lava dome eruptions *Earth and Planetary Science Letters*, **150**, 177–189.

SPARKS, R. S. J. & PINKERTON, H. 1978. Effects of degassing on rheology of basaltic lava. *Nature*, **276**, 385–386.

SPARKS, R. S. J., BURSIK, M. I., CAREY, S. N., GILBERT, J. S., GLAZE, L., SIGURDSSON, H. & WOODS, A. W. 1997. *Volcanic Plumes*. John Wiley, Chichester.

SPARKS, R. S. J., MURPHY, M. D., LEJEUNE, A. M., WATTS, R. B., BARCLAY, J. & YOUNG, S. R. 2000. Control on the emplacement of the andesite lava dome of the Soufrière Hills Volcano by degassing-induced crystallization. *Terra Nova*, **12**, 14–20.

SPARKS, R. S. J., SIGURDSSON, H. & WILSON, L. 1977. Magma mixing: mechanism of triggering explosive acid eruptions. *Nature*, **267**, 315–318.

STASIUK, M. V., BARCLAY, J., CARROLL, M. R., JAUPART, C., RATTE, J. C., SPARKS, R. S. J. & TAIT, S. R. 1996. Decompression of volatile-saturated rhyolitic magma in the Mule Creek vent, New Mexico, U.S.A. *Bulletin of Volcanology*, **58**, 117–130.

STEVENSON, D. S. & BLAKE, S. 1998. Modelling the dynamics and thermodynamics of volcanic degassing. *Bulletin of Volcanology*, **60**, 307–317.

STIX, J., TORRES, C. R., NARVÁEZ, M. L., CORTES, J. G. P., RAIGOSA, J. A., GOMEZ, M. D. & CASTONGUEY, R. 1977. A model of vulcanian eruptions at Galeras volcano, Columbia. *Journal of Volcanology and Geothermal Research,* **77**, 285–304.

SUH, C. E., SPARKS, R. S. J., FITTON, J. G., AYONGHE, S. N., ANNEN, C., NANA, R. & LUCKMAN, A. 2003. The 1999 and 2000 eruptions of Mount Cameroon: eruption behaviour and petrochemistry of lava. *Bulletin of Volcanology* (in press).

SWANSON, D. A. & FABBI, B. P. 1973. Loss of volatiles during fountaining and flowage of basaltic lava at Kilauea volcano, Hawaii. *US Geological Survey Journal of Research*, **1**, 649–658.

TAIT, S. R., JAUPART, C. & VERGNIOLLE, S. 1989. Pressure, gas content and eruption, periodicity in a shallow crystallising magma chamber. *Earth and Planetary Science Letters*, **92**, 107–123.

TAYLOR, B. E., EICHELBERGER, J. C. & WESTRICH, H. R. 1983. Hydrogen isotope evidence for rhyolitic magma degassing during shallow intrusion and eruption. *Nature*, **306**, 541–545.

TURNER, J. S., HUPPERT, H. & SPARKS, R. S. J. 1982. Experimental investigations of volatile exsolution in evolving magma chambers. *Journal of Volcanology and Geothermal Research*, **16**, 263–277.

TUTTLE, O. F. & BOWEN, N. L. 1958. Origin of granite in the light of experimental studies in the system $NaAlSiO_3$–$KAlSiO_3$–SiO_2–H_2O. *Geological Society of America Memoirs*, **74**.

VERGNIOLLE, S. & JAUPART, C. 1986. Separated two-phase flow in basaltic eruptions. *Journal of Geophysical Research*, **91**, 12 840–12 860.

VERGNIOLLE, S. & JAUPART, C. 1990. Dynamics of degassing at Kilauea volcano, Hawaii. *Journal of Geophysical Research*, **95**, 2793–2809.

VOIGHT, B. & SPARKS, R. S. J. *ET AL.* 1999. Magma flow instability and cyclic activity at Soufrière Hills Volcano, Montserrat, British West Indies. *Science*, **283**, 1138–1142.

WALLACE, P. J. 2001. Volcanic SO_2 emissions and the abundance and distribution of exsolved gas in magma bodies. *Journal of Volcanology and Geothermal Research*, **108**, 85–106.

WALLACE, P. J. & ANDERSON, A. T. 1998. Effects of eruption and lava drainback on the H_2O contents of basaltic magmas at Kilauea volcano. *Bulletin of Volcanology*, **59**, 327–344.

WALLACE, P. J., ANDERSON, A. T. & DAVIS, A. M. 1999. Gradients in H_2O, CO_2 and exsolved gas in a large-volume silicic magma system: interpreting the record preserved in melt inclusions from the Bishop Tuff. *Journal of Geophysical Research*, **104**, 20 097–20 122.

WATSON, I. M. & OPPENHEIMER, C. *ET AL.* 2000. The relationship between degassing and deformation at Soufrière Hills volcano, Montserrat. *Journal of Volcanology and Geothermal Research*, **98**, 117–126.

WATTS, R. B., HERD, R. A., SPARKS, R. S. J. & YOUNG, S. R. 2002. Growth patterns and emplacement of the andesite lava dome at the Soufrière Hills Volcano, Montserrat. *In:* DRUITT, T. H. & KOKELAAR, B. P. (eds) *The Eruption of the Soufrière Hills Volcano, Montserrat, 1995 to 1999.* Geological Society, London, Memoirs, **21**, 115–152.

WHALLEY, P. B. 1987. *Boiling, Condensation and Gas–Liquid Flow.* Clarendon Press, Oxford.

WILSON, L. & HEAD, J. 1981. Ascent and eruption of magma on the Earth and Moon. *Journal of Geophysical Research*, **86**, 2971–3001.

WOODS, A. W. & KOYAGUCHI, T. 1994. Transitions between explosive and effusive volcanic eruptions. *Nature*, **370**, 641–644.

Experimental constraints on volatile abundances in arc magmas and their implications for degassing processes

B. SCAILLET & M. PICHAVANT

ISTO-CNRS, UMR 6113, 1A rue de la Férollerie, 45071, Orléans Cedex 02, France.

Abstract: Recent phase equilibrium studies, combined with analytical and petrological data, provide rigorous constraints on the pre-eruptive P–T–fH_2O–fO_2–fS_2–fCO_2 conditions of silicic to mafic arc magmas. Pre-eruptive melts show a broad negative correlation between temperature and melt H_2O contents. Pre-eruptive melt S contents cluster around 100 ppm in residual rhyolitic liquids of silicic to andesitic magmas, and range up to 5000 ppm in more mafic ones. For the entire compositional spectrum, melt sulphur contents are almost independent of prevailing fO_2. In contrast, they are positively correlated to fS_2, in agreement with experimental observations. Using these intensive constraints, the composition of coexisting fluid phases has been modelled through a MRK equation of state. Pre-eruptive fluids in silicic to andesitic magmas have XH_2O (mole fraction of H_2O) in the range 0.65–0.95. XH_2O decreases as pressure increases, whereas XCO_2 increases up to 0.2–0.3. Pre-eruptive fluids in hydrous mafic arc magmas, such as high-alumina basalts, generally have similar mole fractions of H_2O and CO_2 at mid-crustal levels, with XH_2O increasing only for magmas stored at shallow levels in the crust (<1 kbar). The sulphur content of the fluid phase ranges from 0.12 up to 6.4 wt% in both mafic and silicic magmas. For silicic magmas coexisting with 1–5 wt% fluid, this implies that more than 90% of the melt+fluid mass of sulphur is stored in the fluid. Calculated partition coefficients of S between fluid and melt range from 17 up to 467 in silicic to andesitic magmas, tending to be lower at low fO_2, although exceptions to this trend exist. For mafic compositions, the sulphur partition coefficient is constant at around 20. The composition of both melt and coexisting fluid phases under pre-eruptive conditions shows marked differences. For all compositions, pre-eruptive fluids have higher C/S and lower H/C atomic ratios than coexisting melts. Comparison between volcanic gas and pre-eruptive fluid compositions shows good agreement in the high temperature range. However, to reproduce faithfully the compositional field delineated by volcanic gases, silicic to andesitic arc magmas must be fluid-saturated under pre-eruptive conditions, with fluid amounts of at least 1 wt%, whereas mafic compositions require lower amounts of fluid, in the range 0.1–1 wt%. Nevertheless, volcanic gases colder than 700 °C are generally too H_2O-rich and S-poor to have been in equilibrium with silicic to andesitic magmas under pre-eruptive conditions, which suggests that such gases probably contain a substantial contribution from meteoric or hydrothermal water.

Introduction

Understanding how water and sulphur supply by magmas may have varied through geological times, as well as identifying the factors that control the abundances of these species in modern and ancient magmas, has implications for fundamental geological processes, such as the long-term geochemical cycles of these elements or the origin and evolution of the atmosphere. On a shorter observational time-scale, which is of more direct relevance to humankind, water and sulphur are among the most important climate forcing species released by volcanic activity worldwide. In particular, sulphur-rich eruptions, such as El Chichón in 1982 or Mount Pinatubo in 1991, have illustrated how volcanic events of even moderate magnitude may affect the Earth's climate on a global scale (Robock 2000; Blake, 2003, Chapter 22). Quantifying the water and sulphur budgets released by arc magmas during the recent past (e.g. Palais & Sigurdsson 1989; Zielinski 1995) has thus become an important aspect of studies attempting to unravel factors affecting secular climate trends based on climate proxies such as ice-core records (Robock 2000). Understanding the behaviour of these two species in magmatic systems is also fundamental from the perspective of volcanic hazard assessment. It has long been known that because arc magmas are water rich they may erupt explosively. The determination of pre-eruptive magma water

From: OPPENHEIMER, C., PYLE, D.M. & BARCLAY, J. (eds) *Volcanic Degassing.* Geological Society, London, Special Publications, 213, 23–52. 0305–8719/03/$15.00

contents is clearly one, although not the only, vital parameter that needs to be constrained in order to predict the eruptive behaviour of volcanoes. Sulphur contributes little to the eruption explosivity, because its abundance is one to two orders of magnitude lower than that of water. However, although minor, this species plays a central role in the monitoring of active volcanoes because it is easily measured with remote sensing tools and thus offers a potential insight into degassing mechanisms occurring at depth (e.g. Watson *et al.* 2000; McGonigle & Oppenheimer, 2003, Chapter 9). Monitoring of SO_2 fluxes of active volcanoes has yielded promising results for the forecast of volcanic eruptions, such as for the Galeras volcano, where SO_2 fluctuations could be correlated with the seismicity associated with magma ascent (Fischer *et al.* 1994). Correctly interpreting volatile degassing in terms of pre-eruptive signals, however, depends on our knowledge of volatile solubilities and diffusivities in silicate melts and their dependence on pressure, temperature and melt composition. It has been one of the main goals of experimental petrology to place narrow constraints on these critical parameters, as demonstrated by numerous studies over the past 18 years (Rutherford *et al.* 1985; Johnson & Rutherford 1989; Rutherford & Devine 1988, 1996; Luhr 1990; Martel *et al.* 1998, 1999; Scaillet & Evans 1999; Scaillet & Macdonald 2001), as well as to establish empirical or thermodynamical models describing the volatile solubilities in silicate melts (e.g. Silver & Stolper 1985; Dixon *et al.* 1995; Zhang 1999; Clemente *et al.* 2003; Moretti *et al.*, 2003, Chapter 6).

Volatiles released either passively or explosively by volcanoes presumably derive from various depths or structural levels where storage and partial degassing of magma bodies take place. Although the exact geometry and size of these bodies remain poorly constrained, and certainly vary between each volcano, there exists usually one upper-crustal reservoir where magma accumulation rates are high enough to build a sizeable body in which differentiation, mixing, degassing and cooling can take place. This reservoir is usually the main source of the erupted material where part, if not most, of the volatiles to be expelled are stored. The fluid/volatile contents of the upper reaches in the plumbing system may be due to the intrinsically volatile-rich nature of the emplaced magma, but also to the fact that, because most volatiles have high solubilities in silicate melts at high pressures, magma bodies in the upper crust may trap volatiles released at deeper levels and thus the plumbing system may act as a channel or

channels for volatile degassing. To understand volcanic degassing, it is therefore essential to characterize properly the conditions under which these reservoirs evolve – conditions that correspond with the starting point of any eruptive event.

In this report, we first review recent advances concerning our understanding of sulphur solubility in silicate melts, and its dependence on T, fO_2 and fS_2. We then discuss the pre-eruption P, T, melt H_2O, CO_2 and S values and the corresponding volatile fugacities of well-characterized arc-magmas, as constrained by phase equilibrium, melt inclusion and petrological data, building upon previous reviews (Johnson *et al.* 1994; Scaillet *et al.* 1998a, b). These constraints are used to derive, from thermodynamic calculations, the composition of the fluid phase that may coexist with the magma at depth before an eruption starts. We finally compare these fluid compositions against high-temperature volcanic gases collected at open vents of well-characterized active volcanoes (e.g. Symonds *et al.* 1994). The rationale is to estimate to what extent fluids coexisting at depth differ from those measured at the vent and, if so, to identify the factors responsible for these differences.

Sulphur solubility and fluid/melt partioning in arc magmas

Solubility

The solubility of sulphur in silicate melt has been extensively reviewed by Carroll & Webster (1994) for both mafic and silicic compositions, and here we focus mostly on the most recent developments in this field. Unlike water, whose solubility depends primarily on pressure, sulphur solubility is controlled by a number of parameters that include melt composition, temperature, fO_2 and fS_2. Until recently, experimental data for silicic systems were available only for the first three parameters. The magnitude of the control exerted by fS_2, although anticipated from experimental studies on dry (1 atmosphere) synthetic and mafic compositions (Carroll and Webster 1994), was virtually unknown. This gap has been filled by recent experimental work in which the interplay between T–fO_2–fS_2 and dissolved sulphur in a silicic magma (rhyolite) has been systematically explored and modelled at 2 kbar (Clemente *et al.* 2003). This study has shown that fS_2 exerts a control on sulphur solubility in hydrous rhyolitic melts, similar in magnitude to that of fO_2. This is illustrated in Figure 1 for a temperature of 930 °C at which most of the data were acquired, for either sulphide- or sulphate-saturated conditions. Although oxidized conditions need additional constraints in terms of sulphur solubility–fugacity relationships, it can be seen that at any given fixed fS_2, the sulphur solubility exhibits a minimum in the fO_2 range NNO–NNO+1, as shown by many previous studies. For a given T–fO_2, the melt sulphur solubility increases with fS_2, as expected. As a result, the dependence on fO_2 decreases with fS_2 such that at low fS_2 the half bell-shaped curve opens widely to the extent of becoming almost flat (i.e. independent of fO_2). From these experimental data, Clemente et al. (2003) have derived the following empirical expression:

$$\log S_{melt}=0.001\ T(°C)-0.2567\ (\Delta NNO)+ 0.1713\ \Delta FFS+0.0034\ \Delta NNO\ \Delta FFS \quad (1)$$

where S is the total sulphur concentration in ppm, T temperature in °C, ΔNNO is the $\log fO_2$ referenced to that of the Ni–NiO solid buffer (NNO, calculated after Chou 1987), and ΔFFS is the $\log fS_2$ referenced to the Fe–FeS buffer (calculated after Froese and Gunter 1976). The main limitations of equation 1 are that it has been calibrated only for metaluminous rhyolites saturated with H–O–S fluids, and that the effect of pressure remains to be determined. It is, however, the only model yet available and serves as a

useful starting point for the determination of fluid phase composition coexisting at depth, as shown below.

For mafic melt compositions there is as yet no calibrated model for hydrous and oxidizing conditions, which characterize most arc basalts. The only solubility model available for now is that of Wallace and Carmichael (1992), and it has been calibrated on sulphide-saturated and nominally dry compositions up to NNO. In this report we have used a simple empirical model based on the data for MORB glasses of Wallace and Carmichael (1992). To calculate either the melt S ppm or $\log fS_2$, the following polynomial fits have been used:

$$\log fS_2=-3.9829+3.7022\times10^{-2}\ (S_{ppm})- 1.083\times10^{-6}\ (S_{ppm})^2+9.3232\times10^{-11}\ (S_{ppm})^3 \quad (2)$$

and,

$$\log S_{ppm}=3.2211+2.0928\ (\log fS_2)+ 9.5397\times10^{-2}\ (\log fS_2)^2+3.5864\times10^{-2} \quad (3) (\log fS_2)^3 (3)$$

where S_{ppm} is the melt S content in ppm. This model is a mere extension toward oxidizing conditions of the model of Wallace and Carmichael (1992), which is based on the observation that both dry reduced and wet oxidized natural mafic

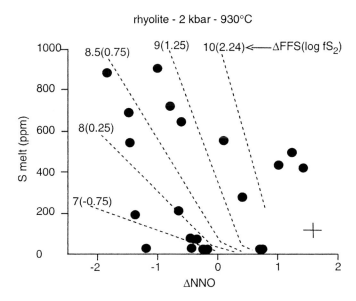

Fig. 1. Sulphur solubility in a sulphide or sulphate-saturated rhyolitic melt at 2 kbar and 930 °C, from Clemente et al. (2003). All charges are saturated in either pyrrhotite or anhydrite. Dashed lines represent contours of constant ΔFFS with values of $\log fS_2$ given in parentheses. The cross in the lower right area of the figure represents the average standard deviation (one sigma) of oxygen fugacity (fO_2) and melt sulphur content (see text).

melts display a single continuous trend relative to fO_2, with only a very weak dependence on redox conditions (see below). Equation 2 calculates log fS_2 within 0.3 log unit of the values reported by Wallace and Carmichael (1992) while equation 3 yields melt S contents to within 14% of those measured by Wallace and Carmichael (1992).

Partitioning

Interest in the partitioning behaviour of sulphur between melt and fluid has essentially been driven by the 'excess sulphur' problem identified for the 1991 Pinatubo eruptions. The huge SO_2 cloud released by Mount Pinatubo cannot be accounted for by the erupted magma volume, considering its pre-eruptive conditions, which were characterized by a low sulphur content of the melt, as represented by matrix and glass inclusions (Westrich & Gerlach 1992). This rules out melt as the main sulphur reservoir at depth. One explanation, put forward by Westrich and Gerlach (1992), is that the excess sulphur resided mostly in a coexisting vapor phase, which implies S_{fluid}/S_{melt} partitioning of about 700–800 (Gerlach *et al.* 1996). Direct determination of the partition coefficients of sulphur in laboratory experiments has been hindered by back reactions in fluids upon quenching, which prevent preservation of the equilibrium compositions of S-bearing magmatic fluids. So far, only two experimental studies have attempted to determine the partition of sulphur between melt and fluid at high P and T. Both used a mass-balance approach where only the S-bearing condensed phases have their sulphur content determined, whereas that of the fluid was calculated by difference (Scaillet *et al.* 1998b; Keppler 1999). Both studies have found that under certain conditions there is indeed a strong preferential partitioning of sulphur in favour of the fluid, yet the defined conditions are different between the two studies: Keppler (1999) found sulphur-enriched fluid under low fO_2, while Scaillet *et al.* (1998b) found the opposite. It has to be stressed that this difference is not due to a particular experimental procedure or to an analytical problem. Instead, the reason lies in the different bulk compositions on which the experiments were carried out. Keppler (1999) used a Ca- and Fe-free haplogranite melt composition, while Scaillet *et al.* (1998b) worked with the dacite from the Mount Pinatubo 1991 eruption. The haplogranite compositions used by Keppler (1999) mean that the experimental results are of limited applicability to understanding the behaviour of sulphur in arc-magmas, because the crystallization of S-bearing phases such as anhydrite or pyrrhotite cannot be

taken into account. The fO_2 dependence of the partition coefficient obtained by Keppler (1999) must be related to the contrasted solubilities of H_2S and SO_2 fluid species in hydrous Fe and Ca-free silicic melts, and suggests that H_2S is less soluble than SO_2. The experiments of Scaillet *et al.* (1998b) have shown that in Fe- and Ca-bearing magmas, part of the sulphur is being locked up by either pyrrhotite or anhydrite. The great affinity of iron and sulphur under reduced conditions results in most sulphur being stored in pyrrhotite and little being available for the fluid phase. Extensive sulphide precipitation makes the coexisting iron-bearing silicate phases (pyroxenes, amphiboles, biotite) becoming richer in magnesium. In contrast, when anhydrite is stable, although this mineral also holds a significant amount of sulphur, its modal proportion is lower than that of pyrrhotite, hence there is more sulphur available for the fluid and melt phases. At low temperatures where the sulphur solubility of silicate melts is low, sulphur resides primarily in the fluid phase. Scaillet *et al.* (1998b) suggested that the lower modal amounts of anhydrite relative to pyrrhotite are due to the fact that calcium needed for anhydrite crystallization in hydrous magmas is limited due to plagioclase and hornblende precipitation. For mafic compositions, there are no experimental constraints on the partitioning behaviour of sulphur between fluid and melt.

Pre-eruptive conditions

Rhyolitic to andesitic compositions

Johnson *et al.* (1994) and Scaillet *et al.* (1998a) have reviewed the available evidence for the pre-eruptive conditions determined for several arc-volcanoes using a variety of approaches including phase equilibria, melt inclusion and mineral equilibria (Fe–Ti oxides). In this work we use the database of Scaillet *et al.* (1998a), excluding all non arc-magma compositions, to which we have added the results of recent phase equilibrium or analytical works (Katmai: Coombs & Gardner 2001; Minoan: Cottrell *et al.* 1999; Michaud *et al.* 2000; Unzen: Sato *et al.* 1999). In the case of chemically zoned eruptions (e.g. Katmai, Bishop, Krakatau, Minoan) we restrict the analysis to volcanic ejecta believed to represent the top portion, or first tapped part, of the magmatic reservoir, except for the Pine Grove where the deepest possible magma (i.e. the CO_2 rich part) has been used in an effort to shed light on the lowest regions of the plumbing system. In the most favourable cases, the combination of phase equilibrium, melt inclusion, and oxide thermobarometry constraints generally allows us to define the pre-eruption temperature to within ±30 °C, melt H_2O content to ±0.5 wt% and fO_2 to ±0.3 log unit. Good examples include the recent eruptions of Mount St Helens, Mount Pelée, Montserrat and Mount Pinatubo. Pressure is the least well-constrained parameter. The spatial resolution of geophysical data (e.g. seismic, gravimetric, magnetotelluric methods) is often too low to image accurately magma bodies that are only a few km across, which is the expected size for the most frequent type of eruptions involving up to a few km^3 of erupted material. Most pressures of magma storage are derived from phase equilibrium constraints (Pinatubo, St Helens, El Chichón, Fish Canyon, Mount Pelée, Montserrat, Mount Unzen, Katmai, and Minoan), coupled, when available, with seismic data (e.g. Pinatubo, St Helens). Melt inclusion barometry can also help to constrain pressures of magma storage, assuming fluid saturation (Wallace *et al.* 1995). Such constraints have been used for the Bishop and Pine Grove eruptions. For other eruptions (Krakatau, Taupo, Toba, Santa Maria) lacking seismic or phase equilibrium constraints on depth of the magma reservoir, the pressure of magma storage before eruption has been assumed to be at 2–3 kbar for amphibole-bearing magmas (Toba, Taupo, Santa Maria) and 1.2 kbar for magmas lacking this phase (Krakatau). We stress, however, that these amphibole-based constraints are only crude estimates that need refinement. Based on available experimental data, there is a general consensus that amphibole presence in andesitic–dacitic magmas requires a minimum of 1–1.5 kbar (e.g. Rutherford & Hill 1993), but recent work has established that amphibole may persist down to 500 bars in some dacitic groundmasses (Sato *et al.* 1999), while in others amphibole crystallization on the liquidus requires at least 4 kbar (Martel *et al.* 1999). The broad chemical similarities of the rocks in these experimental studies show that the compositional control of amphibole stability in andesitic–dacitic magmas is subtle, and additional experimental work is required before amphibole geobarometry can be of general, as well as precise, use in arc settings.

The critical pre-eruption parameters are listed in Table 1, together with the melt atomic C/S, H/S and H/C ratios. Most volcanoes have their upper crustal reservoir, which may correspond with either the top portion of a larger vertical system tapped during eruption (e.g. Pichavant *et al.* 2002a) or to a single isolated magma body with limited vertical dimensions, at a pressure of 2 ± 1 kbar. Pre-eruptive melt water contents range from 4 to 7 wt%, temperatures between 675 and 900 °C, and fO_2 between NNO and NNO+2. A general inverse correlation exists between T and H_2O, such that the drier the magma, the hotter it is. This trend may, in part, reflect the fact that magmatic differentiation is accompanied by a decrease in temperature and a concentration of water in the residual melt (Fig. 2, see also Scaillet *et al.* 1998a). Such a trend does not exist for both the melt CO_2 (calculated as explained below) and S contents, whose abundance seems fairly insensitive to the temperature of magma storage (Fig. 2). In contrast, melt CO_2 contents show a broad positive dependence on pressure, reaching a maximum at around 500 ppm for magmas stored in the middle crust (Pine Grove) (Fig. 3). Melt S concentrations display a remarkably flat trend over nearly two log units of fO_2 (Fig. 3), most magmas having S concentrations at around 100 ppm under pre-eruption conditions. The lack of clear dependence between melt S concentration and fO_2 suggests that variations in fO_2 do not significantly affect the melt sulphur in silicic to andesitic arc magmas, at least in the upper portions of the storage zone. In contrast, there is a gentle positive correlation between melt S concentration and fS_2 (Fig. 3). Overall, calculated fS_2 ranges from 10^{-5} up to a few bars, in agreement with previous work (Whitney 1984).

Basaltic compositions

The number and quality of quantitative constraints on pre-eruptive conditions for mafic systems are more limited than those for silicic systems. The main reason is that, owing to the strong negative dP/dT slopes of crystallizing phases in H_2O-bearing magmas coupled to the low viscosity of hydrous mafic melts, mafic arc-magmas rarely erupt without extensive crystallization. This seriously hampers conventional petrological laboratory studies. Over the last decade, however, major advances have been made (see Johnson *et al.* 1994), largely thanks to experimental studies (e.g. Sisson & Grove 1993a, b; Pichavant *et al.* 2002a, b) or analytical work on melt inclusions (e.g. Sisson & Layne 1993; Sobolev & Chaussidon 1996; Roggensack *et al.* 1997; Luhr 2001; Roggensack 2001). It is important to distinguish MgO-rich arc basalts from MgO-poor ones with which we will be primarily concerned in this study. The former correspond with the most primitive type (i.e. mantle-derived) of magma found in arc settings, albeit very seldom for the reasons just given, and which last equilibrated with mantle rocks. Recent phase equilibria have shown that such primary arc magmas, with MgO contents higher than 10 wt%, have melt H_2O contents of around 2 wt%

Table 1. *Pre-eruptive volatile fugacities of arc magmas*

Eruption	SiO_{2melt} (wt%)	P min[1] (bar)	P_{tot} (bar)	ΔNNO[2]	Log fO_2	H_2O[3] wt%	fH_2O[4] (bar)	fH_2[5] (bar)	S melt (ppm)	fS_2[6] (bar)	fS_2–Po[7] (bar)	fCO_2[8] (bar)	CO_2[9] (ppm)	C/S	H/S	H/C
Silicic to andesitic compositions																
Pinatubo	78	2150	2200	1.70	−12.98	6.0	1517	1.06	75	0.06435	–	201	67	0.32	1422	4378
Bishop	77	1800	1800	0.20	−15.46	5.4	1177	4.53	100	0.00163	0.00200	100	37	0.13	967	7188
Toba	77	2000	3000	0.39	−14.97	5.7	1529	4.49	–	–	0.00088	1817	454	2.01	1236	614
St Helens	74	1450	2200	1.18	−10.10	4.6	1334	2.03	68	0.12747	0.40000	945	329	1.76	1203	684
Krakatau	72	1100	1200	1.20	−10.83	4.0	958	1.42	200	47.3446	0.40000	80	36	0.07	356	5432
El Chichón	70	1600	2000	1.00	−12.79	5.0	1289	2.13	150	0.97917	0.07330	466	162	0.39	593	1509
Fish Canyon	77	1550	2400	1.70	−12.97	5.0	1231	0.85	–	–	1.60000	1135	351	0.95	658	696
Mt Pelée	75	1900	2000	0.60	−11.68	5.5	1593	4.48	100	–	0.09844	120	44	0.16	978	6111
Montserrat	76	1400	1400	1.00	−11.78	4.7	1143	2.04	100	0.09689	–	17	8	0.03	995	28 722
Mt Unzen	77	1050	1100	1.60	−11.19	4.0	872	0.79	50	0.03357	–	84	40	0.29	1422	4889
Taupo	76	1450	2000	0.00	−13.79	5.0	1245	6.50	44	3.7×10^{-5}	–	575	205	1.69	2020	1192
Pine Grove	76	4050	4050	0.79	−15.95	7.0	2176	3.53	60	8.8×10^{-5}	–	2973	491	2.98	2074	697
Katmai	76	1000	1000	0.25	−13.05	4.0	831	3.49	65	0.00158	0.0316	25	12	0.07	1094	16296
Santa Maria	74	1250	2000	−0.50	−13.60	4.2	1032	9.88	198	0.09139	–	920	330	0.61	380	627
Minoan	74	2150	2300	0.50	−12.75	6.0	1747	5.18	90	0.01660	–	169	55	0.22	1185	5333
Basaltic compositions																
Parent	48	5200	–	1.50	−7.80	6.0	3700	3.90	3074	7.0000	–	5101	1007	0.24	69	291
Cerro Negro	49	3000	–	1.50	−7.88	3.8	1400	1.60	800	0.0100	–	2810	881	0.80	169	211
Cerro Negro	48	3000	–	1.50	−7.88	4.2	1700	2.00	1300	0.2100	–	2071	650	0.37	115	316
Cerro Negro	55	2300	–	1.50	−7.90	4.2	1550	1.80	800	0.0100	–	927	337	0.31	187	609
Cerro Negro	52	1600	–	1.50	−7.93	3.0	1050	1.00	600	0.0045	–	865	364	0.43	172	403
Cerro Negro	51	800	–	1.50	−7.96	2.8	700	0.90	300	0.0010	–	63	32	0.08	339	4431

[1]Minimum pressure at which the chemical equilibrium condition is satisfied in a C–O–H–S fluid using the tabulated T, fO_2, fH_2O and fS_2 values.

[2]log fO_2 referenced to the fO_2 value of the Ni–NiO solid buffer (Chou 1987) at the given P and T.

[3]H_2O in melt determined by phase equilibrium, FTIR or VBD approaches. See Scaillet et al. (1998a, b) for sources, and also text.

[4]For silicic to andesitic magmas the fH_2O have been calculated using the melt H_2O content and the model of Zhang (1999). For basaltic compositions, the model of Dixon et al. (1995) has been used, with thermodynamic parameters as listed in Holloway & Blank (1994).

[5]fH_2 calculated from the dissociation equilibrium of water, using fO_2, fH_2O and thermodynamic data from Robie et al. (1978).

[6]fS_2 calculated using the empirical model of Clemente et al. (2003) for silicic to andesitic compositions or equations (2) and (3) for basaltic compositions derived from the data-set of Wallace & Carmichael (1992).

[7]fS_2 calculated using the pyrrhotite composition and the thermodynamical model of Toulmin & Barton (1964) implemented by Froese and Gunter (1976). For Mount Pelée, the pyrrhotite composition used to calculate fS_2 is from Martel (1996).

[8]For silicic to andesitic compositions, fCO_2 have been calculated using the MRK equation of state of Holloway (1977), modified by Flowers (1979), in the C–O–H–S system using listed P, T, fH_2, fH_2O and fS_2 values. When there are two fS_2 available, the calculation has been done using the one corresponding to the pyrrhotite composition. For basaltic compositions, fCO_2 is calculated using the melt CO_2 content and the model of Dixon et al. (1995).

[9]For silicic to andesitic compositions, melt CO_2 contents have been calculated using the thermodynamical model of Blank et al. (1993) and Holloway and Blank (1994). For basaltic compositions, melt CO_2 contents are similar to those measured by Roggensack et al. (1997) on Cerro Negro melt inclusions. Note that only melt inclusions where both H_2O and S were also known have been taken into account.

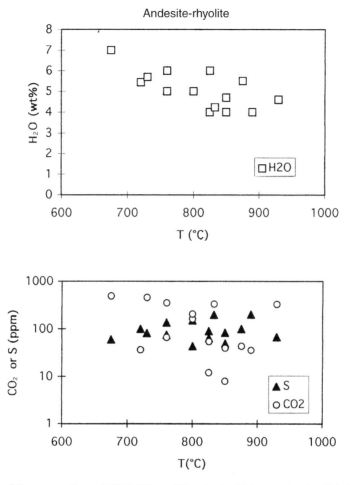

Fig. 2. Variation of the pre-eruptive melt H_2O, CO_2, and S contents with temperature in silicic to andesitic magmas. The SiO_2 content of the melts ranges from 70 up to 78 wt%.

or higher (Fig. 4) and are extracted from the mantle wedge at temperatures around 1200 °C (Pichavant *et al.* 2002*b*).

Arc basalts having MgO contents significantly lower than 7–8 wt% are widely believed to be derivative products of such primary mantle melts (e.g. Sisson & Grove 1993*a*, *b*; Pichavant *et al.* 2002*a*). In particular, high-alumina basalts (HABs), which commonly occur in convergent zones, can be derived by fractionation of these primitive, almost picritic, basalts (e.g. Sisson & Grove 1993*b*). If this scenario is of general validity, because of the largely incompatible behaviour of water in such systems, the melt H_2O contents of HABs must be substantially higher than 1–2 wt%. Both melt inclusion and phase equilibrium constraints have indeed shown that,

in many instances, the melt H_2O content of such magmas at depth is at least 4 wt%, and concentrations as high as 8–9 wt% have been reported (Fig. 4) (Sisson & Grove 1993b; Pichavant *et al.* 2002*a*). There are no direct constraints on temperature, but experimental data show that high-Mg HAB (with 7–8 wt% MgO) are produced within a temperature range 1100–1200 °C from the crystallization of primitive basalts, while the dominant low-Mg HAB type (with 3–5 wt% MgO) is, in turn, produced by crystallization of high-Mg HABs in the temperature range 1000–1100 °C (all under hydrous conditions as required by phase assemblages and compositions). Although the available data show that mafic arc melts display a negative correlation between melt H_2O content and temperature,

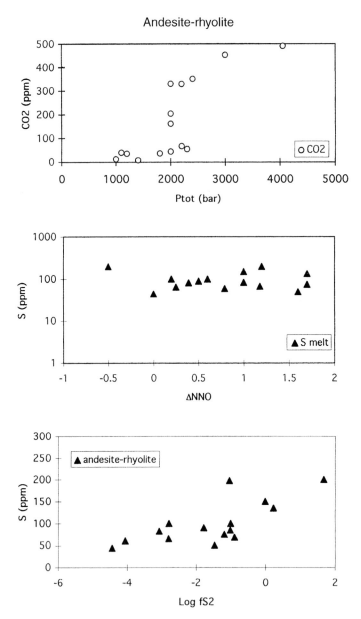

Fig. 3. Variation of pre-eruptive melt CO_2 and S contents with pressure (CO_2), fO_2 (S) and fS_2 (S) in silicic to andesitic magmas.

additional work is needed to confirm this trend. The mafic trend does not join that defined by silicic to intermediate magmas, both groups having clearly distinct fields in the T–H_2O projection (Fig. 4). The few mafic melt inclusions analysed for CO_2 (Roggensack *et al.* 1997; Sisson & Bronto 1998; Luhr 2001; Roggensack 2001) point to pre-eruptive melt CO_2 contents of up to 1000 ppm, with a corresponding H_2O content of up to 6 wt% (Table 1), in agreement with the phase equilibrium constraints detailed above. This indicates that the pressure of magma storage may be as high as 5–6 kbar (Table 1). Although the level of uncertainty is high, since these HAB are parental to most andesite–dacite arc series, they must lie in the deeper part of the plumbing system, which implies pressures in excess of 2–3 kbar, although some may cross-cut

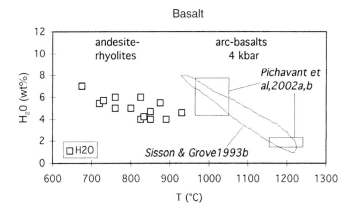

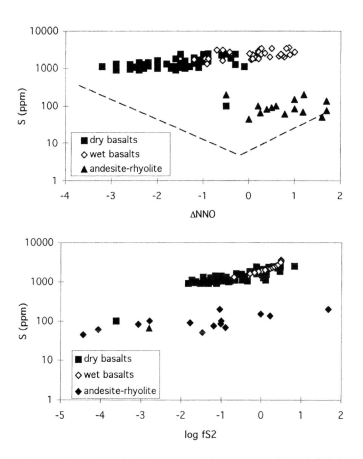

Fig. 4. Variation of pre-eruptive melt H_2O and S contents with temperature, fO_2 and fS_2 in basaltic arc magmas (wet basalts), compared to arc rhyolites–dacites–andesites (Fig. 2) and MORB type basalts (dry basalts) (Wallace & Carmichael 1992). In the T–H_2O diagram, the field corresponds to plagioclase–liquid equilibrium constraints (Sisson & Grove 1993b), while the two boxes are from phase equilibrium constraints on Lesser Antilles arc basalts (Pichavant *et al.* 2002a, b). In the S–ΔNNO plot, the dashed line represents the sulphur solubility of a dry basaltic melt equilibrated with H–C–O–S fluids at 1 bar and 1250 °C, under various fO_2 (see Carroll & Webster 1994). The sulphur fugacities of arc basalts have been calculated using equation 2 and data from Métrich & Clocchiatti (1996).

the silicic reservoirs. With respect to the redox state of these mafic magmas, there are again very few direct constraints, but experimentally produced liquid lines of descent broadly match observed calc-alkaline trends, in particular their low FeO_{tot}/MgO ratio, provided that the fO_2 is higher than NNO (Sisson & Grove 1993a; Pichavant *et al.* 2002a). Both melt and natural mineral compositions suggest that the relatively deep part of some magma reservoirs may be more oxidized than their upper part, with fO_2 in the range NNO+1 to NNO+2, or even higher (Pichavant *et al.* 2002a). Here we have adopted a constant value of NNO+1.5 (Table 1).

The sulphur content of mafic arc melts is known primarily from melt-inclusion studies (e.g. Métrich & Clocchiatti 1996; Roggensack *et al.* 1997; Sisson & Bronto 1998; Métrich *et al.* 1999; Luhr 2001). Mafic arc magmas consistently display S contents similar to or higher than those of mid-ocean ridge basalts (MORB), despite the fact that both types of magma differ widely in their redox states. In fact, the hydrous oxidized mafic arc magmas extend toward high fO_2 the trend defined by MORB melts (Fig. 4). Although there is a slight positive increase in melt S content with fO_2, the redox trend is again remarkably flat over more than 4 log units. This is in spectacular contrast to the laboratory behaviour of basaltic melt compositions undersaturated in sulphide, which shows a prominent solubility minimum around NNO (Fig. 4). As for the H_2O–T projection, there is no overlap between the mafic and silicic–andesitic data-sets in the S–log fO_2 diagram. This gap, however, is mainly due to the preference given in this work to consider only the most fractionated, i.e. with rhyolitic residual melt, magma of a given eruption. For instance, at Krakatau, andesitic melt inclusions have sulphur contents up to 1186 ppm (Mandeville *et al.* 1996).

Composition of the pre-eruptive fluids

Method

The composition of the coexisting fluid phase has been calculated using the modified Redlich–Kwong equation of state of Holloway (1977), as modified by Flowers (1979). Calculations have been performed in the C–O–H–S system, taking into account the following species: H_2O, H_2, CO_2, CO, CH_4, SO_2, H_2S, S_2 and O_2. We therefore ignore the contribution of halogens such as F and Cl, basically because the activity–composition relationships (that is, the relation between solubilities and fugacities) of these volatiles in silicate melts are still not well

established. Because C–O–H–S bearing species account for more than 95 mol.% of the species in magmatic fluids, this approximation is in most cases justified. By the phase rule we have:

$$v = 2 + C - \varphi \qquad (4)$$

where C is the number of constituents (four: C, O, H and S), φ is the number of phases (one: the fluid phase), and v is the degree of freedom (five). If pressure, temperature, and three additional intensive parameters are fixed (i.e. fH_2, fH_2O and fS_2 or fH_2O, fCO_2 and fH_2), the system is invariant and we can calculate the fluid phase composition and the fugacities of all remaining fluid species.

For silicic to andesitic magmas, calculations were performed at the listed pre-eruptive P–T values (Table 1), using as input parameters fH_2O, fH_2 and fS_2. To calculate fH_2O, we use the model of Zhang (1999), together with the melt water content, the anhydrous melt composition and the pre-eruptive P and T. The fH_2 is then calculated knowing fO_2 and fH_2O as calculated above, using the dissociation equilibrium of water (Robie *et al.* 1979). For calculating fS_2 we use the empirical model of Clemente *et al.* (2003). Also listed is the minimum pressure that is needed in order to meet the chemical equilibrium condition in the fluid phase. In other words, calculating the fluid species fugacities at a pressure lower than this minimum would result in fluid pressures being higher than total pressures. An interesting output of such calculations is the derivation of the fugacities of all C-bearing species, even though none is known. Therefore, for each eruption we can also derive the fCO_2 prevailing in the storage region, assuming the presence of a free fluid phase at depth. From this, the melt CO_2 content can be calculated using the Blank *et al.* (1993) thermodynamic model. In cases where the pre-eruptive melt CO_2 contents are also known from melt inclusion data, we thus have an independent constraint on the choice of the input pressure, which is usually the least constrained parameter.

If the fH_2O for a given melt H_2O content is close to that corresponding with H_2O saturation, then the resulting fluid phase must be very poor in C-bearing and S-bearing species. Alternatively, if the calculated fH_2O at the fixed pressure is far from that required to saturate the melt in H_2O (i.e. a melt with 3 wt% H_2O at 2 kbar, at which the saturation in H_2O requires 6–7 wt% H_2O), then the calculated fluid phase must be richer in C- or S-bearing species. Because in our calculations the S-bearing fugacities are fixed by the input fS_2, it follows that the major source of compositional variation of the calculated fluid phase concerns the proportions of C-bearing species that in turn arise from uncertainties in total pressure. Basically, for a given P and T and set of fH_2O, fH_2 and fS_2, the fugacities of C-bearing species are calculated so that the sum of partial pressures of each volatile species equals total pressure, as equilibrium demands.

A useful limiting case is when melt inclusions have CO_2 contents below the detection limit of infrared spectroscopy (e.g. Montserrat and Mount Pelée), which is in the range 10–20 ppm. Because there will always be some, even minor, amounts of CO_2 in a magmatic system, this indicates that the pressure of magma storage must be close to that defined by volatile saturation in the H–O–S system with calculated melt CO_2 (or fCO_2) being lower than the FTIR detection limit. For instance, at Mount Pelée the calculation performed at 2 kbar yields a melt CO_2 content of 120 ppm, while analysed melt inclusions yield contents below detection levels (Martel, pers. comm.). Such low CO_2 contents are attained when the total pressure approaches the minimum required for chemical equilibrium, which is around 1.9 kbar for Mount Pelée (Table 1), or only 100 bar lower than the pressure deduced from phase equilibrium considerations. In other words, the assumption of fluid saturation, coupled with thermodynamic calculations of volatile solubilities in both the melt and fluid phases, provides an extremely precise tool for determination of the minimum depth of magma storage. However, given the level of uncertainty attached to the input parameters, it is clear that the fluid compositions calculated in the way outlined above may have large uncertainties (as illustrated below for the Santa Maria 1902 eruption), which could obscure or hamper their comparison with volcanic gas data. Given the assumption that the uncertainty of each given set of parameters is similar between different eruptions, we have applied the approach to as many eruptive events as possible, including those that clearly deserve additional work but which allow us to explore the effect of a given parameter over a broader range (Santa Maria, Taupo). Because the data-set covers a considerable range in P–T–fO_2–fH_2O–fS_2 conditions, the compositional field of the calculated fluids is believed to represent the maximum possible error associated with any specific single event, although for particularly well-constrained eruptions (Pinatubo, Pelée, St Helens, Montserrat, El Chichón) the uncertainty is much smaller.

As stressed above the existing data-set on pre-eruption conditions for mafic compositions is very limited. To calculate the fluid phase composition coexisting with such melts, we have adopted a slightly different strategy from that for silicic to andesitic magmas. We have considered melt inclusion data from Cerro Negro where H_2O, CO_2 and S have been measured (Roggensack et al. 1997). From these, fH_2O, fCO_2 have been derived at a fixed temperature at 1050 °C. We use the model of Dixon et al. (1995) to calculate fH_2O from the melt H_2O content, and the model of Holloway and Blank (1994) to calculate fCO_2 from the melt CO_2 content. The fO_2 is fixed at NNO+1.5, which permits calculation of fH_2 with fH_2O as outlined above, using the dissociation equilibrium of water. Thus the input parameters are here fH_2O, fCO_2 and fH_2, in addition to T and P. In a similar approach to that used for C-bearing species in silicic to andesitic magmas, the S-bearing species fugacities can be calculated. Knowing fS_2, we can then calculate the melt S content using equation 3, and compare it with measured values. Because there are no independent constraints on the pressure of magma storage, the calculations correspond with the minimum pressure required for chemical equilibrium in the fluid.

The melt inclusions analysed at Cerro Negro record widely different fluid saturation pressures, which range from 0.8 up to 3 kbar (Table 2). Such a dispersion in pressure suggests that the various melt inclusions record magma conditions (and thus fluid conditions if fluid-saturated) last equilibrated at various levels in the upper crust (see for instance Roggensack 2001). In addition to these melt inclusion constraints, we have also calculated the fluid phase composition of a hypothetical mafic melt (termed Parent) having 6 wt% H_2O, 1000 ppm CO_2 and about 3000 ppm of dissolved S (Table 2). The melt H_2O and CO_2 contents are the highest recorded at Cerro Negro, while the S content is within the range of the S concentration of melt inclusions of the Fuego volcano (1700–5200 ppm, Rose et al. 1982; Roggensack 2001), and also similar to the maxima analysed in some alkali-rich and oxidized basaltic arc magmas by Métrich & Clocchiatti (1996). These volatile contents imply a saturation pressure of 5.2 kbar, and can be considered to model a deep and presumably less degassed stage for a mafic arc magma. The whole data-set thus spans 5 kbar in saturation pressures and is used to track the evolution of fluid phases coexisting with mafic arc magmas as they rise through the upper crust.

Silicic to andesitic melt compositions

The results of calculations are listed in Table 2. The fluid phases coexisting at depth are all water-rich with mole fractions of H_2O (XH_2O) higher

Table 2. *Pre-eruptive fluid compositions of arc magmas*

Eruption	P_{tot} (bar)	T (°C)	ΔNNO	X_{H_2O}	X_{H_2}	X_{CO_2}	X_{CH_4}	X_{CO}	X_{SO_2}	X_{H_2S}	X_{S_2}	C/S	H/S	H/C	S_{fluid} (wt%)	S_{melt} (ppm)	S_{fluid}/S_{melt}
Silicic to andesitic compositions																	
Pinatubo	2200	760	1.70	0.933	0.00018	0.063	1.5×10^{-10}	1.3×10^{-5}	0.00148	0.00708	1.3×10^{-5}	7	219	30	1.38	75	184
Bishop	1800	720	0.20	0.955	0.00095	0.044	4.3×10^{-7}	9.8×10^{-5}	4.6×10^{-6}	0.00933	3.8×10^{-7}	4	184	44	1.72	100	172
Toba	3000	730	0.39	0.724	0.00049	0.269	5.6×10^{-7}	0.00024	2.7×10^{-6}	0.00309	9.3×10^{-8}	87	471	5	0.40	–	–
St Helens	2200	930	1.18	0.708	0.00048	0.282	8.9×10^{-10}	0.00035	0.00891	0.00871	9.5×10^{-5}	16	81	5	2.17	68	319
Krakatau	1200	890	1.20	0.912	0.00074	0.062	1.8×10^{-10}	6.8×10^{-5}	0.01549	0.01820	0.00022	2	55	30	5.21	200	261
El Chichon	2000	800	1.00	0.832	0.00047	0.162	5.8×10^{-9}	0.00011	0.00059	0.01230	1.6×10^{-5}	13	131	10	1.83	150	122
Fish Canyon	2400	760	1.70	0.708	0.00014	0.263	6.6×10^{-10}	7.2×10^{-5}	0.00631	0.02818	0.00028	8	42	6	4.31	–	–
Mt Pelée	2000	875	0.60	0.933	0.00105	0.048	4.9×10^{-9}	6.9×10^{-5}	0.00068	0.01549	2.3×10^{-5}	3	117	40	2.68	100	266
Montserrat	1400	850	1.00	0.955	0.00079	0.011	1.7×10^{-10}	1.1×10^{-5}	0.00389	0.02344	0.00011	0	71	170	4.67	100	467
Mt Unzen	1100	850	1.60	0.912	0.00045	0.072	5.0×10^{-11}	4.2×10^{-5}	0.00813	0.00447	1.9×10^{-5}	6	145	25	1.99	50	398
Taupo	2000	800	0.00	0.794	0.00145	0.195	6.6×10^{-7}	0.00045	1.3×10^{-6}	0.00085	8.3×10^{-9}	229	1869	8	0.12	44	27
Pine Grove	4050	675	0.79	0.794	0.00018	0.214	2.3×10^{-7}	6×10^{-5}	3.4×10^{-7}	0.00074	4.2×10^{-9}	288	2145	7	0.10	60	17
Katmai	1000	825	0.25	0.955	0.00219	0.024	1.1×10^{-8}	4.4×10^{-5}	9.3×10^{-5}	0.00832	2.0×10^{-6}	3	229	80	1.45	65	223
Santa Maria	2000	833	-0.50	0.646	0.00251	0.295	5.2×10^{6}	0.00182	3.7×10^{-5}	0.05248	2.4×10^{-5}	6	27	5	6.35	198	321
Minoan	2300	825	0.50	0.933	0.00087	0.052	1.7×10^{-8}	5.9×10^{-5}	8.5×10^{-5}	0.00871	2.8×10^{-6}	6	214	36	1.45	90	161
Basaltic compositions																	
Parent	5200	1050	1.50	0.642	0.00027	0.308	2.7×10^{-10}	0.00037	0.04181	0.00840	0.00043	6	26	4	5.82	3074	19
Cerro Negro	3000	1050	1.50	0.517	0.00028	0.476	1.0×10^{-10}	0.00077	0.00551	0.00033	1.7×10^{-6}	82	177	2	0.61	800	8
Cerro Negro	3000	1050	1.50	0.606	0.00034	0.368	1.2×10^{-10}	0.00056	0.02290	0.00187	3.5×10^{-5}	15	49	3	2.77	1294	21
Cerro Negro	2300	1050	1.50	0.721	0.00044	0.269	6.9×10^{-11}	0.00038	0.00855	0.00055	2.6×10^{-6}	30	159	5	1.15	800	15
Cerro Negro	1600	1050	1.50	0.588	0.00042	0.399	3.8×10^{-11}	0.00068	0.01058	0.00032	1.9×10^{-6}	37	108	3	1.21	619	20
Cerro Negro	800	1050	1.50	0.911	0.00087	0.077	6.3×10^{-12}	0.00014	0.01131	0.00029	1.0×10^{-5}	24	157	24	1.81	304	59

All fluid compositions have been calculated using the MRK equation of state of Holloway (1977) modified by Flowers (1979) and P, T, fO_2, fH_2O and fS_2 values listed in Table 1.

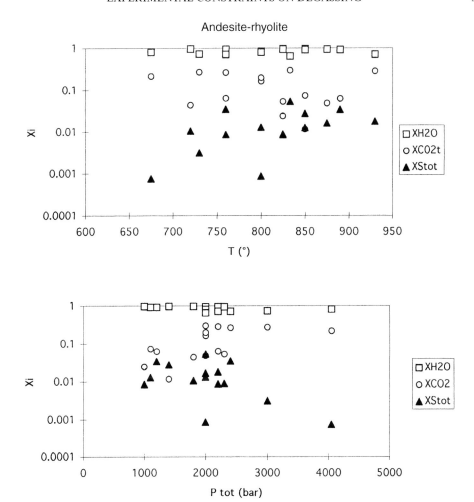

Fig. 5. Variation of the composition (X_i, mole fraction) of the pre-eruptive fluid phase with temperature and pressure in silicic to andesitic magmas.

than 0.6. Carbon dioxide is the second species in terms of molar abundance, with XCO_2 ranging between about 0.3 and 0.01. Other C-bearing species have concentrations 2 to 10 orders of magnitude lower than CO_2. In general XH_2S is the dominant S-bearing species, except in high-temperature oxidized magmas where XSO_2 equals or slightly exceeds XH_2S. The mole fraction of S_{tot} ($XH_2S + XSO_2$) approaches in some instances that of CO_2, but decreases significantly at temperatures below 750 °C (Fig. 5). Apart from this feature, the fluid composition is relatively insensitive to the pre-eruption temperature. The fluid becomes more CO_2-rich and H_2O- and S-poorer with pressure (Fig. 5), although there is a significant dispersion at around 2 kbar.

The compositional range displayed by pre-eruptive fluids can be conveniently described using C/S, H/S and H/C atomic ratios (Fig. 6). Pre-eruptive C/S ratios fall mostly in the range 1–10, while H/S ratios cluster around 100 except for some low-temperature magmas (Taupo, Pine Grove) that display higher values in both ratios due to their exceedingly low melt S contents. The fluid has H/C ratios almost always below 100 (Fig. 6). The comparison between the atomic ratios in both melt and fluid shows clearly that both phases differ significantly in terms of their H–C–S composition. Melts have lower C/S and higher H/S ratios, with the former being below 1 and the latter around 1000. Similarly, in the H/C v. C/S diagram, the two groups define a single trend but with no overlap. This contrasting

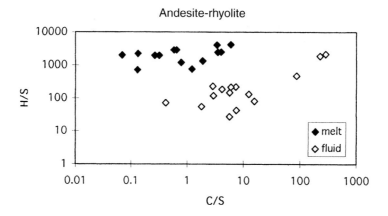

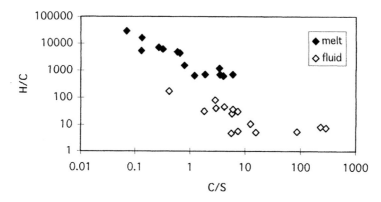

Fig. 6. Atomic compositions of pre-eruptive fluid (open symbols) and melt (closed symbols) phases in silicic to andesitic magmas.

behaviour is obviously due to the preferential partitioning of C- and S-bearing volatiles into the fluid phase. This phenomenon is best illustrated using partition coefficients for the major volatile species H_2O, CO_2 and S (Fig. 7). The three partition coefficients again show no obvious dependence on temperature, being fairly constant, with averages of $DH_2O=14$, $DS=257$ and $DCO_2=2268$. In contrast, all three partition coefficients decrease gently with pressure (Fig. 7), a trend that reflects the increasing solubilities of volatiles in silicate melts as pressure increases. When plotted against log fO_2, the S partition coefficients show no clear dependence on redox state. In particular, the partition coefficient calculated for the most reduced magma of the data-set (Santa Maria) appears to be similar to that obtained for other more oxidized magmas.

This is in contrast with the experimental findings of Scaillet *et al.* (1998*b*) that suggest that the partition coefficients of sulphur in low fO_2 dacitic magmas are in the range 1–10. A possible explanation could be that the chosen pressure for the calculation, which has been fixed arbitrarily at 2 kbar, is too low. Amphiboles in Santa Maria dacite lavas are Al_2O_3-rich (11 wt%; Rose 1987), which could be explained by crystallization under higher pressures than the assumed 2 kbar. Calculations performed at 4 kbar yield a partition coefficient of 89 (instead of 321) which illustrates the sensitivity to pressure. Another possible source of error concerns the pre-eruptive melt sulphur content. If, instead of 198 ppm, a value of 100 ppm is taken, the corresponding S partition coefficient drops from 321 to 82. Although we have considered this

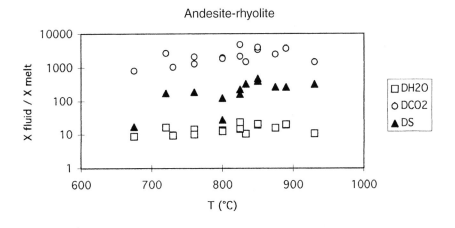

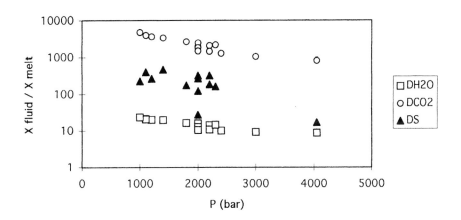

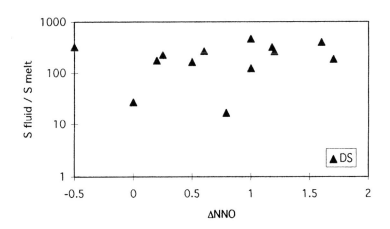

Fig. 7. Variation of the partition coefficients D of H_2O, CO_2 and S between fluid and melt (in wt%) with temperature, pressure, and fO_2 in silicic to andesitic magmas.

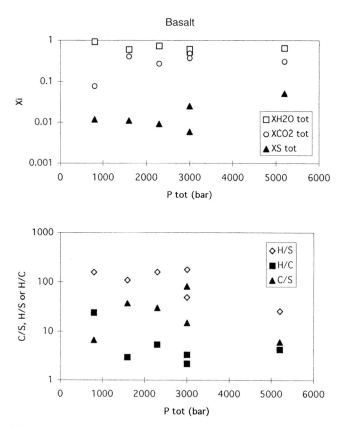

Fig. 8. Variation of the fluid phase composition with pressure (mole fraction of H_2O, CO_2, and S_{tot}, and atomic ratios) in basaltic magmas.

eruption because it allows us to extend the dataset to low fO_2 conditions, the disagreement between experimental and calculated S partition coefficients emphasizes the need for additional experimental work on the partitioning of sulphur between melt and coexisting fluid.

Mafic melt compositions

The calculated fluid phase compositions at equilibrium with mafic melt compositions are listed in Table 2. Compared with silicic to andesitic magmas, the fluid phase compositions display higher mole fractions of CO_2. Only at pressures below 1 kbar does the fluid become significantly richer in H_2O relative to CO_2 (Fig. 8). As with the silicic to andesitic group, both the fluid and melt atomic compositions differ (Fig. 9), with C/S ratios being higher than 10 for pre-eruptive fluids and lower than one for the melts, while both phases have a similar H/S ratio of around 100. A negative correlation also appears

in the C/S v. H/C projection, with fluids displaying lower (<100) H/C ratios than melts (>100) (Fig. 9). The partition coefficients show again a negative dependence on pressure but, in this case, H_2O and S display roughly similar behaviour (Fig. 10) with average partition coefficients of 24 and 13 respectively, whereas CO_2 is always the most strongly volatile species partitioned toward the fluid, with partition coefficients continuously increasing from 473 at 5.2 kbar up to 5139 at 0.8 kbar.

Comparison with volcanic gases

Having computed the equilibrium fluid composition under pre-eruptive conditions, it is now possible to evaluate how this fluid compares with volcanic gas compositions. We restrict the comparison to volcanic gases with equilibrium or collection temperatures higher than 500 °C, since these are the most likely to preserve a large magmatic component (Symonds *et al.* 1994). We

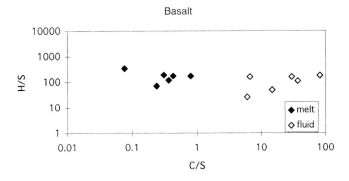

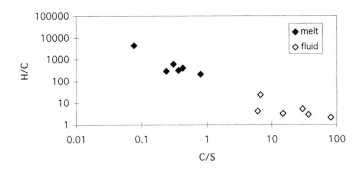

Fig. 9. Atomic compositions of pre-eruptive fluid (open symbols) and melt (closed symbols) phases in basaltic magmas.

use the recent compilation on convergent-plate volcanoes of Symonds *et al.* (1994), complemented by the additional recent data of Ohba *et al.* (1994), Fischer *et al.* (1998), Giggenbach *et al.* (2001), and Taran *et al.* (2001). Of the volcanic sites where gases have been sampled (Merapi, Unzen, St Helens, Showa–Shinzan, Usu, Kudryavi, Colima and Augustine for silicic to andesitic compositions, and Poas and Momotombo for basaltic ones) only two have their pre-eruption fluid composition constrained (Unzen and Mount St Helens). Therefore, a potential limitation of the following exercise results from the fact the volatile behaviour may change from site to site. Also (as stressed by Wallace 2001), for obvious reasons, the volcanic gases of explosive eruptions are extremely difficult to sample, whereas the estimates of pre-eruptive fluid compositions are based on tephra from the explosive phase. Nevertheless, as noted by many previous studies (e.g. Symonds *et al.* 1994), there are systematic trends in the analysed

volcanic gas compositions of arc volcanoes, which presumably are of general significance.

Silicic to andesitic melt compositions

In terms of atomic ratios, volcanic gases display rather constant C/S ratios, mostly in the range 1–30, irrespective of temperature, while their H/S ratios show a general increase as temperature decreases (Fig. 11). High-temperature volcanic gases are extremely H_2O-rich, with XH_2O higher than 0.9, often in the range 0.95–0.99 (Fig. 12). The hottest gases, however, tend to be less H_2O-rich, with XH_2O dropping to near 0.8 (Fig. 12). The comparison with pre-eruptive fluids shows only partial overlap between the two groups, basically at high temperature (Fig. 12). A substantial proportion of volcanic gases are therefore not reproduced by equilibrium pre-eruptive fluids. A similar feature can be noted with respect to S. Both groups overlap at high temperature but, again, low-temperature

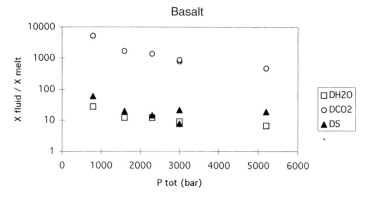

Fig. 10. Variation of the partition coefficients D of H_2O, CO_2 and S between fluid and melt (in wt%) with pressure in basaltic magmas.

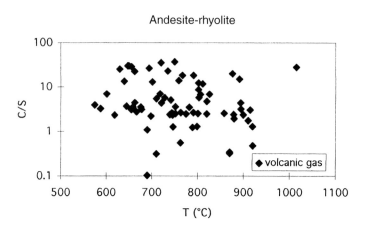

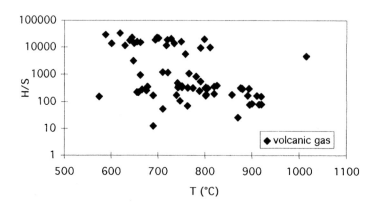

Fig. 11. Atomic compositions of volcanic gases v. temperature in silicic to andesitic volcanoes. See text for data sources.

Andesite-rhyolite

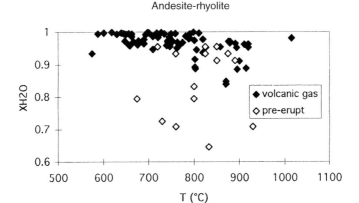

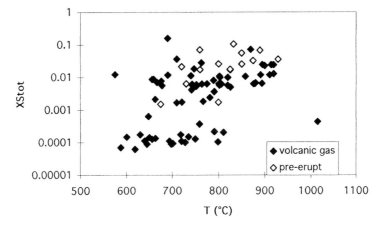

Fig. 12. Comparison of the mole fractions of H_2O and S_{tot} in volcanic gases (closed symbols) and pre-eruptive fluids (open symbols) v. temperature in silicic to andesitic volcanoes. See text for data sources.

volcanic gases tend to be much less S-rich than pre-eruptive ones (Fig. 12). Therefore, although both volcanic gas and pre-eruptive fluid display significant overlap in terms of their atomic compositions, the former show a conspicuous H_2O-enrichment trend, with H/C and H/S ratios notably higher than those calculated for the fluid at storage conditions (Fig. 13).

Mafic melt compositions

The compositional difference between pre-eruptive fluids and volcanic gases is even more apparent in basaltic systems, with no overlap between the two groups (Fig. 14). Although this gap could be due to the restricted number of gas analyses available, such a feature is due to the CO_2-rich character of pre-eruptive fluids in mafic arc magmas relative to those coexisting with more

acid magmas (Table 2). High CO_2 contents shift C/S and H/C ratios to higher and lower values, respectively, relative to the coexisting melt.

The origin of the difference

There are two end-member cases for modelling the degassing processes that affect a magma at depth or during its ascent towards the surface. Degassing can occur with continuous separation of each increment of fluid phase generated from the magma and such that open system degassing takes place. Alternatively, degassing can occur *in situ*, in a closed system, with no separation between the degassing melt and the fluid phase, until perhaps the very late stage of the process, such as during an explosive eruptive event (see Villemant *et al.*, 2003, Chapter 5). Hydrogen isotope studies have shown that both types of

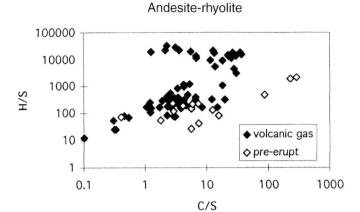

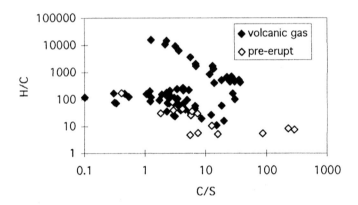

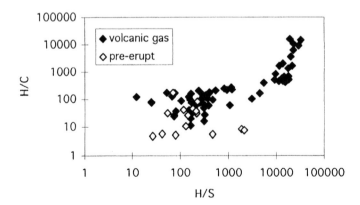

Fig. 13. Atomic composition of volcanic gases (closed symbols) and pre-eruptive fluids (open symbols) in silicic to andesitic magmas. See text for data sources.

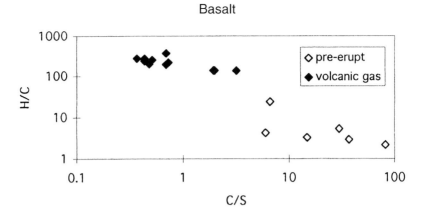

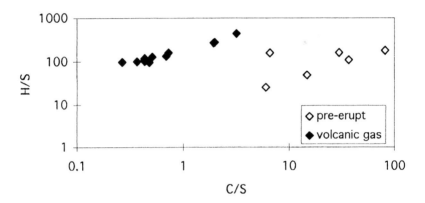

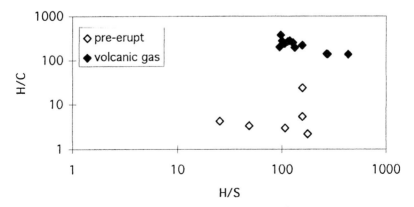

Fig. 14. Atomic composition of volcanic gases (closed symbols) and pre-eruptive fluids (open symbols) in basaltic magmas.

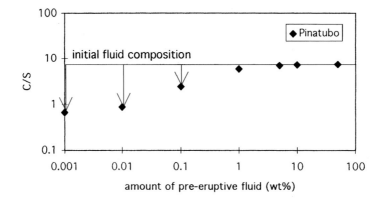

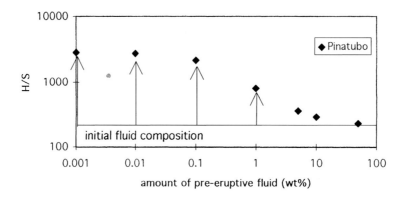

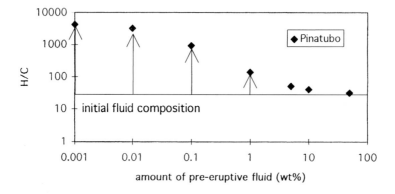

Fig. 15. Evolution of C/S, H/S and H/C atomic ratios of volcanic gases v. the amount of pre-eruptive fluids for the Pinatubo magma, calculated assuming closed-system behaviour. The horizontal lines represent the atomic ratio of the pre-eruptive fluid. Vertical arrows represent the change in atomic ratio followed by the exsolving fluid upon decompression to near-surface conditions, calculated for amounts of pre-eruptive fluid varying between 50 and 0. 001 wt%. See text for additional explanations. Magmas having amounts of pre-eruptive fluid lower than 1 wt% yield atmospheric fluid compositions significantly different from that in the deep reservoir.

degassing occur in silicic magmas (Taylor *et al.* 1983). The contrasted atomic compositions of both fluid and melt phases at depth offer a simple test for the closed-system scenario. In such a case, the final or exit fluid composition will depend on the storage conditions that fix both the compositions of melt and fluid, if any, and on the respective mass proportions of the two phases, according to the following simple mass-balance relations:

$$H_2O_{tot}=aH_2O_{melt}+bH_2O_{fluid} \qquad (5)$$

$$CO_{2tot}=aCO_{2\ melt}+bCO_{2\ fluid} \qquad (6)$$

$$SO_{2tot}=aSO_{2melt}+bSO_{2\ fluid} \qquad (7)$$

with a and b being the mass fractions of the melt and fluid phases (taking into account the crystal content of the magma), and H_2O_{melt} and H_2O_{fluid} are the mass fractions of H_2O in melt and fluid, respectively (the same for CO_2 and SO_2). For the fluid we assume that $H_2O_{fluid}=H_2O+H_2$, $CO_{2\ fluid}=CO_2+CO+CH_4$ and $SO_{2\ fluid}=SO_2+H_2S+S_2$.

Calculations performed on the 1991 Pinatubo eruption illustrate the general evolution of C/S, H/S and H/C fluid atomic ratios following complete degassing (that is the final pressure is 1 bar, at which the H_2O, CO_2 and S solubilities are assumed to be close to zero), for a magma starting with different initial, i.e. pre-eruptive, amounts of fluid phase (Fig. 15). Physically, the calculations reproduce the hypothetical case of a decompressing melt+crystals+fluid mixture in which the melt continuously exsolves its C–O–H–S volatiles into a coexisting fluid phase that remains in contact with the magma until near-surface conditions are reached. As shown for the Pinatubo case, all three ratios undergo dramatic changes during decompression that are not linearly correlated with the initial amount of the fluid phase. The final C/S ratio of the fluid decreases by an order of magnitude if the magma at depth contains significantly less than 1 wt% (i.e. 0.1 wt%) of coexisting fluid phase. In contrast, pre-eruptive amounts of fluid higher than 1 wt% produce a marginal effect on the C/S ratio of the final fluid. In other words, as soon as the magma contains more than 1 wt% pre-eruptive fluid, the final fluid composition (assuming closed-system degassing) is essentially buffered by the starting composition of the fluid phase. The other atomic ratios display similar behaviour, yet the buffered condition is reached for higher amounts of pre-eruptive fluids, closer to 10 wt% (Fig. 15). The results of these simulations are shown for the evolution of the C/S ratio for three well-known eruptions in addition to Pinatubo (Bishop, St Helens and El Chichón). All four systems show the similar pattern of rapid increase in C/S for the first increments of pre-eruptive fluid, with the small inter-sample variations depending on the storage conditions and on the amount of crystallization, which in turn control the mass contribution of melt degassing to the fluid. Therefore, for andesitic to silicic magmas, a pre-eruptive fluid-saturated magma seems to be a necessary condition to reproduce the observed C/S ratios of volcanic gases (Fig. 11), if closed-system degassing holds.

Table 3 lists the results obtained for the silicic

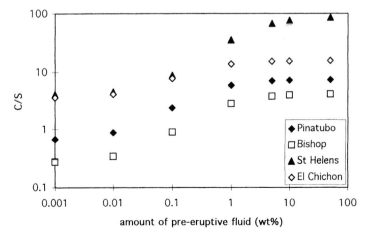

Fig. 16. Evolution of the C/S atomic ratios of volcanic gases v. the amount of pre-eruptive fluids for the Pinatubo, Bishop, St Helens and El Chichón magmas, calculated assuming closed-system behaviour.

Table 3. *Calculated volcanic gas compositions of arc volcanoes*

	$X\text{H}_2\text{O}_{tot}$	$X\text{CO}_{2tot}$	$X\text{S}_{tot}$	C/S	H/S	H/C
Silicic to andesitic compositions, 1 wt% pre-eruptive fluid						
Pinatubo	0.95672	0.03788	0.00541	7	355	51
Bishop	0.97250	0.02179	0.00571	4	343	90
Toba	0.87423	0.12393	0.00184	67	950	14
St Helens	0.83241	0.15742	0.01033	15	162	11
Krakatau	0.94546	0.03447	0.02044	2	94	55
El Chichón	0.88381	0.10714	0.00909	12	196	17
Fish Canyon	0.83465	0.14560	0.02020	7	84	12
Mt Pelée	0.95853	0.03075	0.01076	3	180	63
Montserrat	0.97455	0.00742	0.01823	0	109	267
Mt Unzen	0.93999	0.05095	0.00910	6	207	37
Crater Lake	0.80306	0.13361	0.06819	2	25	13
Taupo	0.90728	0.09206	0.00066	139	2738	20
Pine Grove	0.90089	0.09852	0.00060	165	3019	18
Katmai	0.98117	0.01367	0.00517	3	381	144
Santa Maria	0.77826	0.18775	0.03403	6	48	9
Minoan	0.97020	0.02518	0.00463	5	421	77
Basaltic compositions, 0.1 wt% pre-eruptive fluid						
Parent	0.96223	0.00971	0.02806	0.3	69	198
Cerro Negro	0.96124	0.01608	0.02267	0.7	85	120
Cerro Negro	0.95560	0.01122	0.03318	0.3	58	170
Cerro Negro	0.97176	0.00752	0.02072	0.4	94	258
Cerro Negro	0.96499	0.01267	0.02235	0.6	86	152
Cerro Negro	0.98569	0.00267	0.01165	0.2	169	740

to andesitic magma data-set with 1 wt% fluid under pre-eruptive conditions. In Figure 17, the results of the calculations performed for all magmas coexisting either with 1 wt% or 0.001 wt% fluid in the storage region are shown on a H/S v. H/C diagram. Clearly, again, the presence of 1 wt% fluid helps bridge the gap between volcanic gas compositions and the pre-eruptive compositions. It is also apparent that if the magmas were not fluid-saturated – a situation that is approached with the 0.001 wt% fluid condition, then the final fluid phase would lie clearly outside the field of observations. Yet, there is still a significant portion of the field delimited by natural gases – the H/C- and H/S-rich apex of the domain – that is not reproduced by the simulation. As shown previously, most of these are H_2O-rich, S-poor and low-temperature gases. Possible explanations for the origin of these H_2O-rich and S-poor fluids are that: (1) the colder volcanic gases have been contaminated by meteoric waters; (2) precipitation of C- and S-bearing minerals has altered the original magmatic fluid during cooling; (3) degassing cannot be modelled as a closed system; or (4) the process of segregation of fluid from melt is not an equilibrium one – such that kinetic factors control the composition of the fluid. In particular, it is well known that both S- and C-

bearing volatiles are slow-diffusing species in silicate melts as compared with H_2O which has a diffusivity many orders of magnitude higher than those of S and CO_2 (Watson 1994). This could lead to a selective enrichment in H over S and C during ascent-controlled degassing.

The same simulations have been performed for the mafic data-set and are displayed in Figure 17. The results of calculations for a magma having 0.1 wt% fluid at depth are listed in Table 3. In contrast to silicic–andesitic systems, the simulation nearly perfectly reproduces the natural gas compositional field, and it does so when the magmas coexist with 0.1–1 wt% fluid at depth. Interestingly, the amount of pre-eruptive fluid needed to reproduce the volcanic gas composition is roughly pressure-dependent –being higher at low pressure. For instance, the melt inclusion with an entrapment pressure of 800 bar requires 1 wt% fluid to join the volcanic gas field, while that entrapped at 5.2 kbar needs only 0.1 wt%. To a first approximation, this is in agreement with the fact that, as a volatile-bearing magma decompresses as a closed system, the amount of coexisting fluid must increase. Calculation in the simple basalt–H_2O system shows that at 5 kbar a basaltic magma at H_2O–saturation has about 8.6 wt% H_2O in solution (see Dixon *et al.* 1995). If it

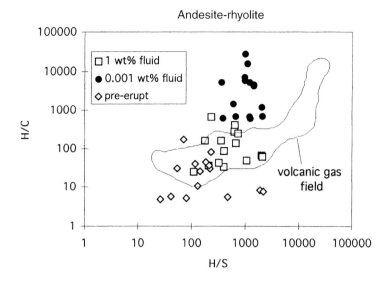

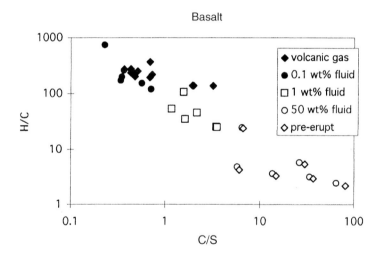

Fig. 17. H/S v. H/C plot showing the effect of the amount of pre-eruptive fluid on the final volcanic gas composition, calculated assuming closed-system behaviour. The calculations are shown for 1 and 0.001 wt% fluid (silicic to andesitic magmas) and 50, 1 and 0.1 wt% fluid (basaltic magmas).

decompresses to 800 bar, where the solubility is only 2.9 wt% H_2O, then it will coexist with 6 wt% fluid, in substantial agreement with our estimate.

Discussion and conclusions

The comparison between calculated fluid phase chemistries under pre-eruptive conditions and volcanic gases shows overall good agreement.

This suggests that thermodynamic models of volatile solubilities in silicic to mafic melts and their coexisting fluids are reasonably well calibrated, with good predictive capabilities at $P–T$ conditions relevant to arc-magma genesis and evolution. It seems clear that silicic to andesitic magmas coexist with fluid at depth, in agreement with a number of independent lines of evidence (Anderson *et al.* 1989; Westrich & Gerlach 1992; Wallace *et al.* 1995; Gerlach *et al.* 1996; Scaillet *et al.* 1998*b*; Wallace 2001). The overlap between pre-eruptive fluid and volcanic gas compositions indicates that, in some instances, this pre-eruptive fluid may escape the reservoir and reach the surface unaltered. Yet, most volcanic gas compositions require a contribution from melt degassing at low pressure. For this to be possible, a physical contact between melt and fluid, or absence of significant segregation, is required over a significant portion of the ascent path. One possible reason lies in the viscous character of the residual melt of most silicic to andesitic magmas, which significantly inhibits fluid fractionation, especially in situations where magma ascent takes place over short time-scales. There is also a population of volcanic gases that is not reproduced by the simple calculations performed in the present paper. The fact that they are, in general, the colder gases, with equilibrium temperatures below the solidus temperatures of any arc magmas (<650 °C), suggests that they may have been significantly modified before collection, such as through interaction with low-temperature hydrothermal fluids. Precipitation of S-bearing minerals during cooling may be an obvious alternative or additional mechanism to remove sulphur from the fluid.

For mafic melt compositions, the amount of pre-eruptive fluid required to reproduce volcanic gases is smaller than for silicic compositions, which is in qualitative agreement with the highly differentiated nature of andesitic to silicic magmas, but clearly there is a need for additional data concerning the volatile contents of mafic arc magmas. The available data point to the existence of two separate trends in the T–H_2O diagram (Fig. 4), which need further discussion. The fact that the high-temperature end of the silicic–andesite trend plots significantly below the low-temperature end of the mafic trend merely reflects the fact that the studied basalt magmas were stored at higher pressures, and thus could reach higher water contents than the more silicic ones. Andesites produced by fractionation of hydrous basalts at around 4 kbar, such as in the Lesser Antilles arc (Pichavant *et al.* 2002*a*), must be fluid-saturated during nearly all their evolution, since their parental basaltic magma starts crystallizing with H_2O contents, at 4 kbar, of 6–8 wt% (Pichavant *et al.* 2002*a*), i.e. close to or even higher than the solubility value at 2–3 kbar. Still, near-liquidus and H_2O-rich andesitic magmas (i.e. at 950 °C and with 6 wt% H_2O) have yet to be sampled. As for H_2O-rich basalts, this absence could indicate that those magmas cannot erupt without massive, decompression-driven, crystallization. In fact, heavily crystallized andesitic magmas near H_2O-saturation seem more common, as illustrated by the Mount Pelée and Montserrat eruptions. In such cases, the magma column feeding the volcano is likely to be fluid-saturated over a substantial depth interval. The evidence summarized above suggests that magma degassing may start at pressures as high as 4 kbar, and not just very late at shallow levels during eruption or within the roof of an upper-crustal reservoir, as was commonly believed.

How this continuous degassing may affect the fluid chemistry and the residual melt still remains to be quantitatively evaluated. However, this is not to say that arc-basalts inevitably stall and fractionate at around 4 kbar, and that all andesite magmas are fluid-saturated. There are certainly many instances, especially during the less-mature stage of arc development where the crust is thinned, in which basalt storage occurs at 2 kbar, or at even lower pressures. Were analytical or experimental data available for such occurrences, they would presumably extend the silicic–andesitic trend toward higher temperatures (see Fig. 4). Similarly, there are andesite occurrences whose pre-eruptive melt water content seems to deviate significantly from saturation values (i.e. the andesite at Katmai if the storage pressure is 2 kbar). This suggests that the degree of H_2O-enrichment in arc magmas, whether mafic or felsic, may vary greatly for both intra- and inter-arc situations.

As previously noted, the weak dependence of S melt contents on fO_2 suggests that fO_2 exerts little control on the sulphur solubility in natural magmas. While this might appear surprising, it mainly reflects the fact that the fS_2 values displayed by natural magmas are in the range where fO_2 control on S solubility is minor (Fig. 1). Maintaining low fS_2 in natural magmas can be achieved through two main mechanisms:

1. Under reduced conditions, the S solubility is controlled via sulphide–melt equilibrium, as discussed by Wallace and Carmichael (1992). The great affinity between iron and sulphur under reduced conditions is a well-established feature, as indicated by the strong positive correlation between the two elements. Despite this affinity, reduced basaltic magmas cannot dissolve large amounts of S, because they soon develop an immiscible sulphide melt which prevents the magma from reaching excessive values, say several bars, of fS_2. Experimental data and theoretical modelling show that natural, sulphide-saturated, basaltic melts have fS_2 generally below 1 bar, corresponding with S melt contents in the order of 1300 ppm (Wallace & Carmichael 1992), apart from some Fe–Ti-rich basalts, which

can have up to 2500 ppm dissolved sulphur (P. Wallace, pers. comm.).

2. Under oxidizing conditions, such as in arc magmas, fluid–melt equilibrium can be an additional controlling factor of the S concentration of the melt, along with solid–melt or melt–melt equilibria. If the amount of pre-eruptive fluid in arc magmas is in the range 1–6 wt% (e.g. Wallace 2001), then most of their sulphur content will be stored in the fluid phase. Indeed, calculated sulphur contents of pre-eruptive fluids are mostly in the range 1–6 wt% S (Table 2), except for low-temperature and reduced silicic magmas. Ignoring the potential contribution of pyrrhotite and anhydrite, a magma with 5 wt% fluid that is half crystallized, with a residual melt S content of 100 ppm, has more than 98.4% of its bulk sulphur stored in the fluid if the latter contains 6 wt% S (91.4% for 1 wt% S in fluid). The fluid phase may therefore effectively buffer the S content of the melt of arc magmas, at least for silicic compositions. It should not be concluded, however, that fO_2 does not affect the sulphur behaviour at all. Clearly, fO_2 will fix the S^{2-}/S^{6+} ratio (Carroll & Webster 1994), but the bulk S content of the melt appears to be controlled by the coexisting fluid phase, otherwise natural magmas should display a pronounced depletion in their S content in the fO_2 range NNO – NNO+1, a trend not observed.

From the standpoint of experimental petrology, the present study shows that additional work is needed for the accurate determination of partition coefficients of S using an experimental procedure where both the fluid and melt have their S contents determined. The determination of the relationships between fS_2 and S in hydrous basaltic melts is another important task if rigorous modelling of the evolution of the fluid phase in hydrous mafic systems is to be attempted. The dependence on P_{tot} of S solubility in both mafic and silicic melts also remains to be evaluated. Finally, in recent years, much effort has been put into measuring Cl solubility and partitioning in felsic to mafic melts (Carroll & Webster 1994; Webster *et al.* 1999), the reason being that many arc magmas display significant Cl concentrations. Studies aimed at quantifying the relationships between $fHCl$ and Cl solubility would therefore be highly valuable.

This paper greatly benefited from helpful reviews of P. Wallace and C. Mandeville, and from the editorial intervention of C. Oppenheimer. J. Lowenstern kindly supplied critical information on pre-eruptive conditions for the Pine Grove eruption. Numerous discussions with F. Costa helped to improve the manuscript.

References

ANDERSON, A. T., NEWMAN, S., WILLIAMS, S. N., DRUITT, T. H., SKIRIUS, C. & STOLPER, E. 1989. H_2O, CO_2, Cl gas in Plinian and ash-flow Bishop rhyolite. *Geology*, **17**, 221–225.

BLAKE, S. 2003. Correlations between eruption magnitude, SO_2 yield and surface cooling. *In:* OPPENHEIMER, C., PYLE, D.M. & BARCLAY, J. (eds) *Volcanic Degassing.* Geological Society, London, Special Publications, **213**, 371–380.

BLANK, J. G., STOLPER, E. M., & CARROLL, M. R. 1993. Solubilities of carbon dioxide and water in rhyolitic melts. *Earth and Planetary Science Letters,* **119**, 27–36.

CARROLL, M. R. & WEBSTER, J. D. 1994. Solubilities of sulfur, noble gases, nitrogen, chlorine and fluorine in magmas. *In:* CARROLL, M. R. & HOLLOWAY, J. R. (eds) *Volatiles in Magmas*, Reviews in Mineralogy, **30**, 231–279.

CHOU, I. M. 1987. Oxygen buffer and hydrogen sensor technique at elevated pressures and temperatures. *In:* BARNES, H. L. & ULMER, G. C. (eds) *Hydrothermal Experimental Techniques.* John Wiley, New York, 61–99.

CLEMENTE, B., SCAILLET, B. & PICHAVANT, M. 2003. The solubility of sulphur in rhyolite. *Journal of Petrology* (in press).

COOMBS, M. L. & GARDNER, J. E. 2001. Shallow-storage conditions for the rhyolite of the 1912 eruption at Novarupta, Alaska. *Geology,* **29**, 775–778.

COTTRELL, E., GARDNER, J. & RUTHERFORD, M. J. 1999. Petrologic and experimental evidence for the movement and heating of the pre-eruptive Minoan rhyodacite (Santorini, Greece). *Contributions to Mineralogy and Petrology,* **135**, 315–331.

DIXON, J. E., STOLPER, E. M. & HOLLOWAY, J. R. 1995. An experimental study of water and carbon dioxide solubilities in mid-ocean ridge basaltic liquids. Part I: calibration and solubility models. *Journal of Petrology,* **36**, 1607–1631.

FISCHER, T. P., MORRISSEY, M. M., CALVACHE, M. L., DIEGO GOMEZ, M., ROBERTO TORRES, C., STIX, J. & WILLIAMS, S. N. 1994. Correlations between SO_2 flux and long period seismicity at Galeras volcano. *Nature* **368**, 135–137.

FISCHER, T. P., GIGGENBACH, W. F., SANO, S. & WILLIAMS, S. N. 1998. Fluxes and sources of volatiles discharged from Kudryavy, a subduction zone volcano, Kurile Islands. *Earth and Planetary Science Letters,* **160**, 81–96.

FLOWERS, G. C. 1979. Correction of Holloway's (1977) adaptation of the Modified Redlich–Kwong equation of state for calculation of the fugacities of molecular species in supercritical fluids of geologic interest. *Contributions to Mineralogy and Petrology,* **69**, 315–318.

FROESE, E. & GUNTER, A. E. 1976. A note on the pyrrhotite–sulfur vapor equilibrium. *Economic Geology,* **71**, 1589–1594.

GERLACH, T. M., WESTRICH, H. R. & SYMONDS, R. B. 1996. Pre-eruption vapor in magma of the climactic Mount Pinatubo eruption: source of the giant stratospheric sulfur dioxide cloud. *In:* NEWHALL, C. G. & PUNONGBAYAN, R. S. (eds) *Fire and Mud. Eruptions and Lahars of Mount Pinatubo, Philippines,* University of Washington Press, 415–434.

GIGGENBACH, W. F., TEDESCO, D. ET AL. 2001. Evaluation of results from the fourth and fifth IAVCEI field workshops on volcanic gases, Vulcano island, Italy and Java, Indonesia. *Journal of Volcanology and Geothermal Research,* **108,** 157–172.

HOLLOWAY, J. R. 1977. Fugacity and activity of molecular species in supercritical fluids. In: FRASER, D. (ed.) *Thermodynamics in Geology.* Riedel, Dordrecht, 161–181.

HOLLOWAY, J. R. & BLANK, J. 1994. Applications of experimental results to C–O–H species in natural melts. *In:* CARROLL, M. R. & HOLLOWAY, J. R. (eds) *Volatiles in Magmas,* Reviews in Mineralogy, **30,** 187–230.

JOHNSON, M. C. & RUTHERFORD, M. J. 1989. Experimentally determined conditions in the Fish Canyon Tuff, Colorado, magma chamber. *Journal of Petrology,* **30,** 711–737.

JOHNSON, M. C., ANDERSON, A. T. & RUTHERFORD, M. 1994. Pre-eruptive volatile contents of magmas. *In:* CARROLL, M. R. & HOLLOWAY, J. R. (eds), *Volatiles in Magmas,* Reviews in Mineralogy, **30,** 281–330.

KEPPLER, H. 1999. Experimental evidence for the source of excess sulfur in explosive volcanic eruptions. *Science* **284,** 1652–1654.

LUHR, J. F. 1990. Experimental phase relations of water- and sulfur-saturated arc magmas and the 1982 eruptions of El Chichón volcano. *Journal of Petrology,* **31,** 1071–1114.

LUHR, J. F. 2001. Glass inclusions and melt volatile contents at Paricutin volcano, Mexico. *Contributions to Mineralogy and Petrology* **142,** 261–283.

MCGONIGLE, A. & OPPENHEIMER, C. 2003. Optical sensing of volcanic gas and aerosol emissions. *In:* OPPENHEIMER, C., PYLE, D. M. & BARCLAY, J. (eds) *Volcanic Degassing.* Geological Society, London, Special Publications, **213,** 149–168.

MANDEVILLE, C. W., CAREY, S. & SIGURDSSON, H. 1996. Magma mixing, fractional crystallisation and volatile degassing during the 1883 eruption of Krakatau volcano, Indonesia. *Journal of Volcanology and Geothermal Research,* **74,** 243–274.

MARTEL, C. 1996. Conditions pré-éruptives et dégazage des magmas andésitiques de la Montagne Pelée (Martinique): étude pétrologique et expérimentale. Unpublished PhD thesis, Université d'Orléans, 299 pp.

MARTEL, C., PICHAVANT, M., BOURDIER, J. L, TRAINEAU, H., HOLTZ, F. & SCAILLET, B. 1998. Magma storage conditions and control of eruption regime in silicic volcanoes: experimental evidence from Mt. Pelée. *Earth and Planetary Science Letters,* **156,** 89–99.

MARTEL, C., PICHAVANT, M., HOLTZ, F., SCAILLET, B., BOURDIER, J. L & TRAINEAU, H. 1999. Effects of

fO$_2$ and H$_2$O on andesite phase relations between 2 and 4 kbar. *Journal of Geophysical Research,* **104,** 29 453–29 470.

MÉTRICH, N. & CLOCCHIATTI, R. 1996. Sulfur abundance and its speciation in oxidized alkaline melts. *Geochimica et Cosmochimica Acta,* **60,** 4151–4160.

MÉTRICH, N., SCHIANO, P., CLOCCHIATTI, R. & MAURY, R. C. 1999. Transfer of sulfur in subduction settings: an example from Batan Island (Luzon volcanic arc, Philippines). *Earth and Planetary Science Letters,* **167,** 1–14.

MICHAUD, V., CLOCCHIATTI, R. & SBRANA, S. 2000. The Minoan and post-Minoan eruptions, Santorini (Greece), in the light of melt inclusions: chlorine and sulphur behaviour. *Journal of Volcanology and Geothermal Research,* **99,** 195–214.

MORETTI, R., PAPALE, P. & OTTONELLO, G. 2003, A model for the saturation of C–O–H–S fluids in silicate melts. *In:* OPPENHEIMER, C., PYLE, D.M. & BARCLAY, J. (eds) *Volcanic Degassing.* Geological Society, London, Special Publications, **213,** 81–101.

OHBA, T., HIRABAYASHI, J. & YOSHIDA, M. 1994. Equilibrium temperature and redox state of volcanic gas at Unzen volcano, Japan. *Journal of Volcanology and Geothermal Research,* **60,** 263–272.

PALAIS, J. & SIGURDSSON, H. 1989. Petrologic evidence of volatile emissions from major historic and prehistoric volcanic eruptions. *In:* BERGER, A. L., DICKINSON, R. E. & KIDSON, J. (eds) *Understanding Climate Change,* AGU, Washington D.C., 31–53.

PICHAVANT, M., MARTEL, C., BOURDIER, J. L. & SCAILLET, B. 2002a. Physical conditions, structure and dynamics of a zoned magma chamber: Mt. Pelée (Martinique, Lesser Antilles arc). *Journal of Geophysical Research,* **107(B5),** 101029/2001JB-000315.

PICHAVANT, M., MYSEN, B. O. & MACDONALD, R. 2002b. Origin and H$_2$O content of high-MgO magmas in island arc settings: an experimental study of a primitive calc-alkaline basalt from St Vincent, Lesser Antilles Arc. *Geochimica et Cosmochimica Acta,* **66,** 2193–2209.

ROBIE, R. A., HEMINGWAY, B. S. & FISHER, J. R. 1979. *Thermodynamic Properties of Minerals and Related Substances at 298.15 K and 1 bar (10^5 pascals) Pressure and at Higher Temperature.* US Geological Survey Bulletin, **1452,** 456 pp.

ROBOCK, A. 2000. Volcanic eruptions and climate. *Reviews of Geophysics,* **38,** 191–219.

ROGGENSACK, K. 2001. Unraveling the 1974 eruption of Fuego volcano (Guatemala) with small crystals and their young melt inclusions. *Geology,* **29,** 911–914.

ROGGENSACK, K., HERVIG, R. L., MCKNIGHT, S. B. & WILLIAMS, S. N. 1997. Explosive basaltic volcanism from Cerro Negro volcano: influence of volatiles on eruptive style. *Science,* **277,** 1639–1642.

ROSE, W. I. 1987. Santa Maria, Guatemala: bimodal soda-rich calc-alkalic stratovolcano. *Journal of Volcanology and Geothermal Research,* **33,** 109–129.

ROSE, W. I., STOIBER, R. E. & MALINCONICO, L. L. 1982. Eruptive gas compositions and fluxes of explosive volcanoes: budget of S and Cl emitted from Fuego volcano, Guatemala. In: Thorpe, R. S. (ed.) Andesites, John Wiley, London, 669–676.

RUTHERFORD, M. J., & DEVINE, J. D. 1988. The May 18, 1980 eruption of Mount St. Helens: 3, Stability and chemistry of amphibole in the magma chamber. Journal of Geophysical Research, 93, 949–959.

RUTHERFORD, M. J. & DEVINE, J. D. 1996. Pre-eruption pressure–temperature conditions and volatiles in the 1991 Mount Pinatubo magma. In: NEWHALL, C. G. & PUNONGBAYAN, R. S. (eds) Fire and Mud. Eruptions and Lahars of Mount Pinatubo, Philippines, University of Washington Press, 751–766.

RUTHERFORD, M. J. & HILL, P. M. 1993. Magma ascent rates from amphibole breakdown: an experimental study applied to the 1980–1986 Mount St. Helens eruptions. Journal of Geophysical Research, 98, 19 667–19 685.

RUTHERFORD, M. J., SIGURDSSON, H. & CAREY, S. 1985. The May 18, 1980 eruption of Mount St. Helens: 1, Melt composition and experimental phase equilibria. Journal of Geophysical Research, 90, 2929–2947.

SATO, H., NAKADA, S., FUJII, T., NAKAMURA, M. & SUZUKI-KAMATA, K. 1999. Groundmass pargasite in the 1991–1995 dacite of Unzen volcano: phase stability experiments and volcanological implications. Journal of Volcanology and Geothermal Research, 89, 197–212.

SCAILLET, B. & EVANS, B. W. 1999. The June 15, 1991 eruption of Mount Pinatubo. I. Phase equilibria and pre-eruption P–T–fO_2–fH_2O conditions of the dacite magma. Journal of Petrology, 40, 381–411.

SCAILLET, B. & MACDONALD, R. 2001. Phase relations of peralkaline silicic magmas and petrogenetic implications. Journal of Petrology, 42, 825–845.

SCAILLET, B., HOLTZ, F. & PICHAVANT, M. 1998a. Phase equilibrium constraints on the viscosity of silicic magmas 1. Volcanic–plutonic comparison. Journal of Geophysical Research, 103, 27 257–27 266.

SCAILLET, B., CLEMENTE, B., EVANS, B. W. & PICHAVANT, M. 1998b. Redox control of sulfur degassing in silicic magmas. Journal of Geophysical Research, 103, 23 937–23 949.

SILVER, L. A. & STOLPER, E. 1985. A thermodynamic model for hydrous silicate melts. Journal of Geology, 93, 161–178.

SISSON, T. W. & BRONTO, S. 1998. Evidence for pressure–release melting beneath magmatic arcs from basalts at Galunggung, Indonesia. Nature, 391, 883–886.

SISSON, T. W. & GROVE, T. L. 1993a. Experimental investigations of the role of H_2O in calc-alkaline differentiation and subduction zone magmatism. Contributions to Mineralogy and Petrology 113, 143–166.

SISSON, T. W. & GROVE, T. L. 1993b. Temperatures and H_2O contents of low-MgO high alumina basalts. Contributions to Mineralogy and Petrology 113, 167–184.

SISSON, T. W. & LAYNE, G. D. 1993. H_2O in basaltic and basaltic andesite glass inclusions from four subduction-related volcanoes. Earth and Planetary Science Letters, 117, 619–635.

SOBOLEV, A. V. & CHAUSSIDON, M. 1996. H_2O concentrations in primary melts from supra-subduction zones and mid-ocean ridges: implications for H_2O storage and recycling in the mantle. Earth and Planetary Science Letters, 137, 45–55.

SYMONDS, R. B., ROSE, W. I., BLUTH, G. J. S. & GERLACH, T. M. 1994. Volcanic gas studies: methods, results, and applications. In: CARROLL, M. R. & HOLLOWAY, J. R. (eds) Volatiles in Magmas, Reviews in Mineralogy, 30, 1–60.

TARAN, Y. A., BERNARD, A., GAVILANES, J. C., LUNEZHEVA, E., CORTES, A. & ARMIENTA, M. A. 2001. Chemistry and mineralogy of high temperature gas discharges from Colima volcano, Mexico. Implications for magmatic gas–atmosphere interaction. Journal of Volcanology and Geothermal Research, 108, 245–264.

TAYLOR, B. E., EICHELBERGER, J. C. & WESTRICH, H. R. 1983. Hydrogen isotopic evidence of rhyolitic magma degassing during shallow intrusion and degassing. Nature, 306, 541–545.

TOULMIN III, P. & BARTON JR, B. P. 1964. A thermodynamic study of pyrite and pyrrhotite. Geochimica et Cosmochimica Acta, 28, 641–671.

VILLEMANT, B., BOUDON, G., NOUGRIGAT, S., POTEAUX, S. & MICHEL, A. 2003 Water and halogens in volcanic clasts: tracers of degassing processes during plinian and dome-forming eruptions. In: OPPENHEIMER, C., PYLE, D.M. & BARCLAY, J. (eds) Volcanic Degassing. Geological Society, London, Special Publications, 213, 63–79.

WALLACE, P. J. 2001. Volcanic SO_2 emissions and the abundance and distribution of exsolved gas in magma bodies. Journal of Volcanology and Geothermal Research, 108, 85–106.

WALLACE, P. J. & CARMICHAEL, I. S. E. 1992. Sulfur in basaltic magmas. Geochimica et Cosmochimica Acta 56, 1863–1874.

WALLACE, P. J. & GERLACH, T. M. 1994. Magmatic vapor source for sulfur dioxide released during volcanic eruptions: evidence from Mount Pinatubo, Science, 265, 497–499.

WALLACE, P. J., ANDERSON, A. T. & DAVIS, A. M. 1995. Quantification of pre-eruptive exsolved gas contents in silicic magmas. Nature 377, 612–615.

WATSON, E. B., 1994. Diffusion in volatile-bearing magmas. In: CARROLL, M. R. & HOLLOWAY, J. R. (eds) Volatiles in Magmas. Reviews in Mineralogy, 30, 371–411.

WATSON, I. M. & OPPENHEIMER, C., ET AL. 2000. The relationship between degassing and ground deformation at Soufriere Hills Volcano, Montserrat. Journal of Volcanology and Geothermal Research, 98, 117–126.

WEBSTER, J., KINZLER, R. J. & MATHEZ, E. 1999. Chloride and water solubility in basalt and andesite melts and implications for magmatic degassing. Geochimica et Cosmochimica Acta, 63, 729–738.

WESTRICH, H. R. & GERLACH, T. M. 1992. Magmatic gas source for the stratospheric SO_2 cloud from the June 15, 1991 eruption of Mount Pinatubo. Geology, 20, 867–870.

WHITNEY, J. A. 1984. Fugacities of sulfurous gases in pyrrhotite-bearing silicic magmas. *American Mineralogist*, **69**, 69–78.

ZHANG, Y. 1999. H_2O in rhyolitic glasses and melts: measurement, speciation, solubility, and diffusion. *Reviews of Geophysics*, **37**, 493–516.

ZIELINSKI, G. A. 1995. Stratospheric loading and optical depth estimates of explosive volcanism over the last 2100 years derived from the Greenland Ice Sheet Project 2 ice core. *Journal of Geophysical Research* **100**, 20 937–20 955.

Water diffusion in natural potassic melts

C. FREDA[1], D. R. BAKER[2], C. ROMANO[3] & P. SCARLATO[1]

[1]*Istituto Nazionale di Geofisica e Vulcanologia, Via di Vigna Murata, 605-00143, Rome, Italy.*
(e-mail: freda@ingv.it)
[2]*Department of Earth and Planetary Sciences, McGill University, 3450 University Street, Montreal H3A 2A7, Canada.*
[3]*Dipartimento di Scienze Geologiche, Università degli Studi di Roma Tre., Largo San Leonardo Murialdo, 1-00146, Rome, Italy.*

Abstract: Water diffusion experiments were performed on a trachytic melt from the Agnano–Monte Spina explosive eruption (Phlegrean Fields, South Italy). Experiments were run in a piston cylinder apparatus at 1 GPa pressure, at temperatures from 1373 to 1673 K and for durations of 0 to 255 s, using the diffusion-couple technique. Water concentration profiles were measured by Fourier transform infrared spectrometry. Water diffusion coefficients at different temperatures and water concentrations were calculated from the total water profiles, using the Boltzmann–Matano technique.

Over the investigated range of temperatures and water concentrations, the diffusivity of water in potassic melts (D_{water}), m²/s can be described by Arrhenius equations that can be generalized for water concentrations between 0.25 and 2 wt% as follows:

$$D_{water} = \exp\left(-11.924 - 1.003 \ln C_{H_2O}\right) \exp\left(\frac{-\left(\exp\left(11.836 - 0.139 \ln C_{H_2O}\right)\right)}{RT}\right)$$

where C_{H_2O} is the water concentration in wt%, R is 8.3145 (J K⁻¹ mol.⁻¹) and T is the temperature in Kelvin. Water diffusivities in trachytic melts were compared with water diffusivities in rhyolitic and basaltic melts. The activation energies for water diffusivity in trachyte and basalt are comparable, and higher than in haplogranitic melt. This results in a convergence of water diffusion coefficients in all melts at lower (magmatic) temperatures.

Introduction

Diffusion of water in silicate melts plays a major role in numerous geological phenomena. In the last few decades, this process has been the subject of many studies, because of its importance in the hydration and dehydration of magmas. Hydration of silicate melts is particularly important, since it has been demonstrated that small amounts of water significantly influence the physical and chemical properties of magmas (cf. Shaw 1963; Watson 1981). On the other hand, the dehydration of magmas by bubble formation and evolution strongly affects magma ascent dynamics. Depending on the style of vesiculation, magma can expand at extreme rates, or degas slowly, producing either explosive eruptions or lava flows, respectively (cf. Sparks *et al.* 1994). Therefore, knowledge of water diffusion is essential for modelling volatile exsolution from

magmas during their ascent to the Earth's surface. Previous experimental studies were devoted to determination of water diffusivity almost exclusively in rhyolitic melts (cf. Zhang & Behrens 2000). However, some extremely dangerous volcanoes belong to the potassic alkaline series (e.g. Vesuvius and the Phlegrean Fields, in Italy), and yet the properties of magmas of these compositions are very poorly known.

As part of a project devoted to the study of the chemical and physical properties of potassic magmas from the Phlegrean Fields, we determined the water diffusivity in a trachyte from the Agnano–Monte Spina (AMS) explosive eruption. This eruption was the largest event at the Phlegrean Fields during the last 5000 years, and can be considered the upper limit for the next explosive episode expected in an area where

From: OPPENHEIMER, C., PYLE, D.M. & BARCLAY, J. (eds) *Volcanic Degassing*. Geological Society, London, Special Publications, **213**, 53–62. 0305–8719/03/$15.00

almost two million people live at present (de Vita
et al. 1999). The occurrence of an eruption as
energetic as the AMS event represents a considerable volcanic hazard, and understanding
this is important for the prediction of eruption
scenarios in the Phlegrean Fields.

Experimental techniques

Starting material preparation

The starting material for the water diffusion
measurements was produced by melting the
trachytic (SiO_2=59.9, TiO_2=0.39, Al_2O_3=18.0,
MgO=0.89, MnO=0.12, FeO=3.86, CaO=2.92,
Na_2O=4.05, K_2O=8.35, P_2O_5=0.21 wt%) glassy
matrix of pumices from the fallout level of
the Agnano–Monte Spina deposit (D1 level,
AMS59) at 1 atm and 1400–1650 °C (for further
details of the synthesis method, see Dingwell *et
al.* 1998). A portion of the glass was reduced to
powder and an aliquot of this powder was
hydrated by melting at 1250 °C, 1.5 GPa for 1
hour in $Au_{75}Pd_{25}$ capsules in a piston-cylinder
apparatus using a 1.91 cm NaCl–pyrex–pyrophyllite–crushable alumina assembly (Freda
et al. 2001). Cores small enough to fit capsules of
3 mm external diameter were drilled from the
same anhydrous glass. Two cores were hydrated
following the above procedure. The two hydrated
starting materials were checked for homogeneity
of water concentration and were found to be
homogeneous, but they contained different water
concentrations. The two cores were not mixed
together, but used separately in different experiments.

Diffusion-couple experiments

Experiments were carried out in a piston-
cylinder apparatus at the Department of Earth
and Planetary Sciences of McGill University
(Montreal, Canada). The experiments were
performed at 1.0 GPa, temperatures from 1100
to 1400 °C, and a time duration from 0 to 255 s
(Table 1).

Previous experimental studies of water diffusion in basaltic and rhyolitic melts used either
internally heated pressure vessels (IHPV), cold
seal vessels (CSV) (e.g. Nowak & Behrens 1997)
or a piston-cylinder apparatus (e.g. Zhang &
Stolper 1991; Zhang & Behrens 2000). Each of
these techniques can produce problems when
studying the diffusion of mobile volatile species.
The most serious problem in using IHPVs and
CSVs is that the heating and cooling rates are
slow; thus, in many cases during water diffusion
experiments, the time to reach the experimental

Table 1. *Run conditions of the starting material and of the diffusion-couple experiments used for determination of diffusivities.*

Sample	T (°C)	Time (s)
Starting material preparation (1.5 GPa)		
AMS59–I	1250	3600
AMS59–X	1250	3600
AMS59–XI	1250	3600
Third set of experiments (1 GPa)		
AMS59–XIX	1400	0
AMS59–XX	1400	120
AMS59–XVII	1300	180
AMS59–XXII	1300	180
AMS59–XXI	1200	210
AMS59–XXXI	1100	255

temperature can be longer than the experimental
duration itself. However, by contrast, the piston
cylinder's heating and cooling rates are very fast
(300 °C min^{-1} and 2000 °C min^{-1}, respectively),
which provide a significant advantage compared
to the other types of apparatus. In addition, in
the piston cylinder both the vertical and radial
temperature gradients were found to be less than
approximately 5 °C (Hudon *et al.* 1994).

One disadvantage of the piston-cylinder
apparatus is that it is not easy to keep samples
undeformed and crack free. Fractures should be
avoided because they alter the shape of the
sample, making the water concentration analyses
very difficult. One of our goals was to test different experimental techniques in order to obtain
minimally deformed and cracked run products.
All the experiments were performed using the
diffusion-couple technique, but were carried out
following three different methods.

The first set of experiments was assembled by
firmly packing the hydrated powdered glass into
the lower half of a graphite capsule (1 mm
internal diameter, 6 mm long). The upper half of
the capsule was filled with the anhydrous
powdered glass, a thin layer of platinum powder
(1 μm or less in size) was introduced between the
two glasses in order to mark the contact area,
then the capsule was closed with a graphite lid.
To avoid water loss the graphite capsule was
placed into a platinum capsule, which was welded
closed in a water bath. Capsules were placed
vertically into 1.91 cm NaCl–pyrex glass–crushable alumina assemblies. Unfortunately, experimental products produced by this technique were
significantly deformed, and contained fractures
that made them unsuitable for Fourier transform

infrared analysis and water diffusion calculations.

The second set of experiments also used powdered hydrous and anhydrous glasses separated by a thin layer of platinum powder, but in 9 mm long, 1 mm diameter, platinum capsules placed horizontally into 1.91 cm NaCl–pyrex glass–pyrophyllite–graphite–crushable alumina assemblies (Fig. 1). By placing the capsule horizontally in this assembly, we managed to prevent fracturing of the samples, but some runs lost their geometry, making calculation of water diffusion from the concentration profile impossible.

The third set of experiments was assembled by first putting coarsely crushed hydrated glass (*c.* 9 mg, from the hydrated core) and then a dry glassy cylindrical core (*c.* 35 mg) in a platinum capsule (3 mm diameter, 9 mm long); the capsule was squeezed, then welded closed and com-pressed at room temperature before the experiment in order to eliminate air and free space between the capsule and the sample. Capsules were placed horizontally into the same assembly (Fig. 1) used for the second set of experiments. This third set of experiments produced the best results in terms of maintaining sample geometry and keeping the samples unfractured (Fig. 2).

Analysis of experimental products by Fourier transform infrared (FTIR) spectroscopy

After quenching, samples were sectioned perpendicular to the contact between hydrous and anhydrous glasses in order to yield a glass slice with the complete diffusion profile. Run products were inspected by optical microscopy and found to be free of crystals and bubbles. Thin sections

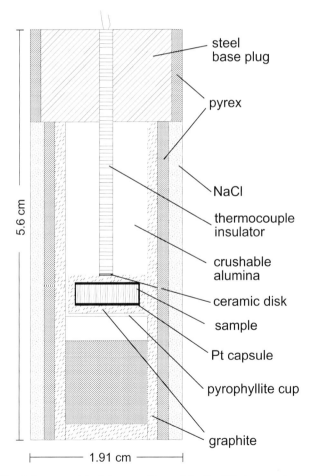

Fig. 1. Sketch (not to scale) of the assembly used for the diffusion-couple experiments.

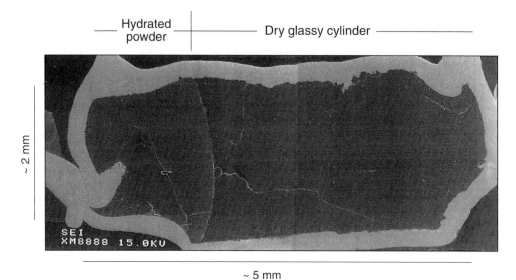

Fig. 2. A typical capsule after an experiment ($T=1300$ °C, $t=180$ s). The sample preserved its geometry, and is unfractured.

were double-polished to a thickness of 200–300 μm. In order to compare the three different experimental techniques the best products of the first two sets of experiments were also prepared for FTIR analysis. As expected, the best concentration profiles were obtained from experiments performed using the third technique, and for this reason they were the only ones used to calculate water diffusion.

Molecular H_2O and OH concentration profiles were determined from transmission infrared spectra measured with a Nicolet Fourier transform spectrophotometer (Nicolet Magna 760) in the NIR region (2500–8000 cm^{-1}), using a W source, CaF_2 beam-splitter and MCT detector at the Dipartimento di Scienze Geologiche (Università di Roma Tre). The infrared beam was delimited by using a circular slit (spot diameter 50 μm). Molecular H_2O and OH concentrations, both expressed as wt% H_2O, were determined from the peak heights of the absorption bands at 5200 cm^{-1} and at 4500 cm^{-1} respectively by the Beer–Lambert law:

$$C_{5200 or 4500} = \frac{A_{5200 or 4500} \times 18.015}{t \times \rho \times \varepsilon_{5200 or 4500}} \quad (1)$$

where A=absorption (height of the absorbance peak), t=sample thickness, ρ=sample density (C. Romano, pers. comm.), and $\varepsilon\gamma$=extinction coefficient.

At present the extinction coefficient for a composition comparable with that considered in this study (alkaline–potassic) is not available. The water concentrations along the profiles were calculated using the extinction coefficient determined by Carroll & Blank (1997) for a phonolitic composition (alkaline–sodic). We are aware that we may have introduced an error in the diffusivity determination. Nevertheless, a comparison of the water concentration along the diffusion profiles calculated using the extinction coefficients determined by Silver & Stolper (1989) for an albitic composition, by Ihinger *et al.* (1994) for a rhyolitic composition, and by Carroll & Blank (1997) demonstrated that all diffusivities are comparable (e.g. at $T=1300$ °C with 1 wt% water in the melt, the diffusion coefficients are 8.59×10^{-11}, 8.85×10^{-11}, and 8.14×10^{-11} m^2 s^{-1} for phonolitic, albitic, and rhyolitic extinction coefficients, respectively). Thus, we assumed that the extinction coefficient determined for a phonolitic composition can be reasonably applied to the trachyte used for this diffusion study.

As demonstrated in previous studies (Nowak & Behrens 1995; Shen & Keppler 1995) the water speciation of the melt cannot be quenched during cooling. Consequently, the diffusivity of individual H_2O_{mol} and OH species cannot be determined directly from their profiles. Therefore, the bulk diffusion coefficient of water at different temperatures and water concentrations has to be calculated from the total water concentration profiles (Fig. 3) obtained by summing H_2O_{mol} and OH concentrations (cf. Nowak & Behrens 1997).

Initial water concentrations in the hydrated starting materials varied somewhat from experiment to experiment, as reflected by the plateau water concentration in the hydrated glass measured by FTIR after the experiment.

Results and discussion

Calculation of water diffusivity from concentration profiles

Diffusion coefficients (D) were calculated from total water concentration profiles using Boltzmann–Matano analysis (Crank 1975). To calculate the diffusion coefficient at any water concentration the following equation was solved:

$$D = -\frac{1}{2t}\frac{dx}{dC}\int_{C_{bkg}}^{C} x\,dC \qquad (2)$$

where D is the diffusivity (in $m^2\,s^{-1}$) at concentration C at position x along the traverse, dx/dC is the derivative of the position respect to concentration, t is the experiment duration (in seconds), C_{bkg}, is the high or the low initial concentration depending on the x location with

respect to the Matano interface (where $x=0$). To perform Boltzmann–Matano analysis the analytical profiles were fitted with polynomials that can be easily integrated and the Matano interface found. The integrations and derivations were performed to calculate the diffusivity at different points along the concentration profile. Because Boltzmann–Matano analysis cannot provide good results for concentrations close to the ends of the profile (cf. Crank 1975), the diffusion coefficients could not be calculated below 0.25 and above 2.0 wt% water for most experiments (Table 2).

Several factors can affect the diffusion coefficient determination (cf. Nowak & Behrens 1997):

1. Uncertainty due to fluctuation in the experimental temperature is minor because the temperature was controlled within 2 °C of the set point, except at the beginning of the run when the overshoot sometimes reached a maximum of 10 °C.
2. Water diffusion in melts can be very rapid. Thus, significant transport may occur during the heating of experiments to run temperatures. A 'zero time' experiment, in which the run is quenched immediately after the experimental temperature is reached, when performed at 1400 °C produced a diffusion profile 0.35 mm long, demonstrating that water diffused during heating. To correct for any diffusion

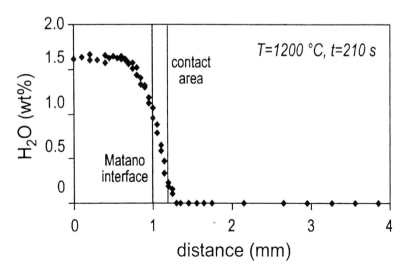

Fig. 3. Total water concentration profile obtained by summing H_2O_{mol} and OH concentrations determined from transmission infrared spectra measured with a Fourier transform spectrophotometer. In the figure, the positions of the Matano interface (see the text for explanation) and of the contact area between hydrous and anhydrous glasses are shown. The two positions do not necessarily coincide (cf. Nowak & Behrens 1997).

Table 2. *Diffusivities of water at P=1 GPa.*

H_2O (wt%)	T_{exp} (°C)	T_{avg} (°C)	D (m^2/s)
0.25	1100	1079	5.99×10^{-12}
	1200	1167	4.04×10^{-11}
	1300	1253	5.48×10^{-11}
	1400	1328	7.02×10^{-11}
0.5	1100	1070	1.19×10^{-11}
	1200	1155	5.50×10^{-11}
	1300	1238	5.04×10^{-11}
	1400	1308	1.09×10^{-10}
1.0	1100	1065	2.35×10^{-11}
	1200	1148	8.91×10^{-11}
	1300	1230	8.59×10^{-11}
	1400	1297	1.77×10^{-10}
2.0	1100	1061	4.46×10^{-11}
	1300	1223	1.05×10^{-10}
	1400	1288	2.77×10^{-10}

that may have occurred during heating to run temperatures, the iterative technique of Yinnon & Cooper (1980) was followed. This technique uses the Arrhenius relationship determined from the measured experimental temperatures, T_{exp}, and diffusion coefficients to calculate an average temperature, T_{avg}, for each diffusion measurement, based upon the integrated diffusion occurring during the experiment. This procedure takes into account the diffusion that occurred during heating. This T_{avg} is then used to recalculate a new Arrhenius relationship, and the procedure for calculating T_{avg} is repeated until T_{avg} reaches a constant value. Diagrams use T_{avg} rather than T_{exp}.

3. The contact area between hydrated and dry glasses was easily recognized under the microscope, and was found to be perfectly flat without any indentation of one glass in the other. This can be considered evidence that there was no convection during the experiments, and so diffusion was the only transport process involved in these experiments.
4. Uncertainty in the FTIR results is about 2%, based on the reproducibility of the measurements and on the error associated with the background subtraction procedure.
5. Based upon previous studies, the uncertainties in diffusion measurements calculated by Boltzmann–Matano analysis are estimated to be within 40% relative (Baker & Bossányi 1994). This can be considered the maximum uncertainty for our diffusion experiments, and was used to define error bars shown in the figures.

Temperature and water content dependence of water diffusivity

Water diffusion coefficients measured in this study for a trachytic melt composition vary from 5.99×10^{-12} m^2 s^{-1} at 1100 °C and 0.25 wt% of H_2O, to 2.77×10^{-10} m^2 s^{-1} at 1400 °C and 2.0 wt% water (Table 2). Water diffusion coefficients display an Arrhenian behaviour (Fig. 4). The relative difference between water diffusion

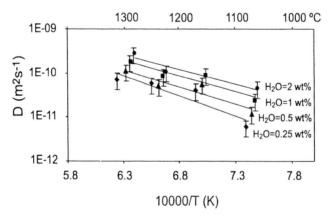

Fig. 4. Arrhenius diagram for water diffusion. Each line represents the effect of temperature on diffusion at given water content. The addition of water to the melt lowers both the activation energy and the pre-exponential coefficient in the Arrhenius equations. Graphically, this results in a family of Arrhenius lines converging at higher temperature. Symbols in figure are as follows: diamonds refer to 0.25 wt% water, triangles to 0.5 wt% water, squares to 1 wt% water, and circles to 2 wt% water.

coefficients at water concentrations of 0.25 and 2.0 wt.% is greater in the 1100 °C experiment than in the 1400 °C experiment.

In the investigated range of temperatures and water content, water diffusion in the trachytic melt can be described by the following Arrhenius equations:

melt with 0.25 wt % H₂O

$$D = 3.83 \times 10^{-5} \left({}^{+2.779 \times 10^{-3}}_{-3.770 \times 10^{-5}} \right) \exp\left(\frac{-171.9 \pm 56.6}{RT} \right) \quad (3)$$

melt with 0.5 wt % H₂O

$$D = 8.01 \times 10^{-6} \left({}^{+2.760 \times 10^{-4}}_{-7.780 \times 10^{-6}} \right) \exp\left(\frac{-147.2 \pm 42.2}{RT} \right) \quad (4)$$

melt with 1 wt % H₂O

$$D = 6.15 \times 10^{-6} \left({}^{+1.240 \times 10^{-4}}_{-5.860 \times 10^{-6}} \right) \exp\left(\frac{-136.7 \pm 36.8}{RT} \right) \quad (5)$$

melt with 2 wt % H₂O

$$D = 4.12 \times 10^{-6} \left({}^{+1.190 \times 10^{-4}}_{-3.980 \times 10^{-6}} \right) \exp\left(\frac{-127.7 \pm 41.1}{RT} \right) \quad (6)$$

where the activation energy is in kJ mol⁻¹, R is 8.314 J mol⁻¹ K⁻¹, and T is in K. The diffusivity of water in the potassic melts was found to increase with the total water content in the melt. This behaviour has been observed for many other melt components (cf. Watson 1994) and is related to the depolymerization of the melt by reaction of water molecules with bridging oxygens (Zhang *et al.* 1991).

The data obtained in this study were then combined (Fig. 5) to yield a general equation for the prediction of water diffusion in trachytic composition at all conditions studied:

$$D_{water} = \exp\left(-11.924 - 1.003 \ln C_{H_2O} \right)$$
$$\exp\left(\frac{-\left(\exp\left(11.836 - 0.139 \ln C_{H_2O} \right) \right)}{RT} \right) \quad (7)$$

where C is the water concentration in the melt in wt %. The average difference between D calculated with this equation and those measured in the experiments is 22% relative.

Comparison with water diffusion in different melt compositions

Water diffusivities in trachytic melt were compared to water diffusivities in rhyolitic and basaltic melts (Figure 6a, b & c).

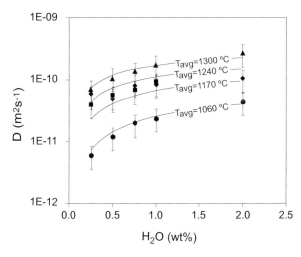

Fig. 5. Diffusion coefficients v. water content. The diffusivity of water increases linearly with the total water content in the melt. Temperatures shown are an average of the T_{avg} for each water content. In the figure, symbols represent the diffusivities obtained from Boltzmann–Matano analysis; curves were calculated using equation 7 in the text. Circles refer to 1060 °C, squares to 1170 °C, diamonds to 1240 °C, and triangles to 1300 °C.

C. FREDA *ET AL.*

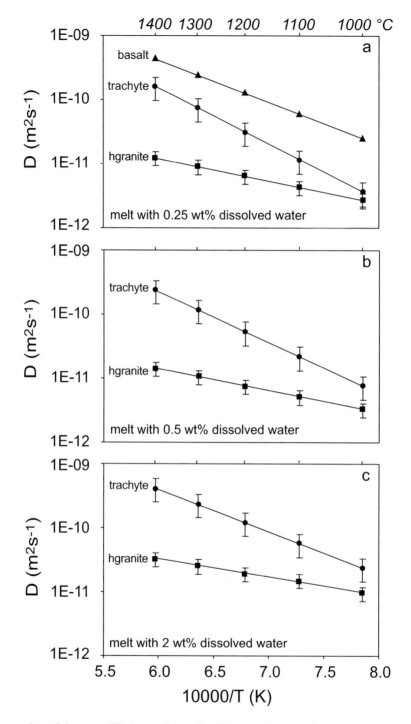

Fig. 6. Comparison of the water diffusion coefficients for different melt compositions: (**a**) basalt (calculated from Zhang & Stolper 1991), trachyte (calculated from equation 7 in the text), and haplogranite (calculated from Nowak & Behrens 1997) for a water content of 0.25 wt%; (**b**) and (**c**) trachyte (calculated from equation 7 in the text) and haplogranite (calculated from Nowak & Behrens 1997) for a water content in the melt of 0.5 and 2 wt%, respectively.

At constant temperature, water diffusion in the trachytic melt (see Fig. 5) appears to increase linearly with water content up to 2 wt%. This behaviour is comparable with that observed in haplogranitic and rhyolitic melts (Nowak & Behrens 1997 and Zhang & Behrens 2000, respectively). In the latter two melts, the diffusivity increases linearly up to a water content of 3 wt% and increases exponentially above this water amount. At present, we have no indication of how water diffusion in trachytic melts behaves at water contents higher than 2 wt%. Further studies must be done on potassic melts to understand the diffusion behaviour at higher water contents.

The activation energies for water diffusion in trachytic (this study) and basaltic melts (Zhang & Stolper 1991) are comparable (172 ± 57 and 126 ± 32 kJ mol^{-1} with 0.25 wt% water in the melt, respectively) and higher than those of haplogranitic melts calculated by Nowak & Behrens (1997), (147 ± 42 and 64 ± 10 kJ mol^{-1} with 0.5 wt% water in the melt, for the trachyte and the haplogranite, respectively). This behaviour is such that diffusion coefficients converge at lower (magmatic) temperatures and significantly diverge at higher temperature.

Conclusions

We report here the first investigation of water diffusion in potassic melts, and obtain a general equation describing water diffusivities at different temperatures and water contents in trachytic melts. Our data show that water diffusivities in trachytic and haplogranitic melts converge at lower (magmatic) temperatures. The difference between water diffusivities in trachytic and haplogranitic melts becomes significant when 2 wt% water is added to the melts.

We suggest that the general equation for water diffusion obtained in this study should be taken into account for volatile exsolution models in potassic magmas, and in particular should be used to model bubble growth in trachytic melts. Magma vesiculation is controlled not only by volatile diffusion, but also by other parameters, including melt viscosity. The viscosity of the AMS trachytic melts (at 1100 K) is within one order of magnitude of that of rhyolites for water contents higher than 1 wt%. It is orders of magnitude less than that of rhyolites if the water content in the melt is lower than 1 wt% (C. Romano, pers. comm.). Therefore, during magma ascent, the bubble growth history in trachytic and rhyolitic liquids should be similar, because diffusivity and viscosity values are comparable, but significant differences can be expected close to the Earth's surface, where the dissolved volatile concentration is expected to be very low and the viscosity of the two melts very different. In such a case, while bubble growth in rhyolitic magmas may be hindered by the very high melt viscosity, such growth may continue in the less-viscous trachytic magmas up to very shallow levels.

We thank an anonymous reviewer for helpful comments. This research was financed by NSERC grants OGP89662 and CPG0183275 and by Italian Civil Protection (GNV project N. 2000–02/17).

References

BAKER, D. R., & BOSSÁNYI, H. 1994. The combined effect of F and H₂O on interdiffusion between peralkaline dacitic and rhyolitic melts. *Contributions to Mineralogy and Petrology*, **117**, 203–214.

CARROLL, M. R. & BLANK, J. G. 1997. The solubility of H₂O in phonolitic melts. *American Mineralogist*, **82**, 549–556.

CRANK, J. 1975. *The Mathematics of Diffusion.* Clarendon Press, Oxford/London.

DE VITA, S. & ORSI, G. *ET AL.*, 1999. The Agnano–Monte Spina eruption (4100 years BP) in the restless Campi Flegrei caldera (Italy). *Journal of Volcanology and Geothermal Research*, **91**, 269–301.

DINGWELL, D. B., HESS, K.-U. & ROMANO, C. 1998. Viscosity data for hydrous peraluminous granitic melts: incorporation in a metaluminous model. *American Mineralogist*, **83**, 236–239.

FREDA, C., BAKER, D. R. & OTTOLINI, L. 2001. Reduction of water loss from gold–palladium capsules during piston–cylinder experiments by use of pyrophyllite powder. *American Mineralogist*, **86**, 234–237.

HUDON, P., BAKER, D. R. & TOFT, P. B. 1994. A high-temperature assembly for 1.91-cm (3/4-in.) piston–cylinder apparatus. *American Mineralogist*, **79**, 145–147.

IHINGER, P. D., HERVIG, R. L. & MCMILLAN, P. F. 1994. Analytical methods for volatiles in glasses. *In:* CARROLL, M. R. & HOLLOWAY, J. R. (eds) *Volatiles in Magmas.* Reviews in Mineralogy, **30**, pp. 67–121.

NOWAK, M. & BEHRENS, H. 1995. The speciation of water in haplogranitic glasses and melts determined by in situ near-infrared spectroscopy. *Geochimica et Cosmochimica Acta*, **59**, 3445–3450.

NOWAK, M. & BEHRENS, H. 1997. An experimental investigation on diffusion of water in haplogranitic melts. *Contributions to Mineralogy and Petrology*, **126**, 365–376.

SHAW, H. R. 1963. Obsidian–H₂O viscosities at 1000 and 2000 bars in the temperature range 700 to 900 °C. *Journal of Geophysical Research*, **68**, 6337–6343.

SHEN, A. & KEPPLER, H. 1995. Infrared spectroscopy of hydrous silicate melts to 1000 °C and 10 kbar: direct observation of H₂O speciation in a diamond-anvil cell. *American Mineralogist*, **80**, 1335–1338.

SILVER, L. A. & STOLPER, E. M. 1989. Water in albitic glasses. *Journal of Petrology*, **30**, 667–709.

SPARKS, R. S. J., BARCLAY, J., JAUPART, C., MADER, H. M. & PHILLIPS, J. C. 1994. Physical aspects of magmatic degassing. I. Experimental and theoretical constraints on vesiculation. *In:* CARROLL, M. R. & HOLLOWAY, J. R. (eds) *Volatiles in Magmas.* Reviews in Mineralogy, **30**, pp. 413–446.

WATSON, E. B. 1981. Diffusion in magmas at depth in the Earth: the effect of pressure and dissolved H_2O. *Earth and Planetary Science Letters*, **52**, 291–301.

WATSON, E. B. 1994. Diffusion in volatile-bearing magmas. *In:* CARROLL, M. R. & HOLLOWAY, J. R. (eds) *Volatiles in Magmas.* Reviews in Mineralogy, **30**, pp. 372–411.

YINNON, H. & COOPER, A. R. J. 1980. Oxygen diffusion in multicomponent glass forming silicates. *Physics and Chemistry of Glasses*, **21**, 204–211.

ZHANG, Y. & BEHRENS, H. 2000. H_2O diffusion in rhyolitic melts and glasses. *Chemical Geology*, **169**, 243–262.

ZHANG, Y. & STOLPER, E. M. 1991. Water diffusion in basaltic melt. *Nature*, **351**, 306–309.

ZHANG, Y., STOLPER, E. M. & WASSERBURG, G. J. 1991. Diffusion of water in rhyolitic glasses. *Geochimica et Cosmochimica Acta*, **55**, 441–456.

Water and halogens in volcanic clasts: tracers of degassing processes during Plinian and dome-building eruptions

B. VILLEMANT[1], G. BOUDON[1,2], S. NOUGRIGAT[1], S. POTEAUX[1]
& A. MICHEL[1]

[1]Physique et Chimie des Systèmes volcaniques, Institut de Physique du Globe de Paris,
Université Pierre et Marie Curie and CNRS-UMR 7046 (Géomatériaux),
Boîte 109, 4 place Jussieu, 75005 Paris, France.
(e-mail: villemant@ipgp.jussieu.fr)
[2]Observatoires Volcanologiques, IPGP, Boîte 89, 4 place Jussieu, 75005 Paris, France.

Abstract: Magma degassing may occur either with no significant gas escape from the magma column, which corresponds with typical Plinian type eruptions, or with gas loss, which corresponds with typical effusive (dome-building) eruptions. Magma degassing may also lead to melt crystallization, which modifies the residual melt composition and, in turn, may significantly affect the degassing conditions. We propose a method for modelling these processes for H_2O-rich rhyolitic melts through measurements of volatiles (H_2O, Cl, Br) in the microcrystalline matrix and glass of erupted volcanic clasts (pumice and dome clasts). This method is applied to two Plinian and dome-building eruptions at Mount Pelée (Martinique) and Santa Maria (Guatemala) volcanoes. Extreme magma degassing and crystallization during dome-building eruptions may explain the contrasts in halogen and H_2O contents of residual melts of dense volcanic clasts: they display very large ranges of Cl contents (few ppm to thousands of ppm), whereas the ranges of H_2O contents are much narrower, and lower than 1%. This method allows prediction of the evolution of volcanic gas chemistry (as HCl content or HCl/HF ratio) as a function of the degassing style of magma at shallow depth.

Eruptive styles of H_2O-rich silicic magmas vary from effusive to highly explosive. Water degassing at shallow depths constitutes the main source of energy in these eruptions, and the eruptive styles are controlled by the evolution of the fluid phase during magma ascent (exsolution, bubble expansion, and gas loss) and the bulk magma rheology (density and viscosity), which are interdependent (Eichelberger et al. 1986; Eichelberger 1995, Jaupart & Allègre 1995; Sparks 1997; Melnik & Sparks 1999; Sparks 2003). In particular, microlite crystallization related to melt degassing may play an important role by increasing melt crystallinity and hence bulk magma viscosity (Lejeune & Richet 1995).

The syn-eruptive evolution of the aqueous fluid phase in magmas is complex and depends on many parameters, such as solubility, diffusivity, and expansion, which are controlled by pressure, temperature, melt composition (particularly the initial fluid content), rate of fluid escape from the magma column (through the wall-rocks or due to differential movement between the gas phase and the magma), and degassing-related microlite crystallization. Based on simple thermo- and hydro-dynamic considerations, it is possible to establish theoretical models that, for different eruptive styles, describe the theoretical evolution of the exsolved and residual fluids (Jaupart & Allegre 1991; Sparks 1997; Villemant & Boudon 1998; Melnik & Sparks 1999). However, applications to real eruptions remain difficult because the determination of the compositions of the exsolved fluids (volcanic gases), or of the fluids dissolved in erupted products, is technically complex and may involve large measurement uncertainties, especially for major components such as H_2O (see e.g. Ihinger et al. 1994; Symonds et al. 1994). The use of halogens to follow degassing processes is of interest because their behaviour is mainly controlled by their partitioning into the H_2O-rich fluid phase, and the analysis of these elements in natural systems (glasses, melt inclusions, and volcanic gases) is generally easier and more accurate than for H_2O. Thus, measurement of halogen contents of primary melt inclusions and in erupted magmas (pumice or dome clasts) allows reconstruction of

From: OPPENHEIMER, C., PYLE, D.M. & BARCLAY, J. (eds) Volcanic Degassing. Geological Society, London, Special Publications, **213**, 63–79. 0305-8719/03/$15.00

the bulk H_2O degassing path during an eruptive event (Villemant & Boudon 1998, 1999). Moreover, the evolution of the bulk gas phase composition may be deduced from these models and compared with compositions of volcanic gas plumes (Villemant & Boudon 1999, Edmonds *et al.* 2001).

Here we present a refinement of the model proposed by Villemant & Boudon (1999) to describe shallow-depth degassing of H_2O-rich silicic melts subject to decompression and crystallization. The model gives consistent interpretations of residual H_2O and halogen contents of magmatic clasts erupted during Plinian and dome-building (effusive) eruptions from different active volcanoes: Mount Pelée (Martinique, Lesser Antilles: 650 years BP eruption) and Santa Maria-Santiaguito (Guatemala: Plinian and dome-building eruptions since 1902).

Modelling degassing processes

Major volatile species (mainly H_2O in the silicic magmas of interest) dissolved in melts may reach saturation in response to a pressure decrease or to variations of the melt composition, due, for example, to crystallization. Then a fluid phase exsolves and the magma vesiculates, decreasing the bulk magma density. If the magma is able to rise, the pressure decrease induces both an expansion of the bubbles and a decrease of the volatile solubility in the melt. In addition, the melt may also crystallize in response to gas loss, increasing, in turn, the volatile content in the residual melt, and hence promoting the degassing process.

Closed- and open-system evolution

If the system remains closed (i.e. there is no significant differential motion between melt and gas phase), bubble expansion and increase of the mass fraction of the exsolved fluid phase lead to an increase in the magma ascent velocity. When the magma contains a large volume fraction of bubbles (60–75%) it can fragment: i.e. the magma, which constitutes a continuous medium containing melt, crystals, and gas bubbles, is transformed into a continuous gas medium containing vesiculated magmatic clasts (pumice). The gas jet then evolves differently in response to an extremely rapid gas expansion (Wilson *et al.* 1980). This model corresponds with an ideal Plinian type eruption. It is generally assumed that, at fragmentation, the melt is quenched, and no further significant volatile exsolution occurs. Moreover, in this model, since eruption rates are high, it is assumed that the melt composition

remains constant over the whole degassing path (in particular, no microlite crystallization occurs). This is consistent with the common observation that pumice glass is generally homogeneous and lacking in microlites. Thus, between H_2O-saturation and fragmentation, the degassing history of a H_2O-rich magma may be described using the well-known solubility law of H_2O in melts and the perfect gas law (gas expansion), if equilibrium is assumed between the melt and the exsolved gas phase (Burnham 1979, 1994; Jaupart & Allegre 1991; Villemant & Boudon 1999).

For open-system evolution models, it is assumed, in addition, that the exsolved gas fraction has had time to escape from the source magma, either through wall-rocks by percolation, or through the volcanic vent itself by differential motion between the more rapidly ascending gas phase and the magma. In this case, eruption rates are much lower than in closed-system evolution. This corresponds with effusive (dome-building) type eruptions. In such cases, H_2O escape may induce melt crystallization (Burnham 1979; Swanson *et al.* 1989; Cashman 1992; Hammer *et al.* 1999). In addition, if gas escapes from the permeable magma by bubble connection (the permeable foam model of Eichelberger *et al.* 1986), the internal gas pressure of these bubbles is no longer maintained, and the bubbles collapse. Highly microlitic groundmass, irregular and flattened vesicles, and low residual gas contents are common features of lava-dome magmas. In models, these processes are taken into account by adding Rayleigh distillation equations for both gas loss and melt crystallization to the closed-system equations (Villemant & Boudon 1998, 1999; Melnik & Sparks 1999). In addition, a relationship between bubble collapse rate and parameters such as decompression rate or magma crystallinity is needed for describing the evolution of the magma vesicularity (Villemant *et al.* 1996).

Erupted magmatic clasts: samples from different degassing steps

It has been shown (Bursik 1993; Gardner *et al.* 1996; Villemant & Boudon 1998) that different magmatic clasts emitted during the same eruptive stage may have followed different degassing histories in the magma conduit. Thus, during a typical Plinian eruption, erupting products mainly consist of vesiculated clasts with glassy matrix (pumice) characteristic of a closed-system evolution, but they may also contain more crystallized and degassed magma fragments corresponding with the evolution of degassing in an open system with significant melt crystallization (Hammer *et al.* 1998; Villemant & Boudon 1998; Blundy & Cashman 2001, among others). Similarly, open-system, effusive dome-building eruptions generally give rise to a highly degassed and microcrystalline matrix, but also to degassed, glassy and unvesiculated obsidians or to less degassed, glassy and highly vesiculated clasts. More rarely, these eruptions are interrupted by short 'Vulcanian' episodes, as on 9 July 1902 at Mount Pelée, Martinique (Bourdier *et al.* 1989), or on 17 September 1996 and August–September 1997 at Soufrière Hills, Montserrat (Robertson *et al.* 1998). Thus, measurement of residual volatile contents in glasses from a large sample of erupted products in the same eruptive unit gives a more or less complete record of the degassing paths characteristic of the eruption dynamics.

Halogens in glasses: a tool for modelling degassing processes

The behaviour of minor volatile species extracted from the melt by the H_2O vapour may be simply deduced from the preceding degassing models by using partition coefficients between vapour and melt. Halogens display a wide spectrum of distribution coefficients between H_2O-rich fluids and melts (d^i_{v-l}). Experimental determinations of halogen partitioning show that d^i_{v-l} values strongly increase from F to I ($d^F_{v-l} < 1 << d^{Cl}_{v-l} < d^{Br}_{v-l} << d^I_{v-l}$; Kilinc & Burnham 1972; Webster & Holloway 1988; Shinohara *et al.* 1989; Métrich & Rutherford 1992; Webster 1992; Bureau *et al.* 2000). These results have been confirmed by modelling F, Cl, and Br behaviour in Plinian eruptions (Villemant & Boudon 1999). Since halogens are highly incompatible elements in magmas, degassing-related melt crystallization induces an increase of their concentration in residual melts which may be simply calculated from the crystallization rate. Degassing-induced crystallization and gas escape have opposite effects on H_2O and halogen contents in the melt, and the net effect is directly dependent on the ratio between crystallization and degassing rates. In addition, experimental studies show that vapour–melt partioning of halogens is also strongly dependent on the melt composition (Shinohara *et al.* 1989; Webster 1992; Signorelli & Carroll 2000, 2001, and discussion below).

Concentrations of halogens in initial and residual melts may be measured by different techniques with accuracies generally better than for H_2O: *in situ* measurements for F and Cl by electron- or ion-probe (residual glasses and melt inclusions) and bulk-rock measurements of F, Cl, and Br by pyrohydrolysis extraction and ion chromatography or ICP–MS (Ihinger *et al.* 1994; Schnetger *et al.* 1998). The H_2O and halogen content of the bulk groundmass (residual melt + microlites) may be simply calculated from bulk rock sample measurements, by correcting for phenocryst contents (see Villemant & Boudon 1998 and below).

Equations for open- and closed-system evolution

The following is a revised and extended formulation of equations given by Villemant & Boudon (1999). The isothermal degassing evolution for H_2O and a minor volatile species (1) characterized by its vapour–melt partition coefficient (d^i_{v-l}) are described by the following two equations:

$$X_{H_2O} = S_{H_2O} P^n_{H_2O} \quad (1)$$
$$(H_2O \text{ solubility law})$$

$$d^i_{v-l} = (x_i^0/x_i - 1)/(X^0_{H_2O} - X_{H_2O}) \quad (2)$$

where S_{H_2O} and n_{H_2O} are constants and P is the pressure. $X^0_{H_2O}$ and x_i^0 are the initial melt contents (i.e. at saturation pressure) of H_2O and element i, and X_{H_2O} and x_i the corresponding residual melt contents at pressure P. Typical values for these parameters in rhyolitic melts are given in Table 1. Initial melt compositions

Table 1. *Thermochemical characteristics of the reference rhyolitic melt.*

Rhyolitic melt	T	S_{H_2O}*	n_{H_2O}	K_R*	Initial melt[†]	H_2O	F	Cl	Br
	900 °C	0.321	0.54	14	d^i_{v-l}	–	<0.1	20	18
					X_0^i	5.5%	270 ppm	2100 ppm	6.2 ppm

S_{H_2O} and n_{H_2O} values are from Villemant & Boudon (1998).
*If P is expressed in MPa and X_{H_2O} in %.
[†]Initial melt composition of the 650 years BP eruption at Mount Pelée (Villemant & Boudon 1998; Martel *et al.* 1999).

$(X^0_{H_2O}, x_i^0)$ may be estimated from melt inclusions or experimental determination and d^i_{v-1} values from experimental determinations or degassing models. The $X^0_{H_2O}$ and x_i values are measured in residual glasses from erupted magmas.

Closed-system evolution

In this degassing model, the exsolved gas fraction remains confined in the magma, and the evolution of the volume of gas in bubbles is also controlled by the perfect gas law:

$$V_g/V_1=K_R (X^0_{H_2O}-X_{H_2O})/P \tag{3}$$

where V_g/V_1 is the ratio between the volumes of gas and melt at pressure P, and K_R is a constant (Table 1).

Open-system evolution

This degassing model assumes that the volatile phase escapes the reference melt volume after exsolution. The composition of the residual melt remains controlled by the H_2O solubility law, and the evolution of minor species may be described using a Rayleigh distillation law, which substitutes into equation (2) (Villemant & Boudon 1999).

If there is no melt crystallization, then the model may be expressed by the following set of equations:

$$x_i=x_i^0 f_v^{\delta i} \text{ with } \delta i=d^i_{v-1}-1 \tag{2b}$$

$$f_v=1-(X^0_{H_2O}-X_{H_2O}) \tag{2c}$$

where $1-f_v$ represents the fraction of exsolved fluid.

If melt crystallization also occurs, then we can write:

$$dm_L=-dm_V-dm_S$$

where m_L, m_V and m_S represent, respectively, the mass of melt, exsolving vapour, and crystallizing solid. It is assumed that crystallization and degassing are directly related (Burnham 1979, 1994; Villemant & Boudon 1998; Cashman & Blundy 2000); hence, we can write an additional equation:

$$dm_S=k_{SV} dm_V$$

If f_m represents the mass fraction of residual melt:

$$f_m=m_L/m^0_L=1-m_V/m^0_L (1+k_{SV})$$
$$\approx1-(X^0_{H_2O}-X_{H_2O}) (1+k_{SV})$$

and $dm_L/m_L=df_m/f_m$

The system of equations describing the degassing–crystallization model is then:

$$dm_L=-dm_V (1+k_{SV})$$

$$dx_i/x_i=(d^i_{v-1}/(1+k_{SV})-1) dm_L/m_L$$

By integration and using the definition of f_m, this system of equations leads to:

$$x_i=x_i^0 f_m^{\Delta i} \text{ with } \Delta i=d^i_{v-1}/(1+k_{SV})-1 \tag{2d}$$

$$f_m\approx1-(X^0_{H_2O}-X_{H_2O}) (1+k_{SV}) \tag{2e}$$

which substitute into equations (2b) and (2c).

Estimations of parameters

Estimation of k_{SV} values cannot be simply inferred from observations. The microlite mass fraction may be estimated on the basis of SEM or TEM measurements with, however, very large uncertainties and interpretation difficulties (see, for example, Cashman 1992). Direct estimates of vapour mass fraction in erupted clasts are impossible if gas loss occurs. However, for some simple melt compositions, phase diagrams in the presence of water are experimentally established. The well-known Q–Ab–Or diagram may be used as a good representation of rhyolitic melts (Tuttle & Bowen 1958; Cashman & Blundy 2000; Blundy & Cashman 2001). By direct measurements on phase diagrams or by using thermodynamic codes, the k_{SV} values may thus be calculated for different cases of interest. Simulations of isothermal decompression of rhyolitic melt, using either direct projections of melt compositions in the Q–Ab–Or diagram or MELTS code (Ghiorso & Sack 1995) – although not strictly valid for these compositions – show that the k_{SV} values vary quite widely over crystallization–decompression paths (5–40 or more, Nougrigat *et al.* in prep.). During isothermal decompression simulations, k_{SV} values are, to a first approximation, constant in steps with P decrease, and rise to higher values when new crystallizing phases (such as silica minerals) appear (Fig. 1). In addition, calculations show that for H_2O saturated rhyolitic melts, the k_{SV} values slightly increase with decreasing initial H_2O content.

Partition coefficients

These may be estimated using experimental data or by using the halogen–H_2O compositions of a

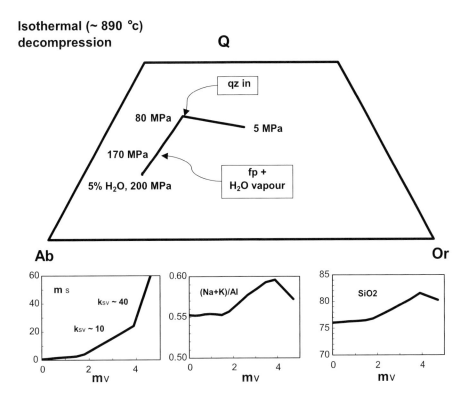

Fig. 1. Isothermal decompression of a H_2O-rich rhyolitic melt: the effects of shallow-depth decompression–crystallization on $k_{SV}=dm_V/dm_S$ (m_V=mass of exsolving vapour and m_S=mass of crystallizing solid), SiO_2 content, and aluminous character of residual melts. The theoretical evolution of a natural rhyolitic melt (melt composition of the 650 years BP eruption at Mount Pelée) during isothermal ($T\ c.890\ °C$) degassing at low pressure (P <200 MPa) calculated using MELTS code (Ghiorso & Sack 1995) is represented in the Q–Ab–Or normative representation. The MELTS code is not established for rhyolitic compositions, and leads to some systematic bias. The comparison of MELT calculations on synthetic systems with experimental data allows correction of these biases, and shows that the relative variations of masses of melt, solid, and vapour formed at given conditions are not modified (Nougrigat *et al.* in preparation). Decompression path in the Q–Ab–Or diagram for a rhyolitic melt with an initial H_2O content of 5% H_2O. This melt is saturated relative to H_2O at $c.$170 MPa, and crystallizes mainly Ab-rich plagioclase (fp). At low pressure ($c.$80 MPa), a silica mineral phase joins plagioclase at the liquidus. The m_S–m_V diagram (the same arbitrary units are used on both axes) shows that the k_{SV} values (given by the slopes) are constant by steps. Crystallization of silica minerals leads to a strong increase in the k_{SV} value. The residual melt composition also strongly varies during degassing-induced crystallization, as shown by the evolution of the (Na+K)/Al ratio and SiO_2 content. The variations of the aluminous character and SiO_2 content of the residual melts may lead to large variations of the partition coefficients of volatile halogens between melt and vapour phase.

series of glasses that have degassed in a closed system (i.e. measured in clasts from Plinian eruptions; see Villemant & Boudon 1999). Experimental data show, however, that d^{Cl}_{v-l} varies in a complex manner with T, P, and melt composition. The d^{Cl}_{v-l} values increase with decreasing T and increasing P, if $P >100$–200 MPa, increasing SiO_2 and Cl contents of the melt (Webster 1992; Webster *et al.* 1999; Signorelli & Carroll 2000, 2001). The d^{Cl}_{v-l} values vary strongly with the aluminous and peralkaline character of the melt, being maximum for (Na+K)/Al values close to 1 (Signorelli & Carroll 2001). For pressures below 100–200 MPa, because most experiments are using NaCl-bearing aqueous solutions, the fluids are in a subcritical condition, in which a NaCl brine and a Cl-poor aqueous fluid coexist. In this case, chlorine partitioning is affected by the phase relations in the fluid (Shinohara *et al.* 1989;

Signorelli & Carroll 2001). On the basis of the available experimental data at pressures <100–200 MPa, it is difficult to infer the actual d^{Cl}_{v-l} values and their dependence on pressure and composition. In addition, the experiments of Kravchuk and Keppler (1994) show that Cl partitioning between melt and H_2O vapour strongly differs in HCl-bearing and in NaCl- or KCl-bearing systems, suggesting that d^{Cl}_{v-l} values also strongly depend on the cation exchange (Na^+, K^+, or H^+) between vapour and melt. Since gaseous acids (HCl, HF, and HBr) are the dominant halogen-bearing species of juvenile magmatic gases, the results of Kravchuk and Keppler suggest that HCl-bearing experimental systems are more suitable than NaCl-bearing systems for measuring Cl partitioning during magma degassing at shallow depth, i.e. in conditions where metal-poor aqueous fluids are exsolved. In addition, some experiments suggest that kinetic effects may play an important role in halogen partitioning during shallow degassing processes (Gardner *et al.* 1998).

For rhyolitic melts at relatively high temperature (T >800 °C) and relatively low Cl contents (<2000 ppm), the available experimental data suggest that the main factors controlling d^{Cl}_{v-l} values are the SiO_2 content and the aluminous character of the residual melts. Calculations of residual melt composition in isothermal degassing experiments using the MELTS code show that (Na+K)/Al ratio and SiO_2 contents display significant variations: for the chosen example (Na+K)/Al ratio and SiO_2 content increase, respectively, from $c.0.55$ to $c.0.60$, and from $c.75\%$ to $c.82\%$ during plagioclase crystallization, and they decrease when silica minerals appear at the liquidus (Fig. 1). Larger ranges of (Na+K)/Al ratios (0.50–0.86) are displayed by residual melt compositions in dome fragments from eruptions at Mount Pelée and Santiaguito (Villemant & Boudon 1999, and S. Poteaux, unpublished data). As suggested by high-pressure (≥200 MPa) experiments, such variations should be able to induce significant increases of d^{Cl}_{v-l} values (typically from $c.10$–20 to values as high as $c.50$ or more; Webster 1992, Signorelli & Carroll 2001).

Vesicularity

In a closed-system evolution, the ratio V_g/V_l (3), which represents the magma vesicularity, may be estimated in erupted volcanic clasts by density measurements (Gardner *et al.* 1996; Villemant & Boudon 1999). However, in an open-system degassing model, gas loss is achieved either by differential motion of bubbles

relative to melt or by the connection of bubbles (followed by flattening of the bubbles and their eventual complete disappearance). This excludes the possibility of establishing simple predictive models for the relationship between the final vesicularity and the residual volatile content of the melts: i.e. for open-system degassing, there is no straightforward equivalent to equation (3). In some cases, however, information on magma ascent rates may be obtained from the measured final vesicularity and the residual volatile contents of dome clasts, and assumptions of magma rheology (Villemant & Boudon 1998).

Correlation diagrams between residual volatile contents

The theoretical evolutions of residual melt compositions corresponding with the different models above are represented in H_2O–Cl, V_g/V_l–H_2O and V_g/V_l–Cl diagrams in Figure 2. For closed-system evolution, initial melt compositions and d^i_{v-l} values determined for the 650 years BP eruption at Mount Pelée have been used (Table 1). Arbitrarily, the open-system degassing processes are assumed to occur after a closed-system evolution step, from H_2O=2% in the residual melt.

Five sets of evolution curves are reported:

1. closed-system evolution from the initial melt composition (grey lines).
2. degassing without crystallization (dotted line).
3. degassing with crystallization, d^{Cl}_{v-l}=20, and k_{SV} varying between 10 and 40 (large open symbols).
4. the same as model (3), but assuming that d^{Cl}_{v-l} increases (20 to 40) in response to the variation of the residual melt composition (small open symbols)
5. same as model (4), but for Cl and H_2O contents of the bulk groundmass (residual glass+microlites; solid symbols).

Water–V_g/V_l diagrams may be used to distinguish closed-system and open-system evolution, as stated by Villemant & Boudon (1999), but they are not good at discriminating between the different open-system degassing models, regardless of which measurements are used (glass or bulk groundmass compositions). If only bulk groundmass compositions are used, it is seen that Cl–V_g/V_l or H_2O–V_g/V_l and Cl–H_2O diagrams cannot discriminate between the different degassing–crystallization models (solid symbols). In addition, if no crystallization occurs, the

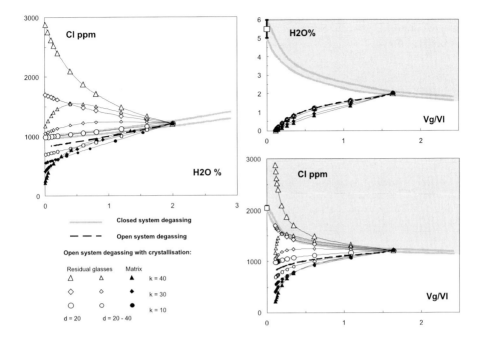

Fig. 2. Theoretical evolution of H_2O, Cl, and V_g/V_l in residual melts or groundmass (melt+microlites) for closed- and open-system degassing models: grey lines: closed-system evolution from initial melt (open square); initial melt compositions and d^i_{v-1} values correspond with those of the 650 years BP eruption at Mount Pelée (Table 1). Open-system degassing models are assumed to begin at $H_2O=2\%$, $Cl=1100$ ppm, and $V_g/V_l=1.7$. The discontinuous line indicates open-system degassing with no melt crystallization. Large open symbols indicate open-system degassing with degassing-induced crystallization ($k_{SV}=10$ to 40). Small open symbols indicate the same models, assuming an increase of the d^{Cl}_{v-1} values ($d=20$ to 40). Solid symbols indicate the same models calculated for the bulk groundmass (residual glass+microlites) compositions. Notice that in V_g/V_l – H_2O or -Cl diagrams, the stippled zone corresponds with the clasts having evolved in a closed system, including the possibility of gas expansion without further H_2O vapour exsolution (see Villemant & Boudon 1999). The lower half of the space (under closed-system evolution lines) corresponds with open-system degassing if no crystallization occurs. However, when degassing-induced crystallization occurs, and for large k_{SV} values, volatile halogen contents may sufficiently increase in residual melts, such that their compositions plot in the 'closed-system evolution domain'. Note, however, that such an effect is never encountered for H_2O.

open-system degassing model is not distinct from closed-system evolution.

On the contrary, when residual melt compositions are measured, very large variations in Cl contents are observed at high degrees of degassing. Halogen contents in residual melts, which may vary by one order of magnitude and may be much greater or lower than initial melt contents, are thus much more sensitive tracers of extreme degassing–crystallization steps than H_2O. Very large increases in halogen contents in residual melts are expected when crystallization rates are high relative to degassing rates (large k_{SV} values): the incompatible behaviour of halogens (enrichment in residual melts due to microlite crystallization) is not counterbalanced by their volatile behaviour (halogen extraction from the melt by the H_2O vapour phase). On the

contrary, when the crystallization rate is low relative to the degassing rate, halogen extraction from the melt by the vapour phase dominates. Thus, the net result of these two opposite effects depends critically on the value of k_{SV}, which relates the degassing and the crystallization rates. For the chosen conditions (expected to act in a rhyolitic melt during a dome-building eruption), a net increase in the Cl content of the residual melt is observed when k_{SV} exceeds c.20. This value typically corresponds with the appearance of silica minerals at the liquidus of H_2O-saturated rhyolitic melts (Fig. 1). Finally, if possible variations of d^{Cl}_{v-l} values with the evolution of residual melt composition are taken into account, complex variations may be observed (see the fourth set of curves with d^{Cl}_{v-l} increasing from 20 to 40; Fig. 2).

Application to natural systems: the examples of Mount Pelée and Santa Maria-Santiaguito

Measurements of H_2O and Cl contents in glasses from dome-building eruptions are relatively abundant in the literature. However, because of the analytical difficulties mentioned above, numerous data-sets do not report halogen and H_2O measurements on the same glasses or melt inclusions. Published values for the Mount Pinatubo, Galeras, Mount St Helens and Soufrière Hills eruptions give some general information on the relative behaviour of H_2O and Cl during shallow degassing of rhyolitic melts during dome-building eruptions (Table 2). The main characteristics of all these eruptions are:

1. The H_2O contents of residual glasses in erupted products are generally significantly lower than estimated initial melt contents, as a result of magma degassing. The lowest measured H_2O contents are $c.0.5\%$, which generally corresponds with the analytical detection limits, and so lower H_2O contents in residual melts may thus be likely.
2. In the same glasses, Cl contents are much more highly variable than H_2O contents, and maximum values are similar to, or even higher than, those estimated in initial melts.
3. Composition ranges for Cl and H_2O are generally narrower in melt inclusions than in corresponding glasses, and the maximum values are close to estimated initial melt contents. It should be noted, however, that in most cases, initial melt content estimates are based on melt inclusion measurements, but these values are generally confirmed by experimental petrology. Such evolution of melt inclusion compositions probably reflects

relatively deep degassing stages with simultaneous melt crystallization.

Water and halogen contents measured in both melt inclusions and residual melts thus provide consistent records of shallow magma degassing. The systematic variations of volatile abundances in volcanic products from different eruptions are qualitatively consistent with the degassing-crystallization models described above, which predict contrasting behaviours between H_2O and Cl.

Here we present H_2O and halogen measurements in both groundmass and residual melts of volcanic clasts from Plinian and dome-building eruptions of two volcanoes: Mount Pelée (Martinique, Lesser Antilles; Table 3) and Santa Maria (Guatemala; Table 4). Groundmass compositions were obtained from bulk-rock analyses, corrected for phenocryst contents as described in Villemant and Boudon (1999). Halogen (F, Cl, and Br) compositions of bulk rocks were measured using pyrohydrolysis and ion chromatography (F, Cl) or ICP–MS (Br) (Michel & Villemant, submitted); crystallinities were measured by both SEM image analysis and mass-balance calculations (Villemant & Boudon 1998). Bulk-rock H_2O contents were measured by H_2 manometry. Mean 2σ errors estimated by reproducibility on repeated analyses (and including errors on crystallinity measurements) are $c.10\%$ for H_2O, Cl, and Br. Spot analyses of H_2O and Cl in glasses (residual melts and melt inclusions) were performed using electron-probe (CAMECA, 15 kV, 5 nA), scanning analysis. Water contents were calculated using the 'difference to 100%' method. Each value represents a mean of three to five individual measurements on the same glassy area (100–200 μm across). Mean errors are $c.15–20\%$ for both H_2O and Cl.

Table 2. *Ranges of H_2O and Cl contents measured in glasses and melt inclusions of different eruptions.*

	Initial contents estimates*		Melt inclusions		Glasses	
	H_2O (%)	Cl (ppm)	H_2O (%)	Cl (ppm)	H_2O (%)	Cl (ppm)
Pinatubo	6	1250	5.5–6.4	1250–880	2.5–0.30	1500–400
Soufrière Hills	4–5	3400	6.6–2	4400–1000	3.6–1.9	3200–10
Mount St Helens	5		7.5?–2.5		3.5–0.45	
Galeras	?	?	2.4–0.3	2700–700	1–0.6	1200–400
Mount Pelée	5.5	2100	6–1.3	2300–1000	2.8–0.1	1700–25

*Estimates from melt inclusion analysis and/or experiments.
References: Pinatubo: Gerlach *et al.* (1996); Rutherford and Devine (1996); Soufrière Hills: Devine *et al.* (1998); Edmonds *et al.* (2001); Mount St Helens: Melson (1983); Rutherford *et al.* (1985); Galeras: Stix *et al.* (1997); Mount Pelée: Martel *et al.* (1998); Villemant and Boudon (1999).

Table 3. *Composition of residual glasses in clasts from the 650 years BP eruption (Mount Pelée).*

	1310K1		ML 801-b		MB 1101				MF 1001A					
H_2O (%)	1.85	3.91	1.22	0.38	3.13	1.02	<0.05	1.02	<0.05	2.81	3.44	0.77	0.39	1.08
Cl (ppm)	1080	1625	1903	1887	1627	1890	1619	1910	1328	1348	1906	2056	1315	1860

Measurements by electron probe (CAMECA, 15 kV, 5 nA, scanning analysis). Water is calculated using the 'difference to 100%' method. Each value represent a mean of three to five individual measurements on a same glassy area (100–200 μm). Mean errors are c.15–20 % for both H_2O and Cl.

Table 4. *Composition of groundmass and residual glasses in clasts from the Plinian- and dome-building eruptions of Santa Maria volcano (Guatemala).*

Dome clasts and lava domes and flows (1929 to present day – Santiaguito)

	C3-1	C3-3	C3-7	SM-8	13	12	10a	10b	11	15
H_2O (%)	0.93	0.36	0.35	0.62	0.38	0.23	0.22	0.07	0.39	0.70
Cl (ppm)	651	344	114	573	396	466	397	343	385	676
Br (ppm)	1.92	1.01	2.14	1.61	1.47	1.41	1.12	1.14	1.48	1.65

Plinian fall (1902 eruption)

	B2-1	C2-1	C2-12	D2-4	D2-8	E2-1	E2-2	E2-9	6-C2a	6-C2b	6-B2a	6-B2b	14	6-E0
H_2O (%)	1.33	1.38	1.32	1.21	1.09	1.04	1.10	1.27	0.55	2.12	1.82	1.00	1.53	7.01
Cl (ppm)	934	1238	780	842	809	875	886	834	937	1258	1397	1195	922	1380
Br (ppm)	1.26	2.07	1.63	2.39	1.24	1.84	1.94	1.75	–	–	–	–	1.89	–

Glasses – Plinian fall (1902 eruption)

	SM6-C2					SM6-B2				
H_2O (%)	0.55	2.12	2.37	2.37	0.80	2.07	1.25	1.25	1.82	1.00
Cl (ppm)	937	1258	1390	1125	937	1397	1155	1235	1397	1195

Groundmass compositions (H_2O, Cl and Br) are calculated from bulk-rock analyses, and the compositions of residual glasses (H_2O, Cl) are measured by electron probe (see Table 3 and text).

Representative major-element compositions of initial melts estimated from melt inclusions measurements are also reported in Table 5.

The 650 years BP eruption at Mount Pelée (Pl eruption) was a complex eruption with a succession of dome-building (Peléean) eruptions and a Plinian eruption in a short interval of time (Villemant *et al.* 1996; Villemant & Boudon 1998). The different evolution paths evidenced by the variation in volatile contents (H_2O, F, Cl, and Br) measured in bulk clasts have been interpreted in terms of closed- and open-system degassing models (Villemant & Boudon 1999). New Cl and H_2O measurements on residual glasses by electron-probe analysis are reported in Table 3. Bulk-rock analyses corrected for phenocryst contents and residual glass analyses are represented in Cl–H_2O–V_g/V_l diagrams (Fig. 3).

Table 5. *Representative major-element compositions of initial melts: measurements on melt inclusions.*

	1310K1	SM6
SiO_2	74.49	72.9
TiO_2	0.32	0.30
Al_2O_3	13.82	14.6
Fe_2O_3	2.58	2.50
MnO	0.09	0.20
MgO	0.42	0.50
CaO	2.60	1.80
Na_2O	3.69	4.90
K_2O	1.99	2.30
Total	100.00	100.0

1310K1: 650 years BP eruption at Mount Pelée, SM6: 1902 Plinian eruption at Santa Maria (from Villemant & Boudon 1999, and Poteaux 1998, unpublished).

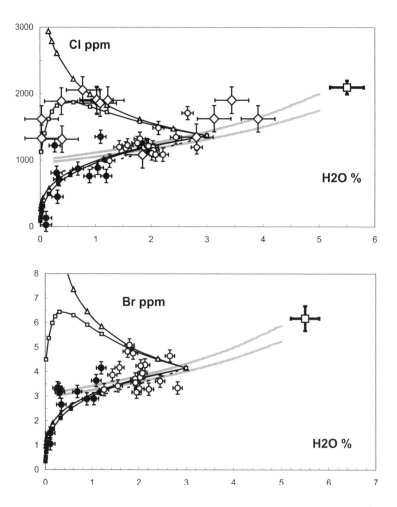

Fig. 3. Matrix and glass analyses of volcanic clasts from the 650 years BP eruption at Mount Pelée, Martinique: closed circles indicate dome clasts (groundmass compositions); open circles indicate Plinian clasts (groundmass compositions); open diamonds represent glass compositions in Plinian- or dome- clasts. Open squares indicate the initial melt composition (from Villemant & Boudon 1998). Evolution lines are the same as in Figure 2. Grey lines

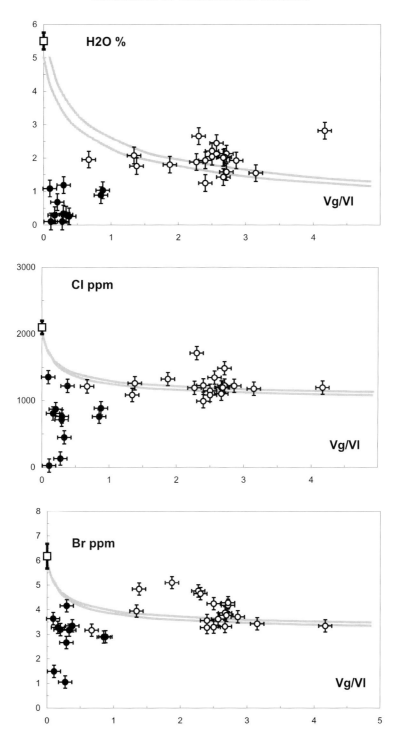

indicate closed-system evolution. Solid lines indicate open-system evolution; solid symbols represent groundmass compositions (data from Villemant & Boudon 1999); open symbols indicate residual melt compositions (see Table 3). Open-system evolution is arbitrarily calculated from initial compositions on the closed-system evolution lines (H_2O=3%); (1) k_{SV}=30, d^{Cl}_{v-1}=20; d^{Br}_{v-1}=18 and (2) k_{SV}=30, d^{Cl}_{v-1}=20 – 40; d^{Br}_{v-1}=18 – 36.

The 1902 Plinian eruption and the
1922–present-day dome-building eruption of
Santa Maria volcano

The recent activity of the Santa Maria volcano
started in 1902 with a climactic Plinian eruption
(Rose 1972; Williams & Self 1983). In 1922, the
construction of successive lava domes and thick
lava flows (called Santiaguito) began in the caldera
resulting from the 1902 eruption. Continuing
activity up to the present has produced numerous
dome collapse events (Rose 1973). Water and
halogen measurements of groundmass and

residual melts in clasts from the 1902 Plinian
eruption, the 1929 block-and-ash flows and in
different lava flows and lava domes of the
1947–present-day period of activity, are reported
in Table 4 and represented in Figure 4.

Correlation diagrams between V_g/V_l and H_2O
or halogen (Cl, Br) contents of groundmasses for
both series clearly show that most Plinian clasts
correspond with closed-system evolution, which
can be simply deduced from the initial melt
compositions and equations 1 to 3. In contrast to
this, dome clast compositions typically correspond with open-system degassing with gas loss,

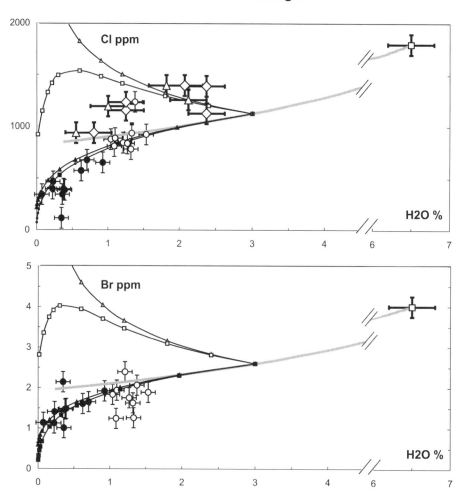

Fig. 4. Matrix and glass analyses of volcanic clasts from the Santa Maria-Santiaguito eruptions (1902–present
day, Guatemala). Symbols and evolution lines as in Figure 3. Closed circles indicate dome clasts or lava flows
(1922–present-day activity), groundmass compositions; open circles represent Plinian clasts (1902 eruption),

evidenced by a large decrease of the V_g/V_l values with decreasing volatile content. As stated above, however, it is not possible to identify more precisely the conditions of these open-system degassing processes in the absence of an independent measurement of the ratio between exsolved and lost vapour.

More complete information is obtained when spot analyses of residual glasses are used. The available analytical techniques only provide information on the H_2O and Cl contents of residual melts. Water–Cl correlation diagrams for both volcanic series clearly show that the effects

of degassing-related crystallization are significant on halogen behaviour. Chlorine enrichment in residual melts is significant, and may be as high as in initial melts as exemplified by clasts of the 650 years BP eruption of Mount Pelée (Fig. 3). Such an enrichment may be modelled using a high k_{SV} value, which corresponds with highly evolved melts, eventually corresponding with crystallization of silica minerals. For the 650 years BP eruption of Mount Pelée, this is consistent with SEM and TEM observations of dome clasts, which show that residual glasses are highly microcrystalline with abundant plagioclase

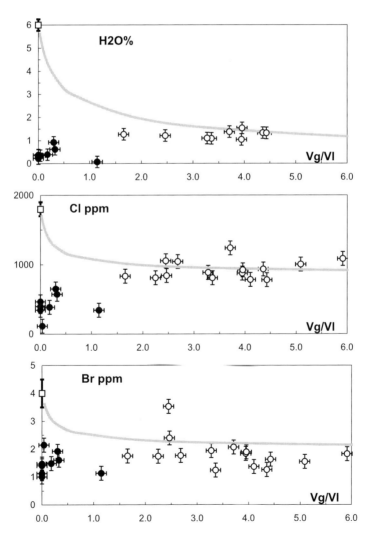

groundmass compositions (Table 4); open squares indicate initial melt compositions estimated from melt inclusions (S. Poteaux, unpublished data).

microlites and the presence of quartz nanolites (Villemant *et al.* 1996; Villemant & Boudon 1998; Nougrigat *et al* in prep.).

If the measured glass compositions represent different steps of the same continuous degassing process, H_2O–Cl diagrams show that crystallization–degassing processes do not occur at constant d^{Cl}_{v-l} and/or k_{SV}. The complex variations of the residual melt compositions may be explained by large k_{SV} values and a significant increase in d^{Cl}_{v-l} values, both related to melt differentiation due to degassing-induced crystallization at shallow depth.

Models of degassing processes at shallow depths are well constrained by the H_2O and halogen contents of residual melts. A combination of both bulk-rock analyses (corrected from phenocryst contents), and spot analyses of glasses and of micro-textural characteristics of erupted clasts (dome or Plinian clasts) allow identification of the relative importance of H_2O degassing and crystallization processes in H_2O-rich rhyolitic melts during their transfer to the surface by volcanic eruptions. The study of well-documented Plinian and dome-building eruptions (the 1902 to present-day eruptions at Santa Maria-Santiaguito volcano, Guatemala, and the 650 years BP eruption at Mount Pelée, Martinique) show that Plinian and dome-building eruptions display distinct signatures for H_2O, halogens (Cl, Br) and vesicularities. In particular, spot analyses of glasses show that during the slow degassing processes characterizing dome-building eruptions, degassing-induced crystallization leads to large variations in halogen contents. These variations are the result of two opposing effects: (1) melt crystallization, which induces an increase of halogens in the residual melt due to their incompatible character, and (2) halogen extraction by the vapour phase. This latter effect depends on the relative mass fractions of crystallizing microlites and exsolving vapour and on the variation in halogen partition coefficients between vapour and melt; both depend on the major-element composition of the residual melt, which may be modelled using experimental data or thermodynamic codes. The main difficulty of these modelling methods involves the determination of halogen partition coefficients and their dependence on *P*, *T*, and melt compositions and on possible kinetic effects. In this study, we show that in order to interpret the variations of Cl contents in residual melts of dome-building eruptions, large variations of d^{Cl}_{v-l} values during the last stages of crystallization–degassing process must be assumed, which is consistent with some experimental results. On the contrary, such large

variations in Cl contents – observed in the residual melts of Soufrière Hills volcano (Montserrat) are considered as incompatible with crystallization–degassing processes alone and, on the basis of hydrogen isotope measurements, have been interpreted as the result of dome leaching by groundwater circulation (Harford 2000). Such divergent interpretations show that, in addition to the fact that both syn-eruptive and late-eruptive processes may affect the volatile contents of residual melts of dome magmas, there is a great need for further experimental work to improve constraints on halogen behaviour during shallow-depth magma degassing.

This modelling shows that the halogen content of the residual melts, and consequently of the exsolved vapour phases, directly depends on the kinetics of melt degassing and magma ascent rate and, for dome-building eruptions, on the extent of melt crystallization–degassing process. Fluid compositions calculated from theoretical residual melt compositions and *d* values show that, with an increasing fraction of extracted H_2O vapour, Plinian eruptions (closed-system) produce Cl-poor vapour, while dome-building eruptions (open-system degassing with crystallization) are much more efficient at extracting volatile halogens (Cl, Br, and probably I), leading to HCl-, HBr- and HI-rich vapours (Fig. 5). Since F is very weakly extracted into vapour phase (d^F_{v-l} < 1), volcanic gases are relatively HF-poor, and the F concentration in the melt should be constant when there is no melt crystallization and should increase with advancing degassing-induced crystallization, because of the incompatible character of halogens. Measurements of HF and HCl contents of volcanic gases thus should provide precise indications of the degassing regime at shallow depth: for example, the above models suggest that volcanic gases should have increasing HCl/HF and decreasing HCl contents when the eruptive style evolves from effusive to explosive. In addition, these models predict that during dome-building eruptions the HCl/HF ratio of gases should vary with the different phases of eruptive activity. However, HCl emission rates and HCl/HF or HCl/SO_2 ratios measured in volcanic plumes by spectroscopic techniques (see e.g. Edmonds *et al.* 2002) display highly variable situations, which indicate that many processes other than those described by the above models at the scale of the residual melts in erupted magma fragments, determine the final composition of the gases expelled by the volcanic vents. In particular, large variations in the degassing conditions, such as the ratio between

Fluid phase composition

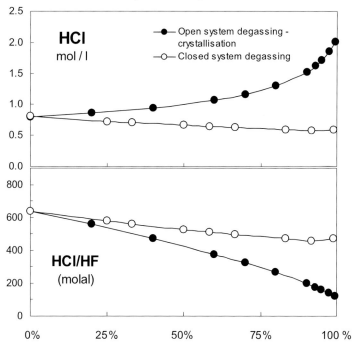

Fig. 5. Theoretical evolution of HCl and HF/HCl ratios of volcanic gases during closed- and open-system degassing. Gas compositions are calculated from residual melt compositions using d^i_{v-1} values (d^{Cl}_{v-1}=20 and d^F_{v-1}=0.1). The initial melt composition (H_2O=3%) and the degassing paths are the same as in Figures 3 and 4 (closed- and open-system degassing). The HCl content and HCl/HF ratio of volcanic gases vary with the eruptive style and the progress of the degassing process.

gas escape and degassing-induced crystallization, are expected to occur over the whole magma body, and are ultimately reflected in the gas composition of the volcanic plume. The relative importance of these different contributions is especially dependent on the variations of conduit geometry and permeability, the magma extrusion and ascent rates, etc. Thus, interpretation of juvenile volcanic gas compositions must integrate various chemical and physical processes acting at different scales, which requires multidisciplinary approaches, among which analytical and experimental petrology and chemistry play a critical role.

J. C. Komorowski, C. Oppenheimer, D. Pyle and an unknown reviewer are thanked for their comments and fruitful discussions. This research was supported by the PNRN programme (CNRS, France) and the Central America Research Programmes of the French Foreign Office.

References

BLUNDY, J. & CASHMAN K.V. 2001. Ascent-driven crystallisation of dacite magmas at Mount St Helens, 1980–1986. *Contributions to Mineralogy and Petrology*, **140**, 631–650.

BOURDIER, J. L., BOUDON, G. & GOURGAUD, A. 1989. Stratigraphy of the 1902 & 1929 nuée ardente deposits, Mt Pelée, Martinique. *In*: BOUDON, G. & GOURGAUD, A. (eds) Mount Pelée. *Journal of Volcanology and Geothermal Research*, **38**, 77–96.

BURNHAM, C.W. 1979. The importance of volatile constituents. *In: The Evolution of Igneous Rocks: Fiftieth Anniversary Perspectives.* Princeton: Princeton University Press, 439–482.

BURNHAM, C.W. 1994. Development of the Burnham model for prediction of H_2O solubility in magmas. *In*: CARROLL, M. & HOLLOWAY, J.R. (eds) *Volatiles in Magmas.* Reviews in Mineralogy, **30**, 123–129, Mineralogical Society of America, Washington D.C.

BUREAU, H., KEPPLER, H. & MÉTRICH, N. 2000. Volcanic degassing of bromine and iodine: experimental fluid/melt partitioning data and application to stratospheric chemistry. *Earth and Planetary Science Letters*, **183**, 51–55.

BURSIK, M. 1993. Subplinian eruption mechanisms inferred from volatile and clast dispersal data. *Journal of Volcanology and Geothermal Research*, **57**, 57–70.

CASHMAN, K.V. 1992. Groundmass crystallisation of Mount St Helens dacite, 1980–1986: a tool for interpreting shallow magmatic processes. *Contributions to Mineralogy and Petrology*, **109**, 441–449.

CASHMAN, K. V. & BLUNDY, J. 2000. Degassing and crystallisation of ascending andesite and dacite. *Philosophical Transactions of the Royal Society of London*, A**358**, 1487–1513.

DEVINE, J. D., MURPHY, M. D., RUTHERFORD, M. J., BARCLAY, J., SPARKS, R. S. J., CARROLL, M. R., YOUNG, S. R. & GARDNER, J. E. 1998. Petrologic evidence for pre-eruptive pressure–temperature conditions, and recent reheating, of andesitic magma erupting at the Soufrière Hills volcano, Montserrat, W.I. *Geophysical Research Letters*, **19**, 3669–3672.

EDMONDS, M., PYLE, D. & OPPENHEIMER, C. 2001. A model for degassing at the Soufrière Hills Volcano, Montserrat, West Indies, based on geochemical data. *Earth and Planetary Science Letters*, **186**, 159–173.

EDMONDS, M., PYLE, D. & OPPENHEIMER, C. 2002. HCl emission at Soufrière Hills Volcano, Montserrat, West Indies, during a second phase of dome building: November 1999 to October 2000. *Bulletin of Volcanology* **64**, 21-30.

EICHELBERGER, J. C. 1995. Silicic volcanism: ascent of viscous magmas from crustal reservoirs. *Annual Review of Earth and Planetary Science Letters*, **23**, 41–63.

EICHELBERGER, J. C., CARRIGAN, C. R., WESTRICH, H. R. & PRICE, R. H. 1986. Non-explosive silicic volcanism. *Nature*, **323**, 598–602.

GARDNER, J. E., THOMAS, R. M. E., JAUPART, C. & TAIT, S. 1996. Fragmentation of magma during Plinian volcanic eruptions. *Bulletin of Volcanology*, **58**, 144–162.

GARDNER, J. E., RUTHERFORD, M. & HORT, M. 1998. Degassing of trace gases during volcanic eruptions. *EOS, Transactions of the American Geophysical Union*, **79**, F936.

GERLACH, T. M., WESTRICH, H. R. & SYMONDS, R. 1996. Preeuption vapour in magma of the climactic Mount Pinatubo eruption: source of the giant stratospheric sulfur dioxide cloud. *In:* NEWHALL, C. & PUNONGBAYAN, R. (eds) *Fire and Mud: Eruptions and Lahars of Mount Pinatubo, Philippines.* University of Washington Press, Seattle, 415–433.

GHIORSO, M. S. & SACK, R. O. 1995. Chemical mass transfer in magmatic processes IV. A revised and internally consistent thermodynamic model for the interpolation and extrapolation of liquid–solid equilibria in magmatic systems at elevated temperatures and pressures. *Contributions to Mineralogy and Petrology*, **119**, 197–212.

HAMMER, J. E., CASHMAN, K.V., HOBLITT, R. P. &

NEWMAN, S. 1999. Degassing and microlite crystallisation during the pre-climactic events of the 1991 eruption of the Mt Pinatubo, Philippines. *Bulletin of Volcanology*, **60**, 355–380.

IHINGER, P. D., HERVIG, R. L. & MCMILLAN, P. F. 1994. Analytical methods for volatiles in glasses. *In:* CARROLL, M. R. & HOLLOWAY, J. R. (eds) *Volatiles in Magmas.* Reviews in Mineralogy, **30**, 66–121, Mineralogical Society of America, Washington D.C.

HARFORD, C. 2000. *The Volcanic Evolution of Montserrat.* PhD Thesis, University of Bristol, 195 pp.

JAUPART, C. & ALLÈGRE, C. J. 1991. Gas content, eruption rate and instabilities in silicic volcanoes. *Earth and Planetary Science Letters*, **102**, 413–429.

KILINC, I. A. & BURNHAM, C. W. 1972. Partitioning of chloride between silicate melts and coexisting aqueous phase from 2 to 8 kbars. *Economic Geology*, **67**, 231–235.

KRAVCHUK, I. F. & KEPPLER, H. 1994. Distribution of chloride between aqueous fluids and felsic melts at 2 kbar and 800°C. *European Journal of Mineralogy*, **6**, 913–923.

LEJEUNE, A.-M. & RICHET, P. 1995. Rheology of crystal bearing silicate melts: an experimental study at high viscosities. *Journal of Geophysical Research*, **100**, 4215–4229.

MARTEL, C., PICHAVANT, M., BOURDIER, J. L., TRAINEAU, H., HOLTZ, F. & SCAILLET, B. 1998. Magma storage and control of eruption regime in silicic volcanoes: experimental evidence from Mt. Pelée. *Earth and Planetary Science Letters*, **156**, 89–99.

MELNIK, O. & SPARKS, R. S. J. 1999. Nonlinear dynamics of lava dome extrusion. *Nature*, **402**, 37–41.

MELSON, W.G. 1983. Monitoring the 1980–1982 eruptions of Mount St. Helens: compositions and abundances of glass. *Science,* **221**, 1387–1391.

MÉTRICH, N. & RUTHERFORD, M. J. 1992. Experimental study of chlorine behaviour in hydrous silicic melts. *Geochimica et Cosmochimica Acta*, **56**, 607–616.

MICHEL, A. & VILLEMANT, B. Determination of halogens (F, CI, Br, I), sulphur and water in 17 reference geological material. *Geostandard Newsletter* (submitted).

NOUGRIGAT, S., VILLEMANT, B., BOUDON, G., BESSON, P. & KOMOROWSKI, J.C. (in preparation). Origin of lava dome explosivity: the 1902 and 1929 eruptions of Montagne Pelée (Martinique, Lesser Antilles).

ROBERTSON, R., COLE, P., SPARKS, R. S. J., HARFORD, C., LEJEUNE, A. M., MCGUIRE, W. J., MILLER, A. D., MURPHY, M. D., NORTON, G., STEVENS, N. F. & YOUNG, S. R.1998. The explosive eruption of Soufrière Hills Volcano, Montserrat, West Indies, 17 September 1996. *Geophysical Research Letters,* **25(18)**, 3429–3432.

ROSE, W. I. 1973. Notes on the 1902 eruption of Santa Maria volcano, Guatemala. *Bulletin of Volcanology*, **36**, 29–45.

RUTHERFORD, M. J. & DEVINE, J. D. 1996. Preeruption pressure temperature conditions and volatiles in the 1991 dacitic magma of Mount Pinatubo. *In:*

NEWHALL, C. & PUNONGBAYAN, R. (eds) *Fire and Mud: Eruptions and Lahars of Mount Pinatubo, Philippines*. University of Washington Press, Seattle, 751–766.

RUTHERFORD, M. J., SIGURDSSON, H., CAREY, S. & DAVIS, A. 1985. The May 18, 1980, eruption of Mount St. Helens. 1. Melt composition and experimental phase equilibria. *Journal of Geophysical Research*, **90**, 2929–2947.

SCHNETGER, B., MURAMATSU, Y. & YOSHIDA, S. 1998. Iodine (and other halogens) in twenty six geological reference materials by ICP–MS and ion chromatography. *Geostandards Newsletter*, **22**, 181–186.

SHINOHARA, H., IIYAMA, J. T. & MATSUO, S. 1989. Partition of chlorine compounds between silicate melt and hydrothermal solutions: I partition of NaCl–KCl. *Geochimica et Cosmochimica Acta*, **53**, 2617–2630.

SIGNORELLI, S. & CARROLL, M. R. 2000. Solubility and fluid-melt partitioning of Cl in hydrous phonolitic melts. *Geochimica et Cosmochimica Acta*, **64**, 2851–2862.

SIGNORELLI, S. & CARROLL, M. R. 2001. Experimental constraints on the origin of chlorine emissions at the Soufrière Hills volcano, Montserrat. *Bulletin of Volcanology*, **62**, 431–440.

SPARKS, R. S. J. 1997. Causes and consequences of pressurisation in lava dome eruptions. *Earth and Planetary Science Letters*, **150**, 177–189.

SPARKS, R. S. J. 2003. Dynamics of magma degassing. *In:* OPPENHEIMER, C., PYLE, D. M. & BARCLAY, J. (eds) *Volcanic Degassing*, Geological Society of London, Special Publications, **213**, 5–22.

STIX, J., TORRES, R. C., NARVAEZ, L. M., CORTÉS, G. P. J., RAIGOSA, J. A., GOMEZ, D. M. & CASTONGUAY, R. 1997. A model for vulcanian eruption at Galeras volcano, Colombia. *Journal of Volcanology and Geothermal Research*, **77**, 285–303.

SWANSON, S. E., NANEY, M. T., WESTRICH, H. R. & EICHELBERGER, J. C. 1989. Crystallisation history of Obsidian dome, Inyo Domes, California. *Bulletin of Volcanology*, **51**, 161–176.

SYMONDS, R.B., ROSE, W.I., BLUTH, G.J.S. & GERLACH, T.M. 1994. Volcanic gas studies: methods, results and applications. *In:* CARROL, M.R. & HOLLOWAY, J.R. (eds) *Volatiles in magmas*. Min. Soc. of Am., Washington DC Reviews in Mineralogy, **30**, 66–121.

TUTTLE, O. F. & BOWEN, N. L. 1958. *Origin of Granite in the Light of Experimental Studies in the System NaAlASi3O8–KAlSi3O8–SiO2–H2O*. Geological Society of America, Memoir, **74**, 153.

VILLEMANT, B. & BOUDON, G. 1998. Transition between dome-building and plinian eruptive styles: H2O and Cl degassing behaviour. *Nature*, **392**, 65–69.

VILLEMANT, B. & BOUDON, G. 1999. H2O and halogen (F, Cl, Br) behaviour during shallow magma degassing processes. *Earth and Planetary Science Letters*, **168**, 271–286.

VILLEMANT, B., BOUDON, G. & KOMOROWSKI, J. C. 1996. U-series disequilibrium in arc magmas induced by water–magma interaction. *Earth and Planetary Science Letters*, **140**, 259–267.

WEBSTER, J. D. 1992. Water solubility and chlorine partitioning in Cl-rich granitic systems: effects of melt composition at 2 kbar and 800°C. *Geochimica et Cosmochimica Acta*, **56**, 679–687.

WEBSTER, J. D. & HOLLOWAY, J. R. 1988. Experimental constraints on the partitioning of Cl between topaz rhyolite melt and H2O and H2O+CO2 fluids: new implications for granitic differentiation and ore deposition. *Geochimica et Cosmochimica Acta*, **52**, 2091–2105.

WEBSTER, J. D., KINZLER, R. J. & MATHEZ, E. A. 1999. Chloride and water solubility in basalt and andesite melts and implications for magmatic degassing. *Geochimica et Cosmochimica Acta*, **63**, 729–738.

WILLIAMS, S. N. & SELF, S. 1983. The October 1902 plinian eruption of Santa Maria volcano, Guatemala. *Journal of Volcanology and Geothermal Research*, **16**, 33–56.

WILSON, L., SPARKS, S. & WALKER, G. 1980. Explosive volcanic eruptions IV: the control of magma properties and conduit geometry on eruption column behaviour. *Geophysical Journal of the Royal Astronomical Society*, **63**, 117–148.

A model for the saturation of C–O–H–S fluids in silicate melts

R. MORETTI[1], P. PAPALE[2] & G. OTTONELLO[3]

[1]Istituto Nazionale di Geofisica e Vulcanologia, Osservatorio Vesuviano, Naples, Italy.
[2]Istituto Nazionale di Geofisica e Vulcanologia, Via della Faggiola 32, I 56126 Pisa, Italy.
(e-mail: papale@pi.ingv.it)
[3]Dipartimento per lo Studio del Territorio e delle sue Risorse, Genoa, Italy.

Abstract: The behaviour of volatile components in magmas is crucial for magmatic and volcanic processes, from the deep regions of magma generation and storage to the shallow regions of magma eruption and emplacement. Water, carbon dioxide, and sulphur compounds are the main volatile components in natural magmas, generally comprising more than 99% of the volcanic gases released before, during, and after eruption. We have set up a method to calculate the chemical equilibrium between a fluid phase in the C–O–H–S system and a silicate liquid with a composition defined by ten major oxides. The method is based on previous models for the saturation of H_2O–CO_2 fluids (Papale 1997, 1999) and sulphur solubility (Moretti 2002) in silicate liquids, and for the fugacities of components in fluids with complex composition (Belonoshko et al. 1992). The model calculations provide estimates of the partitioning of H_2O, CO_2 and S between the silicate liquid and the coexisting fluid, and the composition of the fluid phase in terms of H_2O, CO_2, SO_2, and H_2S, as a function of pressure, temperature, volatile-free liquid composition, oxygen fugacity, and total amount of each volatile component in the system. Model calculations are presented for silicate liquids with tholeiitic and rhyolitic composition, oxygen fugacities in the NNO ± 2 range, and pressures from a few hundred MPa to atmospheric, with the simplifying assumption that no reduced or oxidized sulphur-bearing solid or liquid phases nucleate or separate from the liquid–gas system. The results are in good agreement with the bulk of experimental data from the literature, and show the well-known minima in sulphur saturation contents as a function of oxygen fugacity, the mutual effects of volatiles on their saturation contents, and the complex relationships between the saturation surface of multi-component fluids and the liquid composition, volatile abundance, and pressure–temperature–oxygen fugacity conditions. The new model therefore represents a powerful tool for the prediction of multi-component gas–liquid equilibria in natural magmatic systems, for the simulation of magmatic and volcanic processes, and for the interpretation of data on the degassing of magma bodies and composition of volcanic plumes, provided that the assumptions on which the model rests, first of all that no separation of additional S-bearing phases occurs, are satisfied.

Introduction

The behaviour of volatile components in magmas is crucial for magmatic and volcanic processes from the deep regions of magma generation, segregation, and storage, to the shallow regions of magma ascent and eruption into the atmosphere. Dissolved and exsolved volatiles largely affect the crystallization paths of magma bodies (Tuttle & Bowen 1958; Nicholls & Russell 1990), and magma properties such as viscosity and density, which play major roles in the magma and in eruption dynamics (Lange 1994; Dingwell 1998; Jaupart 1998; Papale 1998). Volatile exsolution from liquid magma, and associated volume increases, are likely to be major factors triggering crack formation in rocks surrounding crustal magma reservoirs (Burnham 1985; Tait et al. 1989), possibly leading to magma ascent and eruption. Volatile exsolution during decompression accompanying magma ascent is responsible for a number of processes that lead to acceleration and fragmentation of the bubbly or foamy magma in a volcanic conduit (Mader 1998; Cashman et al. 2000; Papale 2001).

Water is the most abundant volatile in magmas, followed by carbon dioxide, sulphur, chlorine, fluorine, nitrogen, and noble gases (Johnson et al. 1994). Total carbon dioxide and sulphur estimates in silicic magmas, made solely on the basis of glass-inclusion studies can lead to large underestimation of the actual contents (Newman et al. 1988). In many cases involving eruptions of

From: OPPENHEIMER, C., PYLE, D.M. & BARCLAY, J. (eds) *Volcanic Degassing*. Geological Society, London, Special Publications, **213**, 81–101. 0305–8719/03/$15.00

silicic volcanoes, an exsolved gas phase seems to have been present at magma chamber depths, carrying a large fraction of the low-solubility volatile components (Wallace 2001). Multi-component (H_2O+CO_2) gas–liquid equilibrium modelling supports such a conclusion, showing that the addition of a few tenths of a weight per cent of carbon dioxide to a magma containing a few weight per cent of water can result in an increase of the gas saturation pressure by hundreds of MPa, leading therefore to the separation of a CO_2-rich gas phase at a depth several kilometres greater than that corresponding with separation of a pure H_2O fluid (Holloway & Blank 1994; Papale 1999). Such a gas phase can be at equilibrium with a liquid containing only tens to hundreds of ppm dissolved carbon dioxide. Due to such an important effect in modifying the gas saturation pressure in silicate liquids, relatively small amounts of carbon dioxide in natural magmas can significantly modify the dynamics of magma ascent, affecting the mass flow-rate and the conduit exit flow conditions (Papale & Polacci 1999).

Although, to date, there are a large amount of data available on the solubility of volatiles in silicate liquids, as well as on volatile contents in glass inclusions within crystals, the modelling of multi-component gas–liquid equilibria in silicate systems is still at an early stage, and no comprehensive model has been proposed to account for the large variability of liquid and gas compositions shown by natural magmas.

In this chapter we present a method for the evaluation of the chemical equilibrium between a fluid (gas) phase with composition in the C–O–H–S system, and a silicate liquid with composition defined in terms of ten major oxides. The method is based on previous models for the saturation of H_2O+CO_2 fluids (Papale 1999) and for sulphur solubility (Moretti 2002) in silicate liquids, as well as for the fugacity of components in complex gas mixtures (Belonoshko *et al.* 1992), and it allows calculations of the partitioning between gas and liquid phases of water, carbon dioxide and sulphur, and the composition of the gas phase in terms of H_2O, CO_2, SO_2, and H_2S, as a function of pressure, temperature, liquid composition, total amounts of volatiles, and oxygen fugacity. Applications to cases involving liquids with tholeiitic and rhyolitic composition show that the thermo-dynamic equilibrium between C–O–H–S fluids and silicate liquids can be very complex. Simple trends evidenced in many experimental investigations can be totally hidden, although still effective, as a consequence of the several homogeneous and heterogeneous equilibria that must be simultaneously satisfied due to the multi-component nature of the equilibrium.

Description of the method for multi-component gas–liquid equilibrium in silicate systems

When dealing with the equilibrium between C–O–H–S gases and silicate liquids at conditions relevant for natural magmatic systems, it is necessary to take into account several possible oxidation states of sulphur, either dissolved in the liquid or exsolved in the gas, chemical reactions between the different components in the gas phase, possible precipitation of mineral phases containing reduced (e.g. pyrrhotite) or oxidized (anhydrite) sulphur, and separation of a Fe–S–O–rich immiscible liquid phase (Carroll & Webster 1994).

Here we assume that only one oxidized and one reduced sulphur compound are present in the gas and liquid phases, namely, hydrogen sulphide (H_2S, reduced) and sulphur dioxide (SO_2, oxidized) in the gas, and sulphide (S^{2-}, reduced) and sulphate (SO_4^{2-}, oxidized) ions in the liquid. Furthermore, we assume that the gas phase comprises only H_2O, CO_2, SO_2, and H_2S species. This assumption is evaluated a posteriori below (see Table 3). Experiments on a variety of silicate melt compositions show that sulphide and sulphate ions are the primary sulphur compounds dissolved in silicate liquids (Carroll & Webster 1994), and the thermodynamics of sulphur reactions in C–O–H–S gases at magmatic conditions show that H_2S and SO_2 species are often from one to several orders of magnitude more abundant than SO_3, S_2, SO or COS species (Katsura & Nagashima 1974; Gerlach & Nordlie 1975). Additionally, we neglect the possible precipitation of S-rich minerals or separation of S-rich immiscible liquids. This assumption implies that the method in its present form can only be used at S-undersaturated conditions relative to such mineral or liquid phases. In several cases related to natural volcanism, such condensed (solid or liquid) phases are likely to form. This is the case for the recent eruptions of El Chichón, Pinatubo, and Lascar volcanoes, where anhydrite crystals are present in the mineral paragenesis, and of most primitive ocean ridge basalts that are sulphide saturated (Carroll & Webster 1994). On the contrary, other magmas are undersaturated in S-rich solid or liquid phases. These include the dacitic magma discharged at Mount St Helens in 1980–1982 (Johnson *et al.* 1994), with associated peak sulphur discharges of 2600 t day^{-1} (Casadevall et al. 1983); the Hawaiian basalts, which contain up to 0.2 wt% S in glass inclusions but no sulphide-rich phases (Johnson et al. 1994); the back-arc basalts and basaltic andesites from Lau Basin (southwest Pacific) (Nilsson & Peach 1993); and the shoshonitic basalts from Stromboli (Métrich et al. 2001). For these cases the application of the present method is straightforward. Future work will be aimed at including additional S-bearing phases in the multi-component, multiphase equilibrium modelling.

In the following sections, we present calculations made in the fO_2 range defined by NNO±2, although it is likely that at least in some of the considered conditions, precipitation of S-rich solid phases or separation of immiscible S-rich liquid occurs. This is done with the aim of showing the potential of model calculations and highlighting several features of non-linear behaviour in multi-component volatile saturation.

As stated above, the method is based on previous different models for H_2O+CO_2 and for S saturation in silicate liquids. It must be noted that the two models are different in many respects. The H_2O+CO_2 saturation model is based on the equality of fugacities for dissolved and exsolved water and carbon dioxide. In the case of sulphur, the chemical reactions occurring in the gas phase and leading to an equilibrium between water, hydrogen sulphide, and sulphur dioxide, together with the adoption of a polymeric model to describe the liquid, make it preferable to solve for the equilibrium constants describing the reactive dissolution mechanisms.

The above different approaches are reflected in different thermodynamic model for the liquid phase. The H_2O+CO_2 model adopts a 'classical' thermodynamic description, where the excess Gibbs free energy of the multi-component liquid is expressed as a function of binary interaction coefficients describing the attractive–repulsive behaviour of each pair of liquid components. The interaction coefficients not involving volatiles are taken from previous works mostly aimed at the description of solid–liquid equilibria in silicate systems (Ghiorso et al. 1983; Ghiorso & Sack 1994), while the interaction coefficients involving water and carbon dioxide were obtained by least-squares regression applied to nearly 1000 solubility measurements in silicate liquids with composition from very simple to natural (Papale 1997, 1999). On the contrary, the sulphur model is based on the computation of the equilibrium constants characterizing the reaction of sulphide and sulphate ions with each

metal oxide in the liquid (Moretti 2002; see also the Appendix). The liquid is described within the framework of the Temkin model (Temkin 1945). Anionic and cationic matrixes are computed by means of a generalized polymeric approach (Ottonello et al. 2001) which allows the concentration of three quasi-chemical species of oxygen to be calculated, namely, O^{2-}, O^0, O^-, or free oxygens, bridging oxygens, and non-bridging oxygens, respectively, following the notation given by Fincham and Richardson (1954). Such concentrations are computed by solving the mass balances implicit in the Toop–Samis treatment of silicate melts (Toop & Samis 1962a, b). A description of the physics and mathematics of the two separate H_2O+CO_2 and sulphur saturation models is reported in the Appendix.

In order to allow the two separate models to work together to predict the equilibrium conditions between C–O–H–S fluids and silicate liquids, the following assumptions are made:

1. the dissolved sulphur (either sulphide or sulphate) modifies the activity coefficients of dissolved H_2O and CO_2 only through dilution of such volatiles in the liquid phase;
2. the same holds for the effect of dissolved CO_2 on dissolved sulphur;
3. the dissolved H_2O has a direct (chemical) effect on S saturation in the liquid phase; and
4. the same holds for the relationships between H_2O and CO_2 in the liquid phase.

In order to determine the composition of the gas phase, which defines the fugacity of the major gaseous components H_2O, CO_2, SO_2, and H_2S, we must solve the model equations reported in the Appendix, together with mass-balance equations for the considered volatile species, and a redox equilibrium equation describing the SO_2–H_2S speciation in the gas phase as a function of system conditions, including oxygen fugacity. The mass-balance equations are the following:

$$\frac{w_{CO_2}^T - w_{CO_2}^G}{w_{CO_2}^L - w_{CO_2}^G} = \frac{k_1\left(w_{H_2O}^T - w_{H_2O}^G\right) - k_2 w_{H_2S}^G}{k_1\left(w_{H_2O}^L - w_{H_2O}^G\right) - k_2 w_{H_2S}^G} \quad (1)$$

$$\frac{w_{CO_2}^T - w_{CO_2}^G}{w_{CO_2}^L - w_{CO_2}^G} = \frac{w_S^T - k_3 w_{SO_2}^G - k_4 w_{H_2S}^G}{w_S^L - k_3 w_{SO_2}^G - k_4 w_{H_2S}^G} \quad (2)$$

$$w_{H_2O}^G + w_{CO_2}^G + w_{SO_2}^G + w_{H_2S}^G = 1 \quad (3)$$

In the above equations, w is mass fraction, the superscripts L and G indicate liquid and gas phases, respectively, the superscript T refers to total mass fraction (that is, with respect to the bulk system including liquid and gas phases), and $k_{1...4}$ are stoichiometric coefficients with values of 1/9, 1/17, 1/2, and 16/17, respectively. In the case where sulphur is not present, the system reduces to equations (1) and (3) (Papale 1999).

The redox equilibrium governing the speciation of sulphur in the gas phase is given by the following reaction:

$$2H_2O + 2SO_2 \Leftrightarrow 3O_2 + 2H_2S \qquad (4)$$

with equilibrium constant K from the thermodynamic data in Barin & Knacke (1973) and Barin *et al.* (1977):

$$\ln K_4 = 8.223 - \frac{54209}{T} \qquad (5)$$

where T is absolute temperature. On the basis of the same thermodynamic data, the equilibrium constant of the following reaction can be computed:

$$S_2 + 2O_2 \Leftrightarrow 2SO_2 \qquad (6)$$

$$\ln K_6 = 7.64 - \frac{37794}{T} \qquad (7)$$

Gaseous molecular sulphur and oxygen do not contribute to the mass-balance equations 1–3, since their abundance is normally several orders of magnitude lower than that of the major gas species defined above. The S_2 and O_2 fugacities are, however, necessary in order to solve the multi-component volatile saturation equations (see Appendix). Fugacities of components H_2O, CO_2, SO_2, and H_2S in the gas phase are computed by using the SUPER-FLUID code (Belonoshko *et al.* 1992), which accounts for complex mixtures in a wide P–T range encompassing that of interest for present purposes.

Once the oxygen fugacity is assigned, equations 6 and 7 allow the fugacity of molecular sulphur in the gas phase to be computed, and the polymeric approach used to describe sulphur saturation in the silicate liquid (see the Appendix) allows the redox equilibrium between iron species in the liquid phase as a function of the silicate liquid composition to be calculated (Ottonello *et al.* 2001).

Application to natural systems

In order to explore the potential of the new multi-component volatile saturation model, we have applied it to a few cases of interest for the degassing of magma bodies. We have considered two different volatile-free silicate liquid compositions corresponding with typical natural tholeiite and rhyolite (Table 1), each at its typical eruptive temperature. For each one, we have assumed a given distribution of total volatiles H_2O, CO_2 and S, and have varied the oxygen fugacity (NNO±2) and pressures (200 MPa to atmospheric). The set of conditions considered in the present model applications is reported in Table 2. For each condition, the model calculates the dissolved amount of each volatile, the composition of the gas phase in terms of H_2O,

Table 1. *Composition (wt%) of silicate liquids employed in the model calculations.*

	SiO_2	TiO_2	Al_2O_3	FeO*	MnO	MgO	CaO	Na_2O	K_2O
Tholeiite	49.20	2.29	13.30	11.40	0	10.40	10.90	2.15	0.51
Rhyolite	78.34	0.06	12.76	0.76	0	0.10	1.23	3.60	3.14

*Total iron as FeO. Disproportionation between ferrous and ferric iron in the liquid is accounted for within the model calculations, by the method described in Ottonello *et al.* (2001).

Table 2. *Range of physical conditions employed in the model calculations in Figures 1–10.*

Composition	P (MPa)	T (K)	fO_2 (ΔNNO)	$w^T_{H_2O}$ (wt%)	$w^T_{CO_2}$ (wt%)	w^T_S (wt%)
Tholeiite	0.1–200	1400	−2 – +2	3	1	0.5
Rhyolite	0.1–200	1100	−2 – +2	6	1	0.5

CO_2, SO_2 and H_2S, the proportion of gas and liquid phases, the speciation of dissolved sulphur between S^{2-} and SO_4^{2-}, the amounts of Fe_2O_3 and FeO, and other thermodynamic quantities, including fugacities and activities in the gas and liquid phases.

Actually, in the natural case fO_2 is buffered by several redox equilibria that may occur between components of the various phases in the system (Gerlach & Nordle 1975). Selecting fO_2 as an independent parameter in the calculations is a convenient choice, which simplifies the calculations and which is particularly suitable to illustrate the potential of the present multi-component volatile saturation model.

In the following, we describe the results related to the tholeiitic liquid first, then we move on to the rhyolitic liquid case.

Tholeiitic composition

Figure 1 shows the saturation content of sulphur, and the sulphur speciation, as a function of oxygen fugacity, for several different pressures from 0.1 to 200 MPa. The conditions for this set of simulations are reported in Table 2, and the calculation results are plotted in Figs 1–4. Total H_2O, CO_2 and S are 3, 1, and 0.5 wt%, respectively.

As emerges from Figure 1a, the curves corresponding with pressure equal to, or larger than 10 MPa, show a significant increase of sulphur saturation content with increasing oxygen fugacity. Such an increase is more important at low than at high pressure. On the reduced side of the diagram the dissolved sulphur content markedly decreases with decreasing pressure, whereas on

the oxidized side such a decrease is very little from 200 to 50 MPa, then it becomes appreciable. No dissolved reduced sulphur (S^{2-}) is found in the liquid for oxygen fugacities larger than NNO+1. Conversely, no dissolved oxidized sulphur (SO_4^{2-}) is found for oxygen fugacities less than NNO – 1.5. At 0.1 MPa (1 bar), Figure 1b shows that the sulphur saturation curve displays a well-defined minimum at an oxygen fugacity close to NNO – 0.5. At such low pressure, oxidized sulphur can be found down to nearly NNO – 2, while reduced sulphur disappears around NNO.

Figure 2 shows the calculated dissolved amounts of water and carbon dioxide, as a function of the oxygen fugacity conditions, for the same runs as in Figure 1a. Oxygen fugacity does not affect directly the saturation contents of water and carbon dioxide, but it has an indirect effect due to its role on the homogeneous chemical equilibria in the gas phase, equations (4)–(7), on the sulphide and sulphate capacities governing the dissolution behaviour of sulphur, and on the redox equilibrium governing the ferrous–ferric iron proportions (see the Appendix).

As indicated in the figure, in general the H_2O and CO_2 saturation contents change only slightly with the adopted oxygen fugacity buffer, but some significant variations are possible, the most noticeable one being the increase from about 700 to 850 ppm dissolved CO_2 when moving from the reduced to the oxidized side of the diagram at 200 MPa pressure. Conversely, the variation of dissolved H_2O with oxygen fugacity is larger at low pressure, being slightly less under oxidized conditions.

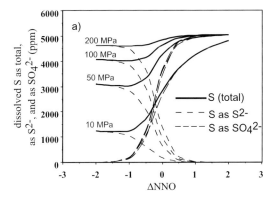
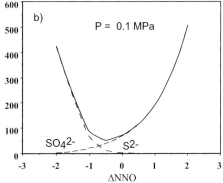

Fig. 1. (**a**) Calculated sulphur saturation content for the tholeiitic case, at different pressures from 10 to 200 MPa. The amount of sulphur present as S^{2-} and as SO_4^{2-} is also shown (dashed lines). Total amounts of H_2O, CO_2, and S in the system are 3, 1, and 0.5 wt%, respectively. Temperature is 1400 K. (**b**) Calculations pertaining to 0.1 MPa pressure. Figures 2–4 report other results pertaining to the same simulations as the present figure.

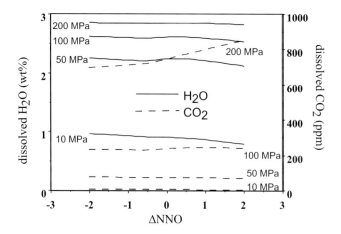

Fig. 2. Calculated water and carbon dioxide saturation contents for the tholeiitic case, at different pressures from 10 to 200 MPa.

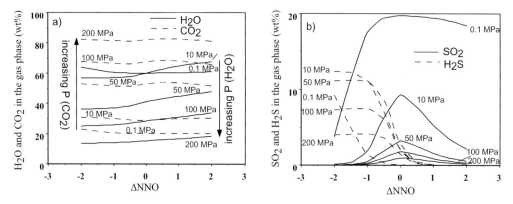

Fig. 3. (a) Calculated water and carbon dioxide proportions in the gas phase for the tholeiitic case, at different pressures from 0.1 to 200 MPa. (b) As for figure (a), for sulphur dioxide and hydrogen sulphide.

Figure 3 shows the calculated composition of the gas phase for the same runs as in Figures 1 and 2, again as a function of fO_2. Gas phase compositions show general trends which agree with those expected on the basis of the existing data, and deviations from such trends which reflect the complexities due to the multi-component nature of the gas–liquid equilibrium. In general, water abundance in the gas phase increases, and carbon dioxide abundance decreases, with decreasing pressure from 200 to 0.1 MPa (Fig. 3a). However, the calculated proportion of water at 0.1 MPa and oxidized conditions (>NNO) is less than the corresponding proportion at 10 MPa, contrary to the common trend invariably found in gas–liquid equilibrium calculations with H_2O+CO_2 volatiles

(Gerlach 1986; Holloway & Blank 1994; Papale 1999). This low-pressure inversion in the common trend of increasing water content in the gas phase with decreasing pressure appears to be related to the complex behaviour of SO_2 and H_2S in the gas phase, as shown in Figure 3b. While at reduced conditions H_2S is the dominant sulphur species in the gas, SO_2 becomes largely dominant under oxidized conditions (at atmospheric pressure SO_2 is found to be the dominant sulphur gas component over nearly all of the considered fO_2 range). However, the curves of SO_2 abundance in Figure 3b are not monotonic, but they show maxima for oxygen fugacities around NNO. At 0.1 MPa, SO_2 is more abundant than H_2S at an oxygen fugacity buffer larger than NNO – 1.8; it becomes about 20% by weight around NNO, then it decreases only very slightly with increasingly oxidizing conditions, still exceeding 18 wt% at the largest employed buffer of NNO+2. If we interpolate from Figure 3b different depressurization paths made at different constant oxygen fugacity buffers, that is, if we look at the intercepts of the curves in the figure with different vertical lines, each corresponding with a given fO_2, we see a very large increase in the proportion of SO_2 in the gas phase when moving from 10 to 0.1 MPa pressure. Such an increase buffers a further increase in the proportion of H_2O with decreasing pressure, which explains the decrease in the H_2O mass ratio with pressure decreasing from 10 to 0.1 MPa (Fig. 3a).

Figure 4 shows the calculated gas mass fraction, and the normalized gas volume fraction, as a function of the assumed oxygen fugacity buffer, for the same runs as in Figures 1–3. The relative variations in the gas mass fraction with fO_2 buffer (Fig. 4a) range from 5 to 15%, increasing with decreasing pressure. The trends of normalized gas volume fraction (Fig. 4b) show a complex behaviour with fO_2, with relative maxima at around NNO–0.5, and relative minima at around NNO+0.5. Highest normalized values (normalization is done for each pressure with respect to the volume fraction at NNO) appear at NNO+2 and intermediate pressures. At 0.1 MPa pressure, only a minor change in the gas volume fraction is visible in Figure 4b, since in this very low-P case almost all of the volume is occupied by the gas phase under any fO_2 conditions.

Rhyolitic composition

In the case of simulations made with rhyolitic composition, we have increased the total amount of H_2O in the system to 6 wt% and have used the same total CO_2 and S, in order to account for the generally larger water contents of chemically evolved silicate liquids (Johnson *et al.* 1994). Figures 5–8 for the rhyolitic case are analogous to Figures 1–4 for the tholeiitic case.

Figure 5 shows the dissolved sulphur content as a function of fO_2. The shapes of lines in this case show important differences with respect to those of the tholeiitic case in Figure 1. First, the amount of dissolved sulphur in the reduced side of the diagram is very low at any considered pressure up to 200 MPa (Fig. 5a), approaching zero below 10 MPa. As in Figure 1, the saturation content of sulphur markedly increases when moving toward higher fO_2. Maximum amounts of dissolved S occur at NNO+2 and largest employed pressure, and are comparable with the corresponding values for the tholeiitic case in Figure 1. At atmospheric pressure (Fig. 5b) maximum amounts of dissolved S correspond with a few ppm, comparing well with the determinations made by Katsura and Nagashima (1974) on rhyodacite.

Figure 6 shows the calculated dissolved water and carbon dioxide contents for the same runs as in Figure 5. The differences with the analogous Figure 2 pertaining to the tholeiitic case are small, mostly regarding the dissolved quantities but not the general trends. In fact, also in this case there is a weak dependency of the amount

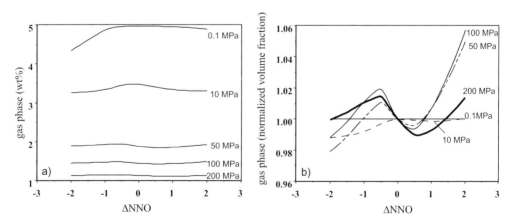

Fig. 4. (**a**) Calculated proportion of gas phase at equilibrium for the tholeiitic case, and at different pressures from 0.1 to 200 MPa. (**b**) Calculated normalized volume fraction of gas phase at equilibrium for the same simulations as in part (**a**). Normalization is done with respect to the gas volume fraction calculated at NNO, corresponding with 0.067 at $P=200$ MPa, 0.154 at $P=100$ MPa, 0.317 at $P=50$ MPa, 0.837 at $P=10$ MPa, and 0.999 at $P=0.1$ MPa.

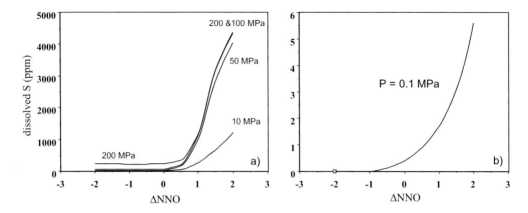

Fig. 5. (**a**) Calculated sulphur saturation content for the rhyolitic case, at different pressures from 10 to 200 MPa. Total amounts of H_2O, CO_2, and S in the system are 6, 1, and 0.5 wt%, respectively. Temperature is 1100 K. (**b**) Calculations pertaining to 0.1 MPa pressure. The amounts of sulphur dissolved as S^{2-} and SO_4^{2-} are not reported in this figure (while they are reported in Fig. 1 pertaining to the tholeiitic case). Figures 5–8 report other results pertaining to the same simulations in the present figure.

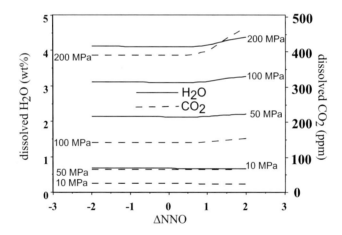

Fig. 6. Calculated water and carbon dioxide saturation contents for the rhyolitic case, at different pressures from 10 to 200 MPa.

of each dissolved volatile on fO_2, the only significant deviation being represented in both Figures 2 and 6 by CO_2 at 200 MPa pressure which increases significantly at ΔNNO greater than 1. The dissolved H_2O slightly increases with increasing oxidation state, while it slightly decreases in the tholeiitic case reported in Figure 2.

Figure 7 shows the calculated composition of the gas phase for the same runs as in Figures 5 and 6, analogous to Figure 3 which pertains to the tholeiitic case. The trends of H_2O and CO_2 in the gas phase (Fig. 7a) are very similar to those

in Fig. 3a, except that in this case the proportion of H_2O is larger than that of CO_2 at any pressure from 200 to 0.1 MPa, due to the larger amount of total water in the system in the rhyolitic (6 wt%) as compared with the tholeiitic (3 wt%) case. As for the tholeiitic case, the 0.1 MPa pressure curve of H_2O crosses lines pertaining to higher pressure at high oxidation state, indicating that in such conditions, as pressure is reduced from 200 MPa, the amount of H_2O in the gas phase increases down to a certain P value, then it decreases (or it remains about constant) approaching atmospheric pressure.

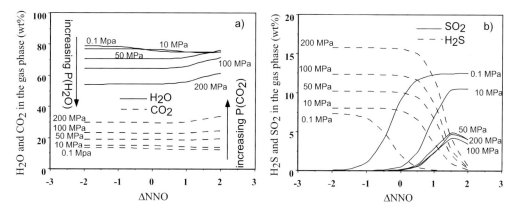

Fig. 7. (**a**) Calculated water and carbon dioxide proportions in the gas phase for the rhyolitic case, at different pressures from 0.1 to 200 MPa. (**b**) As for part (**a**), for sulphur dioxide and hydrogen sulphide.

Figure 7b shows the calculated amounts of SO_2 and H_2S in the gas phase. This figure displays analogies and differences with respect to the similar tholeiitic Figure 3b. Analogies include the prevalent speciation of gaseous sulphur as H_2S on the reduced side of the diagram, and as SO_2 on the oxidized side; the general constancy of H_2S abundance on the reduced side; and the presence of maxima in the distribution of SO_2. Differences include the different trends with pressure of H_2S and SO_2 abundance in the rhyolitic with respect to the tholeiitic case. In particular, the amount of H_2S is found to generally decrease with pressure in the tholeiitic case (Fig. 3b), and to increase with pressure in

the rhyolitic case (Fig. 7b). Other differences include the greater abundance of H_2S, and the lower abundance of SO_2, for the rhyolitic with respect to the tholeiitic case; and the position of maxima in the distribution of SO_2 with fO_2, which occur at around NNO for the tholeiitic case, and NNO+1.5 for the rhyolitic case. Such differences relate to the different trends with pressure evidenced in Figure 5 with respect to Figure 1, and to the larger amount of H_2O in the gas phase for the rhyolitic than for the tholeiitic case (Figs 3a and 7a).

Figure 8 shows the calculated mass (Fig. 8a) and normalized volume (Fig. 8b) of gas at equilibrium. Again, similarities and differences

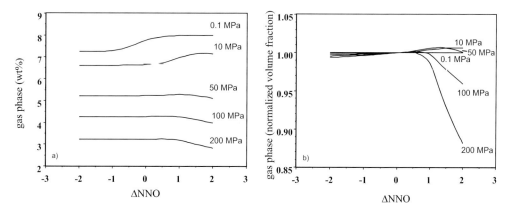

Fig. 8. (**a**) Calculated proportion of gas phase at equilibrium for the rhyolitic case, and at different pressures from 0.1 to 200 MPa. (**b**) Calculated normalized volume fraction of gas phase at equilibrium for the same simulations as in part (**a**). Normalization is done with respect to the gas volume fraction calculated at NNO, corresponding with 0.151 at $P=200$ MPa, 0.299 at $P=100$ MPa, 0.516 at $P=50$ MPa, 0.880 at $P=10$ MPa, and 0.999 at $P=0.1$ MPa.

with Figure 4 for the tholeiitic case emerge. Similarities are mostly evident by comparing Figures 4a and 8a (mass of gas). Here, apart from differences in numbers and spacing between curves referring to different pressures, and from small oscillations in the computed trends, the two tholeiitic and rhyolitic cases appear similar. On the contrary, the normalized volumes (Figs 4b and 8b) show important differences. In fact, in the case of rhyolite, the largest gas volume increase occurs when moving from oxidized to NNO conditions, while from NNO+0.5 to NNO − 2 the volume fraction of gas remains essentially constant. Furthermore, the maximum volume increase is much larger for the rhyolitic case, being about 15% at 200 MPa.

Discussion

The above results on the two-phase multi-component gas–liquid equilibrium in silicate systems clearly evidence the complex relationships between the several factors governing such an equilibrium. The trends shown in Figures 1–8 are in fact the result of relatively simple relationships, which are described above and in the Appendix, and which interact non-linearly, producing results which could not be predicted without the aid of numerical calculations.

In order to illustrate such a concept further, consider the sulphur saturation curves shown in Figures 1 and 5. On the basis of experimental investigation (Fincham & Richardson 1954; Nagashima & Katsura 1973; Katsura & Nagashima 1974) it is well known that sulphur displays a minimum on a log w^L_S v. log fO_2 diagram, implying a progressive decrease of sulphide (S^{2-}), and progressive increase of sulphate (SO_4^{2-}) content, with increasing oxidation state. The way in which such a change in the relative proportion of S^{2-} and SO_4^{2-} occurs, reflects the way in which the experiments are carried out. This can be well understood by combining equilibrium (6) with equilibria (A10) and (A11), respectively:

$$SO_{2(g)} + O^{2-}_{(m)} \Leftrightarrow \frac{3}{2}O_{2(g)} + S^{2-}_{(m)} \qquad (8)$$

$$SO_{2(g)} + \frac{1}{2}O_{2(g)} + O^{2-}_{(m)} \Leftrightarrow SO_4^{2-}_{(m)} \qquad (9)$$

At 0.1 MPa pressure, where most of the experimental determinations of sulphur solubility were made, it is common to maintain the fugacity of gaseous SO_2 constant throughout a large portion of the investigated oxygen fugacity field. Under such conditions, as long as the liquid structure is not significantly affected by dissolution of sulphur, the above equilibria imply that log w^L_S varies as $-3/2$ log fO_2 for sulphide dissolution, equation (8), and as $1/2$ log fO_2 for sulphate dissolution (equation 9). This conclusion, which is valid as long as the fugacity of SO_2 is kept constant, implies that the change of sulphate solubility is less sensitive to changes of log fO_2 than that of sulphide solubility.

The results in Figures 1 and 5 seem to show opposite behaviour, as evidenced by the general constant concentration of dissolved sulphur on the reduced side, and its large increase on the oxidized side of the diagrams. However, contrary to how it might appear, the curves in such figures coincide with the theoretical trends described above and implied by equations (8) and (9). This is evidenced by considering a normalized dissolved sulphur content, obtained by dividing w^L_S by the fugacity of SO_2. As can be seen in Figure 9, the above theoretical trends do emerge.

As a conclusion, although the experiments made at constant fSO_2 are useful and necessary to reveal the mechanisms of sulphur dissolution and to constrain the chemical equilibria describing such mechanisms, their application to the natural case should not be straightforward, since in such a case fSO_2 is governed by the complex multi-component equilibria that must be simultaneously satisfied and that produce non-intuitive dependence of $w^G_{SO_2}$, and therefore of fSO_2, with fO_2 as shown in Figures 3b and 7b. As an example, based on experimental S solubility trends like those in Figure 9, mixing between two liquids having dacitic and basaltic composition, each characterized by different fO_2 conditions, has been suggested to be the origin of an important gas exsolution event leading to eruption at Mount Pinatubo, Philippines, in 1991 (Kress 1997). In such a view, gas exsolution would have occurred as a consequence of a post-mixing oxygen fugacity close to that corresponding with the S solubility minimum in Figure 9, determining the conditions of sulphur supersaturation in the liquid. Figures 4 and 8 show that such a mechanism can be possible, but its efficiency is largely dependent on the specific conditions under consideration. The relatively small but significant changes occurring in the saturation content of water and carbon dioxide (Figs 2 and 6) and the gas compositional changes (Figs 3 and 7), accompanying variations in oxygen fugacity, contribute significantly to determining the amount of gas at equilibrium, the gas volume changes with fO_2, and the relative position of curves in Figures 4 and 8. An interpretation simply based on the trends in Figure 9

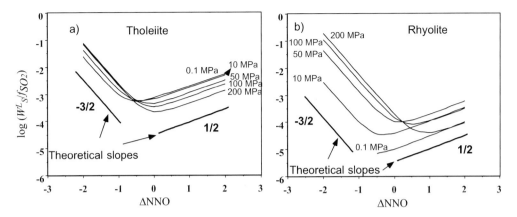

Fig. 9. Calculated normalized sulphur content at equilibrium for the simulations pertaining to (**a**) tholeiitic composition, and (**b**) rhyolitic composition, at different pressures from 0.1 to 200 MPa. Normalization is done in order to reproduce the expected trends corresponding with constant SO_2 fugacity, as explained in the text.

can be largely misleading, since it does not take into account the multi-component nature of gas–liquid equilibrium, which is capable of producing saturation curves that, although consistent with those in Figure 9, can have very different shapes and even totally hide the sulphur saturation minima corresponding with constant fSO_2 conditions. It is worth bearing in mind that using the present model for the Pinatubo case is not recommended, since the magma erupted during the 1991 eruption was saturated in S-rich solid phases (Carroll & Webster 1994; Kress 1997; Scaillet *et al.* 1998; Scaillet & Evans 1999). Such an example is made here as an illustrative case, where direct application of the curves in Figure 9 has been done to interpret the data from a real eruption, and to show how such simple trends can be misleading due to the multi-component nature of gas–liquid equilibrium.

Figure 9 also shows the position of minima in the distribution of dissolved sulphur (normalized as described above) versus the oxygen fugacity buffer. The low value of sulphide solubility for the rhyolitic case (Fig. 5), with only SO_4^{2-} as a dissolved S species at 0.1 MPa (Fig. 5a), explains why at such a pressure only the oxidized side appears in Figure 9b. As indicated by the figure, the minimum moves toward more oxidized conditions with increasing pressure. Such a shift from 0.1 to 200 MPa is less than 1 fO_2 log unit in the tholeiitic case, while it is much larger, at least 1.5 fO_2 log units, in the rhyolitic case. For comparison, Katsura and Nagashima (1974) found in their experiments that there was a minimum in sulphur solubility between QFM+0.5 and QFM+1 for basaltic compositions at 0.1 MPa and 1523 K, and between QFM

and QFM+2 for rhyodacitic compositions at the same *P–T* conditions (Carroll & Webster 1994), in quite good agreement with our calculations reported in Figure 9.

As for the sulphur saturation patterns described above, the variation of SO_2 and H_2S in the gas phase shown in Figures 3b and 7b appears quite complex, with largely opposite trends of H_2S and SO_2 with pressure for the two rhyolitic and tholeiitic cases at the two different temperatures considered. However, also in this case the complexities derive from the multi-component nature of the equilibrium, but they actually embody much simpler behaviours. Figure 10 shows the ratio of SO_2 to H_2S in the gas phase for the simulations in the present chapter, plotted as $\log (w^G_{SO_2}/w^G_{H_2S})$ versus fO_2. In spite of the large differences evidenced above, both the tholeiitic and rhyolitic cases show the same simple trends. At constant fO_2 buffer, SO_2/H_2S increases with decreasing pressure. Such an increase is relatively small for a pressure variation from 200 to 50 MPa, but then it becomes large as atmospheric pressure is approached. From 10 to 0.1 MPa such an increase is as great as almost two orders of magnitude.

The constant slope of the lines in Figure 10 can be understood by considering equilibrium (4) above, rewritten in terms of the equilibrium constant K_4:

$$\log \frac{f_{SO_2}}{f_{H_2S}} = 1.5 \log f_{O_2} - \log K_4 - \log f_{H_2O} \quad (10)$$

Since in the pressure range here considered, the fugacity coefficients of SO_2 and H_2S are nearly

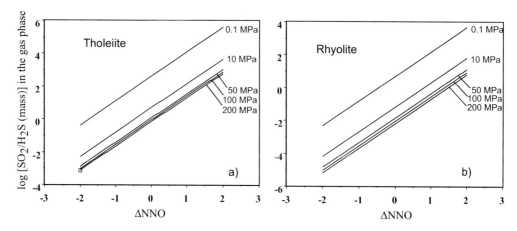

Fig. 10. Calculated mass ratio, on a log scale, of SO_2 over H_2S in the gas phase, for the simulations pertaining to (**a**) tholeiitic composition, and (**b**) rhyolitic composition, at different pressures from 0.1 to 200 MPa.

equal (Reid *et al.* 1988), the term on the left-hand side of equation (10) approximates the molar ratio SO_2/H_2S. The slopes of the lines in Figure 10 will reproduce the resulting theoretical value of 0.64 (= $1.5 - \log p_{H_2S}/p_{SO_2}$, where p is the molecular weight) only if the last term on the right-hand side of equation (8), and the total amount of H_2O+CO_2 in the gas phase, do not change significantly with oxygen fugacity. Figures 3a and 7a show that this is actually the case. Accordingly, the slopes of lines in Figure 10 are very close to the above-mentioned theoretical value.

We can conclude therefore that the multi-component nature of the equilibrium produces trends which appear complex, although they are the result of relatively simple behaviours which act together and interplay in a non-linear way. Numerical modelling is required in order to take into account such non-linearities and to obtain predictions which could not be simply obtained by considering all the effects separately. In this light, we can expect that the future introduction into the modelling of additional S-bearing phases like pyrrhotite, anhydrite or immiscible Fe–O–S liquid, will result in important and still unpredictable changes in the distribution of each volatile component, especially S-bearing species, between the different phases at equilibrium.

Table 3 examines the validity of assumption that the gas phase is composed of only H_2O, CO_2, SO_2, and H_2S. This is evaluated on the basis of chemical equilibria applied at the conditions corresponding with the calculated gas phase compositions and fugacities. From such an analysis it is possible to estimate the amount of gas species other than those considered. In the

Table 3. *Estimated amounts of $COS+CO+S_2+SO+H_2$ (mol.%) in the gas phase, for the range of conditions considered in the calculations in Figures 1–10. Based on thermodynamic data from Barin and Knacke (1973).*

ΔNNO	Tholeiite (1400 K)		Rhyolite (1100 K)	
	200 MPa	0.1 MPa	200 MPa	0.1 MPa
−2	15	9	5.7	6.5
−1	6	2.8	2	2.1
0	2	0.9	0.8	0.7
1	0.5	0.3	0.4	0.2
2	0.1	0.1	< 0.1	< 0.1

range of conditions in Figures 1–10, the molar amounts of such components vary in the following ranges: S_2 0.1–100 ppm; SO 0.1–10 ppm; COS 10^{-3} ppm to 1.5%; CO 40 ppm to 12%; H_2 300 ppm to 7%. From Table 3, it emerges that appreciable errors in neglecting the above gaseous species only emerge for the most reduced conditions encountered in our calculations.

Up to this point, we have discussed the capabilities and internal consistency of the present multi-component volatile saturation model. The reliability of the model's predictions is based on the number and quality of data on which it is calibrated. In the present case, the calibration has been done separately for the H_2O+CO_2 and S saturation parts that make up the C–O–H–S saturation model, as described above and in the Appendix. Unfortunately, at present, the behaviour of the above three volatile species in silicate liquids is not known with the same accuracy. Water solubility is known at a satisfactory level (Papale 1997; Zhang 1999), and it is demonstrated that most of the experimental data are mutually consistent (Papale 1997). This results in the possibility of modelling H_2O solubility with satisfactory confidence. On the contrary, the existing data pertaining to both carbon dioxide and sulphur solubility in silicate liquids are much less exhaustive. Carbon dioxide solubility data produced before the 1980s are largely inconsistent with those produced during the last twenty years (Blank & Brooker 1994; Papale 1999), resulting in a drastic decrease of the quality of data-set for model calibration, and in a significant increase in the uncertainty of predictions regarding the CO_2 or H_2O+CO_2 with respect to H_2O saturation in silicate liquids.

As far as S solubility is concerned, about 90% of the data have been produced at atmospheric pressure, mostly used in the metallurgical and glass industries. As a consequence, only a few data pertain to multi-component volatile conditions. This represents a major limit for the present modelling, as the model itself shows a large influence of dissolved water on the dissolved sulphur at saturation. In order to explore further such dependency, we have performed additional simulations (reported in Figure 11) in which we have fixed the fO_2 buffer at $NNO+1$, and have maintained all the input conditions unchanged apart from total H_2O in the system ($w^T_{H_2O}$ in equations (1)–(3)), which varies from 2 to 8 wt%. Obviously, an increase of $w^T_{H_2O}$ corresponds with an increase in the amount of dissolved water, which varies from 1.9 to 5.3 wt%

at the maximum pressure of 300 MPa considered in Figure 11 (this value being less than the solubility of water at the same conditions, mainly due to the additional presence of carbon dioxide in the system). Closed-system conditions have been assumed in the calculations of Figure 11, although the model can work equally well with open-system conditions (that is, by taking into account a given loss of gas from the system as pressure decreases). As the figure shows, the effect of increasing amounts of water in the system is that of largely decreasing the saturation content of S in the liquid. At the largest amounts of H_2O employed (6 and 8 wt%), the S saturation curve shows nearly constant values from 300 to about 50 MPa.

Conclusions

We have devised a physico-mathematical model for the equilibrium between fluids with C–O–H–S composition and silicate liquids with composition defined in terms of 10 major oxides. The model accounts for many aspects of the two-phase multi-component equilibrium, and is particularly sensitive to compositional variations of the liquid and gas phases. Examples of calculations illustrate the complexities of multi-component equilibrium in silicate systems. Predictions on the amount of dissolved volatiles, particularly sulphur species, as well as on the composition of the gas phase at equilibrium, that do not account for the multi-component nature of magmatic gases, can result in large errors.

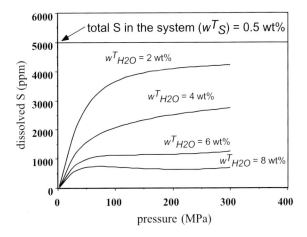

Fig. 11. Calculated sulphur saturation content as a function of pressure for the rhyolitic case, $fO_2=NNO+1$, and four different assumed total water contents from 2 to 8 wt%. Points on the curve labeled '$w^T_{H_2O}=6$ wt%' and corresponding with $P=200$, 100, 50, 10, and 0.1 MPa, correspond with those in Figure 5 at $NNO+1$.

Particularly relevant results include, firstly, the dependency of sulphur saturation on oxygen fugacity, which in the natural case can be very different from the experimental curves, commonly obtained by buffering the fugacity of one sulphur species in the gas phase; and, secondly, the composition of the gas phase at equilibrium with the silicate liquid, which can display very complex and largely opposite trends with pressure, depending on the specific conditions under consideration. The limits of the model include, firstly, the neglect of the presence of additional sulphur-bearing solid or liquid phases, implying a rather narrow range of applicability of the model to natural cases; and secondly, the still unsatisfactory experimental constraints for carbon dioxide solubility and, most importantly, for sulphur saturation under high-pressure, hydrous conditions, increasing significantly the uncertainty associated to the model predictions. A model like the present one, constrained by additional data covering those P–T–fO_2-compositional regions not well represented in the available data-set, would represent an optimum basis for an extension to multi-phase multi-component liquid–solid–gas equilibrium.

APPENDIX

Description of $H_2O + CO_2$ and S saturation models

$H_2O + CO_2$ saturation model

The model for the saturation of $H_2O + CO_2$ fluids in silicate liquids is described in Papale (1999). Only minor modification due to the presence of dissolved sulphur is introduced in the expressions of the activity coefficient of dissolved water and carbon dioxide (equations (A7) and (A8) below), and the chemical interaction between sulphur and other components in the silicate liquid is neglected. Such a simplification (which is obviously not made in the polymeric model for S saturation described below) introduces an uncertainty in the predictions of the $H_2O + CO_2 + S$ saturation when significant amounts of sulphur of the order of several tenths per cent by weight are dissolved in the liquid.

An additional modification with respect to the model presented in Papale (1999) is that now the fugacities of components in the gas phase are computed by means of the SUPERFLUID code (Belonoshko *et al.* 1992) in order to account for complex gas composition including SO_2 and H_2S, determined by mass balance and homogeneous chemical equilibrium in the gas phase (equations (1)–(5)).

The chemical equilibrium between exsolved and dissolved water and carbon dioxide is given by the following equations:

$$f^G_{H_2O} = \gamma_{H_2O} x_{H_2O} f^{oL}_{H_2O} \qquad (A1)$$

$$f^G_{CO_2} = \gamma_{CO_2} x_{CO_2} f^{oL}_{CO_2} \qquad (A2)$$

where f is fugacity, γ is the activity coefficient in the liquid phase, x is mole fraction in the liquid phase, f^o is a reference or standard fugacity, and the superscripts G and L refer to the gas and liquid phases, respectively. The chemical equilibrium equations A1 and A2 are closed by two mass-balance equations expressing conservation of total and exsolved mass of volatiles:

$$y_{H_2O} + y_{CO_2} = 1 \qquad (A3)$$

$$\frac{x^T_{H_2O} - y_{H_2O}}{y_{H_2O} - x_{H_2O}} = \frac{x^T_{CO_2} - y_{CO_2}}{y_{CO_2} - x_{CO_2}} \qquad (A4)$$

where y is mole fraction in the gas phase, and the superscript T means 'total' (that is, with respect to total mass, including liquid and gas phases).

The reference fugacity of each dissolved volatile in the liquid is given by the following equation:

$$\ln f^{oL}_i (P,T) = \ln f^{oL}_i (P^o, T^o) + \int_{P^0}^{P} \frac{v^o_i}{RT}$$
$$dP - \int_{T^0}^{T} \frac{1}{RT^2} \int_{P^0}^{P} \left[v^o_i - T \left(\frac{\partial v^o_i}{\partial T} \right)_P \right] dP dT \qquad (A5)$$

where R is the gas constant, and v^o_i is the molar volume of the ith dissolved volatile (water or carbon dioxide) in its reference state, given by

$$v^o_i = a_1 + a_2 T + a_3 T^2 + $$
$$a_4 T^3 + P \left(a_5 + a_6 T + a_7 T^2 \right) + $$
$$P^2 \left(a_8 + a_9 T \right) + a_{10} P^3 \qquad (A6)$$

with parameters $a_{1...10}$ from Burnham & Davis (1971) for dissolved water, and from Papale (1999) for dissolved carbon dioxide.

The activity coefficients of dissolved water and carbon dioxide are calculated on the basis of a model for the excess Gibbs' free energy of silicate liquids similar to that of Ghiorso *et al.* (1983) and Ghiorso & Sack (1994), but with the difference that the presence of carbon dioxide introduces a non-isometric mixing behaviour with P-dependence of activity coefficients (Papale 1997):

$$RT \ln \gamma_{H_2O} = (1 - x_{H_2O}) x_{CO_2} w_{H_2O CO_2} +$$

$$(1 - x_{H_2O})(1 - x_{H_2O} - x_{CO_2} - x_S) \sum_{i \neq CO_2 = 1}^{n} x_i' w_{H_2O i}^{(0)}$$

$$- x_{CO_2}(1 - x_{H_2O} - x_{CO_2} - x_S)$$

$$\left[\sum_{i \neq H_2O = 1}^{n} x_i' w_{CO_2 i}^{(0)} + \ln \frac{P}{P^o} \sum_{i \neq H_2O = 1}^{n} x_i' w_{CO_2 i}^{(1)} \right]$$

$$- (1 - x_{H_2O} - x_{CO_2} - x_S)^2$$

$$\sum_{i \neq H_2O, CO_2 = 1}^{n-1} \sum_{j \neq H_2O, CO_2 = i+1}^{n} x_i' x_j' w_{ij} \qquad (A7)$$

$$RT \ln \gamma_{CO_2} = (1 - x_{CO_2}) x_{H_2O} w_{H_2O CO_2} - x_{H_2O}$$

$$(1 - x_{H_2O} - x_{CO_2} - x_S) \sum_{i \neq CO_2 = 1}^{n} x_i' w_{H_2O i}^{(0)}$$

$$+ (1 - x_{CO_2})(1 - x_{H_2O} - x_{CO_2} - x_S)$$

$$\left[\sum_{i \neq H_2O = 1}^{n} x_i' w_{CO_2 i}^{(0)} + \ln \frac{P}{P^o} \sum_{i \neq H_2O = 1}^{n} x_i' w_{CO_2 i}^{(1)} \right]$$

$$- (1 - x_{H_2O} - x_{CO_2} - x_S)^2$$

$$\sum_{i \neq H_2O, CO_2 = 1}^{n-1} \sum_{j \neq H_2O, CO_2 = i+1}^{n} x_i' x_j' w_{ij} \qquad (A8)$$

where the w_{ij} values are binary interaction coefficients expressing the attractive–repulsive behaviour of each pair of liquid components, the values of which are taken from Ghiorso et al. (1983) for coefficients not involving volatiles, and from Papale (1997, 1999) for coefficients involving dissolved water and carbon dioxide, and the mole fractions of non-volatile components in the liquid are recalculated according to:

$$x_{i \neq H_2O, CO_2}' = \frac{x_i}{1 - x_{H_2O} - x_{CO_2} - x_s} \qquad (A9)$$

Note that equations (A7)–(A9) contain the mole fractions of dissolved sulphur (x_S), which modifies the activities of dissolved water and carbon dioxide through dilution in the liquid phase (non-reactive effect).

S saturation model

The model for the solubility of sulphur in silicate liquids is described in Moretti (2002), and it is here summarized in some more detail with respect to the above $H_2O + CO_2$ saturation model.

Sulphur solubility is modelled via a thermo-chemical model that allows the calculation of the sulphide and sulphate capacities in simple and complex silicate melts. The model is based on the Toop–Samis polymeric model (Toop & Samis 1962b) combined with a Flood–Grjotheim treatment (Flood & Grjotheim 1952) involving oxide component reactions.

Since the work of Fincham and Richardson (1954), the solubility of sulphur may be described via the following reactions:

$$\frac{1}{2} S_{2(g)} + O^{2-}{}_{(m)} \Leftrightarrow \frac{1}{2} O_{2(g)} + S^{2-}{}_{(m)} \qquad (A10)$$

$$\frac{1}{2} S_{2(g)} + \frac{3}{2} O_{2(g)} + O^{2-}{}_{(m)} \Leftrightarrow SO_4^{2-}{}_{(m)} \qquad (A11)$$

Equations A10 and A11 can be written in terms of any gaseous species of sulphur in the O–S system, e.g. by substituting S_2 with SO_2 through equations (4) and (5), as discussed in the text. Equations A10 and A11 should be intended as being representative of the multiple equilibria between *quasi-chemical ionic* species of sulphur and oxygen in the melt phase (Fincham & Richardson 1954). This means that the equilibrium constants for reactions A10 and A11 depend on the bulk composition, reflecting the various dissociation constants pertinent to equilibria of the type $MA \Leftrightarrow M^{v+}{}_{2/v} + A^{2-}$. Equations (A10) and (A11) may be solved in the framework of the Flood–Grjotheim thermochemical cycle (Flood & Grjotheim 1952), which allows calculation of the contribution of disproportionation equilibria of oxide–sulphide or oxide–sulphate components, i.e.:

$$\frac{1}{2} S_{2(g)} + M_{2/v} O_{(m)} \Leftrightarrow \frac{1}{2} O_{2(g)} + M_{2/v} S_{(m)} \qquad (A12)$$

$$K_{Ox-S^{2-}, M} = \frac{a_{M_{2/v}S}}{a_{M_{2/v}O}} \left(\frac{fO_2}{fS_2} \right)^{\frac{1}{2}} \qquad (A13)$$

$$\frac{1}{2} S_{2(g)} + M_{2/v} O_{(m)} + \frac{3}{2} O_{2(g)} \Leftrightarrow M_{2/v} SO_{4(m)} \qquad (A12a)$$

$$K_{Ox} - SO_4^{2-}, M = \frac{{}^aH_2S_{/v}}{{}^aH_2O_{/v}} fO_2^{-\frac{3}{2}} fS_2^{-\frac{1}{2}}$$

(A13a)

where the subscript Ox–S indicates the disproportionation between oxide and sulphide or sulphate salt. In terms of Flood–Grjotheim extension:

$$\ln K_{A10/A11} = N_{A^{v+}} \ln K'_{O-S,A} +$$
$$N_{A^{v+}} \ln K'_{O-S,B} + ...$$

(A14)

where N is the *electrically equivalent ion fraction* (Flood & Grjotheim 1952):

$$N_{A^{v+}} = \frac{v_A^+ n_A}{v_A^+ n_A + v_B^+ n_B}$$

(A15)

Electrically equivalent fractions are computed by making use of the Temkin notation for fused salts. Therefore, each fraction refers to the amount of each cation (anion) in the corresponding cationic (anionic) matrix (Temkin 1945).

The K quantities in equation (A14) differ from the equilibrium constant A13 or A13a by a constant factor. In fact, the reference state condition for $M_{2/v}S$ consistent with the Toop–Samis theory is that of completely dissociated sulphide in solution, in which the Temkin activity is one. Thus, for instance, in the case of sulphides, although for some particular cation M^{v+} (for example Fe^{2+}), the thermodynamic equilibrium demands:

$$\frac{a_{Fe_{melt}^{2+}} a_{S_{melt}^{2-}}}{a_{FeS_{melt}}} = K_{diss}$$

(A16)

the state of reference is such that K_{diss}, the equilibrium constant for sulphide dissolution, reduces to one (Lewis & Randall 1970; Ottonello *et al.* 2001). This difference represents a contribution of translation from the standard state of completely dissociated (Temkin model) sulphide component $M_{2/v}S^*$, for which (still taking the example of Fe^{2+})

$$\mu_{FeS,melt} = \mu^*_{FeS,melt} +$$
$$RT \ln \left(a_{Fe^{2+}} \cdot a_{S^{2-}} \right)$$

(A17)

to the standard state of the true molten sulphide component for which

$$\mu_{FeS,melt} = \mu^o_{FeS,melt} + RT \ln a_{FeS,melt}$$

(A18)

We have thus

$$\exp \left(\frac{\mu^*_{FeS,melt} - \mu^o_{FeS,melt}}{RT} \right) =$$
$$\frac{a_{FeS,melt}}{a_{Fe^{2+}} \cdot a_{S^{2-}}} = K_{diss}^{-1}$$

(A19)

The oxide–sulphide equilibrium between melt components and a gaseous phase becomes:

$$\frac{(S^{2-})}{(O^{2-})} = K_{O-S,M} \exp$$

$$\left(\frac{\mu^\circ_{M_{2/v}S,melt} - \mu^\circ_{M_{2/v}O,melt} + \mu^*_{M_{2/v}O,melt} - \mu^*_{M_{2/v}S,melt}}{RT} \right)$$

$$\left(\frac{f_{S_2}}{f_{O_2}} \right)^{\frac{1}{2}} = K'_{O-S,M} \left(\frac{f_{S_2}}{f_{O_2}} \right)^{\frac{1}{2}}$$

(A20)

The same concepts apply for sulphate components. The energetic gap represented by the term within the large brackets in equation (A20), may be conceived as an annealing term related to the transfer of sulphide or sulphate component from the state of pure liquid component to its true structural condition in the melt, and must be accounted for in equation (A14).

The concentration of free oxygens (O^{2-}) is computed through a polymeric approach developed by Ottonello *et al.* (2001), which solves the following equilibrium:

$$2O^- \Leftrightarrow O^0 + O^{2-}$$

(A21)

The above equation represents the polymerization reaction between singly bonded (O^-), doubly bonded or bridging oxygen (O^0), and free oxide ions (O^{2-}), following the nomenclature given by Fincham & Richardson (1954). The polymerization constant between the three quasi-chemical species of oxygen involved in equilibrium A21 is related to the contrast of acid–base properties of the constituent oxides in the slag, depending, firstly, on their role as either network formers or network modifiers, established according to their Lux–Flood acidity, and, secondly, on their optical basicity. Ottonello *et al.* (2001) obtained the following relationship:

$$K_{2,melt} = \exp$$

$$\left[4.662 \times \left(\frac{\sum_i X_{M_i^{y+}} \gamma_{M_i^{y+}} -}{\sum_j X_{T_j^{\eta+}} \gamma_{T_{ij}^{\eta+}}} \right) - 1.1445 \right] \quad (A22)$$

where X_M are ion fractions computed over the appropriate matrix, and γ is the *basicity moderating parameter*, which is the reciprocal of the so-called 'optical basicity' (Duffy 1990) and represents the tendency of the oxide-forming cation to reduce the localized donor properties of oxide ions (Duffy & Ingram 1973, 1976; Ottonello *et al.* 2001). The computation of the polymerization constant allows the calculation of the extension of the anionic matrix by solving the mass balances of the Toop–Samis model along the guidelines of Ottonello *et al.* (2001). In other words, from the knowledge of the equilibrium constant for the equilibrium (A21) we can calculate how many polyanions and free anions constitute the anionic matrix. On such a basis, electrically equivalent ion fractions are calculated.

Oxide–sulphide equilibria as well as oxide–sulphate equilibria were then investigated for all cations in terms of an Arrhenian T-dependency and compared with observed quantities, as it follows from equation (A20):

$$\ln K'_{O-S,M} = A'_{O-S,M} + B'_{O-S,M}/T -$$
$$\frac{1}{RT} \int_1^P \Delta V_m dP \quad (A23)$$

where ΔV_m represents the change in molar volume associated with molten couples oxide–sulphide or oxide–sulphate, slopes A' account for the energy gaps (annealing terms) between pure liquid oxides and sulphides and the Temkin standard or reference state. Thermochemical compilations from Barin & Knacke (1973) and Barin *et al.* (1977) allow the determination of some of the terms B'_{O-S} in equation A23. These terms correspond with all those pertaining to metal oxide–metal sulphide exchange reactions, and to a few of those pertaining to metal oxide–metal sulphate exchange reactions, namely, those involving Na^+, K^+, Mg^{2+}. The available data regarding such cations, for which exchange reactions with both sulphide and sulphate are known, show that

$$B'_{MO-MSO_4} - B'_{MO-MS} = const \quad (A24)$$

Equation A24 simply states that the enthalpy of the various sulphide to sulphate reactions ($MS + 2O_2 \Leftrightarrow MSO_4$) is a constant, independently of the coordinating metal cation involved in the reaction, in line with what may be found for solid compounds (Jacob & Jyenger 1982). Therefore, we have assumed that such a relationship holds for any M cation, including those for which only data for sulphide reactions are available.

Volume terms for molten sulphides and sulphates have been estimated on the basis of a generalization based on optical basicity (Ottonello *et al.* 2001; Moretti 2002), and are reported in Table A.1. The oxide–sulphide thermodynamic constants A' in equation (A23) are treated as model parameters in a non-linear minimization routine that compares the computed and measured *sulphide capacity* C_s defined by Fincham & Richardson (1954):

$$C'_S = [S]_{wt\%} \left(\frac{P_{O_2}}{P_{S_2}} \right)^{\frac{1}{2}} \quad (A25)$$

The same procedure has been adopted to determine oxide–sulphate thermodynamic constants

Table A1. *Molar volumes employed in the calculations (Moretti 2002).*

	V (1100 K) (cm^3 mol.$^{-1} \times 10^3$)	V (1400 K) (cm^3 mol.$^{-1} \times 10^3$)
Si(SO$_4$)$_2$	127.50	135.26
Ti(SO$_4$)$_2$	119.67	129.57
Al$_2$(SO$_4$)$_3$	186.60	198.98
Fe$_2$(SO$_4$)$_3$	187.91	202.23
FeSO$_4$	62.31	67.05
MnSO$_4$	60.39	65.07
MgSO$_4$	60.28	64.93
CaSO$_4$	65.23	69.97
Na$_2$SO$_4$	74.86	80.95
K$_2$SO$_4$	89.35	96.78
H$_2$SO$_4$	65.13	70.03
SiS$_2$	78.66	86.42
TiS$_2$	68.96	78.86
Al$_2$S$_3$	66.60	78.98
Fe$_2$S$_3$	67.91	82.23
FeS	22.31	27.05
MnS	20.39	25.07
MgS	20.28	24.93
CaS	25.23	29.97
Na$_2$S	34.86	40.95
K$_2$S	49.35	56.78
H$_2$S	25.13	30.03

98 R. MORETTI *ET AL.*

A' by introducing the *sulphate capacity* C_S'':

$$C_S'' = [S]_{wt\%} P_{O_2}^{-3/2} P_{S_2}^{-1/2} \qquad (A26)$$

The comparison between computed and experimental sulphide and sulphate capacities for the data-set used in the calibration procedure is shown in Figure A1. This figure includes all the data that we could find in the literature up to the middle of 2001, and that contain all the necessary information (composition, temperature, pressure, fO_2 – given or constrained by equilibria, and the fugacity of one sulphur-bearing component in the fluid phase irrespective of its amount) which allows their use in the regression procedure. Experimental data mostly come from work performed for the purposes of metallurgy and glass industry research. For this reason, most of these data refer to 0.1 MPa pressure. A subset of data has been obtained under pressurized, hydrous conditions (indicated in Fig. A1). The temperature-compositional range covered by the data is very large, and the generally good consistency between data and model calculations indicates that the computed electrically equivalent fractions and molar amounts of free oxygen are sufficiently accurate and internally consistent, independent of the chemical complexities of the investigated systems. This provides a further suggestion that the polymerization framework of both artificial slags and natural silicate melts is correlated with the contrasts between the acid–base properties of the various oxide components in the melt.

Figure A2 shows the results of an error propagation analysis, obtained by considering all the standard deviations in the computed A' terms in equation A23 for all metal sulphide and metal sulphate couples describing the silicate liquid with dissolved sulphur. Figure A2a refers to the dissolved sulphide in the tholeiitic liquid at 1400 K and NNO – 1, and Figure A2b refers to dissolved sulphate in the rhyolitic liquid at 1100 K and NNO+1. As shown in Figure A2a, the uncertainty associated with dissolved sulphide calculations is less than half an order of magnitude, i.e. quite small compared with the total range of dissolved sulphide in the figure, which spans about five orders of magnitude. Hydrous S saturation data were obtained by two different authors, and refer to 21 determinations on trachyandesitic liquid (Luhr 1990) and 36 determinations on rhyolitic liquid (Clemente 1998; Clemente *et al.* 2002). In both cases the experimental conditions were unbuffered with respect to fS_2 (but were buffered for fH_2). However, in both cases the presence of pyrrhotite in the data subset employed for model parameter calibration allowed the measurement of fS_2, and therefore the experimental sulphide capacity could be calculated.

The case of sulphate in Figure A2b is quite different. In this case, the uncertainty in calculations (given by the two widest solid lines) is much larger than in the case of sulphide. The origin of the much larger uncertainty for sulphate as compared with sulphide calculations is to be found in the lower number of data available for the former, as well as in the quite limited amount of data referring to sulphate saturation at high-pressure, hydrous conditions. These data refer to only one group of experiments by Luhr (1990) on a trachyandesitic melt.

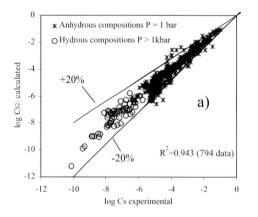 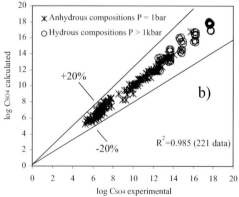

Fig. A1. (a) Comparison between calculated and experimental sulphide capacities for 794 data from literature involving large composition and temperature ranges. Data at pressurized, hydrous conditions are reported with a different symbol. (b) As for part (a), for sulphate capacities (221 data).

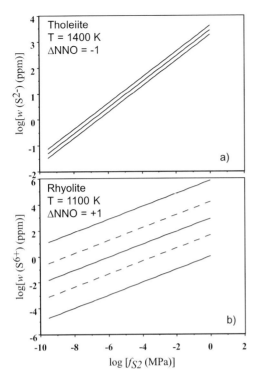

Fig. A2. Uncertainties in the calculation of dissolved sulphide (**a**) and sulphate (**b**), for the tholeiitic and rhyolitic cases. Uncertainties result from the standard deviations associated with calibrated model parameters.

As for the experiments by Carroll & Rutherford (1985, 1987) on a similar composition, the experimental determinations by Luhr (1990) refer to unconstrained fugacity conditions. However, while the former authors did not include the necessary data to evaluate the S_2 (or SO_2) fugacity in the gas phase, the latter includes an estimate made on the basis of solid–gas equilibrium involving clinopyroxene, titanomagnetite, anhydrite, O_2, and S_2, allowing the use of such data for the calibration in the sulphur saturation model of the parameter in equation (A12a) corresponding with H_2O–SO_4^{2-} reaction in the liquid. Actually, these data were the only ones useful for this purpose. Since no measurement of the dissolved amount of water in the trachy-andesitic melt at the various experimental conditions was made, although the coexisting gas phase was estimated to be close to pure H_2O (Luhr 1990), the calibration has been done assuming an H_2O saturation content corresponding with the solubility of water at those P–T–composition conditions, calculated using the model of Papale (1997).

In the light of the above discussion, it must be stressed that the calibration of the model parameter for H_2O–SO_4^{2-} reaction in equation (A12a) still relies on too few experimental data, containing probably quite large approximations. The consequence is that the model predictions on sulphur saturation at hydrous oxidized conditions should be considered cautiously, and that additional data are required for a better calibration of the model parameter involving H_2O–SO_4^{2-} reaction.

References

BARIN, I. & KNACKE, O. 1973. *Thermochemical Pro-perties of Inorganic Substances.* Springer-Verlag, Berlin/Heidelberg/New York.

BARIN, I., KNACKE, O. & KUBASCHEWSKY, O. 1977. *Thermochemical Properties of Inorganic Substances, Supplement.* Springer-Verlag, Berlin/Heidelberg/New York.

BELONOSHKO, A. B., SHI, P. & SAXENA, S. K. 1992. SUPERFLUID: a FORTRAN 77 program for calculation of Gibbs free energy and volume of C–H–O–N–S–Ar mixtures. *Computers and Geoscience,* **18,** 1267–1269.

BLANK, J.G. & BROOKER, R.A. 1994. Experimental studies of carbon dioxide in silicate melts: solubility, speciation, and stable carbon isotope behaviour. *In:* CARROLL, M.R. & HOLLOWAY, J.R. (eds) *Volatiles in Magmas.* Reviews in Mineralogy, **30,** 157–186.

BURNHAM, C.W. 1985. Energy release in subvolcanic environments: implications for breccia formation. *Economic Geology,* **80,** 1515–1522.

BURNHAM, C. W. & DAVIS, N. F. 1971. The role of H_2O in silicate melts. 1. P–V–T relations in the system $NaAlSi_3O_8$–H_2O to 10 kbars and 1000°C. *American Journal of Science,* **270,** 54–79.

CARROLL, M. R. & RUTHERFORD, M. J. 1985. Sulfide and sulfate saturation in hydrous silicate melts. *Journal of Geophysical Research,* **90,** C601–C612.

CARROLL, M. R. & RUTHERFORD, M. J. 1987. The stability of igneous anhydrite: experimental results and implications for sulfur behaviour in the 1982 El Chichon trachyandesite and other evolved magmas. *Journal of Petrology,* **28,** 781–801.

CARROLL, M. R. & WEBSTER, J. D. 1994. Solubilities of sulfur, noble gases, nitrogen, chlorine, and fluorine in magmas. *In:* CARROLL, M. R. & HOLLOWAY, J. R. (eds) *Volatiles in Magmas. Reviews in Mineralogy,* **30,** 187–230.

CASADEVALL, T., ROSE, W., GERLACH, T., GREENLAND, L. P., EWERT, J., WUNDERMAN, R. & SYMONDS, R. 1983. Gas emissions and the eruptions of Mount St. Helens through 1982. *Science,* **221,** 1383–1385.

CASHMAN, K. V., STURTEVANT, B., PAPALE, P. & NAVON, O. 2000. Magmatic fragmentation. *In:* SIGURDSSON, H., HOUGHTON, B., MCNUTT, S. R., RYMER, H. & STIX, J. (eds) *Encyclopedia of Volcanoes,* Academic Press, San Diego, 421–430.

CLEMENTE, B. 1998. *Etude expérimentale et modélis-*

ation de la solubilité du soufre dans les liquides magmatiques. PhD thesis, University of Orleans.

CLEMENTE, B., SCAILLET, B. & PICHAVANT, M. 2003. The solubility of sulfur in hydrous rhyolitic melts. *Journal of Petrology* (in press).

DINGWELL, D. B. 1998. Recent experimental progress in the physical description of silicic magma relevant to explosive volcanism. *In:* GILBERT, J. S. AND SPARKS, R. S. J. (eds) *The Physics of Explosive Volcanic Eruptions.* Special Publication, Geological Society of London, **145**, 9–26.

DUFFY, J. A. 1990. *Bonding, Energy Levels and Bands.* Longman, London.

DUFFY, J. A. & INGRAM, M. D. 1973. Nephelauxetic effect and Pauling electronegativity. *Journal of the Chemical Society, Chemical Communications,* **17**, 635–636.

DUFFY, J. A. & INGRAM, M. D. 1976. An interpretation of glass chemistry in terms of the optical basicity concept. *Journal of Non-Crystalline Solids,* **21**, 373–410.

FINCHAM, C. J. B. & RICHARDSON, F. D. 1954. The behaviour of sulphur in silicate and aluminate melts. *Proceedings of the Royal Society of London,* **A223**, 40–62.

FLOOD, H. & GRJOTHEIM, K. 1952. Thermodynamic calculation of slag equilibria. *Iron and Steel Institute Journal,* **171**, 64–80.

GERLACH, T.M. 1986. Exsolution of H_2O, CO_2, and S during eruptive episodes at Kilauea volcano, Hawaii. *Journal of Geophysical Research,* **91**, 12 177–12 185.

GERLACH, T. M. & NORDLIE, B. E. 1975. The C–H–O–S gaseous systems, Part II: temperature, atomic composition, and molecular equilibria in volcanic gases. *American Journal of Science,* **275**, 377–394.

GHIORSO, M. S. & SACK, R. O. 1994. Chemical mass transfer in magmatic processes IV. A revised internally consistent thermodynamic model for the interpolation and extrapolation of liquid–solid equilibria in magmatic systems at elevated temperatures and pressures. *Contributions to Mineralogy and Petrology,* **119**, 197–212.

GHIORSO, M. S., CARMICHAEL, I. S. E., RIVERS, M. L. & SACK, R. O. 1983. The Gibbs free energy of mixing of natural silicate liquids; an expanded regular solution approximation for the calculation of magmatic intensive variables. *Contributions to Mineralogy and Petrology,* **84**, 107–145.

HOLLOWAY, J. R. & BLANK, J. G. 1994. Application of experimental results to C–O–H species in natural melts. *In:* CARROLL, M. R. & HOLLOWAY, J. R. (eds) *Volatiles in Magmas. Reviews in Mineralogy,* **30**, 187–230.

JACOB, K. T. & JYENGAR, G. N. K. 1982. Oxidation of alkaline earth sulfides to sulfates: thermodynamic aspects. *Metallurgical Transactions B,* **17B**, 387–390.

JAUPART, C. 1998. Gas loss from magmas through conduit walls during eruption. *In:* GILBERT, J. S. & SPARKS, R. S. J. (eds) *The Physics of Explosive Volcanic Eruptions.* Geological Society, London, Special Publications, **145**, 73–90.

JOHNSON, M. C., ANDERSON, A. T. JR & RUTHERFORD, M. J. 1994. Pre–eruptive volatile contents of magmas. *In:* CARROLL, M. R. & HOLLOWAY, J. R. (eds) *Volatiles in Magmas. Reviews in Mineralogy,* **30**, 281–330.

KATSURA, T. & NAGASHIMA, S. 1974. Solubility of sulfur in some magmas at 1 atmosphere. *Geochimica et Cosmochimica Acta,* **38**, 517–531.

KRESS, V. 1997. Magma mixing as a source for Pinatubo sulphur. *Nature,* **389**, 591–593.

LANGE, R. A. 1994. The effect of H_2O, CO_2 and F on the density and viscosity of silicate melts. *In:* CARROLL, M. R. & HOLLOWAY, J. R. (eds), *Volatiles in Magmas, Reviews in Mineralogy,* **30**, 331–369.

LEWIS, G. N. & RANDALL, M. 1970. *Termodinamica.* Leonardo Edizioni Scientifiche, Rome.

LUHR, J. F. 1990. Experimental phase relations of water and sulfur-saturated arc magmas and the 1982 eruption of El-Chichon volcano. *Journal of Petrology,* **31**, 1071–1114.

MADER, H. M. 1998. Conduit flow and fragmentation. *In:* GILBERT, J. S. & SPARKS, R. S. J. (eds) *The Physics of Explosive Volcanic Eruptions.* Geological Society, London, Special Publications, **145**, 51–71.

MÉTRICH, N., BERTAGNINI, A., LANDI, P. & ROSI, M. 2001. Crystallization driven by decompression and water loss at Stromboli volcano (Aeolian Islands, Italy). *Journal of Petrology,* **42**, 1471–1490.

MORETTI, R. 2002. *Solubility of volatiles in silicate melts with particular regard to sulphur species: theoretical aspects and application to Etnean volcanics.* PhD thesis, University of Pisa.

NAGASHIMA, S. & KATSURA, T. 1973. The solubility of sulfur in Na_2O–SiO_2 melts under various oxygen partial pressures at 1100°C, 1250°C and 1300°C. *Bulletin of the Chemical Society of Japan,* **46**, 3099–3103.

NEWMAN, S., EPSTEIN S. & STOLPER, E. 1988. Water, carbon dioxide, and hydrogen isotopes in glasses from the ca. 1340 A.D. eruption of the Mono Craters, California: constraints on degassing phenomena and initial volatile content. *Journal of Volcanology and Geothermal Research,* **35**, 75–96.

NICHOLLS, J. & RUSSELL, J. K. (eds) 1990. *Modern Methods of Igneous Petrology: Understanding Magmatic Processes. Reviews in Mineralogy,* **24**, Mineralogical Society of America, Washington D.C.

NILSSON, K. & PEACH, C. L. 1993. Sulfur speciation, oxidation state, and sulfur concentration in backarc magmas. *Geochimica et Cosmochimica Acta,* **57**, 3807–3813.

OTTONELLO, G., MORETTI, R., MARINI, L. & VETUSCHI ZUCCOLINI, M. 2001. On the oxidation state of iron in silicate melts and glasses: a thermochemical model. *Chemical Geology,* **174**, 157–179.

PAPALE, P. 1997. Modeling of the solubility of one component H_2O or CO_2 fluid in silicate liquids. *Contributions to Mineralogy and Petrology,* **126**, 237–251.

PAPALE, P. 1998. Volcanic conduit dynamics. *In:* FREUNDT, A. & ROSI, M. (eds) *From Magma to Tephra, Modelling Physical Processes of Explosive Volcanic Eruptions.* Developments in Volcanology Series, **4**, 55–89, Elsevier, New York.

PAPALE, P. 1999. Modeling of the solubility of a two-component H_2O+CO_2 fluid in silicate liquids. *American Mineralogist*, **84**, 477–492.

PAPALE, P. 2001. Dynamics of magma flow in volcanic conduits with variable fragmentation efficiency and nonequilibrium pumice degassing. *Journal of Geophysical Research*, **106**, 11 043–11 065.

PAPALE, P. & POLACCI, M. 1999. Role of carbon dioxide in the dynamics of magma ascent in explosive eruptions. *Bulletin of Volcanology*, **60**, 583–594.

SCAILLET, B. & EVANS, B. W. 1999. The June 15, 1991 eruption of Mount Pinatubo. I: Phase equilibria and pre-eruption $P–T–fO_2–fH_2O$ conditions of the dacite magma. *Journal of Petrology*, **40**, 381–411.

SCAILLET, B., CLEMENTE, B., EVANS, B. W. & PICHAVANT, M. 1998. Redox control on sulfur degassing in silicic magmas. *Journal of Geophysical Research*, **103**, 23 937–23 949.

TAIT, S., JAUPART, C. & VERGNIOLLE, S. 1989. Pressure, gas content and eruption periodicity of a shallow, crystallising magma chamber. *Earth and Planetary Science Letters*, **92**, 107–123.

TEMKIN, M. 1945. Mixtures of fused salts as ionic solutions. *Acta Physicochimica USSR*, **20**, 411–420.

TOOP, G. W. & SAMIS, C. S. 1962a. Some new ionic concepts of silicate slags. *Canadian Metallurgist Quarterly*, **1**, 129–152.

TOOP, G. W. & SAMIS, C. S. 1962b. Activities of ions in silicate melts. *Transactions of the Metallurgical Society of AIME*, **224**, 878–887.

TUTTLE, O. F. & BOWEN, N. L. 1958. Origin of granites in the light of experimental studies in the system $NaAlSi_3O_8–KAlSi_3O_8–SiO_2–H_2O$. *Geological Society of America Memoirs*, **74**, 1–153.

WALLACE, P. J. 2001. Volcanic SO_2 emissions and the abundance and distribution of exsolved gas in magma bodies. *Journal of Volcanology and Geothermal Research*, **108**, 85–106.

ZHANG, Y. 1999. H_2O in rhyolitic glasses and melts: measurement, speciation, solubility, and diffusion. *Reviews in Geophysics*, **37**, 493–516.

Sulphur release from flood lava eruptions in the Veidivötn, Grímsvötn and Katla volcanic systems, Iceland

T. THORDARSON[1], S. SELF[1,2], D. J. MILLER[3], G. LARSEN[4]
& E. G. VILMUNDARDÓTTIR[5]

[1]*Department of Geology and Geophysics, School of Ocean and Earth Sciences and Technology, University of Hawaii at Manoa, Hawaii 96822, USA.*
(e-mail: moinui@soest.hawaii.edu)
[2]*Department of Earth Sciences, The Open University,*
Milton Keynes MK7 6AA, UK.
[3]*Ocean Drilling Program, Texas A & M University Research Park,*
1000 Discovery Drive, College Station, Texas 77845–9547, USA.
[4]*Science Institute, University of Iceland, Dunhagi 6, Reykjavík, IS101, Iceland.*
[5]*National Energy Authority, Grensásvegur 9, Reykjavík, IS–108, Iceland.*

Abstract: Emissions of SO_2 by volcanic eruptions have been shown to be important for short-term environmental and climate changes. Stratospheric sulphur mass-loading by explosive silicic eruption is commonly considered to be the principal forcing factor for these changes. The SO_2 emissions from basaltic flood lava eruptions have not featured strongly in the discussions on volcano–climate interactions, notwithstanding the fact that basaltic magma is typically richer in sulphur (by a factor of two to four), than silicic magmas, as well as the evidence of widespread atmospheric impact associated with historical flood lava eruption.
    Fourteen Holocene flood lava eruptions are known from the Veidivötn, Grímsvötn, and Katla volcanic systems of the Eastern Volcanic Zone in South Iceland, which include the three largest of its kind in Iceland; the 1783–1784 Laki, 934–40 Eldgjá, and *c.*8600 years BP Thjórsá events. We present new data on the sulphur content in melt inclusions from the Veidivötn system and use this information, along with existing inclusion data from the Grímsvötn and Katla volcanic systems, to establish an empirical method for estimating the sulphur mass release from these basaltic flood lava eruptions. The results show that these eruptions released a total of *c.*700 Mt SO_2 into the atmosphere in four 600- to 850-year-long eruption periods. During each period, between 98 and 328 Mt SO_2 were emitted into the atmosphere, and the mass loadings from individual eruptions ranged from 5 to 210 Mt SO_2. These flood lava eruptions are likely to have resulted in widespread atmospheric perturbations and, by analogy with the 1783–1784 Laki eruption, the effects of the largest eruptions may have been felt on a hemispheric scale.

Introduction

Sulphur emissions from volcanic eruptions have resulted in significant atmospheric perturbations on a hemispheric to global scale and are often cited as an important forcing element in short-term climate changes (e.g. Self *et al.* 1981; Rampino & Self 1984; Robock 1991, 2000). Stratospheric mass-loading of sulphur by explosive silicic eruptions is commonly cited as the principal source of these volcano-induced forcings. Basaltic flood lava eruptions, defined here as effusive eruptions with magma volumes ≥1 km^3 and >90% of the erupted material emplaced

as lava (Thorarinsson 1982), have not featured heavily in discussions on volcano–climate interactions, despite abundant knowledge of the atmospheric effects of the 1783–1784 Laki flood lava eruption in Iceland (e.g. Sigurdsson 1982; Wood 1992; Grattan 1995, 1998; Thordarson 1995; Thordarson & Self, 2001, 2003).
    Fissure-fed, flood lava eruptions are prolonged events, lasting months to years (e.g. Self *et al.* 1996*a*, 1997). They are characterized by recurring eruption episodes featuring an initial explosive phase that is capable of producing 7–15-km high eruption columns (e.g. Stothers *et al.* 1986; Woods 1993; Thordarson & Self 1993,

From: OPPENHEIMER, C., PYLE, D.M. & BARCLAY, J. (eds) *Volcanic Degassing.* Geological Society, London, Special Publications, **213**, 103–121. 0305-8719/03/$15.00

1996). Large amounts of sulphur gases are released into the atmosphere because of the high sulphur yield of basaltic magmas coupled with efficient vent degassing mechanisms. Consequently, prolonged high-discharge flood lava eruptions can maintain elevated atmospheric concentrations of H_2SO_4 aerosols because the eruption plumes are continually replenished with SO_2. Historical flood lava eruptions have produced atmospheric perturbations on a hemispheric scale, lasting for months to years, suggesting that such eruptions may be equally as important as their explosive counterparts when evaluating the atmospheric impact of volcanic eruptions in the past (e.g. Rampino *et al.* 1988; Stothers 1996 1998; Thordarson & Self 2003).

One of the critical factors for assessing the environmental and climatic impact of volcanic eruptions in the past, present and future is the atmospheric mass loading of sulphur gases, because this information can be used to estimate the potential H_2SO_4 aerosol burden generated by individual eruptions (e.g. Self *et al.* 1981, Rampino & Self 1984; Robock 1991, 2000). The petrological method (e.g. Devine *et al.* 1984) is one of three methods (the others being ice-core acidity records and historic records on atmospheric turbidity) used for assessing the H_2SO_4 aerosol loading of volcanic eruptions in the past. The petrological method is based on measuring the sulphur concentration in pristine melt (or glass) inclusions and in quenched eruption products, which represent undegassed and degassed melt, respectively. The method assesses the potential atmospheric sulphur yield from individual eruptions by mass-balance calculations using the mass of erupted melt and the difference between sulphur values in undegassed and degassed melt. It has been shown that the petrological method gives reliable results for divergent margin and hot-spot basalt eruptions (e.g. Andres *et al.* 1989; Thordarson *et al.* 1996), whereas it often underestimates the sulphur mass released by eruptions at many convergent margin volcanoes (e.g. Wallace 2001). In the case of basaltic fissure eruptions the petrological method is a fairly straightforward procedure for estimating the atmospheric sulphur yield from prehistoric explosive and effusive eruptions, and it has some distinct advantages over the other two methods. Firstly, it involves direct analysis of the eruption products, and thus can be used to obtain information on eruptions much further back in time (up to 20 Ma as opposed to <0.1 Ma and 0.002 Ma for the other two). Secondly, it does not involve correlation between unrelated records, whereas the other two require matching between two independent data series, the

volcanic and the ice core (or historical) records (e.g. Hammer 1977, 1984; Zielinski *et al.* 1994, 1995; Stothers 1996, 1998). Some of the disadvantages of the petrological method are: (1) that it requires unaltered samples of glass (melt) inclusions and quenched (glassy) eruption products, and (2) it involves lengthy sample preparation and analysis.

In this paper we focus on the sulphur yield of Holocene flood lava eruptions from the Veidivötn, Grímsvötn and Katla volcanic systems (Fig. 1). We introduce an empirical approach, which is based on the petrological method and the two-stage degassing model of Thordarson *et al.* (1996), to estimate the amount of sulphur released into the atmosphere by these eruptions. This approach provides a simple procedure for estimating the sulphur yield by utilizing the observed linear correlation between the pre-eruption sulphur content and TiO_2/FeO_{total} values in melt (glass) inclusions representative of the magmas erupted by each system. Its main advantage is that estimates of the sulphur yield from past eruptions can be obtained from an analysis of a few (or even a single) representative samples, reducing the time-consuming sampling and analytical procedures of the petrological method. Also, the TiO_2/FeO_{total} values of basaltic magmas are typically unaffected by cooling and crystallization at the surface. Therefore, unlike the petrological method, the empirical approach is not dependent on preservation of glassy eruption products, which are very susceptible to post-eruption alteration. Consequently, it can be applied to Veidivötn, Grímsvötn and Katla eruptions reaching further back in time.

Geological setting

The Veidivötn and Grímsvötn and Katla volcanic systems are located within the Eastern Volcanic Zone (EVZ). Each system features a glacier-covered central volcano, as well as narrow, elongate segments (i.e. fissure swarms) of volcanic fissures, tensional cracks and graben structures (Fig. 1). The EVZ is a young (<3 Ma old), rift zone in south-central Iceland developing by southwest propagation through older crust (Sæmundsson 1978, 1979). It is characterized by tholeiitic magmatism in the northeast grading into transitional to mildly alkaline magmatism in the southwest, and contains nine volcanic systems (Jakobsson 1979). The Veidivötn, Grímsvötn, and Katla volcanic systems have been by far the most productive systems during the Holocene (Table 1a). EVZ volcanoes have erupted ≥200 km^3 of basaltic magma in the

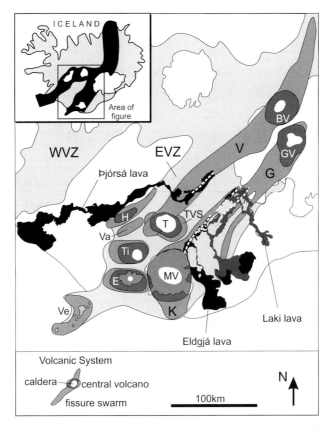

Fig. 1. Map of the Eastern Volcanic Zone (EVZ) in Iceland, showing the position of the Veidivötn (V), Grímsvötn (G) and Katla (K) volcanic systems and the location of the corresponding Bárdarbunga (BV), Grímsvötn (GV), and Mýrdalsjökull (MV) central volcanoes. Also shown is the distribution of the Laki, Eldgjá and Thjórsá vent systems and lava flows. The other six volcanic systems of the EVZ are indicated as follows: Vestmannaeyjar (Ve), Eyjafjöll (E), Tindfjöll (Ti), Torfajökull (T), Vatnafjöll (Va), and Hekla (H). Inset shows the volcanotectonic setting of the EVZ in relation to other volcanic zones in Iceland. Modified from Jakobsson (1979).

last 9000 years (Table 1a). About 60% ($c.125$ km³) of this magma volume was erupted by subaerial fissure eruptions, mostly within the Veidivötn, Grímsvötn, and Katla volcanic systems ($c.104$ km³). The bulk of the remaining volume ($c.80$ km³) was expelled by subglacial eruptions at the Mýrdalsjökull, Grímsvötn and Bárdarbunga central volcanoes.

During the Holocene the Veidivötn, Grímsvötn, and Katla systems have produced at least 14 fissure-fed flood lava eruptions, including the three largest of their kind on Earth; the 1783–1784 Laki, 934–940 Eldgjá, and $c.8600$ years BP Thjórsá events (Table 1b). The magnitude of these three eruptions was such that the combined volume of erupted magma (57 km³) is $c.28\%$ of the total Holocene basalt magma output from the EVZ. All of the Holocene flood lava eruptions occurred on the

ice-free fissure swarm of each system, and in total they account for $c.44\%$ ($c.91$ km³) of the Holocene basalt magma volume in the EVZ. The basalts of the Veidivötn and Grímsvötn volcanic systems range in composition from olivine tholeiite to tholeiite, whereas those from the Katla system are FeTi basalts. These basalts are well characterized in terms of their chemical composition (e.g. Jakobsson 1979) and exhibit well-defined Fe and Ti enrichment trends when plotted against magma evolution indices such as Mg# and K_2O (Fig. 2).

Sulphur release in flood lava eruptions – the two-stage degassing model

The atmospheric mass loading of sulphur in explosive Plinian eruptions can be regarded as instantaneous, because the volatiles are released

Table 1(a). *Estimates of basaltic magma volume erupted from the Veidivötn, Grímsvötn and Katla volcanic systems and the Eastern Volcanic Zone (EVZ) during the Holocene.*

Volcanic system	Subaerial eruption volume (km³)	Explosive subglacial eruption volume (km³)*
Veidivötn	57	*c.*10*
Grímsvötn	22	*c.*35*
Katla	25	*c.*35*
Total	104	80
Total EVZ	*c.*125	*c.*83

*This column shows the estimated magma volume expelled by explosive subglacial eruptions at the Mýrdalsjökull, Grímsvötn, and Bárdarbunga central volcanoes during the Holocene. These estimates are obtained by extrapolating data from Thorarinsson (1975) and Larsen *et al.* (1998) on the average eruption volume and eruption frequency at these central volcanoes in historic times. The value for the Veidivötn system also includes the magma volume from the 874 Vatnaöldur and 1477 Veidivötn eruptions (Larsen 1984), the two largest phreatomagmatic fissure eruptions in Iceland during the Holocene.

Table 1(b). *Timing and magma volume of flood lava eruptions in the Veidivötn, Grímsvötn, and Katla volcanic systems.*

Volcanic system	Eruption	Age (years BP)	Calendar age	Volume (km³)
Veidivötn	Thjórsá lava (THa&b)	*c.*8600		22
Veidivötn	Raudhóll–Flögd lava	>8000		1
Veidivötn	Háganga lava	>8000		1
Veidivötn	Háa–Botnar lava	>8000		1.1
Veidivötn	Tungnaá lava (THc)	6800		1.4
Veidivötn	Tungnaá lava (THd)	6700		3.8
Veidivötn	Sigalda lava (THf)	6200		3.4
Veidivötn	Brydja lava	*c.*4000		1
Veidivötn	Búrfell–Dreki lava (THi)	3200		6.5
Grímsvötn	Hálsar–Botnar lava	*c.*6000?		>3
Grímsvötn	Núpar lava	3800		7
Grímsvötn	Laki Fires	217	AD1783–1784	15.1
Katla	Hólmsá Fires	*c.*6800		>5
Katla	Eldgjá Fires	*c.*1060	AD934–40	19.6
			Total:	90.9

The compilations in Tables 1(a) and 1(b) were made by using information from the following sources: Thorarinsson (1974, 1975); Vilmundardóttir (1977), Jakobsson (1979), Larsen (1984, 2000), Vilmundardóttir *et al.* (1983, 1988, 1990, 1997, 1999 *a, b*), Hjartarson (1988), Larsen *et al.* (1998), Thordarson and Self (1993), and Thordarson *et al.* (2001), and unpublished data by the authors. Years BP are calculated from AD 2000.

in a single event or a series of explosive events lasting from several hours up to a few days. However, this approach is not directly applicable to flood lava eruptions, which can last for months to years and are characterized by sequential eruption episodes resulting from periodic injections of fresh magma batches into the conduit system. These episodes may be separated by significant time intervals (days to years) and usually begin with a short-lived explosive phase that leads to a longer lasting effusive phase (Thordarson & Self 1993, 1998; Larsen 2000). Detailed studies of the Laki and Eldgjá eruptions show that the magma degassing in flood

lava eruptions occurs in two stages: (1) as the magma moves up through the conduit and erupts from the vents and (2) during and immediately after lava emplacement (Fig. 3). Thus, in order to estimate the total sulphur output from flood lava eruptions the degree of degassing during each of the two stages needs to be determined (the procedure is given in Thordarson *et al.* 1996).

Data presentation and analysis

The data-set used in this study concerns the products of 10 eruptions within the Veidivötn (4), Grímsvötn (2), and Katla (4) volcanic

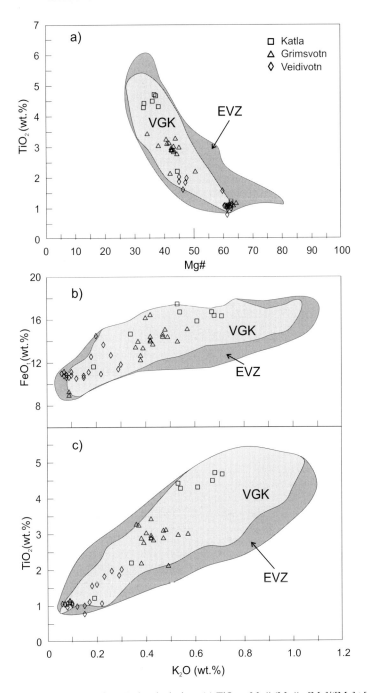

Fig. 2. Major-element composition of EVZ glass inclusions (a) TiO_2 v. Mg# (Mg#=[Mg]/([Mg]+[Fe]) * 100. Fe calculated from total FeO), (b) FeO v. K_2O, and (c) TiO_2 v. K_2O. The compositional fields of basaltic eruption products from the Veidivötn, Grímsvötn and Katla volcanic systems (VGK, light grey) and EVZ eruptives (grey) are also shown. These fields are based on data from Jakobsson (1979), Steinthorsson (1977), Vilmundardóttir, (1977), Oskarsson *et al.* (1982), Devine *et al.* (1984), Grönvold and Jóhannesson, (1984), Meyer *et al.* (1985), Steinthorsson *et al.* (1985), Miller (1989), Thordarson *et al.* (1996, 1998, 2001), and unpublished data by Thordarson, 2002. Inclusion data are from Metrich *et al.* (1991), Thordarson *et al.* (1996, 2001), and this study. Key (top right) shows plotting symbols for glass inclusions from each system.

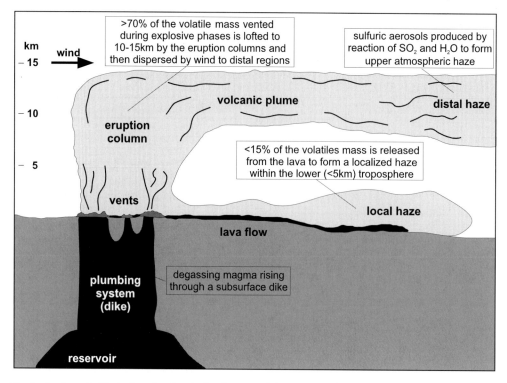

Fig. 3. A schematic illustration showing the key features of the two-stage degassing in flood lava eruptions (modified from Thordarson *et al.* 1996).

systems. It includes microprobe measurements of major-element and sulphur concentrations in more than 50 glass (melt) inclusions and in groundmass glass from tephra and quenched lava lobe margins of 42 samples (>700 analyses). The data from the Veidivötn system are a new contribution (Table 2), but the data on the Grímsvötn and Katla volcanic system are mostly from previous studies on the Laki and Eldgjá flood lava eruptions (Metrich *et al.* 1991; Thordarson 1995; Thordarson *et al.* 1996, 2001). These data are supplemented by 22 new whole-rock analyses (by ICP) of sulphur, providing a better constraint on the residuals in crystalline lava from all three systems.

Glass inclusions – pre-eruption sulphur content

The major phenocryst phases in the basalts from the Veidivötn, Grímsvötn and Katla volcanic systems are plagioclase and olivine (±clinopyroxene). All of these phases contain glass inclusions, which correspond with undegassed

melt fractions incorporated by the phenocrysts during growth in the subsurface magma reservoir. We have measured the sulphur concentration in 55 inclusions, split as follows between the three volcanic systems: Veidivötn (20), Grímsvötn (22) and Katla (13), and hereafter referred to as VGK inclusions. These analyses include measurements of melt inclusions in phenocrysts which, according to their mineral composition, were in equilibrium with their host magma. These VGK inclusions represent crystals growing from the magma at reservoir depth shortly before the onset of eruption. The data-set also includes inclusions contained within phenocrysts that are clearly foreign to their host magma (i.e. xenocrysts that grew from pre-existing melts of more primitive composition) and were physically incorporated into the magma prior to, or during, its ascent toward the surface. The equilibrium phenocryst assemblages typically contain glass inclusions that have melt compositions compatible with their host magma, whereas the inclusions in the xenocrysts invariably have less-evolved compositions (i.e. higher

Table 2. *Major element and sulphur content in glass inclusions from the Veidivötn volcanic system.*

Glass inclusions (2–4 analyses per inclusion)

Sample No.	Host	SiO$_2$	TiO$_2$	Al$_2$O$_3$	FeO	MnO	MgO	CaO	Na$_2$O	K$_2$O	P$_2$O$_5$	Sum	Mg#	S
ThB–i3b	Cpx	50.82	1.98	13.60	11.62	0.20	5.33	11.74	2.41	0.29	0.20	98.19	44.98	1252
ThB–i3a	Cpx	51.62	1.84	13.86	11.27	0.19	5.17	11.88	2.52	0.29	0.16	98.80	44.98	1261
Th4–i1	Plag	50.39	1.97	13.72	12.63	0.19	6.42	11.42	2.26	0.26	0.20	99.46	47.53	1489
Th4–i5	Plag	49.68	1.82	13.58	13.63	0.22	6.81	11.25	2.27	0.23	0.17	99.65	47.11	1661
Th4–i10	Plag	48.00	1.56	13.30	14.11	0.26	6.83	10.86	2.11	0.20	0.17	97.38	46.31	1583
ThB–i2a	Plag	50.46	0.78	13.94	10.56	0.20	9.38	11.73	2.20	0.15	0.05	99.45	61.28	1090
Th4–i3	Plag	49.82	1.01	13.03	10.77	0.16	9.49	13.15	1.79	0.15	0.22	99.57	61.09	
Th4–i9	Plag	50.20	1.09	13.16	11.23	0.19	9.67	13.21	1.76	0.10	0.00	100.61	60.54	1021
Th4–i2	Plag	49.96	1.04	13.03	10.80	0.22	9.72	12.89	1.73	0.10	0.13	99.60	61.59	1005
Th4–i7	Plag	49.54	1.05	12.85	11.10	0.17	9.74	13.18	1.71	0.07	0.05	99.46	60.99	962
Th4–i6	Plag	50.54	1.08	13.10	10.98	0.21	9.77	13.37	1.78	0.08	0.03	100.94	61.32	1090
Th4–i8	Plag	50.19	0.97	13.02	10.91	0.25	9.77	13.11	1.81	0.08	0.08	100.19	61.48	371
ThB–i2b	Plag	50.20	0.99	13.96	10.52	0.22	9.86	11.72	2.15	0.12	0.08	99.82	62.55	1033
Th4–i11	Plag	49.61	1.06	12.96	10.56	0.23	9.92	13.13	1.69	0.08	0.07	99.29	62.61	1143
Th4–i1	Plag	49.75	1.04	12.93	10.74	0.21	9.95	13.02	1.75	0.07	0.12	99.57	62.27	1055
Th4–i4	Plag	49.92	1.07	13.11	11.08	0.19	10.04	13.20	1.72	0.07	0.08	100.46	61.77	1071
Th4–i12	Plag	49.84	1.11	12.99	10.59	0.21	10.05	13.15	1.43	0.09	0.12	99.55	62.85	1128
Th1–i2	Olivine	48.99	1.20	13.10	10.72	0.21	11.24	12.14	1.77	0.13	0.10	99.62	65.14	787
Th1–i3	Olivine	48.11	1.55	13.70	12.52	0.16	10.40	10.86	2.01	0.18	0.14	99.62	59.68	1038
Th1–i6	Plag	50.97	1.07	13.79	10.94	0.29	9.31	11.74	1.39	0.22	0.08	99.81	60.26	1226
Th1–i0	Plag	50.92	1.12	12.33	11.25	0.23	10.29	12.96	1.54	0.17	0.14	100.95	61.98	1163

Samples ThB and Th4 are from the Brandur tuff cone at the southeast shores of Lake Thórisvatn (64°16.8'N, 18°34.65'W), and sample Th1 was collected from the Thjórsá lava flow in an outcrop along the west bank of the River Thjórsá, just short of the bridge on Highway 1 in South Iceland (64°00'N, 20°42'W). The glass inclusions were analysed by Cameca SX50 microprobe at the University of Hawaii at Manoa using the instrument set-up and analytical procedure of Thordarson et al. (1996). Compositions in wt%, S in p.p.m.

MgO, as well as lower K_2O, TiO_2 and FeO_t contents; Table 2, see also Metrich *et al.* 1991; Thordarson *et al.* 1996, 2001).

The major-element composition of the VGK inclusions matches the known compositional range of basalts in the corresponding volcanic systems and falls well within the compositional field of EVZ basalts (Fig. 2a–c), indicating adequate sampling of the erupted magmas and their pre-eruption sulphur content. The sulphur content in the inclusions varies from 914 to 2435 ppm by mass (Fig. 4a). This variability reflects the compositional difference of the magmas that characterize each of the three volcanic systems, as well as compositional differences within each system. Furthermore, VGK inclusions with high sulphur content correspond to the most evolved basaltic magma produced by each system, whereas those with lower sulphur contents have compositions consistent with more primitive parental magmas (Fig. 4b). As shown in Figure 4c, sulphur and Fe are positively correlated in the VGK inclusions, and they delineate a trend that falls just below the sulphur saturation line of mid-ocean ridge basalts (MORBs) as defined by Mathez (1976). The sulphur content of the VGK inclusions is, on average, 15–25% lower than in these MORB glasses at equivalent Fe contents. This relationship implies that the Veidivötn, Grímsvötn and Katla magmas are under-saturated with respect to sulphur at reservoir depths, a conclusion that is supported by the observed positive correlation between sulphur and potassium (Fig. 4d). The co-variance of sulphur and Fe in VGK inclusions is consistent with the dependence of sulphur solubility on the FeO content in basaltic magmas (Haughton *et al.* 1974; Wallace & Carmichael 1992).

Quenched and crystalline eruption products – sulphur degassing

We have measured sulphur in degassed eruption products representing the key phases of flood lava eruptions from all three volcanic systems. These include samples from vent and tephra-fall deposits as well as samples of quenched margins glassy selvages and crystalline interiors of the lava flows. Evaluating the data obtained from the products of individual eruptions, the magmatic pyroclastic deposits and the lavas are character-ized by low and uniform sulphur concentrations compared with the corresponding glass inclu-sions, as shown by the example given in Figure 5. The difference between the sulphur content in the glass inclusions from each volcanic system and corresponding groundmass glasses implies that $\geq 70\%$ of the sulphur was released by

degassing at the vents (Fig. 6a). On the other hand, the difference between the measured sulphur concentrations in the matching ground-mass glasses and crystalline lavas indicates that an additional 5–15% was released during lava emplacement and crystallization after flow stagnation (Fig. 6b).

Empirical method for estimating atmospheric venting of sulphur

As predicted by the observed Ti and Fe trends in the Veidivötn, Grímsvötn and Katla basalts (Figs 2 and 7a), the sulphur content in glass inclusions exhibits a strong positive correlation with the corresponding TiO_2/FeO_t values (Fig. 7b). In fact, all three data-sets, that is sulphur in glass inclusions, magmatic tephra, and crystalline lava, define distinct trends when plotted against the Ti–Fe ratio. This relationship makes the TiO_2/FeO_t value a good proxy for estimating the original and the residual sulphur content in the magmas from these systems. Furthermore, this ratio is fairly resilient to post-emplacement alteration processes. Titanium is highly resistant to alteration, and therefore in the case of mildly altered basalts it can serve as a measure of Fe mobility (e.g. Rollinson 1993).

In order to establish an empirical method for estimating the sulphur yield of basaltic flood lava eruptions from the Veidivötn, Grímsvötn, and Katla volcanic systems, we have calculated the best linear fit (by regressing S on TiO_2/FeO_t) for each of the three trends in Fig. 7b. These calculations give the following expressions for determining the sulphur content dissolved in the magma prior to eruption and the residual sulphur after degassing upon eruption:

$$c_S = 516 + 5806 TiO_2/FeO \text{ [glass inclusions]} \quad (1)$$

$$c_S = 359 + 493 TiO_2/FeO \text{ [magmatic tephra]} \quad (2)$$

$$c_S = 183 + 479 TiO_2/FeO \text{ [crystalline lava]} \quad (3)$$

The calculated sulphur concentrations (c_S) are in ppm by mass.

The concentration of sulphur (c_S) released by vent degassing is determined by subtracting equation 2 from 1 (expression 4), whereas the difference between equations 2 and 3 gives the fraction released by the lava (expression 5).

$$c_S = 157 + 5313 TiO_2/FeO$$
$$\text{[S released at the vents]} \quad (4)$$

$$c_S = 176 + 14 TiO_2/FeO$$
$$\text{[S released by the lava]} \quad (5)$$

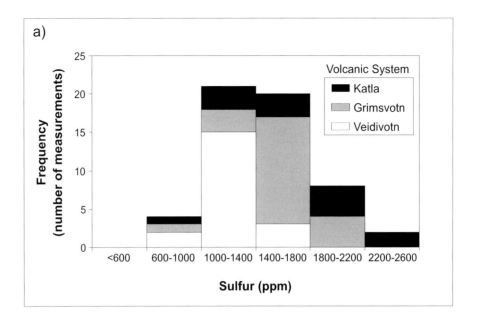

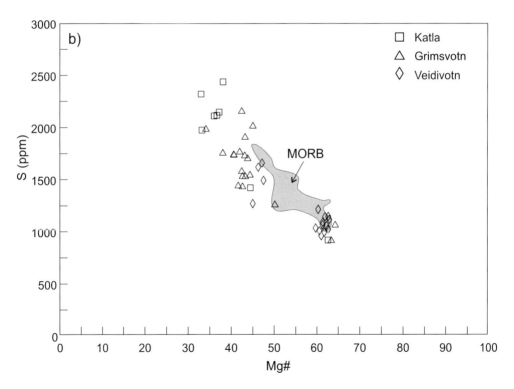

Fig. 4. Sulphur in VGK glass inclusions, (**a**) distribution of measured sulphur content within an individual volcanic system; (**b**) sulphur v. Mg# (see Fig. 3 for definition). The grey shaded area in (b) and (c) shows the compositional field of mid-ocean ridge basalt used by Mathez (1976).

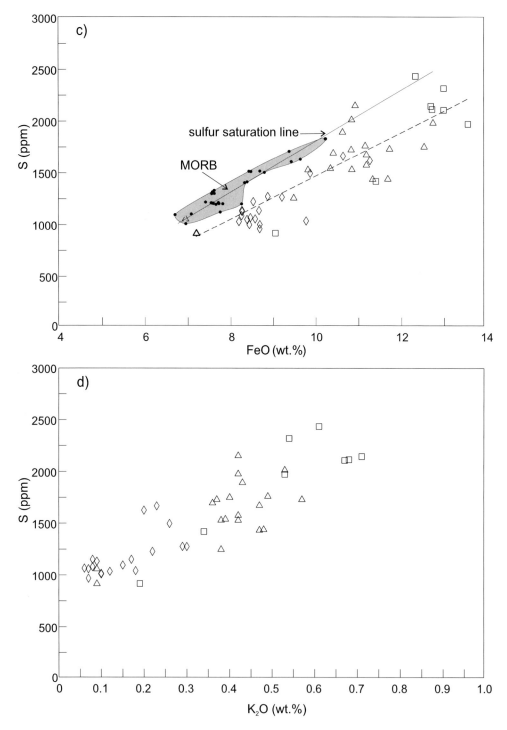

Fig. 4. (continued) Sulphur in VGK glass inclusions, (**c**) sulphur v. FeO; also shown is the mid-ocean ridge basalt sulphur saturation line ($y=230x-520$; $r^2=0.90$) of Mathez (1976) and the line of best fit by regression through the VGK inclusion data ($y=214x-686$; $r^2=0.77$); (**d**) sulphur v. K$_2$O. The grey shaded area in (b) and (c) shows the compositional field of mid-ocean ridge basalt used by Mathez.

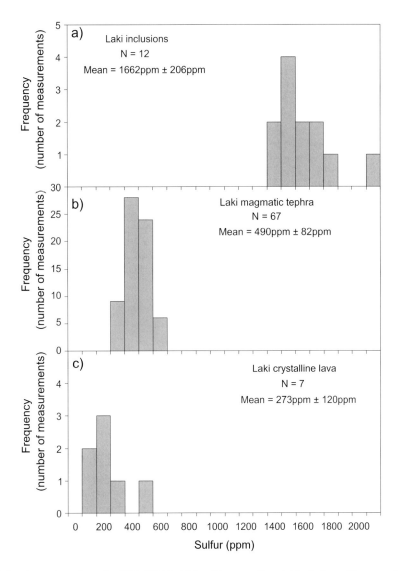

Fig. 5. Sulphur in products from the 1783–1784 Laki flood lava eruption: (**a**) inclusions; (**b**) magmatic vent and tephra-fall deposit; and (**c**) crystalline lava. Data are from Thordarson *et al.* (1996).

The SO$_2$ mass (in megatonnes, 1 Mt$=10^9$ kg) in, or released from, the magma at any stage is given by:

$$M_{SO_2}=\rho e\ V_e\ x_S \qquad (6)$$

where V_e is total magma volume in km^3, ϵ is the magma density (kg/m^3), x_S is the mass fraction of sulphur ($x_S=c_S \times 10^{-6}$) and e is the constant required to convert the pure element to the species assumed to be present in the magma (e $\approx$

2 for converting S into SO$_2$). Substituting expressions 1, 4 and 5 for x_S in equation 6 gives the following expressions for calculating the original SO$_2$ mass (in Mt) dissolved in the magma, as well as the mass released by the degassing at the vents (stage 1) and the lava (stage 2):

$$M_{SO_2}\ \text{magma}=V_e\ \rho(10.3+116$$
$$TiO_2/FeO)\times10^{-4}.[\text{pre-eruption SO}_2] \qquad (7)$$

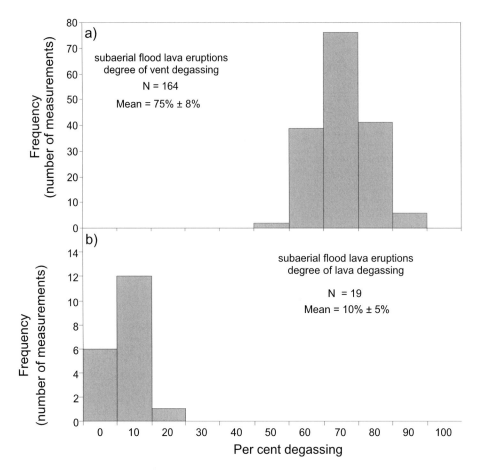

Fig. 6. Degree of vent and lava degassing in the 1783–1784 Laki, 934–940 Eldgjá, and *c.*8600 years BP Thjórsá flood lava eruptions as determined by the difference in sulphur contents between (**a**) melt inclusions and magmatic tephra and (**b**) magmatic tephra and crystalline lava.

$$M_{SO_2} \text{ vents} = V_e \, \rho(3.1 + 106 \, TiO_2/FeO) \times 10^{-4}.\text{[degassing stage 1]} \quad (8)$$

$$M_{SO_2} \text{ lava} = V_e \, \rho(35.2 + 2.8 TiO_2/FeO) \times 10^{-5} \quad \text{[degassing stage 2]} \quad (9)$$

The petrological method has been used to estimate SO_2 budgets for three flood lava eruptions in the EVZ, the 1783–1784 Laki (Thordarson *et al.* 1996), 934–940 Eldgjá (Thordarson *et al.* 2001), and *c.*8600 years BP Thjórsá events (Thordarson 1995). The SO_2 masses for these eruptions obtained by the above equations are typically within 4% of those obtained from the petrological method (Fig. 8). The exceptions are the values obtained for the SO_2 mass released by the lava flows, which are underestimated by the petrologic method by as much as 50%. However, the values used here to establish the empirical relationship for residual sulphur in crystalline lava are obtained from new whole-rock analyses, which are on average higher, by a factor of two, than the sulphur values used in the original studies. This difference in the sulphur values used to derive SO_2 mass released by the lavas explains most of the observed variance between the two methods. Therefore, we can conclude that the empirical approach gives a reasonable estimate of the SO_2 mass released from flood lava eruptions in these three volcanic systems. The error margins on these estimates are ±15%.

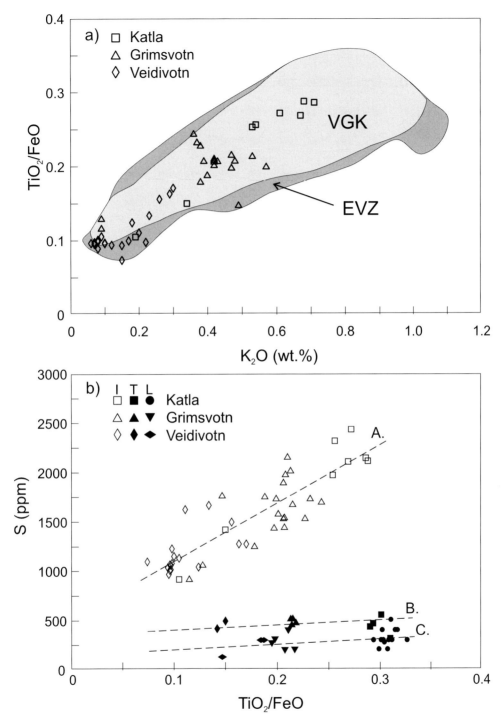

Fig. 7. (**a**) TiO$_2$/FeO v. K$_2$O, symbols and data sources as in Figure 3; (**b**) Sulphur v. TiO$_2$/FeO. Broken lines show best fit by regression for glass inclusions (A), magmatic tephra (B), and crystalline lava (C). Symbols indicate inclusion (I), tephra (T), and lava (L) for each of the three volcanic systems. Data are from Metrich *et al.* (1991), Thordarson *et al.* (1996, 2001), and this study.

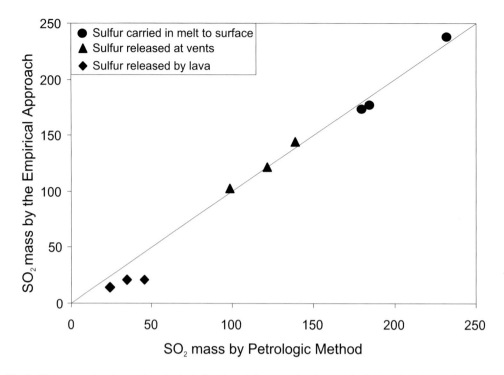

Fig. 8. Plot comparing the results of calculating the sulphur mass by the petrological method versus the empirical approach for the Laki, Eldgjá, and Thjórsá flood lava eruptions. The line has a slope=1.

Application and results

The SO$_2$ emission budgets for Holocene flood lava eruptions at the Veidivötn, Grímsvötn and Katla volcanic systems have been estimated by the procedures outlined in the previous section and the results are listed in Table 3. In the last 9000 years these flood eruptions have carried about 840 Mt (= 8.4 × 10^{11} kg) of SO$_2$ to the surface and released *c.*700 Mt into the atmosphere, of which 87% (*c.*608 Mt) was emitted directly from the vents and only 13% (90 Mt) was released from the lava flows (Table 3). However, these values for the total SO$_2$ contribution by flood lava eruptions from the Veidivötn, Grímsvötn, and Katla systems should be taken as minimum estimates, because: (1) the figures used here for the volume of erupted magma are conservative estimates, and (2) the method ignores possible SO$_2$ contributions from degassing of unerupted magma now residing as dykes in the volcano conduits.

The magnitude and temporal distribution of these sulphur emissions were highly variable and divided among 14 eruptions with erupted magma volumes ranging from 1 to 22 km^3 and SO$_2$ emissions from 5 to 210 Mt. The occurrences of these flood eruptions appear to have been confined to four discrete time periods (Fig. 9). In the first eruption period (8600–8000 years BP) the activity was confined to the Veidivötn system and a total of four flood lava eruptions released *c.*186 Mt SO$_2$ into the atmosphere, *c.*150 Mt of which was released in a single event (i.e. the Thjórsá eruption). In the second period (6800–6000 years BP) all three systems produced eruptions of flood lava magnitude with a cumulative SO$_2$ emission of *c.*120 Mt and, in the third period (4000–3200 years BP), three eruptions released *c.*98 Mt SO$_2$ into the atmosphere. Although the fourth period (1066–217 years BP) only featured two eruptions, they were giants; the first was the Eldgjá eruption with an atmospheric mass loading of about 210 Mt SO$_2$, and 850 years later the Laki event released *c.*120 Mt SO$_2$ into the atmosphere (Fig. 9). Alone, the three largest eruptions (i.e. Laki, Eldgjá, and Thjórsá), account for *c.*65% (457 Mt SO$_2$) of the total atmospheric SO$_2$ mass loading from Holocene flood lava eruptions on the Veidivötn, Grímsvötn, and Katla volcanic systems.

Table 3. *Sulphur released by Holocene flood lava eruptions in the Veidivötn, Grímsvötn, and Katla volcanic systems.*

Volcanic system	Lava flow or eruption	Age (BP)	Volume* (km³)	TiO₂/ FeO	S in magma	SO₂ in magma (Mt)	SO₂ released at vents (Mt)	SO₂ released by lava (Mt)
Veidivötn	Thjórsá lava	8600	22	0.183	1542	173	121	21
	Thjórsá lava[†]				1575	179	122	46
Veidivötn	Raudhóll–Flögd lava	>8000	1.1	0.123	1230	7	5	1.1
Veidivötn	Háganga lava	>8000	1	0.107	1137	6	4	1
Veidivötn	Háa–Botnar lava	>8000	1.1	0.146	1364	8	6	1.1
Veidivötn	Tungnaá lava (THc)	6800	1.4	0.155	1418	11	7	1.3
Veidivötn	Tungnaá lava (THd)	6700	3.8	0.139	1324	27	18	4
Veidivötn	Sigalda lava	6500	3.4	0.112	1166	21	14	3
Veidivötn	Brydja lava	c.4000	1	0.166	1480	8	6	1
Veidivötn	Búrfell–Dreki lava	3200	6.5	0.135	1300	46	31	6
Grímsvötn	Laki Fires	217	15.1	0.207	1718	143	102	15
	Laki Fires[†]				1675	139	99	24
Grímsvötn	Hálsar–Botnar lava	6000?	>3	0.195	1648	>27	>19	>3
Grímsvötn	Núpar lava	3800	7	0.205	1706	66	47	7
Katla	Hólmsá Fires	6800	>5	0.288	2188	>61	>46	>5
Katla	Eldgjá Fires	1066	19.6	0.291	2171	238	177	20
	Eldgjá Fires[†]				2155	232	184	35

*The densities used to convert the magma volume to mass are as follows: Veidivötn (ρ=2700 kg/m³); Grímsvötn (ρ=2750 kg/m³); Katla (ρ=2800 kg/m³). No attempt was made to correct the volume figures for phenocryst contents of these lavas, which in most cases are low, <1 modal % in Katla system lavas, <3 modal % (range 1–12%) in the Grímsvötn system lavas; and ≤12 modal % (range 4–25%) in the Veidivötn system lavas.
[†]Values obtained by the petrological method (Thordarson 1995; Thordarson *et al.* 1996, 2001).

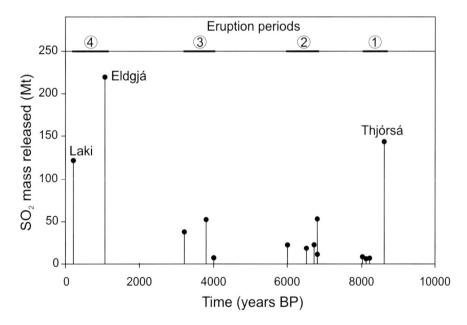

Fig. 9. Mass of sulphur dioxide released by Holocene flood lava eruptions in the Veidivötn, Grímsvötn, and Katla volcanic systems plotted against time. The four flood lava eruption periods mentioned in the text are indicated by the numbers and bars at the top: (1) 8600–8000 years BP; (2) 6800–6000 years BP; (3) 4000–3200 years BP; (4) 1066–217 years BP. Other labels refer to the 1783–1784 Laki, 934–940 Eldgjá and c.8600 years BP Thjórsá flood lava

Discussion

The results presented here indicate that flood lava eruptions at the Veidivötn, Grímsvötn and Katla volcanic systems discharged $c.700$ Mt SO_2 into the atmosphere. These emissions were confined to four 600- to 850-year-long eruption periods (e.g. Table 3, Fig. 9) and the atmospheric SO_2 mass loading during each of these periods ranged from $c.100$ to $c.330$ Mt. When averaged across each eruption period these SO_2 emissions are equivalent to a sulphur flux of 1.2 to 3.9 Mt per decade, rates that correspond with $c.5–15\%$ of the present global volcanic sulphur flux (Graf *et al.* 1998). Therefore it is expected that these eruptions contributed significantly to the contemporary atmospheric sulphur budgets, at least on regional to hemispheric scales.

Each of these flood lava eruptions represent an event pumping tens to hundreds of Mt of SO_2 into the upper troposphere and the lower stratosphere over periods of months to years, and therefore very probably resulted in widespread atmospheric perturbations. The magnitude of the atmospheric SO_2 mass loading by these eruptions is perhaps best appreciated by comparison with recent large-scale explosive silicic eruptions. Nine of the fourteen flood lava eruptions considered here released more than 17 Mt SO_2 into the atmosphere (Table 3), and thus, match or exceed the SO_2 emissions from the 1991 Mount Pinatubo eruption in the Philippines, which is the most recent climatically significant volcanic event (e.g. Self *et al.* 1996*b*). Furthermore, the largest eruptions, the Laki, Eldgjá, and Thjórsá events, released between 100–210 Mt SO_2 into the atmosphere. This is significantly greater than the SO_2 output ($c.85$ Mt) from the 1815 Tambora eruption in Indonesia (e.g. Sigurdsson & Carey 1992), which makes these three eruptions some of the greatest pollution events on Earth during the Holocene. Consequently, they most probably had a notable, but short-lived impact on the climate and the natural habitat in the Northern Hemisphere. For example, the 1783–1784 Laki flood lava eruption in Iceland produced a $c.200$ Mt sulphuric aerosol veil that hung over the Northern Hemisphere for more than five months. About $c.175$ Mt of H_2SO_4 aerosols were removed almost instantly as acid precipitation and caused the extreme volcanic pollution (i.e. dry fog) that affected Europe in 1783. The remaining $c.25$ Mt stayed aloft at tropopause level for more than a year. It has been suggested (Thordarson & Self 2003), that the longer lasting aerosol cloud from Laki disrupted the thermal balance of the Arctic regions for two summers and caused the observed surface cooling in Europe and North America that followed the Laki eruption, which was about $-1.3\ °C$ on an annual basis and lasted for two to three years. Judging from the widespread environmental and climatic effects of the 1783–1784 Laki (e.g. Grattan 1995, 1998; Thordarson & Self 2003) and the 934–940 Eldgjá eruptions (e.g. Stothers 1998; Thordarson *et al.* 2001), the effects of the other large-scale EVZ flood lava eruptions were most likely felt on a hemispheric scale. Of those listed in Table 3, the prime suspects are the Thjórsá, Hólmsá, Núpar and Búrfell–Dreki events. However, when compared with major explosive eruptions in the tropics, the global atmospheric effects of these eruptions are offset to an extent by the lower levels of SO_2 injection, higher rates of aerosol deposition, and the high latitude of Iceland.

It is important to note that here we have only considered the sulphur mass loadings from flood lava eruptions within the Veidivötn, Grímsvötn, and Katla volcanic systems, which only account for about half of the basaltic magma volume produced by these systems during the Holocene. The bulk of the remaining magma volume ($c.85\%$) was emitted by explosive subglacial eruptions (venting subaerially) at the associated central volcanoes (Table 1a). Similar basalt compositions suggest that the potential sulphur yield of these subglacial eruptions is probably of the same magnitude as found for the flood lava eruptions. However, it is not possible at this stage to estimate the total atmospheric SO_2 mass loading from these eruptions because of insufficient knowledge of magma degassing and eruption column processes for these hydromagmatic eruptions. The style and pattern of these explosive central volcano eruptions are also very different from those of the flood lava eruptions; the eruption frequency is much higher (2–10 eruptions per century) and the volume of magma erupted in each event is much smaller ($\leq 0.1\ km^3$) (e.g. Larsen *et al.* 1998). Consequently, the sulphur emissions from these eruptions are likely to have been spread more evenly in time, and thus mostly contributed to the background SO_2 flux from EVZ volcanoes.

Concluding remarks

Our results suggest that the sulphur emissions from nine Holocene flood lava eruptions within the Veidivötn, Grímsvötn, and Katla volcanic systems were large enough to have resulted in atmospheric perturbations on a regional to a hemispheric scale. However, the flood lava eruptions considered here represent <20% of the total basalt magma output from Icelandic volcanoes during the Holocene, and at least 10 other volcanic systems in Iceland have produced one or more eruptions of flood lava magnitudes in this time. If the SO_2 output from these eruptions is any indication of the sulphur flux from Icelandic basalt eruptions, then basalt volcanism in Iceland must have contributed significantly to the global atmospheric sulphur budget during the Holocene. Many of these eruptions must have been responsible for widespread environmental and climate change. Consequently, an important task for the future is to obtain reasonable estimates of the atmospheric SO_2 yield from other Holocene basaltic eruptions in Iceland.

This study is in part based on earlier work that was supported by the NASA Global Change Fellowship Fund and by the National Science Foundation grants no. EAR-9118755. We thank S. Blake for constructive comments on an early version of the manuscript. Our thanks also go to N. Óskarsson, J. Grattan, and C. Oppenheimer for their helpful reviews and suggestions. This is Hawaii Institute of Geophysics Contribution No. 6017.

References

ANDRES, R. J., KYLE, P. R., STOKES, J. B. & ROSE, W. I. 1989. SO_2 from episode 48A eruption, Hawaii: sulfur dioxide emissions from the episode 48A East Rift Zone eruption of Kilauea volcano, Hawaii. *Bulletin of Volcanology*, **52**, 113–117.

DEVINE, J. D., SIGURDSSON, H., DAVIS, A. N. & SELF, S. 1984. Estimates of sulphur and chlorine yield to the atmosphere from volcanic eruptions and potential climatic effects. *Journal of Geophysical Research*, **89(B7)**, 6309–6325.

GRAF, H.-F., LANGMANN, B. & FEICHTER, J. 1998. The contribution of Earth degassing to the atmospheric sulphur budget. *Chemical Geology*, **147**, 131–145.

GRATTAN, J. P. 1995. The distal impact of volcanic gases and aerosols in Europe: a review of the phenomenon and assessment of vulnerability in the late 20th century. *In:* PENN, S. & CULSHAW, M. G. *Geohazards and Engineering Geology.* Geological Society, London, 123–133.

GRATTAN, J. P. 1998. The Distal Impact of Volcanic Gases and Aerosols in Europe: a Review of the 1783 Laki Fissure Eruption and Environmental Vulnerability in the Late 20th Century. *In:* MAUND, J. G. & EDDLESTON, M. *Geohazards in Engineering Geology.* Geological Society, London, Engineering Geology Special Publications, **15**, 7–53.

GRÖNVOLD, K. & JÓHANNESSON, H. 1984. Eruption in Grímsvötn 1983. *Jökull*, **34**, 1–11.

HAMMER, C. U. 1977. Past volcanism revealed by Greenland ice sheet impurities. *Nature*, **270**, 482–486.

HAMMER, C. U. 1984. Traces of Icelandic eruptions in the Greenland ice sheet. *Jökull*, **34**, 51–65.

HAUGHTON, D. R., ROEDER, P. L. & SKINNER, B. J. 1974. Solubility of sulphur in mafic magmas. *Economic Geology*, **69**, 451–467.

HJARTARSON, Á. 1988. Thjórsárhraunid mikla – stærsta nútímahraun jardar. (The Great Thjórsá lava – the largest Holocene lava on Earth.) *Náttúrufæding-urinn*, **58(1)**, 16.

JAKOBSSON, S. P. 1979. Petrology of recent basalts of the Eastern Volcanic Zone, Iceland. *Acta Naturalia Islandica*, **26**, 1–103.

LARSEN, G. 1984. Recent volcanic history of the Veidivötn fissure swarm, southern Iceland – an approach to volcanic risk assessment. *Journal of Volcanology and Geothermal Research*, **22**, 33–58.

LARSEN, G. 2000. Holocene eruptions within the Katla volcanic system, south Iceland. *Jökull*, **49**, 1–28.

LARSEN, G., GUDMUNDSSON, M. T. & BJORNSSON, H. 1998. Eight centuries of periodic volcanism at the centre of the Iceland hotspot revealed by glacier tephrostratigraphy. *Geology*, **26**, 943–946.

MATHEZ, E. A. 1976. Sulfur solubility and magmatic sulfides in submarine glass. *Journal of Geophysical Research*, **81(23)**, 4269–4276.

METRICH, N., SIGURDSSON, H., MEYERS, P. S. & DEVINE, J. D. 1991. The 1783 Lakagigar eruption in Iceland, geochemistry, CO_2, and sulfur degassing. *Contributions to Mineralogy and Petrology*, **107**, 435–447.

MEYER, P. S., SIGURDSSON, H. & SCHILLING, J.-G. 1985. Petrological and geochemical variations along Iceland's neovolcanic zones. *Journal of Geophysical Research*, **90(B12)**, 10 043–10 072.

MILLER, D. J. 1989. *The 10th Century Eruption of Eldgjá, Southern Iceland.* Nordic Volcanological Institute, University of Iceland, Reykjavík, 30 pp.

OSKARSSON, N., SIGVALDASON, G. E. & STEINTHORSSON, S. 1982. A dynamic model of rift zone petrogenesis and the regional petrology of Iceland. *Journal of Petrology*, **23(1)**, 28–74.

RAMPINO, M. R. & SELF, S. 1984. Sulphur-rich volcanic eruptions and stratospheric aerosols. *Nature*, **310**, 677–679.

RAMPINO, M. R., SELF, S. & STOTHERS, R. B. 1988. Volcanic winters. *Annual Review of Earth and Planetary Sciences* **16**, 73–99.

ROBOCK, A. D. 1991. The Volcanic Contribution to Climate Change of the Past 100 Years. *In:* M. E. Schesinger (ed.) *Greenhouse-Gas-Induced Climate Change: a Critical Appraisal of Simulations and Observations.* Elsevier, Amsterdam, 429–444.

ROBOCK, A. 2000. Volcanic eruptions and climate. *Reviews of Geophysics*, **38**, 191–219.

ROLLINSON, H. 1993. *Using geochemical data: evaluation, presentation, interpretation.* Longman, Essex, UK.

SÆMUNDSSON, K. 1978. Fissure swarms and central volcanoes of the neovolcanic zones of Iceland. *Geological Journal Special Issue*, **10**, 415–432.

SÆMUNDSSON, K. 1979. Outline of the geology of Iceland. *Jökull*, **29**, 7–28.

SELF, S., RAMPINO, M. R. & BARBERA, J. J. 1981. The possible effects of large 19th and 20th century volcanic eruptions on zonal and hemispheric surface temperatures. *Journal of Volcanology and Geothermal Research* **11**, 41–60.

SELF, S., THORDARSON, T. & KESZTHELYI, L. 1997.

Emplacement of continental flood basalt lava flows. *In:* MAHONEY, J. J. & COFFIN, M. F. *Large Igneous Provinces: Continental, Oceanic, and Planetary Flood Volcanism,* Geophysical Monograph, **100,** 381–410, American Geophysical Union, Washington D. C.

SELF, S., THORDARSON, T., KESZTHELYI, L., WALKER, G.P.L., HON, K. MURPHY, M. T., LONG, P. & FINNEMORE, S. 1996a. A new model for the emplacement of the Columbia River Basalt as large, inflated pahoehoe sheet lava flow fields. *Geophysical Research Letters,* **23,** 2689–2692.

SELF, S., ZHAO, J.-X., HOLASEK, R. E., TORRES, R. C. & KING, A. J. 1996b. The atmospheric impact of the 1991 Mount Pinatubo eruption. *In:* PUNONGBAYAN, R. S. & NEWHALL, C. G. (eds) *Fire and Mud. Eruptions and Lahars of Mount Pinatubo, Philippines.* Philippine Institute of Volcanology and Seismology and University of Washington Press, Quezon City and Seattle, pp. 1089–1116.

SIGURDSSON, H. 1982. Volcanic pollution and climate: the 1783 Laki eruption. *Eos,* **63,** 601–602.

SIGURDSSON, H. & CAREY, S. 1992. The eruption of Tambora in 1815: environmental effects and eruption dynamics. *In:* HARINGTON C. R. (ed.) *The Year Without Summer: World's Climate in 1816.* Canadian Museum of Nature, Ottawa, pp. 16–45.

STEINTHORSSON, S. 1977. Tephra layers in a drill core from the Vatnajökull ice cap. *Jökull,* **27,** 2–27.

STEINTHORSSON, S., OSKARSSON, N. & SIGVALDASON, G. E. 1985. Origin of alkali basalts in Iceland: a plate tectonic model. *Journal of Geophysical Research,* **90(B12),** 10 027–10 042.

STOTHERS, R. B. 1996. The great dry fog of 1783. *Climate Change,* **32,** 79–89.

STOTHERS, R. B. 1998. Far reach of the tenth century Eldgjá eruption, Iceland. *Climatic Change,* **39,** 715–726.

STOTHERS, R. B., WOLFF, J. A., SELF, S. & RAMPINO, M. R. 1986. Basaltic fissure eruptions, plume height and atmospheric aerosols. *Geophysical Research Letters,* **13,** 725–728.

THORARINSSON, S. 1974. *Vötnin Stríd: saga Skeidarárhlaupa og Grímsvatnagosa. (The swift flowing rivers: history of Grímsvötn eruptions and jökulhlaups.)* Bókaútgáfa Menningarsjóds, Reykjavík, 254 pp.

THORARINSSON, S. 1975. Katla og annáll Kötlugosa (The annals of historical Katla eruptions). *Árbók Ferdafélags Íslands,* **1975,** 125–149.

THORARINSSON, S. 1982. Jardeldasvædi á Nútíma (Holocene volcanic regions in Iceland). *In: Náttúra Íslands,* Almenna Bókafélagid, Reykjavík, 81–120.

THORDARSON, T. 1995. *Volatile Release and Atmospheric Effects of Basaltic Fissure Eruptions.* Department of Geology and Geophysics, Honolulu, University of Hawaii, unpublished PhD thesis, 570 pp.

THORDARSON, T. & SELF, S. 1993. The Laki (Skaftár Fires) and Grímsvötn eruptions in 1783–1785. *Bulletin of Volcanology,* **55,** 233–263.

THORDARSON, T. & SELF, S. 1996. Sulphur, chlorine and fluorine degassing and atmospheric loading by

the Roza eruption, Columbia River Basalt group, Washington, USA. *Journal of Volcanology and Geothermal Research,* **74,** 49–73.

THORDARSON, T. & SELF, S. 1998. The Roza Member, Columbia River Basalt Group: a gigantic pahoehoe lava flow field formed by endogenous processes? *Journal of Geophysical Research,* **103 (B11),** 27 411–27 445.

THORDARSON, T. & SELF, S. 2001. Real-time observations of the Laki sulfuric aerosol cloud in Europe 1783 as documented by Professor S. P. van Swinden at Franeker, Holland. *Jökull,* 50, 65–72.

THORDARSON, T. & SELF, S. 2003. Atmospheric and environmental effects of the 1783–84 Laki eruption, Iceland: a review and reassessment. *Journal of Geophysical Research,* **108(D1),** 10.1029/2001JD 002042.

THORDARSON, T., SELF, S., ÓSKARSSON, N. & HULSEBOSCH, T. 1996. Sulphur, chlorine, and fluorine degassing and atmospheric loading by the 1783–1784 AD Laki (Skaftár Fires) eruption in Iceland. *Bulletin of Volcanology* **58,** 205–225.

THORDARSON, T., MILLER, D. J., & LARSEN, G. 1998. New data on the age and origin of the Leidólfsfell cone group in south Iceland. *Jökull,* **46,** 3–15.

THORDARSON, T., MILLER, J. D., LARSEN, G., SELF, S. & SIGURDSSON, H. 2001. New estimates of sulphur degassing and atmospheric mass-loading by the AD934 Eldgjá eruption, Iceland.

VILMUNDARDÓTTIR, E. G. 1977. *Tungnaárhraun (Tugnaá lavas), Geological Report. OS ROD 7702,* Orkustofnun, Reykjavík, 156.

VILMUNDARDÓTTIR, E. G., GUDMUNDSSON, Á. & SNORRASON, S. P. 1983. *Geological Map, Búrfell– Langalda, 3540 B,* National Energy Authority and National Power Company, Reykjavík.

VILMUNDARDÓTTIR, E. G., SNORRASON, S. P., LARSEN, G. & GUDMUNDSSON, Á. 1988. *Geological Map, Sigalda–Veidivötn, 3340 B,* National Energy Authority and National Power Company, Reykjavík.

VILMUNDARDÓTTIR, E. G., GUDMUNDSSON, Á., SNORRASON, S. P. & LARSEN, G. 1990. *Geological Map Botnafjöll 1913 IV, 1:50 000, Iceland Geodetic Survey,* National Energy Authority and National Power Company: Reykjavík.

VILMUNDARDÓTTIR, E. G., LARSEN, G. & SNORRASON, S. P. 1999a. *Geological Map Nyrdri Háganga 1914 II, 1:50 000. Iceland Geodetic Survey,* National Energy Authority and National Power Company, Reykjavík.

VILMUNDARDÓTTIR, E. G., SNORRASON, S. P., LARSEN, G. & ADALSTEINSSON, B. 1999b. *Geological Map, Tungnaárjökull 1913 I, 1:50 000, Iceland Geodetic Survey,* National Energy Authority and National Power Company, Reykjavík.

WALLACE, P. & CARMICHAEL, I. S. E. 1992. Sulphur in basaltic magmas. *Geochimica et Cosmochimica Acta,* **65,** 1863–1874.

WALLACE, P. J. 2001. Volcanic SO_2 emissions and the abundance and distribution of exsolved gas in magma bodies. *Journal of Volcanological and Geothermal Research,* **108,** 85–106.

WILSON, L. & HEAD, J. W. 1981. Ascent and eruption

of basaltic magma on the Earth and Moon. *Journal of Geophysical Research*, **86,** 2971–3001.

WOOD, C. A. 1992. *Climatic Effects of the 1783 Laki Eruption. The Year Without a Summer? In*: C. R. Harington (ed.). Ottawa, Canadian Museum of Nature, 58–77.

WOODS, A. W. 1993. A model of the plumes above basaltic fissure eruptions. *Geophysical Research Letters* **20**, 1115–1118.

ZIELINSKI, G. A. 1994. A continuous record of volcanism (present–7000 BC) and volcano–climate implications. *Science*, **264**, 948–952.

ZIELINSKI, G. A., GERMANI, M. S. 1995. Evidence of the Eldgjá (Iceland) eruption in the GISP2 Greenland ice core: relationship to eruption processes and climatic conditions in the tenth century. *The Holocene*, **5**, 129–140.

Particles from the plume of Popocatépetl volcano, Mexico – the FESEM/EDS approach

J. H. OBENHOLZNER[1], H. SCHROETTNER[2], P. GOLOB[2] & H. DELGADO[3]

[1]Naturhistorisches Museum/Mineralogie, Postfach 417, A-1014 Vienna, Austria.
(e-mail: obenholzner@a1.net)
[2]Zentrum fuer Elektronenmikroskopie, TU-Graz, Steyrerg. 17, A-8010 Austria.
(hartmuth.schroettner@felmi-zfe.at)
[3]Instituto de Geofisica, UNAM, Coyoacan 04510, Mexico D.F., Mexico.
(e-mail: hugo@tonatiuh.igeofcu.unam.mx)

Abstract: Magma–wall-rock interaction contributes gases to evolving magmatic systems, and removes volatiles into the country rock. These processes happen at depth, far away from direct observation. Micro-analysis of particles collected from volcanic plumes can provide information about these processes. For Popocatépetl volcano, scanning electron microscope (SEM) and field emission gun SEM (FESEM/EDS) analysis of contact-metamorphosed particles from fallout ash reveal the presence of wollastonite, hercynite and glass of non-volcanic, contact-metamorphic origin. Condensates from the passively degassing plume show a wide variety of chemical elements and are rich in phosphorus, indicating a possible non-magmatic source for this element.

Volcanic eruptions inject considerable quantities of fine particles of volcanic and non-volcanic origin into the atmosphere. Such particles may act as nuclei for condensation processes, or as sites for heterogeneous chemical reactions in the atmosphere. The abundance of chlorine and other trace species in these particles makes a significant but under-evaluated contribution to the environmental impacts of volcanic eruptions.

Aerosols are suspensions of solid or liquid particles in a gas. Aerosols are usually stable for at least a few seconds, and in some cases may last a year or more. In the plume environment, magmatic, non-magmatic (contact-metamorphic, CM) gases and entrained air will mix. Particles may form by a number of processes, and have widely differing origins (Table 1 summarizes the nomenclature). Liquid droplets may form by condensation, grow by coagulation and scavenge other materials from the plume. Dust particles may arise from breakage, or resuspension; may act as nuclei for heterogeneous surface processes, and form clusters or aggregates with other particles. Particles may be primary (having already existed in the volcanic emission as it was released), or secondary (formed in the plume, perhaps by gas-to-particle conversion). Particles may range from homogeneous crystalline minerals, to heterogeneous or amorphous substances.

The volcanic production of aerosols, dust and gases is difficult to assess, because of the scarcity of data. In addition to primary tephra particles, volcanic activity releases significant quantities of reactive gases including H_2S, SO_2, HCl, and HF. Over the past few decades, stratospheric and tropospheric aerosols have been studied at a number of volcanoes, and in the aftermath of several significant volcanic eruptions. Notable among these include studies on the explosive eruptions of Mount St Helens (1980; Hobbs et al. 1981; Oberbeck et al. 1982; Phelan et al. 1982) and Pinatubo (1991; Sheridan et al. 1992, Hamill et al. 1996); studies of passive emissions from Erebus (Meeker et al. 1991) and Kilauea (Zoller et al. 1983) and the plumes of Pacaya, Fuego (Rose et al. 1980; Ammann & Burtscher 1993) and Mount Etna (Andres et al. 1993).

This study presents new data from particles collected in a plume. The analytical possibilities of state-of-the-art SEM techniques provide a unique opportunity for cooperation between the analyst and the modeller, and results provide important constraints for models of stratospheric chemistry. Particles smaller than several millimetres in diameter are candidates for scanning electron microscope (SEM) analysis. Recent developments in SEM techniques, like the field emission gun SEM (FESEM) have improved morphological, mineralogical, and textural examinations. Modern SEM systems are equipped with energy dispersive X-ray detectors (EDS) for chemical analysis.

From: OPPENHEIMER, C., PYLE, D.M. & BARCLAY, J. (eds) *Volcanic Degassing*. Geological Society, London, Special Publications, **213**, 123–148. 0305–8719/03/$15.00

Table 1. *Particle-size terms used in volcanology and aerosol sciences.*

Volcanic particles (Fisher & Schmincke 1984)	(diameter)	Aerosol particles (Hinds 1982; Seinfeld & Pandis 1998)	(diameter)
Lapilli	64–2 mm		
Coarse ash	2–1/16 mm		
Fine ash	< 1/16 mm (=62.5 μm)	Dust	1–10 000 μm
		Fine sand	20–200 μm
		Coarse particle	> 2μm
		Fine particle	< 2μm
		Clay	c. 0.01–2 μm
		Fume	c. 0.001–1 μm
		Hazes	< 1 μm
		Aitken size range (particle radius)	0.1–0.001 μm

A variety of contact-metamorphic and related minerals indicate the interaction of magma and magmatic fluids with carbonate-bearing rocks and other sediments beneath the volcano. Contact metamorphism may occur around a magma chamber, within magma storage zones at higher levels or as a wall-rock–magma inter-action during ascent. These processes may contribute a variety of volatile species, especially CO_2, SO_2, F, and Cl, to the original magmatic gas.

Complex condensation processes in the plume lead to the formation of a wide variety of fluffy (semi-solid?), and spherical (solid?) particles. The latter are sometimes coated by crystallites of S-bearing Mg-chlorides. Using EDS techniques, we have been able to characterize the chemical composition of individual aerosols. Elements detected in fluffy aerosols are Si, Al, Ca, Na, Mg, K, Fe, Ti, P, Cu, Zn, *Bi*, Pb, *Mo, Sn*, S, Cl, O. Elements detected in spherical particles are Si, Al, Ca, Na, K, Mg, Fe, Ti, P, *Mn*, Cu, Zn, S, *V*, Cl, *Ni*, O, Pb, (*Cr*) (italics indicate species found only in one type of aerosol; Cr only as shown in Fig. 8d). Individual spheres may have distinct chemical compositions. The variety of chemical compositions may reflect different sources, or different micro-environments in the plume and at the magma-plume–atmosphere interfaces.

Evidence for contact metamorphism associated with the eruptions at Popocatépetl volcano

Popocatépetl is a stratovolcano situated in the central part of the Trans Mexican Volcanic Belt. Popocetépetl is the youngest active volcano of a N–S trending chain of volcanoes (Popocatépetl, Iztaccíhuatl, Tláloc) above the subducting Cocos plate. The basement beneath Popocatépetl comprises metamorphosed Palaeozoic rocks: c.3 km of Cretaceous carbonates, and 500 m of Tertiary sediments with intercalated evaporites

(Fries 1965*a*, *b*), including gypsum. The volcanic history of Popocatépetl volcano is described by Siebe *et al.* (1996, 1999), and the major Holocene and younger Pleistocene volcanic events are summarized in Table 2.

Past explosive eruptions of Popocatépetl (e.g. the c.14 ka BP Plinian eruption) contain blocks of calc-silicate rocks with diopside and grossular garnet as the predominant minerals. Some dolo-mite marble xenoliths contain clinohumite ((Mg, Fe^{2+})$_9(SiO_4)_4(OH, F)_2$). As the F content of most sediments is rather low, clinohumite may reflect the migration of F from magma into the wall rock. Millimetre-sized inclusions in pumice of the Tocuila lahar (derived from the c.14 ka Plinian eruption; Siebe *et al.* 1999) contain grossular with droplet-shaped haüyne ((Na, Ca)$_{4-8}[Al_6Si_6 O_{24}](SO_4,S)_{1-2}$), diopside, K-feldspar, quartz,

Table 2. *Major Holocene and younger Pleistocene volcanic events at Popocatépetl*

Present eruption	1994–?	(CM)
Upper Ceramic Plinian Eruptive Sequence	675–1095 AD	
Intermediate Ceramic Eruptive Sequence	125–255 AD	
Nealtican andesite flow	c. 2300 BP	(CM)
Lower Ceramic Plinian Eruptive Sequence	215–800 BC	
Upper Pre-Ceramic Plinian Eruptive Sequence	2830–3195 BC	
Tocuila lahar (redeposited Plinian eruption of c.14 000 BP)	11 000–12 000 BP	(CM)
Plinian eruption	c.14 000 BP	(CM)

Dates based on conventional ^{14}C dating (BP=years before present); from Siebe *et al.* (1996, 1999).
(CM) refers to contact metamorphosed xenoliths or particles observed in lava flows, pyroclastic deposits or volcanic ash.

and sylvite. These altered wall-rock fragments were mixed throughout the magma prior to eruption. One sample (P 97-02) from the 'ochre surge' beneath the 'pink pumice' (Upper Ceramic Plinian Eruptive Sequence, *c.* AD 800) contains abundant euhedral to anhedral anhydrite. The origin of this anhydrite (whether hydrothermal or magmatic) is unknown.

Contact-metamorphic particles from on-going eruptions

Calc-silicates

Ash from the eruptions of winter 1995 (2 January 1995), spring 1995 (20 March 1995 and winter 1996 (28 November 1996) contains a variety of contact-metamorphosed rock fragments. The November 1996 ash contains dome fragments and vesiculated or moss-shaped aggregates of a calc-silicate whose composition is close to $CaSiO_3$, probably wollastonite. Most of the observed calc-silicates are highly heterogeneous at a small scale, and difficult to characterize chemically with either EDS or electron probe microanalysis (EMPA). The wollastonite particles are unusually rich in Fe. Back-scattered (BSE) images do not show the typical fibrous features known from light microscopy. As there is no volcanic glass associated with the wollastonite particles, they may have formed without direct interaction with the melt. One microclast appears vesicular and glassy, but comprises quartz, Ca-feldspar and calc-silicate. Wollastonite aggregates contain randomly distributed pyrite (?) with rare molybdenite (MoS_2).

Textural and compositional varieties of wollastonite

Micro-clasts are texturally very different. Type 1 clasts have *c.*20 μm veins of massive, chemically homogeneous, non-vesicular wollastonite, intergrown with K-feldspar and quartz (Fig. 1). One micro-clast appears vesicular and glassy, and comprises an Si-rich glass (?) with Ca-feldspar and type 2 wollastonite. The wollastonite is massive, and up to *c.*40 μm (Fig. 2), with inclusions of quartz and rare sulphides. One 5-μm vug is surrounded by massive, chemically homogeneous wollastonite. Vugs in the glassy (?) region are open, or filled with sulphide.

Type 3 wollastonite has a variable Fe-content (Figs 3 & 4) and shows intergrowths of 1–10 μm Fe-rich (FeO *c.*12%) and Fe-poor (FeO *c.*3%) patches with randomly distributed pyrite (?) and rare molybdenite (MoS_2). Type 3 wollastonite is

vesicular, with 1–10 μm vesicles, suggesting that wollastonite formation was accompanied by vigorous gas release. The gas may have been CO_2 (from calcite+quartz=wollastonite+CO_2) or SO_2 (from anhydrite+quartz=wollastonite +SO_2+O; Wood 1994). While neither reaction explains the high Fe-content of wollastonite, a Cretaceous Fe–Ca carbonate protolith is considered more likely than an Fe–Ca-sulphate component from an evaporitic succession or hydrothermally altered volcanic rocks. Type 4 wollastonite is Fe-poor and occurs in 10–20 μm, chemically homogeneous, non-vesicular intergrowths with quartz (Fig. 5).

The November 1996 ash contains wollastonites of several grain sizes (A: 32–65 μm; B: 20–32 μm; C: 20–32 μm (particles float on water according to low density or surface tension)). Wollastonite B1 is a 20×40 μm vesicular, rounded grain, which shows a reaction rim at the outermost edge. This zone is slightly Mg-rich relative to the core, may be indicating interaction with a fluid. Vesicles are heterogeneously distributed, and up to 10 μm. One vesicle is partially filled with a glassy P-rich material (15–28% P_2O_5). Grain B2 is a 20×50 μm vesicular fragment with a glassy rim (SiO_2: 80–95%). Sphene crystals are abundant at the interface between wollastonite and glass, and vesicles are <5 μm size. B3 is a subangular clast comprising vesiculated wollastonite with inclusions of Cl-rich glass (SiO_2: 75–80%, Cl: *c.*3%), plagioclase-like inclusions and irregularly distributed Fe-oxides, and a glass (SiO_2: 60–65%) vesiculated towards the boundary with wollastonite and a pyroxene inclusion. Vesicle shapes sometimes resemble crystals, and may be remnants of dissolved minerals. Particles rich in calc-silicates (11-28-96 ash) may also contain 1 μm fluorite crystals. Other particles from November 1996 are Si-rich glasses of contact metamorphic origin ('buchites') containing anhydrite crystals and inherited zircons. The vesicularity is typically bimodal with coalescing vesicles (*c.*10 μm) and a spongy vesiculation (*c.*1 μm). EDS analysis of the glass gives Na_2O=1.93, MgO=0.19, Al_2O_3=4.37, SiO_2=85.6, K_2O=0.30, CaO=0.35, TiO_2=0.48, MnO=0.16, FeO=0.53, P_2O_5=0.95, SO_3=4.41, Cl=0.13.

Apart from B1, none of the wollastonite types show alteration or signs of retrograde metamorphism (e.g. growth of hydrous calc-silicates). This is considered to reflect the young age of wollastonite and the absence of water. Wollastonite particles (B1) are rounded, suggesting physical abrasion, with alteration rims due to interaction with a liquid or gas phase (Table 3). Calc-silicate particles have been found in the

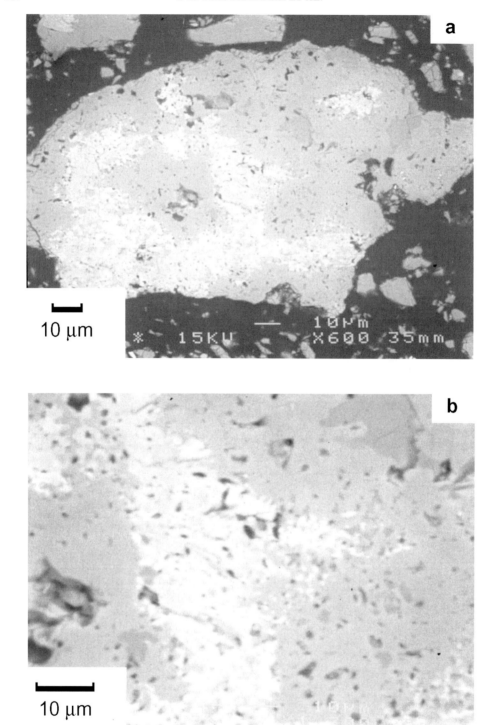

Fig. 1. BSE images, (**a**) Type 1 wollastonite, massive Fe-poor wollastonite (white) surrounded by K-feldspar (grey), dark grey patches are quartz (wo–A). (**b**) Close-up of central part of (a). Wollastonite is almost homogeneous; the surrounding K-feldspar shows many small inclusions of quartz (dark grey).

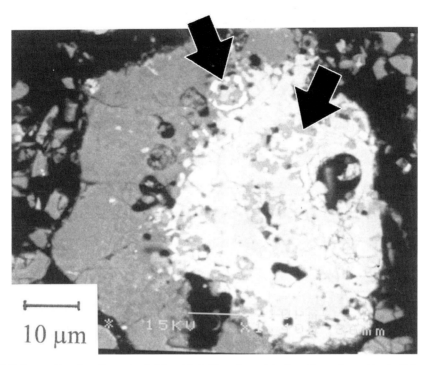

Fig. 2. BSE image: Type 2 wollastonite (bright white). Note the vesicles in wollastonite and in the SiO_2-rich matrix (grey). Some vesicles seem to be annealed by another generation of wollastonite and quartz (arrows).

troposphere, and can act as ice-forming nuclei (Parungo *et al.* 1976)

Spinel, buchites, and other indicators of contact metamorphism

Hercynite (Fe–Al-spinel)-bearing particles are also recognized. Euhedral hercynite (clast 1: H1, H2; clast 2: H3; Table 4) is scattered in a BSE homogeneous matrix that may be glassy (clast 1: M1-4; Table 5). Individual spinel crystals range from <1 to 2–3 µm, and typically form clusters. The SiO_2 and other element contents of H1-H3 probably derive from background or interstitial matrix. Hercynite may derive from metamorphosed argillaceous rock, and has been reported from the *c.* 900 °C section of a silica tube experiment from Merapi (Le Guern & Bernard 1982a).

Other fragments comprise phlogopite and sphene, with widespread small magnetite crystals between the euhedral sphene crystals. Possible reactions to form sphene and phlogopite are:

$$TiO_2 + calcite + quartz \leftrightarrow sphene + CO_2$$

$$2\ dolomite + K\text{-feldspar} + H_2O \leftrightarrow$$
$$phlogopite + 3\ calcite + 3CO_2$$

Both reactions would contribute CO_2 to the gas phase. As most marine limestones have $\delta^{13}C$ values close to zero, one would expect that limestone decarbonation would yield CO_2 with $\delta^{13}C \approx +5.0\text{‰}$ (Shieh & Taylor 1969).

The 20 March 1995 ash contains lithic fragments. They consist mostly of euhedral pyroxenes (Table 5). The crystals are free from adhering melt, but there are relics of an Si-rich homogeneous, interstitial matrix (Table 5). Cavities between the pyroxene crystals host rounded Ni-rich minerals, with a maximum diameter of 5 µm. The Ni-bearing minerals, with Fe:Cu:Ni:S ≈ 1:1:1:4, are heterogeneous in the BSE image. Very bright small (*c.* 1 µm) crystals are embedded in a bright P_2O_5–rich matrix, indicating a contact-metamorphic origin. Fe–Ni-sulphides are widespread in hornfels-type xenoliths (#95/73). The surface of this xenolith has pseudo-concentric patches of an Mn–Fe–(Ni?)-coating, and shows dehydration cracks. The genesis of these patches might be related to post-depositional processes.

The January 1995 volcanic ash contains fragments of anhydrite crystals in a chemically heterogeneous matrix rich in Al, P and S, comprising 1–5 µm intergrowths of Fe-rich and

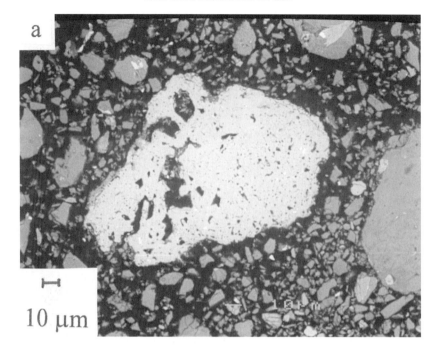

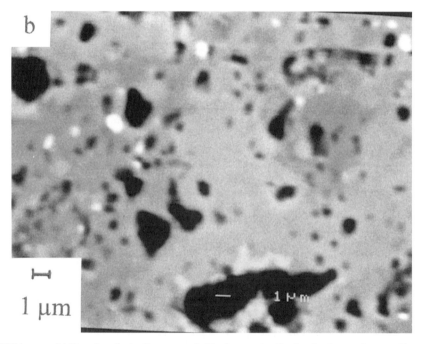

Fig. 3. BSE images: (**a**) Type 3 wollastonite surrounded by fragments of volcanic glass and magmatic crystals. The wollastonite grain (white) is slightly rounded and vesiculated. Vesicles are black. (**b**) Close-up of (a). Note the different grey levels of the vesiculated wollastonite, reflecting the different Fe contents: lighter patches have higher Fe. Bright white dots are sulphides. For interpretation see p. 125.

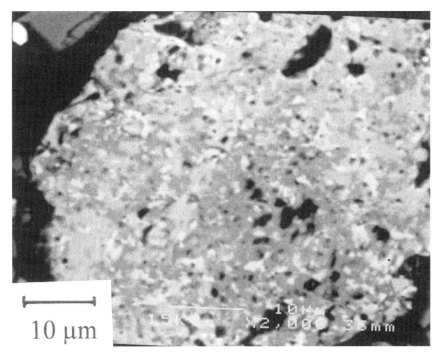

10 μm

Fig. 4. BSE image: Type 3 wollastonite. This grain is highly heterogeneous and vesiculated. Dark grey areas are Fe-poor; light grey areas are Fe-rich. Vesicles are black; sulphides are white.

Fe-poor patches. This texture may reflect the spinodal decomposition of an originally homogeneous phase, or the quenched products of a reaction process. Chemical analysis of this material by EDS gives $Na_2O=1.93$, $MgO=0.69$, $Al_2O_3=48.9$, $SiO_2=5.35$, $K_2O=1.89$, $CaO=6.95$, $FeO=1.32$, $P_2O_5=14.2$, $SO_3=17.8$, $Cl=0.76$ (oxides of Ti, Mn and Ni are not present).

The significance of contact-metamorphic minerals in the Popocatépetl plume

The occurrence of contact-metamorphic and related minerals in the plume reflects changes in the recent eruptive process. The interpretation of the age of the CM-minerals is crucial: does Popocatépetl erupt old CM-minerals? Is CM an on-going process when magma is sitting at shallow levels, or are the CM fragments alien to the volcanic ash collected in the vicinity of Mexico DF? Wollastonite can be the product of a variety of processes not related to volcanoes for example from pyrometamorphic rocks associated with naturally burned coal beds (Cosca *et al.* 1989, Matthews & Gross 1980).

There are a number of occurrences of wollastonite in volcanic xenoliths. Notable examples are listed in Table 6. Porous wollastonite (with bustamite, hercynite, sphene and other CM-minerals) is present in xenoliths of the recent dome of Merapi, Java (Clocchiatti *et al.* 1982). The cavities in this case are interpreted as formerly CO_2 filled. Wollastonite is also reported as a sublimate phase from Merapi volcano (Symonds *et al.* 1987).

At Vesuvius, another volcano situated on massive carbonates, wollastonite-bearing xenoliths have been ejected at the end of some shorter periods of activity that terminate with a more energetic, clast-clearing phase: for example in 1822, 1872, 1906 and 1944 (Zambonini 1935; Del Moro *et al.* 2002). Isotopic studies of fumarolic CO_2 of Mount Vesuvius demonstrate an input of metamorphic CO_2 (Chiodini *et al.* 2001).

Wollastonite can form under a wide range of conditions, depending on the composition of the pore fluid. Experimental data report wollastonite formation at 2 kbar (4–6 km) at >700 °C and only 500 bars (1–2 km) at 600 °C. Popocatepetl erupts dacite lavas at temperatures between 750 and 950 °C. The formation of wollastonite indicates the highest grades of contact metamorphism against the magma, but not necessarily in immediate contact with the melt. Fluids can

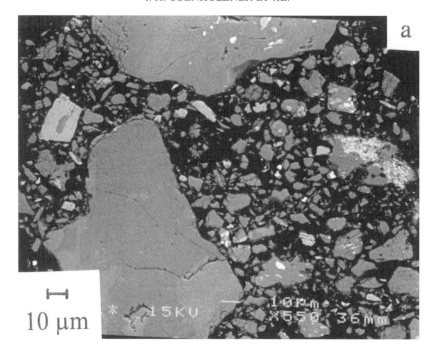

Fig. 5. BSE images: Type 4 wollastonite. (**a**) Large, grey fragments are feldspars embedded in glassy matrix; upper left: white mineral is a pyroxene with a glass inclusion (grey). At the centre right there are wollastonite-bearing fragments, white is wollastonite. Scattered fragments are volcanic glass and magmatic crystals. (**b**) Close-up of (a). Wollastonite (white) showing blocky inclusions of quartz (?). The grey part of the fragment is SiO_2.

Table 3. *Chemical composition (EDS) of wollastonites (28 Nov. 96 volcanic ash)*

Sample	15	wo-f1	wo-f2	wo-f3	woP	wo-A	B1-1	B1-2	B2-1	B2-2	B3-1	B3-2
Composition, wt%												
SiO_2	45.12	46.7	47.75	47.84	45.26	44.44	45.17	45.63	45.51	46.52	45.91	44.65
CaO	39.71	40.5	48.17	47.46	50.18	52.43	40.43	39.4	47.96	48.88	50.88	50.37
FeO	13.29	12.39	3.15	03.35	1.54	2.38	12.55	12.99	2.75	3.15	1.23	1.73
MnO	1.21	0.02	0.00	0.00	0.11	0.17	0.00	0.62	0.50	0.25	0.00	0.00
MgO	0.22	0.21	0.08	0.00	0.00	0.00	0.00	0.08	0.28	0.10	0.27	0.32
K_2O	0.19	0.11	0.41	0.11	0.24	0.00	0.00	0.07	0.00	0.06	0.01	0.00
TiO_2	0.26	0.06	0.08	0.00	0.00	0.10	0.51	0.00	0.54	0.08	0.07	0.27
Na_2O									0.00	0.22	0.25	0.19
Al_2O_3			0.34		2.17	0.04			0.36	0.23	0.12	0.53
NiO			0.02									
P_2O_5				0.54	0.14	0.01						
Cr_2O_3				0.20	0.08							
SO_3					0.11	0.42						
CuO									0.30	0.30	0.02	1.33
Zn									0.20	0.20	1.24	0.00
Sum	99.00	99.99	100.0	99.50	99.79	99.99	98.66	98.79	98.40	99.99	100.0	99.39

Cations per formula unit, based on 24 oxygen atoms												
Si	7.429	7.591	7.597	7.570	7.220	7.188	7.411	7.497	7.272	7.433	7.427	7.191
Ca	7.006	7.053	8.211	8.049	8.577	9.085	7.107	6.935	8.211	8.368	8.821	8.692
Fe	1.831	1.684	0.419	0.443	0.205	0.322	1.722	1.785	0.367	0.421	0.166	0.233
Mn	0.168	0.003	0.000	0.000	0.014	0.023	0.000	0.087	0.067	0.034	0.000	0.000
Mg	0.054	0.052	0.019	0.000	0.000	0.000	0.000	0.019	0.067	0.024	0.064	0.077
K	0.04	0.023	0.082	0.022	0.049	0.000	0.000	0.014	0.000	0.012	0.002	0.001
Ti	0.032	0.008	0.009	0.000	0.000	0.012	0.063	0.000	0.065	0.010	0.009	0.032
Na									0.000	0.069	0.059	0.059
Al			0.063		0.409	0.008			0.067	0.043	0.022	0.101
Ni			0.003									
P				0.072	0.019							
Cr				0.025	0.010							
S					0.013	0.051						
Cu									0.036	0.000	0.003	0.162
Zn									0.030	0.000	0.185	0.000

Blank spaces=not determined.

transport ions deep into the country rock. Examples are known of wollastonitized cherts intercalated within limestones, where the cherts operated as metamorphic aquifers (Romer and Heinrich 1998).

Wollastonite growth in aureoles may be very fast. The 20-μm thick wollastonite (type 1) could grow in just 1–2 years at >800°C (Kridelbaugh 1973). Experiments document that diffusion-controlled growth of wollastonite on quartz through CO_2-filled fractures is possible (Milke & Heinrich 2002). Harker and Tuttle (1956) grew wollastonite in half an hour at 660 °C and *c*.340 bars in the presence of water. Tanner *et al.* (1985) report replacement of calcite by wollastonite (100 μm) in 1.1 years at 850 °C and 1 kbar.

Goff *et al.* (2001) measured CO_2/SO_2 excursions at Popocatépetl of up to 30 times higher than the typical CO_2/SO_2 values. These events were considered to reflect active assimilation of limestones into the magma chamber. Given the long-lasting activity of Popocatépetl and its eruptive history (the last major degassing phase happened in the 1920s), it is hard to imagine that a new batch of magma could reactivate contact metamorphism and related degassing of already more or less metamorphosed country rocks. Fracturing might be necessary to expose unmetamorphosed carbonates to the

Table 4. *Chemical composition (by EDS) of the matrix (M1-4) and hercynite (H1-3), wt%*

Sample	M1	M2	M3	M4	H1	H2	H3
SiO_2	41.73	45.0	46.48	60.71	5.26	4.35	1.01
TiO_2	0.01	0.00	0.00	0.14	0.24	0.38	0.95
Al_2O_3	39.07	36.9	34.8	26.98	46.19	47.38	49.29
FeO	12.65	12.17	12.44	2.60	43.43	42.96	43.06
MgO	3.48	3.56	3.74	0.27	1.56	1.54	3.68
CaO	0.15	0.10	0.23	2.02	0.50	0.67	
Na_2O	0.00	0.00	0.34	2.30	0.00	0.00	2.01
K_2O	0.53	0.59	0.23	3.73	0.43	0.23	
SO_3	0.00	0.00	0.00	0.19	0.24	0.14	
Cl	0.16	0.00	0.25	0.00	0.02	0.23	
Cr_2O_3	0.00	0.00	0.10	0.22	0.94	0.23	
NiO	0.32	0.00	0.00	0.25	0.00	0.00	
CuO	0.00	0.12	0.35	0.00	0.15	0.12	
Zn	1.05	0.43	0.00	0.00	0.00	0.43	
MnO	0.04	0.59	0.10	0.00	1.03	0.28	
P_2O_5	0.80	0.51	0.91	0.60	0.00	0.29	
Sum	99.99	99.95	99.98	100.01	99.99	99.23	99.23

Table 5. *EDS analysis of pyroxenes (pyx 1-2) and matrix (M1-2), wt%*

Sample	M1	M2	pyx1	pyx2
SiO_2	76.12	74.09	51.47	53.1
TiO_2	0.41	0.47	0.63	0.51
Al_2O_3	12.59	12.85	0.73	3.52
FeO	3.60	3.93	24.48	28.91
MnO	0.00	0.00	1.00	0.72
MgO	0.00	0.42	18.26	8.85
CaO	0.94	1.14	2.23	3.14
Na_2O	1.83	3.01	0.00	0.55
K_2O	3.49	3.57	0.13	0.50
Cr_2O_3	0.12	0.00	0.00	0.05
P_2O_5	0.75	0.49	0.34	0.00
Cl	0.10	0.00	0.00	0.02
Ni	0.00	0.01	0.54	0.00
Cu	0.00	0.00	0.00	0.12
Sum	99.95	99.98	99.81	99.99

replenished magma chamber to release these huge quantities of CM-derived gas.

Seismicity beneath Popocatépetl since 1994 extends to 170 km depth, but is concentrated between 5 to 10 km, roughly defining a volume of 25 km³ (Shapiro *et al.* 2000). Volcanotectonic earthquakes from 1994 to 1996 were concentrated between 0 and 3.5 km beneath the edifice (Valdes *et al.* 1995; Arciniega-Ceballos *et al.* 2000). Even if the magma chamber lies beneath the 3-km thick Cretaceous limestones, magma will still interact with the carbonate complex on its route to the surface. Volcanotectonic earthquakes in the brittle rocks around the magma reservoir and conduits may relate to stresses induced by magma movement. This may lead to fracturing of the surrounding rocks which may be added to the moving magma (Arcienega-Ceballos, pers. comm.).

Decarbonation reactions decrease the volume of the country rock, releasing large volumes of gas. Escaping gases and fluids may cause hydrofracture and may enter the magmatic system. The long-lasting volcanic activity at Popocatépetl might have formed a magmatic 'karst' or other erosional features linked to magma turbulence (Kille *et al.* 1986). Continuous contact metamorphism would create a shell of decarbonated rocks, as known from many plutons. Nevertheless, the transfer of heat and

Table 6. *Selected occurrences of wollastonite-bearing ejecta in volcanic rocks.*

Volcano	Host material	Reference
Asama, Japan (1783–recent?)		Aramaki (1961)
Ettringer Bellerberg (Mayen, Eifel)	Lava flows	Jasmund & Hentschel (1964)
Kanpu volcano, Japan (Fe-wollastonite)		Isshiki (1954).
La Soufrière, St Vincent	Lava flows	Devine& Sigurdson (1980)
Merapi, Java	Dome lavas and sublimates	Clocchiatti *et al.* (1982) Symonds *et al.* (1987)
Mt Etna, Sicily (1892, 1986)		Michaud (1995), Michaud *et al.* (1988)
Pacaya volcano, Guatemala (March 1989, July 1990)	Lava flows	Janik *et al.* (1992)
Popocatépetl volcano.	Andesite lava flow	Goff *et al.* (2001)
Southern Burgenland and Styria, Austria (Pliocene)	Basaltic peperite, basanites and basalts	Schoklitsch (1934), Postl *et al.* (1996)
Santorini, Greece	Dacite lavas	Nicholls (1971)
Semeru, Java, 15 November 1911		Brouwer (1920
Tarumai volcano, Hokkaido	Lavas	Ishikawa (1953)
Vesuvius	Lava flows and ejecta	Zambonini (1935), Barberi *et al.* (1980), Del Moro *et al.* (2001)
White Island 25 July 1987 and Ruapehu, New Zealand		Wood (1994), Wood *et al.* (1996)
Alban Hills volcano (0.2–0.02 Ma)	Tephrite, phonolite	Federico & Peccerillo (2002)

Table 7. *Complex and simple particles – shape, size, and chemical composition*

FESEM image no.	Single particle (s), Aggregated particles (a)	Diameter (d), Length (l) (μm)	Spherical (s), Crystalline (c), Fluffy (f), Complex (co)	Elements	Interpretation
–	s		c?	S	elemental sulphur
–	s		c	Ba, S, O	barite
Popoc04	s	$l=3$	c	Sr, Ba, S, Fe,O	Sr-bearing barite, Fe-bearing rim
Popoc12	s	$l=6$	co	Fe, Ba, S, O	Fe-oxide/hydroxide and barite
Popo06	s	$l=10$	c	S & Si, Al, Ca	sulphur
Popo03	s	$l=7$	c?	Ca, O & Si, Al, Mg, K	Ca-carbonate/ oxide/hydroxide
Popo02	a	$l=7$	co	Si, Al, O & Na, Mg, K, Ca, Ti, Fe, P, S, Cl	
Popo04	s	$l=2$	c	Si, Mg, Ca, O & Na, Al, Fe	
Pop2-1	s	$d=0.5$	c?	Ca, Cr, Mn, Cu, Zn, O	
–	s			Ca, Mg, O	Ca–Mg carbonate?
–	s			Ca, O	Ca-carbonate?
Pop5-1/6	s	$d=7$	c?	Si, Al, K, O & Na, Mg, P, S, Cl	
Pop7-1	a	$d=0.7$	co	Al, Si, Ti, Fe, O & Na, Mg, P, S, Cl	
12941	s	$d=8$		Zn, O	

fluids could cause further decarbonation reactions. Injections of basaltic melts into the magma chamber would cause convection, heat transfer, and eruption. Fenitization may have progressed at rising temperature and pressure, causing shattering of the surrounding country rock. Mechanical stress, however, which generally precedes metasomatism, can be widespread and locally intensive, and brecciation is a common feature.

At well-studied aureoles, like Ballachulish (Scotland, diameter: 5.8 km) or the Monzoni Complex (northern Italy, diameter: 2.5 km), decarbonation reactions in the limestones extend up to 500 m from the magma intrusion (Masch & Heuss-Aßbichler 1991; Heuss-Aßbichler & Masch 1991). At Ballachulish, fluid flow during CM is well documented (Holness & Watt 2001). Applying these data to the subsurface structure of Popocatépetl, a gigantic reservoir for CO_2 release would be available.

Since 1 kg of natural limestone contains *c.*0.44 kg CO_2 (Schoklitsch 1935), decarbonation of intruded limestone will be an important source of CO_2. A 2.5-km diameter cylindrical intrusion would release *c.*10^5 Mt of CO_2, assuming a 20-m wide zone of total decarbonation around a 500-m high intrusion; these estimates are conservative when compared with the known subsurface structure of Vesuvius or Popocatépetl. Time is another parameter limiting the value of such a model, i.e. is magma stored long enough to drive the necessary decarbonation reactions? While contact-metamorphic gases might enter the magmatic system, they may also dissolve in secondary melts and fluids. Melt and fluid inclusion studies of skarn xenoliths yield insights into the complex interaction between melt and carbonate host rocks, as documented at Vesuvius (Gilg *et al.* 2001; Fulignati *et al.* 2001).

Aerosol particles from the passively degassing plume

Aerosol particles from Popocatépetl volcano were obtained on 14 March 1997 by flying across the plume in a fixed-wing Cessna. Containers with 1 μm Teflon filters, and filters impregnated with 3M LiOH/20% glycerin (to absorb acidic gases) were placed outside the craft, 10 cm above the plane's fuselage, and connected by Teflon piping to an air pump controlled from inside the plane. The filters were uncovered at about 5790 m, and the pump turned on with an average flow rate of 30 ml/min. The plume traverse crossed the southeastern side of the volcano with an azimuth of 200°. The volcano's plume was moving outwards with a rough direction of 290°. At this

altitude the ambient temperature was –3° C. Ten traverses were made at evenly spaced altitudes between 5640 and 3690 m, each spanning 12.7 km, normal to the plume. At 5640 m the plume was detected by COSPEC and LI-COR instruments, yielding SO_2 burdens as high as 236 ppm m^{-1} and volcanic CO_2 concentrations of 0.5 μmol/mol SO_2 (445 ppm m^{-1}), and CO_2 concentrations (8 μmol/mol) both peaked at 5213 m. Integration of the plume cross-section yielded emission rates of 6530 ± 790 t/day SO_2 and 13 630 ± 1000 t/day CO_2 (Delgado *et al.* 2001).

Results from standard SEM analysis

The March 1997 filters were analysed by wet chemical techniques at the Los Alamos National Laboratory (EES-1). Only a few gas species were sufficiently concentrated to be detected, including CO_2 (2400 ppm), S (2ppm) and Hg (1ppb) (Counce, pers. comm. 1997). Particles show a wide range of composition. Solid aerosols include volcanic glass, magmatic silicates, Cu-, Zn-, Cl-, P- and S-bearing minerals/particles. We identified mercallite ($KHSO_4$), known from fumaroles of Vesuvius (Imbo 1965), and indicating a formation temperature <650 °C. Ca-chloride is also present (antarcticite: $CaCl_2.6H_2O$ or sinjarite: $CaCl_2.2H_2O$), and CaO or $Ca(OH)_2$. Galindo *et al.* (1998) used standard TEM and XRF techniques to analyse solid aerosols from an impactor filter collected from beneath the plume at Popocatépetl (Dec. 1994–Jan 1995). They reported various spherical or blocky and fragmental particles and detected a wide range of elemental components.

Results from field emission gun SEM analysis

Given the much better resolution of FESEM than SEM, we did not continue with standard SEM investigations. FESEM EDS analysis allowed us to detect more elements than by XRF, and to relate elements to certain particles.

Preliminary FESEM analysis was used to investigate the micro-morphology and microchemistry of very small particles (<5 μm) on the impactor filter. As Teflon filters were used, EDS spectra do not permit characterization of C and F. Preliminary results show that chemical characterization of particles does not necessarily define minerals. Instead, we introduce a micro-morphological rather than a chemical/mineralogical scheme to describe the particles. For illustration, we describe some particles in more detail in the following sections (Tables 7–10 and Figs 6–10). Complex or simple particles are observed as aggregates or clusters; in addition, tiny spheres (S?) are often found adhering to particle surfaces. The overall appearance is blocky or fragmental (Table 7).

A pseudohexagonal particle shows network-like structure in a composite image. (Fig. 9 c & d). Other particles are irregular, with bumpy surfaces derived by coagulation of numerous small spheres (Fig. 10 c). Pop9 and Popoc18 are slightly elongate aggregates (length $c.20$ μm), comprising hundreds of mineral or glassy fragments. Popoc16 and Popoc28 (not listed in Table 7) are $c.10$ μm aggregates comprising several tens of smaller fragments.

While individual particles often appear chemically homogeneous, morphologically they may be fluffy, botryoidal, flaky, spongy, or gel-like; also they may be the remnants of collapsed or decrepited short-lived particles. Some particles listed in Table 8 are described in the following section. One 3 μm particle shows a rough surface, which appears to have formed by coagulation of smaller (50–100 nm) spheres. Aluminium, Si and Fe are the dominant elements, with minor P, K, Ca and Ti. The particle edges suggest that it was broken off a larger particle, and might have been a part of a fumarolic deposit (Fig. 10 a & b).

Popoc17 has a cloud-shape with a core surrounded by a ring. Popoc22 ($c.$ 10 μm) has a feathery appearance (Fig. 6a). Popoc25 shows two 1 μm particles side by side: one has defined edges, the other is fluffy. Other fluffy particles include Popoc26 (two adjacent 10 μm particles, Fig. 6d); Popoc27 ($c.7$ μm, Fig. 6b) and Popoc10 (Fig. 6c).

One type of particle has been observed several times: Popo11 (Fig. 7a) consists of Ca, P, Mg, and Cl, with minor K, S, Si, Al, and Na. Popo 10 shows a very similar morphology and composition (Fig. 7b). The surface of a Ca-phosphate (apatite or collophane?) sphere is scattered with anhedral crystallites of a complex S-bearing Mg-chloride (i.e. bischofite: $MgCl_2.6H_2O$; carnallite: $KMgCl_3.6H_2O$; chloromagnesite: $MgCl_2$; d'ansite: $Na_{21}Mg(SO_4)_{10}Cl_3$; kainite: $MgSO_4.KCl.3H_2O$).

Other spherical particles are rich in Fe, Si, and Cl, with a few Ca sulphate crystals on the surface (popoc01, close-up: popoc02). The sphere shows part of a subsurface layer or core (Si?), beneath an Fe-chloride surface layer. Another sphere is Zn-bearing, and irregularly covered with clustering Mg-chlorides (popoc07, close-up: popoc08; Fig. 7c and d). This particle may be an

Table 8. *Fluffy and botryoidal particles – shape, size and chemical composition.*

FESEM image no.	Single particle (s), aggregated particles (a)	Diameter (d), length (l) (μm)	Spherical (s), Crystalline (c), Fluffy (f), Complex (co)	Elements	Interpretation
Popoc03	s	$l=5$	f	Fe, Cl, O & Si	Fe-chloride
Popoc11	s	$d=2$	f	Fe, Si, Al, Mg, O & Ca	
Popoc10	s	$d=2$	f	Pb, S, P, Ca, Si, Al, Mg, Na, O & Cu	galena, apatite?
Popoc05	s	$d=1.5$	f	Ti, Fe, Mg, Al, O & Si	
Popoc07	s	$d=5$	f	Si, Al, Ca, S, O, & Na, Mg, K, Fe, Cl	
Popoc13	a	$d=5$	co	Si, Al, Mg, Na, K, Fe, O & S, Cl, Ti	
Popoc09			f	Cu, Zn, S & Si, Al	
Popoc14				Ca, O & S, Cl, P, Mg	Ca-oxide?
Popoc06				Mo, S	molybdenite
Popoc15	s	$d=5$	f/co	Si, Al, Ca, Na, O & Fe	
–				Si, Al, O	mullite?
Pop11/12	a(?)	$d=3$	co	Al, Si, Fe, O & P, K, Ca, Ti	
Popoc17	s	$d=5$	f	Fe, Al, Si, P, S, Ca, O & Cl, K, Cu	
Popoc22	a	$l=10$	f	Fe, Al, Si, O & P	
Popoc25	s	$d=2$	c/f	Bi, Cu, O & Si, Al	
Popoc26	s	$d=10$	f	Si, Al, Mg, Na, Ca, P, S, Cl, O & K, Fe	
Popoc27	s	$d=10$	f	Fe, Cl, O & Si	
12946	a(?)	$d=1.5$	f/a	Sn, O	

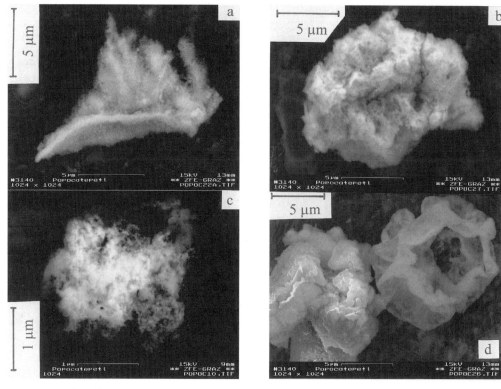

Fig. 6. Examples of fluffy particles. Note the feathery, or membrane-like textures. For chemical composition, see Table 8. Images from upper left to lower right: (**a**) Popoc22A; (**b**), Popoc27; (**c**) Popoc10; (**d**) Popoc26.

apatite+anhydrite sphere, trapping Si, Al and Zn during condensation.

Pop 14-1 is a 1.5 μm sphere, enclosing a dozen small crystals rich in Pb, Cr, or Ti with minor Cu. The particle itself comprises Al and Si (Fig. 8d). Figures 8a and b show rare CaSO$_4$ crystals growing on top of spherical particles (popoc01/02). This may reflect a reaction between sulphuric acid droplets and Ca-bearing particles within the plume. Figure 8c shows a 1.5 μm spherical particle, composed of Na, Mg, S, and minor amounts of Ca (pop3-1). The surface of this sphere is scattered with rings of droplets, in the centre of which larger (100 nm) droplets are visible. The host sphere appears homogeneous, while the droplets are partly to totally embedded in this material.

Popo09 (Fig. 9b) shows coagulated Ca and P-rich spheres and collapsed (?) particles. Popoc20 shows several coagulated spheres embedded in a matrix, to form a 1.5 μm particle. Popoc21 is a morphologically similar 4 μm particle (comprising Fe, Si, Ca, S, and Cl with minor Mg), with coagulated spheres that form worm-like structures. Popo 12 is an aggregate of tiny spheres (<2

μm) and bladed crystals (Fig. 9a). Pop8-1 is an example of a larger (3 μm) P, K rich spherical particle that coagulated with smaller particles. As pop13 shows (Fig. 10d), particles can be deformed. Pop13 is a 3 μm pseudo-spherical particle, with a wrinkled (desiccated?) surface.

Several particles appear compact and crystalline but anhedral (Table 10), and have spectra that indicate mono- or polymineralogical compositions. Feldspar fragments, some highly corroded, and were identified, as well as Fe–Ti oxides. Other particles include 20–30 μm fragments of vesiculated glass with adhering dust particles.

On January 11, 2002 new samples were collected with a borosilicate and Al–P ceramic filter. The particle spectrum is very different from that of 14 March 1997. Alkali halides (Na–Cl, K–Cl; >1 μm); 250 nm Ca-, K- and Ba-sulphates, Na–O (nahcolite, NaHCO$_3$?), Fe-, Fe–Ti, Si–Ti minerals and Ni–Ca–Na particles are common. A 5 μm agglomerated particle contains euhedral crystals of a Pb chloride (diameter <1 μm) in a K, Ca, Fe, (Si, Al, Na, O ?) matrix. Aggregated soot particles are widespread. Individual particle

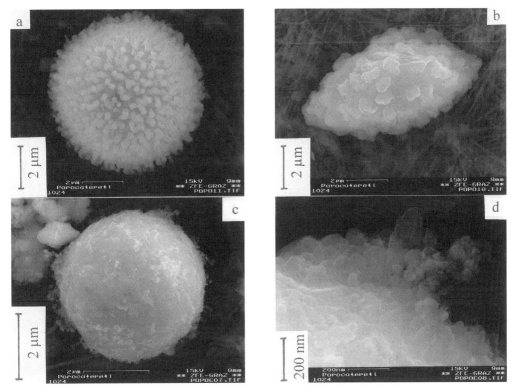

Fig. 7. Examples of spherical particles. Popo11 (**a**) and Popo10 (**b**) are a P-rich sphere and an ellipsoidal body covered by almost regularly scattered Mg chlorides. Popoc 07 (**c**) is another sphere, (**d**) is a close-up of (c), showing chlorides growing on top of the sphere. For chemical composition see Table 9.

diameters vary around 50 nm. Spherical and fluffy particles were absent, as were mineral overgrowths.

Discussion

Various microphysical processes affect aerosols, for example nucleation, coagulation, growth by condensation and sedimentation. Theoretical models of nucleation of stratospheric aerosols after large volcanic eruptions assume that newly formed particles are droplets of condensed sulphuric acid, which may be modelled as a homogeneous nucleation process. Problems in these assumptions are discussed by Hamill *et al.* (1996). The spectrum of observed particles and their chemical composition cannot simply be the product of such processes. As soon as environmental humidity exceeds about 60%, water accumulates on most aerosol particles, transforming them to coated spheres (Bakan & Hinzpeter 1988). Assuming a constant growth rate (several nm per hour) for particle formation, either nucleation must have started several times

to produce different size and chemical categories of particles, reflecting changing chemical and physical parameters in the plume, or the particle-size spectrum reflects formation by a variety of processes.

The appearance of P-bearing spheres suggests that they formed by condensation without subsequent particle–particle collision. We suggest that these might form first by condensation of Ca-phosphate, trapping minor amounts of Si and Al. Later this sphere might act as a nucleus for further condensation of a fluid phase coating the micro-sphere. Later fluid evaporation then caused the crystallization of magnesium chloride. These three steps of particle formation could be attributed to changes in the chemical environment and processes within the plume. Parameters such as temperature, gas composition, dilution, particle velocity and pressure will all change along the path of this particle.

Most spherical particles do not show internal structure, as the surfaces appear smooth and none of the studied particles showed breakage. Only one particle contains internal Ti-, Pb- and

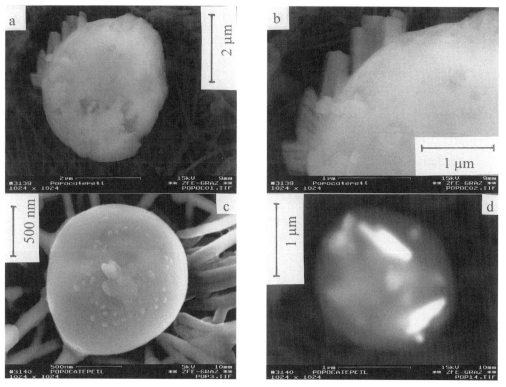

Fig. 8. Examples of spherical particles. Popoc01 (**a**), (**b**) close-up of (a), showing Ca sulphates growing on top of the sphere. Pop3 (**c**) shows the corona-like distribution of smaller particles on the otherwise smooth surface. Pop14 (**d**) is an internally mixed spherical particle. Crystallites inside the sphere are Ti- and Cr-rich. For chemical composition, see Table 9.

Cr-rich crystallites (see the BSE image, Fig. 8d). Many of the coagulated or aggregated particles are internally mixed according to different chemical/mineralogical components. FESEM analysis by Heinrichs (University of Göttingen, Germany; pers. comm. 1999) has documented the stability of spheres and Mg–Cl crystallites on a filter stored in a sealed plastic box in an evacuated desiccator. EBSD (electron back-scatter diffraction) of spherical particles did not provide results, due to surface roughness, shape, and/or lack of crystallinity. A re-examination of the filter in 2001 by Schroettner and in 2002 by Poelt (both ZFE, Graz, pers. comm.) revealed that most of the spherical and fluffy particles disappeared.

Vertical transport of pollutants may be a problem when interpreting airborne filter samples (Dewan 1981). Galindo (1984) documented the increasing turbidity above Mexico City during the 20th century, and showed that turbidity peaks at the end of the dry season in March and April. This coincides with our date of sampling

(14 March 1997). Northeasterly trade winds, which prevail in Mexico City during February and March, should drain most of the aerosol layer. Since Popocatépetl lies SE of Mexico City, particles from Mexico City should be blown away from the crater.

Le Guern and Bernard (1982b) collected spherical aerosols by condensing gases above an Etnaen lava flow in a silica tube. SEM investigations demonstrated that these spherical aerosols were droplets which crystallized as c. 300 µm aphthitalite aggregates ($K_2Na(SO_4)_2$), preserving the shape of the droplet from which fluid evaporated. Bernard (1985) described <100 to c. 1000 µm spherical particles from a fumarole. Using the high resolution of the FESEM, we have detected many types of spherical particles, none of which appear to be the crystallized remains of desiccated droplets.

Spherical particles have a variety of chemical compositions and may be coated with a chemically distinct population of more or less well-crystallized minerals (Table 9). We do not

Fig. 9. Popo12 (**a**) and Popo09 (**b**) are examples of coagulated spheres. Popo12 might have formed during aggregation; see blade-like particles at the right side. For chemical composition, see Table 9. Pop5 (**c**) is a pseudo-hexagonal particle with a network-like surface structure; (**d**) is a close-up of (c), showing the network-like structure in the BSE image. The smooth surface is covered by adhering dust particles. For chemical composition see Table 7.

know yet if the chemically different spheres are hollow or massive. Processes forming spherical particles are known, but little studied in the context of volcanic plumes. Nucleation, adsorption, desorption, condensation, coagulation, condensation, evaporation, or diffusion (deposition across a boundary layer) are well modelled (Whitby & McMurry 1997). At this point of data collection it is difficult to imagine processes like sintering (Seto *et al.* 1997) or spray pyrolysis (Jain *et al.* 1997) happening in plumes. Wohletz and McQueen (1984) produced spherical particles in water–melt interaction experiments. They found hollow spheres (cenospheres) and filled hollow spheres (plerospheres). Spherical particles are also known from phreatomagmatic ash deposits around Kilbourne Hole, New Mexico. Wohletz (pers. comm. 2000) mentions metallic spherical particles from the Bishop Tuff.

Metals in volcanic gas are postulated to exist as halide, sulphate, and oxide compounds. Chloride and fluoride compounds are considered to be the primary transporters of metals in volcanic gas, but bromide compounds may also play a role in the metal transport (Gemmell 1987). Copper partitions strongly into the magmatic vapor phase in pantellerites (Lowenstern *et al.* 1991). Copper, Zn and other metallic trace elements are known in fumarolic condensates and as soluble material on ash from Central American volcanoes (Gemmell 1987; Taylor & Stoiber 1973), and both Cu and Zn are strongly enriched over Al in tropospheric aerosols (Rahn *et al.* 1979). The highest enrichment factors are reported for Sb (1430), Cd (1920) and Se (3100). These elements could not be detected by FESEM/EDS in this study. Continuous measurements of Pb, Cd, Zn, Cu, and other metals from Kilauea show the high metal outputs from quiescent degassing volcanoes (Hinkley *et al.* 1999). Vanadates are rare, but known from sublimates (Hughes *et al.* 1987). Vanadium-bearing Na–K sulphates and V–W–Co phases are described from Colima volcano, Mexico (Taran *et al.* 2000, 2001). Lead and Bi can easily be volatilized, as outlined by Stimac *et al.* (1996)

Fig. 10. Pop11 (**a**) is a botryoidal particle, maybe coagulated by smaller spheres, which 'welded' together. Note tiny, coagulated spheres in upper left of the image; (**b**) is a close-up of (a). For chemical composition, see Table 8. Pop7 (**c**) shows a rough surface, which looks like thousands of small spheres have coagulated. For chemical composition see Table 7. Pop13 (**d**) is a wrinkled particle, indicating desiccation. The surface is not smooth, and may have been built from very small spheres. For chemical composition see Table 9.

and Symonds *et al.* (1987). Galena (?) and PbO (massicot) might be present in aerosol particles, while cotunnite ($PbCl_2$) is known from recent sublimates of Vesuvius (Houtermans *et al.* 1964).

The origin of Mg-chlorides might relate to the reaction: $MgSiO_3 + 2HCl = MgCl_2 + H_2O + SiO_2$ (Stoiber & Rose 1970). Similar reactions can be assumed for the formation of $CaCl_2$ ($CaSiO_3 + 2HCl = CaCl_2 + H_2O + SiO_2$; $CaAl_2Si_2O_8 + 8HCl + 8H_2O = CaCl_2 + 2SiO_2 + 2AlCl_3 . 6H_2O?$). Chloraluminate is known as a sublimate at Cerro Negro volcanic fumarole (Stoiber & Rose 1973). High concentrations of Mg were observed in snow samples influenced by the Redoubt volcano (Jaffe *et al.* 1994). The high contents of Mg are unusual, as the usual order of abundance for cations in volcanic gas from calc-alkaline magma is Na > K > Al > Fe > Ca > Zn > Mg, with Mg 10–20 times lower than Na or K.

The fraction of elements, like S and Cl, in solid particles and in minerals growing on top of particles compared to these elements in volcanic

gases is not yet known. Quantification of S and Cl by automatic EDS analysis is possible, if the filter surface is plain (nuclepore filters are recommended). The collection efficiency of different filters should be tested for the volcanic plume environment). The efforts of plume and fumarole monitoring could be obscured by ignoring the chemical composition of condensing particles. Chemical analysis of aerosol collection on filters compared with analysis of lava leads to enrichment factors for elements in the plume. Normalization against highly volatile elements, like bromine, helps distinguish elements hosted in glass and magmatic crystals, from elements hosted in condensates (Allard *et al.* 2000). This FESEM/EDS study detected Si and Al, typical for silicate melts and a variety of magmatic crystals, as constituents of condensed particles.

Several elements observed in particles are also important components of volcanic gases, like S and Cl. These preliminary results do not constrain how much S and Cl are present in the

Table 9. *Spherical particles – shape, size, chemical composition.*

FESEM Image no.	Single particle (s), aggregated particles (a)	Diameter (d), length (l) (μm)	Spherical (s), Crystalline (c), Fluffy (f), Complex (co)	Elements	Interpretation
Popo11	s	d=8	s/co	Ca, P, Mg, Cl, O & K, S, Si, Al, Na	apatite?, Mg-chloride
Popo10	s	l=8	s/co	Mg, Cl, Ca, P, O & S, Si, Al, Na	
Popo12	a	l=10	s/co	Si, Al, Na, S, Cl, Ca & Mg, P, K, Ti, Fe, Cu, Zn	
Popoc01/02	s	d=5	s/co	Fe, S, Ca, Si, Cl, O	Ca-sulphate on top of sphere
Popoc07/08	s	d=5	s/co	Ca, S, P, O & Si, Al, Zn	
Popo09	a	l=10	s/co	Ca, P, O & K, Si, S, Cl, Na, Mg, Al	
Popoc20	a	l=2	s/co	Fe, Zn, Si, Mg, Al, Ca, S, Cl, O & K, Mn	
Popoc21	a	l=5	s/co	Fe, Si, Ca, S, Cl, O & Mg	
–	s	d=1.5	s	Si, O & Al	
–	s	d=1	s	Na, Mg, S, O & Ca	
–	s	d=1.5	s	Al, Si, O	
–	s	d=2.5	s	Si, Al, O	
–	s	d=2	s	Fe, O	
–	s	d=1.5	s	Si, Al, O	
–	s	d=1.5	s	C?	soot?
Pop3-1	s	d=1	s	Na, Mg, S, O & Ca	
Pop8-1	s	d=3	s	P, K, O & Cu, Si, S, Cl	
Pop13-1	s	d=3	s	Mg, O & Si, Al	
Pop14-1	s	d=1.5	s/co	Pb, Cr, Ti, O & Al, Si, Cu	
Pop4-1	s	d=1	s	S, Ca, V, Fe, Ni, O & Si, K	
Pop1-1	s	d=2	s	S, V, O & Al, Si	
-		d=0.2		Pb, O	massicot (?)

Table 10. *Crystalline particles – shape, size, chemical composition*

FESEM Image no.	Single particle (s), aggregated particles (a)	Diameter (d), length (l) (μm)	Spherical (s), Crystalline (c), Fluffy (f), Complex (co)	Elements	Interpretation
Popoc15	s	d=5	c	Ca, Si, Al, Na, O & Fe	feldspar
Popo01	s	d=7	co	Si, Al, Ca, O & Na, S, Cl, Ti, Fe	
Popo05	s	d=5	c?	Ca, O & Si, S, Cl	
Popo08	a	d=4	c?	Fe, Ti, O & Si, Al, Mg	
Popoc24	s	d=20	c	Ca, Na, Al, Si, O & K	feldspar
Pop10	s	l=8	c	Si, Al, K, O	feldspar

aerosol, rather than the gas phase. COSPEC and FTIR spectrometers detect only gaseous phases, and estimates of S fluxes from volcanoes refer only to the gas emissions (Bluth *et al.* 1993; Malinconico 1987; Stoiber *et al.* 1987; Graf *et al.* 1998). The sulphur in the aerosol phase may be an important contribution to the total S budget of the atmosphere.

The phosphorus in the samples might be related to contact metamorphism, as mobilization of P is documented in P-rich buchite particles. Red clays derived from volcanic detritus can be highly phosphatic (7–20% P_2O_5; Blackburn *et al.* 1969), and may be intercalated with limestones beneath Popocatépetl. Ivlev *et al.* (1995) found high concentrations of S (4300–11 4000 ng/m^3),

Cl (1000–4100 ng/m^3) and P (700 to <4000 ng/m^3) in ash collected between December 1994 and January 1995 at Hnos. Serdán airport (Mexico, DF).

Particles with low P-contents were detected at the degassing lava flow of Mount Etna (2001), Italy. Phosphorus-rich buchites are also known from Mount Etna (Michaud *et al.* 1988). The bulk chemical composition of aerosol from Mt. Etna (1980) also reveals high contents of phosphorus (Quisefit *et al.* 1982). Particles with P$_2$O$_5$ contents of c.1 wt. % arc documented from Mt. Etna (1981) and Mt. S. Helens (1980; Varekamp *et al.* 1986) Silica tube experiments from the fumaroles of Colima volcano, Mexico document crystallization of euhedral apatite at temperature ranges from 600 to 650 °C (Taran, pers. comm.). Data for P in volcanic gases are rare. Taran *et al.* (1995) report 2–30 ppm from fumarolic condensates of Kudryavy volcano, Kurile Islands, Russia. Carmichael *et al.* (1974) mention P from the Showa-shinzan fumarole (Usu volcano, Japan; <0.005 vol % P$_2$O$_5$).

At Popocatépetl we investigated the possibility of contamination of the plume by P-fertilizer. FESEM study of the fertilizer demonstrated that even very small particles are always blocky. The P-containing volcanic particles are fluffy or spherical, showing smooth surfaces. A coagulation or aggregation of wind-blown, blocky fertilizer particles can be excluded.

Phosphorus is known to exist as a compound of a variety of gaseous molecules. Remote-sensing methods and direct sampling techniques and subsequent analysis should focus on the detection of these molecules. This would help to explain the high abundance of P in observed aerosol particles.

To assess particle compositions from an air mass unpolluted by volcanic activity, we sampled the troposphere north of the Alps in Austria (February 2002). Particles are morphologically different from the spectrum of particles from Popocatépetl, but particles rich in P, Zn, Cu, S, Cl, Si, Al, Na, K, Mg, Ca, Cr, and O are present. Earlier studies by Obenholzner and Wieser (unpublished) document aerosol particles from a refuse incinerator (Austria) containing Pb, Zn, Ca, Fe, Al, Si, Mg, Ti, K, Ni, Cl, Cr, Mn, Ag, Cu, S, and O. Volcanic plumes intrude air masses which might be polluted pre-volcanically. High-resolution electron microscopy on particles from different environments is needed to differentiate volcanic from non-volcanic particles. Chemical characterization alone does not distinguish between volcanic and non-volcanic particles.

Conclusions

Models of the geochemical C and S cycles (Arthur 2000) do not differentiate between volcanic gases derived from mantle and/or subducted rocks, and gases derived from the basement of volcanoes. Volcanoes situated on massive carbonates or evaporites should be considered separately, as such materials are implicated in the recent emissions from El Chichón (Mexico, Cochéme *et al.* 1982) and Lascar, Chile (Risacher *et al.* 2001).

The 16 Mt of CO$_2$ released from Popocatépetl between December 1994 and November 1996 (Goff *et al.* 1998; Love *et al.* 1998) may be a mixture of magmatic and basement-derived CO$_2$. The remaining questions include: how does the release of gases from metamorphosed country rock affect the style and dynamics of eruptions of volcanoes situated on massive carbonate platforms? Could the monitoring value of CO$_2$ become reduced by such assumptions? How many volcanoes are situated on massive carbonate platforms, and what role have metamorphosed carbonate and evaporite sequences played in contributing gases to volcanic eruptions and the atmosphere throughout Earth's history?

Volcanic rocks associated with massive carbonates during the Triassic (Southern Alps) has been investigated and earlier work has been reviewed by Obenholzner (1991). Investigation of lithic clasts deserves more attention in the examinations of pyroclastic rocks, as CM clasts might be present at the microscopic level in many deposits of volcanoes situated on massive carbonate platforms. Studies of fumarolic gases, CM clasts in volcanic deposits, and the dating of contact metamorphic events would improve models for magma–carbonate/evaporite-interaction in time and space.

> While direct experimental investigations of magmatic gases and thermodynamic modelling have revealed a large set of possible reaction mechanisms, little is known about the actual plume formation processes where the complexity of the fully heterogeneous system must be considered. (Ammann *et al.* 1993)

More FESEM/EDS data for particles from fumaroles, degassing lava flows and plumes are needed. Automated sizing and chemical analysis can reduce FESEM time, but with the disadvantage of a loss of information on individual particles and their morphological features. To develop SEM analysis of volcanic ash particles and aerosol as a monitoring tool, it would be necessary to sample in a continuous, time-resolved way.

This study documents the presence of particles of different origins collected in a volcanic plume. The spectrum of particles ranges from the products of magmatic fragmentation (vesiculated volcanic glass shards, magmatic crystals), through contact-metamorphosed rocks, to particles from air pollution and crystals from evaporated liquids, and fragments of fumarolic incrustations. Photochemical reactions may lead to particle formation within the plume. The presence of such particles modifies the optical properties of a plume, in ways that can be modelled. Andres *et al.* (2001) remark that 'the COSPEC does not discriminate between light added to its field-of-view by ambient aerosols or light scattered from its field-of-view by in-plume aerosols. Thus, these competing effects on the true SO_2 burden are not quantified under most field conditions.' Volcanic plume measurements should be accompanied by remote sensing of aerosols, by LIDAR (Winker *et al.* 1992) or other instruments (Shaw 1982). *In situ* plume sampling and FESEM analysis could provide necessary data for correction procedures. FESEM/EDS studies of particles from plumes and surrounding air masses are needed to improve interpretation of bulk chemical data from traditional filter studies.

Investigation should be extended to marine and lacustrine deposits, and ice cores post-dating major volcanic eruptions, in order to seek relicts of sedimented spherical particles. At the moment, we have to consider the possibility that many of the analysed particles are anthropogenic. Eruption plumes will entrain and transport these particles, possibly into the stratosphere, with potentially important consequences.

EDS is not the ultimate tool for chemical analysis of single particles in the submicron region. Mass spectrometric methods (Peter 1996), like time-of-flight secondary mass spectrometry (TOF SIMS), might be used to analyse for stable isotopes of S, Cl, and C; or particle-induced X-ray emission (PIXE) for trace elements. While techniques like instrumental neutron activation analysis (INAA) or ICP–MS are excellent instruments for chemical analysis, the disadvantage is that these are bulk techniques. Allard *et al.* (2000) analysed bulk elements by a combination of INAA and ICP–MS on a filter from the plume of Stromboli. Analytical transmission electron microscopy (TEM) would be another approach, but sample preparation is difficult. TEM analysis should be performed on spherical particles to define their physical state (crystallized or amorphous). Glass created by vapour condensation is theoretically possible (Vogel 1994). Progress in atomic force microscopy (AFM) (e.g. Pethica & Egdell 2001) might also open new doors. M. Pfeffer (UNM, Albuquerque, New Mexico) has successfully applied SEM, TEM, and AFM to aerosol particles collected at fumaroles of the Poas volcano (pers. comm. 2002).

Air pollution is a global problem (Elsom 1992). Plumes can easily mix with polluted air, which may add aerosol particles to the plume or to fall-out ash. Aerosol particles containing a variety of chemical elements are present in tropospheric air masses all over the world. The known environmental problems of Mexico DF make it especially difficult to obtain volcanologically relevant data. This study presents preliminary data on a variety of particles which cannot be attributed to a certain process, but could influence gas measurements, chemical analysis, and modelling of physical parameters like electrical charging of plume particles (James *et al.* 2000). Aerosol particles can be charged (Rapp & Lübken 1999) and lightning, common in volcanic plumes, can contribute to ultrafine aerosol formation (Yu & Turco 2001).

Satellite-borne aerosol particle monitoring of plumes, like NASA's LIDAR In-space Technology Experiment (LITE) and/or ESA's SCIAMACHY instrument of ENVISAT would be synergetic. It would be of value to develop an impactor which can be used directly to sample stratospheric aerosol. Rocket-borne *in situ* aerosol measurements have been tested positively to study noctilucent clouds (Rapp & Lübken 1999) and vertical distribution of aerosols (Jayaraman & Subbaraya, 1988). Rocket-borne data from plumes could be an important contribution to atmospheric chemistry and volcanism and climate change.

SEM and FE SEM studies of volcanic ash and aerosols from Popocatépetl volcano, Mexico were sponsored by the Naturhistorisches Museum (NHM)/Mineralogie, Vienna, and the Zentrum für Elektronenmikroskopie (ZFE), TU Graz. Data collection was possible due to cooperation with S. Hughes, C. Siebe, G. Kurat, and F. Brandstätter. Mr Enthammer (HELIOS Ges. mbH., Anthering, Austria) helped to obtain filter samples from north of the Alps. Airborne aerosol collection at Popocatépetl volcano was supported by the Centro Nacional de Prevención de Desastres of the Secretaría de Gobernación, México. We are also grateful to Y. Taran and F. Goff, who critically reviewed earlier versions of the manuscript. Further reviews were provided by M. James, T. Jones, and M. Holness. D. Pyle has been a very constructive reviewer and editor.

APPENDIX 1

Explanations for Tables 7 to 10

The filter was obtained on 14 March 1997, from a passively degassing plume. Fragments of magmatic crystals and glass shards must have been blown from the crater by strong winds, or were suspended in the air by earlier small explosions. Diameter (*d*) and length (*l*) were measured in μm. Elements listed after the '&'-sign are present in minor amounts. Elements listed are detected by a peak in the spectrum. Further FESEM images can be obtained from Obenholzner and Schroettner. All samples were C-coated and analysed at 10–15 keV. A four-quadrant BSE detector and an SE in-lens detector were used for imaging.

Several particles are not documented as images. The category, single or agglomerated particle, describes the overall appearance according to chemical composition and morphology. Larger agglomerated particles (*l*=10–30 μm) consisting of dozens or hundreds of fragments are not mentioned in the tables. For these particles, EDS analysis is problematical, as X-rays would derive from too many individual, smaller 1–5 μm fragments. Size, morphology, and chemical elements detected by EDS are listed for all other particles. Interpretation of the detected elements refers to known minerals and their chemical composition. For most of the particles such an interpretation is highly speculative. The morphology does not show typical crystal structures. This has to be kept in mind for all particles categorized as fluffy, spherical or complex.

APPENDIX 2

Abbrevations used in this chapter

AFM – atomic force microscopy
BSE – back-scattered electron
CM – contact metamorphism
COSPEC – Correlation spectroscopy
EBSD – Electron back-scatter diffraction
EDS – Energy-dispersive spectrometry
EMPA – electron microprobe analysis
FESEM – field emission scanning electron microscopy
FTIR – Fourier transform infrared spectroscopy
ICP–MS – inductively coupled plasma mass spectrometry
INAA – instrumental neutron activation analysis
LI-COR – CO_2 analyser by LI-COR company
LIDAR – Light Detection and Ranging

PIXE – particle induced X-ray emission
SCIAMACHY – Scanning Imaging Absorption SpectroMeter for Atmospheric Cartography
SE – secondary electron
SEM – scanning electron microscopy
TEM – transmission electron microscopy
TOF SIMS – time-of-flight secondary ion mass spectrometry
Wo – wollastonite
XRF – X-ray fluorescence

References

ALLARD, P., AIUPPA, A., LOYER, H., CARROT, F., GAUDRY, A., PINTE, G., MICHEL, A. & DONGARRA, G. 2000. Acid gas and metal emission rates during long-lived basalt degassing at Stromboli volcano. *Geophysical Research Letters*, **27**, 1207–1210.

AMMANN, M. & BURTSCHER, H. 1993. Aerosol dynamics and light-scattering properties of a volcanic plume. *Journal of Geophysical Research*, **98**, 19 705–19 711.

ANDRES, R. J., KYLE, P. R. & CHUAN, R. L. 1993. Sulphur dioxide, particle and elemental emissions from Mount Etna, Italy during July 1987. *Geologische Rundschau*, **82**, 687–695.

ANDRES, R.J. & SCHMID, J. W., 2001.The effects of volcanic ash on COSPEC measurements. *Journal of Volcanology and Geothermal Research*, **108**, 237–244.

ARAMAKI, S. 1961. Sillimanite and cordierite from volcanic xenoliths. *American Mineralogist*, **46**, 1154–1165.

ARCINIEGA-CEBALLOS, A., VALDES-GONZALES & DAWSON, P. 2000. Temporal and spectral characteristics of seismicity observed at Popocatépetl volcano, central Mexico. *Journal of Volcanology and Geothermal Research*, **102**, 207–216.

ARTHUR, M. J. 2000. Volcanic contributions to the carbon and sulphur geochemnical cycles and global change. *In:* SIGURDSSON, H. (ed.) *Encyclopedia of Volcanoes*, 1045–1056.

BAKAN, S. & HINZPETER, H. 1988. Atmospheric radiation. *In:* FISCHER, G. (ed.) *Landolt-Börnstein: Zahlenwerte und Funktionen aus Naturwissenschaft und Technik – Gruppe V: Geophysik und Weltraumforschung.* Band 4 Meteorologie. Teilband b: Physikalische und chemische Eigenschaften der Luft, 110–186, Springer-Verlag.

BARBERI, F. & LEONI, L. 1980. Metamorphic carbonate ejecta from Vesuvius Plinian eruptions: Evidence of the occurrence of shallow magma chamber. *Bulletin Volcanologique*, **43-1**, 107–120.

BERNARD, A. 1985. *Les méchansimes de condensation des gaz volcaniques (chimie, minéralogie et équilibres des phases condensées majeures et mineures).* These, Universite Libre de Bruxelles, Tomes 1 & 2, 1–412.

BLACKBURN, G. & TAYLOR, R. M. 1969. Limestones and red soils of Bermuda. *Geological Society America Bulletin*, **80**, 1595–1598.

BLUTH, G. J. S., SCHNETZLER, C. C., KRUEGER, A. J. & WALTER, L. S. 1993. The contribution of explosive volcanism to global atmospheric sulphur dioxide concentrations. *Nature*, **366**, 327–329.

BROUWER, H.A., 1920. *Studien ueber Kontaktmetamorphose in Niederl.-Ostindien. VI. Ein Kalksilikatauswuerfling des Vulkans Semeru (Java)*. Centralblatt fuer Mineralogie, Geologie und Palaeontologie, 37–45.

CARMICHAEL, I. S. E., TURNER, F. J. & VERHOOGEN, J. 1974. *Igneous Petrology*. McGraw-Hill, New York.

CHIODINI, G., MARINI, L. & RUSSO, M. 2001. Geochemical evidence for the existence of high-temperature hydrothermal brines at Vesuvio volcano, Italy. *Geochimica et Cosmochimica Acta*, **65**, 2129–2147.

CLOCCHIATTI, R., JORON, J.-L., KERINEC, M. & TREUIL, M. 1982. Quelques données préliminaires sur la lave du dôme actuel du volcan Mérapi (Java, Indonésie) et sur ses enclaves. *Comptes Rendus de l'Académie des Sciences, Paris*, **295(II)**, 817–822.

COSCA, M. A., ESSENE, E. J., GEISSMAN, J. W., SIMMONS, W. B. & COATES, D. A., 1989. Pyrometamorphic rocks associated with naturally burned coal beds, Powder River Basin, Wyoming. *American Mineralogist*, **74**, 85–100.

COCHÉME, J.-J., DEMANT, A., DUFFIELD, W.A., GUERRERO, J., SILVA, L. & TILLING, R.I. 1982. L'éruption du Volcan Chichonal (mars–avril 1982) dans l'État de Chiapas, Mexique. *Comptes Rendus de l'Académie des Sciences, Paris*, **295(II)**, 737–744.

DELGADO-GRANADOS, H., CARDENAS GONZALES, L. & PIEDAD SANCHEZ, N. 2001. Sulphur dioxide emissions from Popocatépetl volcano (Mexico): case study of a high-emission rate, passively degassing erupting volcano. *Journal of Volcanology and Geothermal Research*, **108**, 107–120.

DEL MORO, A., FULIGNATI, P., MARIANELLI, P. & SBRANA, A. 2002. Magma contamination by direct wall rock interaction: constraints from xenoliths from the wall of a carbonate-hosted magma chamber (Vesuvius 1944 eruption). *Journal of Volcanology and Geothermal Research*, **112**, 15–24.

DEVINE, J. D. & SIGURDSON, H. 1980. Garnet–fassaite calc-silicate nodule from La Soufriere, St. Vincent. *American Mineralogist*, **65**, 302–305.

DEWAN, E. M. 1981. Turbulent vertical transport due to thin intermittent mixing layers in the stratosphere and other fluids. *Science*, 211, 1041–1042.

ELSOM, D. M. 1992. *Atmospheric Pollution – a Global Problem*. Blackwell.

FEDERICO, M. & PECCERILLO, A., 2002. Mineral chemistry and petrogenesis of granular ejecta from the Alban Hills volcano (Central Italy). *Mineralogy and Petrology*, **74**, 1–2, 223–252.

FISHER, R. V. & SCHMINCKE, H.-U., 1984. *Pyroclastic Rocks*. Springer-Verlag, 472 pp.

FRIES, K. 1965a. *Resumen de la geologia de la hoja Cuernavaca, Estados Morelos, Mexico, Guerrero y Puebla*. UNAM, Instituto de Geologia, Mexico, DF.

FRIES, K. 1965b. *Hoja Cuernavaca 14Q-h (8). Carta Geologica de Mexico, Serie de 1:100 000*. UNAM, Instituto de Geologia, Mexico, DF.

FULIGNATI, P., KAMENETSKY, V. S., MARIANELLI, P., SBRANA, A. & MERNAGH, T. P. 2001. Melt inclusion record of immiscibility between silicate, hydrosaline, and carbonate melts: application to skarn genesis at Mount Vesuvius. *Geology*, **29(11)**, 1043–1046.

GALINDO, I., 1984. Anthropogenic aerosols and their regional scale climatic effects. *In:* GERBER, H.E. & DEEPAK, A. (eds) *Aerosols and Their Climatic Effects*, 245–260. Deepak Publishing, Hampton, VA.

GALINDO, I., IVLEV, L. S., GONZALEZ, A. & AYALA, R. 1998. Airborne measurements of particle and gas emissions from the December 1994–January 1995 eruption of Popocatépetl volcano, Mexico. *Journal of Volcanology and Geothermal Research*, **83**, 197–217.

GEMMELL, J. B. 1987. Geochemistry of metallic trace elements in fumarolic condensates from Nicaraguan and Costa Rican volcanoes. *Journal of Volcanology and Geothermal Research*, **33**, 161–181.

GILG, H.A., LIMA, A., SOMMA, R., BELKIN, H. E., DE VIVO, B. & AYUSO, R. A. 2001. Isotope geochemistry and fluid inclusion study of skarns from Vesuvius. *Mineralogy and Petrology*, **73**, 145–176.

GOFF, F., JANIK, C. J., DELGADO, H., WERNER, C., COUNCE, D., STIMAC, J. A., SIEBE, C., LOVE, S. P., WILLIAMS, S. N., FISCHER, T. & JOHNSON, L. 1998. Geochemical surveillance of magmatic volatiles at Popocatépetl volcano, Mexico. *Geological Society America Bulletin*, **110**, 695–710.

GOFF, F., LOVE, S. P., WARREN, R., COUNCE, D., OBENHOLZNER, J., SIEBE, C. & SCHMIDT, S. 2001. Passive infrared remote sensing evidence for large, intermittent CO_2 emissions at Popocatépetl volcano, Mexico. *Chemical Geology*, **177**, 133–156.

GRAF, H.-F., LANGMANN, B. & FEICHTNER, J. 1998. The contribution of Earth degassing to the atmospheric sulfur budget. *Chemical Geology*, **147**, 131–145.

HAMILL, P., HOUBEN, H., YOUNG, R., TURCO, R. & ZHAO, J. 1996. Microphysical processes affecting the Pinatubo plume. *In:* FIOCCO, G., FUA, D. & VISCONTI, G. (eds.) *The Mount Pinatubo Eruption*. NATO ASI Series I; Global Environmental Change, **42**, 49–59.

HARKER, R. I. & TUTTLE, O. F. 1956. Experimental data on the P_{CO_2}–T curve for the reaction: Calcite+Quartz ↔ Wollastonite+Carbon Dioxide. *American Journal of Science*, 254, 239–256.

HEUSS-ABBICHLER, S. & MASCH, L. 1991. Microtextures and reaction mechanisms of carbonate rocks: a comparison between the thermoaureoles of Ballachulish and Monzoni (N. Italy). In: VOLL, G., TÖPEL, J., PATTISON, D.R.M & SEIFERT, F. *Equilibrium and Kinetics in Contact Metamorphism: the Ballachulish Igneous Complex and its Aureole*, 229–250. Springer Verlag, Berlin.

HINDS, W. C. 1982. *Aerosol Technology*. John Wiley, New York.

HINKLEY, T. K., LAMOTHE, P. J., WILSON, S. A., FINNEGAN, D. L. & GERLACH, T. M. 1999. Metal emissions from Kilauea, and a suggested revision of the estimated worldwide metal output by quiescent degassing volcanoes. *Earth and Planetary Science Letters*, **170**, 315–325.

HOBBS, P. V., RADKE, L., ELTGROTH, M. & HEGG, D.

1981. Airborne studies of the emissions from the volcanic eruptions of Mount St. Helens. *Science*, **211**, 816–818.

HOLNESS, M. B. & WATT, G. R. 2001. Quartz recrystallization and fluid flow during contact metamorphism: a cathodoluminescence study. *Geofluids*, **1**, 215–228.

HOUTERMANS, F.G., EBERHARDT, A. & FERRARA, G. 1964. Lead of volcanic origin. *In*: CRAIG, H., MILLER, S. L. & WASSERBURG, G. J. (eds) *Isotopic and Cosmic Chemistry*, 233–243.

HUGHES, J. M., CHRISTIAN, B. S., FINGER, L. W. & MALICONICO, L. L. 1987. McBirneyite, $Cu_3(VO_4)_2$, a new sublimate mineral from the fumaroles of Izalco Volcano, El Salvador. *Journal of Volcanology and Geothermal Research*, **33**, 183–190.

IMBO, G. 1965. *Catalogue of the Active Volcanoes of The World Including Solfatara Fields. Part XVIII*, Italy, 6–19.

ISHIKAWA, T. 1953. Xenoliths included in the lavas from volcano Tarumai, Hokkaido, Japan. *Journal of the Faculty of Science, Hokkaido University, Series 4*, **8**, 225–244.

ISSHIKI, N. 1954. On iron-wollastonite from Kanpu volcano, Japan. *Proceedings of the Japanese Academy*, **30**, 869–872.

IVLEV, L. S., GALINDO, I. & KUDRYASHOV, V. I. 1995. *Estudio de aerosoles y cenizas. In: Volcan Popocatépetl–Estudios realizados durante la crisis de 1994–1995*, CENAPRED. MEXICO D.F.

JAFFE, D.A., CERUNDOLO, B. & KELLEY, J. 1994. The influence of Redoubt Volcano emissions on snow chemistry. *Journal of Volcanology and Geothermal Research*, **62**, 359–367.

JAIN, S., SKAMSER, D. J. & KODAS, T. T. 1997. Morphology of single-component particles produced by spray pyrolysis. *Aerosol Science and Technology*, **27**, 575–590.

JAMES, M. R., LANE, S. J. & GILBERT, J. S., 2000. Volcanic plume electrification: experimental investigation of a fracture-charging mechanism. *Journal of Geophysical Research*, **105**, 16 641–16 649.

JANIK, C. J., GOFF, F., FAHLQUIST, L., ADAMS, A. I., ROLDAN, M. A., CHIPERA, S. J., TRUJILLO, P. E. & COUNCE, D. 1992. Hydrogeochemical exploration of geothermal prospects in the Tecuamburro volcano region, Guatemala. *Geothermics*, **21**, 447–481.

JASMUND, K. & HENTSCHEL, G., 1964. Seltene Mineralparagenesen in den Kalksteineinschlüssen der Lava des Ettringer Bellerberges bei Mayen (Eifel). *Beiträge zur Mineralogie und Petrographie*, **10**, 296–314.

JAYARAMAN, A. & SUBBARAYA, B. H., 1988. Rocket and balloon measurements of the vertical distribution of aerosols in the Indian tropical region. *In:* HOBBS, P. V. & MCCORMICK, M. P. (eds) *Aerosols and Climate*, 117–124, Deepak.

KILLE, I. C., THOMPSON, R. N., MORRISON, M. A. & THOMPSON, R. F. 1986. Field evidence for turbulence during flow of basalt magma through conduits from southwest Mull. *Geological Magazine*, **123(6)**, 693–697.

KRIDELBAUGH, S. J. 1973. The kinetics of the reaction:

calcite+quartz↔wollastonite+CO_2 at elevated temperatures and pressures. *American Journal of Science*, **273**, 757–777.

LE GUERN, F. & BERNARD, A. 1982*a*. A new method for sampling and analyzing volcanic sublimates – application to Merapi Volcano, Java. *Journal of Volcanology and Geothermal Research*, **12**, 133–146.

LE GUERN, F. & BERNARD, A. 1982*b*. Etude des mecanismes de condensation des gaz magmatiques – exemple de l'Etna. *Bulletin of Volcanology*, **45**, 161–166.

LOVE, S. P., GOFF, F., COUNCE, D., SIEBE, C. & DELGADO, H. 1998. Passive infrared spectroscopy of the eruption plume at Popocatépetl volcano, Mexico. *Nature*, **396**, 563–567.

LOWENSTERN, J. B., MAHOOD, G. A., RIVERS, M. L. & SUTTON, S. R. 1991. Evidence for extreme partitioning of copper into a magmatic vapor phase. *Science*, **252**, 1405–1409.

MALINCONICO, L. L. 1987. On the variation of SO_2 emission from volcanoes. *Journal of Volcanology and Geothermal Research*, **33**, 231–237.

MASCH, L. & HEUSS-AßBICHLER, S. 1991. Decarbonation reactions in siliceous dolomite and impure limestone. *In*: VOLL, G., TÖPEL, J., PATTISION, D. R. M & SEIFERT, F. *Equilibrium and Kinetics in Contact Metamorphism: the Ballachulish Igneous Complex and its Aureole*, 211–228, Springer Verlag, Berlin.

MATTHEWS, A. & GROSS, S. 1980. Petrologic evolution of the 'Mottled Zone' (Hatrurim) metamorphic complex of Israel. *Israeli Journal of Earth Sciences*, **29**, 93–106.

MEEKER, K. A., CHUAN, R. L., KYLE, P. R. & PALAIS, J. M. 1991. Emission of elemental gold particles from Mount Erebus, Ross Island, Antarctica. *Geophysical Research Letters*, **18**, 1405–1408.

MICHAUD, V. 1995. Crustal xenoliths in recent hawaiites from Mount Etna, Italy: evidence for alkali exchanges during magma–wall rock interaction. *Chemical Geology*, **122**, 21–42.

MICHAUD, V., CLOCCHIATTI, R. & JORON, J.–L. 1988. Approche des phénomènes d'interaction magma/ encaissant par l'étude des enclaves énallogènes. L'éruption paroxysmale du 24 september 1986 de l'Etna (Sicile). *Comptes Rendus de l'Académie des Sciences, Paris*, **307(II)**, 1527–1533.

MILKE, R. & HEINRICH, W. 2002. Diffusion-controlled growth of wollastonite rims between quartz and calcite: comparison between nature and experiments. *Journal of Metamorphic Geology*, **20**, 467–480.

NICHOLLS, I. A. 1971. Calcareous inclusions in lavas and agglomerates of Santorini volcano. *Contributions to Mineralogy and Petrology*, **30**, 261–276.

OBENHOLZNER, J.H. 1991. Traissic volcanogenic sediments from the Southern Alps (Italy, Austria, Yugoslavia) – a contribution to the 'Pietra verde' problem, *Sedimentary Geology*, **74**, 147–171.

OBERBECK, V. R., FARLOW, N. H., FONG, W., SNETSINGER, K. G., FERRY, G. V. & HAYNES, D. M. 1982. Mount St. Helens aerosol evolution. *Geophysical Research Letters*, **9**, 1089–1092.

PARUNGO, P., ACKERMAN, E. & PROULX, H. 1976. Natural ice nuclei. *J. Rech. Atmos.* **X(1)**, 45–60.

PETER, T. 1996. Airborne particle analysis for climate studies. *Science*, **273**, 1352–1353.

PETHICA, J. B. & EGDELL, R. 2001. The insulator uncovered. *Nature*, **414**, 27–28.

PHELAN, J. M., FINNEGAN, D. L., BALLANTINE, D. S., ZOLLER, W. H., HART, M. A. & MOYERS, J. L. 1982. Airborne aerosol measurements in the quiescent plume of Mount S. Helens: September, 1980. *Geophysical Research Letters*, **9**, 1093–1096.

POSTL, W., TAUCHER, J. & MOSER, B. 1996. Neue Mineralfunde im oststeirischen Vulkangebiet. *Mitteilungen für Mineralogie am Landesmuseum Joanneum*, **60/61**, 3–86.

QUISEFIT, J.-P., BERGAMETTI, G., VIÉ LE SAGE, R., MARTIN, D., ZETTWOOG, P., CARBONELLE, J. & FAIVRE-PIERRET, R., 1982. Nouvelle évaluation des flux particulaires de l'Etna-1980. *Comptes Rendus de l'Académie des Sciences, Paris*, **295(II)**, 943–945.

RAHN, K. R., BORYS, G., SHAW, L., SCHULTZ, L. & JAENICKE, R. 1979. Long-range impact of desert aerosol on atmospheric chemistry: two examples. *In:* Morales (ed.) *Saharan Dust: Mobilization, Transport, Deposition*, SCOPE 14, 243–266. Chichester, UK.

RAPP, M. & LÜBKEN, F.-J. 1999. Modelling of positively charged aerosols in the polar summer mesopause region. *Earth, Planets, Space*, **51**, 799–807.

RISACHER, F. & ALONSO, H. 2001. Geochemistry of ash leachates from the 1993 Lascar eruption, northern Chile. Implications for recycling of ancient evaporites. *Journal of Volcanology and Geothermal Research*, **109**, 319–337.

ROMER, R. L. & HEINRICH, W. 1998. Transport of Pb and Sr in leaky aquifers of the Bufa del Diente contact metamorphic aureole, north-east Mexico. *Contributions to Mineralogy and Petrology*, **131**, 155–170.

ROSE, W. I., JR, CHUAN, R. L., CADLE, R. D. & WOODS, D. C. 1980. Small particles in volcanic eruption clouds. *American Journal of Science*, **280**, 671–696.

SCHOKLITSCH, K. 1934. Pyrometamorphose an Einschlüssen in Eruptiven am Alpen-Ostrand. *Tschermaks Mineralogische und Petrographische Mitteilungen*, 127–152

SCHOKLITSCH, K. 1935. Beitrag zur Physiographie steirischer Karbonspaete (Gitterkonstanten, physikalische Angaben und chemische Zusammensetzung). *Zeitschrift für Kristallographie*, **90(4)**, 433–445.

SEINFELD, J. H. & PANDIS, S. N. 1998. *Atmospheric Chemistry and Physics – From Air Pollution to Climate Change*. A Wiley Interscience Publication.

SETO, T., HIROTA, A., FUJIMOTO, T., SHIMADA, M. & OKUYAMA, K. 1997. Sintering of polydisperse nanometer-sized agglomerates. *Aerosol Science and Technology*, **27**, 422–438.

SHAPIRO, N. M., SINGH, S. K., IGLESIAS-MENDOZA, A., CRUZ-ATIENZA, V. M. & PACHECO, J. F., 2000. Evidence of low Q below Popocatépetl volcano, and its implication to seismic hazard in Mexico City. *Geophysical Research Letters*, **27**, 2753–2756.

SHAW, G. E., 1982. Remote sensing of aerosol in the free atmosphere by passive optical techniques. *In:* GERBER, H. E. & HINDMANN, E. E. *Light Absorption by Aerosol Particles*, 335–355, Spectrum Press.

SHERIDAN, P. J., SCHNELL, R. C., HOFMANN, D. J. & DESHLER, T. 1992. Electron microscope studies of Mount Pinatubo aerosol layers over Laramie, Wyoming, during summer 1991. *Geophysical Research Letters*, **19**, 203–206.

SHIEH, Y. N. & TAYLOR, H. P. 1969. Oxygen and carbon isotope studies of contact metamorphism of carbonate rocks. *Journal of Petrology*, **10**, 307–331.

SIEBE, C., ABRAMS, M., MACIAS, J. L. & OBENHOLZNER, J. H. 1996. Repeated volcanic disasters in Prehispanic time at Popocatépetl, central Mexico: past key to the future? *Geology*, **24**, 399–402.

SIEBE, C., SCHAAF, P. & URRUTIA-FUCUGAUCHI, J. 1999. Mammoth bones embedded in a late Pleistocene lahar from Popocatépetl volcano, near Tocuila, central México. *Geological Society of America Bulletin*, **111**, 1550–1562.

STIMAC, J., HICKMOTT, D., ABELL, R., LAROCQUE, A. C. L., BROXTON, D., GARDNER, J., CHIPERA, S., WOLFF, J. & GAUERKE, E. 1996. Redistribution of Pb and other volatile trace metals during eruption, devitrification, and vapor-phase crystallization of the Bandelier Tuff, New Mexico. *Journal of Volcanology and Geothermal Research*, **73**, 245–266.

STOIBER, R. E. & ROSE, W. I. 1970. The geochemistry of Central American volcanic gas condensates. *Geological Society America Bulletin*, **81**, 2891–2912.

STOIBER, R. E. & ROSE, W. I. 1973. Sublimates at volcanic fumaroles of Cerro Negro volcano, Nicaragua. *Publ. Geol. del ICATI*, **4**, 63–68.

STOIBER, R. E., WILLIAMS, S. N. & HUEBERT, B. 1987. Annual contribution of sulphur dioxide to the atmosphere by volcanoes. *Journal of Volcanology and Geothermal Research*, **33**, 1–8.

SYMONDS, R. B., ROSE, W. I., REED, M. H., LICHTE, F. E. & FINNEGAN, D. L. 1987. Volatilization, transport and sublimation of metallic and non-metallic elements in high temperature gases at Merapi Volcano, Indonesia. *Geochimica et Cosmochimica Acta*, **51**, 2083–2101.

TANNER, S. B., KERRICK, D. M. & LASAGA, A. C. 1985. Experimental kinetic study of the reaction: Calcite+Quartz↔Wollastonite+Carbon Dioxide, from 1 to 3 kilobars and 500° to 850°C. *American Journal of Science*, **285**, 577–620.

TARAN, Y. A., HEDENQUIST, J. W., KORZHINSKY, M. A., TKACHENKO, S. I. & SHMULOVICH, K. I. 1995. Geochemistry of magmatic gases from Kudryavy volcano, Iturup, Kuril Islands. *Geochimica et Cosmochimica Acta*, **59(9)**, 1749–1761.

TARAN, Y.A., BERNARD, A., GAVILANES, J.-C., & AFRICANO, F. 2000. Native gold in mineral precipitates from high-temperature volcanic gases of Colima volcano, Mexico. *Applied Geochemistry*, **15**, 337–346.

TARAN, Y. A., BERNARD, A., GAVILANES, J.-C., LUNEZHEVA, E., CORTES, A. & ARMIENTA, M. A. 2001. Chemistry and mineralogy of high-temperature gas discharges from Colima volcano, Mexico. Implications for magmatic gas–atmosphere interaction. *Journal of Volcanology and Geothermal Research*, **108**, 245–264.

TAYLOR, P. S. & STOIBER, R. E. 1973. Soluble material on ash from active Central American volcanoes. *Geological Society America Bulletin*, **84**, 1031–1042.

VALDES C., GONZALES, G., ARCINIEGA, A, GUZMAN, M., NAVA, E., GUTIERREZ, C. & SANTOYO, M. 1995. Sismicidad del volcan Popocatépetl a partir del 21 de diciembre de 1994 al Marzo de 1995. *In: Volcan Popocatépetl–Estudios realizados durante la crisis de 1994–1995*, CENAPRED. MEXICO D.F.

VAREKAMP, J. C., THOMAS, E., GERMANI, M. & BUSECK, P. R. 1986. Particle geochemistry of volcanic plumes of Etna and Mt. St. Helens. *Journal of Geophysical Research*, **91 B12**, 12 233–12 248.

VOGEL, W. 1994. *Glass Chemistry*. Springer-Verlag.

WHITBY, E. R. & MCMURRY, P.H. 1997. Modal aerosol dynamics modeling. *Aerosol Science and Technology*, **27**, 673–688.

WINKER, D. M. & OSBORN, M. T. 1992. Airborne LIDAR observations of the Pinatubo volcanic plume. *Geophysical Research Letters*, **19/2**, 167–170.

WOHLETZ, K. H. & MCQUEEN, R. G. 1984. Volcanic and stratospheric dustlike particles produced by experimental water–melt interactions. *Geology*, **12**, 591–594.

WOOD, C. P. 1994. Mineralogy at the magma–hydrothermal system interface in andesite volcanoes, New Zealand. *Geology*, **22**, 75–78.

WOOD, C. P. & BROWNE, P. R. L. 1996. Chlorine-rich pyrometamorphic magma at White Island volcano, New Zealand. *Journal of Volcanology and Geothermal Research*, **72**, 21–35.

YU, F. & TURCO, R. P., 2001. On the contribution of lightning to ultrafine aerosol formation. *Geophysical Research Letters*, **28**, 155–158.

ZAMBONINI, F. 1935. Mineralogia vesuviana ed appendice alla mineralogia vesuviana. *Atti. Acc. Sc. Fis. e Mat. di Napoli*, **XIV**, 2a edizione, a cura di Quercigh E., Napoli, SIEM.

ZOLLER, W. H., PARRINGTON, J. R. & KOTRA, J. M. P. 1983. Iridium enrichment in airborne particles from Kilauea volcano: January 1983. *Science*, **222**, 1118–1119.

Optical sensing of volcanic gas and aerosol emissions

A. J. S. McGONIGLE & C. OPPENHEIMER

Department of Geography, University of Cambridge, Downing Place,
Cambridge CB2 3EN, UK.
(email: ajsm2@cam.ac.uk)

Abstract: Volcanic gas and aerosol surveillance yield important insights into magmatic, hydrothermal, and atmospheric processes. A range of optical sensing and sampling techniques has been applied to measurements of the composition and fluxes of volcanic emissions. In particular, the 30-year worldwide volcanological service record of the Correlation Spectrometer (COSPEC) illustrates the point that robust, reliable, straightforward optical techniques are of tremendous interest to the volcano observatory and research community. This chapter reviews the field, in particular the newer and more versatile instruments capable of augmenting or superseding COSPEC, with the aim of stimulating their rapid adoption by the volcanological community. It focuses on sensors that can be operated from the ground, since they generally offer the most flexibility and sensitivity. The success of COSPEC underlines the point, however, that such devices should be comparatively cheap, and easy to use and maintain, if they are to be widely used.

Volcanoes emit gases (principal components include H_2O, CO_2, SO_2, HCl, HF, H_2, S_2, H_2S, CO and SiF_4) and aerosols to the atmosphere, both during and between eruptions. By monitoring the chemistry, isotopic composition, and flux of these emissions, information can be gleaned about subsurface magmatic conditions and higher-level fluid–rock interactions. For instance, temporal variations in the ratios of emitted CO_2/SO_2 and HCl/SO_2 have been used to infer changes in magmatic systems feeding volcanoes (e.g. Noguchi & Kamiya 1963; Gerlach & Casedevall 1986), while gas flux measurements have been used to constrain the masses of degassing magmas (Symonds *et al.* 1996). Such data are valuable for hazard assessment because volcanic activity is strongly controlled by the dynamics of degassing.

Volcanic plumes are also studied in order to understand their hemispheric to global scale atmospheric and climatic impacts. The sulphur emissions from major explosive eruptions have been implicated in tropospheric cooling, stratospheric heating, stratospheric ozone depletion, and an alteration of stratospheric global circulation patterns, due to the radiative and chemical properties of erupted gas and aerosol (e.g. Robock 2000; Grainger and Highwood 2003). From local to regional scales, volcanic emissions can result in severe environmental (Delmelle 2003) and environmental health consequences,

including destruction of agricultural crops, contamination of pasture, and human respiratory morbidity and cardiovascular mortality, for example, during and in the aftermath of the 1783 eruption of Laki in Iceland (Thordarson *et al.* 1996, 2003, Chapter 7; Grattan *et al.* 2003).

The conventional way to measure volcanic emissions is by direct sampling, either by close-range collection of samples from fumarole vents and active lava bodies using 'Giggenbach bottles', filter packs and condensing systems, or within atmospheric plumes from aircraft using various kinds of sampling apparatus and on-board analysers. A range of spectroscopic, gravimetric, isotopic and chromatographic techniques is available to determine chemical concentrations in real time or subsequently in the laboratory (Symonds *et al.* 1994). While direct sampling is capable of delivering very detailed and accurate analyses, it is difficult to sustain routine surveillance in this way, and to compete with geophysical and geodetic monitoring techniques in terms of temporal resolution of the data streams. Arguably, the primary reason for this is the risk involved, which often restricts gas geochemical studies to low-temperature, possibly subordinate vents (that may not provide good indicators of the magmatic system). Additionally, chemical reactions between the container material or reagents and the collected gas sample

From: OPPENHEIMER, C., PYLE, D.M. & BARCLAY, J. (eds) *Volcanic Degassing*. Geological Society, London, Special Publications, **213**, 149–168. 0305-8719/03/$15.00

may mask the original chemical composition (Symonds *et al.* 1994). While the use of electrochemical sensors to monitor and telemeter continuous (near real-time) gas data avoids many of these complications (McGee & Sutton 1994), this approach is not yet widespread and is also not ideal since sensors may be destroyed in the event of an eruption.

Over the last thirty years ground-based optical remote-sensing techniques have been increasingly used for volcanic gas and aerosol monitoring. In particular, the Correlation Spectrometer (COSPEC) has been used routinely by volcano observatories. Such techniques possess many of the advantages of seismic and deformation monitoring over direct sampling, such as the ability to obtain measurements in reasonable safety, allowing semi-continuous monitoring even through violent eruptive periods. Because remote-sensing techniques measure integrated gas concentrations through cross sections of the plume, in contrast to *in situ* sampling, they can potentially yield a more representative picture of bulk plume composition and flux. Additionally remote sensing is non-invasive, eliminating the possibility of sample contamination. In parallel with the development of much improved models of the complex chemical behaviour of multi-component gases in high-temperature volcanic environments (e.g. Symonds *et al.* 2001), these remote-sensing approaches have contributed significantly to raising the profile of geochemical gas surveillance relative to the traditionally favoured geodetic and seismological volcano monitoring techniques. While not all of the techniques discussed in this paper are capable of remote sensing, even those that directly sample still offer the advantage over conventional direct sampling approaches of being able to retrieve data in near-real time.

Several spectroscopic techniques, including Thermal Infrared Multispectral Scanner imaging for SO_2 measurements (Realmuto *et al.* 1994, 1997), closed-path infrared CO_2 analysis (Gerlach *et al.* 1997; Harris *et al.* 1981) and closed-path Fourier transform infrared (FTIR) spectroscopy for SO_2 (McGee & Gerlach 1998a) have been successfully deployed on aircraft. However, high costs and the potential for adverse conditions in or around plumes (especially ashy ones) mitigate against frequent airborne campaigns. Satellite-based remote sensing has also yielded important results for volcanic emission measurements, not least in quantification of SO_2 releases by major explosive eruptions, using the Total Ozone Mapping Spectrometer (TOMS) and similar instruments operating in the ultraviolet region (e.g. Krueger *et al.* 1995; Rose *et al.* 2001; Carn

et al. 2003). However, despite the potential of instruments such as ASTER to measure SO_2 in tropospheric volcanic plumes (e.g. Realmuto *et al.* 1997), space-borne remote sensing is unlikely, in the near future, to provide routine and frequent measurements of most of the weaker volcanic plumes (from quiescent degassing, in particular). This is due to the demanding spatial and spectral resolution requirements of the sensors and poorly constrained radiative transfer models for the infrared region of interest, which are complicated by accounting for thermal emission from the ground beneath the plume.

The focus of this chapter is, therefore, on techniques capable of ground-based deployment. We discuss optical methods within the following six categories: correlation spectroscopy, differential optical absorption spectroscopy (DOAS), Fourier transform spectroscopy, laser techniques, optical particle counters, and Sun photometry. While the boundaries between these techniques in terms of measurement principles (i.e. absorption or emission spectroscopy, wavelength-dependent scattering) overlap considerably, it is easier to make sense of the literature by this instrument-based division. Our intention is to highlight available technologies that are suitable for volcano surveillance, and to stimulate further development of novel optical sensing technologies that will meet key volcanological requirements, including low cost, low maintenance, low weight and bulk, high temporal resolution, and multi-component gas and aerosol detection and measurement. Appendices are included at the end of the article to provide a summary of the characteristics of the instruments discussed here as well as sources of further information.

Correlation spectroscopy

Arguably, the most widely applied instrument for ground-based remote-sensing of volcanic plumes is the Barringer Research COSPEC, which was originally developed during the 1960s to measure industrial SO_2 and NO_2 emissions (Moffat & Millán 1971), and was first used in a volcanological context in 1971 at Mount Mihara, Japan (Moffat *et al.* 1972). Since that time, most of the credit for establishing the popularity and credibility of the COSPEC as a volcanological tool is due to Dick Stoiber (1911–2001) and his co-workers (e.g. Stoiber *et al.* 1983). Over the last thirty years, COSPEC SO_2 measurements have been performed by numerous research teams at a variety of volcanoes worldwide, including sites in the United States, Central and South America, Italy, Japan, Indonesia, New Zealand and

Antarctica (see, for example, Caltabiano *et al.* 1994; Stoiber *et al.* 1986; Casadevall *et al.* 1984; Allard *et al.* 1991; Gerlach *et al.* 1998, and references therein). This section reviews operating principles and results of COSPEC surveillance, and introduces some similar instruments.

Operation and accuracy of COSPEC

The COSPEC is typically operated in a passive mode during volcanological studies, viewing the zenith sky and recording the absorption of diffuse ultraviolet sky radiation between 300 and 315 nm by SO_2 in the plume (Millán & Hoff 1978). A grating disperses the incident skylight on to a spinning correlation disc, which contains four masks (each corresponding to a quarter disc segment), that are consecutively placed in the optical path (Figure 1). Correlation is achieved because these masks are etched with slits at radii that correspond with peaks or troughs of the SO_2 absorption spectrum, so that radiation is sampled alternately at regions of relatively high and low SO_2 absorption. Consequently, the photomultiplier electrical output is modulated according to the amount of SO_2 in the plume. The instrument is calibrated by placing quartz cells containing known amounts of SO_2 in the internal optical path of the spectrometer. Measurements are reported as mixing ratios (in units of ppm m), which can be misleading due to the pressure and temperature dependence of these units (see Gerlach 2003, this volume, for a discussion).

While the COSPEC can be used from a fixed position, it is typically carried on a moving platform (vehicle, boat or aircraft) that traverses under the plume, recording SO_2 concentrations as a function of position (often measured using a GPS receiver) along a route approximately perpendicular to the plume axis (see Figure 2). When these data are combined with measurements of wind speed, SO_2 fluxes (typically expressed in tonnes per day, t d^{-1}, or kg/s) can be derived, as can the fluxes of other gases (such as HCl and CO_2) if gas concentration ratios are known (e.g. via direct sampling or FTIR spectroscopy, Horrocks *et al.* 1999; Burton *et al.* 2000).

The COSPEC possesses many advantages as a tool for volcanic surveillance. As this device operates using scattered skylight, alignment is trivial and measurements are possible even in overcast conditions. In contrast, techniques that rely on direct sources of light normally require more complex configurations, involving solar tracking or installation of an artificial light source at another point on the crater. COSPEC has modest power requirements, is robust, and does not require a specialist operator or subsequent spectral analysis because the SO_2 retrieval is achieved with the calibration cells. There are problems with the procedure, however, not least that SO_2 fluxes are subject to large errors (up to 40%, e.g. Stoiber *et al.* 1983), arising principally from uncertainty in the plume velocity (though this issue is, of course, not restricted to COSPEC observations). Often the speed of the moving plume is assumed to be equal to wind-speed measurements obtained close to the ground (e.g. at the volcano summit or on the traverse route), or is based on visual observations of the moving plume, or on distant radiosonde data. More accurate wind data can

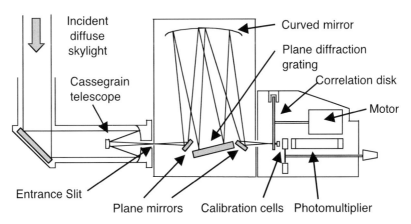

Fig. 1. Configuration of the COSPEC optical assembly, showing the optical path of light, at a particular wavelength, as it is focused on to a particular radius of the rotating correlation disc.

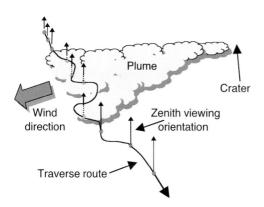

Fig. 2. Schematic diagram of a traverse route along a road beneath a volcanic plume, showing points at which zenith sky measurements are taken (plume is under-sampled here for clarity).

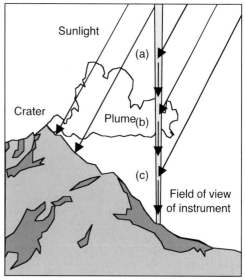

Fig. 3. Illustration of the various paths of light that are ultimately scattered into the field of view of the COSPEC instrument, from (a) above, (b) within, and (c) below the volcanic plume.

be obtained by videography, or from aircraft navigational equipment in the case of airborne traverses.

Further errors are introduced as a result of using a diffuse skylight source (Moffat & Millán 1971; Millán 1980) (see Fig. 3). For instance, light can be scattered into the field of view of the COSPEC from below the plume, above the plume or within the plume, complicating the radiative transfer problem. Significant concentrations of ash in the plume can also have an impact on SO_2 retrievals as a result of scattering effects (Andres & Schmid 2001).

Volcanological interpretation of SO_2 fluxes

The COSPEC was originally applied in a volcanological context to assess whether changes in SO_2 gas fluxes could be associated with changes in eruptive activity of open conduit volcanoes. It was postulated that these flux measurements could be used to indicate masses of degassing magmas, whether these magmas were rising or falling, and whether the magma chambers were being sealed off or opened (through fracturing of the overlying rock). Positive correlations of increasing SO_2 flux with activity were observed during initial experiments on Mount Etna (Malinconico et al. 1979), and more recently, for instance, on Mount Pinatubo, where COSPEC measurements contributed significantly to hazard assessment prior to the 1991 eruption (Hoff 1992; Daag et al. 1996). Immediately prior to the Pinatubo eruption, the measured SO_2 flux increased by an order of magnitude over two weeks, in parallel with

seismic unrest. These observations were interpreted as evidence of shallow intrusion of magma, increasing the expectation of an impending eruption. Decreasing SO_2 fluxes in parallel with decreasing post-eruptive activity have also been observed on many volcanoes, notably at Mount St. Helens from 1980 to 1988 (McGee 1992) (see Fig. 4), where a decline in CO_2 flux and increase in H_2O flux were also observed following the 1980 eruption. This decrease in the CO_2 and SO_2 gas fluxes suggested that the magma reservoir was not being replenished, consistent with the decreased eruption rates. The increase in water vapour emission was interpreted as the result of ground water permeating the conduit system.

The catalogue of SO_2 flux measurements obtained at many active and passively degassing volcanoes is one of the major contributions to volcanology that has been made possible by the COSPEC. It is only recently that other ground-based optical techniques have been successfully configured to measure flux values. Of particular note, COSPEC measurements revealed that many volcanoes emit SO_2 in excess of levels that could be sustained by degassing of erupted magma, highlighting the so-called 'excess sulphur' issue (Wallace 2001). Indeed, passive fluxes from volcanoes such as Popocatépetl (up to 50 000 to 60 000 t day^{-1} of SO_2) rival emission rates from

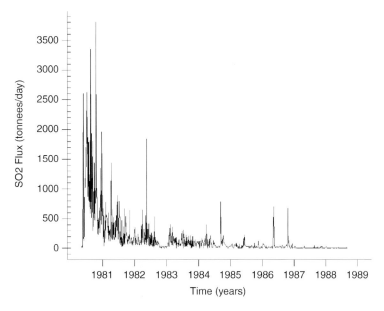

Fig. 4. Measurements of SO_2 flux from Mount St Helens volcano for the period May 1980 to September 1988 obtained using a COSPEC. Note the decrease in flux that accompanied the waning activity following the 18 May 1980 eruption. Modified from U.S. Geological Survey Open-File Report 94-212 authors: K. A. McGee & T. J. Casadevall (http://pubs.usgs.gov/openfile/of94-212/Derived/report.html).

many erupting volcanoes. By extrapolating these and other flux data, estimates of around 20 Mt year^{-1} have been obtained for the total volcanic SO_2 flux to the atmosphere (Stoiber & Jepsen 1973; Berresheim & Jaeschke 1983; Stoiber *et al.* 1987; Andres & Kasgnoc 1998). Based on these values, estimates of global annual fluxes of other volcanic gases such as CO_2 have also been derived (e.g. Williams *et al.* 1992).

Interpreting COSPEC SO_2 flux data is not always straightforward. For instance, in the past, both increasing *and* decreasing flux signatures have been recorded prior to volcanic eruptions (Symonds *et al.* 2001). Additionally, chemical conversion of SO_2 to H_2SO_4 can occur on the surface of aerosols (Malinconico *et al.* 1979; Oppenheimer *et al.* 1998*a*), as can scrubbing of SO_2 by the hydrothermal systems that the gases are released through (Oppenheimer 1996; Doukas & Gerlach 1995; Symonds *et al.* 2001). Consequently, in order to gain a fuller understanding of a volcano's behaviour, it is desirable to make simultaneous measurements of multiple gases, as is possible using FTIR spectroscopy. A final, more practical problem with COSPEC is that the instrument is no longer in routine production, and servicing and sourcing replacement parts is becoming increasingly costly and difficult.

Other correlation spectrometers

Another correlation approach is to use cells containing known concentrations of the target gases, to provide the most accurate possible fits to the absorption spectra of the species in question. These cells are mounted on a rotating chopper disc or discs in the optical path(s) of the instrument so that the plume gas concentrations may be determined from the modulated detector output(s). This approach has been implemented to remotely sense volcanic CO and OCS concentrations using a technique called gas correlation filter spectrometry (GASCOFIL) (Stix *et al.* 1996).

Based on the same principle, the LI-COR Inc. LI-COR spectrometer has been used to measure extractively both diffuse CO_2 emissions from the ground (McGee & Gerlach 1998*b*; McGee *et al.* 2000), and CO_2 fluxes by in-plume sampling (Gerlach *et al.* 1997; Brantley & Koepenick 1995). These time-consuming ground surveys have provided unique data on distributed sources of CO_2 degassing, although Rogie *et al.* (2001) and Gerlach *et al.* (2001) highlight some of the meteorological factors that influence such measurements and complicate interpretation. A third application of LI-COR is based on eddy correlation or covariance, which involves measurements of vertical windspeed and CO_2 concentration (e.g. Anderson & Farrar 2001).

Volcanic CO_2 emissions are generally more difficult to quantify than SO_2 because they may only result in small enhancements above ambient concentrations in the atmosphere at the point of measurement. Nevertheless, CO_2 is considered an especially important diagnostic magmatic gas because of its deep exsolution, limited interaction with volcano–hydrothermal systems, and comparatively inert behaviour in the atmosphere (Symonds *et al.* 2001).

A further correlation technique, called gas correlation imaging, is capable of recording two-dimensional concentration maps of target gases in real time (Sandstern *et al.* 2000). This technique has already been applied to monitor industrial gas leaks, suggesting some potential for mapping volcanic plumes.

Differential optical absorption spectroscopy

Although not widely used for volcanological work to date, another ultraviolet remote sensing technique, differential optical absorption spectroscopy (Platt 1994) offers some very attractive possibilities for surveillance of plumes. One advantage of DOAS over the COSPEC is that it yields atmospheric spectra as opposed to merely

column amounts of SO_2, thus permitting more rigorous data analysis (including quantification of other atmospheric trace gases).

Operation

The major difference between DOAS and correlation spectroscopy is the order in which 'correlation' to the target gas absorption spectrum and measurement of the optical signal is performed. A diagram of the experimental configuration of a DOAS spectrometer is shown in Figure 5. Light, from the source (either ambient sky, direct solar, or artificial lamp), which has passed through the volcanic plume, is collected using a telescope, and coupled into the spectrometer using an optical fibre. A grating is used to disperse this light and spectra are measured using either a CCD array or a photomultiplier tube and scanning mechanism.

In order to reduce interferences caused by background atmospheric absorption and the solar spectral structure (Fraunhofer lines), each plume absorption spectrum is divided by a spectrum taken outside the plume, under otherwise identical conditions. SO_2 retrievals can be obtained by scaling a reference spectrum (known column amount) to fit the observed spectrum. The potential to scrutinize the spectral quality

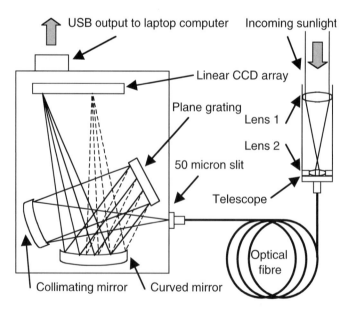

Fig. 5. Experimental configuration of an Ocean Optics USB 2000 DOAS spectrometer, coupled to a telescope via an optical fibre (drawing not to scale). Rays traced within the spectrometer, denoted by dashed and non-dashed lines, correspond with the optical paths of light at two distinct wavelengths, demonstrating how the spectrometer disperses light on to the CCD array.

provides a safeguard against systematic errors that can occur in COSPEC measurements (e.g. due to mechanical distortions, thermal variations and the poorly defined light source) and are not readily discernible because of the 'black box' nature of the correlation process.

Measurements

The first DOAS volcano measurements were performed from 1992 to 1997 (Edner *et al.* 1994; Weibring *et al.* 1998), on Etna, Stromboli, and Vulcano (using diffuse sky radiation as a light source) in parallel with differential absorption LIDAR (Light Detection and Ranging) monitoring. The problems arising from use of the diffuse signal can be overcome by using direct sunlight as the source. This has recently been attempted successfully at Mount Etna (J. Mellqvist *et al.* pers. comm.).

A particularly promising development has been the recent demonstration that a commercial, ultra-compact and lightweight DOAS spectrometer out-performed a COSPEC during side-by-side volcanic SO_2 measurements (Galle *et al.* 2003). This device provided a minimum detection limit of 2.5 ppm m for a 3 s integration time (standard deviation). Given the advantages of DOAS over COSPEC, it is likely that this miniature DOAS will be of considerable interest to those struggling to maintain valuable long-term degassing data-sets with ageing COSPEC instruments. The instrument can also be readily configured for automated scanning measurements yielding high temporal resolution observations of gas flux for the first time. Such a

system has recently been installed by the Montserrat Volcano Observatory (B. Galle and M. Edmonds, pers. comm., 2002). An example of 'mini-DOAS' data acquired at Masaya volcano is shown in Figure 6.

Fourier transform infrared spectroscopy

Prior to the early 1990s, ground-based remote sensing of volcanic gases was confined almost exclusively to measurements of SO_2. To a great extent this was because SO_2 is the only volcanic gas that COSPEC is capable of measuring. Up to that time there was a scarcity of field-portable spectroscopic technologies operating within spectral windows suitable for detecting other volcanic gases (e.g. <240 nm for H_2S, and the fundamental region of the infrared for HCl, HF, CO and CO_2). However, there are compelling reasons why SO_2 itself is a natural volcanic target gas. For example, SO_2 is often the third most abundant gas species in a volcanic plume, behind H_2O and CO_2. Unlike the latter gases, which have atmospheric background concentrations that can be significantly higher than the volcanological contributions, ambient levels of SO_2 are typically less than a few ppb. Moreover, SO_2 has several strong absorption signatures in the ultraviolet (electronic) and infrared (rotation–vibration) regions of the spectrum. However, there are important limitations in relying on SO_2 as a tracer of magmatic activity, due principally to its solubility in, and availability from, hydrothermal systems (Oppenheimer 1996; Symonds *et al.* 2001), highlighting the importance of measurements of other volcanic species.

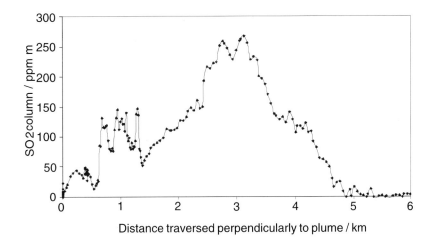

Fig. 6. Traverse data obtained by the authors using the mini-DOAS spectrometer, at Masaya volcano, Nicaragua, during December 2001. The flux value obtained in this case was 8 kg/s.

The desire for multiple gas species detection and measurement spurred volcanological interest in FTIR spectroscopy. While laboratory spectrometers had been used in atmospheric research observatories for many years, field-based volcanological applications of the technology had to wait for the commercial availability of rugged, compact FTIR spectrometers (originally designed for battlefield chemical weapon sensing) in the early 1990s. Operating in the fundamental infrared region (2.4–25 μm) at spectral resolutions of up to 0.5 cm^{-1}, these devices opened up the possibility of measuring many volcanic species of interest (including HCl, H_2O, SO_2, HF, CO_2, SiF_4, OCS, and CO) using their rotation–vibration line structures.

Operation

FTIR spectrometers are based on the Michelson, or moving-mirror interferometer (Fig. 7), in which incoming light is split into two beams using an optical beam-splitter. This beam-splitter is also used to recombine these beams after they are reflected from two mirrors. By moving one of the mirrors backwards and forwards along the axis of the beam, a variable path difference is introduced, which results in a temporally varying detector signal due to constructive and destructive interference of the different wavelengths of the incident light. Application of an inverse Fourier transform to the resulting interferograms yields atmospheric absorption spectra in the wavelength domain. These can be fitted using radiative transfer codes and atmospheric transmittance databases such as HITRAN, in order to determine column amounts of the trace gases present, and hence concentration ratios of the volcanic species of interest. Because these spectrometers measure a wide wavelength interval simultaneously and can operate with large entrance ports (providing high optical throughput), FTIR spectroscopy offers a number of advantages over dispersive spectrometers (such as the DOAS instruments) in which narrow entrance slits are required and measurements are made over narrow wavelength increments. Horrocks *et al.* (2001) have demonstrated accuracies of better than 5–10 % for FTIR spectroscopic measurements of SO_2 using infrared lamps.

While Fourier transform spectroscopy is also possible in the ultraviolet spectral region, few instruments are available, and they are far less field portable due to the bulky, precise mirror positioning systems required at the short ultraviolet wavelengths (factor of 10 to 100 shorter than infrared) (Cageao *et al.* 2001). However, a recently developed Fourier transform ultraviolet spectrometer, which achieves beam interference without recourse to mirror scanning (Courtial *et al.* 1997; Patterson *et al.* 1998), may be suitable for volcanic SO_2 and H_2S measurements.

Measurements

Field deployments of FTIR spectrometers can take many forms, exploiting natural or artificial infrared sources, and adapting to the dictates of volcanic activity, access and terrain (Figure 8). The first demonstration of their potential to measure volcanic gas emissions was carried out in 1991 at Asama volcano, Japan, although only SO_2 was identified (Notsu *et al.* 1993). This research team extended the range of measured species during subsequent campaigns at Unzen, Japan (SO_2 and HCl; Mori *et al.* 1993), Aso, Japan (CO, OCS, CO_2, SO_2, and HCl; Mori & Notsu 1997), and Vulcano, Italy (SO_2 and HCl; Mori *et al.* 1995). During the Vulcano campaign, SO_2/HCl ratios were measured for individual fumaroles, revealing variations of a factor of two between closely spaced vents. For the Aso campaign, the CO/CO_2 ratio was used to constrain plume gas temperatures.

Additional development of FTIR spectroscopy for volcanic gas measurements has been undertaken by a UK-based group (Oppenheimer *et al.* 1998c, 2002a; Francis *et al.* 2000). During

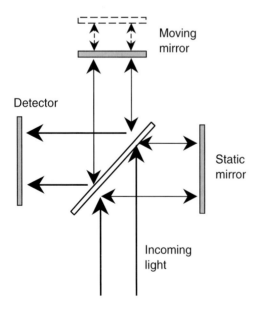

Fig. 7. Diagram of a Michelson interferometer, illustrating the optical paths of light through the instrument.

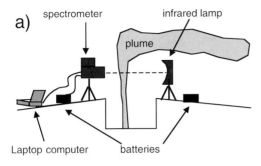

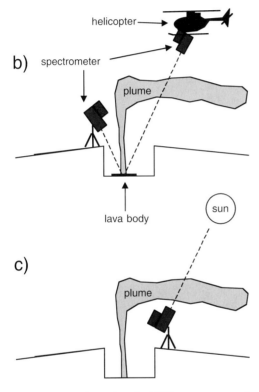

Fig. 8. Field configurations for FTIR spectroscopy of volcanic gases: (**a**) active cross-crater or flank measurements using an infrared lamp; (**b**) passive sensing using hot rocks (Sun- or fumarole heated) or active lava bodies as natural infrared sources; (**c**) Passive solar occultation at locations downwind of the vent.

initial campaigns at Mount Etna and Vulcano, SO_2, HCl, and SiF_4 concentrations were measured (Francis *et al.* 1995; Francis *et al.* 1996). The latter result permitted plume temperature estimates based on the estimated HF/SiF_4 ratio. Later work on Mount Etna, where the solar occultation geometry (Fig. 8(c)) was used

for the first time, resulted in the first FTIR spectroscopic measurements of volcanic HF (Francis *et al.* 1998).

Since 1998, this group has carried out annual campaigns at Masaya volcano, Nicaragua, which represents an excellent laboratory volcano for development of remote gas surveillance methods. A road around the summit crater of Masaya permits straightforward measurements across the crater using an artificial infrared source (as in Fig. 8(a)). At this proximity to the gas vent, the concentrations of volcanic gases are very high, permitting retrieval of volcanic CO_2 and H_2O, despite the high atmospheric background concentrations of these species (Burton *et al.* 2000). Both cross-crater and solar occultation measurements indicated consistent SO_2/HCl and HCl/HF molar ratios of 1.6 and 5, respectively, during 1998–2000, indicating steady-state, open-system degassing (Horrocks *et al.* 1999). In contrast, in 2001 a SO_2/HCl ratio of 4.5 was observed, coinciding with reduced SO_2 fluxes, descent of the magma column in the vent on the crater floor, and preceding a small explosive eruption on the 23rd April (H. Duffell *et al.*, pers. comm.).

By comparing solar and lunar occultation measurements at Masaya, Burton *et al.* (2001) observed that the plume SO_2/HCl ratio was higher at night-time, which was interpreted to be due to the greater solubility of HCl than SO_2 in water, and increased plume condensation and high liquid water content of the cooler nocturnal atmosphere. Horrocks *et al.* (2003) point out that, by day there is no evidence for significant loss of either HCl or SO_2 from the gas phase. Solar occultation FTIR spectroscopic measurements of the plume of Mount Erebus, Antarctica (Keys *et al.* 1998), have also revealed that no rapid scavenging of HCl occurs in the dry Antarctic spring atmosphere.

Burton *et al.* (2000) reported fluxes of HCl, CO_2, H_2O and HF from Masaya volcano based on the FTIR spectroscopy, but these relied on scaling the retrieved gas ratios by SO_2 fluxes obtained with a COSPEC. Subsequently, Duffell *et al.* (2001) have shown that by optically joining an FTIR spectrometer to an automatic solar tracker, and carrying the assembly on the back of a vehicle while traversing under the plume, measurements of HCl, SO_2, and possibly HF fluxes can be obtained directly (combined with appropriate plume speed estimates), in a similar manner to COSPEC operation.

Soufrière Hills Volcano, Montserrat, has been another target for Fourier transform spectroscopy (Oppenheimer *et al.* 1998*d*; Edmonds *et al.* 2001, 2002, 2003; Oppenheimer *et al.* 2002*b*). In summary, these investigations have indicated that HCl/SO_2 molar ratios of 1–5 typify dome-building episodes, and that lower ratios (down to 0.1) characterize non-eruptive periods. This behaviour has been explained in terms of an andesitic HCl source that exsolves on ascent from the magma chamber, and a deeper SO_2 reservoir (probably derived from intruded mafic magma) that degasses to the atmosphere discontinuously, depending on the plumbing system's permeability. Based on this interpretation, Edmonds et al. (2002) have identified the potential degassing signals that might herald the end of this eruption. Oppenheimer et al. (1998b) demonstrated the application of FTIR spectroscopy from a helicopter at distances of c.100 m from the lava dome. Although these spectra were of very poor quality due to various sources of noise, it was possible to detect HCl, and helicopter deployments have subsequently been used to measure emissions from the summit craters of Mount Etna (M. Burton pers. comm. 2000).

While the previously described FTIR spectroscopic investigations have measured volcanic gases in absorption using a warm background, Love et al. (1998, 2000) have shown it is possible also to measure volcanic gases in emission against a cold sky background. This requires a means to calibrate the detector signal to radiance values, which was achieved by placing temperature-controlled black-body ovens in the field of view of the spectrometer. At Popocatépetl volcano, Mexico, Love et al. (1998) observed a steady increase in SiF_4/SO_2 ratio prior to an eruption on 25–26 February 1997, followed by a tenfold decrease within a few hours. These results suggested a cooling of the gas prior to the eruption, attributed to adiabatic gas expansion on release of a conduit plug. More recently, Goff et al. (2001) identified an extreme emission rate for CO_2 at Popocatépetl sometimes exceeding 10^5 t day^{-1}, suggesting the possible sourcing of a significant fraction of the CO_2 from carbonate basement rocks.

These studies on very different volcanoes in varying eruptive states highlight the flexibility of FTIR spectroscopy for volcanological applications. Data collection strategies can be adapted to suit varying field conditions, taking into account accessibility and safety on and around the volcano, and distribution, speciation and flux of emitted volatiles (Fig. 8). For example, at Soufrière Hills volcano, where safety is a major concern in the field, the spectroscopic measurements have been obtained by solar occultation several km from the summit. At Masaya, the road around the rim of the degassing crater

permits straightforward cross-crater measurement using an artificial lamp. Burton et al. (2003, Chapter 17) have shown that lava flows and lava fountains are also suitable infrared sources, which enabled them to obtain unique gas geochemical data for erupting and passively degassing vents prior to and during the 2001 Mount Etna eruption. In particular, they observed a doubling of the SO_2/HCl ratio prior to the eruption, and clear geochemical trends in SO_2/HCl, CO_2/SO_2, and HCl/HF for different active vents at different elevations through the course of the eruption (M. Burton, pers. comm. 2001). These kinds of data would have been impossible to collect in real time by any conventional technique.

While the operation of FTIR spectrometers is relatively straightforward (the MIDAC instrument used in many of the field campaigns at Soufrière Hills volcano and Masaya does not even have an on–off switch), processing the spectra and retrieving gas column amounts requires some expertise. To date, retrievals have not been effected in real time, and while this should be achievable, it is not a straightforward matter since fully automated routines would need to be sufficiently 'intelligent' to screen out low quality spectra, recognize poor spectral fits, identify baseline offsets, and other instrumental effects. This is clearly a fruitful area for further development since the multi-species capability of FTIR spectroscopy makes it a very valuable adjunct to COSPEC or DOAS surveillance of SO_2 fluxes. The first routine FTIR surveillance has been running since April 2000, at Mount Etna, under the auspices of the Istituto Internazionale per Geofisica e Vulcanolgia (Burton et al. 2003). The results of the team responsible for the measurements to date serve as an excellent advertisement for the value of the technique in the routine work of a volcano observatory, and its complementarity with other geophysical and geodetic monitoring efforts (Calvari 2001).

Laser techniques

By virtue of the short pulse lengths, high powers and narrow spectral bandwidths that lasers can deliver laser based techniques are unique amongst optical remote-sensing methods and are being increasing applied to measure volcanic gas and aerosol emissions.

LIDAR

To date, the most commonly applied laser-based technique for measurement of volcanic plumes is

LIDAR. A pulsed laser source acts as the radiation source, and the back-scattered light returned to the instrument and collected by telescope is sensed by a detector. Measurements of the two-way travel time of the laser pulses yield range-resolved information on the amounts and location of trace gases or aerosols. This can represent a considerable advantage over the passive infrared and ultraviolet techniques already described, which only indicate the amounts of gas present (e.g. molecules cm^{-2}), and not their distribution or concentration. LIDAR is very useful, therefore, for defining plume structure (Chuan *et al.* 1986; Hobbs *et al.* 1982). By scanning or profiling the plume it is even possible to obtain three-dimensional distributions of gases or particles.

The LIDAR technique has been used to measure concentrations and fluxes of volcanic sulfate aerosol (Casadevall *et al.* 1984; Edner *et al.* 1994; Porter *et al.* pers. comm.), and ash (Hobbs *et al.* 1991). In the cases of particulate mapping, longer laser wavelengths are used (532 nm to 1064 nm) as the ratio of scattering from volcanic particles to ambient gas and aerosol is enhanced at these wavelengths. Parallel gas sampling and aerosol measurements can enable estimation of gas to particle conversion rates (e.g. for sulphur dioxide to sulphate, Stith *et al.* 1978; Radke 1982; Rose *et al.* 1986). This is an important topic since, although numerous studies of anthropogenic plumes indicate SO_2 to SO_4^{2-} conversion rates of a few per cent per hour in the lower troposphere (e.g. see Eatough *et al.* 1994 for a review), very few comparable investigations of volcanic plumes have been undertaken. The wide variation in their composition (e.g. gas and ash content, liquid water content) may result in distinct gas scavenging processes and rates (e.g. Horrocks *et al.* 2003; Oppenheimer *et al.* 1998a; Rose *et al.* 2001).

A variation on the LIDAR method involves rapid switching of the frequency of laser pulses to probe absorption lines of gases of interest. By dividing the LIDAR curves (returned signal versus height) obtained at the two wavelengths (Fig. 9) and then applying Beer's law, range-resolved gas concentrations may be derived. The technique, known as Differential Absorption LIDAR (DIAL), has been tested on the Southern Italian volcanoes by Edner *et al.* (1994) and Weibring *et al.* (1998). Their ultraviolet DIAL measurements of SO_2 are instructive, as they were carried out in parallel with COSPEC and DOAS traverses. This revealed significant discrepancies in retrieved SO_2 column amounts between the different techniques, with the passive measurements yielding up to 50 % higher values than the

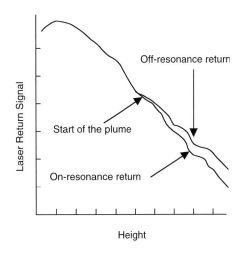

Fig. 9. On- and off-resonance LIDAR signals (DIAL) for a given gas species as a function of height from which the beam is backscattered by the atmosphere (determined from the travel time of the laser pulses). The difference is due to the presence of the gas molecules concerned, reducing the return signal at the wavelength coinciding with strong absorption by the gas.

LIDAR. This probably reflects multiple scattering effects within the plume (i.e. SO_2 molecules are effectively counted more than once by the measurement) and other radiative transfer complexity in the passive sensing case (see Fig. 3).

While simple LIDAR systems can be relatively inexpensive, compact, and transportable, the DIAL apparatus is very costly, heavy and bulky, and has a high power requirement. For example, the system used by Edner *et al.* (1994) and Weibring *et al.* (1998) was housed in a 10 tonne truck. Laser ranging and spectroscopic techniques offer unique capabilities but require further innovation before they are likely to become a regular tool in volcano observatories.

Other approaches

Alternative sensing strategies based on overtone spectroscopy using near-infrared distributed feedback (DFB) lasers (Gianfrani *et al.* 2000; De Natale *et al.* 2001) and mid-infrared difference frequency generation (DFG) lasers (Richter *et al.* 2002) have been evaluated for direct sampling of volcanic gas. In the latter study, volcanic SO_2 was measured with a sensitivity of 3 ppm. Measurements are performed by monitoring the laser's absorption following numerous transits of a multipass cell, into which the volcanic gas sample is pumped.

A further approach relies on transmitting the laser output through a fibre with no cladding, which is placed in a fumarole, and monitoring the absorption of the evanescent field due to the molecules adsorbed on to the fibre (W. Schade pers. comm. 2001). Recent developments in both quantum cascade lasers and cavity ringdown spectroscopy also hold out promise for future field measurements of volcanic gases (e.g. Kostarev *et al.* 2001).

Operating in the infrared spectral region, as opposed to the near ultraviolet (used in the DOAS and COSPEC techniques), delivers access to the absorption features of many gases of interest other than SO_2, including CO_2, SO_2, H_2O, H_2S, CH_4, and HCl. A potential advantage of lasers over other optical techniques currently applied to volcanic gas sensing, is a more realistic potential to measure isotopic ratios, due to the narrow (tens of MHz) line-width of these laser sources. (FTIR spectroscopy has been applied to isotopic measurement of atmospheric trace gases (e.g. Meier & Notholt 1996) but, at present, instruments too bulky to be field portable are required to attain adequate spectral resolution.) Richter *et al.* (2002) have described a laser system capable of measuring all isotopes of CO_2, although the equipment has yet to be field tested at a volcano.

An additional laser based technique that shows potential to perform volcanic isotopic measurements, but which has yet to be applied within this field, is photoacoustic spectroscopy, in which the sound waves, generated by resonant laser light exciting the target species, are measured (Meyer & Sigrist 1990).

Optical particle counters

Quantifying volcanic airborne particle size distributions and concentrations is of especial significance in assessing environmental health impacts of volcanism, given the respiratory conditions such as silicosis that such emissions may give rise to (e.g. Baxter *et al.* 1999). The TSI Inc. DUSTTRAK optical particle counter is the only optical instrument yet used for *in situ* aerosol measurements in this context. This device determines particle data by measuring the light, from a 780 nm diode laser, scattered on to a detector by the airborne aerosols suspended in the ambient air sample pumped into the instrument's sampling chamber (Chung *et al.* 2001; Moosmuller *et al.* 2001). Calibration is obtained against a gravimetric reference dust with a broad quantified particle size distribution. The DUSTTRAK has been used routinely to monitor the respirable fraction of ash on Montserrat

(Allen *et al.* 2000), in order to quantify the risk presented due to ash at various sites.

Sun photometry

Sun photometry is routinely applied in atmospheric research to measurement of aerosol properties, including concentration and size distribution. Characterization of volcanic aerosol is important in studies of plume chemistry, atmospheric radiation, and the environmental and health impacts of particle emissions. Such measurements can also improve the accuracy and interpretation of gas phase plume measurements by indicating the importance of in-plume gas–particle interaction (which could modify the primary magmatic gas ratios), and by permitting modelling of aerosol scattering effects (that can cause significant errors in techniques such as DOAS and COSPEC).

Operation

Sun photometry operates by viewing the Sun through the plume and measuring the solar irradiance in a number of narrow wavelength channels (typically spanning the ultraviolet, visible, and near-infrared). Plume effects can be isolated by subtracting background (without plume) measurements from the plume spectra, then determining particle-size distributions by inversion using a Mie code and assumed extinction coefficients for each size class per wavelength increment (King *et al.* 1978; Asano *et al.* 1985, 1993; Asano 1989; Lienert *et al.* 2001). The instrument requires calibration for solar exoatmospheric irradiance, which is usually achieved by a Langley routine, involving high-altitude measurements at sunrise or sunset. There are potential uncertainties in results due to the dependence of retrievals on, often assumed, optical properties of the scattering medium (e.g. refractive index and shape of particles), and their sensitivity to wavelength limits of inversions.

One instrument used for volcanological research is the Cimel 318-2 solar tracking Sun photometer (Holben *et al.* 1998). It has eight channels between 0.44 and 1.02 mm in five bands centered on 0.44, 0.67, 0.87, 0.936, and 1.02 mm, with three additional polarizing-filtered channels at 0.87 mm. The 0.936 mm channel permits water vapour measurements.

Measurements

Sun photometry has been used to measure stratospheric (Asano *et al.* 1993; Beyerle *et al.*

1995; Schmid *et al.* 1997) and, more recently, tropospheric volcanic aerosols (Watson & Oppenheimer 2000*a*, *b*, 2001). In the latter case, during work performed at Mount Etna, it was observed that different plume types possessed distinct aerosol optical signatures and that the particles appeared to be coagulating as the plume aged. Relatively inexpensive, hand-held Sun photometers are available as off-the-shelf products (e.g. Porter *et al.* 2001). Porter *et al.* (pers. comm.) have obtained sunphotometer data for the plume from Pu'u 'O'o vent on Kilauea, Hawaii from a moving vehicle in order to build profiles of sulfate concentration. By integrating these and using appropriate wind speed values, they calculated a flux of 58 t d^{-1} of sulphate from the vent.

Future directions

The potential of optical methods for volcanic gas and aerosol sensing is clearly considerable. But there are further innovations that are required to ensure that the best are adopted by the volcanological community. If they are to be widely used, new sensing and sampling techniques should adhere to some guiding principles: they should be cheap, easy to operate and maintain, have minimal power requirements, be lightweight and low bulk. Ideally, they should run autonomously and provide real-time data streams with the minimum of post-processing, at high temporal resolution, and continue to provide measurements even during higher levels of volcanic activity.

Simplified retrievals

An attractive characteristic of the COSPEC is the ability to calibrate raw voltages recorded by the photomultiplier tube into SO$_2$ column amounts by rotating the calibration cells into the optical path. This makes retrievals possible by simple graphical scaling, obviating the need for complex processing. Currently, processing of the high spectral resolution data from FTIR, DOAS, and laser spectrometers is not entirely straightforward, and intercalibration with data obtained via alternative optical techniques has yet to be fully explored. There is a clear need, therefore, for development of generally available software tools that will simplify and standardize retrievals and modelling of field spectra.

Longer-term and multi-instrumental monitoring

To date, remotely sensed gas data have been generally limited to discrete campaigns lasting weeks to months (that are too short to observe changes between quiescent and eruptive states) and/or sampling frequencies too low to permit meaningful correlations with geodetic and seismic data (sampling time-scales <<1 min). Because of these factors, gas geochemistry is still widely considered to be less important than geodetic or seismic monitoring. This, in turn, has hindered attempts to develop modelling frameworks in which to interpret gas data and to understand in detail the role of degassing in magma dynamics and eruptive style (Sparks 2003). Given the increasing evidence for the interrelationship between degassing, crystallization, ground deformation, seismicity and switches in eruptive style, to which this volume bears reference (also see Watson *et al.* 2000*b*; Jousset *et al.* 2000; Voight *et al.* 2000), it is important to overcome these limitations. As technology is further developed, we can conceive of semi-permanently installed, automated remote-sensing stations measuring and telemetering high temporal resolution, real-time, long-term volcano gas and aerosol data. (Of particular interest would be the simultaneous deployments of multiple optical technologies, for instance automated solar tracking FTIR and scanning DOAS which would provide unprecedented data streams of SO$_2$, HF, and HCl fluxes.) Such automated configurations, installed in parallel with geodetic and seismic monitoring networks, would more fully exploit the capacities of the remote sensing techniques, enabling new possibilities for multi-parameter volcanological analysis.

Error reduction and quantification

Further potential future developments in this field would include the application of aerosol monitoring techniques, such as Sun photometry and LIDAR, to help model the scattering effects that can distort diffuse skylight measurements of SO$_2$ by COSPEC or DOAS. Such measurements could also help to assess the potential chemical changes in a volcanic plume due to aerosol scavenging effects. An additional area for improvement would be the reduction in the large errors induced in gas or aerosol flux estimates due to uncertainties in plume speed. Many COSPEC campaigns on volcanoes have relied on measurements of wind-speed close to the ground (e.g. by hand-held anemometer) or for the correct plume altitude but at a distant meteorological station (e.g. using radiosondes). A major problem with these approaches is that because the plume velocity itself is not being measured, it is extremely difficult even to apply a meaningful error budget analysis to the SO_2 flux determinations. Multi-angle videography has been used successfully to measure plume speeds, and other more sophisticated techniques are available (e.g. Doppler RADAR and LIDAR systems), but no-one has yet come up with a simple solution to this deceptively straightforward requirement for accurate flux calculations. Application of meteorological models that predict wind speed across the topography in the vicinity of the volcano could be of use.

A further issue is that the increasing utilization of optical techniques within volcanology has not always been accompanied by rigorous analysis of the accuracy of the exploited techniques. In order to foster the greatest confidence in the utility of the derived data, it is imperative that the task of validation is undertaken more seriously than in the past.

Concluding remarks

We have described in this article the optical techniques that have been applied in ground-based volcanic gas and aerosol sensing and sampling, alongside some of the volcanological insights that they have yielded. Such methods are capable of providing real-time measurements of plume composition and flux, even during eruptions. The miniaturization and ruggedization of many optical technologies has led to a great diversification in the spectroscopic techniques available. Perhaps the most striking example of this is the recent demonstration that a miniature DOAS spectrometer (the size of a pack of cigarettes) out-performed the 15 kg and considerably more expensive COSPEC (Galle *et al.* 2003). The 30 years of outstanding service rendered by COSPEC is a perfect illustration of just how valuable optical methods can be for volcanology. Now is the time to capitalize on a range of novel sensor technologies to provide the tools for the next three decades.

This work has been supported by the EC 5th Framework programme 'MULTIMO', NERC grant GR9/4655, GNV grant 'Development of an integrated spectroscopic system for remote and continuous monitoring of volcanic gas', and NASA grant NAG5-10640. We are grateful to L. Horrocks and J. Porter for their constructive reviews of the manuscript.

APPENDIX 1

Summary of the instruments described in this paper

Technique (spectral region)	Typical volcanological application*	Advantages	Disadvantages
COSPEC (UV)	SO_2 fluxes	Black-box technology – simple to operate and retrieve SO_2 columns; data reduction achievable without computers if chart recorders used	Dated technology, difficult to obtain replacement parts, new instrument costs *c.* US$60 000. If chart recorder used, counting squares can be time consuming. Errors arise from atmospheric scattering effects.
GASCOFIL (IR)	CO, OCS abundances and ratios	Use of cells containing gases of interest facilitate relatively simple retrievals	Not yet widely tested on volcanoes
LI-COR (IR)	CO_2 concentrations and fluxes	Sensitive CO_2 measurements of airborne plumes and diffuse emissions from the ground permit flux estimations that are otherwise difficult because of high atmospheric background CO_2 concentrations	Flux measurements of airborne plumes require costly aircraft traverses within plumes, not possible during violent eruptive episodes. Surveys of diffuse emissions are time-consuming and sensitive to seasonal and meteorological effects (soil moisture, etc)

Appendix 1 (continued)

Technique (spectral region)	Typical volcanological application*	Advantages	Disadvantages
DOAS (UV)	SO_2, *H_2S* fluxes concentrations	Mini-DOAS system very light, easy to operate and comparatively inexpensive (in region of US$5000), well suited for automated, long-term deployments. Real-time retrievals possible.	Requires computer processing and specialist software. Errors arise from atmospheric scattering
FTIR (IR)	H_2O, CO_2, SO_2, OCS, CO, HCl, HF, CH_4, SiF_4 concentrations, ratios and fluxes	Very versatile in terms of field deployment configurations. Can measure greatest range of species, enhancing volcanological interpretations of data. Real-time retrievals possible.	Equipment can be bulky, especially when it includes IR lamps, tripods, solar trackers, etc., and relatively power consuming (needing multiple batteries or a generator). Requires computer processing and specialist software. Cost of new instrument in region of US$40 000
FTUV (UV)	*SO_2, H_2S* concentrations	Capable of remote measurements of H_2S – not yet achieved on a volcano	Not yet tested on a volcano; requires a UV lamp.
LIDAR (UV–Visible–IR)	Aerosol, SO_2 concentrations, fluxes	Only technique capable of providing range resolved data.	Systems are expensive, bulky, and not widely available.
Lasers – DFG, DFB, (IR)	H_2O, CO_2, CH_4, H_2S, HCl, SO_2, *OCS, CO, HF, CH_4, SiF_4* concentrations	Very high sensitivity and selectivity may permit isotope ratio measurements	Complex operation and data reduction; not widely available.
Optical particle counters (near IR)	Aerosol concentration and size distributions	Measurement of respirable ash concentrations allows local risk assessments	Direct sampling is less suited for studies of total aerosol emissions from a volcano
Sun photometry (near UV, visible, near IR)	Aerosol size distributions and fluxes	Measurements made remotely, results important for investigating aspects of plume chemistry, dynamics and radiative impacts	Errors arise from uncertainties in optical properties of aerosol. Relatively complex retrieval

* Italicized species have yet to be measured on a volcano, but are in principle measurable in this context using the techniques in question.

APPENDIX 2

Information sources

1. SO₂ flux measurements

COSPEC, Resonance Inc.:
    http://www.resonance.on.ca/
DOAS: http://www.uphys.uni-
    heidelberg.de/urmel/atmos_e.html
Ocean Optics spectrometer:
    http://www.oceanoptics.com/

2. CO2 flux measurements

LI-COR: http://www.licor.com/
West Systems: http://www.westsystems.com/

3. Multicomponent gas measurements (ratios and/or fluxes)

Gascofil:
    http://www.resonance.on.ca/ReTrace.
    html

MIDAC FTIR Air monitoring systems:
   http://www.midac.com/
Bruker OPAG 22 FTIR:
   http://www.bruker.com/
Bomem 100 FTIR: http://www.bomem.com/

4. LIDAR (aerosol and gas measurements)

General information: http://asd-
   www.larc.nasa.gov/lidar/lidar.html
Q-Peak Applied Photonics Systems:
   http://www.qpeak.com/
ELIGHT laser systems: http://www.elight.de/

5. Optical particle counters (aerosol measurements)

DUSTTRAK:
   http://www.tsi.com/iaq/products/dusttrak/
   dusttrak.htm

6. Sun photometers (aerosol measurements)

Cimel: http://www.cimel.fr/photo/sunph_us.htm
Microtops: http://www.solar.com

References

ALLARD, P., CARBONELLE, J., METRICH, N. &
   ZETTWOOG, P. 1991. Eruptive and diffuse emissions
   of carbon dioxide from Etna volcano. *Nature*, **351**,
   387–391.
ALLEN, A. G., BAXTER, P. J. & OTTLEY, C. J. 2000. Gas
   and particle emissions from Soufriere Hills
   Volcano, Montserrat, West Indies: characterization
   and health hazard assessment. *Bulletin of
   Volcanology*, **62**, 8–19.
ANDERSON, D. E. & FARRAR, C. D. 2001. Eddy
   covariance measurement of CO_2 flux to the
   atmosphere from an area of high volcanogenic
   emissions, Mammoth Mountain, California.
   Chemical Geology, **177**, 31–42.
ANDRES, R. J. & KASGNOC, A. D. 1998. A time-
   averaged inventory of subaerial volcanic sulfur
   emissions. *Journal of Geophysical Research*, **103**, 25
   251–25 261.
ANDRES, R. J. & SCHMID J. W. 2001. The effects of
   volcanic ash on COSPEC measurements. *Journal of
   Volcanology and Geothermal Research*, **108**,
   237–244.
ASANO, S. 1989. Aircraft measurements of the radiative
   effects of tropospheric aerosols: II. Estimation of
   aerosol optical properties. *Journal of the
   Meteorological Society of Japan*, **67**, 1023–1034.
ASANO, S., SEKINE, M., KOBAYASHI, M. & MUARI, K.
   1985. Atmospheric turbidity and aerosol size
   distribution in winter at Tsukuba. Effects of the El
   Chichon Eruption. *Journal of the Meteorological
   Society of Japan*, **63**, 453–463.
ASANO, S., UCHIYAMA, A. & SHIOBARA, M. 1993.
   Spectral optical thickness and size distribution of
   the Pinatubo volcanic aerosols as estimated by
   ground based Sunphotometry. *Journal of the
   Meteorological Society of Japan*, **71**, 165–173.
BAXTER, P. J., BONADONNA, C. ET AL. 1999. Cristobalite
   in volcanic ash of the Soufriere Hills Volcano,
   Montserrat, British West Indies. *Science*, **283**,
   1142–1145.
BERRESHEIM, H. & JAESCHKE, W. 1983. The
   contribution of volcanoes to the global atmospheric
   sulphur budget. *Journal of Geophysical Research*,
   88, 3732–3740.
BEYERLE, G., HERBER, A., NFUBER, R. & GERNANDT,
   H. 1995. Temporal development of Mt. Pinatubo
   aerosols as observed by lidar and sun photometer at
   Ny-Alesund, Spitsbergen. *Geophysical Research
   Letters*, **22**, 2497–2500.
BRANTLEY, S. L. & KOEPENICK, K. W. 1995. Measured
   carbon dioxide emissions from Oldoinyo Lengai
   and the skewed distribution of passive volcanic
   fluxes. *Geology*, **23**, 933–936.
BURTON, M. R., OPPENHEIMER, C., HORROCKS, L. A. &
   FRANCIS, P. W. 2000. Remote sensing of CO_2 and
   H_2O emission rates from Masaya volcano,
   Nicaragua. *Geology*, **28**, 915–918.
BURTON, M. R., OPPENHEIMER, C., HORROCKS, L. A. &
   FRANCIS, P. W. 2001. Diurnal changes in volcanic
   plume chemistry observed by lunar and solar
   occultation spectroscopy. *Geophysical Research
   Letters*, **28**, 843–846.
BURTON, M., ALLARD, P. MURÉ, F. & OPPENHEIMER, C.
   2003. Observations of secondary degassing on Mt.
   Etna, Sicily. *In*: OPPENHEIMER, C., PYLE, D. M.
   & BARCLAY, J. (eds) *Volcanic Degassing*. Geological
   Society, London, Special Publications, **213**, 281–
   293.
CAGEAO, R. P., BLAVIER, J. F., McGUIRE, J. P., JIANG,
   Y. B., NEMTCHINOV, V., MILLS, F. P. & SANDER, S. P.
   2001. High-resolution Fourier-transform ultraviolet–
   visible spectrometer for the measurement of
   atmospheric trace species: application to OH.
   Applied Optics, **40**, 2024–2030.
CALTABIANO, T., ROMANO, R. & BUDETTA, G. 1994.
   SO_2 flux measurements at Mt.Etna. *Journal of
   Geophysical Research*, **99**, 12 809–12 819.
CALVARI, S. 2001. Multidisciplinary approach yields
   insight into Mt. Etna eruption. *EOS Transactions*,
   82, 653–656.
CARN, S. A., KRUEGER, A. J., BLUTH, G. J. S.,
   SCHAEFER, S. J., KROTKOV, N. A., WATSON, I. M. &
   DATTA, S. 2003. Volcanic eruption detection by the
   Total Ozone Mapping Spectrometer (TOMS)
   instruments: a 22-year record of sulfur dioxide
   emissions. *In*: OPPENHEIMER, C., PYLE, D. M. &
   BARCLAY, J. (eds) *Volcanic Degassing*. Geological
   Society, London, Special Publications **213**, 177–202.
CASADEVALL, T. J., ROSE, W. I. ET AL. 1984. Sulfur
   dioxide and particles in quiescent volcanic plumes
   from Poas, Arenal, and Colima volcanoes, Costa
   Rica and Mexico. *Journal of Geophysical Research*,
   89, 9633–9641.
CHUAN, R. L., PALAIS, J., ROSE, W. I. & KYLE, P. R.
   1986. Fluxes, sizes, morphology and compositions
   of particles in the Mt. Erebus volcanic plume.
   Journal of Atmospheric Chemistry, **4**, 467–477.

CHUNG, A., CHANG, D. P. Y. *ET AL.* 2001. Comparison of real-time instruments used to monitor airborne particulate matter. *Journal of the Air and Waste Management Association,* **51**, 109–120.

COURTIAL, J., PATTERSON, B. A., HIRST, W., HARVEY, A. R., DUNCAN, A. J., SIBBETT, W. & PADGETT, M. J. 1997. Static Fourier-transform ultraviolet spectrometer for gas detection. *Applied Optics,* **36**, 2813–2817.

DAAG, A. S., TUBIANOSA, B. S. *ET AL.* 1996. Monitoring sulfur dioxide emission at Mount Pinatubo. *In:* NEWHALL, C. G. & PUNONGBAYAN, R. S. (eds) *Fire and Mud: Eruptions and Lahars of Mount Pinatubo Philippines,* Philippine Institute of Volcanology and Seismology, Quezon City, and University of Washington Press, Seattle, 409–434.

DELMELLE, P. 2003. Monitoring and environmental impacts of tropospheric volcanic gas plumes. *In:* OPPENHEIMER, C., PYLE, D. M. & BARCLAY, J. (eds) *Volcanic Degassing.* Geological Society, London, Special Publications **213**, 381–399.

DE NATALE, P., GIANFRANI, L. & DE NATALE, G. 2001. Optical methods for monitoring volcanoes: techniques and new perspectives. *Journal of Volcanology and Geothermal Research,* **109**, 235–245.

DOUKAS, M. P. & GERLACH, T. M. 1995. Sulfur dioxide scrubbing during the 1992 eruptions of Crater Peak, Mount Spurr Volcano, Alaska. *In:* KEITH, T. E. C. (ed.), *The 1992 Eruptions of Crater Peak Vent, Mount Spurr volcano, Alaska.* US Geological Survey Bulletin, 2139, 47–57.

DUFFELL, H., OPPENHEIMER, C. & BURTON, M. R. 2001. Volcanic gas emission rates measured by solar occultation spectroscopy. *Geophysical Research Letters,* **28**, 3131–3134.

EATOUGH, D. J., CAKA, F. M. & FARBER, R. J., 1994. The conversion of SO₂ to sulfate in the atmosphere, *Israel Journal of Chemistry,* **34**, 301–314.

EDMONDS, M., PYLE, D. & OPPENHEIMER, C. 2001. A model for degassing at the Soufrière Hills Volcano, Montserrat, West Indies, based on geochemical data. *Earth and Planetary Science Letters,* **186**, 159–173.

EDMONDS, M., PYLE, D. & OPPENHEIMER C. 2002. HCl emissions at Soufrière Hills Volcano, Montserrat, West Indies, during the second phase of dome-building: November 1999 to October 2000. *Bulletin of Volcanology,* **64**, 21–30.

EDMONDS, M., OPPENHEIMER, C., PYLE, D. M. & HERD, R. 2003. Rainwater and ash leachate analysis as proxies for plume chemistry at Soufrière Hills Volcano, Montserrat. *In:* OPPENHEIMER, C., PYLE, D. M. & BARCLAY, J. (eds) *Volcanic Degassing.* Geological Society, London, Special Publication **213**, 203–218.

EDNER, H., RAGNARSON, S. *ET AL.* 1994. Total fluxes of sulfur dioxide from the Italian Volcanoes Etna, Stromboli and Vulcano measured by differential absorption lidar and passive differential optical absorption spectroscopy. *Journal of Geophysical Research,* **99**, 18 827–18 838.

FRANCIS, P., MACIEJEWSKI, A., OPPENHEIMER, C., CHAFFIN, C. & CALTABIANO, T. 1995. SO₂:HCl ratios in the plumes from Mt. Etna and Vulcano

determined by Fourier transform spectroscopy. *Geophysical Research Letters,* **22**, 1717–1720.

FRANCIS, P., CHAFFIN, C., MACIEJEWSKI, A. & OPPENHEIMER, C. 1996. Remote determination of SiF₄ in volcanic plumes: a new tool for volcano monitoring. *Geophysical Research Letters,* **23**, 249–252.

FRANCIS, P., BURTON, M. & OPPENHEIMER, C. 1998. Remote measurements of volcanic gas compositions by solar FTIR spectroscopy. *Nature,* **396**, 567–570.

FRANCIS, P., HORROCKS, L. & OPPENHEIMER, C. 2000. Monitoring gases from andesite volcanoes. *Philosophical Transactions of the Royal Society,* **358**, 1567–1584.

GALLE, B., OPPENHEIMER, C., GEYER, A., McGONIGLE, A. J. S., EDMONDS, M. & HORROCKS, L. A. 2003. Ultraviolet remote sensing of SO₂ fluxes: a new tool for volcano surveillance. *Journal of Volcanology and Geothermal Research* **119**, 241–254.

GERLACH, T. M. 2003. Altitude effects on COSPEC measurements of volcanic SO₂ emission rates. *In:* OPPENHEIMER, C., PYLE, D. M. & BARCLAY, J. (eds) *Volcanic Degassing.* Geological Society, London. Special Publications **213**, 169–175.

GERLACH, T. M. & CASADEVALL T.M. 1986. Fumarole emission at Mount St Helens volcano, June 1980 to October 1981 – degassing of a magma–hydrothermal system. *Journal of Volcanology and Geothermal Research,* **28**, 141–160.

GERLACH, T. M., DELGADO, H., McGEE, K. A., DOUKAS, M. P., VENEGAS, J. J. & CÁRDENAS, L. 1997. Application of the LI–COR CO₂ analyser to volcanic plumes: a case study, volcán Popocatépetl, Mexico, June 7 and 10, 1995. *Journal of Geophysical Research,* **102**, 8005–8019.

GERLACH, T. M., McGEE, K. A., SUTTON, A. J. & ELIAS. T. 1998. Rates of volcanic CO₂ degassing from airborne determinations of SO2, emission rates and plume CO₂/SO₂: Test study at Pu'u'O'o cone, Kilauea volcano, Hawaii. *Geophysical Research Letters,* **25**, 2675–2678.

GERLACH, T. M., DOUKAS, M. P., McGEE, K. A. & KESSLER, R. 2001. Soil efflux and total emission rates of magmatic CO₂ at the Horseshoe Lake tree kill, Mammoth Mountain, California, 1995–1999. *Chemical Geology,* **177**, 101–116.

GIANFRANI, L., DE NATALE, P. & DE NATALE, G. 2000. Remote sensing of volcanic gases with a DFB-laser-based fiber spectrometer. *Applied Physics B,* **70**, 467–470.

GOFF, F., LOVE, S. P., WARREN, R. G., COUNCE, D., OBENHOLZNER, J., SIEBE, C. & SCHMIDT, S. C. 2001. Passive infrared remote sensing evidence for large, intermittent CO₂ emissions at Popocatepetl volcano, Mexico. *Chemical Geology,* **177**, 133–156.

GRAINGER, R. & HIGHWOOD, E. 2003. Changes in stratospheric composition, chemistry, radiation and climate caused by volcanic eruptions. *In:* OPPENHEIMER, C., PYLE, D. M. & BARCLAY, J. (eds) *Volcanic Degassing.* Geological Society, London, Special Publications **213**, 329–347.

GRATTAN, J., DURAND, M. & TAYLOR, S. 2003. Illness and elevated human mortality in Europe coincident with the Laki fissure eruption. *In*: OPPENHEIMER, C., PYLE, D. M. & BARCLAY, J. (eds) *Volcanic Degassing*. Geological Society, London, Special Publications **213**, 401–414.

HARRIS, D. M., SATO, M., CASADEVALL, T. J. & HUNT, W. H. 1981. Airborne lidar measurements of the Soufrière eruption of 17 April 1979. *Science*, **216**, 1113–1115.

HOBBS, P. V., TUELL, J. P., HEGG, D. A., RADKE, L. F. & ELTGROWTH, M. W. 1982. Particles and gases in the emissions from the 1980–1981 volcanic eruptions of Mt. St. Helens. *Journal of Geophysical Research*, **87**, 11 062–11 086.

HOBBS, P. V., RADKE, L. F., LYONS, J. H., FEREK, R. J., COFFMAN, D. J. & CASADEVALL, T. J. 1991. Airborne measurements of particle and gas emissions from the 1990 volcanic eruptions of Mount Redoubt. *Journal of Geophysical Research*, **96**, 18 735–18 752.

HOFF, R. M. 1992. Differential SO_2 Column Measurements of the Mt. Pinatubo Volcanic Plume. *Geophysical Research Letters*, **19**, 175–178.

HOLBEN, B. H., ECK, T. F. *ET AL*. 1998. AERONET: A federated instrument network and data archive for aerosol characterisation. *Remote Sensing of Environment*, **66**, 1–16.

HORROCKS, L., BURTON, M., FRANCIS, P. & OPPENHEIMER, C. 1999. Stable gas plume composition measured by OP–FTIR spectroscopy at Masaya volcano, Nicaragua, 1998–1999. *Geophysical Research Letters*, **26**, 3497–3500.

HORROCKS, L. A., OPPENHEIMER, C., BURTON, M. R., DUFFELL, H. J., DAVIES, N. M., MARTIN, N. A. & BELL, W. 2001. Open-path Fourier transform infrared spectroscopy of SO_2: an empirical error budget analysis, with implications for volcano monitoring. *Journal of Geophysical Research*, **106**, 27 647–27 659.

HORROCKS, L., OPPENHEIMER, C., BURTON, M. & DUFFELL, H. 2003. Compositional variation in tropospheric volcanic gas plumes: evidence from ground-based remote sensing. *In*: OPPENHEIMER, C., PYLE, D. M. & BARCLAY, J. (eds) *Volcanic Degassing*. Geological Society, London, Special Publications **213**, 349–369.

JOUSSET, P., DWIPA, S., BEAUDUCEL, F., DUQUESNOY, T. & DIAMENT, M. 2000. Temporal gravity at Merapi during the 1993–1995 crisis: an insight into the dynamical behaviour of volcanoes. *Journal of Volcanology and Geothermal Research*, **100**, 289–320.

KEYS, J. G., WOOD, S. W., JONES, N. B. & MURCRAY, F. J. 1998. Spectral measurements of HCl in the plume of the Antarctic volcano Mount Erebus. *Geophysical Research Letters*, **25**, 2421–2424.

KING, M. D., BYRNE, D. M., HERMAN B. M. & REAGAN, J. A. 1978. Aerosol size distributions obtained by inversion of spectral optical depth measurements. *Journal of Atmospheric Sciences*, **35**, 2153–2168.

KOSTAREV, A. A., TITTEL, F. K. *ET AL*. 2001. Cavity ringdown spectroscopy of NO with a single frequency quantum cascade laser. *Applied Optics*, **40**, 5522–5529.

KRUEGER, A. J., WALTER, L. S., BHARTIA, P. K.,

SCHNETZLER, C. C., KROTKOV, N. A., SPROD, I. & BLUTH, G. J. S. 1995. Volcanic sulfur dioxide measurements from the total ozone mapping spectrometer instruments. *Journal of Geophysical Research*, **100**, 14 057–14 076.

LIENERT, B. R., PORTER, J. N. & SHARMA, S. K. 2001. Repetitive genetic inversion of optical extinction data. *Applied Optics*, **40**, 3476–3482.

LOVE, S. P., GOFF, F., COUNCE, D., SIEBE, C. & DELGADO, H. 1998. Passive infrared spectroscopy of the eruption plume at Popocatepetl volcano, Mexico. *Nature*, **396**, 563–567.

LOVE, S. P., GOFF, F., SCHMIDT, S. C., COUNCE, D., PETTIT, D., CHRISTENSON, B. W. & SIEBE, C. 2000. Passive infrared spectroscopic remote sensing of volcanic gases: ground-based studies at White Island and Ruapehu, New Zealand, and Popocatepetl, Mexico. *In*: MOUGINIS-MARK, P., Crisp, J. & Fink, J. (eds) *Remote Sensing of Active Volcanism*, Geophysical Monograph **116**, American Geophysical Union, Washington, D.C., 117–138.

McGEE, K. A. 1992. The structure, dynamics and chemical composition of non-eruptive plumes from Mt. St. Helens, 1980–88. *Journal of Volcanology and Geothermal Research*, **51**, 269–282.

McGEE, K. A. & GERLACH, T. M. 1998a. Airborne volcanic plume measurements using a FTIR spectrometer, Kilauea volcano, Hawaii. *Geophysical Research Letters*, **25**, 615–618.

McGEE, K. A. & GERLACH, T. M. 1998b. Annual cycle of magmatic CO_2 in a tree-kill soil at Mammoth Mountain, California: implications for soil acidification. *Geology*, **26**, 463–466.

McGEE, K. A. & SUTTON, A. J. 1994. Eruptive activity at Mount St. Helens, Washington, USA 1984–1988: a gas geochemistry perspective. *Bulletin of Volcanology*, **56**, 435–446.

McGEE, K. A., GERLACH, T. M., KESSLER, R. & DOUKAS, M. P. 2000. Geochemical evidence for a magmatic CO_2 degassing event at Mammoth Mountain, California, September–December 1997. *Journal of Geophysical Research*, **105**, 8447–8456.

MALINCONICO, L. L. 1979. Fluctuations in SO_2 emission during recent eruptions of Etna: *Nature*, **278**, 43–45.

MEIER, A. & NOTHOLT. J., 1996. Determination of the isotopic abundances of heavy O-3 as observed in arctic ground-based FTIR-spectra. *Geophysical Research Letters*, **23**, 551–554.

MEYER, P. L. & SIGRIST, M. W. 1990. Atmospheric monitoring using CO_2-laser photoacoustic–spectroscopy and other techniques. *Review of Scientific Instruments*, **61**, 1779–1807.

MILLÁN, M. M. 1980. Remote sensing of air pollutants. a study of some atmospheric scattering effects. *Atmospheric Environment*, **14**, 1241–1253.

MILLÁN, M. M. & HOFF, R. M. 1978. Remote sensing of air pollutants by correlation spectroscopy–instrumental response characteristics. *Atmospheric Environment*, **12**, 853–864.

MOFFAT, A. J. & MILLÁN, M. M. 1971. The application of optical correlation techniques to the remote sensing of SO_2 plumes using skylight. *Atmospheric Environment*, **5**, 677–690.

MOFFAT, A. J., KAKARA, T., AKITOMO, T. & LANGAN, L. 1972. *Air Note.* Environmental measurements, San Francisco.

MOOSMULLER, H., ARNOTT, W. P. *ET AL.* 2001. Time resolved characterization of diesel particulate emissions. 1. Instruments for particle mass measurements. *Environmental Science and Technology*, **35**, 781–787.

MORI, T. & NOTSU, K. 1997. Remote CO, COS, CO_2, SO_2 and HCl detection and temperature estimation of volcanic gas. *Geophysical Research Letters*, **24**, 2047–2050.

MORI, T. NOTSU, K., TOHJIMA, Y. & WAKITA, H. 1993. Remote detection of HCl and SO_2 in volcanic gas from Unzen volcano, Japan. *Geophysical Research Letters*, **20**, 1355–1358.

MORI, T., NOTSU, K., TOHJIMA, Y., WAKITA, H., NUCCIO, P. M. & ITALIANO, F. 1995. Remote detection of fumarolic gas chemistry at Vulcano, Italy, using an FT-infrared spectral radiometer. *Earth and Planetary Science Letters*, **134**, 219–224.

NOGUCHI, K. & KAMIYA, H. 1963. Prediction of volcanic eruption by measuring the chemical composition and amounts of gases. *Bulletin of Volcanology*, **26**, 367–378.

NOTSU, K., MORI, T., IGARASHI, G., TOHJIMA, Y. & WAKITA, H. 1993. Infrared spectral radiometer: A new tool for remote measurement of SO_2 of volcanic gas, *Geochemical Journal*, **27**, 361–366.

OPPENHEIMER, C. 1996. On the role of hydrothermal systems in the transfer of volcanic sulfur to the atmosphere. *Geophysical Research Letters*, **23**, 2057–2060.

OPPENHEIMER, C., FRANCIS, P. & STIX., J. 1998a. Depletion rates of SO_2 in tropospheric volcanic plumes. *Geophysical Research Letters*, **25**, 2671–2674.

OPPENHEIMER, C., FRANCIS, P. & MACIEJEWSKI, A. 1998b. Volcanic gas measurements by helicopter-borne fourier transform spectroscopy. *International Journal of Remote Sensing*, **19**, 373–379.

OPPENHEIMER, C., FRANCIS, P., BURTON, M., MACIEJEWSKI, A. & BOARDMAN, L. 1998c. Remote measurement of volcanic gases by Fourier transform infrared spectroscopy. *Applied Physics B*, **67**, 505–515.

OPPENHEIMER, C., FRANCIS, P. & MACIEJEWSKI, A. 1998d. Spectroscopic observation of HCl degassing from Soufrière Hills volcano, Montserrat. *Geophysical Research Letters*, **25**, 3689–3692.

OPPENHEIMER, C., BURTON, M. R., DURIEUX, J. & PYLE, D. M. 2002a. Open-path Fourier transform spectroscopy of gas emissions from a carbonatite volcano: Oldoinyo Lengai, Tanzania. *Optics and Lasers in Engineering*, **37**, 203–214.

OPPENHEIMER, C., EDMONDS, M., FRANCIS, P. & BURTON, M. R. 2002b. Variation in HCl/SO_2 gas ratios observed by Fourier transform spectroscopy at Soufrière Hills Volcano, Montserrat. *In:* DRUITT, T. H. & KOKELAAR, P. (eds) *The eruption of Soufrière Hills Volcano, Montserrat, from 1995 to 1999.* Geological Society, London, Memoirs, **21**, 621–639.

PATTERSON, B. A., LENNEY, J. P., SIBBETT, W., HIRST, B., HEDGES, N. K. & PADGETT, M. J. 1998. Detection of benzene and other gases with an open-path static Fourier-transform ultraviolet spectrometer. *Applied Optics*, **37**, 3172–3175.

PLATT, U. 1994. Differential optical absorption spectroscopy (DOAS). *In: Air Monitoring by Spectroscopic Techniques.* SIGRIST, M. W. (ed.), Chemical Analysis Series, **127**, John Wiley, Chichester, UK.

PORTER, J., MILLER, M. & PIETRAS, C. 2001. Use of the MicroTops Sunphotometer on ships. *Journal of Atmospheric and Oceanic Technology*, **18**, 765–774.

RADKE, L. F. 1982. Sulphur and sulphate from Mt. Erebus. *Nature*, **299**, 710–712.

REALMUTO, V. J., ABRAMS, M. J., BUONGIORNO, M. F. & PIERI, D. C. 1994. The use of mulitispectral thermal infrared image data to estimate the sulfur-dioxide flux from volcanoes – a case-study from Mount Etna, Sicily, July 29, 1986. *Journal of Geophysical Research*, **99**, 481–488.

REALMUTO, V. J., SUTTON, A. J. & ELIAS, T. 1997. Multispectral thermal infrared mapping of sulfur dioxide plumes: a case study from the East Rift Zone of Kilauea Volcano, Hawaii. *Journal of Geophysical Research*, **102**, 15 057–15 072.

RICHTER, D., ERDELYI, M., CURL, R. F., TITTEL, F. K., OPPENHEIMER, C., DUFFELL, H. J. & BURTON, M. 2002. Field measurement of volcanic gases using tunable diode laser based mid-infrared and Fourier transform infrared spectrometers. *Optics and Lasers in Engineering*, **37**, 171–186.

ROBOCK, A. 2000. Volcanic eruptions and climate. *Reviews of Geophysics*, **38**, 191–219.

ROGIE, J. D., KERRICK, D. M., SOREY, M. L., CHIODINI, G. & GALLOWAY, D. L. 2001. Dynamics of carbon dioxide emission at Mammoth Mountain, California. *Earth and Planetary Science Letters*, **188**, 535–541.

ROSE, W. I., CHUAN, R. L., GIGGENBACH, W. F., KYLE, P. R. & SYMONDS, R. B. 1986. Rates of sulfur dioxide and particle emissions from White Island volcano, New Zealand, and an estimate of the total flux of major gaseous species. *Bulletin of Volcanology*, **48**, 181–188.

ROSE, W. I., BLUTH, G. J. S. , SCHNEIDER, D. J., ERNST, G. G. J., RILEY, C. M., HENDERSON, L. J. & McGIMSEY, R. G. 2001. Observations of volcanic clouds in their first few days of atmospheric residence: the 1992 eruptions of Crater Peak, Mount Spurr volcano, Alaska. *Journal of Geology*, **109**, 677–694.

SANDSTERN, J., WEIBRING, P., EDNER, H. & SVANBERG, S. 2000. Real-time gas-correlation imaging employing thermal background radiation. *Optics Express*, **6**, 92–103.

SCHMID, B., MÄTZLER, C., HEIMO, A. & KÄMPFER, N. 1997. Retrieval of the optical depth and particle size distribution of tropospheric and stratospheric aerosols by means of Sun photometry. *IEEE Transactions on Geoscience and Remote Sensing*, **35**, 172–182.

SPARKS, R. S. J. 2003 Dynamics of magma degassing. *In*: OPPENHEIMER, C., PYLE, D. M. & BARCLAY, J. (eds) *Volcanic Degassing.* Geological Society, London, Special Publication **213**, 5–22.

STITH, J. L., HOBBS, P. V. & RADKE, L. F. 1978. Airborne particles and gas measurements in the emissions from six volcanoes. *Journal of Geophysical Research*, **83**, 4009–4017.

STIX, J., MORROW, W. H., NICHOLLS, R. & CHARLAND, A. 1996. Infrared remote sensing of CO and COS gas emitted by the Galeras volcano, Colombia, 8–10 January 1993. *Canadian Joural of Remote Sensing*, **22**, 297–304.

STOIBER, R. E. & JEPSEN, A. 1973. Sulfur dioxide contribution to the atmosphere by volcanoes. *Science*, **182**, 577–578.

STOIBER, R. E., MALINCONICO, L. L. & WILLIAMS, S. N. 1983. Use of the correlation spectrometer at volcanoes. *In:* TAZIEFF, H. AND SABROUX, J.-C. (eds) *Forecasting Volcanic Events.* Elsevier, Amsterdam, 425–444.

STOIBER, R. E., WILLIAMS, S. & HUEBERT, B. J. 1986. Sulfur and halogen gases at Masaya caldera complex, Nicaragua: total flux and varations with time. *Journal of Geophysical Research*, **91**, 12 215–12 231.

STOIBER, R. E., WILLIAMS, S. N. & HUEBERT, B. 1987. Annual contribution of sulfur dioxide to the atmosphere by volcanoes. *Journal of Volcanology and Geothermal Research*, **33**, 1–8.

SYMONDS, R. B., ROSE, W. I., BLUTH, G. J. S. & GERLACH T. J. 1994. Volcanic-gas studies: methods, results and applications. *Reviews in Mineralogy*, **30**, 1–66.

SYMONDS, R. B., MIZUTANI, Y. & BRIGGS, P. H., 1996. Long-term geochemical surveillance of fumaroles at Showa–Shinzan dome, Usu volcano, Japan. *Journal of Volcanology and Geothermal Research*, **73**, 177–211.

SYMONDS, R. B., GERLACH, T. M. & REED, M. H. 2001. Magmatic gas scrubbing: implications for volcano monitoring. *Journal of Volcanology and Geothermal Research*, **108**, 303–341.

THORDARSON, T., SELF, S., OSKARSSON, N. & HULSEBOSCH, T. 1996. Sulfur, chlorine and fluorine degassing and atmospheric loading by the 1783–784 AD Laki (Skaftar fires) eruption in Iceland. *Bulletin of Volcanology*, **58**, 205–225.

THORDARSON, T., SELF, S., MILLER, D. J., & LARSEN, G. 2003. Sulphur release from flood lava eruptions in the Veidivötn, Grímsvötn and Katla volcanic systems, Iceland. *In:* OPPENHEIMER, C., PYLE, D. M. & BARCLAY, J. *Volcanic Degassing.* Geological Society, London. Special Publications **213**, 103–121.

VOIGHT, B., YOUNG, K. D. *ET AL.* 2000. Deformation and seismic precursors to dome-collapse and fountain-collapse nuees ardentes at Merapi Volcano, Java, Indonesia, 1994–1998. *Journal of Volcanology and Geothermal Research*, **100**, 261–287.

WALLACE, P. J. 2001, Volcanic SO_2 emissions and the abundance and distribution of exsolved gas in magma bodies. *Journal of Volcanology and Geothermal Research*, **108**, 85–106

WATSON, I. M. & OPPENHEIMER, C. 2000a. Particle size distributions of Mt. Etna's aerosol plume constrained by sun-photometry. *Journal of Geophysical Research – Atmospheres*, **105**, 9823–9830.

WATSON, I. M. & OPPENHEIMER, C. 2001. Particle-size distributions of ash-rich volcanic plumes determined by sun photometry. *Atmospheric Environment*, **35**, 3561–3572.

WATSON, I. M., OPPENHEIMER, C. *ET AL.* 2000. The relationship between degassing and deformation at Soufriere Hills volcano, Montserrat. *Journal of Volcanology and Geothermal Research*, **98**, 117–126.

WEIBRING, P., EDNER, H., SVANBERG, S., CECCHI, G., PANTANI, L., FERRARA, R. & CALTABIANO, T. 1998. Monitoring of volcanic sulphur dioxide emissions using differential absorption LIDAR (DIAL), Differential Optical Absorption Spectroscopy (DOAS) and Correlation Spectroscopy. *Applied Physics (B)*, **64**, 419–426.

WILLIAMS, S. N., SCHAEFER, S. J., CALVACHE, V. M. L. & LOPEZ, D. 1992. Global carbon dioxide emission to the atmosphere by volcanoes. *Geochimica et Cosmochimica Acta*, **56**, 1765–1770.

Elevation effects in volcano applications of the COSPEC

T. M. GERLACH

US Geological Survey, Cascades Volcano Observatory, 1300 SE Cardinal Court #100, Vancouver, WA 98683-9589, USA.
(e-mail:tgerlach@usgs.gov)

Abstract: Volcano applications commonly involve sizeable departures from the reference pressure and temperature of COSPEC calibration cells. Analysis shows that COSPEC SO_2 column abundances and derived mass emission rates are independent of pressure and temperature, and thus unaffected by elevation effects related to deviations from calibration cell reference state. However, path-length concentrations are pressure and temperature dependent. Since COSPEC path-length concentration data assume the reference pressure and temperature of calibration cells, they can lead to large errors when used to calculate SO_2 mixing ratios of volcanic plumes. Correction factors for COSPEC path-length concentrations become significant (c.10%) at elevations of about 1 km (e.g. Kilauea volcano) and rise rapidly to c.80% at 6 km (e.g. Cotopaxi volcano). Calculating SO_2 mixing ratios for volcanic plumes directly from COSPEC path-length concentrations always gives low results. Corrections can substantially increase mixing ratios; for example, corrections increase SO_2 ppm concentrations reported for the Mount St Helens, Colima, and Erebus plumes by 25–50%. Several arguments suggest it would be advantageous to calibrate COSPEC measurements in column abundance units rather than path-length concentration units.

Introduction

Earlier investigations have examined the sensitivity of COSPEC results to processes associated with radiation transfer, especially atmospheric scattering effects (Millán et al.1980; Millán et al. 1985). Pressure and temperature dependent line broadening effects on absorption bands for sulphur dioxide, have also been examined (M. Millán, pers. comm. 2002). This study considers effects related to departures from the reference pressure and temperature of calibration cells in volcanological applications of the COSPEC. The goals of this study are to clarify the kinds of COSPEC data that are sensitive to these effects (hereafter denoted simply as 'elevation effects'), to give guidelines for evaluating how significant the effects may be in volcanological applications, and to provide equations for estimating their correction. The study begins with an analysis of pressure and temperature dependence of column abundances and path-length concentrations. Examples follow of calculating elevation effects and estimating corrections in volcano applications. Finally, corrections for elevation effects are applied to SO_2 mixing ratios reported for volcanic plumes of Mount St Helens, Colima, and Erebus.

Pressure and temperature dependence of column abundances and path-length concentrations

Column abundances

COSPEC output voltages are proportional to the optical density of SO_2, or absorbance ($\ln I_0/I$), where I_0 is the intensity (in photons/m²/s) of background UV radiation and I is the intensity of UV radiation for background plus volcanic plume. Absorbance is related to the concentration density of SO_2 c_{SO_2} and the optical path-length (L) by the Beer–Lambert law:

$$\ln \frac{I_0}{I} = \varepsilon\, c_{SO_2} L \qquad (1)$$

where ε is the absorption coefficient. The average concentration density of SO_2 along L is given by:

$$c_{SO_2} = \frac{m_{SO_2}}{V} = \frac{m_{SO_2}}{AL} = \frac{B_{SO_2}}{L} \qquad (2)$$

where m_{SO_2} is the mass of SO_2 in the column volume (V) defined by L and the light-gathering cross-section of the instrument (A). B_{SO_2} is the mass abundance of SO_2 per unit area in the

From: OPPENHEIMER, C., PYLE, D.M. & BARCLAY, J. (eds) *Volcanic Degassing*. Geological Society, London, Special Publications, **213**, 169–175. 0305–8719/03/$15.00

optical path column, or simply the SO_2 column abundance defined by:

$$B_{SO_2} \equiv \frac{m_{SO_2}}{A} \qquad (3)$$

Since m_{SO_2} can be expressed as the product of the number of moles of SO_2 in the column (n_{SO_2}) and the molecular weight of SO_2 (M_{SO_2}), equation (3) can be written in several forms by introducing the ideal gas law, ($PV = NRT$) as follows:

$$B_{SO_2} = \frac{n_{SO_2} M_{SO_2}}{A} = \frac{x_{SO_2} N M_{SO_2}}{A} =$$
$$\frac{x_{SO_2} PVM_{SO_2}}{ART} = \frac{x_{SO_2} PLM_{SO_2}}{RT} \qquad (4)$$

where x_{SO_2} is the average column mixing ratio (or mole fraction) for SO_2.

It is clear from equations (1) and (2) that column abundance, B_{SO_2}, is the natural variable actually measured by the COSPEC. While it seems apparent that B_{SO_2} would be independent of pressure and temperature, this fact can be made readily explicit. The pressure and temperature dependence of B_{SO_2} is given by the total derivative

$$d B_{SO_2} = \left(\frac{\partial B_{SO_2}}{\partial P}\right)_T dP + \left(\frac{\partial B_{SO_2}}{\partial T}\right)_P dT \qquad (5)$$

Since the mole fraction of SO_2 (x_{SO_2}) in a volume of gas is independent of pressure and temperature changes, it follows from equation (4) that:

$$\left(\frac{\partial B_{SO_2}}{\partial P}\right)_T = \left(\frac{x_{SO_2} M_{SO_2}}{R}\right)\left[\frac{L}{T} + \frac{P}{T}\left(\frac{\partial L}{\partial P}\right)_T\right] \qquad (6)$$

For the column volume V containing N moles of gas, the ideal gas law gives:

$$L = \frac{NRT}{PA} \qquad (7)$$

Thus,

$$\left(\frac{\partial L}{\partial P}\right)_T = -\frac{NRT}{P^2 A} = -\frac{L}{P} \qquad (8)$$

and

$$\left(\frac{\partial L}{\partial T}\right)_P = \frac{NR}{PA} = \frac{L}{T} \qquad (9)$$

Substituting equation (8) into (6) gives:

$$\left(\frac{\partial B_{SO_2}}{\partial P}\right)_T =$$
$$\left(\frac{x_{SO_2} M_{SO_2}}{R}\right)\left[\frac{L}{T} + \frac{P}{T}\left(\frac{\partial L}{\partial P}\right)_T\right] = 0 \qquad (10)$$

And likewise:

$$\left(\frac{\partial B_{SO_2}}{\partial T}\right)_P =$$
$$\left(\frac{x_{SO_2} M_{SO_2}}{R}\right)\left[-\frac{PL}{T^2} + \frac{P}{T}\left(\frac{\partial L}{\partial T}\right)_P\right] = 0 \qquad (11)$$

The total derivative, dB_{SO_2} by equation (5) is therefore zero, and SO_2 column abundances are clearly independent of pressure and temperature, and thus elevation effects.

Path-length concentrations

In volcanological applications (and commonly elsewhere) COSPEC output voltages are calibrated in SO_2 path-length concentrations b_{SO_2} instead of column abundances. The ppm-based path-length concentration is defined by:

$$b_{SO_2} \equiv 10^6 x_{SO_2} L \qquad (12)$$

Thus, for L in m, b_{SO_2} is in path-length concentration units of ppm m. The total derivative of b_{SO_2} with respect to pressure and temperature is given by:

$$d b_{SO_2} = \left(\frac{\partial b_{SO_2}}{\partial P}\right)_T dP + \left(\frac{\partial b_{SO_2}}{\partial T}\right)_P dT \qquad (13)$$

It follows from equations (8), (9), and (12) that:

$$\left(\frac{\partial b_{SO_2}}{\partial P}\right)_T = 10^6 x_{SO_2}\left(\frac{\partial L}{\partial P}\right)_T =$$
$$-\frac{10^6 x_{SO_2} L}{P} = -\frac{b_{SO_2}}{P} \qquad (14)$$

and:

$$\left(\frac{\partial b_{SO_2}}{\partial T}\right)_P = 10^6 x_{SO_2}\left(\frac{\partial L}{\partial T}\right)_P =$$
$$\frac{10^6 x_{SO_2} L}{T} = \frac{b_{SO_2}}{T} \qquad (15)$$

Substituting the results of equations (14) and (15) into (13) gives:

$$d b_{SO_2} = -\left(\frac{b_{SO_2}}{P}\right) dP + \left(\frac{b_{SO_2}}{T}\right) dT \quad (16)$$

The solution to equation (16), obtained by separating variables and integrating from the reference path-length concentration ($b_{SO_2,r}$) at the reference pressure and temperature (P_r and T_r) to the b_{SO_2}, P, and T of interest, i.e.

$$\int_{b_{SO_2,r}}^{b_{SO_2}} \frac{d b_{SO_2}}{b_{SO_2}} = -\int_{P_r}^{P} \frac{dP}{P} + \int_{T_r}^{T} \frac{dT}{T} \quad (17)$$

gives the following expression for b_{SO_2} at P and T:

$$b_{SO_2} = \left(\frac{TP_r}{T_r P}\right) b_{SO_2,r} \quad (18)$$

Thus, unlike column abundances, SO_2 path-length concentrations are indeed pressure and temperature dependent, and thus sensitive to elevation effects.

Relationship of path-length concentration to column abundance

Substituting equations (12) and (18) into (4) gives the relationship between b_{SO_2} and B_{SO_2},

$$B_{SO_2} = \left(\frac{10^{-6} M_{SO_2}}{R}\right)\left(\frac{P}{T}\right) b_{SO_2} = \left(\frac{10^{-6} M_{SO_2} P_r}{R T_r}\right) b_{SO_2,r} \quad (19)$$

confirming again the pressure and temperature independence of B_{SO_2}.

Applications

Example calculations

COSPEC calibration cells are constructed at a reference temperature (T_r) of 20 °C (293.15 K) and reference pressure (P_r) of 1 atm (101.325 kPa) with calibration values stated in path-length concentration units (ppm m SO_2). COSPEC path-length concentrations based on curves fit to

calibration cell data are therefore $b_{SO_2,r}$ values referenced to these conditions. These *reference* path-length concentrations can be transformed to b_{SO_2} values at the P and T of interest from equation (18), as follows:

$$b_{SO_2} = \left(\frac{T(101.325\,kPa)}{(293.15\,K)P}\right) b_{SO_2,r} \quad (20)$$

(Note that the ratio P_r/T_r of COSPEC calibration cells is not affected by the ambient conditions of measurements, since it is equivalent to the constant $N_c R/V_c$, where N_c and V_c are respectively the fixed molar gas content and volume of the rigid cell.)

Column abundances can be calculated directly from COSPEC reference path-length concentrations without pressure and temperature corrections. Evaluating M_{SO_2} (64.063×10^{-3} kg mol^{-1}) and (8.3145×10^{-3} kPa m^3 mol^{-1} K^{-1}) in equation (19) for $b_{SO_2,r}$ in ppm m units gives

$$B_{SO_2} = \left(2.663 \times 10^{-6}\,kg\,ppm^{-1}\,m^{-3}\right) b_{SO_2,r} \quad (21)$$

Thus, a unit ppm m COSPEC result for SO_2 is always equivalent to a column abundance of 2.663×10^{-6} kg m^{-2}, no matter what the pressure and temperature.

The above equations permit ready calculation of most quantities of interest, as illustrated in the following example: an upward viewing COSPEC measurement made in airborne mode directly under a 100-m thick volcanic plume gives a path-length concentration of 600 ppm m for SO_2. The average P and T of the plume are 0.6 atm (60.795 kPa) and $-13°$ C (260.15 K), respectively. For this example, the 600-ppm m path-length concentration is a $b_{SO_2,r}$ value referenced to the P_r and T_r of the calibration curve. The path-length concentration at *in situ* conditions is given by equation (20):

$$b_{SO_2} = \left(\frac{T(101.325\,kPa)}{(293.15\,K)P}\right) b_{SO_2,r} =$$

$$\left(\frac{(260.15\,K)(101.325\,kPa)}{(293.15\,K)(60.795\,kPa)}\right)$$

$$(600\,ppm\,m) = 887\,ppm\,m$$

The corresponding average SO_2 ppm concentration along the vertical path through the plume is:

$$\frac{b_{SO_2}}{100\,m} = \frac{887\,ppm\,m}{100\,m} = 8.9\,ppm$$

compared with a value of 6 ppm calculated directly from the COSPEC reference path-length concentration of 600 ppm m. The column abundance B_{SO_2} can be calculated directly from the 600-ppm m COSPEC reading by equation (21), giving:

$$B_{SO_2} = \left(2.663x10^{-6}\,kg\,ppm^{-1}\,m^{-3}\right)b_{SO_{2,r}} =$$

$$\left(2.663x10^{-6}\,kg\,ppm^{-1}\,m^{-3}\right)$$

$$600\,ppm\,m = 1.6x10^{-3}\,kg\,m^{-2}$$

Finally, the SO_2 concentration density, c_{SO_2}, is calculated from equation (2), as follows:

$$c_{SO_2} = \frac{B_{SO_2}}{100\,m} = \frac{1.6x10^{-3}\,kg\,m^{-2}}{100\,m} =$$

$$1.6x10^{-5}\,kg\,m^{-3}$$

Estimated corrections for path-length concentrations

It is best to base corrections of calibration cell-referenced path-length concentrations on pressures and temperatures measured directly at plume elevations (e.g. Gerlach et al. 1999). When these are not available, estimates can be made of pressure and temperature at plume elevations from the US Standard Atmosphere (US Committee on Extension to the Standard Atmosphere 1976), a composite atmosphere model used widely in scientific studies and technical applications. The model is based on rocket and satellite data and perfect gas theory. It represents pressures and temperatures from sea-level to 1000 km. Below 32 km, the US Standard Atmosphere is identical with the Standard Atmosphere of the International Civil Aviation Organization. Several WWW sites provide output values of model pressures and temperatures (and other atmospheric parameters) at user specified input elevations (e.g. http://www.digitaldutch.com/atmoscalc/). Figure 1 displays pressures and temperatures of the US Standard Atmosphere up to elevations of 6 km, the range of interest for most volcanological applications of the COSPEC.
Figure 2 shows the estimated correction factor ($b_{SO_2}/b_{SO_{2,r}}$) for calibration cell-referenced path-length concentrations calculated from equation (20) and pressures and temperatures at

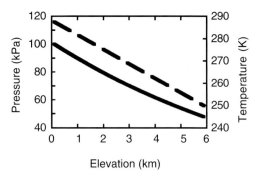

Fig. 1. Pressure (solid line) and temperature (dashed line) for the US Standard Atmosphere as a function of elevation above sea level over the range of elevations of interest in most volcanological applications of the COSPEC.

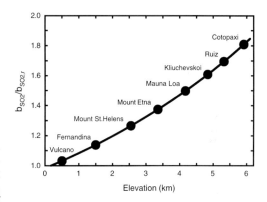

Fig. 2. Path-length concentration correction factors ($b_{SO_2}/b_{SO_{2,r}}$) based on equation (20) and pressures and temperatures as a function of elevation above sea level for the US Standard Atmosphere (Figure 1). Points illustrate estimated correction factors based on summit elevations for several volcanoes (Simkin & Siebert 1994). The correction factor at sea level is 0.983 instead of unity, because the model atmosphere temperature (15 °C) is less than the COSPEC calibration cell reference temperature (20 °C).

elevation for the US Standard Atmosphere. For convenient calculation, the following exponential equation gives a nearly exact fit to $b_{SO_2}/b_{SO_{2,r}}$ directly as a function of elevation, h (in m), from 0 to 6 km:

$$b_{SO_2}\Big/b_{SO_{2,r}} = 0.265 + 0.719\exp\left(\frac{h}{7740.49}\right) \quad (22)$$

At plume elevations greater than about one kilometre, correction factors rise rapidly and are clearly significant, as b_{SO_2} values become 10–80% larger than calibration cell-referenced path-length concentrations. Roughly 70% of the volcanoes listed by Simkin & Siebert (1994) have elevations above 1 km. When plume elevations are not known, satisfactory estimates of correction factors can usually be made from volcano summit elevations. Figure 2 illustrates examples of estimated correction factors for several volcano summit elevations. It is underscored that correction factors obtained with equation (22) and Figure 2 are estimates because of the mismatch between model and actual atmospheric pressures and temperatures at elevation; the degree of mismatch varies somewhat with season and latitude (US Committee on Extension to the Standard Atmosphere 1976).

Example corrections applied to reported plume SO_2 mixing ratios

Reported COSPEC-based mixing ratios for SO_2 in volcanic plumes have generally been calculated from calibration cell-referenced path-length concentrations by simply dividing $b_{SO_2,r}$ values by plume thickness. As indicated above, however, the $b_{SO_2}/b_{SO_2,r}$ correction factors, and thus the inferred SO_2 mixing ratios at plume P and T, can increase significantly for higher elevation plumes. The only reported COSPEC-based volcanic plume mixing ratios (known to the author) that take elevation effects into account are those reported by McGee (1992). Applying equation (20) (supplied by the author), McGee found increases of c.27% in the corrected SO_2 mixing ratios for a 29 July 1980 Mount St Helens plume (K.A. McGee, pers. comm.). These corrections are based on airborne altimeter readings; for comparison, equation (22) gives a closely agreeing increase of 26% for the 2550-m summit elevation (Fig. 2).

Stoiber *et al.* (1983) used calibration cell-referenced path-length concentrations from COSPEC measurements on a 19 September 1980 Mount St Helens plume to derive average SO_2 mixing ratios (Table 1) for plume elevation intervals determined from airborne altimeter readings. The downwind distance from the source was not reported. Correcting the reported results with equation (22) at the stated elevations increases the SO_2 mixing ratios by 24% to 28% (Table 1).

Casadevall *et al.* (1984) present average SO_2 mixing ratios (Table 2) based on calibration cell-referenced path-length concentrations from COSPEC measurements for vertical sectors of margin and core areas of a plume cross-section

at Colima volcano on 20 February 1982. Plume elevation and thickness were obtained from altimeter readings and LIDAR measurements. The downwind distance from the source was not reported. The SO_2 mixing ratios increase by 47% (Table 2) when the reported results are corrected with equation (22) for the average plume elevation of 4000 m.

Rose *et al.* (1985) report several average total plume SO_2 mixing ratios (uncorrected) for Erebus volcano on four days in December 1983, based on COSPEC traverses under the plume and plume thickness data (Table 3). Typical downwind distances were 2–3 km. Plume elevations were not reported, so the corrected SO_2 mixing ratios in Table 3 are based on equation (22) at the summit elevation of 3794 m (Simkin & Siebert 1994). The corrected SO_2 mixing ratios are 44% larger than reported values.

Table 1. *Average plume SO_2 mixing ratios, Mount St Helens, 19 September 1980*[*]

Elevation range (m)	SO_2 (uncorrected) (ppm)	$b_{SO_2}/b_{SO_2,r}$[†]	SO_2 (corrected) (ppm)
2590–2743	0.12	1.280	0.154
2438–2590	0.09	1.260	0.113
2286–2438	0.05	1.241	0.062
Total plume	0.08	1.260	0.101

[*]Elevation and uncorrected SO_2 data from Stoiber *et al.* (1983).
[†]From equation (22) for median elevation of given range.

Table 2. *Average plume SO_2 mixing ratios, Colima volcano, 20 February 1982*[*]

Location	SO_2 (uncorrected) (ppm)	SO_2 (corrected) (ppm)[†]
Plume margin	0.027	0.040
Plume margin	0.078	0.115
Plume margin	0.078	0.115
Plume margin	0.051	0.075
Plume margin	0.051	0.075
Plume margin	0.022	0.032
Plume core	0.156	0.229
Plume core	0.317	0.466
Plume core	0.217	0.319

[*]Uncorrected SO_2 data from Casadevall *et al.* (1984).
[†]From uncorrected SO_2 data and $b_{SO_2}/b_{SO_2,r}$ of 1.471 by equation (22) for an average plume elevation of 4000 m (Casadevall *et al.* 1984).

Table 3. *Average total plume SO₂ mixing ratios, Erebus volcano, December 1983*

Date	Distance down-wind (km)	SO₂ (uncor-rected) (ppm)	SO₂ (corrected) (ppm)[†]
9 December 1983	3	0.30	0.432
9 December 1983	6	0.26	0.374
9 December 1983	6	0.26	0.374
9 December 1983	6	0.26	0.374
9 December 1983	3	0.26	0.374
9 December 1983	3	0.18	0.259
14 December 1983	2	0.13	0.187
14 December 1983	2	0.11	0.158
14 December 1983	2	0.12	0.173
14 December 1983	2	0.11	0.158
14 December 1983	2	0.13	0.187
14 December 1983	2	0.07	0.101
14 December 1983	2	0.08	0.115
17 December 1983	3	0.10	0.144
17 December 1983	3	0.13	0.187
17 December 1983	3	0.10	0.144
17 December 1983	3	0.08	0.115
17 December 1983	3	0.07	0.101
17 December 1983	3	0.11	0.158
17 December 1983	3	0.10	0.144
19 December 1983	3	0.20	0.288
19 December 1983	3	0.11	0.158
19 December 1983	3	0.19	0.273
19 December 1983	3	0.18	0.259
19 December 1983	4	0.17	0.245
19 December 1983	3	0.27	0.389
19 December 1983	3	0.24	0.345

*Downwind distances and uncorrected SO₂ data from Rose *et al.* (1985).

[†]From uncorrected SO₂ data and $b_{SO_2}/b_{SO_2,r}$ of 1.439 by equation (22) for summit elevation of 3794 m (Simkin & Siebert 1994).

Concluding remarks

The SO_2 column abundances from COSPEC measurements are independent of pressure and temperature. There is thus no need to correct COSPEC column abundances for elevation effects. By implication, COSPEC-based SO_2 emission rates (kg/s) are similarly independent of these elevation effects, since they are derived from column abundances (kg/m²) integrated over wind-normalized traverses (m) and multiplied by wind speed (m/s). COSPEC SO_2 path-length concentration data, however, are pressure and temperature dependent, and they may – depending on volcano height – benefit appreciably from corrections for elevation effects. COSPEC path-length concentrations, being referenced to 293.15 K and 1 atm, are not equivalent to path-length concentrations at the elevations of most

COSPEC applications in volcanology. *In situ* SO_2 mixing ratios of volcanic plumes based on dividing COSPEC path-length concentrations by plume thickness are only approximations, i.e. always lower than actual values. Accurate *in situ* volcanic plume mixing ratios require correction of COSPEC path-length concentration data for departure from the reference pressure and temperature of calibration cells. These corrections become important for volcanic plumes at elevations above about a kilometre; such plumes can have mixing ratios 10–80% higher than the mixing ratios calculated directly from COSPEC path-length concentrations.

Since column abundance is the natural variable measured by the COSPEC and independent of pressure and temperature, it seems appropriate to calibrate the output signal of the instrument in column abundance units, instead of the commonly used ppm m path-length concentration units. Calibration cells in path-length concentration units are easily rescaled to column abundance units by equation (21). With the output voltage calibrated in column abundance units, emission rates are directly and simply calculated as indicated above, without involving potentially confusing conversions of path-length concentrations. To obtain plume concentration densities of SO_2, column abundance is simply divided by plume thickness (equation (2)). If SO_2 mixing ratios are of interest, they can be easily obtained from the concentration density, the ideal gas law, and measured or estimated plume pressures and temperature. Calibration in column abundance units would reduce the complexity and confusion that, in the author's opinion, often results from calibration in path-length concentration units.

COSPEC measurements are of course subject to elevation effects additional to those considered here. Among these are pressure- and temperature-dependent line broadening effects on SO_2 absorption bands. These effects have been evaluated for the 18 May 1980 Mount St. Helens eruption cloud as it drifted at an elevation of *c.*12 km over a ground-based COSPEC in southern Ontario (Milán *et al.* 1985). Analysis shows that the COSPEC SO_2 path-length concentrations at this elevation would be *c.*16% too high, due mainly to sharpened absorption bands in a less pressure-broadened spectrum (M.Milán pers. comm. 2002). Equation (20) indicates COSPEC SO_2 path-length concentrations would be *c.*74% too low ($b_{SO_2}/b_{SO_2,r}$ of 3.9 for Standard Atmosphere temperature of 216.65 K and pressure of 19.33 kPa at 12 km). From this example, it appears that COSPEC line-broadening elevation effects would be a great deal smaller in magnitude than the elevation effects examined in this study, and in the opposite direction.

Finally, the need to correct for elevation effects may arise in applications of other spectroscopic methods based on the Lambert-Beer law to volcanic gases (e.g. open-path FTIR). The equations for doing so can be developed by analogy with those presented above for COSPEC SO_2 measurements.

My interest in the topics of this study began several years ago as a result of stimulating discussions with T. J. Casadevall and R. L. Chuan. I thank M. P. Doukas, B. Galle, K. A. McGee, and M. Millán for constructive reviews of the draft manuscript. I am grateful to M. Millán for providing unpublished results of line-broadening effects on SO_2 absorption bands for the Mount St Helens eruption cloud of 18 May 1980. The US Geological Survey Volcano Hazards Program supported the work. Finally, I want to acknowledge the important contributions of Peter Francis to understanding the chemistry and role of volcanic gases. I am one of many impressed by how quickly and fundamentally Peter changed this field of research.

References

CASADEVALL, T. J., ROSE, W. I., FULLER, W. H., HUNT, W. H., HART, M. A., MOYERS, J. L., WOODS, D. C., CHUAN, R. L. & FRIEND, J. P. 1984. Sulfur dioxide and particles in quiescent volcanic plumes from Poás, Arenal, and Colima Volcanoes, Costa Rica and Mexico. *Journal of Geophysical Research*, **89**, 9633–9641.

GERLACH, T. M., DOUKAS, M. P., McGEE, K. A. & KESSLER, R. 1999. Airborne detection of diffuse carbon dioxide emissions at Mammoth Mountain, California. *Geophysical Research Letters*, **26**, 3661–3664.

McGEE, K. A. 1992. The structure, dynamics, and chemical composition of noneruptive plumes from Mount St. Helens, 1980–88. *Journal of Volcanology and Geothermal Research*, **51**, 269–282.

MILLÁN, M. M. 1985. COSPEC observation of Mt. St. Helens volcanic SO_2 eruption cloud of 18 May 1980 over southern Ontario. *Atmospheric Environment*, **19**, 255–263.

MILLÁN, M. M., GALLANT, A. J., CHUNG, Y.-S. & FANAKI, F. 1980. Remote sensing of air pollutants. A study of some atmospheric scattering effects. *Atmospheric Environment*, **14**, 1241–1253.

ROSE, W. I., CHUAN, R. L. & KYLE, P. R. 1985. Rate of sulphur dioxide emission from Erebus volcano, Antarctica, December 1983. *Nature*, **316**, 710–712.

SIMKIN, T. & SIEBERT, L. 1994. *Volcanoes of the World*. Geoscience Press, Tucson, Arizona.

STOIBER, R. E., MALINCONICO, L. L. & WILLIAMS, S. N. 1983. Use of the correlation spectrometer at volcanoes. *In:* TAZIEFF, H. & SABROUX, J. C. (eds) *Forecasting Volcanic Events*. Elsevier, Amsterdam, 425–444.

US Committee on Extension to the Standard Atmosphere. 1976. US Standard Atmosphere. US Government Printing Office, Washington, D.C.

Volcanic eruption detection by the Total Ozone Mapping Spectrometer (TOMS) instruments: a 22-year record of sulphur dioxide and ash emissions

S. A. CARN[1], A. J. KRUEGER[1], G. J. S. BLUTH[2], S. J. SCHAEFER[1], N. A. KROTKOV[3], I. M. WATSON[2] & S. DATTA[1]

[1]*Joint Center for Earth Systems Technology (NASA/UMBC), University of Maryland Baltimore County, 1000 Hilltop Circle, Baltimore, MD 21250, USA.*
(e-mail: scarn@umbc.edu)
[2]*Department of Geological Engineering and Sciences, Michigan Technological University, 1400 Townsend Drive, Houghton, MI 49931, USA.*
[3]*Goddard Earth Sciences and Technology (GEST) Center, Code 916, NASA Goddard Space Flight Center, Greenbelt, MD 20771, USA.*

Abstract: Since their first deployment in November 1978, the Total Ozone Mapping Spectrometer (TOMS) instruments have provided a robust and near-continuous record of sulphur dioxide (SO_2) and ash emissions from active volcanoes worldwide. Data from the four TOMS satellites that have flown to date have been analysed with the latest SO_2/ash algorithms and incorporated into a TOMS volcanic emissions database that presently covers 22 years of SO_2 and ash emissions. The 1978–2001 record comprises 102 eruptions from 61 volcanoes, resulting in 784 days of volcanic cloud observations. Regular eruptions of Nyamuragira (DR Congo) since 1978, accompanied by copious SO_2 production, have contributed material on approximately 30% of the days on which clouds were observed. The latest SO_2 retrieval results from Earth Probe (EP) TOMS document a period (1996–2001) lacking large explosive eruptions, and also dominated by SO_2 emission from four eruptions of Nyamuragira. EP TOMS has detected the SO_2 and ash produced during 23 eruptions from 15 volcanoes to date, with volcanic clouds observed on 158 days. The EP TOMS instrument began to degrade in 2001, but has now stabilized, although its planned successor (QuikTOMS) recently failed to achieve orbit. New SO_2 algorithms are currently being developed for the Ozone Monitoring Instrument, which will continue the TOMS record of UV remote sensing of volcanic emissions from 2004 onwards.

Volcanic eruptions vary greatly in style, duration and vigour, but all sub-aerial eruptions involve the emplacement of material, typically including water vapour and other gases, silicate ash, and aerosols, into the atmosphere above the eruption vent. The detection, analysis and tracking of the ensuing volcanic clouds and plumes is crucial for effective mitigation of volcanic hazards such as airborne ash (e.g. Casadevall 1994), understanding of magmatic degassing processes (e.g. Scaillet *et al.* 1998; Wallace 2001) and quantifying effects of volcanic emissions on the Earth's atmosphere-climate system (e.g. Robock 2000). Satellite remote sensing has made an indispensable contribution to volcanic cloud studies over the past few decades, by providing regular, synoptic views of gas and ash clouds, and quantitative information on their composition, as they are erupted and dispersed over areas that may range from hundreds to millions of square kilometres (e.g. Oppenheimer 1998*a*).

One of the first space-borne instruments to provide quantitative data on the mass and spatial distribution of two important volcanic cloud components (sulphur dioxide (SO_2) and volcanic ash) was the Total Ozone Mapping Spectrometer (TOMS), which was first deployed on the Nimbus-7 (N7) satellite in 1978 (Heath *et al.* 1975). TOMS was developed to produce daily global maps of the spatial variation of column

From: OPPENHEIMER, C., PYLE, D.M. & BARCLAY, J. (eds) *Volcanic Degassing*. Geological Society, London, Special Publications, **213**, 177–202. 0305–8719/03/$15.00
© The Geological Society of London 2003.

ozone amounts in the Earth's atmosphere using absorption bands in the ultraviolet (UV) spectral region from 300 to 340 nm (Krueger 1984). However, SO_2 and ozone have similar molecular structures, and hence SO_2 also has absorption bands in the UV region exploited by TOMS. When present in significant amounts, as in volcanic eruption clouds, SO_2 produces an 'apparent' ozone signal in the TOMS data which can be converted into a quantitative measurement of column SO_2 amounts (see Krueger et al. 1995 for a detailed description of the TOMS SO_2 algorithm). UV wavelengths measured by TOMS can also be used to locate and quantify the mass of UV-absorbing aerosols (e.g. silicate ash, desert dust, smoke from biomass burning) in the atmosphere and can also detect non-absorbing aerosols such as sulphate (Seftor et al. 1997; Torres et al. 1998). The TOMS Aerosol Index (AI) data can be used to derive ash masses in drifting volcanic clouds (Krotkov et al. 1997, 1999).

Although not the most abundant volcanic gas (water vapour (H_2O), carbon dioxide (CO_2) and occasionally hydrogen chloride (HCl) are produced in greater amounts; e.g. Delmelle & Stix 2000), SO_2 is one of the most important species, since SO_2 clouds in the atmosphere are ultimately converted into sulphate aerosol (over a period of minutes to weeks depending on altitude; e.g. Bluth et al. 1997; Oppenheimer et al. 1998a), which can have significant radiative effects especially if present in the stratosphere (e.g. Andres & Kasgnoc 1998; Stenchikov et al. 1998). Stratospheric sulphate aerosol layers scatter and absorb incident solar radiation and absorb emitted terrestrial radiation (Stenchikov et al. 1998), warming the upper atmosphere while cooling the lower atmosphere, and also promote heterogeneous chemical reactions that deplete the Earth's protective ozone layer (Prather 1992). Of all volcanic gases, SO_2 is also the principal species that is not subject to interference by other large sources or high background concentrations, making it an obvious target for remote sensing. Models predict background SO_2 values of less than 0.5 Dobson Units (DU; 1 $DU = 2.687 \times 10^{16}$ molecules/$cm^2 = 10$ parts per million metres or ppm m at STP) over much of the globe, with less than 3 DU over polluted regions of the Northern Hemisphere (Chin et al. 2000). In contrast, SO_2 column amounts in volcanic clouds can range from 30 to 1000 DU, with the maximum amounts observed in the centres of large, very fresh eruption clouds (Fig. 1).

The ability of TOMS to map SO_2 in addition to ozone was not realized until 1982, when the SO_2-rich clouds produced by the eruption of the Mexican volcano El Chichón (Fig. 1) were serendipitously detected in TOMS Ozone data (Krueger 1983). In 1984, during real-time processing of TOMS data for the Mauna Loa eruption in Hawaii, SO_2 clouds were discovered emerging from the volcanic Isla Fernandina (Galápagos Islands), and later verified as the result of an effusive eruption, marking the first instance of an eruption 'early warning' using TOMS. These discoveries initiated two decades of SO_2 algorithm development and research into volcanic emissions using TOMS data, resulting in significant contributions to our understanding of volcanic degassing, volcanic hazards, and the impact of volcanic eruptions on the Earth's atmosphere (see Krueger et al. 2000 for a review).

N7 TOMS operated for almost 15 years (Table 1), and its lifetime spanned a period of heightened volcanic activity that included the major explosive eruptions of Mount St Helens (USA) in 1980, El Chichón in 1982, and most notably Pinatubo (Philippines) in 1991 (Fig. 1; Bluth et al. 1992). Data collected by N7 TOMS allowed the first quantitative assessments of the contribution to the atmospheric sulphur budget from individual volcanic eruptions (Krueger et al. 1990; Bluth et al. 1992, 1994, 1995; Schnetzler et al. 1994; Constantine et al. 2000) and from long-term explosive volcanism (Bluth et al. 1993, 1997; Pyle et al. 1996). Meteor-3 (M3) TOMS flew in tandem with N7 until the latter failed in 1993. Then, following the end of the M3 mission in December 1994, there was a gap of approximately 19 months before the Earth Probe (EP) satellite recommenced the TOMS program in July 1996 (Table 1). A fourth TOMS was launched on the Japanese Advanced Earth Observing Satellite (ADEOS) in September 1996, but unfortunately the satellite failed prematurely the following year. EP TOMS had initially been flown in a low orbit (500 km, producing a nadir footprint of 24×24 km; Table 1) to provide increased sensitivity, at the expense of gaps between successive orbits in equatorial latitudes, whilst ADEOS TOMS (in a higher orbit at c.800 km) provided global coverage. However, following the demise of ADEOS, EP's orbit was raised (to 739 km, producing a nadir footprint of 39×39 km; Table 1) with its remaining fuel in order to maximize the coverage of the one remaining TOMS satellite. EP TOMS is still operational at the time of writing (June 2002), although its orbit is not sufficiently high to provide contiguous daily coverage in equatorial latitudes (between c.30°N and c.30°S). A fifth TOMS launch was attempted in September 2001, but the QuikTOMS satellite

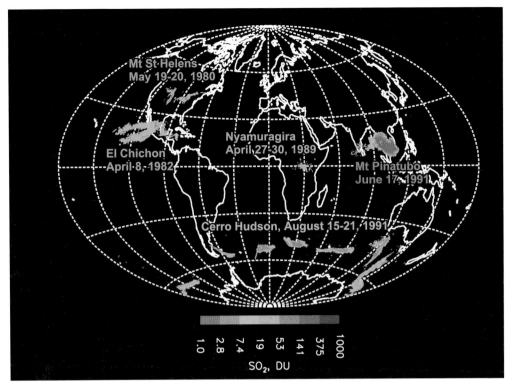

Fig. 1. Composite map of several large volcanic SO$_2$ clouds measured by Nimbus-7 TOMS between 1978 and 1993 (Krueger *et al.* 2000). The SO$_2$ clouds shown were produced by eruptions of Mount St Helens (USA; 18 May 1980; *c.*1 Mt SO$_2$), El Chichón (Mexico; 4 April 1982; *c.*7 Mt), Nyamuragira (DR Congo; 24 April 1989), Pinatubo (Philippines; 15 June 1991; *c.*20 Mt) and Cerro Hudson (Chile; 15 August 1991; *c.*2.7 Mt). Scale is in Dobson Units (DU).

which had been due to replace the aging EP TOMS regrettably failed to achieve orbit.

In this chapter we present the latest results of a complete re-analysis of the TOMS database using the latest algorithms, covering 22 years of volcanic emissions. TOMS data have been analysed for all eruptions listed in the available historic records of volcanism (e.g. Simkin & Siebert 1994), and all detected eruptions have been documented. The only potential omissions are eruptions or volcanic clouds from remote volcanoes that remain undetected or observed by other means. Such emissions could yet emerge from the daily TOMS record, though this would involve detailed analysis of each day's data for each active volcano since 1978. We stress, therefore, that the database does not represent a definitive record of volcanic activity between 1978 and 2001, but rather a record of all significant emissions of SO$_2$ and/or ash to the upper troposphere and stratosphere in that period.

On-going development and updating of the TOMS algorithms has produced some variability in retrieved volcanic cloud characteristics depending on the algorithm version that is employed. Most previously published work by the TOMS volcanic emissions group has utilized version 6 data from N7 TOMS (e.g. Bluth *et al.* 1992, 1993, 1997), whereas the algorithms currently in use are the version 7 production algorithms (also referred to as the sulphur dioxide index or SOI, and the AI for ash and aerosols; McPeters *et al.* 1998) and a more accurate iterative SO$_2$ retrieval scheme developed within our group (Krueger *et al.* 1995). For this paper, to establish which eruptions were detected, TOMS data from all 4 satellites have been analysed using the version 7 algorithms. The principal factor governing whether a volcanic cloud is detected or not is thus the differing sensitivity of the 4 TOMS satellites (Table 1): a result of varying footprint size and slight shifts in measured wavelengths. The iterative SO$_2$ algorithm is used to accurately

Table 1. *TOMS missions 1978-2001.*

Satellite	Activation/ Ending dates	Nadir footprint (km)	SO₂ detection limit (t)*	Eruptive events detected[†]	Days tracked[‡]
Nimbus-7	November 1, 1978 6 May 1993	50	10 700 (1σ=6 DU)	135	557
Meteor-3	22 August 1991 24 December 1994	62	16 460 (1σ=6 DU)	29	110
Earth Probe	17 July 1996 Operating, June 2002	24 (Launch – Sept 97) 39 (Nov 9– present)	1440 (1σ=3.5 DU) 3800 (1σ=3.5 DU)	39	158
ADEOS	11 September , 1996 June 30, 1997	42	3780 (1σ=3 DU)	4	24
QuikTOMS	Failed at launch, 21 September, 2001	42	–	–	–

*Computed for a cluster of 5 nadir pixels at 5σ (1σ is defined as the standard deviation of the combined noise due to instrument, measurement, retrieval, and random errors); DU=Dobson Units or milli atm cm.
[†]Gives the total number of eruptive events detected by each TOMS mission. 'Eruptive events' are defined as discrete eruptive episodes that are clearly separable in time from preceding or subsequent episodes, while 'eruptions' are classified according to Simkin & Siebert (1994) for pre-1994 eruptions and similarly for post-1994 eruptions.
[‡]Gives the total number of days of TOMS volcanic cloud observations for each mission.

calculate SO₂ tonnages contained in volcanic clouds. Tonnages have been calculated in this way for all EP TOMS volcanic cloud data, but have yet to be completed for N7 and M3 TOMS data. Our long-term goal is to retrieve SO₂ tonnages for all eruptions detected by N7 and M3 TOMS using the iterative algorithm, to produce a fully consistent time-series of volcanic SO₂ loading from 1978 onwards.

Hence our aim in this paper is to catalogue every eruption detected by TOMS in the period 1978–2001, and also to focus in more detail on recent results from EP TOMS since its launch in 1996. A subsidiary aim is to refute any notion that TOMS detects only the large, stratospheric volcanic clouds such as those produced by the eruption of Pinatubo in 1991 (Fig. 1; Bluth *et al.* 1992). Although uniquely able to image these huge clouds, TOMS is also able to provide useful quantitative information on the SO₂ and ash released by eruptive events of lower magnitude or explosivity, such as those with a Volcanic Explosivity Index (VEI) of 3 (Newhall & Self 1982; for a more detailed comparison between VEI and SO₂ emissions see Schnetzler *et al.* (1997)), that occur far more frequently, and is thus an important source of data for volcanic emissions research, hazard assessments and airborne hazard mitigation.

We also look ahead to the next generation of UV remote-sensing instruments and consider the potential capabilities of the Ozone Monitoring Instrument (OMI), due to be launched on the EOS/Aura satellite in 2004, with regard to volcanic emissions. OMI and other UV instruments such as the Scanning Imaging Absorption Spectrometer for Atmospheric Cartography (SCIAMACHY; launched on the European Space Agency's Envisat-1 satellite in March 2002) will offer many improvements over TOMS and will build on the 22-year heritage of the TOMS instruments that is discussed in this chapter.

The TOMS volcanic emissions database

Overview

The TOMS volcanic emissions database is an archive of eruption data amassed by current and previous members of our group over the lifetime of the TOMS instruments. It is by no means a comprehensive list of all the volcanic eruptions that have occurred in this period, as such lists have been exhaustively compiled elsewhere (e.g. Simkin & Siebert 1994), but an inventory of all eruptions that produced sufficient SO₂ and/or ash to be detected in TOMS imagery (TOMS images and an eruption inventory can be viewed on the TOMS volcanic emissions website; http://skye.gsfc.nasa.gov).

TOMS detection limits

TOMS detection limits have varied over time, as the four satellites that have carried a TOMS instrument to date have been flown at different altitudes, producing different footprint areas (Table 1). EP and ADEOS TOMS wavelengths were also optimized for SO_2 detection, resulting in lower noise levels (Table 1; Gurevich & Krueger 1997), and SO_2 absorption cross-section data have improved over the years. Smaller footprint areas result in increased sensitivity, such that smaller amounts of SO_2/ash can be detected, and lower instrument noise levels mean that less SO_2/ash is required to produce a recognizable signal above the background. These concepts are discussed in greater detail in Krueger *et al.* (1995) and Gurevich & Krueger (1997).

Detection limits in Table 1 are computed for a representative volcanic SO_2 cloud signal of 5 anomalous TOMS nadir pixels, each at 5σ (5 sigma) above the background. Such a signal observed close to a volcano near the time of a known eruption would be easily identifiable as a volcanic cloud, although in practice smaller signals may also be classified as volcanic in origin. This is largely dependent on the data analyst and the noise level of the data in the area of interest, thus the limits in Table 1 are given as a guide to the size of signal that would be unambiguously identified as volcanic for each of the TOMS satellites, in nadir-view data. The TOMS footprint increases in size considerably towards the edges of each swath (e.g. McPeters *et al.* 1998), increasing the detection limit of the sensor. The EP TOMS footprint increases in area by a factor of 6 from nadir to the swath edges, with a commensurate increase in the detection limit. A more detailed study of TOMS SO_2 retrieval accuracy and error analysis was carried out by Krueger *et al.* (1995).

Detection limits for ash clouds are more difficult to quantify, since ash mass retrievals are not routinely performed using TOMS data. TOMS AI data are mainly used for the detection and tracking of ash and aerosols (e.g. Seftor *et al.* 1997), although quantitative information on ash/aerosol properties can be retrieved (Krotkov *et al.* 1997, 1999). The TOMS AI is a dimensionless quantity, for which meteorological (water) clouds yield approximately zero, and ash clouds yield increasingly positive values. The densest ash clouds produce AI values of 10 or higher, with a noise level of c. 0.2 AI units for N7 TOMS (Krotkov *et al.* 1999).

Timing is also a factor that impacts the likelihood of TOMS detection of an eruption. In mid-latitudes TOMS overpasses occur once per day, typically around local noon, whilst at higher latitudes the successive TOMS orbits converge and increase the frequency of coverage. TOMS does not function at night, being a UV sensor that measures backscattered solar radiation. Thus a mid-latitude eruptive event occurring just after the daily TOMS overpass will be missed, unless it is of sufficient magnitude to produce a cloud that persists for at least 24 hours. Similarly, a small eruption occurring just a few hours before the TOMS overpass may be missed if the resulting cloud disperses quickly. These issues are mainly applicable to smaller events, many of which are missed by TOMS simply due to unfortunate timing.

Description of the database

We have categorized the current TOMS volcanic emissions database in a number of ways to illustrate the distribution of TOMS-detected eruptions by satellite, volcano, geographic location, volcano type and tectonic setting (Tables 1–6). Note the distinction between 'eruptive events' and 'eruptions' that is explained in Table 1. Thus a single (usually explosive) eruption may comprise many discrete events (e.g. the 1982–1983 eruption of Galunggung, Java; Bluth *et al.* 1994), whereas effusive eruptions, which typically involve continuous activity for a period of days or weeks precluding separation of individual events, may be classified as a single event/eruption. We use this distinction to convey a sense of the number of individual volcanic clouds detected by TOMS, particularly for prolonged eruptions that may actually involve multiple significant SO_2 and/or ash emissions. 'Days tracked' gives a sense of the longevity of effusive eruptions, being simply a count of the number of days on which volcanic clouds were observed, and of the lifetime of explosively released volcanic clouds as SO_2 is scavenged or converted to sulphate aerosol and ash sediments out.

Tables 2–6 integrate data from each of the 4 TOMS satellites that have operated to date (Table 1). As mentioned above, calculation of actual SO_2 loadings from N7 and M3 TOMS data is on-going, and hence SO_2 tonnages are not given for all eruptive events in these tables. For completeness and as a guide to the magnitude of emissions between 1978 and 1994, in Table 3 we reproduce earlier TOMS version 6 SO_2 data (published by Bluth *et al.* (1997)) for a subset of

Table 2. *TOMS volcanic emissions database (1978–2001), organized by volcano.*

Volcano[1]	Latitude	Type[2]	Events[3] (%)	SO₂ events[4]	Dates[5]	Ash events[6]	Dates[5]	Eruptions*	Days tracked† (%)
Alaid	50.9° N	St	2 (1.0)	2	4/28, 5/8/81	0		1	14 (1.8)
Ambrym	16.3° S	St	2 (1.0)	2	11/15/86, 4/24/89	0		2	7 (0.9)
Augustine	59.4°N	LD	1 (0.5)	1	3/27/86	0		1	1 (0.1)
Banda Api	4.5°N	C	1 (0.5)	1	5/9/88	0		1	3 (0.4)
Bezymianny	56.0°N	St	5 (2.5)	2	10/13/84, 6/12/85	3	2/12/79, 4/18/80, 5/8/97	5	7 (0.9)
Bulusan	12.8°N	St	1 (0.5)	0		1	2/7/80	1	1 (0.1)
Cameroon	4.2°N	St	2 (1.0)	2	10/18/82, 3/30/99	0		2	5 (0.6)
Canlaon	10.4°N	St	1 (0.5)	1	3/14/85	0		1	1 (0.1)
Cerro Azul	16.3° S	Sh	2 (1.0)	2	2/1/79, 9/16/98	0		1	1 (0.1)
Cerro Hudson	45.9° S	St	3 (1.5)	3	1991: 8/9, 8/13, 8/15	0		2	34 (4.3)
Cerro Negro	12.5°N	CC	1 (0.5)	0		1	4/10/92	1	20 (2.6)
Chikurachki	50.3°N	St	1 (0.5)	1	11/20/86	0		1	6 (0.8)
Cleveland	52.8°N	St	3 (1.5)	1	2/19/01	2	3/11, 3/20/01	3	8 (1.0)
Colo	0.2° S	St	10 (5.1)	2	1983: 7/24, 8/2	8	1983: 7/26, 7/28, 7/31, 8/4, 8/7, 8/11, 8/18, 8/26		3 (0.4)
El Chichón	17.4°N	LD	4 (2.0)	4	1982: 3/29, 4/2, 4/3, 4/4	0		1	14 (1.8)
Etna	37.7°N	Sh	3 (1.5)	3	9/2/80, 9/6/80, 7/25/01	0		2	33 (4.2)
Fernandina	0.4° S	Sh	3 (1.5)	3	3/30/84, 9/15/88, 4/20/91	0		3	6 (0.8)
Galunggung	7.3° S	St	24 (12.2)	24	Apr–Sept 1982‡	0		1	16 (2.0)
Gamalama	0.8° N	St	2 (1.0)	1	8/9/83	1	4/26/90	2	33 (4.2)
Heard	53.1° S	St	1 (0.5)	1	1/14/85	0		1	2 (0.3)
Hekla	64.0°N	St	2 (1.0)	2	8/18/80, 2/27/00	0		2	1 (0.1)
Karkar	4.6° S	St	2 (1.0)	2	3/8/79, 5/30/79	0		1	5 (0.6)
Kelut	7.9° S	St	1 (0.5)	1	2/11/90	0		1	5 (0.6)
Kliuchevskoi	56.1°N	St	3 (1.5)	3	2/19/87, 1/30/90, 10/1/94	0		2	2 (0.3)
Krafla	65.7°N	C	3 (1.5)	3	7/11/80, 10/19/80, 9/5/84	0		3	6 (0.8)
Langila	5.5° S	CV	1 (0.5)	1	2/14/97	0		1	23 (2.9)
Lascar	23.3° S	St	1 (0.5)	1	4/19/93	0		1	1 (0.1)
Lonquimay	38.4° S	St	1 (0.5)	0		1	12/27/88	1	7 (0.9)
Lopevi	16.5° S	St	1 (0.5)	1	10/25/82	0		1	21 (2.7)
Makian	0.3° N	St	1 (0.5)	1	7/29/88	0		1	1 (0.1)
Makushin	53.9°N	St	1 (0.5)	1	5/1/80	0		1	7 (1.1)
Manam	4.1° S	St	2 (1.0)	2	2/8/97, 10/5/98	0		2	1 (0.2)
Marchena	0.3° N	Sh	1 (0.5)	1	9/26/91	0		1	3 (0.4)
Mauna Loa	19.5°N	Sh	1 (0.5)	1	3/25/84	0		1	3 (0.4)
Mayon	13.3°N	St	1 (0.5)	1	9/13/84	0		1	15 (1.9)
Merapi	7.5° S	St	2 (1.0)	0		2	6/15/84, 11/23/94	1	4 (0.5)
Miyake-jima	34.1°N	St	1 (0.5)	1	8/19/00	0		2	14 (1.8)
Mount St Helens	46.2°N	St	6 (3.1)	3	1980: 5/18, 5/25, 6/13	3	1980: 7/23, 8/8, 10/17	1	12 (1.5)

Volcano[1]	Latitude	Type[2]	No.[3]	SO₂[4]	Dates[5]	Ash[6]	Dates[5]	No.*	Days†
Nyamuragira	1.4°S	Sh	12 (6.1)	12	2/1/80, 12/26/81, 2/24/84, 7/17/86, 12/31/87, 4/25/89, 9/24/91, 7/5/94, 12/1/96, 10/18/98, 1/28/00, 2/6/01	0		12	208 (26.5)
Oshima	34.7°N	St	1 (0.5)	1	11/20/86	0	3/9/89	1	1 (0.1)
Pacaya	14.4°N	CV	1 (0.5)	0		1		1	2 (0.3)
Pagan	18.1°N	St	1 (0.5)	1	5/15/81	0		1	2 (0.3)
Pavlof	55.4°N	St	4 (2.0)	2	11/15/83, 4/19/86	2	11/11/80, 12/15/83	3	6 (0.8)
Pinatubo	15.1°N	St	3 (1.5)	3	1991: 6/12, 6/13, 6/15	0		1	60 (7.7)
Popocatépetl	19.0°N	St	5 (2.5)	5	7/3/97, 11/25/98, 12/15/00, 12/19/00, 4/29/01	0		1	6 (0.8)
Rabaul	4.3°S	PS	1 (0.5)	1	9/19/94	0		1	5 (0.6)
Redoubt	60.5°N	St	8 (4.1)	2	12/16/89, 3/9/90	6	1990: 1/8, 2/15, 3/5, 3/23, 4/15, 4/21	1	9 (1.2)
Rinjani	8.4°S	St	17 (8.6)	7	1994: 6/7–6/12, 6/15	10	1994: 6/14, 6/18, 6/19, 6/22, 6/26, 7/2, 7/4, 7/18, 8/3	1	23 (2.9)
Ruiz	4.9°N	St	3 (1.5)	3	9/12/85, 11/14/85, 9/1/89	0		1	7 (0.9)
Sangeang Api	8.2°S	CV	1 (0.5)	0		1	7/31/85	1	1 (0.1)
Shishaldin	54.8°N	St	3 (1.5)	1	4/19/99	0		1	3 (0.4)
Shiveluch	56.7°N	St	3 (1.5)	0		3	6/18/81, 4/22/93, 5/21/01	3	4 (0.5)
Sierra Negra	0.8°S	Sh	1 (0.5)	1	11/13/79	0		1	24 (3.1)
Soputan	1.1°S	St	8 (4.1)	5	8/27/82, 11/10/82, 5/24/84, 8/31/84, 5/20/85	3	9/17/82, 9/18/82, 4/23/89	5	15 (1.9)
Soufrière Hills	16.7°N	St	10 (5.1)	4	12/26/97, 7/3/98, 7/20/99, 7/30/01	6	1997: 8/7, 8/8, 9/25, 9/27, 10/18, 10/19	5	10 (1.3)
Souf. St Vincent	13.3°N	St	2 (1.0)	1	4/13/79	1	4/18/79	1	2 (0.3)
Spurr	61.3°N	St	3 (1.5)	3	1992: 6/27, 8/18, 9/17	0		1	21 (2.7)
Tungurahua	1.5°S	St	3 (1.5)	3	10/17/99, 11/16/99, 8/6/01	0		1	3 (0.4)
Ulawun	5.1°S	St	4 (2.0)	4	10/7/80, 11/20/85, 9/28/00, 4/30/01	0		4	12 (1.5)
Westdahl	54.5°N	St	1 (0.5)	0		1	2/8/79	1	1 (0.1)
Wolf	0°	Sh	1 (0.5)	1	8/29/82	0		1	12 (1.5)

[1]Volcanoes in italics indicate the weakest volcanic cloud signals (typically 1–2 anomalous pixels slightly above noise levels in the region of the volcano on dates of known eruptive events).

[2]Follows the classification of Simkin & Siebert (1994). C, caldera; CC, cinder cone(s); CV, complex volcano; LD, lava dome(s); PS, pyroclastic shield; Sh, shield volcano; St, Stratovolcano.

[3]Gives the number of eruptive events detected by TOMS for each volcano. Percentage of the total (197) given in parentheses.

[4]Gives the number of eruptive events that produced detectable SO₂ for each volcano. These events may have produced SO₂ only, or SO₂ and ash.

[5]Gives the date of first detection of each eruptive event by TOMS; a date range implies detection of an eruptive event on each consecutive day between the two dates (inclusive).

[6]Gives the number of eruptive events that only produced detectable ash (in TOMS AI data) for each volcano (i.e. no detectable SO₂).

*Gives the number of eruptions detected by TOMS for each volcano (total = 102).

†Gives the total number of days of TOMS volcanic cloud observations for each volcano. Percentage of the total (784) given in parentheses.

‡For full list of dates see Bluth et al. (1994).

Table 3. *TOMS SO₂ tonnages for VEI ≥ 3 eruptions, 1979-1994**

Volcano	Eruption date[†]	VEI	TOMS SO₂ (Mt)
Sierra Negra	11/13/79	3	1.2
Nyamuragira	1/30/80	3	0.2
Mount St Helens	5/18/80	5	1.0
Hekla	8/17/80	3	0.5
Ulawun	10/6/80	3	0.2
Alaid	4/27/81	3	1.1
Pagan	5/15/81	4	0.3
Nyamuragira	12/25/81	3	4.0
El Chichón	4/4/82	5	7.0
Galunggung	6/24/82	3	0.4
Galunggung	7/13/82	3	0.4
Colo	7/23/83	4	0.2
Pavlof	11/14/83	3	0.05
Soputan	5/24/84	3	0.2
Ruiz	11/13/85	3	0.7
Ulawun	11/20/85	3	0.08
Augustine	3/27/86	4	<0.05
Nyamuragira	7/16/86	4	0.8
Chikurachki	11/19/86	3	0.7
Banda Api	5/9/88	3	0.2
Makian	7/17/88	3	0.05
Redoubt	12/14/89	3	0.2
Kelut	2/11/90	4	<0.05
Pinatubo	6/15/91	6	20
Cerro Hudson	8/8/91	3	0.7
Cerro Hudson	8/12/91	5	3.3
Spurr	6/27/92	3	0.2
Spurr	8/18/92	3	0.4
Spurr	9/17/92	3	0.23
Láscar	4/19/93	3	0.4
Rabaul	9/19/94	4	0.2
Kliuchevskoi	10/1/94	4	0.1

*All data from Bluth *et al.* (1997), using version 6 of the TOMS SO₂ algorithm, except that for the 1991 Cerro Hudson eruptions, which is combined version 6 and 7 data from Constantine *et al.* (2000). Some eruption dates have been updated.
[†]Eruption date = date of eruption associated with the SO₂ emissions measured by TOMS (does not always correspond with the date of TOMS detection of SO₂).

Using the criteria defined above, the 1978–2001 TOMS database currently comprises 197 eruptive events and 102 eruptions from 61 volcanoes, producing a total of 784 days of volcanic cloud observations. Figure 2 charts the yearly totals of these parameters through the TOMS era to date. The 197 events can be further broken down into 141 (*c.*72%) involving detectable SO₂ emission and 56 (*c.*28%) lacking detectable SO₂ that were detected in TOMS AI data by virtue of ash emission only. Of the 197 events, 151 (*c.*77%) are associated with predominantly explosive eruptions and 46 (*c.*23%) with eruptions of a predominantly effusive nature (NB: slow effusion of viscous, silicic magma as in lava dome eruptions is not regarded as effusive in this case). This reflects the generally higher altitudes reached by explosively released volcanic clouds, which renders them more conducive to detection by TOMS (e.g. Krueger *et al.* 1995); explosive eruption clouds are more likely to penetrate meteorological cloud decks that hinder detection of lower-level clouds, and to reach sufficient altitudes above the mean penetration level of UV light to produce high signal to noise ratios. In terms of VEI, which is predominantly based on tephra mass and eruption column height (Newhall & Self 1982), using Simkin & Siebert's (1994) compilation of VEI data for eruptions between 1978 and 1993 indicates that TOMS instruments have detected 100% of eruptions of VEI 4 or above (consisting of 1 VEI=6, 3 VEI=5 and 10 VEI=4 eruptions) and *c.*60% of eruptions (or eruptive events) with a VEI of 3. Of the eruptions listed with VEIs of 2, 1 and 0 from 1978–1993, TOMS detected 3.8%, 1.4%, and 2.6% respectively. Although these eruptions are classed as being of low explosivity (typically effusive eruptions), the few eruptions in this class that TOMS detects probably involve sufficient thermal energy (perhaps from fire-fountaining activity) to loft large amounts of SO₂ to the upper troposphere (Stothers *et al.* 1986).

Volcanoes with TOMS-detected eruptions

Table 2 lists the 61 volcanoes responsible for the 102 eruptions detected by TOMS since 1978. A more complete list of dates of volcanic cloud observations and many volcanic cloud images can be viewed on our group website (http://skye.gsfc.nasa.gov). The geographical distribution of these volcanoes exhibits a significant bias towards the Northern Hemisphere, with 37 (61%) situated north of the equator and 24 (39%) to the south (Wolf volcano in the Galápagos Islands, listed with a latitude of 0° (Table 2), is in

the pre-1995 events listed in Table 2. However, combining version 6 SO₂ tonnages from N7/M3 (e.g. Bluth *et al.* 1993, 1997) with the new EP TOMS tonnages will not be strictly valid until the N7 and M3 data are processed with the iterative SO₂ algorithm, although analysis to date suggests that, in the majority of cases, the iterative SO₂ tonnages will only differ from the version 6 data by a few per cent at most. In any case, this will not affect the inventory of TOMS-detected eruptions presented here. EP TOMS SO₂ data since 1996 are presented in a later section of this chapter.

Table 4. *TOMS volcanic emissions database (1978–2001) organized by volcano region.*

Subregion/region[1]	Volcanoes[2] (%)	Events[3] (%)	Eruptions[4]	Days tracked[5] (%)
Italy	1 (1.6)	3 (1.5)	2	6 (0.8)
Europe to Caucasus – total	**1 (1.6)**	**3 (1.5)**	**2**	**6 (0.8)**
Africa – W and N	1 (1.6)	2 (1.0)	2	5 (0.6)
Africa – Kenya to Zaire	1 (1.6)	12 (6.1)	12	208 (26.5)
Africa and Red Sea – total	**2 (3.3)**	**14 (7.1)**	**14**	**213 (27.2)**
Indian Ocean	1 (1.6)	1 (0.5)	1	1 (0.1)
Mid-East & Indian Ocean – total	**1 (1.6)**	**1 (0.5)**	**1**	**1 (0.1)**
New Zealand to Fiji – total	0	0	0	0
Vanuatu and S	2 (3.3)	3 (1.5)	3	8 (1.0)
Offshore New Guinea & Admiralty Is.	2 (3.3)	4 (2.0)	3	8 (1.0)
New Britain	3 (4.9)	6 (3.1)	6	18 (2.3)
Melanesia & Australia – total	**7 (11.4)**	**13 (6.6)**	**12**	**34 (4.3)**
Sulawesi	2 (3.3)	18 (9.1)	6	29 (3.7)
Lesser Sunda Islands	2 (3.3)	18 (9.1)	2	24 (3.1)
Java	3 (4.9)	27 (13.7)	4	37 (4.7)
Halmahera	2 (3.3)	3 (1.5)	3	9 (1.2)
Banda Sea	1 (1.6)	1 (0.5)	1	3 (0.4)
Indonesia and Andaman Islands – total	**10 (16.4)**	**67 (34.0)**	**14**	**102 (13.0)**
Philippines – N	3 (4.9)	5 (2.5)	3	65 (8.3)
Philippines – Central	1 (1.6)	1 (0.5)	1	1 (0.1)
Philippines and SE Asia - total	**4 (6.6)**	**6 (3.1)**	**4**	**66 (8.4)**
Mariana Islands	1 (1.6)	1 (0.5)	1	2 (0.3)
Izu and Volcano Islands	2 (3.3)	2 (1.0)	2	15 (1.9)
Japan, Taiwan, and Marianas – total	**3 (4.9)**	**3 (1.5)**	**3**	**17 (2.2)**
Kuriles – total	2 (3.3)	3 (1.5)	2	22 (2.8)
Kamchatka – total	3 (4.9)	11 (5.6)	10	17 (2.2)
Aleutian Islands	4 (6.6)	6 (3.1)	6	8 (1.0)
Alaska – Peninsula and SW	4 (6.6)	16 (8.1)	6	37 (4.7)
Alaska – total	**8 (13.1)**	**22 (11.2)**	**12**	**45 (5.7)**
USA – W Coast states	1 (1.6)	6 (3.1)	1	12 (1.5)
Canada and Western USA – total	**1 (1.6)**	**6 (3.1)**	**1**	**12 (1.5)**
Hawaii	1 (1.6)	1 (0.5)	1	15 (1.9)
Hawaii & Pacific Ocean – total	**1 (1.6)**	**1 (0.5)**	**1**	**15 (1.9)**
Nicaragua	1 (1.6)	1 (0.5)	1	6 (0.8)
Mexico – S	1 (1.6)	4 (2.0)	1	33 (4.2)
Mexico – Central Belt and Durango	1 (1.6)	5 (2.5)	1	6 (0.8)
Guatemala	1 (1.6)	1 (0.5)	1	2 (0.3)
Mexico and Central America – total	**4 (6.6)**	**11 (5.6)**	**4**	**47 (6.0)**
Galápagos Islands	5 (8.2)	8 (4.1)	8	89 (11.4)
Ecuador	1 (1.6)	3 (1.5)	1	3 (0.4)
Colombia	1 (1.6)	3 (1.5)	1	7 (0.9)
Chile – S and Argentina	1 (1.6)	3 (1.5)	1	20 (2.6)
Chile – N, Bolivia and Argentina	1 (1.6)	1 (0.5)	1	7 (0.9)
Chile – C and Argentina	1 (1.6)	1 (0.5)	1	21 (2.7)
South America – total	**10 (16.4)**	**19 (9.6)**	**13**	**147 (18.8)**
West Indies – total	**2 (3.3)**	**12 (6.1)**	**2**	**12 (1.5)**
Iceland – S	1 (1.6)	2 (1.0)	2	5 (0.6)
Iceland – NE	1 (1.6)	3 (1.5)	3	23 (2.9)
Iceland and Arctic Ocean – total	**2 (3.3)**	**5 (2.5)**	**5**	**28 (3.6)**
Atlantic Ocean – total	**0**	**0**	**0**	**0**
Antarctica and S Sandwich Islands – total	**0**	**0**	**0**	**0**

[1]Volcano regions and named subregions correspond with those in Simkin & Siebert (1994).
[2]Gives the number of volcanoes in each region/subregion responsible for eruptions detected by TOMS. Percentage of the total (61) given in parentheses.
[3]Gives the number of eruptive events in each region/subregion detected by TOMS. Percentage of the total (197) given in parentheses.
[4]Gives the number of eruptions in each region/subregion detected by TOMS.
[5]Gives the total number of days of TOMS volcanic cloud observations for each region/subregion. Percentage of the total (784) given in parentheses.

Table 5. *TOMS volcanic emissions database (1978–2001) organized by volcano type*

Volcano type[1]	Volcanoes[2] (%)	Events[3] (%)	Eruptions[4]	Days tracked[5] (%)
Stratovolcanoes	44 (72)	159 (81)	68	390 (50)
Shields	8 (13)	24 (12)	23	318 (41)
Lava domes	2 (3.3)	5 (2.5)	2	34 (4.3)
Calderas	2 (3.3)	4 (2.0)	4	26 (3.3)
Complex volcanoes	3 (4.9)	3 (1.5)	3	4 (0.5)
Cinder cones	1 (1.6)	1 (0.5)	1	6 (0.8)
Pyroclastic shields	1 (1.6)	1 (0.5)	1	5 (0.6)

[1]Volcano classification corresponds with that in Simkin & Siebert (1994).
[2]Gives the number of volcanoes of each type responsible for eruptions detected by TOMS. Percentage of the total (61) given in parentheses.
[3]Gives the number of eruptive events detected by TOMS for each volcano type. Percentage of the total (197) given in parentheses.
[4]Gives the number of eruptions detected by TOMS for each volcano type.
[5]Gives the total number of days of TOMS volcanic cloud observations for each volcano type. Percentage of the total (784) given in parentheses.

Table 6. *TOMS volcanic emissions database (1978–2001) organized by tectonic setting*

Volcano type[1]	Volcanoes[2] (%)	Events[3] (%)	Eruptions[4]	Days tracked[5] (%)
Subduction zones	50 (82)	168 (85)	73	438 (56)
Hot-spots	11 (18)	29 (15)	29	346 (44)
Rifts	4 (6.6)	19 (9.6)	19	241 (31)
Pacific Rim (including Indonesia)	47 (77)	153 (78)	69	419 (53)
Pacific Rim (excluding Indonesia)	37 (61)	86 (44)	53	317 (40)
Atlantic Region	4 (6.7)	17 (8.7)	7	40 (5.1)
Pacific Region	53 (87)	162 (82)	78	523 (67)

[1]*Hot-spots* covers Hawaii, Iceland, Galápagos Islands, DR Congo, Cameroon and the Indian Ocean; *Rifts* covers Iceland, DR Congo and Cameroon; *Atlantic Region* covers Iceland and the West Indies; *Pacific Region* covers the Pacific Rim (including Indonesia) plus Hawaii and the Galápagos Islands.
[2]Gives the number of volcanoes in each tectonic setting responsible for eruptions detected by TOMS. Percentage of the total (61) given in parentheses.
[3]Gives the number of eruptive events detected by TOMS for each tectonic setting. Percentage of the total (197) given in parentheses.
[4]Gives the number of eruptions detected by TOMS for each tectonic setting.
[5]Gives the total number of days of TOMS volcanic cloud observations for each tectonic setting. Percentage of the total (784) given in parentheses.

fact marginally in the southern hemisphere). Their distribution is furthermore biased towards tropical latitudes, with 38 (*c.*62%) situated between the Tropics of Cancer and Capricorn and 30 (c.49%) between 15° N and 15° S. Only 3 volcanoes (5%) lie further than 30° S, whereas 19 (*c.*31%) lie further than 30° N, of which 15 (25%) are at latitudes of 50° N or more (volcanoes in the Kuriles, Kamchatka, Aleutians, Alaska, and Iceland). The extremes of the distribution are occupied by Heard Island (in the southern Indian Ocean) and Krafla (Iceland).

Although volcanoes in high northern latitudes already comprise a significant proportion of the list, their contribution to the TOMS database would probably be greater were it not for the under-representation of eruptions in this region in the boreal winter months. High-latitude volcanoes suffer from insufficient UV levels during the winter, and thus a shorter TOMS detection 'window' (e.g. the December 1989 eruption cloud from Redoubt volcano, Alaska, was not detected until it drifted further south; Schnetzler *et al.* 1994), and persistent cloud cover may also be a problem. Furthermore, if eruption clouds from these volcanoes drift further north beyond the light terminator (the boundary between day and night) then they will also elude detection. High ozone levels at these latitudes may also obscure lower-level SO_2, though stratospheric plumes should still be detected. On the other hand, the decrease in the altitude of the

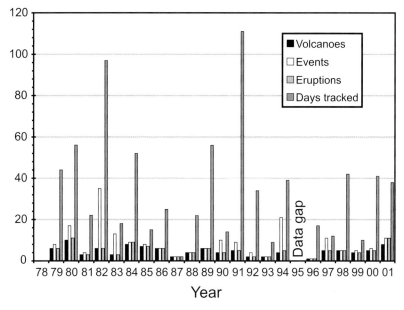

Fig. 2. Plot showing the number of: volcanoes with TOMS-detected eruptions, TOMS-detected eruptive events, TOMS-detected eruptions, and days of TOMS volcanic cloud observations for each year between 1978 and 2001. There was a data gap between Meteor-3 TOMS and EP TOMS in 1995.

tropopause from the equator (*c.*17 km) to the poles (*c.*11 km) may enhance detection in some circumstances, and the convergence of TOMS orbits towards the poles produces more frequent images at high latitudes.

Ranked in order of number of events, the list is dominated by the Indonesian volcanoes Galunggung, Rinjani, Colo, and Soputan, with 59 events (*c.*30% of the total) between them. With the exception of Rinjani, which was active in 1994, this is largely due to a remarkably active period of the early 1980s in Indonesia (mainly 1982–1983) when Galunggung, Colo and Soputan experienced multiple explosive eruptions, producing ash and SO_2 clouds that severely disrupted air traffic over Southeast Asia (Tootell 1985; Gourgaud *et al.* 1985), at a time when smoke from forest fires in Kalimantan was also creating large aerosol clouds over the region. Nyamuragira (Democratic Republic of Congo) has erupted every 1–2 years on average since 1978, giving a total of 12 eruptions (also classified as 12 events due to the continuous nature of most Nyamuragira eruptions), each involving production of copious SO_2 without any significant amounts of ash. The remainder of the volcanoes with at least five eruptive events in the database (Soufrière Hills, Redoubt, Mount St Helens, Popocatépetl, and Bezymianny) have all experienced, or are currently undergoing, dome-forming eruptions. This type of eruption is notorious for producing intermittent and often unpredictable explosive activity (e.g. Christiansen & Peterson 1981; Newhall & Melson 1983; Miller & Chouet 1994), as gas pressures within a growing lava dome periodically exceed the strength of the magma, precipitating explosive disruption of the dome (Sparks 1997). These volcanoes have thus produced multiple events in the TOMS database, although many have only one listed eruption (Table 2).

In terms of days tracked, the data-set is clearly dominated by Nyamuragira, which has 208 days (*c.*27% of the total) of observed clouds (Table 2). This is a result of Nyamuragira's frequent, long-lived eruptions, each of which have involved, on average, 17–18 days of continuous SO_2 emission. It does not imply that the SO_2 clouds produced by Nyamuragira have long atmospheric residence times, since much of this SO_2 remains in the troposphere and is typically only tracked by TOMS for a maximum of 2–3 days before dispersing, although a small proportion of SO_2 from Nyamuragira may reach the stratosphere during its larger eruptions (e.g. Krueger *et al.* 1996). The high totals for Galunggung and Rinjani are also due to frequent eruptive events rather than long cloud lifetimes, and eruptions involving continuous emission of SO_2 or ash for several days or weeks contribute to high totals for Krafla, Cerro Azul and Sierra Negra (Galápagos Islands) and Lonquimay (Chile). Conversely, the high totals for Pinatubo and El Chichón, and to a lesser extent Mount Spurr and Cerro Hudson, are due to the production of single, large, stratospheric SO_2 clouds that were tracked by TOMS for many days as the slow conversion to sulphate aerosol proceeded (Table 3; Krueger 1983; Bluth *et al.* 1992, 1995; Constantine *et al.* 2000).

Regions with TOMS detected eruptions

Table 4 divides the database into regions, following the classification of Simkin & Siebert (1994). South America and Indonesia head the list of regions when ranked by number of volcanoes with TOMS-detected eruptions (10, or *c.*16% of the total). For South America, this is due largely to the inclusion of the 5 Galápagos Island volcanoes that erupted between 1978 and 2001. These volcanoes also contribute significantly to the 147 days of volcanic cloud observations recorded for South America (Table 4). Indonesia dominates the list of events (67, or *c.*34% of the total) due to the activity of Galunggung (Java), Colo (Sulawesi), Soputan (Sulawesi), and Rinjani (Lesser Sunda Islands) during the TOMS era. Volcanoes of the Alaskan peninsula and SW Alaska have also produced a significant number of eruptive events (16, or *c.*8% of the total) over the 22-year period, principally during the 1989–1990 eruption of Redoubt (Miller & Chouet 1994) and the 1992 eruptions of Mount Spurr (Bluth *et al.* 1995). Nyamuragira's contribution gives Africa the highest total of days tracked from only 2 volcanoes (Table 4), and South America (predominantly the Galápagos Islands, Cerro Hudson and Lonquimay which between them produced 88% of South America's total) and Indonesia also have significant totals. Despite the large contribution of the 1991 Pinatubo and 1982 El Chichón eruptions to the respective total days tracked for the Philippines and Mexico, the data in Table 4 underline the prevalence of frequent explosive activity (e.g. Galunggung 1982–1983) and long-duration effusive eruptions (e.g. Nyamuragira, Galápagos Islands) in the TOMS database, and highlights Africa (i.e. Nyamuragira) as the site of most persistent volcanic cloud emission (all of which were SO_2 clouds; Table 2) in the 1978–2001 period.

Only three of the 19 regions in Simkin & Siebert (1994) have no listed eruption in the TOMS database for 1978–2001 (Table 4). The Atlantic Ocean and Antarctica regions have relatively few active volcanoes and have not seen

significant recorded eruptions in this period (Simkin & Siebert 1994), and in any case much of the Antarctic suffers from insufficient UV light levels for much of the year. New Zealand is covered adequately by TOMS, but the most significant eruption of recent times in this region, that of Ruapehu in September 1995 (GVN 1995) unfortunately fell in the 19-month gap between M3 and EP TOMS. This eruption would almost certainly have been detected had there been a TOMS satellite operating at the time. Ruapehu also erupted in June-July 1996, producing a substantial plume on 16 July 1996 (GVN 1996*a*) just one day before the activation of EP TOMS.

Volcano types with TOMS-detected eruptions

Expressing the TOMS database in terms of volcano type (following Simkin & Siebert 1994) reveals the expected predominance of stratovolcanoes as the source of over 80% of the eruptive events and *c.*67% of the eruptions detected by TOMS (Table 5). Shield volcanoes, such as Nyamuragira and the Galápagos Island volcanoes, have produced over 40% of the total days tracked from only 13% of contributing volcanoes, reflecting the long durations of eruptions from this volcano type. Lava domes and calderas only achieve significant total days tracked due to the inclusion of El Chichón and Krafla, respectively, in these categories (Table 2). Note that, in this case, eruptions from volcanoes classed as calderas (Krafla and Banda Api (Indonesia)) do not imply caldera-forming eruptions. In fact these data are somewhat misleading in that a significant proportion of eruptions in the database have involved lava dome-forming eruptions of volcanoes classed as stratovolcanoes rather than lava domes. If the data from all dome-forming eruptions are collated irrespective of volcano type, the result is 50 eruptive events, 21 eruptions and 105 days tracked from 14 volcanoes, representing *c.*25%, 21%, *c.*13% and *c.*23% of the respective totals. This comprises dome-forming eruptions of Augustine (Alaska), Bezymianny (Kamchatka), El Chichón, Langila (Papua New Guinea), Lascar (Chile), Makian (Indonesia), Mayon (Philippines), Merapi (Indonesia), Mount St Helens (USA), Popocatépetl (Mexico), Redoubt, Shiveluch (Kamchatka), Soufrière Hills and Soufriere St Vincent (West Indies), several of which are on-going at the time of writing. The TOMS record demonstrates the hazardous nature of this type of volcanism, which can produce a series of significant SO_2 and ash clouds over a protracted period and threaten aircraft operations (e.g. Casadevall 1994).

Tectonic settings with TOMS-detected eruptions

The final database summary considers the tectonic setting of the eruptions that constitute the 1978–2001 TOMS database (Table 6). Subduction zone volcanoes, which produce volatile-rich magmas and are thus most prone to explosive eruptions, represent c.82% of the total number of volcanoes in the database, and are responsible for c.85% of recorded events, c.72% of recorded eruptions and c.56% of the total days tracked. However, the significant contribution from effusive volcanism in hot-spot and rift settings is once more in evidence, with the former responsible for c.44% of the total days tracked from c.18% of listed volcanoes. Although only c.15% of TOMS-detected eruptive events are attributable to hot-spot-related volcanism, the latter accounts for c.21% of events involving SO_2 production (Table 2), reflecting the relatively high sulphur content of the basaltic magma erupted in this setting (e.g. Wallace & Carmichael 1992).

Although the most prolific contributor to the TOMS database since 1978 (Nyamuragira) is in central Africa, it is clear from Table 6 that the Pacific Rim and Indonesia experience by far the greatest frequency of major eruptive activity of any region of the globe. This is not surprising, as most of the world's sub-aerial volcanoes are situated in these regions (Simkin & Siebert 1994). As one of the longest satellite-derived records of volcanic emissions, the 22-year TOMS volcanic emissions database demonstrates the need for continuous surveillance of the Pacific region using space-borne instruments, to enable rapid detection, location, and tracking of volcanic clouds as they impinge on aircraft flight paths. Near real-time 24-hour surveillance could be achieved using combined UV and IR sensors on a geostationary platform situated over the Pacific, although such a mission has yet to be approved.

Results from Earth Probe TOMS (1996–2001)

EP TOMS was launched in mid-1996 in a low earth orbit, providing increased sensitivity to SO_2 and aerosols, due to a reduced footprint area and a slight wavelength shift (Table 1). The improved sensitivity of EP TOMS was exploited for validation experiments, wherein ground-based correlation spectrometry (COSPEC) was used to measure passive SO_2 emissions from Popocatépetl concurrently with EP TOMS operating in a special 'stare mode' (fixed scan position) over the volcano (Schaefer *et al.* 1997).

However, increased sensitivity came at the expense of gaps between adjacent EP TOMS pixels and between successive orbit tracks (McPeters *et al.* 1998), and thus an increased probability of missing smaller or more fleeting volcanic eruptions. Consequently, although the EP TOMS detection limit for volcanic clouds (prior to September 1997) was up to 11 times smaller than previous TOMS instruments (Table 1), the non-contiguous coverage of EP TOMS meant that some events would be missed and that larger volcanic cloud signals would be truncated if they intersected a data gap.

The EP TOMS orbit has since been raised (Table 1), although gaps still exist between pixels (towards the centre of each swath) and between orbits (in equatorial latitudes). Despite these caveats, the ability of EP TOMS to detect smaller eruptive events enhances its utility as a hazard mitigation tool. The coarse spatial resolution (Table 1) means that information on the location of SO_2 or ash is relatively imprecise, but the data can warn of the presence of volcanic clouds. In fact, the EP TOMS spatial resolution is probably good enough for adequate location for the purposes of airborne ash warnings.

The EP TOMS database

The inventory of eruptions and eruptive events detected by EP TOMS between its launch and the end of 2001 is presented in chronological order in Table 7. Note that these data were incorporated into the analysis of the entire TOMS database discussed above and presented in Tables 2 and 4–6. Since the cut-off for the current database is the end of 2001, an eruption of Nyiragongo (DR Congo) that was detected by EP TOMS in January 2002 (NASA Earth Observatory Newsroom 2002) is excluded from the list. Results from ADEOS TOMS are also excluded; although ADEOS provided contiguous coverage in tandem with EP TOMS, the satellite failed prematurely after c. nine months of operation. ADEOS TOMS only detected four eruptive events during its short life (Table 1), although one of these, an eruption of Langila (Papua New Guinea) in February 1997, was missed by EP TOMS due to data gaps. Contiguous data from ADEOS TOMS were used to supplement EP TOMS during the 1996 eruption of Nyamuragira (Table 7), which was affected by data gaps in EP TOMS data.

Two dates are given for each eruption in Table 7; the actual eruption date as given in available sources, and the date of first detection by EP TOMS. These dates are often coincident, signifying an eruption that occurred before the

Table 7. *Volcanic eruptions detected by the Earth Probe TOMS, 1996–2001.*

Volcano (region)	Latitude	Eruption date[1]	EP TOMS first detection date	Days tracked	Retrieved SO_2 (kt)[2]	Aerosol index[3]
Nyamuragira (DR Congo)	1.41° S	1 Dec 1996	2 Dec 1996	*c.*17	*c.*380	Negative
Manam (Papua New Guinea)[4,5]	4.1° S	9 Feb 1997	9 Feb 1997	1	Low	–
Bezymianny (Kamchatka)[4]	55.98°N	9 May 1997	9 May 1997	2	0	1.9
Popocatépetl (Mexico)[4]	19.02°N	30 June 1997	3 July 1997	1	7	–
Soufrière Hills (Montserrat)[4]	16.72°N	7 Aug 1997	7 Aug 1997	1	0	2.4
Soufrière Hills[5]	16.72°N	8 Aug 1997	8 Aug 1997	1	0	2.3
Soufrière Hills[4]	16.72°N	25 Sept 1997	25 Sept 1997	1	0	0.9
Soufrière Hills[4]	16.72°N	27 Sept 1997	27 Sept 1997	1	0	2.3
Soufrière Hills[4]	16.72°N	18 Oct 1997	18 Oct 1997	1	0	2.0
Soufrière Hills[4]	16.72°N	19 Oct 1997	19 Oct 1997	1	Low	2.4
Soufrière Hills[4]	16.72°N	26 Dec 1997	26 Dec 1997	1	31[6]	5.2
Soufrière Hills[4]	16.72°N	3 July 1998	3 July 1998	1	2	–
Cerro Azul (Galápagos Is)	0.9° S	15 Sept 1998	16 Sept 1998	*c.*25	435	Negative
Manam[4]	4.1° S	5 Oct 1998	5 Oct 1998	1	17	–
Nyamuragira	1.41° S	17 Oct 1998	18 Oct 1998	*c.*14	*c.*1100	Negative
Popocatépetl[4]	19.02°N	25 Nov 1998	25 Nov 1998	1	10	–
Mount Cameroon (Cameroon)	4.20° N	28 March 1999	30 March 1999	4	45	–
Shishaldin (Aleutian Islands)	54.75°N	19 Apr 1999	19 Apr 1999	3	63	8.7
Soufrière Hills[4]	16.72°N	20 July 1999	20 July 1999	1	16	2.6
Tungurahua (Ecuador)[4]	1.47° S	17 Oct 1999	17 Oct 1999	1	0	2.0
Tungurahua[4]	1.47° S	16 Nov 1999	16 Nov 1999	1	6	3.7
Nyamuragira	1.41° S	27 Jan 2000	28 Jan 2000	*c.*18	*c.*300	–
Hekla (Iceland)	63.98°N	26 Feb 2000	27 Feb 2000	3	180	Negative
Miyake-jima (Japan)	34.08°N	18 Aug 2000	18 Aug 2000	14	270	4.9
Ulawun (Papua New Guinea)	5.05° S	28 Sept 2000	29 Sept 2000	3	37	8.7
Popocatépetl[4]	19.02°N	15 Dec 2000	15 Dec 2000	1	23	–
Popocatépetl[4]	19.02°N	18–19 Dec 2000	19 Dec 2000	2	26	2.3
Nyamuragira	1.41° S	6 Feb 2001	6 Feb 2001	*c.*25	960	Negative
Cleveland (Aleutian Islands)	52.82°N	19 Feb 2001	19 Feb 2001	1	6	4.6
Cleveland	52.82°N	11 March 2001	11 March 2001	1	Low	3.9
Cleveland	52.82°N	19 March 2001	20 March 2001	1	0	2.1
Popocatépetl[4]	19.02°N	28–29 Apr 2001	29 Apr 2001	1	4	1.7
Ulawun	5.05° S	30 Apr 2001	30 Apr 2001	2	30[6]	–
Shiveluch (Kamchatka)[4]	56.65°N	22 May 2001	22 May 2001	1	0	2.8
Etna (Italy)[5]	37.73°N	17 July 2001	25 July 2001	3	Low	–
Soufrière Hills[4]	16.72°N	29 July 2001	30 July 2001	1	33	–
Tungurahua[4]	1.47° S	5 Aug 2001	6 Aug 2001	1	32	1.6

[1]Data sources: GVN (1996b, 1997a, b, c, 1998b, c, d, e, 1999a, b, c, 2000a, b, c, d, e, 2001a, b, c, d, e, f, g); Montserrat Volcano Observatory (MVO) unpublished data; Etna reports (http://www.ct.ingv.it/etna2001/main.htm).
[2]Gives current best estimate of the SO_2 mass detected by TOMS. *Low* denotes possible signals in SOI or ozone data that are close to detection limits.
[3]Volcanic ash returns a positive Aerosol Index (AI) value; AI increases with increasing ash cloud optical depth and ash cloud altitude (e.g. Krotkov *et al.* 1999). Negative AI indicates the presence of non UV-absorbing aerosols such as sulphate (Seftor *et al.* 1997). The maximum observed AI is given for each eruption that produced aerosols detected by TOMS, unless negative.
[4]Denotes volcanoes displaying intermittent eruptive activity over a number of years. In this case, *Eruption date* refers to the date of the eruptive event considered most likely to have produced the cloud detected by TOMS, and not the date when unrest began.
[5]Denotes eruptions that were detected in EP TOMS Ozone data only.
[6]Denotes SO_2 clouds truncated at the edge of a TOMS swath; hence these are minimum estimates of total SO_2 production.

TOMS overpass on that particular day. Where the TOMS detection date trails the recorded eruption date by a day or more, this may signify an eruption that occurred after the daily TOMS overpass, an eruption that fell in an EP TOMS data gap on the preceding day, or an eruption that did not produce sufficient SO_2 and/or ash in its early phase to exceed the TOMS detection limits. To date, there are no recorded occurrences of detection of precursory activity (i.e. the TOMS detection date preceding the recorded eruption date) by EP TOMS, or any other TOMS instrument.

The latest EP TOMS SO_2 retrieval results are also given for each eruption in Table 7. Retrievals presented in this chapter have been generated using an iterative four-band matrix inversion method detailed in Krueger et al. (1995). We typically quote an error of 30% on these retrievals, though for a full discussion of the errors involved the reader is referred to Krueger et al. (1995). Generating the SO_2 tonnages listed in Table 7 is a two-step process. First, a retrieval is performed using 4 bands of TOMS data for a subset of the image containing the volcanic cloud under scrutiny. To then derive the SO_2 tonnage contained in the cloud, an empirical background correction is applied by subtracting the SO_2 tonnage contained in background regions adjacent to the volcanic cloud from the SO_2 tonnage contained in a box surrounding the cloud. Background boxes are chosen to be of similar size to the box containing the volcanic cloud, and areas are normalized to the area of the cloud box (see Krueger et al. 1995 for a detailed description). To account for the small gaps between adjacent EP TOMS pixels, the data are interpolated on to a regular, contiguous grid (typically $0.5° \times 0.5°$) before the tonnage calculation procedure. The above method has been complicated recently (since 2001) by the appearance of a cross-track bias in EP TOMS data (see below), which results in a variation of background SO_2 with scan position across each TOMS swath. We have attempted to compensate for this by selecting the band combination that produces the lowest retrieval noise, and by adjusting the calibration of individual bands before performing the retrieval.

It should be noted that retrieved SO_2 does not equate to total SO_2 production in the majority of cases. This applies especially to effusive eruptions involving continuous emission (and coincident removal) of SO_2 (e.g. Nyamuragira eruptions; Fig. 3), where it is necessary to account for SO_2 remaining from the previous day along with any new SO_2 produced in the interim (Krueger et al. 1996). The procedure is complicated for EP

TOMS data due to the data gaps that often bisect large clouds; an interpolation method must then be used to estimate the amount of 'missing' SO_2. We are currently investigating ways to produce estimates of total SO_2 production by continuously emitting volcanoes using the daily satellite 'snapshots' from polar orbiting platforms such as TOMS, and hence the SO_2 data in Table 7 may be revised as these techniques are refined. Explosively released eruption clouds can be corrected for SO_2 removal between the time of eruption and the time of the TOMS overpass, if more than one day's worth of data is available (and no data gaps intervene) and if a constant SO_2 removal rate (integrating SO_2 removal through conversion to sulphate and dry/wet deposition processes) can be assumed, by extrapolation of the TOMS-derived tonnages back to the time of eruption to estimate the erupted mass. However, many of the explosive events listed in Table 7 were relatively short-lived and were only tracked by TOMS for a single day, precluding the aforementioned approach. The technique is also not applicable when the eruption plume is still being fed at the time of the first TOMS overpass.

A significant feature of the EP TOMS era to date has been the lack of major explosive eruptions, with the most significant emissions in Table 7 being produced by predominantly effusive events. Two of the most significant explosive eruptions of the last five years occurred at Shishaldin on 19 April 1999 and at Hekla on 26 February 2000 (an effusive eruption which involved an initial explosive phase; Fig. 4; GVN 2000b); independent data suggest that both of these eruptions produced a small stratospheric aerosol signal (Rizi et al. 2000; GVN 2000b) and this seems likely considering the high northern latitudes of these volcanoes (Table 7).

The total retrieved SO_2 in Table 7 amounts to c. 4 Mt, of which c. 3.2 Mt (c. 80%) was produced during eruptions of primarily effusive or non-explosive nature (not including lava dome eruptions) and c. 2.7 Mt (c. 68%) was emitted by Nyamuragira alone, which has erupted four times since 1996 (e.g. Fig. 3). Of a total of 158 days of EP TOMS volcanic cloud observations, Nyamuragira is responsible for 74 days or c. 47% of the total. It is interesting to note that Bluth et al. (1993) found that non-explosive volcanism contributes around 70% of the total annual volcanogenic SO_2 flux to the atmosphere, based on N7 TOMS data for 1978–1993, a period that saw several very large explosive eruptions (Table 3). If an estimate of the annual flux of SO_2 from passive volcanic degassing (e.g. 9 Mt; Stoiber et al. 1987) is added to our EP TOMS results for 1996–2001, the contribution of non-explosive

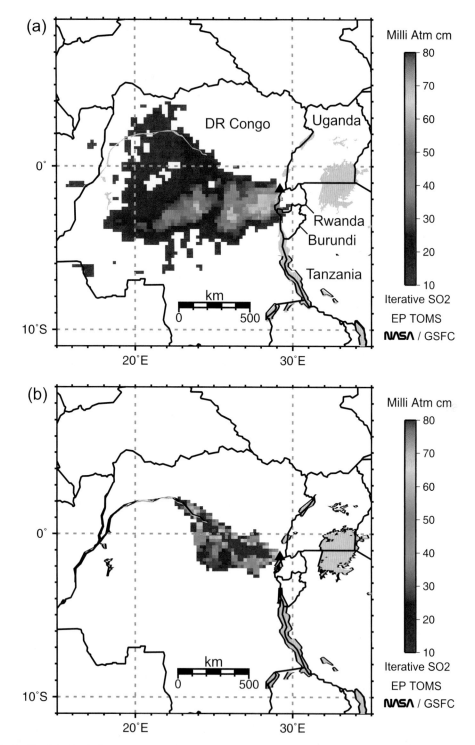

Fig. 3. The SO$_2$ clouds from recent eruptions of Nyamuragira, DR Congo (*triangle*) observed by EP TOMS. (**a**) 19 October 1998; (**b**) 6 February 2001. The data have been interpolated on to a 0.2°×0.2° grid to eliminate gaps between TOMS pixels

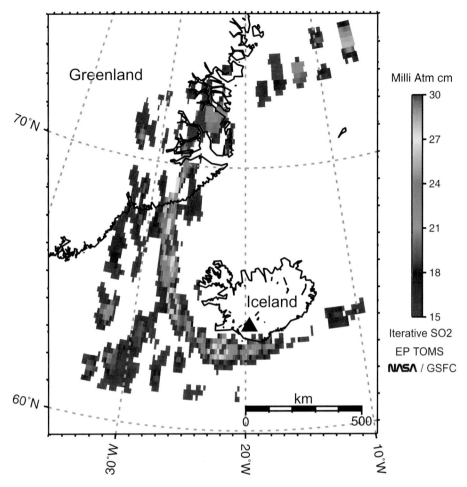

Fig. 4. The SO$_2$ cloud from the 26 February 2000 eruption of Hekla, Iceland (*triangle*) as measured by EP TOMS on 27 February. The data have been interpolated on to a 0.2°×0.2° grid to eliminate gaps between TOMS pixels. The cloud, which was wrapped around a rotating weather system, contained an estimated SO$_2$ mass of *c.*180 kt at this time. Note the problem of relatively high background SO$_2$ in the region of the cloud, and that the data are cut off by the light terminator at the top of the image.

volcanism amounts to *c.*98% of the total. This is clearly an artefact of the lack of Pinatubo- or El Chichón-scale events since 1996, but there is also a semantic difference, as Bluth *et al.* (1993) include effusive eruptions such as those of Mauna Loa (Hawaii) in 1984, Krafla in 1984, Sierra Negra in 1979 and several Nyamuragira eruptions in their total explosive flux.

Also included in Table 7 are several volcanic clouds which were close to EP TOMS detection limits, but which still produced an identifiable signal in the data. Such signals are typically noticed in TOMS ozone data as small regions of abnormally high ozone, which can be attributed to SO$_2$ if other potential causes of high ozone can be disregarded. Low-level SO$_2$ plumes can occasionally be seen in ozone data (e.g. Manam 1997, Etna 2001; Fig. 5) when they are absent from SOI images; this is a useful tool for locating weaker clouds and quantitative estimates of the implied SO$_2$ mass can also be derived. This is achieved by first isolating the volcanic signal by subtracting an average background ozone value, and then using the ratio of the absorption cross-sections of ozone and SO$_2$ to calculate an effective amount of SO$_2$ that would produce the observed signal in TOMS ozone data. This is performed for each anomalous pixel, and then the results are summed to produce an estimate of the total SO$_2$ mass.

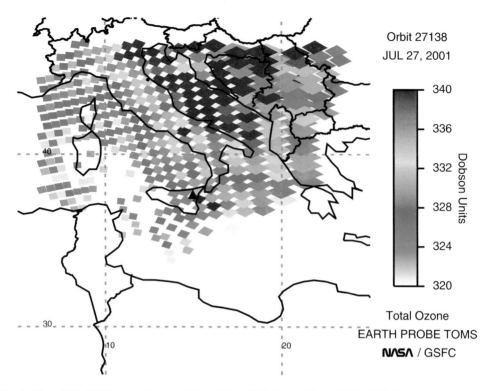

Fig. 5. Plot of EP TOMS ozone data over Mount Etna, Sicily (*triangle*) on 27 July 2001. Note the relatively high ozone values over mainland Europe and the 'ozone' plume emerging from Etna, a result of SO_2 absorption. We estimate that this plume contained $c.3$ kt of SO_2.

Eruption case studies

Nyamuragira

Eruptions of Nyamuragira dominate the short-term EP TOMS record (Table 7; Fig. 3) as they do the whole 1978–2001 TOMS database, both in terms of number of days of observed clouds and total SO_2 tonnage (2.7 Mt between 1996 and 2001). Nyamuragira's total is at least an order of magnitude greater than that of any other volcano, and its total SO_2 production in 12 eruptions over 22 years may even be comparable with the 20 Mt produced by Pinatubo in 1991. Nyamuragira (and neighbouring Nyiragongo) is difficult to monitor in the field, due partly to its frequent eruptions of extensive lava flows (GVN 1996*b*, 1998*c*, 2000*a*, 2001*b*) but mainly due to persistent regional instability in the eastern DR Congo since the 1994 Rwandan civil war, and badly funded monitoring resources (Oppenheimer 1998*b*). Thus the TOMS satellite record provides an extremely valuable data-set documenting the SO_2 emissions from this exceptional volcano (Fig. 3).

The size of the Nyamuragira data-set derived from the 22 years of TOMS data is too large to permit a detailed analysis in this chapter; such analyses are on-going and will be documented in due course. No detailed analysis of the sulphur contents of Nyamuragira lavas has been published to date (although S-bearing pyrrhotites have been found in the groundmass of some lavas; Aoki *et al.* 1985), but we speculate that the voluminous SO_2 emissions from the volcano are somehow related to the unique characteristics of the erupted lavas. Both Nyamuragira and nearby Nyiragongo erupt highly potassic (K_2O rich) lavas (Aoki *et al.* 1985) which have very low viscosities due to their low silica contents (Hayashi *et al.* 1992). This low viscosity results in exceedingly high lava flow rates, such as those recorded during the devastating 1977 eruption of Nyiragongo (Tazieff 1977). Low-viscosity lavas may also promote highly efficient separation of magma and gas as magma batches rise to the surface during eruptions, allowing large gas clouds to develop. Furthermore, studies of earthquakes beneath Nyamuragira indicate that the erupted magma may originate from a storage region at considerable depth (between 4 and 7 km; Aoki *et al.* 1985), suggesting that there is little inter-eruptive degassing that would deplete the available SO_2 reservoir.

Another characteristic of the EP TOMS data for Nyamuragira is the frequent occurrence of negative AI values associated with the volcanic clouds, which indicates the presence of sulphate aerosol (Table 7). This suggests efficient removal of emitted SO_2 through conversion to sulphate in the moist tropical atmosphere of central Africa.

Popocatépetl

EP TOMS has detected at least five eruptive events from Popocatépetl since the volcano awoke from dormancy in December 1994 (Table 7), in a period which has seen the volcano record exceptionally high passive SO_2 degassing rates (up to 9–13 kt/day; Delgado-Granados *et al.* 2001). These high SO_2 fluxes were exploited in a TOMS validation campaign in collaboration with COSPEC operators (Schaefer *et al.* 1997). Popocatépetl's high altitude summit (*c.* 5400 m) means that degassed SO_2 is released well above the boundary layer, making it an ideal target for validation campaigns, as the rate of SO_2 removal is lower and the high altitude is more conducive to detection of emissions by TOMS.

Since 1994, Popocatépetl has undergone phases of lava dome growth and destruction in its summit crater (GVN 1997c, 1998e, 2000e, 2001g; Delgado-Granados *et al.* 2001). A large explosion on 30 June 1997 partially destroyed a pre-existing lava dome but unfortunately coincided with a data gap in EP TOMS data and followed the failure of ADEOS TOMS by one day. A new dome subsequently began to extrude on 4 July 1997 (GVN 1998a), one day after an SO_2 plume from Popocatépetl (containing no detectable ash) was detected by EP TOMS (Table 7). We believe that the EP TOMS SO_2 signal on 3 July may represent vigorous gas venting associated with the emplacement of this new dome.

Most, if not all, of the other instances when emissions from Popocatépetl have been detected by EP TOMS, coincide with phases of dome growth. The highest dome growth rates recorded at Popocatépetl since 1994 occurred in mid-December 2000, when magma extrusion rates of *c.* 180–200 m³/s were inferred and exceptionally high SO_2 fluxes (up to 100 kt/day) were measured (GVN 2000e). The largest TOMS-detected SO_2 emission from Popocatépetl in our data-set (26 kt) coincided with these other geophysical maxima on 19 December 2000 (Table 7). GVN

(2000e) states that seismic tremor amplitude at Popocatépetl in mid-December 2000 was the highest observed since the volcano began erupting in 1994, with amplitudes on 30 June 1997 the next highest. Although the event on 30 June 1997 was unfortunately missed by EP and ADEOS TOMS, the presence of a measurable SO_2 plume 3 days later on 3 July 1997 suggests that the 30 June event would have produced a sizeable signal. If so, then it may be possible to positively correlate tremor amplitudes (and hence dome growth rates) with the satellite-derived SO_2 flux, which would provide a valuable alternative means of monitoring the volcano (and others like it) and, potentially, assessing the volatile content of the magma supplying the lava domes.

Soufrière Hills, Montserrat

The Soufrière Hills volcano (SHV) on Montserrat (West Indies) is currently undergoing an andesitic dome-forming eruption that began in July 1995 (Young *et al.* 1998). The most vigorous phase of the eruption to date occurred in 1997, which is reflected in the incidence of EP TOMS-detected events (Table 7). Beginning in August 1997 and continuing in September–October 1997, SHV produced a series of powerful Vulcanian explosions that lofted ash to altitudes of up to *c.* 15 km (Druitt *et al.* 2002). EP TOMS succeeded in detecting only six of a total of 88 eruption clouds (Table 7), with the timing of the explosions relative to the TOMS overpass being the most critical factor; many explosions occurred in the evening or early morning, and thus the ash produced had dispersed before TOMS flew over. An interesting observation made by EP TOMS is that only one of the 4 explosions (on 19 October 1997) produced measurable SO_2, albeit a very small signal (Table 7). This was towards the end of the Vulcanian explosion sequence (Druitt *et al.* 2002), signifying a possible impending change in the eruptive conditions. Another possible explanation is that SO_2 may have been efficiently scavenged in the ash-rich clouds (e.g. Rose 1977), impeding its detection by TOMS.

The largest SO_2 masses in the SHV volcanic clouds detected by EP TOMS to date have been measured in clouds arising from large dome collapse events during periods of active lava dome growth, e.g. 26 December 1997 and 29 July 2001 (Table 7). However, between March 1998 and November 1999 no lava dome growth was recorded at SHV, yet dome collapses still occurred periodically (Norton *et al.* 2002). Two of these events were detected by EP TOMS, including one that produced significant SO_2 (20 July 1999; Table 7). This indicates that high gas pressures within the quiescent dome may have influenced the timing of this particular dome collapse, but more generally it highlights the fact that even 'quiescent' domes can produce substantial gas/ash clouds, and that they require constant surveillance to mitigate associated hazards.

Volcanic clouds produced by SHV are typically small, and pose problems for detection even for sensors with higher spatial resolution than EP TOMS such as GOES (Rose & Mayberry 2000). Our EP TOMS data demonstrate that, although detection of these small clouds occurs less frequently, important quantitative information on the compositions of these clouds can still be obtained.

Tungurahua

Tungurahua is a similar case to Popocatépetl, being a volcano at high altitude (*c.*5000 m) that, in its current phase of unrest, has been erupting sporadically for several years (since 1999, with the first explosive activity recorded on 5 October; GVN 1999*c*). It is situated near the equator (Table 7) and so is susceptible to EP TOMS data gaps which may intersect the volcano on two out of every three days. The first recorded detection of a Tungurahua eruptive event by EP TOMS that has been discovered in the database to date occurred on 17 October 1999 (Table 7). This coincided with increased activity and the raising of the alert level to orange for the first time, along with evacuations on Oct 16 (GVN 1999*c*). The 16 November 1999 event registered by EP TOMS (Table 7) corresponded with a further increase in volcanic activity at Tungurahua; specifically an increase in number of daily explosions which probably increased the likelihood of detection by TOMS (GVN 1999*c*). The present data-set therefore indicates that EP TOMS succeeds in detecting eruptive events associated with significant changes in activity at the volcano.

Miyake-jima

Nyamuragira and Cerro Azul notwithstanding, Miyake-jima has the highest retrieved SO_2 mass (270 kt) of the remaining volcanoes in the EP TOMS data-set (Table 7). This volcanic island south of Tokyo experienced a large phreatic eruption from the Mount Oyama vent on 18 August 2000, following several months of increasing unrest (GVN 2000*c*). The eruption produced a volcanic cloud containing *c.*23 kt of

SO_2 and significant ash, and may have produced a small stratospheric aerosol signal over southern Japan (GVN 2000*c*). Shortly after this explosive event, the volcano entered into an extended phase of voluminous passive SO_2 release, peaking on 7 December 2000 when SO_2 fluxes (measured by COSPEC) of *c.*230 kt per day were recorded, which may be the highest passive SO_2 flux measured at any volcano to date (K. Kazahaya, pers. comm. 2001). At the end of 2001, 14 days of volcanic cloud observations had been made at the volcano, spanning the period from the August 18 explosion until 14 September 2000. This presumably represents the most vigorous period of degassing, when plumes were reaching sufficient altitudes to be detected easily by EP TOMS. With the exception of the August 18 cloud, no ash has been detected by EP TOMS in Miyake-jima emissions, and to date no further SO_2 emissions from the volcano (after 14 September 2000) have been found in TOMS data, including the period around 7 December 2000, when the maximum SO_2 flux was measured using ground-based techniques.

Etna

Etna is known for its persistent summit degassing that has been maintained for many years (e.g. Allard 1997), but SO_2 emissions from Etna have only rarely been detected by TOMS. Recent analysis of notable eruptive events in Etna's past (such as the September 1980 eruptions) which were detected in TOMS data suggest that there may be several more such events as yet undiscovered in the database. To verify this will require more detailed analysis of the daily TOMS images.

Etna's most recent eruption (at the time of writing), and one of its most spectacular of recent times, occurred in July–August 2001, when lava flows descended the southern flanks of the volcano and a new cinder cone was constructed (INGV 2001). Despite the impressive eruptive plumes produced by the volcano during July 2001, EP TOMS only detected weak signals associated with this eruption. These signals appeared in EP TOMS Ozone data (indicative of SO_2 emissions close to TOMS detection limits) on three (or possibly four) days in late July (25, 27, 28 (possibly) and 31 July), and consisted of small plumes extending from Etna towards the SE (e.g. Fig. 5), except on 31 July, when the signal was NE of Etna over mainland Italy. The first detection on July 25 corresponded with increasing magmatic activity and rates of growth at the Piano del Lago cone that was created during the 2001 eruption. The period from 27 to

31 July was perhaps the most vigorous phase of the eruption, after which activity began to diminish until the eruption ceased on 10 August (INGV 2001). Thus, as is often the case, EP TOMS succeeded in detecting the emissions associated with the most vigorous phase of a relatively non-explosive eruption.

We have attempted to derive quantitative estimates of the SO_2 masses that were implied by the observed EP TOMS ozone signals. This assumes that the apparent increase in ozone over the volcano is entirely due to SO_2, which masquerades as ozone due to the similar absorption bands of the two gases in the UV. Biomass burning is another potential source of tropospheric ozone, but we can discount this as a source of the signal due to the relatively unvegetated slopes of Etna, and we assume no local variations in stratospheric and upper tropospheric ozone due to other causes. Using the procedure briefly outlined above, we arrive at estimated SO_2 masses of c.1.8 kt and c.2.7 kt on 25 and 27 July, respectively. These are rather modest values, but may represent a small amount of SO_2 reaching higher altitudes than the bulk of the emissions from the eruption, with the latter 'lost' in the background TOMS signal.

The future of EP TOMS

EP TOMS, in its fifth year of operation, continues to function at the time of writing (July 2002) and is still able to detect volcanic clouds, as evidenced by the January 2002 eruption of Nyiragongo (NASA Earth Observatory Newsroom 2002). Nevertheless, the instrument has developed technical problems since 2000, which may impact on its long-term future. A major degradation in the throughput of EP TOMS has been noticed since late 2000, with more than 70% of the original transmission lost to date. However, recently the instrument seems to have stabilized at around 25% of its original throughput, with signal to noise still very good (see the TOMS project website for updates: http://toms.gsfc.nasa.gov). The instrument has also developed a serious cross-track spectral bias that results in shifts of the retrieved background SO_2 of 10–20 DU over most latitudes. This offset increases the uncertainty of our eruption tonnage estimates.

Furthermore, the planned successor to EP TOMS failed to achieve orbit in September 2001 (Table 1). It is believed that the launch rocket released the QuikTOMS satellite at a lower altitude and velocity than intended and that for this reason it did not achieve a stable orbit. The failure of QuikTOMS to achieve orbit has cast

doubt on the plan to continue measuring volcanic emissions without interruption until the next generation of UV sensor is launched, and has expedited the need to prolong the life of the ageing EP TOMS. The recent stabilization of the instrument is encouraging and, barring further degradation, should allow its life to be prolonged until the launch of OMI in 2004.

UV remote sensing of volcanic emissions in the post-TOMS era

The next few years will see the launch of instruments with the capabilities to build on and enhance the extensive heritage of the TOMS satellites with regard to volcanic emissions monitoring (Table 8). Most important of these will be OMI, which will be launched on EOS Aura in 2004 to serve its primary purpose of continuing the global ozone mapping mission begun by the TOMS instruments. Our group is currently involved with the development of SO_2 retrieval algorithms for OMI, based on experience gained over the 22-year TOMS era. A long OMI mission could extend the volcanic record until the National Polar-orbiting Operational Environmental Satellite System (NPOESS) Ozone Mapping and Profiler Suite (OMPS) instruments operationally measure volcanic eruptions starting in 2008 (Table 8).

OMI will offer several improvements over TOMS which will greatly reduce the detection limits of the instrument (Table 9), including a smaller footprint area, measurement of multiple wavelengths (740 compared with six on TOMS) and reduced radiometric noise levels. Footprint area is unimportant when the cloud is larger than the footprint, but sub-pixel clouds produce absorption equivalent to the average amount of SO_2 distributed across the full pixel. This effect limits the minimum SO_2 mass that can be detected. Thus, decreasing the footprint area allows detection of smaller eruption clouds. OMI will have one-fifth the footprint area of EP TOMS (Table 8), and will also offer a special 13×13 km mode for occasional use, which will permit detection and tracking of even smaller SO_2 clouds and, potentially, passive degassing signals (Table 9). Parallel wavelength sampling with OMI will produce greater signal to noise than the serial sampling TOMS, and OMI will measure many more wavelengths. In principle, these two factors can produce a lower noise level in OMI SO_2 retrievals. The potential capabilities of multiple wavelength UV sensors such as OMI have been demonstrated by retrievals using data from the Global Ozone Monitoring Experiment (GOME) on ERS-2 (Table 8). With an SO_2 noise

Table 8. *Current and future space-borne instruments capable of detecting SO$_2$ clouds.*

Instrument	Satellite	Data coverage dates	Spectral type	Features
GOME I	ERS-2	April 1995– present	UV	960-km swath; not contiguous daily global coverage, 40×320 km ground resolution
EP TOMS	Earth Probe	July 1996–present	UV	Contiguous daily global coverage, 39×39 km ground resolution
MODIS	EOS Terra, Aqua	Feb 2000– present	IR	2330-km swath; contiguous global coverage every 1–2 days, 1 km ground resolution (IR)
ASTER	EOS Terra	Feb 2000–present	IR	60-km swath; selective data acquisition, 90 m ground resolution (TIR)
SCIAMACHY	ENVISAT-1	Mid-2002–	UV	960-km swath; not contiguous daily global coverage; 25×240 km ground resolution
OMI	EOS Aura	2004–	UV	Contiguous daily global coverage; 13×24 km ground resolution
GOME II	EUMETSAT MetOp 1, 2, 3	2005–2020	UV	See GOME I
ODUS	GCOM-A1	2007–	UV	Non-Sun-synchronous orbit; 20×20 km ground resolution
OMPS	NPOESS	2008–2020	UV	Contiguous daily global coverage, 50×50 km ground resolution

Table 9. *Detection limit (3σ above background) of passive SO$_2$ flux from a 5000-m volcano for OMI and EP TOMS (post-November 1997) nadir pixels.*

	Minimum detectable SO$_2$ flux, t day^{-1}		
Instrument	Plume velocity 1 m/s	Plume velocity 5 m/s	Plume velocity 10 m/s
EP TOMS (1σ = 3.5 DU)	1010	5050	10100
OMI (plume traverses 13 km pixel width; 1σ = 0.2 DU)	36	180	360
OMI (plume traverses 25 km length of pixel; 1σ = 0.2 DU)	19	95	190
COSPEC	10	52	104
Typical volcano	100–5000	100–5000	100–5000

standard deviation of 0.4 DU, Eisinger & Burrows (1998) obtained the first detection of industrial SO$_2$ from space. We are also evaluating the possibilities of the recently launched SCIAMACHY sensor (Table 8) for use in remote sensing of volcanic emissions.

Although procedures to quantitatively retrieve SO$_2$ from infrared (IR) satellite data, such as that collected by the Moderate Resolution Imaging Spectroradiometer (MODIS) and Advanced Spaceborne Thermal Emission Spectrometer (ASTER), both on the EOS/Terra platform (Table 8), are being developed (e.g. Realmuto *et al.* 1997; Realmuto 2000), they have yet to achieve the sensitivity of UV techniques. These IR methods exploit SO$_2$ absorption bands at 7.3 and 8.7 μm, but suffer from problems due to competing water vapour absorption in the same wavelength region, and the background emissivity must also be characterized, although they do offer higher spatial resolution than UV sensors (Table 8). Unlike UV methods, IR techniques fail if the target is opaque, as for very fresh eruption clouds. However, IR sensors offer the potential of SO$_2$ detection by day and night (UV instruments only work by day), and so a combination of UV and IR instruments is necessary to enable detection of volcanic clouds under all possible conditions.

Summary

During approximately 5300 days of operation between 1978 and 1993, N7 TOMS detected volcanic clouds on 557 days, or one cloud every 9–10 days on average. EP TOMS operated for around 1600 days between its launch in 1996 and the end of 2001, detecting volcanic clouds on 158 days; also an average of one cloud every *c.*10 days. The vast majority of SO$_2$ and ash clouds originate from volcanoes of the Pacific Rim and Indonesia, although the African volcano Nyamuragira (along with Nyiragongo) is clearly a target that requires constant surveillance. Although the N7 TOMS era saw a higher incidence of major explosive eruptions (Bluth *et al.* 1993, 1997), the EP TOMS results to date suggest that, even during relatively quiescent periods, a more sensitive instrument will detect volcanic events at a similar frequency by capturing eruptions of smaller size. Such eruptions can be as hazardous to aircraft as much larger events, making detection and tracking of small volcanic clouds crucial for effective hazard mitigation. The success of EP TOMS in detecting smaller events bodes well for the next generation of higher-resolution UV instruments such as OMI, although the best scenario for future volcanic cloud remote sensing would be the concurrent operation of UV and IR sensors, ideally from geostationary platforms, thus enabling detection of volcanic emissions within minutes of eruption by day and night.

We acknowledge NASA's Earth Science Enterprise programs for funding of TOMS volcanic emissions research. Two anonymous reviewers provided many useful suggestions for improvements to the paper.

References

ALLARD, P. 1997. Endogenous magma degassing and storage at Mount Etna. *Geophysical Research Letters*, **24**, 2219–2222.

ANDRES, R. J. & KASGNOC, A. D. 1998. A time-averaged inventory of subaerial volcanic sulfur emissions. *Journal of Geophysical Research*, **103**, 25 251–25 261.

AOKI, K.-I., YOSHIDA, T., YUSA, K. & NAKAMURA, Y. 1985. Petrology and geochemistry of the Nyamur-agira volcano, Zaire. *Journal of Volcanology and Geothermal Research*, **25**, 1–28.

BLUTH, G. J. S., DOIRON, S. D., SCHNETZLER, C. C., KRUEGER, A. J. & WALTER, L. S. 1992. Global tracking of the SO$_2$ clouds from the June 1991 Mount Pinatubo eruptions. *Geophysical Research Letters*, **19**, 151–154.

BLUTH, G. J. S., SCHNETZLER, C. C., KRUEGER, A. J. & WALTER, L. S. 1993. The contribution of explosive volcanism to global atmospheric sulfur dioxide concentrations. *Nature*, **366**, 327–329.

BLUTH, G. J. S., CASADEVALL, T. J., SCHNETZLER, C. C., DOIRON, S. D., WALTER, L. S., KRUEGER, A. J. & BADRUDDIN, M. 1994. Evaluation of sulfur dioxide emissions from explosive volcanism: the 1982–1983 eruptions of Galunggung, Java, Indonesia. *Journal of Volcanology and Geothermal Research*, **63**, 243–256.

BLUTH, G. J. S., SCOTT, C. J., SPROD, I. E., SCHNETZLER, C. C., KRUEGER, A. J. & WALTER, L. S. 1995. Explosive emissions of sulfur dioxide from the 1992 Crater Peak eruptions, Mount Spurr, Alaska. *In:* KEITH, T. E. C. (ed.) *The 1992 eruptions of Crater Peak vent, Mount Spurr Volcano, Alaska.* US Geological Survey Bulletin, **2139**, 37–45.

BLUTH, G. J. S., ROSE, W. I., SPROD, I. E. & KRUEGER, A. J. 1997. Stratospheric loading from explosive volcanic eruptions. *Journal of Geology*, **105**, 671–683.

CASADEVALL, T. J. 1994. The 1989–1990 eruption of Redoubt Volcano, Alaska – impacts on aircraft operations. *In:* MILLER, T. P. & CHOUET, B. A. (eds) *The 1989–1990 eruptions of Redoubt Volcano, Alaska.* Journal of Volcanology and Geothermal Research, **62(1-4)**, 301–316.

CHIN, M., ROOD, R. B., LIN, S.-J., MULLER, J.-F. & THOMPSON, A. M. 2000. Atmospheric sulfur cycle simulated in the global model GOCART: model description and global properties. *Journal of Geophysical Research*, **105(D20)**, 24 671–24 687.

CHRISTIANSEN, R. L. & PETERSON, D. W. 1981. Chronology of the 1980 eruptive activity. *In:* LIPMAN, P. W. & MULLINEAUX, D. R. (eds) *The 1980 Eruptions of Mount St. Helens, Washington.* US Geological Survey Professional Paper, *1250,* 17–30.

CONSTANTINE, E. K., BLUTH, G. J. S. & ROSE, W. I. 2000. TOMS and AVHRR observations of drifting volcanic clouds from the August 1991 eruptions of Cerro Hudson. *In:* MOUGINIS-MARK, P. J., CRISP, J. A. & FINK, J. H. (eds) *Remote Sensing of Active Volcanism.* Geophysical Monograph **116**, AGU, Washington, DC, 45–64.

DELGADO-GRANADOS, H., CÁRDENAS GONZÁLEZ, L. & PIEDAD SÁNCHEZ, N. 2001. Sulfur dioxide emissions from Popocatépetl volcano (Mexico): case study of a high-emission rate, passively degassing erupting volcano. *Journal of Volcanology and Geothermal Research*, **108**, 107–120.

DELMELLE, P. & STIX, J. 2000. Volcanic Gases. In: SIGURDSSON, H., HOUGHTON, B. F., McNUTT, S. R., RYMER, H. & STIX, J. (eds) *Encyclopedia of Volcanoes.* Academic Press, San Diego, CA, 803–815.

DRUITT, T. H., YOUNG, S. R. *ET AL.* 2002. Episodes of cyclic volcanian explosive activity with fountain callapse at Soufrière Hills Volcano, Montserrat. *In:* DRUITT, T. H. & KOKELAAR, B. P. (eds) *The Eruption of the Soufriere Hills Volcano from 1995 to 1999, Montserrat, Lesser Antilles.* Geological Society, London, Memoirs, **21**, 281–306.

EISINGER, M. & BURROWS, J. P. 1998. Tropospheric sulfur dioxide observed by the ERS-2 GOME instrument. *Geophysical Research Letters*, **25**, 4177–4180.

GOURGAUD, A., TJETJEP, W., RAMLI, L., SUDRADJAT, A., VINCENT, P. M. & CAMUS, G. 1985. Volcanic risks and air navigation – case-study of the 1982-1983 eruption of Galunggung volcano (Java, Indonesia). *Comptes Rendus de l'Académie des Sciences Série II*, **301(5)**, 351–353.

GUREVICH, G. S. & KRUEGER, A. J. 1997. Optimization of TOMS wavelength channels for ozone and sulfur dioxide retrievals. *Geophysical Research Letters*, **24(17)**, 2187–2190.

GVN 1995. Ruapehu. *Smithsonian Institution Global Volcanism Network Bulletin*, **20(9)**.

GVN 1996*a*. Ruapehu. *Smithsonian Institution Global Volcanism Network Bulletin*, **21(6)**.

GVN 1996*b*. Nyamuragira. *Smithsonian Institution Global Volcanism Network Bulletin*, **21(10)**.

GVN 1997*a*. Manam. *Smithsonian Institution Global Volcanism Network Bulletin*, **22(2)**.

GVN 1997*b*. Bezymianny. *Smithsonian Institution Global Volcanism Network Bulletin*, **22(4)**.

GVN 1997*c*. Popocatépetl. *Smithsonian Institution Global Volcanism Network Bulletin*, **22(7)**.

GVN 1998*a*. Popocatépetl. *Smithsonian Institution Global Volcanism Network Bulletin*, **23(2)**.

GVN 1998*b*. Cerro Azul. *Smithsonian Institution Global Volcanism Network Bulletin*, **23(8)**.

GVN 1998*c*. Nyamuragira. *Smithsonian Institution Global Volcanism Network Bulletin*, **23(10)**.

GVN 1998*d*. Manam. *Smithsonian Institution Global Volcanism Network Bulletin*, **23(11)**.

GVN 1998*e*. Popocatépetl. *Smithsonian Institution Global Volcanism Network Bulletin*, **23(11)**.

GVN 1999*a*. Mt. Cameroun. *Smithsonian Institution Global Volcanism Network Bulletin*, **24(3)**.

GVN 1999*b*. Shishaldin. *Smithsonian Institution Global Volcanism Network Bulletin*, **24(3)**.

GVN 1999*c*. Tungurahua. *Smithsonian Institution Global Volcanism Network Bulletin*, **24(11)**.

GVN 2000*a*. Nyamuragira. *Smithsonian Institution Global Volcanism Network Bulletin*, **25(1)**.

GVN 2000*b*. Hekla. *Smithsonian Institution Global Volcanism Network Bulletin*, **25(2)**.

GVN 2000*c*. Miyake-jima. *Smithsonian Institution Global Volcanism Network Bulletin*, **25(7)**.

GVN 2000*d*. Ulawun. *Smithsonian Institution Global Volcanism Network Bulletin*, **25(8)**.

GVN 2000*e*. Popocatépetl. *Smithsonian Institution Global Volcanism Network Bulletin*, **25(12)**.

GVN 2001*a*. Cleveland. *Smithsonian Institution Global Volcanism Network Bulletin*, **26(1)**.

GVN 2001*b*. Nyamuragira. *Smithsonian Institution Global Volcanism Network Bulletin*, **26(1)**.

GVN 2001*c*. Cleveland. *Smithsonian Institution Global Volcanism Network Bulletin*, **26(4)**.

GVN 2001*d*. Shiveluch. *Smithsonian Institution Global Volcanism Network Bulletin*, **26(4)**.

GVN 2000*e*. Ulawun. *Smithsonian Institution Global Volcanism Network Bulletin*, **26(5)**.

GVN 2001*f*. Tungurahua. *Smithsonian Institution Global Volcanism Network Bulletin*, **26(7)**.

GVN 2001*g*. Popocatépetl. *Smithsonian Institution Global Volcanism Network Bulletin*, **26(8)**.

HAYASHI, S., KASAHARA, M., TANAKA, K., HAMAGUCHI, H. & ZANA, N. 1992. Major element chemistry of recent eruptive products from Nyamuragira volcano, Africa (1976–1989). *Tectonophysics*, **209**, 273–276.

HEATH, D. F., KRUEGER, A. J., ROEDER, H. A. & HENDERSON, B. D. 1975. The Solar Backscatter Ultraviolet and Total Ozone Mapping Spectrometer (SBUV/TOMS) for Nimbus G. *Optical Engineering*, **14**, 323.

INGV 2001. Etna reports (in Italian). Istituto Nazionale di Geofisica e Vulcanologia, Sezione di Catania. World Wide Web Address: http://www.ct.ingv.it/etna2001/main.htm

KROTKOV, N. A., KRUEGER, A. J. & BHARTIA, P. K. 1997. Ultraviolet optical model of volcanic clouds for remote sensing of ash and sulfur dioxide. *Journal of Geophysical Research*, **102(D18)**, 21 891–2 1904.

KROTKOV, N. A., TORRES, O. *ET AL.* 1999. Comparison of TOMS and AVHRR volcanic ash retrievals from the August 1992 eruption of Mt. Spurr. *Geophysical Research Letters*, **26(4)**, 455–458.

KRUEGER, A. J. 1983. Sighting of El Chichón sulphur dioxide clouds with the Nimbus-7 Total Ozone Mapping Spectrometer. *Science*, **220**, 1377–1379.

KRUEGER, A. J. 1984. The observation of atmospheric structure with TOMS and some potential advancements. *In:* ZEREFOS, C. S. & GHAZI, A. (eds) *Atmospheric Ozone.* Reidel, Dordrecht, 239–242.

KRUEGER, A. J., WALTER, L. S., SCHNETZLER, C. C. & DOIRON, S. D. 1990. TOMS measurement of the sulfur dioxide emitted during the 1985 Nevado del Ruiz eruptions. *Journal of Volcanology and Geothermal Research*, **41**, 7–15.

KRUEGER, A. J., WALTER, L. S., BHARTIA, P. K., SCHNETZLER, C. C., KROTKOV, N. A., SPROD, I. & BLUTH, G. J. S. 1995. Volcanic sulfur dioxide measurements from the total ozone mapping spectrometer instruments. *Journal of Geophysical Research*, **100(D7)**, 14 057–14 076.

KRUEGER, A. J., SCHNETZLER, C. C. & WALTER, L. S. 1996. The December 1981 eruption of Nyamuragira volcano (Zaire), and the origin of the 'mystery cloud' of early 1982. *Journal of Geophysical Research*, **101(D10)**, 15 191–15 196.

KRUEGER, A. J., SCHAEFER, S. J., KROTKOV, N., BLUTH, G. & BARKER, S. 2000. Ultraviolet remote sensing of volcanic emissions. *In:* MOUGINIS-MARK, P. J., CRISP, J. A. & FINK, J. H. (eds) *Remote Sensing of Active Volcanism.* Geophysical Monograph **116**, AGU, Washington, DC, 25–43.

MCPETERS, R. D., BHARTIA. P. K. *ET AL.* 1998. Earth Probe Total Ozone Mapping Spectrometer (TOMS) Data Products User's Guide. NASA Technical Publication 1998-206985. World Wide Web Address:

ftp://daac.gsfc.nasa.gov/data/toms/documentation/eptoms_userguide.pdf

MILLER, T. P. & CHOUET, B. 1994. The 1989–1990 eruptions of Redoubt Volcano: an introduction. *Journal of Volcanology and Geothermal Research*, **62**, 1–10.

NASA EARTH OBSERVATORY NEWSROOM 2002. Sulfur dioxide emissions from Congo volcanoes. World Wide Web Address: *http://earthobservatory.nasa.gov/Newsroom/NewImages/images.php3?img_id=7274*

NEWHALL, C. G. & MELSON, W. G. 1983. Explosive activity associated with the growth of volcanic domes. *Journal of Volcanology and Geothermal Research*, **17**, 111–131.

NEWHALL, C. G. & SELF, S. 1982. The volcanic explosivity index (VEI): an estimate of explosivity magnitude for historic volcanism. *Journal of Geophysical Research*, **87**, 1232–1238.

NORTON, G. E., WATTS, R. *ET AL*. 2002. Pyroclastic flow and explosive activity of the lava dome of Soufrière Hills Volcano, Montserrat, during a period of no magma extrusion (March 1998 to November 1999). *In:* DRUITT, T. H. & KOKELAAR, B. P. (eds) *The Eruption of the Soufriere Hills Volcano from 1995 to 1999, Montserrat, Lesser Antilles.* Geological Society London, Memoirs, **21**, 664.

OPPENHEIMER, C. 1998*a*. Volcanological applications of meteorological satellites. *International Journal of Remote Sensing*, **19(15)**, 2829–2864.

OPPENHEIMER, C. 1998*b*. Satellite observations of lava lake activity at Nyiragongo volcano, Ex-Zaire, during the Rwandan refugee crisis. *Disasters*, **22(3)**, 268–281.

OPPENHEIMER, C., FRANCIS, P. & STIX, J. 1998. Depletion rates of sulfur dioxide in tropospheric volcanic plumes. *Geophysical Research Letters*, **25(14)**, 2671–2674.

PRATHER, M. 1992. Catastrophic loss of stratospheric ozone in dense volcanic clouds. *Journal of Geophysical Research*, **97**, 10 187–10 191.

PYLE, D. M., BEATTIE, P. D. & BLUTH, G. J. S. 1996. Sulphur emissions to the stratosphere from explosive volcanic eruptions. *Bulletin of Volcanology*, **57**, 663–671.

REALMUTO, V. J. 2000. The potential use of earth observing system data to monitor the passive emission of sulfur dioxide from volcanoes. *In:* MOUGINIS-MARK, P. J., CRISP, J. A. & FINK, J. H. (eds) *Remote Sensing of Active Volcanism.* Geophysical Monograph **116**, AGU, Washington, D.C., 101–115.

REALMUTO, V. J., SUTTON, A. J. & ELIAS, T. 1997. Multispectral thermal infrared imaging of sulfur dioxide plumes: a case study from the East Rift Zone of Kilauea Volcano, Hawaii. *Journal of Geophysical Research*, **102**, 15 057–15 072.

RIZI, V., MASCI, F., REDAELLI, G., DI CARLO, P., IARLORI, M., VISCONTI, G. & THOMASON, L. W. 2000. Lidar and SAGE III observations of Shishaldin volcano aerosols and lower stratospheric transport. *Geophysical Research Letters*, **27(21)**, 3445–3448.

ROBOCK, A. 2000. Volcanic eruptions and climate. *Reviews of Geophysics*, **38**, 191–219.

ROSE, W. I. 1977. Scavenging of volcanic aerosol by ash: atmospheric and volcanologic implications. *Geology*, **5**, 621–624.

ROSE, W. I. & MAYBERRY, G. C. 2000. Use of GOES thermal infrared imagery for eruption scale measurements, Soufriere Hills, Montserrat. Geophysical Research Letters, **27(19)**, 3097–3100.

SCAILLET, B., CLEMENTE, B., EVANS, B. W. & PICHAVANT, M. 1998. Redox control of sulfur degassing in silicic magmas. *Journal of Geophysical Research*, **103**, 23 937–23 949.

SCHAEFER, S. J., KERR, J. B. *ET AL*. 1997. Geophysicists unite to validate volcanic SO₂ measurements. *EOS, Transactions of the American Geophysical Union*, **78**, 217.

SCHNETZLER, C. C., DOIRON, S. D., WALTER, L. S. & KRUEGER, A. J. 1994. Satellite measurements of sulfur dioxide from the Redoubt eruptions of 1989–1990. *In:* MILLER, T. P. & CHOUET, B. A. (eds.) The 1989–1990 eruptions of Redoubt Volcano, Alaska. *Journal of Volcanology and Geothermal Research*, **62(1-4)**, 353–357.

SCHNETZLER, C. C., BLUTH, G. J. S., KRUEGER, A. J. & WALTER, L. S. 1997. A proposed volcanic sulfur dioxide index (VSI). *Journal of Geophysical Research*, **102(B9)**, 20 087–20 091.

SEFTOR, C. J., HSU, N. C., HERMAN, J. R., BHARTIA, P. K., TORRES, O., ROSE, W. I., SCHNEIDER, D. J. & KROTKOV, N. 1997. Detection of volcanic ash clouds from the Nimbus 7/total ozone mapping spectrometer. *Journal of Geophysical Research*, **102(D14)**, 16 749–16 759.

SIMKIN, T. & SIEBERT, L. 1994. *Volcanoes of the World*, 2nd edn, Geoscience Press, Tucson, AZ.

SPARKS, R. S. J. 1997. Causes and consequences of pressurization in lava dome eruptions. *Earth and Planetary Science Letters*, **150**, 177–189.

STENCHIKOV, G. L., KIRCHNER, I. *ET AL*. 1998. Radiative forcing from the 1991 Mount Pinatubo volcanic eruption. *Journal of Geophysical Research*, **103**, 13 837–13 857.

STOIBER, R. E., WILLIAMS, S. N. & HUEBERT, B. 1987. Annual contribution of sulfur-dioxide to the atmosphere by volcanos. *Journal of Volcanology and Geothermal Research*, **33(1–3)**, 1–8.

STOTHERS, R. B., WOLFF, J. A., SELF, S. & RAMPINO, M. R. 1986. Basaltic fissure eruptions, plume heights, and atmospheric aerosols. *Geophysical Research Letters*, **13(8)**, 725–728.

TAZIEFF, H. 1977. An exceptional eruption: Mt Nyiragongo, Jan 10th, 1977. *Bulletin of Volcanology*, **40**, 189–200.

TOOTELL, B. 1985. All Four Engines Have Failed: the True and Triumphant Story of Flight BA009 and the 'Jakarta Incident'. Andre Deutsch, London.

TORRES, O., BHARTIA, P. K., HERMAN, J. R., AHMAD, Z. & GLEASON, J. 1998. Derivation of aerosol properties from satellite measurements of back-scattered ultraviolet radiation: Theoretical basis. *Journal of Geophysical Research*, **103**, 17 099–17 110.

WALLACE, P. J. 2001. Volcanic SO_2 emissions and the abundance and distribution of exsolved gas in magma bodies. *Journal of Volcanology and Geothermal Research*, **108**, 85–106.

WALLACE, P. & CARMICHAEL, I. S. E. 1992. Sulfur in basaltic magmas. *Geochimica et Cosmochimica Acta*, **56**, 1863–1874.

YOUNG, S. R., SPARKS, R. S. J., ASPINALL, W. P., LYNCH, L. L., MILLER, A. D., ROBERTSON, R. E. A. & SHEPHERD, J. B. 1998. Overview of the eruption of Soufriere Hills volcano, Montserrat, 18 July 1995 to December 1997. *Geophysical Research Letters*, **25(18)**, 3389–3392.

Rainwater and ash leachate analysis as proxies for plume chemistry at Soufrière Hills volcano, Montserrat

M. EDMONDS[1], C. OPPENHEIMER[2], D. M. PYLE[3] & R. A. HERD[1]

[1]*Montserrat Volcano Observatory, Mongo Hill, Montserrat, West Indies*
(email: marie@mvo.ms)
[2]*Department of Geography, University of Cambridge, Downing Place,*
Cambridge CB2 3EN, UK.
[3]*Department of Earth Sciences, University of Cambridge, Downing Street,*
Cambridge CB2 3EQ, UK.

Abstract: Chloride and sulphate concentrations in rainwater and water-soluble leachates from volcanic ash samples track the compositions of gas emissions at the Soufrière Hills Volcano, Montserrat, from 1996 to 2001. There are both systematic spatial and temporal variations in the chloride/sulphate ratio (expressed as the equivalent HCl/SO_2 mass ratio) in rainwater and ash leachates. Temporal variations reflect changes in eruption rate and eruptive style. Mass ratios of HCl/SO_2 in ash leachates correspond closely with those obtained by open-path Fourier transform infrared (OP–FTIR) spectroscopy, and reflect changes in volatile emissions throughout the eruption. Both leachate and OP–FTIR spectroscopic analyses show mass ratios of $HCl/SO_2 > 1$ during dome growth, and $HCl/SO_2 < 1$ during non-eruptive periods.

The HCl/SO_2 mass ratios in rainwater samples from 1996 and 1997 show temporal variations that correlate with changes in extrusion rate. The HCl/SO_2 ratios in plume-affected rainwater and ash leachates from June and July 2001 correlate positively with increasing rock-fall energy, and with increasing eruption rate prior to a dome collapse event. The HCl/SO_2 mass ratios in water-soluble ash leachates and rainwater samples collected at the same time and from the same sites, are linearly correlated, with rainwater HCl/SO_2 ratios systematically two to three times higher than ash leachate ratios. Spatial patterns of rainwater pH, and HCl/SO_2 in rainwater and ash leachates are principally influenced by the proximity of the sampling sites to the active dome, and to the typical pattern of dispersion of the plume by tropospheric winds. These results demonstrate that rainwater chemistry and ash leachate analysis provides a useful indicator of volcanic activity, and represents a valuable supplement to volcano surveillance efforts.

The sustained eruptive activity at the Soufrière Hills Volcano, Montserrat, since 1995, has provided an unprecedented opportunity to investigate the processes that accompany the continuous release of volcanic gases from degassing and erupting magma. Here we investigate the temporal and spatial variability of the compositions of plume-affected rainwater, and water-soluble leachates from freshly deposited ash, and show how these reflect both changing magmatic conditions and the local plume-related processes.

The onset of volcanic unrest at Soufrière Hills Volcano, Montserrat, began with an earthquake swarm in 1992, which intensified in November 1994 (Young *et al.* 1998*a*; Robertson *et al.* 2000). Steam venting and phreatic explosions commenced in July 1995, accompanied by volcano-

tectonic earthquakes (Aspinall *et al.* 1998). Extrusion of andesite lava to form a dome began in November 1995 and proceeded more-or-less continuously, at rates from <1 to 10 m^3/s, until mid-March 1998. During the first dome-building period, the lava dome reached a maximum volume of *c.*113×10^6 m^3 (MVO archived data). Periodically, gravitational or fluid-pressure-driven collapse of the dome gave rise to pyroclastic flows (Cole *et al.* 1998; Voight *et al.* 1999). In August 1997, effusive dome building gave way to explosive activity, when cycles of hybrid earthquakes culminated in Vulcanian explosions and subsequent fountain collapse (Druitt *et al.* 2002).

Dome growth ceased in mid-March 1998, and the volcano entered a 20-month period of residual activity. As the dome and upper conduit cooled,

From: OPPENHEIMER, C., PYLE, D.M. & BARCLAY, J. (eds) *Volcanic Degassing*. Geological Society, London, Special Publications, **213**, 203–218. 0305–8719/03/$15.00

a groundwater aquifer developed and activity was characterized by shallow-level phreatic explosions and gravitational dome collapses (Norton *et al.* 2002). A swarm of hybrid earthquakes and phreatic explosions in September and October 1999 preceded the onset of a second phase of continuous lava effusion and dome growth in November 1999. Two major dome collapses have occurred during this second stage of dome growth up to the present time (July 2002): one, on 20 March 2000, removed *c.* 30×10^6 m^3 of lava, while a larger collapse on 29 July 2001 removed $40–50 \times 10^6$ m^3.

Monitoring activity on Montserrat

Activity at the Soufrière Hills has been monitored by the Montserrat Volcano Observatory (MVO) using many different techniques, including short period and broad-band seismic networks; ground deformation surveys (differential GPS networks, electronic distance meter measurements, electronic tiltmeters); dome and deposit volume surveying; petrological and environmental monitoring (including airborne dust and sulphur dioxide levels) and gas monitoring. The compositions and mass fluxes of gas emissions have been assessed both by direct sampling and remote-sensing techniques. Early in the eruption, gases were sampled directly from the fumaroles around the volcano and from cracks in the dome itself (Hammouya *et al.* 1998). This continued until February 1996, when the first pyroclastic flows occurred and this methodology was abandoned.

The SO$_2$ emissions have been measured intermittently since 1995, using a correlation spectrometer (COSPEC) and, more recently, using a miniature differential optical absorption spectrometer (DOAS; Galle *et al.* 2003). Open-path Fourier transform infrared (OP–FTIR) spectroscopy has been used sporadically on Montserrat to measure the gas phase HCl/SO$_2$ ratio in the plume and thereby to estimate HCl emission rates. Rainwater collection and ash sampling, for water-soluble leachate analysis, have been carried out intermittently since 1995. Figure 1 summarizes the method and timing of gas data collection at Soufrière Hills Volcano for the period 1995–2001. These data have yielded valuable insights into magma chemistry, degassing processes, and the fate of volcanic gases in the atmosphere (Oppenheimer *et al.* 1998*a*, *b*, 2002; Young *et al.* 1998*b*; Watson *et al.* 2000; Edmonds *et al.* 2001, 2002).

The composition of plume-affected rainwater and ash leachates

The compositions of species adsorbed on to ash particles and rainwater samples that are derived from, or have passed through, volcanic gas plumes will reflect, among other things, the composition of the gas-phase plume species (e.g. Delmelle 2003; Horrocks *et al.* 2003; Stevenson *et al.* 2003). While the details of the chemical interactions that take place in tropospheric plumes remain poorly understood, we may nevertheless elucidate a few general principles (Fig. 2). The Montserrat plume comprises a mixture of solid particulates (ash) released from the vent, together with gas-phase species released from the volcano (principally H$_2$O, CO$_2$, SO$_2$, HCl), diluted by ambient tropospheric gases; and a variety of solid and liquid condensates, which may be volcanic in origin, derived from sea spray or condensed water droplets. Orographic clouds are almost ever-present around the Soufrière Hills summit region, and it is likely that much of the volcanic ash within the plume is coated with liquid water. Gas-phase species, such as HCl and SO$_2$, will undergo dissolution into the aqueous phase (depending on, for example, the local concentration of liquid water; the pH of the aqueous phase; cf. Delmelle 2003) followed, in the case of sulphur, by conversion to sulphate.

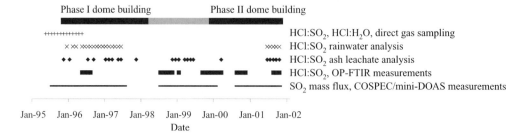

Fig. 1. Time-line summarizing gas sampling techniques employed during the eruption of the Soufrière Hills Volcano, Montserrat.

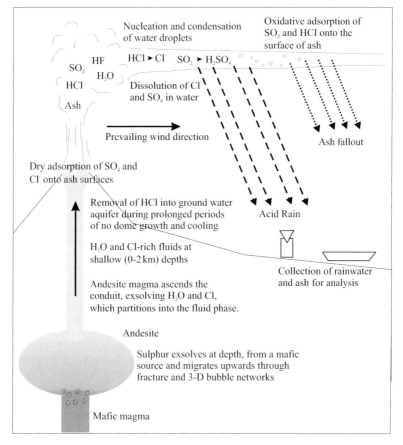

Fig. 2. A schematic diagram to show how HCl and SO$_2$ gases reach the atmosphere, to be scavenged from the volcanic plume at Soufrière Hills Volcano, Montserrat.

Volcanic aerosol may also be removed by interaction with water droplets and ash particles. Up to 30% of the gases emitted during an explosive eruption may be scavenged from the eruption column by these processes (Varekamp *et al.* 1984; de Hoog *et al.* 2001; Textor *et al.* 2003).

Removal of chlorine and sulphur species from the plume will be by a combination of 'dry deposition' and 'wet deposition'. The relative importance of these scavenging and removal processes is expected to vary seasonally (with local meteorological and environmental conditions), and from species to species. This has been demonstrated at Sakurajima (Japan), which receives 0.5–2 metres of rain per year. At one site 6 km from the vent, Kawaratani & Fujita (1990) found that wet deposition (by rain) dominated the removal flux of chloride during the wet season (50–75%), but was of lesser importance during the dry season. Overall, during seven months of

measurement, wet deposition accounted for just 36% of chloride deposition in total (Kawaratani & Fujita 1990). For sulphate, dry deposition (on volcanic dust, ash) accounted for 90% of the total removal flux over the same period of time. At Etna, which also receives 0.5–1.5 m of rainfall per year, dry depositional processes are considered to dominate over wet depositional processes, except during rainy periods, close to the plume source (Martin *et al.* 1986; Aiuppa *et al.* 2001). The sampling technique adopted thus far on Montserrat, and the limited range of anions and cations analysed, do not permit precise quantification of the balance between wet and dry depositional processes, or of the influence of sea-water (cf. Aiuppa *et al.* 2001).

The compositions of water-soluble species adsorbed on to the surfaces of volcanic ash particles ('ash leachates') are thought to reflect, at least to some extent, the composition of the same species in the volcanic plumes. Analyses of Cl/S ratios in ash leachates (quoted here in terms of the equivalent HCl/SO_2 mass ratio) have been reported from a number of volcanoes during both quiescent and eruptive activity, including Arenal, Costa Rica, during phreatic explosive and pyroclastic flow activity in July 1968 (HCl/SO_2 *c.*1.9, Taylor & Stoiber 1973; Simkin *et al.* 1981); Irazú (Costa Rica) during continuous eruptive activity in 1963–1965 (HCl/SO_2 *c.*0.7, Taylor & Stoiber 1973), and at Mount St Helens (USA, 18 May 1980, HCl/SO_2, *c.*0.4–0.9, Stoiber & Williams 1990). A time series of ash leachate data from the 1982–1983 explosive eruptions of Galunggung, Indonesia, has shown that this technique may record temporal changes in volcanic gas emissions (de Hoog *et al.* 2001). Six separate analyses of ash leachates collected over six months at Galunggung appear to show two peaks in S/Cl mass ratio, which were ascribed to the progressive degassing and recharge of a magma chamber (de Hoog *et al.* 2001).

Analyses of rainwater samples collected on Mount Etna from 1997 to 1999 reveal HCl/SO_2 mass ratios of 1 to 20 (Aiuppa *et al.* 2001). Increased sulphate and halogen concentrations were recorded in rainwater during the 1997–1998 Strombolian activity and lava fountaining, when plume HCl and SO_2 fluxes measured by COSPEC and filter packs were high (Pennisi and Le Cloarec 1998; Bruno *et al.* 1999; Aiuppa *et al.* 2001).

We present here the results of a systematic study of rainwater and ash leachate concentrations, measured on samples collected at various locations beneath and away from the volcanic plume at Soufrière Hills Volcano between May 1996 and September 2001. Our aims are to compare these proxies for plume Cl/S ratios with other available geochemical information, to consider their relationship to eruption parameters, and thereby to consider whether these simple and low-cost techniques offer reliable indicators of volcanic activity. The sustained eruption of the Soufrière Hills Volcano presents an ideal opportunity to test the validity of this simple monitoring method over a long time scale. In particular, our goals are:

1. To ascertain whether HCl/SO_2 in these samples correlates with observed changes in volcanic activity, or other measurable volcanic parameters (e.g. seismicity);
2. To investigate the extent to which the results compare with other measures of plume chemistry;
3. To establish the nature of the relationship between ash leachate and rainwater compositions.

Methodology

Sampling sites

A weather station in the Centre Hills provided a database of wind speeds and directions for the period March 1996 to March 1997 (Fig. 3). The prevailing wind direction over the island is from the east-southeast, and therefore the plume generally disperses over Plymouth or the Garibaldi Hill area, and this information was used to guide the selection of accessible rain and ash collection sites beneath the plume (Fig. 3). For rain collection, several sites were set up away from the area affected by plume fallout, in order to evaluate the background chloride concentrations in the rainwater. Ash-collecting trays were positioned in areas that were beneath the plume for approximately 90% of the time.

Ash leachate analysis

Samples of ash have been collected throughout the 1995–2001 eruption at Soufrière Hills Volcano by MVO staff. Samples were usually collected between one and 6 days after deposition. The grain-size distributions of the ash fallout have been consistent throughout the eruption, with 80% of the particles 10–125 μm in diameter. Small fractions of these samples were analysed at the British Geological Survey at Keyworth, UK, for water-soluble species adsorbed on to the surface of the ash particles, including sulphates and chlorides, by ion chromatography. Leaching was carried out by adding 5 g of ash to 25 ml de-ionized water, which was agitated for 1 hour before being allowed to settle for six to eight hours. After isolating the ash from the water extract solution, the solution was passed through a 0.45 μm nylon filter (to remove fine suspended sediment). The solutions obtained were analysed for sulphate and chloride by ion chromatography using a Millipore Waters 510 ion chromatograph with a conductivity detector and a 0.3 M LiOH solution as an eluent. One sample was extracted in duplicate for each extractant. The relative standard deviation of the analytical method is less than 3.5% for all chemical determinations. The results (Table 1) are given in mg analyte per kg of ash, i.e. ppm by mass.

Rainwater analysis

Rainwater samples were collected regularly throughout 1996 and 1997 and then from June 2001 through 2002 (Fig. 1). Water samples were collected between one and six days after the rain fell, and stored in 125 ml Nalgene bottles at

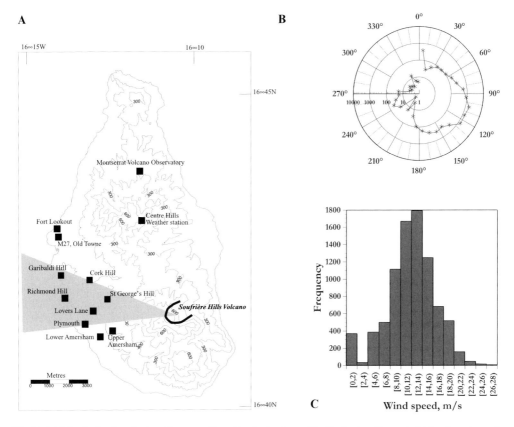

A

B

C

Fig. 3. (**a**) Map indicating the locations mentioned in the text, specifically the locations at which rainwater and ash samples were collected from 1995 to 2001. (**b**) The rose diagram shows wind directions (the bearing from which the wind blows) for the period March 1996 to March 1997, measured at Centre Hills, elevation 650 m. Note the logarithmic frequency scale. (**c**) The histogram shows the distribution of wind speeds over the same period, in m/s.

temperatures <15 °C until analysis. The storage of samples >0 °C could lead to sulphate reduction due to microbial activity, but this effect is considered negligible in this study. Analyses were carried out by the Montserrat Water Authority. Samples were filtered to extract organic matter, and analysed for sulphate and chloride using a photometer operating at 520 nm wavelength. The sulphate in a 10 ml sample of rainwater was reacted with a controlled amount of barium chloride (with a small amount of acid) to form insoluble barium sulphate. The turbidity of the resulting mixture was measured by the photometer and is proportional to the concentration of sulphate in the sample, with a range of 1–500 mg/l and a resolution of better than 1%. Chlorides are measured using silver nitrate, which reacts with chloride to form insoluble silver chloride. The degree of turbidity is proportional to the chloride concentration. The test is carried out under acidic and oxidizing conditions to prevent interference from complexing agents such as EDTA, polyphosphates, and any reducing agents that might also be present in the sample rainwater. Rainwater analyses of samples collected away from the volcanic plume (in the north of the island) were analysed in order to obtain background chloride concentrations, possibly derived from sea-water spray. The background was subtracted from all the rainwater analyses collected at the same time.

Errors and uncertainties

In considering whether the rainwater and ash-leachate analyses provide realistic proxies for gas-phase chemistry in the volcanic plume, understanding both analytical errors and the complexity of plume chemical and physical processes is important. Uncertainties in ash leachate analysis

Table 1. *Chloride and sulphate concentrations derived from ash leachate analysis for samples collected during 1995- 2001 at Soufrière Hills Volcano, Montserrat.*

Date	Location	Chloride (ppm)	Sulphate (ppm)	HCl/ SO₂ (mass)	Date	Location	Chloride (ppm)	Sulphate (ppm)	HCl/ SO₂ (mass)
30 Oct95		1000	9280	0.17	20 Mar 00	Old Towne	149	180	1.3
19 Jan 96	Plymouth	1780	1420	1.9	13 June 01	Richmond Hill	1190	5680	0.32
22 July 96	U.Amersham	1210	671	2.8	22 June 01	Plymouth	651	1080	0.93
19 Sept 96	Plymouth	499	303	2.5	22 June 01	St George's	1410	1750	1.2
22 Sept 96		600	800	1.2	22 June 01	Richmond Hill	2270	1650	2.1
16 Mar 97	Plymouth	24.2	30.4	1.2	26 June 01	St George's	2160	2300	1.5
11 May 97	L.Amersham	350	314	1.7	26 June 01	Garibaldi Hill	811	3080	0.41
27 May 97		111	471	0.36	2 July 01	Lovers Lane	2010	437	7.1
9 June 97	U.Amersham	655	1040	0.97	2 July 01	Richmond Hill	1580	506	4.8
25 June 97	L.Amersham	783	388	3.1	10 July 01	Plymouth	709	1150	0.95
25 June 97		526	198	4.1	21 July 01	Plymouth	591	527	1.7
27 June 97	Richmond Hill	17.2	42.7	0.62	21 July 01	Lovers Lane	1170	189	9.6
30 June 97		116	59.8	3.0	21 July 01	Richmond Hill	1250	253	7.6
20 Nov 97	Old Towne	1410	1040	2.1	25 July 01	Plymouth	1100	667	2.5
20 Nov 97	Old Towne	47.1	34.2	2.1	25 July 01	Lovers Lane	1190	221	8.3
5 May 98	U.Amersham	215	54.3	6.1	25 July 01	Richmond Hill	1480	276	8.3
26 Oct 98	St George's	1110	2980	0.58	2 Aug 01	Plymouth	693	798	1.3
12 Nov 98	MVO	924	2180	0.65	2 Aug 01	Lovers Lane	951	1150	1.3
3 Dec 98		22.5	163	0.21	2 Aug 01	St George's	429	1230	0.54
13 Nov 98	Richmond Hill	187	3000	0.096	2 Aug 01	Richmond Hill	342	622	0.85
3 Dec 98	St George's	9.85	1940	0.0078	2 Aug 01	Cork Hill	891	1180	1.2
14 Jan 99	Richmond Hill	580	3560	0.25	2 Aug 01	Fort Lookout	1560	806	3.0
23 Jan 99	Old Towne	199	1287	0.24	13 Aug 01	Garibaldi Hill	27	179	0.23
26 Mar 99		63.8	540	0.18	28 Aug 01	Garibaldi Hill	481	790	0.94
10 Apr 99	St George's	124	2060	0.093	21 Sept 01	Plymouth	646	516	1.9
10 Apr 99	Cork Hill	37.8	1990	0.029	21 Sept 01	Lovers Lane	440	642	1.1
14 Apr 99	Cork Hill	230	1220	0.29	21 Sept 01	St George's	1298	3430	0.58
28 Apr 99	Cork Hill	49.9	1310	0.059	21 Sept 01	St George's	578	658	1.4
11 June 99	Garibaldi Hill	197	1960	0.16	21 Sept 01	Richmond Hill	272	496	0.85
17 June 99	Old Towne	403	955	0.65					

All concentrations are in mg/kg (i.e. ppm) and are given to three significant figures. Dates and locations of sample collection are shown.

result from variations in the ash/water ratio. The sulphate concentrations are particularly sensitive to this ratio, and supersaturation with respect to gypsum occurs for high concentrations on the ash surfaces. High ash/water ratios may give mis- leadingly low concentrations if the sulphate is prevented from attaining complete dissolution. This error was reduced by performing repeated extractions of some samples in order to ensure complete dissolution of the sulphate adsorbed to the ash particles of the sample. Since chlorides tend to be more soluble in water than sulphates, rain falling on to ash samples before collection may cause preferential leaching of chloride from the ash surfaces, resulting in reduced HCl/SO₂ ratios in the leachate. Similarly, ash mingled with rain may lead to enhanced HCl/SO₂ in rain samples for the same reason. These effects have been minimized by collecting samples regularly and by rejecting visibly ash-contaminated water samples and wet ash samples. The authors are satisfied that the methods of analysis used here sufficiently reduce the significance of these potential errors for our purposes.

Results from rainwater and ash leachate analysis

The ash leachate and rainwater analyses are presented in Tables 1–3. Background rainwater concentrations of chloride, derived from analyses of precipitation at four points away from the plume (the observatory in the north of the island, Fort Lookout, M27 and Old Towne; Table 3, Fig. 3) have been subtracted from the data in Tables 2 and 3. Background sulphate is considered negligible. In each table, the measured chloride and sulphate concentrations have been used to calculate equivalent HCl/SO₂ mass ratios. The outline results are summarized graphically in Figures 4–7.

Table 2. *Chloride and sulphate concentrations (mg/litre) and equivalent (HCl/SO_2) mass ratios in rainwater collected 1996-1997 at Lower and Upper Amersham and Plymouth, Montserrat.*

Location	Upper Amersham			Lower Amersham			Plymouth		
Date	Chloride mg/l	Sulphate mg/l	HCl/SO_2 (mass)	Chloride mg/l	Sulphate mg/l	HCl/SO_2 (mass)	Chloride mg/l	Sulphate mg/l	HCl/SO_2 (mass)
10 Dec 95	21	2.2	15						
15 Dec 95	40	11	5.6						
25 Dec 95	380	28	21						
1 Feb 96	110	6.4	27						
8 Feb 96	1300	71	28						
16 Feb 96	140	13	17						
22 Feb 96	190	8.3	35						
6 Mar 96	190	8.3	35						
6 Mar 96	100	7.7	20						
13 Mar 96	99	7.8	20						
22 Mar 96	0.4	N.D.							
22 Mar 96	190	84	35						
28 Mar 96	500	15	51						
6 May 96	300	26	18						
13 May 96	500	140	5.5						
20 May 96	41	42	1.5						
27 May 96	120	46	4.0						
3 June 96	21	2.2	15						
10 June 96	38	16	3.7						
12 June 96	66	N.D.		68	10	11	68	12	8.7
14 June 96	210	77	4.2						
15 June 96	110	15	11						
17 June 96	36	49	1.1	94	5	30	140	3	72
24 June 96	290	39	12						
24 June 96	4.2	N.D.		120	18	10	130	21	9.6
1 July 96	110	21	8.1				94	N.D.	
7 July 96	64	N.D.		66	5	20	42	3	22
15 July 96	83	5	26	23	3	12	17	5	5.3
22 July 96	100	39	4.0	41	25	2.5	70	3	36
28 July 96	130	120	1.7				25	N.D.	
9 Aug 96	210	29	11	140	33	6.6	160	25	9.9
20 Aug 96	80	N.D.		74	14	8.2	38	10	5.9
30 Sept 96	360	160	3.5				410	190	3.3
20 Oct 96	100	36	4.3	12	9	2.1	5.2	N.D.	
26 Oct 96	58	7	13	18	5	5.6	15	3	7.7
4 Nov 96	20	3	10	17	N.D.		7.8	N.D.	
10 Nov 96	38	3	20	78	18	6.7	17	3	8.7
17 Nov 96	80	3	41	25	N.D.		27	3	13
24 Nov 96	23	8	4.4	7.2	5	2.2	0.7	3	0.36
1 Dec 96	23	12	3.0	17	3	8.7	8.5	3	4.4
8 Dec 96	26	10	4.0	17	5	5.3	18	5	5.6
15 Dec 96	26	3	13	30	N.D.		17	N.D.	
23 Dec 96	24	19	2.0	12	7	2.6	3	N.D.	
29 Dec 96	130	10	20	85	N.D.		8.7	50	0.27
6 Jan 97	13	15	1.3	140	31	7.0	170	59	4.5
26 Jan 97	32	93	0.53	1000	N.D.		230	N.D.	
2 Feb 97	140	13	17	66	N.D.		34	3	17
9 Feb 97	380	54	11	190	160	1.8	230	200	1.8
16 Feb 97	570	87	10	190	52	5.6	340	22	24
23 Feb 97	170	16	16	420	17	38	45	N.D.	
2 Mar 97	160	24	10	58	3	30	53	3	27
9 Mar 97	250	25	15	120	16	12	97	N.D.	
16 Mar 97	230	34	10	100	8	19	68	3	35
23 Mar 97	210	36	9.0						
31 Mar 97	16	39	0.63	160	50	4.9	17	20	1.3
12 Apr 97	140	20	11	64	32	3.1	29		
11 May 97	170	37	7.1						
17 May 97	320	110	4.5	760	97	12	710	560	2.0
25 May 97	1000	93	17						
1 June 97		12			18				
22 June 97	450	200	3.5	220	79	4.3			

N.D. – not detected.

Table 3. *Chloride and sulphate concentrations in rainwater from June to October 2001, Soufrière Hills Volcano, Montserrat*

Rainwater samples collected beneath the plume						Rainwater samples collected away from the plume				
Sample number	Date	pH	Chloride (mg/l)	Sulphate (mg/l)	(HCl/SO$_2$) (mass)	Sample number	Date	pH	Chloride (mg/l)	Sulphate (mg/l)
PLY130601	13 June 01	2.39	63	43	2.26	M27220601	22 June 01	5.32	12	N.D.
LL130601	13 June 01	2.61	60	190	0.49	GH270601	27 June 01	3.09	30	N.D.
SGH130601	13 June 01	3.36	61	150	0.63	M27270601	27 June 01	6.95	4.4	N.D.
RH130601	13 June 01	2.53	58	180	0.50	FLO270601	27 June 01	5.57	9.4	N.D.
PLY220601	22 June 01	3.03	60	35	2.64	MVO270601	27 June 01	7	34	5
LL220601	22 June 01	2.62	59	26	3.50	GH20701	02 July 01	6.41	24	8
SGH220601	22 June 01	3.32		5		MVO20701	02 July 01	7.19	32	8
RH220601	22 June 01	2.8	58	31	2.89	FLO110701	11 July 01	6.69	13	3
PLY260601	26 June 01	2.37	54	13	6.41	MVO110701	11 July 01	6.92	50	3
LL20701	02 July 01	2.56	60	8	11.6	GH250701	25 July 01	3.6	26	8
SGH20701	02 July 01	3.45	21	15	2.16	MVO260701	26 July 01	7.19	25	3
RH20701	02 July 01	2.74	50	7	11.0	FLO270701	27 July 01	6.65	7	N.D.
GH20701	02 July 01	6.41	24	8	4.63	M27150801	15 Aug 01	5.79	3	3
PLY100701	10 July 01	3.15	160	150	1.65	FLO150801	15 Aug 01	6.72	11	N.D.
LL100701	10 July 01	3.1	110	7	24.2	MVO150801	15 Aug 01	7.28	13	3
SGH100701	10 July 01	5.56	41	12	5.27	GH280801	28 Aug 01	3.65	38	10
RH100701	10 July 01	3.42	45	3	23.1	FLO280801	28 Aug 01	6.67	8.3	N.D.
PLY210701	21 July 01	3.09	170	26	10.1	MVO290801	29 Aug 01	4.3	23	N.D.
LL210701	21 July 01	2.82	230	19	18.7	GH100901	10 Sept 01	4.19	3.7	N.D.
RH210701	21 July 01	2.85	230	21	16.9	MVO240901	24 Sept 01	6.28	9	N.D.
GH250701	25 July 01	3.6	26	8	5.01	M27250901	25 Sept 01	3.57	14.8	9
LL020801	02 Aug 01	3.96	250	17	22.7	FLO260901	26 Sept 01	4.01	18.2	N.D.
SGH020801	02 Aug 01	3.75	410	300	2.11	M27280901	28 Sept 01	4.92	3.2	3
RH020801	02 Aug 01	3.95	230	100	3.55	GH121001	12 Oct 01	3.55	29.9	N.D.
PLY150801	15 Aug 01	2.69	290	120	3.73	MVO161001	16 Oct 01	7.25	7.2	N.D.
LL150801	15 Aug 01	2.88	150	30	7.71					
SGH150801	15 Aug 01	4.03	30	40	1.16					
RH150801	15 Aug 01	3.04	230	79	4.49					
GH180801	18 Aug 01	4.02	170	120	2.18					
LL250801	25 Aug 01	2.9	120	26	7.12					
RH250801	25 Aug 01	2.98	3	22	0.21					
SGH100901	10 Sept 01	3.76	41	29	2.18					
RH100901	10 Sept 01	3.46	45	16	4.34					
PLY110901	11 Sept 01	3.43	100	56	2.75					
PLY280901	28 Sept 01	3.04	182	46	6.10					
RH280901	28 Sept 01	3.19	118	12	15.2					
RH121001	12 Oct 01	3.45	50	19	4.06					

Also shown are background rainwater analyses (these were not affected by the plume before precipitation). These background concentrations were averaged and subtracted from the plume-affected rainwater sample analyses.
N.D. not detected; all concentrations in mg/l, to two significant figures.
Key to sampling locations indicated by sample numbers (see also Fig. 3): FLO – Fort Lookout; GH – Garibaldi Hill; LL – Lovers Lane; M – 'M27' Old Towne; MVO – Montserrat Volcano Observatory; PLY – Plymouth; RH – Richmond Hill; SGH – St George's Hill.

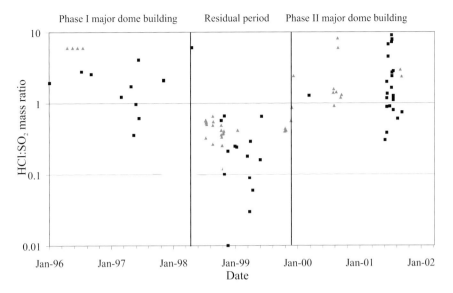

Fig. 4. The HCl/SO$_2$ mass ratio time series for ash leachate data (black squares) and open-path Fourier transform infrared spectroscopy data (grey triangles) from May 1996 up to September 2001. The timing of phases I and II of dome building, and the residual period, are indicated on the time-scale.

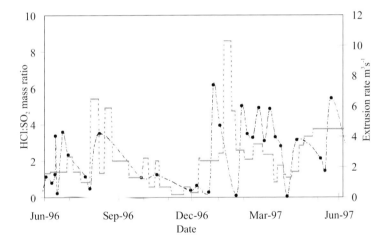

Fig. 5. The HCl/SO$_2$ mass ratios in rainwater collected at Upper Amersham, Montserrat, plotted for the period May 1996 to June 1997 (black circles). Also shown is the time-averaged extrusion rate of andesite lava for the same period, in m^3/s, calculated from dome and deposit surveying (grey dashed–dotted line).

The long-term record of HCl/SO$_2$ in ash leachates

Figure 4 compares the HCl/SO$_2$ mass ratios determined by ash leachate analysis (Table 1), from May 1996 up to September 2001, with remote-sensing measurements (by OP–FTIR spectroscopy) of the gas phase HCl/SO$_2$. The two phases

of dome building, and the intervening period of residual activity, are also indicated. The first four FTIR measurements are minimum estimates of the HCl/SO$_2$ mass ratio, as the amount of SO$_2$ absorption was at the detection limits of the instrument in May 1996 (Oppenheimer *et al.* 1998*a*). The trends of the two data-sets are similar,

(a)

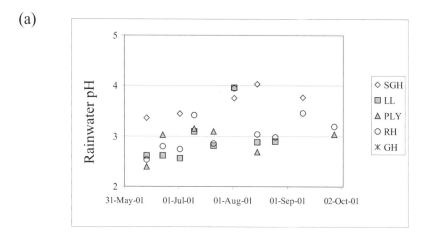

(b)

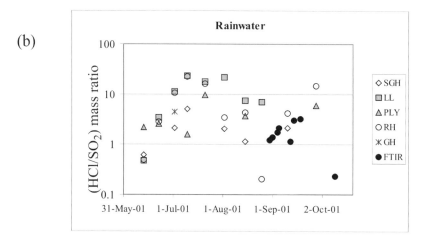

(c)

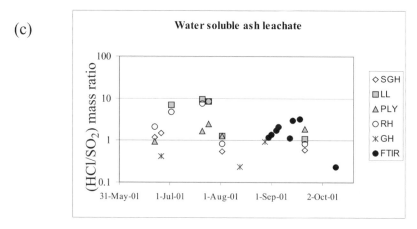

Fig. 6. Time-series of the compositional variation of rainwater and water-soluble ash leachates on Montserrat between June and September 2001. (**a**) Rainwater pH determined on precipitation at 5 sites (SGH, St George's Hill; LL, Lover's Lane; PLY, Plymouth; RH, Richmond Hill; GH, Garibaldi Hill). (**b**) and (**c**) Equivalent HCl/SO_2 mass ratios for these same sites based on measurements of chloride and sulphate in rainwater (b) and ash leachates (c), and compared with OP–FTIR measurements (solid circles).

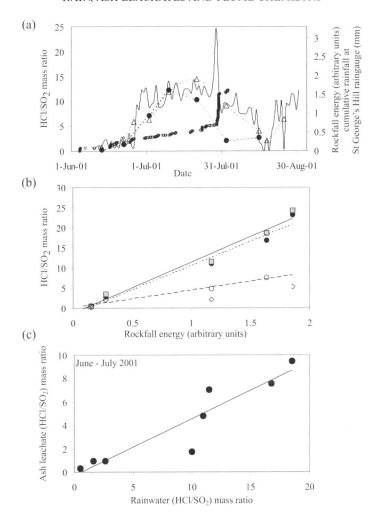

Fig. 7. (**a**) The HCl/SO_2 mass ratio in rainwater for June–September 2001, Montserrat. Filled circles show the results from rain collected at Richmond Hill, open triangles represent the mean HCl/SO_2 mass ratio for the sites at Plymouth, St George's Hill, Richmond Hill, and Lover's Lane. Also shown is rock-fall energy (solid black line) and the cumulative rainfall (small open circles), in mm, from a rain gauge on St George's Hill. (**b**) Graph showing the positive correlation between rock-fall energy and HCl/SO_2 mass ratios in rainwater (RH, Richmond Hill; LL, Lover's Lane; SGH, St George's Hill) and ash leachates (Richmond Hill) for the period June–July 2001. Three linear regression lines are shown for Lover's lane rainwater ($y=12.7x-1.2$; $R^2=0.98$); Richmond Hill rainwater ($y=12.0x-1.4$; $R^2=0.97$), and Richmond Hill ash leachates ($y=4.4x+0.2$; $R^2=0.96$). (c) Comparison of HCl/SO_2 mass ratios in rainwater and ash leachate samples collected from the same sites over the same dates, during June and July 2001. The best-fit line is described by $y=0.49x-0.31$; $R^2=0.86$.

with HCl/SO_2 mass ratios generally >1 during the main dome building phases and HCl/SO_2 <1 during the residual period, when the mass flux of andesite lava to the surface was zero. The large scatter in the ash leachate analyses reflects the fact that samples have been collected at a number of sites, representing deposition from both the centre and periphery of the plume, and at different distances from the vent.

Rainwater results for 1996–1997

Rainwater samples were collected from up to three sites for periods during 1996 and 1997 (Table 2). These samples show little systematic spatial variation in composition (Table 2), presumably because at some times (e.g. June–July 1996; February–March 1997) the plume dispersed directly over Plymouth, with lesser impact on the Amersham sites; and at other times dispersed predominantly south of Plymouth, with relatively more impact on Amersham (e.g. August–December 1996). Peak concentrations of chloride and sulphate reach 10^2–10^3 mg/litre, and show significant variability between sites on any given date; and at any one site through time.

In Figure 5, we compare temporal variations in the HCl/SO_2 mass ratio in rainwater collected between May 1996 and June 1997 from Upper Amersham, with the lava extrusion rate calculated by MVO staff from dome and deposit surveys. The two time series are remarkably similar. From August to December 1996, a decrease in the HCl/SO_2 mass ratio accompanies decreasing lava extrusion; a peak in HCl/SO_2 coincides with a peak in extrusion rate during January/February 1997, and April 1997 shows both reduced rainwater HCl/SO_2 and diminished lava output.

Changes in eruption rate are reflected in rapid increases or decreases in this ratio over periods of weeks. This is consistent with suggestions that the HCl emission rate is proportional to lava extrusion rate (Signorelli & Carroll 2001; Edmonds *et al.* 2002). This result is particularly encouraging in terms of monitoring, as it suggests that we can use changes in this mass ratio as a proxy for dome growth rate.

Data from 13 March 1996, from Upper Amersham, coincide with a period when there was direct sampling of the ambient air at Amersham (Allen *et al.* 2000). Allen and co-workers sampled the air using a filter pack assembly, with pre-filters used to collect particulate material, and base-saturated filters to collect acidic gases. Filter pack measurements from 11–13 March gave HCl/SO_2 mass ratios of 2–16 at Amersham (0.5–4 at Plymouth), and showed considerable, but systematic, decreases of concentrations of both airborne HCl and SO_2 (and HCl/SO_2) away from the volcano. The time-averaged HCl/SO_2 mass ratio in the air at Amersham for this period was $c.4.9$ (Allen *et al.* 2000), compared with a rainfall value of 20 (Table 2). Particulates, collected at the same time and differentiated into coarse (D_{50}=2.5 μm) and fine fractions, had mass-equivalent HCl/SO_2 ratios of 4.7 and 0.06, respectively. These observations suggest that rainwater compositions have significantly higher (Cl/S) ratios than the ambient (plume) gas phase, a feature that is consistent with the higher solubility of HCl over SO_2 (or sulphate) in the aqueous phase.

Rainwater and ash leachate data from June to September 2001

Rainwater data from June to September 2001 (Table 2) show significant spatial and temporal

variability. The spatial patterns identify the sites that are most influenced by the passage of the plume, and the same patterns are evident in the time series of both pH and HCl/SO_2 measurements (Fig. 6 *a*, *b*). In terms of rainwater acidity, many of the plume-affected sites receive acidic precipitation – with a pH from 2.5 to 3 (Fig. 6a). The sites at Lover's Lane and Plymouth (at distances of $c.4.4$ and 4.8 km due west from the dome, respectively) systematically receive rainfall with the lowest pH, followed by Richmond Hill (5.9 km from the dome); while precipitation at St George's Hill (3.7 km WNW from the dome) is significantly less acidic (often 0.5–1 pH unit higher).

Closely similar patterns are recorded in the site-by-site HCl/SO_2 rainwater (Fig. 6b) and ash leachate data (Fig. 6c). While there is considerable day-to-day variability in the HCl/SO_2 ratio at any one site (reflecting variations in the source conditions at the dome), on any day of measurement HCl/SO_2 ratios tend systematically to be highest at Lover's Lane and Richmond Hill, followed by Plymouth. The HCl/SO_2 ratios tend to be lowest at St George's Hill.

Temporal variability again correlates strongly with measures of dome activity and extrusion rate, such as the seismic energy release due to rock-falls. Figure 7a shows rainwater HCl/SO_2 mass ratios for the period June to September 2001, along with rock-fall energy extracted from the MVO seismic network data. The peak in rock-fall energy on 29 July 2001 represents a large dome collapse, when 40–50 million m^3 of the lava dome was removed. The cumulative rainfall record for this period, from a rain gauge on St George's Hill (data from the University of East Anglia, UK), shows that there is no correlation between rainwater composition and amount of rainfall. Over this same period, changes in the HCl/SO_2 mass ratio of rainwater correspond closely with rock-fall energy. The peak in the rainwater HCl/SO_2 mass ratio occurs directly before (10 days) the large dome collapse of 29 July 2001. A sharp decline in rock-fall energy around 20 August coincides with a minimum in the HCl/SO_2, after which both the rock-fall energy and rainwater HCl/SO_2 began to increase once again.

As Figure 7b shows, the most remarkable feature of the period June–July 2001 is the striking positive correlation between rock-fall energy and HCl/SO_2 ratios at a number of plume-affected sites in both rainwater and ash leachates. For this period, the correlations (based on up to five data points at each of four sites) appear to be linear, and site-dependent such that there are generally lower Cl/S ratios at greater distances, or on the margins of, the plume. The patterns seen here are no longer evident from the data after the end of July. This may in part reflect the paucity of data from August and September 2001, but may also reflect a change in prevailing conditions following the large collapse of the dome on 29 July, and the associated rainfall event (Fig. 7a).

Another important feature of the data that is clear from Figure 7b is the nature of the relationship between ash leachate and rainfall compositions. Data from Richmond Hill samples show that in the period June to July 2001 both rainwater and ash leachate HCl/SO_2 ratios correlate linearly with rock-fall energy. Therefore the rainwater/ash leachate relation is also approximately linear, with $(HCl/SO_2)_{rain, RH}$ $c. 2.7 \times (HCl/SO_2)_{ash leachate, RH} - 2$. This approximate relation is borne out when all of the ash leachate and rainwater data collected from the same sites and on the same dates are compared (Fig. 7c). Despite the variability that will presumably reflect the spatial variability of the data-sets, the general correlation is described by $(HCl/SO_2)_{rain} \sim 2.1 \times (HCl/SO_2)_{ash leachate} + 0.6$. In summary, during June and July 2001, rainwater (HCl/SO_2) ratios at any given point were two to three times the (HCl/SO_2) ratios in ash leachates sampled at the same point, and time.

The spatial patterns of HCl/SO_2 variability recognized in these data-sets are consistent with the patterns recognized in acid rainfall at other volcanoes (e.g. Johnson & Parnell 1986; Kawaratani & Fujita 1990; Aiuppa et al. 2001; Delmelle 2003). The HCl/SO_2 ratios tend to be highest (at any given point in time) at sites closest to the dome; and are systematically lower both at more distal sites, or at sites closer to the margins of the plume-influenced area (e.g. St George's Hill, for much of June and July 2001). This is consistent with removal of both HCl and SO_2 from the plume principally by wet-depositional processes: the more readily soluble HCl being extracted more efficiently into hydrometeors, or on to the surface of ash, than SO_2 (see also Horrocks et al. 2003; Delmelle 2003).

Discussion

Discussion of rainwater and ash leachate results

The new data from Montserrat show that the temporal variation of Cl/S ratios in ash leachates and rainwater, when collected in a systematic manner, principally reflect variations in plume chemistry. The consistent differences in the mass ratios between rain and ash leachate cannot be ascribed to processes such as condensation and/or evaporation in the collecting trays and bottles, as these processes would not have a differential effect on these species, unless solubility limits in water were approached, which is not the case. One possibility is that while the species concentrations in rainwater are entirely dependent on the partitioning of Cl and S species between the gas phase and the aqueous phase, the water-soluble fraction on ash particles represents a mixture of species adsorbed 'dry' within the vent, and an additional contribution from dissolution of species into any surficial aqueous phase. Resolution of this matter could be achieved by a program of wet/dry precipitation sampling, coupled with filter pack analysis, and simultaneous analysis of the plume composition by remote-sensing techniques.

Geochemical and remote-sensing data

In parallel with spectroscopic determinations of SO_2 and HCl emission from Soufrière Hills Volcano, chemical analyses of melt inclusions and matrix glasses in the andesite lavas have provided constraints on the sources of sulphur and chlorine in the Montserrat plume. Melt inclusions trapped in phenocrysts contain less sulphur than is needed to account for emissions of SO_2 at the surface (Barclay et al. 1998; Edmonds et al. 2001); a phenomenon well documented at other volcanoes (e.g. Stoiber & Jepson 1973; Rose et al. 1982; Wallace 2001). On Montserrat, the source of the 'excess' sulphur needed to balance the emission budget is attributed to the degassing of a sulphur-rich mafic intrusion at depth, for which there is considerable petrological and geochemical evidence (e.g. Murphy et al. 1998; Murphy et al. 2000; Couch et al. 2001; Edmonds et al. 2001).

In contrast, Cl concentrations in melt inclusions and matrix glass suggest that chlorine is progressively degassed on ascent (Edmonds et al. 2001, 2002). This inference has been corroborated experimentally (Signorelli & Carroll 2001). The rate of chlorine exsolution from the melt is dependent on the rate of water degassing and, consequently, ascent rate (Villemant & Boudon 1999; Villemant et al. 2003). The expectation that chlorine emissions correlate positively with lava extrusion rate is confirmed by measurements of HCl emission rates, which are greater during periods of active dome growth (400–13 000 t d^{-1}), than during periods of no lava extrusion (<100 t d^{-1}, Edmonds et al. 2001). During times such as the residual period when there is no evidence for magma migration within the conduit, a groundwater aquifer may develop, with liquid condensates, which would promote dissolution ('scrubbing') of the soluble HCl gas (Giggenbach & Matsuo 1991; Oppenheimer 1996; Symonds *et al.* 2001).

Conclusions

The monitoring of HCl/SO_2 by analysis of sulphate and chloride in rainwater and ash leachates provides an effective, low-budget means of monitoring broad changes in eruptive activity, at least under the volcanic and meteorological conditions prevalent on Montserrat. When used in conjunction with other monitoring data, this ratio may be used as a reliable indicator of changes in volcanic activity, most notably of changes in eruption rate. While rainwater chemistry records changes in plume chemistry very well, mass HCl/SO_2 is two to three times higher than that recorded by the ash leachates. Gas–ash–rain interactions are clearly complex, and our understanding of these processes will inevitably improve the use of these techniques to monitor volcanic activity. The data suggest that ash leachates provide a reliable means to measure HCl/SO_2 mass ratios in the absence of OP–FTIR spectroscopic data, provided that the ash is uncontaminated by water after reaching the ground.

From 1996 to 2001, there is a clear correspondence between HCl/SO_2 ratios measured by OP–FTIR spectroscopy and ash leachates. The HCl/SO_2 mass ratio exceeds one during dome building periods. Changes in mass ratio recognized in rainwater and ash leachate samples correlate strongly with eruption rate, both on long (month–year) and short (day–week) time-scales. During 1996 and 1997, extrusion rate calculated by independent methods correlates with mass HCl/SO_2 in rainwater, and this ratio may be used as a tool for assessing changes in growth rates over time-scales of weeks to months. In 2001, this mass ratio correlates with rock-fall energy, suggesting a link with dome growth rate. During periods of high magma ascent rate and high dome growth rate, HCl/SO_2 mass ratios are high. Chlorine exsolves rapidly on ascent, partitioning into a water-rich vapour phase. When magma flux to the surface is zero, chlorine cannot exsolve as effectively from the melt and so remains *in situ*. This has the effect of decreasing the HCl/SO_2 mass ratio of the plume gas.

This chapter is submitted with the permission of the Director, British Geological Survey, NERC. Past and present MVO staff are gratefully acknowledged for the collection of rainwater and ash samples for leachate analysis during 1996 and 1997. The British Geological Survey, Keyworth, UK, carried out the leachate analyses presented here, and W. Tonge of the Montserrat Water Authority carried out the rainwater analyses. We are grateful for rainfall gauge data, supplied to the MVO by J. Barclay, of the University of East Anglia, UK; and to P. Delmelle for an incisive review. Much of this work was funded by the Department for International Development, UK, and a NERC studentship awarded to ME. FTIR spectroscopic measurements have been supported by the NERC (grants GR9/03608 and GR9/4655) and the Gruppo Nazionale per la Vulcanologia.

References

AIUPPA, A., BONFANTI, P., BRUSCA, L., D'ALESSANDRO, W., FREDERICO, C. & PARELLO, F. 2001. Evaluation of the environmental impact of volcanic emissions from the chemistry of rainwater: Mount Etna (Sicily). *Applied Geochemistry*, **16**, 985–1000.

ALLEN, A. G., BAXTER, P. J. & OTTLEY, C. J. 2000. Gas and particle emissions from Soufriere Hills Volcano, Montserrat, West Indies: characterization and health hazard assessment. *Bulletin of Volcanology*, **62**, 8–19.

ASPINALL, W. P., MILLER, A. D., LYNCH, L. L., LATCHMAN, J. L., STEWART, R. C., WHITE, R. A. & POWER, J. A. 1998. Soufrière Hills eruption, Montserrat 1995–1997: volcanic earthquake locations and fault plane solutions. *Geophysical Research Letters*, **25**, 3397–3400.

BARCLAY, J., RUTHERFORD, M. J., CARROLL, M. R., MURPHY, M. D., DEVINE, J. D., GARDNER, J. & SPARKS, R. S. J. 1998. Experimental phase equilibria constraints on preeruptive storage conditions of the Soufrière Hills magma. *Geophysical Research Letters*, **25**, 3437–3440.

BRUNO, N., CALTABIANO, T. & ROMANO, R. 1999. SO_2 emissions at Mt Etna with particular reference to the period 1991–1995. *Bulletin of Volcanology*, **60**, 405–411.

COLE, P. D., CALDER, E. S., DRUITT, T. H., HOBLITT, R., ROBERTSON, R., SPARKS, R. S. J. & YOUNG, S. R. 1998. Pyroclastic flows generated by gravitational instability of the 1996–1997 lava dome of Soufrière Hills Volcano, Montserrat. *Geophysical Research Letters*, **25**, 3425–3428.

COUCH, S., SPARKS, R. S. J. & CARROLL, M. R. 2001. Mineral disequilibrium in lavas explained by convective self-mixing in open magma chambers. *Nature*, **411**, 1037–1039.

DE HOOG, J. C. M., KOETSIER, G. W., BRONTO, S., SRIWANA, T. & VAN BERGEN, M. J. 2001. Sulphur and chlorine degassing from primitive arc magmas: temporal changes during the 1982–1983 eruptions of Galunggung (West Java, Indonesia). *Journal of Volcanology and Geothermal Research*, **108**, 55–83.

DELMELLE, P. 2003. Environmental impacts of tropospheric gas plumes. *In*: OPPENHEIMER, C., PYLE, D. M. & BARCLAY J. (eds) *Volcanic Degassing*. Geological Society, London, Special Publications, **213**, 381–399.

DELMELLE, P., STIX, J., BOURQUE, C. P.-A., BAXTER, P.

J., ALVAREZ, J. G. & BARQUERO, J. 2001. Dry deposition and heavy acid loading in the vicinity of Masaya Volcano, a major sulphur and chlorine source in Nicaragua. *Environmental Science and Technology*, **35**, 1289–1293.

DRUITT, T. H., YOUNG, S. R. *ET AL*. 2002. Episodes of Vulcanian explosive activity with fountain collapse at Soufrière Hills Volcano, Montserrat. *In:* DRUITT, T. H. & KOKELAAR, B. P. (eds) The eruption of the Soufrière Hills Volcano from 1995 to 1999, Montserrat, Antilles. *Geological Society, London, Memoirs*, **21**, 281–306.

EDMONDS, M., PYLE, D. M. & OPPENHEIMER, C. M. 2001. A model of degassing at the Soufrière Hills Volcano, Montserrat, West Indies, based on geochemical data. *Earth and Planetary Science Letters*, **186**, 159–173.

EDMONDS, M., PYLE, D. M. & OPPENHEIMER, C. M. 2002. Chlorine degassing during the second phase of dome building at Soufrière Hills Volcano, Montserrat, West Indies. *Bulletin of Volcanology*, **64**, 21–30.

GALLE, B., OPPENHEIMER, C. M., GEYER, A., MCGONIGLE, A. & EDMONDS, M. (2003). A mini-DOAS spectrometer applied in remote sensing of volcanic SO_2 emissions, *Journal of Volcanology and Geothermal Research*, **119**, 241–254.

GIGGENBACH, W. F. & MATSUO, S. 1991. Evaluation of results from second and third IAVCEI field workshop on volcanic gases, Mt Usu, Japan and White Island, New Zealand. *Applied Geochemistry*, **6**, 125–141.

HAMMOUYA, G., ALLARD, P., JEAN-BAPTISTE, P., PARELLO, F., SEMET, M. P. & YOUNG, S. R. 1998. Pre- and syn-eruptive geochemistry of volcanic gases from Soufrière Hills of Montserrat, West Indies. *Geophysical Research Letters*, **25**, 3685–3688.

HORROCKS, L. A., OPPENHEIMER, C., BURTON, M. R. & DUFFELL, H. J. 2003. Compositional variation in tropospheric volcanic gas plumes: evidence from ground-based remote sensing. *In:* OPPENHEIMER, C., PYLE, D. M. & BARCLAY J. (eds) *Volcanic Degassing*. Geological Society, London, Special Publications, **213**, 349–369.

JOHNSON, N. & PARNELL, R. A. 1986. Composition, distribution and neutralization of 'acid rain' derived from Masaya volcano, Nicaragua. *Tellus*, **38**, 106–117.

KAWARATANI, R. K. AND FUJITA, S.-I. 1990. Wet deposition of volcanic gases and ash in the vicinity of Mount Sakurajima. *Atmosphere and Environment*, **24**, 1487–1492.

MARTIN, D., ARDOUIN, B., BERGAMETTI, G., CARBONELLE, J., FAIVRE-PERRET, R., LAMBERT, G., LE CLOAREC, M. F. AND SENNEQUIER, G. 1986. Geochemistry of sulphur in Mt Etna plume. *Journal of Geophysical Research*, **91**, 12 249–12 254.

MURPHY, M. D., SPARKS, R. S. J. *ET AL*. 1998. The role of magma mixing in triggering the current eruption at the Soufrière Hills Volcano, Montserrat, West Indies. *Geophysical Research Letters*, **25**, 3433–3436.

MURPHY, M. D., SPARKS, R. S. J., BARCLAY, J., CARROLL, M. R. & BREWER, T. S. 2000. Remobili-sation of andesite magma by intrusion of mafic magma at the Soufrière Hills Volcano, Montserrat, West Indies. *Journal of Petrology*, **41**, 21–42.

NORTON, G. E., ASPINALL, W. P. *ET AL*. 2002. Pyroclastic flow and explosive activity of the lava dome of the Soufrière Hills Volcano, Montserrat, during a period of no magma extrusion (March 1998 to November 1999). *In:* DRUITT, T. H. & KOKELAAR, B. P. (eds) *The Eruption of the Soufrière Hills Volcano from 1995 to 1999, Montserrat, Antilles*. Geological Society, London, Memoirs, **21**, 467–482.

OPPENHEIMER, C. 1996. On the role of hydrothermal systems in the transfer of volcanic sulphur to the atmosphere. *Geophysical Research Letters*, **23**, 2057–2060.

OPPENHEIMER, C. M., EDMONDS, M., FRANCIS, P. & BURTON, M. 2002. Variation in $HCl:SO_2$ gas ratios at Soufrière Hills Volcano observed by Fourier Transform Spectroscopy 1996–1999. *In:* DRUITT, T. H. & KOKELAAR, B. P. (eds) The eruption of the Soufriere Hills Volcano from 1995 to 1999, Montserrat, Antilles. *Geological Society, London, Memoirs*, **21**, 621–639.

OPPENHEIMER, C. M., FRANCIS, P. & MACIEJEWSKI, A. J. H. 1998*a*. Spectroscopic observation of HCl degassing from Soufrière Hills Volcano, Montserrat. *Geophysical Research Letters*, **25**, 3689–3692.

OPPENHEIMER, C. M., FRANCIS, P. W. & STIX, J. 1998*b*. Depletion rates of SO_2 in tropospheric plumes. *Geophysical Research Letters*, **25**, 2671–2674.

PENNISI, M. & LE CLOAREC, M. F. 1998. Variations of Cl, F and S in Mount Etna's plume, Italy, between 1992 and 1995. *Journal of Geophysical Research*, **103**, 5061–5066.

ROBERTSON, R. E. A., ASPINALL, W. P., HERD, R. A., NORTON, G. E., SPARKS, R. S. J. & YOUNG, S. R. 2000. The 1995–1998 eruption of the Soufrière Hills Volcano, Montserrat, WI. *Philosophical Trans-actions of the Royal Society of London*, **A358**, 1619–1637.

ROSE, W. I., STOIBER, R. E. & MALINCONICO, L. L. 1982. Eruptive gas compositions and fluxes of explosive volcanoes: budget of S and Cl emitted from Fuego Volcano, Guatemala. *In:* THORPE, R. S. (ed.) *Andesites: Orogenic Andesites and Related Rocks*. Wiley, New York, 669–676.

SIGNORELLI, S. & CARROLL, M. R. 2001. Experimental constraints on the origin of chlorine emissions at the Soufrière Hills Volcano, Montserrat. *Bulletin of Volcanology*, **62**, 431–440.

SIMKIN, T., SIEBERT, L., MCCLELLAND, L., BRIDGE, D., NEWHALL, C. & LATTER, J. H. 1981. *Volcanoes of the World*, Smithsonian Institution/Hutchison Ross, Stroudsberg, Pennsylvania.

STEVENSON, D. S., JOHNSON, C. E., COLLINS, W. J. & DERWENT, F. G. 2003 The tropospheric sulphur cycle and the role of volcanic SO_2. *In:* OPPENHEIMER, C., PYLE, D. M. & BARCLAY, J. (eds) *Volcanic Degassing*. Geological Society, London, Special Publication, **213**, 295–305.

STOIBER, R. E. & JEPSON, A. 1973. Sulphur dioxide contributions to the atmosphere by volcanoes. *Science*, **182**, 577–578.

STOIBER, R. E. & WILLIAMS, S. N. 1990. Monitoring active volcanoes and mitigating volcanic hazards: the case for including simple approaches. *Journal of Volcanology and Geothermal Research*, **42**, 129–149.

SYMONDS, R. B., GERLACH, T. M. & ROSE, W. I. 2001. Magmatic gas scrubbing: implications for volcano monitoring. *Journal of Volcanology and Geothermal Research*, **108**, 303–341.

TAYLOR, P. S. & STOIBER, R. E. 1973. Soluble material on ash from active Central American volcanoes. *Geological Society of America Bulletin*, **84**, 1031–1042.

TEXTOR, C., SACHS, P. M. & GRAF, H.-F. 2003. The scavenging of sulphur and halogen gases in a plinian volcanic plume similar to the Laacher See eruption 12900 yr BP. *In:* OPPENHEIMER, C., PYLE, D.M. & BARCLAY, J. (eds) *Volcanic Degassing.* Geological Society, London, Special Publications, **213**, 307–328.

VAREKAMP, J. C., LUHR, J. F. & PRESTEGAARD, K. L. 1984. The 1982 eruptions of El Chichon volcano (Chiapas, Mexico): character of the eruptions, ashfall deposits and gas phase. *Journal of Volcanology and Geothermal Research*, **23**, 39–68.

VILLEMANT, B. & BOUDON, G. 1999. H_2O and halogen (F, Cl, Br) behaviour during shallow level magma degassing processes. *Earth and Planetary Science Letters*, **168**, 271–286.

VILLEMANT, B., BOUDON, G., NOUGRIGAT, S.,

POTEAUX, S. & MICHEL, A. 2003. H_2O and halogens in volcanic clasts: tracers of degassing processes during plinian and dome-forming eruptions. *In:* OPPENHEIMER, C., PYLE, D. M. & BARCLAY, J. (eds) *Volcanic Degassing.* Geological Society, London, Special Publications, **213**, 63–79.

VOIGHT, B., SPARKS, R. S. J. *ET AL.* 1999. Magma flow instability and cyclic activity at Soufrière Hills Volcano, Montserrat, British West Indies. *Science*, **283**, 1138–1142.

WALLACE, P. J. 2001. Volcanic SO_2 emissions and the abundance and distribution of exsolved gas in magma bodies. *Journal of Volcanology and Geothermal Research*, **108**, 85–106

WATSON, I. M., OPPENHEIMER, C. M. *ET AL.* 2000. The relationship between degassing and ground deformation at Soufrière Hills Volcano, Montserrat. *Journal of Volcanology and Geothermal Research*, **98**, 117–126.

YOUNG, S. R., SPARKS, R. S. J., ASPINALL, W. P., LYNCH, L. L., MILLER, A. D., ROBERTSON, R. E. A. & SHEPHERD, J. B. 1998*a*. Overview of the eruption of Soufrière Hills Volcano, Montserrat, 18 July 1995 to December 1997. *Geophysical Research Letters*, **25**, 3389–3392.

YOUNG, S. R, FRANCIS, P. W. *ET AL.* 1998*b*. Monitoring SO_2 emission at the Soufrière Hills Volcano: implications for changes in eruptive conditions. *Geophysical Research Letters*, **25**, 3681–3684.

Magma extrusion dynamics revealed by high-frequency gas monitoring at Soufrière Hills volcano, Montserrat

S. R. YOUNG[1], B. VOIGHT[2] & H. J. DUFFELL[3]

[1]'Dunoon', Dayrells Road, Rockley, Barbados
(e-mail: sry2@psu.edu)
[2]Department of Geosciences, Penn State University, University Park,
PA16802, USA.
[3]Department of Earth Sciences, University of Cambridge,
Cambridge CB2 3EQ, UK.

Abstract: Andesitic to dacitic dome-building volcanoes often present a problem for eruption forecasting because signs of impending activity can be minimal or ambiguous. Gas monitoring is one of a number of techniques used to assist in eruption forecasting. However, a variety of explanations have been offered for the large variations in gas release that are commonly reported from erupting volcanoes. Difficulties in interpretation can arise because gas-flux measurements are generally acquired at lower sampling rates than other geophysical observations. Here, we report SO_2 flux measurements, by correlation spectroscopy, recorded semi-continuously during December 1999 to January 2000 at the Soufrière Hills Volcano, Montserrat. We compare these data to continuously recorded seismic records, and interpret the results in terms of conduit dynamics. We demonstrate two- to six-fold variations in gas flux over a few hours, and show that these variations can be systematic and directly correlated with long-period swarm seismicity. For the period of study, we find that the gas-flux peak lags several tens of minutes behind the peak in seismic energy release. These features are consistent with models of oscillating magma flow, where magma viscosity is dependent on melt volatile content. We propose that seismicity reflects conduit pressurization, and find that gas flux directly reflects magma flow rate. Although other volcanoes might behave differently, our results suggest that it can be possible to use continuous gas measurements to monitor conduit behaviour, perhaps providing short-term warnings of impending eruptions.

Island-arc volcanoes, whose magmas often are highly viscous, gas rich, and relatively slowly extruded, often represent a problem for eruption forecasting, because signs of impending activity can be minimal or ambiguous. Monitoring of seismicity, ground deformation and gas release are the most commonly used methods for identifying pre- and syn-eruptive signals. Seismic activity often precedes and accompanies eruptions, allowing, in favourable circumstances, some conclusions to be drawn on magma movement (McNutt 1996). Ground deformation also often precedes an eruption, but may not always occur in measurable amounts during an eruption (Van der Laat 1996). Gas flux often changes prior to and during eruptions, but interpretation of these changes can be problematic. It is the character of changes in gas flux measured by correlation spectroscopy (COSPEC) at the Soufrière Hills Volcano, Montserrat that is the subject of this chapter.

Variations in gas release at Mount St. Helens have been recognized and attributed to changes in the permeability of lava, with rapid reductions in gas emission rate attributed to sealing of the system (Casadevall et al. 1983). Similar interpretations have been given for Pinatubo (Hoblitt et al. 1996) and Galeras (Fischer et al. 1994), but in other circumstances, large apparent variations in gas flux may indicate inaccuracy and unreliability in the methods (Young et al. 1998b). Some further difficulties in interpretation arise because gas-flux measurements are generally acquired at much lower frequency than other geophysical parameters, and sometimes even at lower frequency than the short-term variations in behaviour of a volcano. Emergence of the 'Millennium' lava dome in November 1999 at the Soufrière Hills Volcano (SHV) on the Caribbean island of Montserrat provided an opportunity for high-frequency gas-flux monitoring by COSPEC synchronous with cyclic seismicity.

From: OPPENHEIMER, C., PYLE, D.M. & BARCLAY, J. (eds) *Volcanic Degassing*. Geological Society, London, Special Publications, **213**, 219–230. 0305-8719/03/$15.00

The recent history of the SHV eruption is as follows. Extruded andesite lava formed an important dome complex at SHV over the period November 1995 to March 1998 (Young *et al.* 1998*a*, Robertson *et al.* 2000). Then, over the next 20 months, 'residual volcanic activity' occurred, i.e. sporadic ash-venting explosions and gravity collapses of remnants of old altered dome rock, but without significant extrusion of magma (Norton *et al.* 2002). Following several relatively large explosions in the last week of October 1999, a swarm of hybrid earthquakes occurred on 3–8 November 1999, and the Montserrat Volcano Observatory (MVO) anticipated that magma was then moving towards the surface. Poorly vesicular pumice, erupted in explosions on 8–9 November, confirmed the rise of fresh magma. A new lava dome was first observed on 27 November 1999, although its initial emergence was suspected 1–2 weeks earlier. The new dome was elongate in plan and rose above the eastward-sloping base of the 1998–1999 collapse scar, facing the Tar River valley (Fig. 1a). After approximately four months of growth, the new lava dome collapsed on 20 March 2000, producing vigorous pyroclastic flows in Tar River valley and a 10-km high ash cloud. Lava dome growth restarted immediately, and the largest dome yet to grow during the current SHV eruption occupied the crater until July 2001, when it too collapsed. At the time of writing (May 2002), another new dome continues to grow at SHV.

Characterizing the renewal of dome growth

At the onset of the second phase of dome growth at SHV, a wide variety of monitoring data was being collected by MVO. Seismic monitoring was undertaken through two telemetered networks, one analogue, with short-period seismometers, and the other digital, with both short-period and broad-band seismometers (Miller *et al.* 1998; Neuberg *et al.* 1998). Ground deformation was monitored by continuous GPS (Mattioli *et al.* 2000; Norton *et al.* 2002), and dome growth by a sophisticated volume estimation method involving photometric and theodolite surveying (Herd 1998; Sparks *et al.* 1998; Watts *et al.* 2002). Rock and ash sampling and analysis, gas measurement by COSPEC and Open-Path Fourier Transform Infrared Spectroscopy (FTIR), and various other short- and long-term monitoring operations provided a large volume of data relating to the behaviour of the volcano.

A systematic cyclic pattern of volcanic tremor (2–3 Hz) was recognized every few hours from 23 November 1999 to 8 January 2000, indicating periodic changes in pressurization. Observations of the lava dome at this time suggested increased venting of ash, and especially gas, associated with the peak of the cycle (Fig. 1b). A typical seismic tremor cycle built gradually over a few hours, and then declined rapidly and stopped (Fig. 2), as revealed by seismograph helicorder records and Real-time Seismic Amplitude Measurement (RSAM; Endo & Murray 1991). Rock-fall activity (including, at times, pyroclastic flows) often occurred near or soon after the peak in RSAM, and is indicated on a spectrogram by an increase in high frequency energy.

Overall, these patterns are very similar to the cyclic patterns observed earlier, throughout much of the eruption (Voight *et al.* 1999). For example, for the period of cyclic activity following the large dome collapse of 21 September 1997, there were 75 cycles, each cycle culminating in a Vulcanian explosion (Druitt *et al.* 2002), averaging nine hours apart. The November 1999–January 2000 period yielded 120 tremor cycles at an average of 8.5 hours apart.

Initial extrusion rates during late-1999 were c.1.4 m^3/s (R. Herd pers. comm. 2001), well below the overall average for the 1995–1998 period (Sparks *et al.* 1998), but similar to rates observed in early 1996. The resumption of growth at such rates suggested that the conduit feeding magma from the chamber was still open in November 1999, despite the lack of significant emergent lava in 20 months. Explosions may have contributed to keeping the conduit open.

Other evidence, such as rock and gas geochemistry (Murphy *et al.* 2000; Edmonds *et al.* 2001) supports the notion that fundamental aspects of magma flow behaviour, including conduit geometry and magma properties, were similar to those observed during the first phase of dome growth: e.g. chamber depth of c.5–6 km, estimated conduit diameter of 30 m, rhyolite melt with water content of 4–5 wt%, magma temperature at 850 °C, magma crystal content of 60–65%, viscosity from 10^6 to about 10^{14} Pa s (Melnik & Sparks 1999; Voight *et al.* 1999; Sparks *et al.* 2000).

Measurements of SO$_2$ flux during dome growth in 1996–1997 were mainly carried out during periods of suppressed cyclicity and inferred small pressurization (Young *et al.* 1998*b*; Watson *et al.* 2000). We used the opportunity, in December 1999–January 2000, to measure SO$_2$ fluxes during an episode of long-lived, consistent cyclic seismicity, good atmospheric conditions, a fully operational instrument and an availability of manpower. During other periods of cyclic seismicity, matching cycles in proximal ground deformation (Voight *et al.* 1998, 1999) and

Fig. 1. (a) Aerial photograph looking towards the SW, showing the November–December 1999 lava dome at SHV. The vent is towards the top of the picture, and the dome is being emplaced on to the eastward-facing floor of the collapse scar within the 1995–1998 dome. The width of the collapse scar is approximately 300 m. Photograph by S. R. Young, 13 December 1999. (b) Photographs to show changes in the vigour of the gas plume during a typical seismic cycle. Each photograph immediately precedes a set of semi-continuous measurements of the SO_2 content of the plume made using the COSPEC instrument in the set-up as shown (see text for details). This sequence is from 15 December, with the local time shown. See Figure 5 for the measured fluxes.

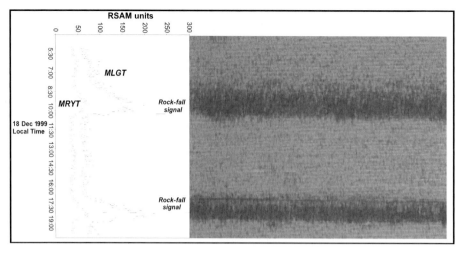

Fig. 2. RSAM records for short-period, single-component seismic stations located at 2 km to the NE (MLGT) and 2.5 km to the SE (MRYT) of the vent. To the right is the equivalent helicorder record for MLGT. Cyclic tremor episodes are defined by RSAM peaks that coincide with increasingly closely spaced long-period seismic events. A typical cycle builds slowly over *c.*3 h, and then stops abruptly. Rock-fall activity often coincides with the peak of the tremor cycle and during the rapid drop-off.

surficial activity on the lava dome have been recorded. We aimed to test current models and explain this behaviour by obtaining semi-continuous gas-flux measurements.

Gas measurement methods

During December 1999 and January 2000, a series of SO_2 flux measurements were taken by MVO staff using a COSPEC instrument on loan from the Geological Survey of Canada. Two different operational modes were utilized (Fig. 3): horizontal traverses (by boat and by helicopter, at 6–10 km and *c.*5 km from the vent, respectively) and vertical scanning of the plume from a fixed location 5 km from the vent and 2 km from the plume.

Horizontal traverses beneath the plume have been the standard method of collecting SO_2 flux data from volcanoes ever since COSPEC was first utilized for volcano monitoring (Stoiber *et al.* 1983). The method is described in detail by Sutton *et al.* (1992) and its application to Montserrat is described by Young *et al.* (1998*b*) and Watson *et al.* (2000). Gas-flux measurements are usually reported in tonnes/day SO_2; on Montserrat, the daily flux was routinely deduced from the average of two to six individual 'runs'. Thus, the reported daily gas flux for Montserrat (and almost all other volcanoes) is an extrapolation of data measured over a few tens of minutes, up to a daily mass emission of SO_2.

For the purposes of this work, we have utilized the 'daily' flux measurements in a manner which, apart from earlier work on Montserrat (Watson *et al.* 2000), has not previously been reported. We have used the horizontal traverse data during the period in question as a snapshot of SO_2 flux during different parts of the pressurization cycle as defined by the seismic data. Voight *et al.* (1999) show that during similar cyclic activity, the peak in long-period seismicity coincides with the peak in pressurization, as measured by proximal tiltmeters as the peak of inflationary deformation. On-going work (T. Powell, G. Thompson pers. comm. 2002) is focused on better defining the exact relationship between seismic and tilt cycles for different periods at SHV. In the absence of tilt data for the period in question, we use seismicity as the best available proxy for upper-conduit pressurization.

Over the course of approximately six weeks, some 27 traverses were made, on 11 different days, during all stages of the seismic cycle (Table 1). We have temporally normalized these data using a representative seismic cycle as a time-line. First, the seismic cycle on-going during any particular gas-measuring run was scaled in both time and amplitude to match the representative cycle, and then COSPEC data was similarly scaled. A final correction was made by negatively offsetting the time of each gas-flux measurement, so that each SO_2 flux data point is plotted at the time that it is emitted at the vent, rather than the

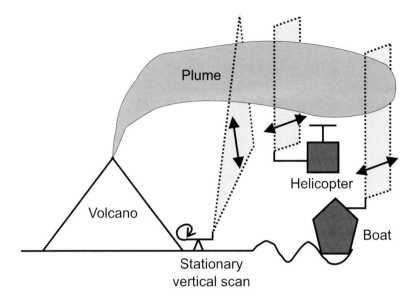

Fig. 3. Schematic diagram showing the three operating modes of the COSPEC instrument used during the study at SHV.

Table 1. *Results of COSPEC surveys by horizontal traverse methods, using helicopter and boat, during the study period.*

Date and time of survey	SO$_2$ flux (t day^{-1})	Method of survey
26/11/99 11:00	128	Helicopter
26/11/99 11:10	117	Helicopter
26/11/99 11:20	213	Helicopter
29/11/99 10:30	457	Helicopter
29/11/99 10:40	544	Helicopter
29/11/99 10:50	119	Helicopter
29/11/99 11:00	258	Helicopter
30/11/99 14:00	398	Helicopter
30/11/99 14:10	279	Helicopter
30/11/99 14:20	212	Helicopter
2/12/99 11:30	680	Helicopter
2/12/99 11:40	515	Helicopter
3/12/99 11:30	909	Helicopter
3/12/99 11:40	1518	Helicopter
3/12/99 11:50	941	Helicopter
13/12/99 15:00	572	Helicopter
13/12/99 15:10	993	Helicopter
13/12/99 15:20	767	Helicopter
20/12/99 14:30	738	Boat
20/12/99 14:45	866	Boat
22/12/99 10:15	370	Boat
22/12/99 10:30	354	Boat
27/12/99 15:00	1484	Helicopter
29/12/99 10:45	254	Boat
31/12/99 14:45	454	Helicopter
31/12/99 14:55	344	Helicopter
31/12/99 15:05	306	Helicopter

time at which it was measured at a downwind point. This correction procedure involves a simple calculation of dividing the downwind distance from the vent to the measurement point by the estimated average wind-speed. The normalized SO$_2$ flux was then plotted against a normalized time axis, as shown for all traverses on Figure 4. The representative seismic cycle is also shown.

Separate and independent sets of stationary SO$_2$ measurements were taken on a number of days during this period. Semi-continuous vertical traverses were made with a scanning azimuth normal to the plume. The fixed scanning location was 2 km from the plume, and measured the plume 4 km from the vent. A pair of scans (a down-scan, immediately followed by an up-scan) was carried out every 15 to 20 minutes for periods of 3.5 to 7 hours on five days during December 1999 and January 2000. Each pair of scans was averaged to produce one data point. Wind-speed measurements were taken before and after each pair of scans, using a hand held anemometer on a local high-point. These data are shown on Figure 5 for the four days for which full, or nearly full, seismic cycles were sampled. The actual seismic cycle, as seen in RSAM data, is also shown. We have again corrected the time axis of the gas-flux data so that each data point is plotted at the time at which the gas left the vent (this offset is typically 15 minutes).

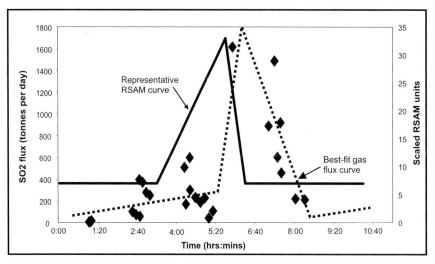

Fig. 4. Normalized gas flux from 27 boat and airborne traverses (diamonds), November–December 1999, compared with the representative RSAM curve (solid line). The best-fit gas flux is shown by the dotted line. Note the many-fold change in gas flux during the cycle, and the time-lag between the gas and RSAM peaks.

Errors

The SO_2 flux data from COSPEC measurements are subject to significant errors, whichever data-collection method is utilized. On Montserrat, Young *et al.* (1998*b*) suggested a ±30% accuracy for SO_2 flux measurements by ground or boat traverse. Sources of error include instrument calibration (±2%), operator-related variables (±5%) and errors in data reduction (±5%). However, the largest contributor to error is inaccurate wind-speed data. For the ground and boat traverses, wind-speed was measured by handheld anemometer 2 m above the ground on a hill 500 m above sea level, at least 500 m lower than the plume altitude. Also, wind-speed was often measured many tens of minutes before or after the actual survey took place. For helicopter surveys, the measurement of wind-speed is done from the helicopter during the survey at an altitude close to that of the plume and, most significantly, far above any ground turbulence effects. This significantly reduces the largest source of error for the helicopter traverse method, and we estimate error on COSPEC measurements from a helicopter to be better than ±20%.

Our use of the data in this study is mainly in relative rather than absolute terms, so data accuracy is less important than data precision. Measurement independent variables include fluctuations in wind-speed and cloud cover and degree of scattering by ash and aerosols in the plume. Meteorological conditions during our study period were generally stable, and ash generation was low, even during cycle peaks. However, variable amounts of ash and aerosols were present in the plume, and this provides the largest source of precision error for our data. We estimate the precision of the horizontal traverse data to be better than ±20%.

The fixed vertical traverse method is subject to larger errors in accuracy than the horizontal traverse method, due mainly to atmospheric scattering as the scan approaches the bottom of its arc (Shannon *et al.* 2001). However, we have used the fixed vertical traverse data for relative, rather than absolute comparisons (i.e. we have not compared or mixed absolute flux data from different methods). The methodology we employed, the continuity of operators, and the stable atmospheric conditions through each of the four days that we measured SO_2 using the vertical traverse method lead us to believe that the precision of these data is better than ±15%. Most of this error is again due to variable amounts of ash and aerosol in the plume.

Discussion

The key findings of this study are that SO_2 fluxes can vary greatly on an hourly time-scale, and that these variations can be systematic and closely associated with cyclic pressurization of the upper conduit, as indicated by seismic data. We infer that various factors influence the relationship between magma flux and SO_2 flux.

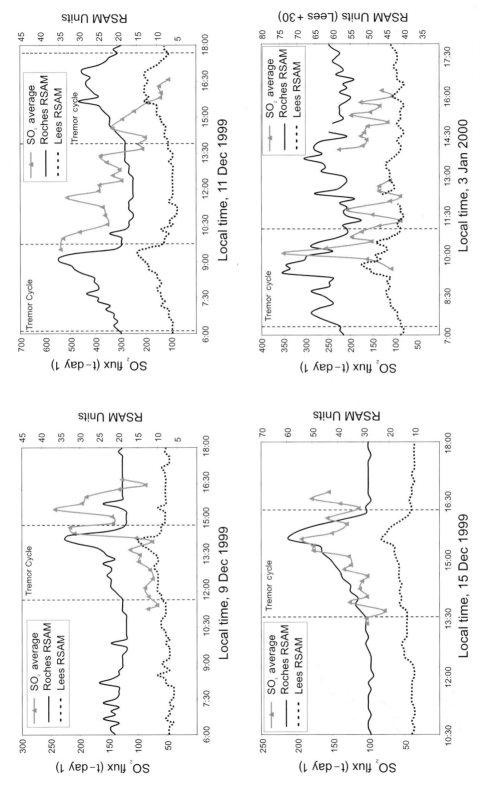

Fig. 5. The SO_2 flux from fixed-position COSPEC scanning on 9, 11 and 15 December 1999 and 3 January 2000. The data show a strong correlation with the RSAM at two stations (solid and dashed lines). Note the threefold changes in flux between the peak and troughs of the cycle, and the c. one-hour lag between the SO_2 peak and the RSAM peak (except 15 December – see text).

Short-term variations in SO₂ flux

The established methods of measuring SO_2 flux from volcanoes, utilizing the COSPEC instrument for short time periods and extrapolating results to represent much longer time periods, have long been thought prone to large inaccuracies. This has led some scientists to distrust the method and the value of SO_2 flux measurements. This study demonstrates that much of the inaccuracy in reported daily fluxes can derive from the low frequency of flux sampling undertaken. We have demonstrated two- to six-fold changes in SO_2 flux at SHV during periods of a few hours – changes that far exceed any estimates of measurement error, and must therefore be considered real. The strong cyclic seismicity recorded at the time of this study is not representative of the style of activity at most volcanoes most of the time, but there is good evidence to suggest that eruptions involving viscous, gas-rich magma will act cyclically at least some of the time (Voight *et al.* 1998, 1999; Denlinger & Hoblitt 1999; Melnik & Sparks 1999; Nakada & Motomura 1999; Sparks *et al.* 2000).

In their review of SO_2 flux data for the first two and a half years of the SHV eruption, Young *et al.* (1998*b*) suggested that SO_2 fluxes could be used as a proxy for magma supply rate. They were able to make this assertion, despite the poor fit for many individual SO_2 flux measurements (see Young *et al.* 1998*b*, Fig. 3) because of the quantity of gas data collected at SHV and the detailed database of erupted magma volume. The study reported here provides a reason other than measurement error for the scatter of data, namely that SO_2 fluxes were taken at many different stages of the pressurization cycle during periods of cyclic activity (e.g. December 1996–January 1997, May–August 1997; Voight *et al.* 1998, Watson *et al.* 2000), creating the potential for five-fold variations in flux for readings taken only hours apart.

The cyclic nature of gas exhalations

This study demonstrates a temporal relationship between cyclic long-period seismicity and gas exhalations. On three of the four days during which semi-continuous vertical-scan gas measurements were made across a clear peak in seismic activity, the peak in gas flux lagged the seismic peak by several tens of minutes. On 15 December (Fig. 5), there are two gas-flux peaks, one synchronous with the seismic cycle peak and the second, less defined, lagging by *c.*60 minutes. The compiled and normalized horizontal traverse data also define a gas-flux cycle, with the gas peak lagging 30–60 minutes after the seismic peak.

Our interpretation of these insights into gas dynamics is enhanced by recent improvements in scientific understanding of the SHV and comparable systems (Sparks 1997; Stix *et al.* 1997; Voight *et al.* 1999; Hammer *et al.* 1999; Melnik & Sparks 1999; Sparks *et al.* 2000, Sparks & Young 2002; Sparks 2003, this volume). Shallow seismicity, short-lived explosive eruptions, and ground deformation patterns previously observed at SHV indicated overpressures of several MPa in the uppermost few hundred metres of the magma conduit. These phenomena may be explained by the non-linear effects of crystallization and gas loss by permeable flow. Crystallization can introduce strong feedback mechanisms which amplify the effect on average extrusion rates of small changes in chamber pressure and conduit viscosity (Melnik & Sparks 1999). Such non-linear dynamics can cause pulsing patterns of dome growth.

Our data support aspects of models recently advanced to explain cyclic pressurization and seismicity, and yield new insights on gas monitoring. A cycle starts when the increased viscosity of conduit magma, due to degassing and microlite crystallization, leads to flow stagnation (Fig. 6). Conduit pressure then builds gradually (as earlier proved by tiltmetry; Voight *et al.* 1998, 1999), and gas flux is low. The gradually building seismicity directly reflects the gradually building pressure, but pressure drops, and seismicity ceases, when the magma plug 'yields' and a slug of magma is extruded from the conduit into the dome. This causes a sharp increase in gas flux through enhanced permeability in the dome, and, by disturbing the dome carapace, promotes an increase in rock-fall activity. Relaxation of driving pressure encourages magma flow to stagnate, viscosity increases, and the flow cycle repeats.

A quantitative model of flow instability (Wylie *et al.* 1999) indicates that the flow-rate peak lags behind the pressure peak. Magma flow-rate variations cannot be directly measured on the short time-scales required to test theory. However, our gas-flux measurements provide a proxy for magma emission rates at this time-scale, as permeability will be greatly enhanced during magma flow as opposed to magma stagnation. Figure 7 compares the model results of Wylie *et al.* (1999) with the actual results from this study. Cycle lengths from the modelled SHV system as illustrated by Wylie *et al.* (1999, Fig. 3) are *c.*50% longer than the long-term average of the November 1999–January 2000 cycles; however, their paper shows that parameters in

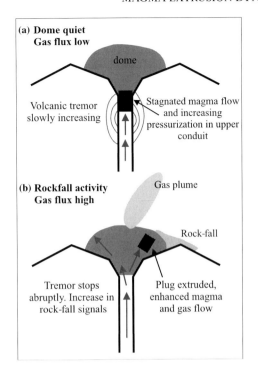

Fig. 6. Schematic diagram of the upper conduit and lava dome. (**a**) Gas-flux low, associated with stagnated magma flow, building conduit pressure, and increasing tremor. (**b**) Lava plug extrudes, gas pulse released, pressure and tremor declines.

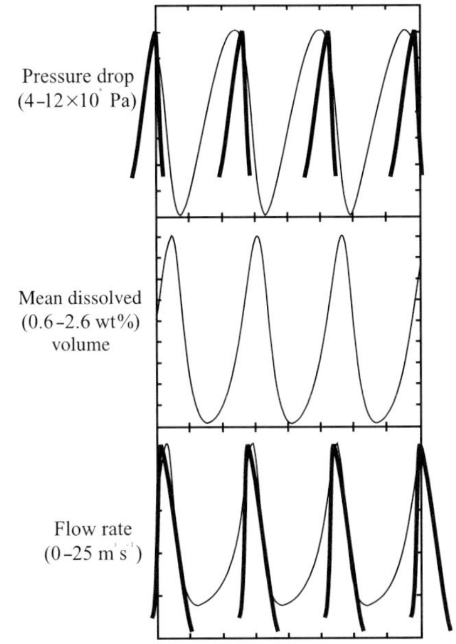

Fig. 7. Comparison of the modelled cyclicity of the Montserrat system, from Wylie *et al.* (1999), and the actual cyclicity as described in this work (taken from Fig. 4) shown with thicker lines. We use seismicity (RSAM) as a proxy for pressure drop (top), and SO_2 flux as a proxy for flow rate (bottom, SO_2 flux scale is 0–2000 t day^{-1}). We have 'stretched' the cycle length of the actual data to match that of the model data, in order to aid comparison.

the model can be adjusted within observed limits to alter the length of cycles. The behaviour of magma flow (or in this case its proxy in the real system – gas flux) in relation to pressure drop (or in this case its proxy in the real system, seismicity as measured by RSAM) follows closely that of the real system.

The relationship between magma flux and SO_2 flux

As stated earlier, Young *et al.* (1998*b*) suggested that SO_2 fluxes could be used as a proxy for magma-supply rate, subject to certain limitations. Following the method of Young *et al.* (1998*b*), the sulphur yield per tonne of magma erupted is estimated for the December 1999–January 2000 period. Repetitive dome volume measurements indicated that the magma eruption rate averaged 1.4 m^3/s during this period. This translates to *c.*42 000 m^3, or 1.0×10^5 tonnes of magma erupted during each nominal eight-hour cycle. From Figure 4, we can calculate the gas flux for this typical cycle (which is, in effect,

an average for all of the horizontal traverse gas-flux measurements). We find that the segment of the cycle where gas flux is high yields 130 t SO_2, and the remainder of the cycle yields about 20 t for a total of 150 t per cycle. These results suggest that *c.*1500 g of SO_2 were erupted per tonne of magma during this period – a ratio that is more than double the average estimated by Young *et al.* (1998*b*) for the 1996–1997 period.

The apparent similarity in eruptive conditions, physical properties of the upper conduit and dome as well as the geochemistry of the erupting magma between the two phases of dome growth was discussed earlier. Although within uncertainties, the doubling of SO_2 flux per unit of magma erupted between the first phase of dome growth, and the start of the second phase is worthy of consideration, especially in light of the conclusion of Young *et al.* (1998*b*) that SO_2 flux can be used as a proxy for magma flux. Edmonds *et al.* (2001) suggest that SO_2 degassing rate at SHV is influenced by near-surface permeability and magma chamber recharge, while HCl degassing rate is a good proxy for magma

eruption rate. Geochemical data (Edmonds *et al.*
2001) show that SO$_2$ is removed from the melt
into a vapour phase at magma chamber depths,
rather than during its rise to the surface.
Consequently, SO$_2$ would be susceptible to
leakage at varied depths, and not simply and
exclusively to magma discharge from the vent at
the end of the conduit.

This study tends to support the view that SO$_2$
degassing rate is not necessarily a good proxy for
magma eruption rate during periods when significant changes in eruptive activity occur.
However, in the absence of HCl data, and
providing that a long baseline of SO$_2$ data can be
established, we believe that short- to medium-
term (hours to months) changes in SO$_2$ flux can
be a good proxy for magma eruption rate.

The relatively high SO$_2$ production rate during
the early stages of renewed dome growth at SHV
may be due in part to changes in vent and conduit
permeability during the 'residual' volcanic
activity between the two phases of dome growth
(Norton *et al.* 2002). A more permeable conduit
system would be likely to enhance SO$_2$ release
from the vapour phase through the conduit and
vent system rather than as leakage from the
chamber. The cyclic nature of activity may also
enhance SO$_2$ release through the vent compared
with when activity is not strongly cyclic. Both of
these factors would tend to increase the amount
of SO$_2$ measured per unit magma flux.

However, the most likely cause of the twofold
increase in SO$_2$ production per unit magma
erupted is a probable increase in SO$_2$ abundance
in the hydrous gas phase in the magma chamber
due to substantial recharge of basaltic magma
during the period of residual activity. This
recharge perhaps prompted the restart of magma
supply to the surface in November 1999.

Conclusions

1. We have demonstrated the value of semi-
continuous gas measurements at volcanoes
where cyclic activity on an hourly time-scale
may be present. Conventional daily gas-flux
measurements by COSPEC provide just a
snapshot of SO$_2$ flux, which may change two-
to six-fold within hours of the measurement
being made. This creates significant inaccuracies in extrapolating these measurements
into daily fluxes, and such inaccuracies can
exceed the instrumental error. We urge
caution in the interpretation of isolated gas-
flux measurements where cyclic activity may
be occurring.
2. This study has quantified the variations in gas
flux during a period of cyclic pressurization of

an andesitic lava dome. Quantitative evidence
for cyclic seismicity, ground deformation, and
dome growth has previously been collected at
SHV, and there was considerable qualitative
observational data from SHV for associated
cyclic gas exhalations. We find that during
cyclic phases of dome growth, the release of
gas peaks tens of minutes after the seismic
peak. The flux at peak exhalation is two- to
six times greater than the flux during the
remainder of the cycle.
3. The results of this study have been compared
with recently developed models of cyclic
dome growth. We find that there is good
agreement between model results and SO$_2$
data, with the SO$_2$ emission rate showing a
consistent lag of 30–60 minutes after the
pressurization peak.
4. The study supports recent work showing that
SO$_2$ flux is not inherently controlled by
magma eruption rate, especially if a magmatic
system changes significantly in eruptive
activity. However, the coincidence of gas-flux
peak with magma extrusion shows a strong
short-term linkage between magma eruption
rate and SO$_2$ flux. We suggest that the
increased SO$_2$ flux per unit magma erupted in
the early stages of renewed dome growth at
SHV is due to enhanced conduit and vent
permeability, more effective gas release during
periods of strong cyclic activity and, most
importantly, an increase in the SO$_2$ reservoir
within the magma chamber due to mafic
recharge.
5. Remote sensing of volcanic gases provides an
opportunity to enhance monitoring and
warning considerably at andesitic and dacitic
dome-forming volcanoes. We have shown that
gas-flux peaks, on a short time-scale, coincide
with magma flow peaks and dome disruption,
which, on Montserrat, coincide with the most
dangerous events, namely pyroclastic flow
generation and explosions.

We thank all colleagues at the MVO for assistance with
this work, especially M. Edmonds, R. Herd, B. Baptie,
T. Syers, G. Thompson, and A. Jolly. The UK
Department for International Development (through
the British Geological Survey) and the Government of
Montserrat provided funding for MVO. B. Voight
acknowledges support from the US National Science
Foundation. We thank C. Hickson, J. Stix and the
Geological Survey of Canada for extended loan of the
COSPEC instrument used in this work.

References

CASADEVALL, T. J., ROSE, W. I., GERLACH, T. M.,
GREENLAND, L. P., EWERT, J., WUNDERMAN, R. &

SYMONDS, R. 1983. Gas emissions and the eruptions of Mount St. Helens through 1982. *Science*, **221**, 1383–1385.

DENLINGER, R. P. & HOBLITT, R. P. 1999. Cyclic eruptive behavior of silicic volcanoes. *Geology*, **27**, 459–462.

DRUITT, T. H., YOUNG, S. R. ET AL. 2002. Episodes of cyclic Vulcanian explosive activity with fountain collapse at Soufrière Hills Volcano, Montserrat. *In:* DRUITT, T. H. & KOKELAAR, B. P. (eds) *The Eruption of Soufrière Hills Volcano, Montserrat, from 1995 to 1999.* Geological Society, London, Memoirs, **21**, 281–306.

EDMONDS, M., PYLE, D. & OPPENHEIMER, C. 2001. A model for degassing at the Soufrière Hills Volcano, West Indies, based on geochemical data. *Earth and Planetary Science Letters*, **186**, 159–173.

ENDO, E. T. & MURRAY, T. 1991. Real time seismic amplitude measurement (RSAM): a volcano monitoring and prediction tool. *Bulletin of Volcanology*, **53**, 533–545.

FISCHER, T. P., MORRISSEY, M. M., CALVACHE, M. L., GÓMEZ, M. D., TORRES, C. R., STIX, J. & WILLIAMS, S. N. 1994. Correlations between SO_2 flux and long-period seismicity at Galeras Volcano, Colombia. *Nature*, **368**, 135–137.

HAMMER, J. E., CASHMAN, K. V., HOBLITT, R. P. & NEWMAN, S. 1999. Degassing and microlite crystallization during pre-climactic events of the 1991 eruption of Mt. Pinatubo, Philippines. *Bulletin of Volcanology*, **60**, 355–380.

HERD, R. A. 1998. *Methods used to survey the lava dome and associated products of the Soufrière Hills Volcano, Montserrat.* Montserrat Volcano Observatory, Open-File Report 98/16.

HOBLITT, R. P., WOLFE, E. W., SCOTT, W. E., COUCHMAN, M. R., PALLISTER, J. S. & JAVIER, D. 1996. The preclimactic eruptions, June 1991, Mount Pinatubo, Philippines. *In:* NEWHALL, C. G. & PUNONGBAYAN, R. S. (eds) *Fire and Mud: Eruptions and Lahars of Mount Pinatubo, Philippines.* Philippine Institute of Volcanology and Seismology, Quezon City and University of Washington Press, Seattle, 457–511.

MCNUTT, S. R. 1996. Seismic monitoring and eruption forecasting of volcanoes: a review of the state-of-the-art and case histories. *In:* SCARPA, R. & TILLING, R. I. (eds) *Monitoring and Mitigation of Volcano Hazards.* Springer-Verlag, Berlin, 99–146.

MATTIOLI, G. S., RODRIGUEZ, L., SMITH, A. L., JANSMA, P. E. & HERD, R. A. 2000. *Changes in magmatic flux recorded by campaign and continuous GPS geodesy of Soufrière Hills, Montserrat, BWI.* Proceedings, Geosciences 2000, Geological Society of London, p. 153.

MELNIK, O. & SPARKS, R. S. J. 1999. Nonlinear dynamics of lava dome extrusion. *Nature*, **402**, 37–41.

MILLER, A. D., STEWART, R. C., WHITE, R. A., LUCKETT, R., BAPTIE, B. J., ASPINALL, W. P., LATCHMAN, J. L., LYNCH, L. L. & VOIGHT, B. 1998. Seismicity associated with dome growth and collapse at the Soufrière Hills Volcano, Montserrat. *Geophysical Research Letters*, **25**, 3401–3404.

MURPHY, M. D., SPARKS, R. S. J., BARCLAY, J., CARROLL, M. R. & BREWER, T. S. 2000. Remobilization of andesitic magma by intrusion of mafic magma at the Soufrière Hills Volcano, Montserrat, West Indies. *Journal of Petrology*, **41**, 21–42.

NAKADA, S. & MOTOMURA, Y. 1999. Petrology of the 1991–1995 eruption at Unzen: effusion pulsation and groundmass crystallization. *Journal of Volcanology and Geothermal Research*, **89**, 173–196.

NEUBERG, J., BAPTIE, B. J., LUCKETT, R. & STEWART, R. C. 1998 Results from the broadband seismic network on Montserrat. *Geophysical Research Letters*, **25**, 3661–3664.

NORTON, G. E., YOUNG, S. R. ET AL. 2002. Pyroclastic flow and explosive activity of the lava dome of Soufrière Hills volcano, Montserrat, during the period of no magma extrusion (March 1998 to November 1999). *In:* DRUITT, T. H. & KOKELAAR, B. P. (eds) *The Eruption of Soufrière Hills Volcano, Montserrat, from 1995 to 1999.* Geological Society, London, Memoirs, **21**, 467–481.

ROBERTSON, R. E. A., ASPINALL, W. P., HERD, R. A., NORTON, G. E., SPARKS, R. S. J. & YOUNG, S. R. 2000. The 1995–1998 eruption of the Soufrière Hills volcano, Montserrat, WI. *Philosophical Transactions of the Royal Society of London*, **A358**, 1619–1637.

SHANNON, J. M., WATSON, I. M., BLUTH, G. J. S. & CARN, S. A. 2001. Investigating errors in Static COSPEC Measurements of Volcanic SO_2 Plumes. *EOS, Transactions of the American Geophysical Union*, **82 (47)**, F1370.

SPARKS, R. S. J. 1997. Causes and consequences of pressurization in lava dome eruptions. *Earth and Planetary Science Letters*, **150**, 177–189.

SPARKS, R. S. J. 2003. Dynamics of magma degassing. *In:* OPPENHEIMER, C., PYLE, D. M. & BARCLAY, J. (eds) *Volcanic Degassing.* Geological Society, London, Special Publications **213**, 5–22.

SPARKS, R. S. J. & YOUNG, S. R. 2002. The eruption of Soufrière Hills Volcano, Montserrat: overview of scientific results. *In:* DRUITT, T. H. & KOKELAAR, B. P. (eds) *The eruption of Soufrière Hills Volcano, Montserrat, from 1995 to 1999.* Geological Society, London, Memoirs, **21**, 45–69.

SPARKS, R. S. J., YOUNG, S. R. ET AL. 1998. Magma production and growth of the lava dome of the Soufrière Hills Volcano, Montserrat, West Indies: November 1995 to December 1997. *Geophysical Research Letters*, **25**, 3421–3424.

SPARKS, R. S. J., MURPHY, M. D., LEJEUNE, A.-M., WATTS, R. B., BARCLAY, J. & YOUNG, S. R. 2000. Control on the emplacement of the andesite lava dome of the Soufrière Hills volcano, Montserrat by degassing-induced crystallization. *Terra Nova*, **12**, 14–20.

STIX, J., TORRES, R. C., NARVAEZ, M. L., CORTÉS, G. P., RAIGOSA, J. A., GOMEZ, D. M. & CASTONGUAY, R. 1997. A model of Vulcanian eruptions at Galeras Volcano, Colombia. *Journal of Volcanology and Geothermal Research*, **77**, 285–304.

STOIBER, R. E., MALINCONICO JR, L. L. & WILLIAMS, S. N. 1983. Use of the correlation spectrometer at volcanoes. *In*: TAZIEFF, H. & SABROUX, J.-C. (eds) *Forecasting Volcanic Eruptions*. Elsevier, Amsterdam, 425–444.

SUTTON, A. J., MCGEE, K. A., CASADEVALL, T. J. & STOKES, B. 1992. Fundamental volcanic-gas-study techniques: an integrated approach to monitoring. *In*: EWERT, J. W. & SWANSON, D. A. (eds) *Monitoring Volcanoes: Techniques and Strategies Used by the Staff of the Cascades Volcano Observatory, 1980–90*. US Geological Survey Bulletin, 1966, 181–188.

VAN DER LAAT, R. 1996. Ground-deformation methods and results. *In*: SCARPA, R. & TILLING, R. I. (eds) *Monitoring and Mitigation of Volcano Hazards*. Springer-Verlag, Berlin, 147–168.

VOIGHT, B., HOBLITT, R. P., CLARKE, A. B., LOCKHART, A. B., MILLER, A. D., LYNCH, L. L. & MCMAHON, J. 1998. Remarkable cyclic ground deformation monitored in real time on Montserrat and its use in eruption forecasting. *Geophysical Research Letters,* 25, 3405–3408.

VOIGHT, B., SPARKS, R. S. J. *ET AL*. 1999. Magma flow instability and cyclic activity at Soufrière Hills volcano, Montserrat, British West Indies. *Science,* 283, 1138–1142.

WATSON, I. M., OPPENHEIMER, C. M. M. *ET AL*. 2000. The relationship between degassing and ground deformation at Soufrière Hills Volcano, Montserrat. *Journal of Volcanology and Geothermal Research,* 98, 117–126.

WATTS, R. B., HERD, R. A., SPARKS, R. S. J. & YOUNG, S. R. 2002. Growth patterns and emplacement of the andesitic lava dome at Soufrière Hills Volcano, Montserrat. *In:* DRUITT, T. H. & KOKELAAR, B. P. (eds) *The eruption of Soufrière Hills Volcano, Montserrat, from 1995 to 1999*. Geological Society, London, Memoirs, 21, 115–152.

WYLIE, J. J., VOIGHT, B. & WHITEHEAD, J. A. 1999. Instability of magma flow from volatile-dependent viscosity. *Science,* 285, 1883–1885.

YOUNG, S. R., SPARKS, R. S. J., ASPINALL, W. P., LYNCH, L. L., MILLER, A. D., ROBERTSON, R. E. A. & SHEPHERD, J. B. 1998a. Overview of the eruption of the Soufrière Hills volcano, Montserrat, July 18, 1995 to December 1997. *Geophysical Research Letters,* 25, 3389–3392.

YOUNG, S. R., FRANCIS, P. W. *ET AL*. 1998b. Monitoring SO_2 emission at the Soufrière Hills volcano: implications for changes in eruptive conditions. *Geophysical Research Letters,* 25, 3681–3684.

Carbon dioxide emissions from fumarolic ice towers, Mount Erebus volcano, Antarctica

L. J. WARDELL, P. R. KYLE & A. R. CAMPBELL

Department of Earth and Environmental Science, New Mexico Institute of Mining and Technology, Socorro, NM 87801, USA.
(e-mail: wardell@nmt.edu)

Abstract: Degassing at Mount Erebus occurs as a plume from a persistent convecting anorthoclase phonolite lava lake, and by flank degassing through warm ground and fumarolic ice towers within the summit caldera. The fumarolic ice towers offer a unique and simple approach to quantifying the flank CO_2 emissions. Carbon dioxide effluxes were determined at openings in the ice towers by measuring the CO_2 concentration, air-flow velocity, and size of the exit orifice. Fluxes ranged from <0.0001 to 0.034 kg s^{-1} at 43 actively degassing ice towers. Small patches of steaming warm ground contributed 0.010 kg s^{-1}. The $\delta^{13}C$ isotopic compositions of the CO_2 samples ranged from –2.1 to –4.7‰, suggesting a magmatic origin for the CO_2. Fumarolic ice towers allow diffuse degassing to be visually identified, providing a strong advantage in determining the total flux rate of these passive emissions. The estimated output of flank CO_2 degassing is 0.46 kg s^{-1} (40 Mg d^{-1}). Compared with direct airborne measurements of the volcanic plume, passive flank emissions constitute less than 2% of the total volcanic CO_2 budget emitted from Mount Erebus.

In recent years it has become apparent that degassing of magma within a volcanic edifice occurs not only by emissions from a summit crater but also by diffusive degassing around the flanks of a volcano. This is particularly true for CO_2. Significant flank degassing of CO_2 has been observed at Mount Etna (Allard *et al.* 1991), Kilauea (Gerlach & Graeber 1985) and Vulcano (Chiodini *et al.* 1996). Therefore, flank degassing through fumaroles and by soil gas emissions must be evaluated when quantifying the volatile budget of a volcano. Although some volcanoes lose only minor amounts of CO_2 via their flanks, in many others diffuse degassing is an important part of the volcanic CO_2 budget.

Diffuse CO_2 emissions have been examined at numerous volcanic and geothermal areas over the last 15 years (Mori *et al.* 2001). At Mammoth Mountain, California, diffuse CO_2 emissions were of such magnitude that they killed large areas of trees and posed a hazard to people in the area (Farrar *et al.* 1995). Soil gas studies have been conducted to examine the extent and nature of the emission source and its ties to an underlying magmatic system (Rahn *et al.* 1996; Gerlach *et al.* 1998, 1999, 2001; McGee *et al.* 1998, 2000; Sorey *et al.* 1998; Rogie *et al.* 2001). Soil gas CO_2 effluxes measured at Usu volcano, Japan, showed an increase prior to an eruption on 31 March 2000, followed by a sudden

decrease in June 2000 following the eruptive activity (Hernandez *et al.* 2001).

Soil gas emissions can reflect the degassing of an underlying magmatic system. It has been suggested that periodic monitoring of sites distant from the eruptive vents can assist in understanding the temporal evolution of the volcanic activity and the associated magmatic system (Giammanco *et al.* 1998). Monitoring of the diffuse CO_2 degassing at sites distant from an erupting vent may also be safer for scientists tasked with volcanic hazard surveillance.

Soil gas emanations, such as CO_2, are also useful for identifying faults and/or areas of subsurface thermal activity (Baubron *et al.* 1991 and Chiodini *et al.* 1998). A number of studies used soil gas CO_2 efflux measurements to identify faults and other volcanotectonic features that were not visible at the surface (Sugisaki *et al.* 1983; Giammanco *et al.* 1997; Azzaro *et al.* 1998). Soil gas CO_2 studies were employed to develop the structural map at Mount Etna and to define fault structures that did not have visible surface expression (Giammanco *et al.* 1998).

Mount Erebus, Antarctica, the world's southernmost active volcano, is mostly snow and ice covered and ambient temperatures are always well below freezing. A convecting persistent anorthoclase phonolite lava lake with a characteristic gas plume is the most obvious sign of

From: OPPENHEIMER, C., PYLE, D.M. & BARCLAY, J. (eds) *Volcanic Degassing*. Geological Society, London, Special Publications, **213**, 231–246. 0305–8719/03/$15.00

volcanic activity (Kyle *et al.* 1982; Kyle 1994). Diffuse flank degassing occurs through steaming warm ground (>0°C) and as fumarolic ice towers, many of which are underlain by ice caves (Lyon & Giggenbach 1974). Flank degassing localities are likely restricted to fractures, as much of the volcano is covered by permanently frozen ground (permafrost) which serves as an impermeable barrier to gas migration.

Here we report on passive CO_2 flank emissions from the summit caldera of Mount Erebus using measurements performed at ice towers and areas of warm ground. Carbon dioxide emission has been detected in all actively degassing features measured on Mount Erebus. The objective of this study was to quantify the total output of volcanic CO_2 from flank degassing and develop a further understanding of the sub-surface systems within the summit caldera. Using fumarolic ice towers is a unique way to estimate CO_2 efflux and offers a new tool to understand flank degassing at Mount Erebus.

Background

Steaming ice towers have been observed at a number of active volcanoes in Antarctica. They show the presence of local geothermal activity and therefore should be considered as signatures of the volcanic activity in the area. Mount Melbourne, 350 km north of Mount Erebus on the Victoria Land coast, has ice towers (Lyon & Giggenbach 1974; Keys *et al.* 1983; Broady 1993). In Marie Byrd Land, Mount Berlin, the only active volcano in West Antarctica, has an active steaming ice tower and an underlying cave, similar to Mount Erebus, with a soil temperature of 12 °C (McIntosh & Dunbar, pers. comm. 1999).

Mount Erebus, a 3,794-metre high composite alkaline volcano, is the dominant feature of Ross Island, Antarctica. It is the world's southernmost active volcano and has a persistent convecting lava lake of anorthoclase phonolite magma that continuously degasses. Small eruptions were occurring at Mount Erebus at the time of its discovery in January 1841 (Ross 1847). Over the last 30 years the volcano has produced small strombolian eruptions typically at a frequency of 2 to 6 events per day (Kyle *et al.* 1982; Dibble *et al.* 1984; Kyle 1994). A plume of volcanic gas is constantly emitted from the lava lake. The flux of various acid gas species and trace metals (Zreda-Gostynska *et al.* 1993; Zreda-Gostynska *et al.* 1997), SO_2 (Kyle *et al.* 1994) and CO_2 (Wardell & Kyle 1998) have been measured.

Fumarolic ice towers form when water vapour diffusing and percolating through the subsurface reaches ground level and condenses and freezes in the cold atmosphere. Ice towers form in a range of shapes and sizes that can rise up to 15 m as simple chimney-like structures. The earliest reference regarding active fumarolic ice towers on Mount Erebus was noted by David and Priestley (1909) during the first ascent of Mount Erebus (Shackleton expedition 1908). Holdsworth and Ugolini (1965) ascended the northwest side of the volcano in 1962 and 1964 and found a number of large ice towers (6 to 10 m tall), but reported that many were inactive with no open steaming vents. During periods of low relative humidity it is extremely difficult to see emissions from the ice towers, so it is possible that the apparently inactive towers were in fact active. Lyon and Giggenbach (1974) gave detailed descriptions of the ice towers and found the majority of towers to be active. However, they did observe eroded remnants of inactive towers.

There are an unknown number of ice caves on the summit plateau of Mount Erebus, and only a few have been explored. Giggenbach (1976) reported on a 400 m-long ice cave system near the summit crater of Mount Erebus that closely resembled the one at Mount Rainier, USA. Although this cave has partially collapsed and may no longer exist, the largely horizontal extent of the cave is attributed to the geometry of diffuse zones of heat release that are similar to the localized thermal activity used to explain the horizontality of the cave on Mount Rainier (Giggenbach 1976). Other ice caves on Mount Erebus also exhibit this horizontal geometry.

In addition to ice towers and their associated ice caves, flank emissions can be observed in areas of warm ground. These areas are free of snow and ice cover and can be seen steaming during optimum atmospheric conditions. The largest and most thermally active area of warm ground is found at the bottom of Tramway Ridge (Fig. 1). Access to this 'Site of Special Scientific Interest (SSSI)' is restricted by the Antarctic Conservation Act. Being 'one of only two known high-altitude areas of fumarolic activity and associated vegetation' makes it a rare environment on the continent (NSF 1995). The whole Tramway warm ground area covers less than 1 hectare (NSF 1995) and only half of the area is accessible by permit regulations as a precautionary measure to protect the biota. Biological studies in the area report surface temperatures ranging from 0 to 46°C (Broady 1993). During the 1972–1973 Austral summer season, Lyon and Giggenbach (1974) reported the surface temperature on red algal growth to be 42–43°C and 34–36°C on the green algal mat with a high temperature of 65°C measured at 15 cm depth.

Sheppard *et al.* (1994) observed CO_2 flank

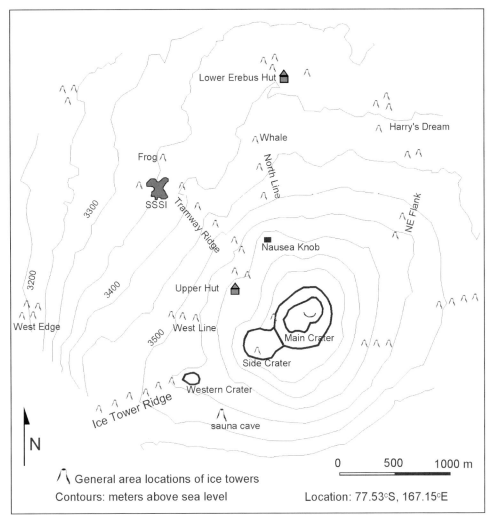

Fig. 1. Sketch map of the summit of Mount Erebus, showing the general locations of ice towers. The ice tower symbols represent general locations of ice towers and not the individual towers.

degassing in two ice towers and in several soil areas on Mount Erebus, but were unable to obtain efflux measurements. The emission rate of CO_2 in the plume of the volcano was measured by direct airborne techniques in December 1997, December 1999 and January 2001. The total CO_2 emission rate from the plume source is a consistent 1930 Mg d^{-1} (22.3 kg s^{-1}) (Wardell & Kyle 2003).

Methods

Flux from ice towers

Carbon dioxide effluxes were determined by measuring the CO_2 concentration, exit gas velocity, and orifice diameter from vents on individual ice towers. For each tower, the total air-flow rate emitted was calculated by multiplying the air exit velocity by the moist air density at 0 °C (CRC 1971–1972) times the cross-sectional area of the exit orifice. The CO_2 efflux is the air flux rate multiplied by the CO_2 concentration in the exit gas (Figure 2).

$$\text{Efflux} = Q \cdot A \cdot C$$

Q = air flow rate (m s^{-1}) multiplied by air density (kg m^{-3})

A = cross-sectional area of the exit orifice (m^2)

C = CO_2 concentration in the exit gas (vol. %)

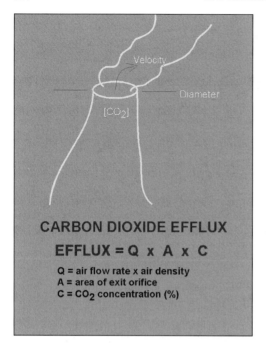

CARBON DIOXIDE EFFLUX

EFFLUX = Q x A x C

Q = air flow rate x air density
A = area of exit orifice
C = CO_2 concentration (%)

Fig. 2. A simple method was used to calculate the efflux of CO_2 emitted from ice towers. This required measuring the CO_2 concentration, exit velocity of the escaping gas and the orifice diameter on each tower.

Towers were measured during three Austral field seasons between 1997 and 2001. Relative humidity and temperature were also measured.

Carbon dioxide was measured with a portable Dräger Multigas IR detector with a standard range of 0 to 5 vol.% (reported accuracy ± 2% of the measured value). Additional chemical sensors were used to monitor SO_2 (0 to 20 ppmv), H_2S (0 to 100 ppmv), and CO (0 to 500 ppmv). Air velocity was measured with an Omega HHF571 digital anemometer of range 0.2 to 40 m/s with accuracy of ±0.25% and equipped with a relative humidity sensor. Dimensions of the orifice were measured with a standard tape measure except when the diameter had to be visually estimated due to difficult access. Temperature was measured with a digital thermocouple.

Although the ice towers have a chimney-like configuration, each one is uniquely shaped. The exit orifice is usually at the top, but many ice towers have openings on their base or sides. Some towers have very large exit diameters or possibly multiple holes. An attempt was made to measure one or more towers from each grouping shown on Figure 1. One series of towers on the far eastern side of the main crater was not measured because it was difficult to reach. Towers with walls too thin to support the weight of a person were drilled into by hand with an ice auger, as illustrated in Figure 3. Instruments were inserted into the throat of the tower via the hole, and the exit orifice diameter was estimated visually.

Measurements on ice towers were only made on days when there was little or no wind. Turbulence caused by outside wind blowing across the ice tower exit can disturb the exit velocities so that measurements were proportional to wind gusts. Some of the exit orifices were large (>1 m diameter), and the exit gas velocity would not be uniform across the cross-section of the orifice. For large openings or where irregular exit geometries created heterogeneous velocity patterns, multiple measurements were performed and averaged.

Soil gas efflux

Soil CO_2 gas efflux was measured by the accumulation chamber technique (Norman *et al.* 1992) by means of a LI-COR 6262 IR portable analyser. A portable computer was used for data logging. Only several measurements per day could be performed at most sites, due to instrument problems from high vapour condensation at high efflux sites or instrument displays freezing at the low temperatures.

Warm ground areas higher up on Tramway Ridge and near the Upper Hut were included in the flux measurements. However, warm ground areas in the Side Crater and Main Crater are not included due to their difficult accessibility. Soil CO_2 efflux measurements were conducted at each site on frozen ground and ice, as background checks to verify that CO_2 degassing was limited to warm thermally active areas. Total CO_2 efflux from warm ground areas was calculated by taking the average emission rate multiplied by the area for the corresponding warm ground section. This method was chosen since the areas were relatively small and the degassing was visible such that representative sampling locations could be selected on site.

Carbon isotope samples

Gas samples for isotopic analysis were collected from ice towers, ice caves, and warm ground. During the 1997–1998 field season, samples were collected in towers and caves by inserting a tygon tube into the fractured rock floor in places where warm gas could be felt blowing out. The gas sample was pumped into polyvinyl fluoride (TEDLAR) gas sampling bags. Soil gas samples

Fig. 3. The top section of this ice tower is too fragile to climb. Therefore a hole is being drilled into the wall of the ice tower with an ice auger so that instruments can be inserted to measure the escaping gas.

from warm ground areas were collected by inserting a hollow steel probe 40 cm into the warm soil and pumping gas into a sample bag. During the 2000–2001 field season, two towers and one cave were sampled using evacuated gas sampling bottles. All samples were transported to New Mexico Tech (Socorro, NM, USA) for analysis. The gas samples were prepared for isotopic analysis by cryogenically separating the CO_2. The sample was introduced into the vacuum line via a needle fitting. Sequential aliquots were admitted to a liquid nitrogen trap to freeze CO_2, and non-condensable gases were pumped away. This was repeated until the gas sampling vessel was empty. The collected CO_2 was cleaned of water using a dry ice–ethylene glycol bath and analysed on a Finnigan MAT delta E mass spectrometer using Oz-Tech gas standards. The $^{13}C/^{12}C$ ratios ($\delta^{13}C$) are reported in parts per thousand deviation (per mil, ‰) from the PDB standard.

Results

Ice tower CO_2 flux

The estimated efflux for passive CO_2 flank emissions from Mount Erebus is 0.46 kg s^{-1} (40 Mg d^{-1}). The CO_2 effluxes determined for 43 ice towers are shown in Table 1. A mean flux value of 0.002 kg s^{-1} (0.22 Mg d^{-1}) for all ice tower data on Mount Erebus was computed. Near the rim of the caldera, close to Harry's Dream (Fig.1), a set of ice towers contributed the largest CO_2 efflux 0.19 kg s^{-1} (16.8 Mg d^{-1}). The CO_2 fluxes from individual towers in this area are all anomalously high in comparison to the observed overall average. Four towers near Harry's Dream averaged 0.031 kg s^{-1} (2.7 Mg d^{-1}). Ice Tower Ridge is the second largest contributor of CO_2 in the investigated areas (Table 1 & Fig. 1). This ridge contains the largest number of ice towers and also exhibits some of the highest air-flow velocities measured. The linear configuration for

Table 1. *Summary of CO₂ efflux measurements for individual fumarolic ice towers*

General Location	Temp (°C)	Relative humidity	CO₂ (vol %)	V m/s (average)	Size m²	Date	Flux ×1000 kg/s
West edge	−1.5	98.1	0.08	0.5	10.0	31/12/00	4.00
West edge	−1.6	100	0.07	0.5	0.8	31/12/00	0.30
West edge	−1.5	100	0.07	0.8	1.2×10^{-2}	31/12/00	0.01
Ice Tower Ridge (1/2)	1.0	93	0.07	1.32	1.8×10^{-3}	16/12/00	0.16
Ice Tower Ridge (2/2)	−	−	0.06	0.8	1.5	16/12/00	0.69
Ice Tower Ridge	−5.0	94	0.06	1.5	0.8	16/12/00	0.69
Ice Tower Ridge	−	94.5	0.08	1.5	3.1	16/12/00	3.82
Ice Tower Ridge	−	−	0.12	0.7	3.1	16/12/00	2.66
Sauna Cave (1/2)	−	−	0.1	0.4	1.3	15/12/99	0.08
Sauna Cave (2/2)	−	−	0.1	0.4	2.0	15/12/99	0.03
West Line	−1.2	94	0.17	1.3	4.0	04/12/99	8.80
West Line	−0.3	96.7	0.14	1.3	1.0	04/12/99	1.85
West Line	−1.9	95.8	0.14	1.8	1.6	04/12/99	4.05
West Line	−1.0	96	0.13	2	1.0	04/12/99	2.55
West Line	−0.1	96	0.17	1.5	9.0	04/12/99	23.15
Tramways	−1.0	95.4	0.13	0.54	6.0	30/12/00	4.21
Tramways	−1.5	97.8	0.15	3.1	1.8	30/12/00	8.37
Tramways (1/2)	−1.7	96.4	0.22	0.9	3.1	31/12/00	6.19
Tramways (2/2)	−1.5	95	0.22	0.7	2.5	31/12/00	3.85
Tramways	−1.7	96.9	0.14	0.36	17.5	31/12/00	0.88
Frog	−4.4	95	0.15	1.5	0.3	05/12/99	0.69
Whale	−1.0	95.4	0.1	0.4	8.0	12/12/99	3.24
North Line	−	−	0.16	0.4	4.0	31/12/00	2.55
North Line	−	−	0.12	0.8	1.1	29/12/00	1.04
North Line	−	−	0.11	0.4	1.7	29/12/00	0.69
North Line	−0.5	94.8	0.14	0.8	3.3	29/12/00	4.24
North Line (1/3)	−1.2	94.7	0.13	1.58	6.0×10^{-4}	12/12/99	0.12
North Line (2/3)	−1.0	94.6	0.15	0.95	4.0×10^{-4}	12/12/99	0.06
North Line (3/3)	−3.3	96	0.13	1.1	3.0×10^{-3}	12/12/99	0.43
North Line (1/2)	−	−	0.08	0	2.8×10^{-3}	12/12/99	0.00
North Line (2/2)	−3.0	93	0.12	0.35	2.4	12/12/99	1.01
North Line	−1.9	97.2	0.13	0.4	3.9×10^{-2}	12/12/99	0.02
Harry's Dream	−1.0	96.6	0.34	0.2	5.3	11/12/99	3.59
Harry's (uphill)	−0.7	94.9	1.35	1.3	0.6	16/12/00	0.11
Harry's (uphill)	−	−	0.82	0.5	1.7	16/12/00	6.97
Harry's (uphill)	−1.7	96.9	1.28	0.26	2.3	16/12/00	7.49
Harry's (uphill)	−2.0	94	1.05	0.76	2.0	11/12/99	15.97
Harry's (downhill)	−1.0	94	0.56	1.0	6.0	15/12/00	33.60
Harry's (downhill)	−1.0	85	0.75	1.2	3.1	15/12/00	28.24
NE Flank	−11.0	95	0.7	0.2	1.4	15/12/00	1.97
NE Flank	−3.0	96.2	1.55	0.8	0.2	15/12/00	2.20
Near Upper Hut	−6.0	93.9	0.18	0.1	5.0×10^{-4}	15/12/00	0.01
Near Upper Hut	−2.0	95.7	0.18	1.0	1.5	15/12/00	2.77
Near Upper Hut	−6.8	92.9	0.16	0.1	3	15/12/00	0.47
LEH	−	−	0.16	0.8	0.9	14/12/99	1.39
LEH	−1.5	96	0.14	0.8	12.0	14/12/99	13.43
LEH	1.3	95.1	0.18	0.5	20.0	14/12/99	18.00
LEH (1/2)	2.4	96	0.12	0.4	1.0	28/12/00	0.46
LEH (2/2)	−	−	0.14	1.2	2.0	28/12/00	3.36
LEH	−	−	0.1	0.4	8.0	01/12/99	0.28
LEH (Helo Cave)	−7.0	91.4	0.07	0.3	1.5	28/12/00	0.03
LEH (Helo Cave)	−4.2	93.4	0.08	0.2	0.5	28/12/00	0.01
LEH (Helo Cave)	−2.0	102.2	0.07	0.4	1.5	01/12/99	0.04
LEH (Rabbit Hole)	−1.0	96.6	0.19	0.6	2.9	01/12/99	0.28

See Figure 1 for general locations. Note that some of the ice towers have more than one measurement, indicating more than one opening.

this group of ice towers is illustrated in Figure 4. Effluxes for the 43 ice towers ranged from below the quantification limit (estimated at 0.0001 kg s^{-1} or 0.01 Mg d^{-1}) up to 0.034 kg/s (2.9 Mg d^{-1}) (Table 1). The propagation error for the ice tower efflux measurements is 12%, assuming that the area of the orifice and exit flow velocities are accurate to 10% and the CO_2 concentration is measured within 2% of the true value. The relative humidity in ice tower emissions ranged from 85% to 100%, while the temperature ranged from –7°C to 1°C. No odours were detected in the towers, except for one tower in the vicinity of Harry's Dream. The odour did not smell like H_2S or SO_2 and is presumed to be organic in nature.

Monitoring inside ice towers and caves

Annual monitoring of air in an ice cave close to the Lower Erebus Hut (LEH) (Fig. 1) showed the highest concentrations in 1997 (0.24% CO_2). During the following seasons in 1999 and 2000, a lower and more stable concentration ranging from 0.16% to 0.18% was observed. Three measurements, spaced approximately a week apart, showed stable CO_2 concentrations coming from the cave during December 1999. An ice tower known as Frog, located below Tramway Ridge, exhibited a CO_2 concentration of 0.15% in December 1997. In December 1999, the ice tower adjacent to Frog, connected by an underlying cave, yielded the same CO_2 concentration value.

Harry's Dream is a noticeable landmark on the summit plateau (Fig. 5). This tower stands approximately 7 m high and contains a small room approximately 5 by 5 m in size. Harry's Dream stands alone and is not interconnected by ice caves. The shape and entrances of this tower have varied from season to season. A sample taken from Harry's Dream in 1997, collected in a similar method to the isotope samples by insertion of a tube into the fractured rock floor, was analysed at McMurdo Station, Antarctica, and yielded a concentration of 1.49% CO_2. Measurements with the Dräger Multigas analyser at the same position showed a decrease in value to 0.47% CO_2 during 1999.

Slightly north of Harry's Dream there is a grouping of ice towers from where the *North Fumarole* sample was collected (Table 2). A single reading from this area in 1997 shows a

Fig. 4. This aerial photograph shows the linear discontinuity on which the fumarolic ice towers of Ice Tower Ridge are located. The alignment is radial to the main crater of Mount Erebus.

Fig. 5. Harry's Dream is a fumarolic ice tower that is a noticeable landmark on the summit caldera of Mount Erebus. Gas samples collected from inside the small room at the base of the tower in 1997 and 1999 showed a decrease in CO_2 concentration.

Table 2. *Results of carbon isotope analyses from CO₂ gas samples*

Location	Gas temperature	δ¹³C raw data (‰)[3]	δ¹³C (average)
Tramways 1[1]	45.3°C at 10 cm	−3.65±0.05	
		−3.68±0.04	−3.7‰
Tramways 2[1]	51.2°C at 20 cm	−3.80±0.05	
		−3.81±0.06	−3.8‰
Tramways 3[1]	61.9°C near surface	−3.40±0.07	
		−3.34±0.10	
		−3.32±0.08	−3.4‰
Tramways 6[1]	35.9°C near surface	−4.32±0.03	−4.3‰
Crater Rim[1]	32.9°C near surface	−3.70±0.05	
		−3.69±0.11	
		−3.63±0.05	−3.7‰
North Fumarole	6°C	−2.06±0.07	
		−2.08±0.05	
		−2.04±0.01	−2.1‰
Harry's Dream	11.8°C	−3.53±0.01	
		−3.51±0.02	−3.5‰
LEH-97	11.5°C	−4.60±0.06	
		−4.71±0.06	−4.7‰
LEH-00[2]	1.3°C	−6.68±0.05	−6.7‰
Way Point 232[2]	−0.5°C	−4.10±0.04	−4.1‰
Way Point 240[2]	−1.7°C	−4.47±0.06	−4.4‰

[1] Denotes soil gas samples from warm ground, all others are from ice towers and caves.
[2] Denotes data collected in December, 2000 in which the collection method differed slightly than in previous years.
[3] Raw data include repeat measurements on the same samples..

CO₂ concentration of 0.28%, which is above the median concentration of 0.14%. An average of four CO₂ concentrations measured at different ice towers in this same area yielded a concentration of 0.55% CO₂, which may imply an increase in the CO₂ concentration for this area between 1997 and 2000.

Ice cave observations

Carbon dioxide concentrations measured in ice caves were above ambient atmospheric values. Carbon dioxide concentrations ranged from 0.06 to 1.55% CO₂. Numerous cave systems exist in the summit caldera, but only a few have been explored. Cave sizes range from small rooms beneath ice towers to caverns as long as 400 m and heights of 20 m. Carbon dioxide was the only gas species detected during field observations. In spite of the low odour threshold recognition level for H₂S (0.00047 ppm, Cheremisinoff and Young 1981), no sulphur odours were recognized in any of the visited caves. Ice crystals and stalactites can be found as transient features inside the ice caves. Temperatures as high as an estimated 35°C can consistently be found inside Sauna Cave, although most caves show temperatures close to 0°C. Warm air, usually enriched in CO₂, can be felt

blowing from beneath fractured lava flow blocks in many of the cavern floors. Entrances to the caves can be marked by large towers such as the one above the Sauna Cave (Figure 6) or be barely noticeable beneath ice hummocks.

Soil gas data

Soil gas emissions from warm ground areas contributed 0.01 kg s⁻¹ (0.9 Mg day⁻¹) of CO₂ to the total flank emissions. Twenty-eight soil gas efflux measurements were performed on the summit area (Table 3). The restricted area at Tramways (SSSI), the warmest and largest warm ground area, yielded the largest soil CO₂ gas contribution (1300 g m⁻² d⁻¹). Efflux values ranged from 0 to 4400 g m⁻² d⁻¹ (Table 3), although several measurements were outside the linear calibration range of our instrument. Due to the irregular shape of the degassing area within the SSSI (1 hectare), only 500 m² of steaming warm ground was used for calculations. The median CO₂ efflux value times the estimated area of active degassing, yielded a total CO₂ flux of 0.008 kg s⁻¹ (0.66 Mg d⁻¹) at Tramway Ridge. Temperatures less than 5 cm below the surface on the section accessible by permit, ranged from below zero (on the permafrost) to 62 °C. Both red and green algal mats were present on some of

Fig. 6. The largest fumarolic ice tower sits above Sauna Cave, an ice cave that is approximately 400 m long. Large blocks of ice can be seen in the foreground, where sections of the tower have collapsed.

the warmer areas. The warmer areas do exhibit higher CO_2 efflux, although there is not a spatial correlation between CO_2 efflux and soil temperature. The area *Below Upper Hut* (Table 3), located near the very top on Tramway Ridge (southeast of the SSSI), exhibits the highest average CO_2 efflux (4760 g m^{-2} d^{-1}) but contributes only 0.003 kg s^{-1} (0.24 g m^{-2} d^{-1}), much less than the SSSI, due to its small area. No measurable CO_2 efflux was observed on snow/ice surfaces or on frozen ground. A short traverse, running north to south on the exposed ground at Nausea Knob, revealed no CO_2

emissions, and soil temperatures below 0°C (Table 3). Other areas of warm ground that were not measured include the Septum (between the Main Crater and the Side Crater), inside the Side Crater and inside the Main Crater. These areas are neglected in our estimates. The Main Crater is not safely accessible and the emissions from areas within the Main Crater are assumed to be included in the plume. Efflux from the Septum and Side Crater were not included due to the difficult access and short field season. The CO_2 emissions from these two areas are assumed to be small compared with the efflux of the warm

Table 3. *Soil CO$_2$ efflux measurements from barren and warm ground areas*

General location	Soil Temp. (°C)	Flux g m^{-2} d^{-1}
Tramway (SSSI)	45.3	917
Tramway (SSSI)	62.4	768
Tramway (SSSI)	39.8	20
Tramway (SSSI)	57.5	4424
Tramway (SSSI)	39.0	481
East Edge Tramway	–	571
East Edge Tramway	–	171
East Edge Tramway	–	192
East Edge Tramway	31.8	458
East Edge Tramway	51.7	70
East Edge Tramway	45.5	450
East Edge Tramway	19.3	82
East Edge Tramway	24.5	236
N–NW side Tramways	–	ldl
N–NW side Tramways	–	ldl
N–NW side Tramways	–	15
Nausea Knob	−11.7	ldl
Nausea Knob	−10.3	ldl
Nausea Knob	−17.0	ldl
Below Upper Hut	–	4329
Below Upper Hut	–	4155
Below Upper Hut	–	5808
Below Upper Hut	–	ldl
Western Crater	−11.6	ldl
Western Crater	24.4	80
Western Crater	28.0	408
Ice Tower Ridge	-7.8	ldl
Ice Tower Ridge	26.1	ldl

ldl: lower than detection limit.

ground in the SSSI, since these areas are smaller, exhibit lower temperatures and do not emit as much visible steam as the SSSI.

Isotopes

Gas samples for carbon isotope analysis were collected from warm ground, on the crater rim, within ice caves, and ice tower/cave outlets. The gas temperature ranged from –1.7 °C to 61.9 °C (Table 2). Carbon dioxide concentrations in the isotope sampling locations ranged from 0.14 to 1.49%. Values of δ^{13}C ranged from –2.04‰ to –4.71‰, with a mean of –3.57‰ and a standard deviation of 0.05 (Table 2). This average excludes an anomalously low value of –6.68‰ for *LEH-00* collected in December 2000. This anomalous value is believed to have significant atmospheric contamination due to its low CO$_2$ concentration and sampling technique. The δ^{13}C of atmospheric CO$_2$ measured in the Ross Sea between Cape Adare and Cape Roberts is –8.06 to –8.21‰ (Longinelli *et al.* 2001) and –7.75‰ for

South Pole Station in 1993 (Ciais *et al.* 1995). These atmospheric compositions of δ^{13}C could account for the downward shift in the contaminated sample. The 1997 sample *LEH-97* is from the same cave as the *LEH-00* sample but yielded a δ^{13}C of –4.71‰ in 1997. This cave still remains the location of the lightest δ^{13}C value, even when the *LEH-00* analysis is discarded.

Samples labelled *Tramways 1, 2, 3 and 6* (in Table 2) are soil gas samples from the warm ground area, labelled SSSI near Tramway Ridge on Figure 1. Carbon dioxide concentrations of the soil gas exceeded the range of the LICOR analyser (>5000 ppmv). Ambient air temperature during the measurements was –34.4°C. *Tramways 6* is from a shallow ice tower adjacent to the SSSI site that exhibited elevated temperatures. It is also included in the soil gas measurements, since the steel probe was inserted into the soil floor of this fumarole and collected in the same manner as the soil gas samples. The sample labeled *Crater Rim* was also collected in a similar manner, except that the probe could only be inserted to 20 cm depth. This location was on the outer rim of the Main Crater, next to some ice hummocks toward the eastern side. The sample labelled *LEH-97* is from inside the cave nearest Lower Erebus Hut (LEH). The CO$_2$ concentration was considerably lower for this sample as compared with others collected from inside the towers or caves. The samples labelled *Harry's Dream* and *North Fumarole* on Table 2 were also collected from ice caves in the same manner, but showed much higher CO$_2$ concentrations (exceeding the instrument range).

The last three samples in Table 2 were collected later and by a slightly different method. For *Way Points 240* and *232*, evacuated glass gas sample bottles were held in the mouth of the ice tower and opened. These samples were collected from outside by leaning into the opening of the ice tower, because CO$_2$ concentrations exiting the structure were high (*c.* 1.5%). Concentrations on the floor of the enclosed structure were assumed to potentially be higher than that observed at the exit, and thus posed a potential health concern. These high concentrations were measured in 1999 and 2000 with the Dräger Multigas instrument, which was not available during the previous 1997 sampling campaign.

The final sample, *LEH-00*, is the same cave as the *LEH-97* sample which was collected three seasons before. The *LEH-00* sample was collected by holding an evacuated gas bottle adjacent to an area of the rock floor that was expelling warm gas. It is likely that this sample was mixed with air, as earlier samples employed a nylon tube that was inserted into the fractured rock area where the warm gas was emanating. As the CO_2 concentration of this sample was relatively low compared with the rest of the samples, atmospheric contamination would have a greater effect, thus also accounting for its anomalously low $\delta^{13}C$ value.

Discussion

According to these results, the total CO_2 efflux from passive flank degassing on Mount Erebus is 0.46 kg s^{-1} (40 Mg d^{-1}). The total contribution of volcanic CO_2 from ice tower fumaroles and soil gas emissions compared to the plume emission rate from Mount Erebus implies that flank degassing is a minor contributor (<2%). At Oldoinyo Lengai volcano, Tanzania, the small contribution of flank degassing (<2%) suggested a small magma chamber or the lack of a hydrogeological system (Koepenick *et al.* 1996). The lack of flank CO_2 emissions on Popocatépetl volcano, Mexico, was unexpected, but such gas migration is dependent on variables that include 'position and size of the magma chamber, the morphology of the edifice, the hydrogeological system and the development of a hydrothermal system within the edifice...'(Varley and Armienta 2001). Ambient environmental conditions at Mount Erebus preclude the input of meteoric water into the system. No indication of thermal springs has been observed in any of the ice caves. As the extreme Antarctic environment is not conducive to liquid water, ice caves could provide conditions for such a feature because they maintain temperatures near or above freezing (0 °C) and have warmer gases emanating from floor features.

The radial alignment of ice towers on the summit cone of Mount Erebus (Fig. 4), as well as clusters of degassing towers at the edges of the caldera, suggests that these are surface expressions of underlying faults and fractured zones. Soil gas studies at Mount Etna suggest that deep gases can only be brought to the surface by zones of strain (Giammanco *et al.* 1998), and a number of studies have associated flank degassing with the location of faults (Koepenick *et al.* 1996). The ability of a volcano to have passive flank emissions may be dependent on the presence or absence of faults having surface expressions (Delmelle & Stix 2000).

Data presented here establish baseline values for areas of flank degassing at Mount Erebus. However, the current data are insufficient to relate CO_2 efflux to concurrent volcanic activity. Surface degassing features are presumed to be indicators of subsurface discontinuities. Results indicate that these distinct groups do not offer uniform emission characteristics. For example, highest gas sample temperatures are from the SSSI soil gases, but the highest concentrations of CO_2 are found in a small cluster of ice towers near Harry's Dream. Variations in CO_2 concentration have been observed in some of the ice caves. These ice caves can be compared with those at found on Mount Rainier. Zimbelman *et al.* (2000) found elevated concentrations of CO_2 in some of the ice caves within the 'world's largest volcanic ice-cave system' at Mount Rainier. They suggested that such ice caves could act as condensers, traps, and calorimeters for magmatic volatiles and heat. Therefore, their monitoring and characterization could provide good indicators of changes in the hydrothermal system, which could elude surface surveillance. Continuous monitoring in ice towers and ice caves is needed to evaluate relationships to volcanic activity on Mount Erebus, if they do exist.

Carbon isotopes

The carbon isotopic composition of CO_2 sampled from Mount Erebus ice towers and warm ground provides an insight into the origin of the gas. The generally recognized carbon isotopic composition of magmatic CO_2 is –8 to –5‰, although other ranges for this mantle signature are reported in the literature (Taylor 1986). Measurements from the summit area of Mount Erebus yielded a $\delta^{13}C$ range of –4.7 to –2.1‰ (excluding the anomalous value of –6.7‰). The spread in values for this range is larger than analytical error. One possible explanation for seeing this spread in values is that the true isotopic composition is enriched ($\geq$ –2‰), as in the *North Fumarole* sample (Table 2), and that the lighter observed values represent varying degrees of mixing with air (*c.* –8‰). This may be particularly true for the 2000 data (*Way Points 232* and *240*, Table 2) where samples were drawn from the mouth of the ice tower and not from the cavern floor beneath it. Therefore, assuming that air is at –8.0‰ and the uncontaminated $\delta^{13}C$ at Mount Erebus is –2.1‰, the anomalous sample at –6.7‰ contains 88% air. The next lightest sample, LEH-97 at –4.7‰, would be 44% air. Therefore, the efflux from the ice towers is likely to contain a large percentage of air, and so the estimated total CO_2 emission rate for flank degassing should be considered a maximum value.

Being unable to collect samples from the plume source in the Main Crater, we are currently assuming that the most representative $\delta^{13}C$ value for Mount Erebus CO_2 emissions is close to –2.1‰. The carbon isotopic signature for Mount

Erebus would then appear enriched relative to the mantle signature. This enrichment appears evident when Mount Erebus is compared to other intra-plate volcanoes such as Kilauea (–8 to –7‰) (Gerlach & Taylor 1990) and Mount Etna (–4.00‰) (D'Alessandro *et al.* 1997*b*). This also appears true for values from spreading axes, including Erta 'Ale (–6.4‰) (Allard & Javoy 1976), Ardoukoba (–6.0‰) (Allard *et al.* 1979), Galapagos (–6.4 to –5.8) (Sakai *et al.* 1984), and the Mid-Atlantic Ridge (–7.6‰) (Pineau & Javoy 1983). The carbon isotopic composition from subduction-related volcanism is more variable, due largely to contamination from subducted and crustal material (Delmelle & Stix 2000). A number of these volcanoes exhibit $\delta^{13}C$ values close to the –2.1‰ measured at Mount Erebus, such as Mount Vesuvius (–2.00‰) (Tedesco 1997), Izu–Oshima (–2.97 to –1.15‰) (Sano *et al.* 1995), Momotombo (–2.6‰) (Allard 1983), and White Island (–2.0‰) (Marty & Giggenbach 1990). The $\delta^{13}C$ ratio is an indicator of the degree of contamination of deep-seated CO_2 (Allard 1983). CIROS-1 drill cores from McMurdo Sound indicate positive $\delta^{13}C$ values for carbonates in the upper sediment layers on which the edifice of Ross Island and Mount Erebus sits (Wada & Okada 1990). The enriched $\delta^{13}C$ value may be an indication of thermo-carbonation processes occurring beneath Mount Erebus. However, D'Alessandro *et al.* (1997*b*) describe the carbon isotopic character for Mount Etna to be a range of –4 to –2‰, similar to that for Mount Erebus. The authors noted that the values for Mount Etna are slightly more positive than what is normally viewed as deep-origin CO_2, and suggested that this could imply crustal contamination of the magmatic source, but proposed that it is more likely to be typical of alkaline volcanoes such as Mount Etna (D'Alessandro *et al.* 1997*b*). Mount Erebus isotopic samples were not collected from the active crater or high-temperature fumaroles, but rather from warm diffuse emissions at the flanks. Although there is no evidence of a hydrothermal system on Mount Erebus, the possibility of isotopic fractionation, exchange, or other interactions during the gaseous migration to the surface may exist. Some passive flank emissions may be dominated by organic carbon sources, as seen at Galeras volcano (Heiligmann *et al.* 1997). Measuring carbon isotopes from various sources of flank emissions (e.g. soil gas, fumaroles, and springs) will commonly yield a wide range of values like that seen at Mount Etna (D'Alessandro *et al.* 1997*a*). Composition is known to vary with temperature, so emanations from high-temperature fumaroles are considered

to be closest to the original character of the magmatic gases (Sano & Marty 1995). Deviations from the values found at the active vent or high-temperature fumaroles are often explained by the lighter $\delta^{13}C$ values having volcanic gas interaction with organic CO_2 and/or cold groundwater, and the more enriched values show interaction with hot groundwater (Giammanco *et al.* 1998). As we are currently lacking data from the active vent, we cannot be sure that the reported isotopic data are truly representative of the $\delta^{13}C$ character of the Mount Erebus magma. However, gases from Mount Erebus have little opportunity to acquire contributions from biogenic carbon sources or interactions from meteoric infiltration that are often seen at other volcanoes.

Conclusions

In contrast to other volcanoes, passive flank emissions are visible on the edifice of Mount Erebus. This type of degassing cannot be seen on other volcanoes, and is sometimes overlooked (Delmelle & Stix 2000). Having a visible surface expression for all degassing features, such as those on Mount Erebus, yields a unique advantage in evaluating the location and flux of the entire soil gas system.

A total of 0.46 kg s⁻¹ (40 Mg d⁻¹) of volcanic CO_2 is contributed from the flanks of Mount Erebus and is confined to the caldera area at the top of the edifice. This represents less than 2% of the total CO_2 budget of this volcano. Such a relatively minor flank emission could be attributed to characteristics such as a small magma chamber or lack of a hydrothermal system. Observations in caves thus far have failed to find an indication of a hydrothermal system. The method for measuring CO_2 flux from ice towers is simple, and being able to visually account for all actively degassing features is a distinct advantage on this volcano in establishing a more accurate emission rate. As volcanic activity can sometimes be related to this form of passive degassing, the data here provide a baseline for geochemical monitoring. Isotopic results verify the magmatic origin of the CO_2. Degassing features on volcanic flanks are normally associated with fault features. The position of the degassing features in radial alignments or in clusters at the caldera edge also suggests that these are locations of faults or zones of strain.

This work was supported by grants from the Office of Polar Programs, National Science Foundation and a fellowship from the Department of Energy, Global Change Education Program. We thank N. Dunbar who provided reviews on the early drafts of the manuscript.

Over the three field seasons on Mount Erebus we were kindly assisted by N. Dunbar, J. Crain, W. McIntosh, J. Pennycook, R. Karstens, K. Panter, A. Eshenbacher, C. Harpel, and also C. Day and F. McCarthy of Raytheon Polar Services. Our gratitude also goes to Drs K. Notsu and J. Salazar for their helpful reviews of the manuscript.

References

ALLARD, P. & JAVOY, M. 1976. Composition isotopique du CO_2, SO_2, et de l'eau, dans les gaz volcaniques éruptifs. *Reunion Annuelle des Sciences de la Terre*, **4**, 4.

ALLARD, P., TAZIEFF, H. & DAJLEVIC, D. 1979. Observations of seafloor spreading in Afar during the November 1978 fissure eruption. *Nature*, **279**, 30–33

ALLARD, P. 1983. The origin of hydrogen, carbon, sulphur, nitrogen and rare gases in volcanic exhalations: evidence from isotope geochemistry. *In:* TAZIEFF, H. & SABROUX, J. C. (eds) *Forecasting Volcanic Events.* Amsterdam, Elsevier, 337–386.

ALLARD, P., CARBONNELLE, J. *ET AL.* 1991. Eruptive and diffuse emissions of CO_2 from Mount Etna. *Nature*, **351**, 387–391.

AZZARO, R., BRANCA, S., GIAMMANCO, S., GURRIERI, S., RASA, R. & VALENZA, M. 1998. New evidence for the form and extent of the Pernicana Fault system (Mt. Etna) from structural and soil-gas surveying. *Journal of Volcanology and Geothermal Research*, **84**, 143–152.

BAUBRON, J.-C., ALLARD, P., SABROUX, J.-C., TEDESCO, D. & TOUTAIN, J-P. 1991. Soil gas emanations as precursory indicators of volcanic eruptions. *Journal of the Geological Society, London*, **148**, 571–576.

BROADY, P. 1993. Soils heated by volcanism. *In:* FRIEDMANN, E. I (ed.) *Antarctic Microbiology*, Wiley-Liss, New York, 413–432.

CHEREMISINOFF, P. N. & YOUNG, R. A. (eds) 1981. *Pollution Engineering Practice Handbook.* Ann Arbor, Ann Arbor Science Publishers.

CHIODINI, G., FRONDINI, F. & RACO, B. 1996. Diffuse emissions of CO_2 from the Fossa Crater, Vulcano Island (Italy). *Bulletin of Volcanology*, **58**, 41–50.

CHIODINI, G., CIONI, R., GUIDI, M., RACO, B. & MARINI, L. 1998. Soil CO_2 flux measurements in volcanic and geothermal areas. *Applied Geochemistry*, **13**, 543–552.

CIAIS, P., TANS, P. P. & TROLIER, M. 1995. A large Northern Hemisphere terrestrial CO_2 sink indicated by the $^{13}C/^{12}C$ ratio of atmospheric CO_2. *Science*, **269**, 1098–1102.

CRC 1971–1972. *In:* WEAST, R. C. (ed.) *Handbook of Chemistry and Physics*, 52nd edn, Cleveland, Chemical Rubber Company, F9–11.

D'ALESSANDRO, W. 1997. Soil gas prospection of He, ^{222}Rn and CO_2: Vulcano Porto area, Aeolian Islands, Italy. *Applied Geochemistry*, **12**, 213–224.

D'ALESSANDRO, W., DE GREGORIO, S., DONGARRA, G., GURRIERI, S., PARELLO, F. & PARISI, B. 1997a. Chemical and isotopic characterization of the gases of Mount Etna (Italy). *Journal of Volcanology and Geothermal Research*, **78**, 65–76.

D'ALESSANDRO, W., GIAMMANCO, S., PARELLO, F. & VALENZA, M. 1997b. CO_2 output and $\delta^{13}C(CO_2)$ from Mount Etna as indicators of degassing of shallow asthenosphere. *Bulletin of Volcanology*, **58**, 455–458.

DAVID, T. W. E. & PRIESTLEY, R. E. 1909. Notes in regard to Mount Erebus. *In:* E. H. SHACKLETON. *The Heart of the Antarctic.* William Heinemann, London, Vol. 2, 308–310.

DELMELLE, P. & STIX, J. (2000). Volcanic gases. *In:* SIGURDSSON, H., HOUGHTON, B., MCNUTT, S., RYMER, H. & STIX, J. (eds) *Encyclopedia of Volcanoes.* San Diego, Academic Press, 803–815.

DIBBLE, R. R., KIENLE, J., KYLE, P. R. & SHIBUYA, K. 1984. Geophysical studies of Erebus volcano, Antarctica, from 1974–1981. *New Zealand Journal of Geology and Geophysics*, **27**, 425–455.

FARRAR, C. D., SOREY, M. L. *ET AL.* 1995. Forest-killing diffuse CO_2 emission at Mammoth Mountain as a sign of magmatic unrest. *Nature* **376**, 675–678.

GERLACH, T. M. & GRAEBER, E. 1985. Volatile budget of Kilauea volcano. *Nature*, **313**, 273–277.

GERLACH, T. M. & TAYLOR, B. E. 1990. Carbon isotope constraints on degassing of carbon dioxide from Kilauea Volcano. *Geochimica et Cosmochimica Acta*, 54, 2051–2058.

GERLACH, T. M., DOUKAS, M., MCGEE, K. & KESSLER, R. 1998. Three-year decline of magmatic CO_2 emissions from soils of a Mammoth Mountain tree kill: Horseshoe Lake, CA 1995–1997. *Geophysical Research Letters*, **25**, 1947–1950.

GERLACH, T. M., DOUKAS, M. P., MCGEE, K. A. & KESSLER, R. 1999. Airborne detection of diffuse carbon dioxide emissions at Mammoth Mountain, California. *Geophysical Research Letters* **26**, 3661–3664.

GERLACH, T. M., KESSLER, R., DOUKAS, M. P. & MCGEE, K. A. 2001. Soil efflux and total emission rates of magmatic CO_2 at the Horseshoe Lake tree kill, Mammoth Mountain, California 1995–1999. *Chemical Geology*, **1–2**, 101–116.

GIAMMANCO, S., GURRIERI, S. & VALENZA, M. 1997. Soil CO_2 degassing along tectonic structures of Mount Etna (Sicily): the Pernicana fault. *Applied Geochemistry*, **12**, 429–436.

GIAMMANCO, S., GURRIERI, S. & VALENZA, M. 1998. Anomalous soil CO_2 degassing in relation to faults and eruptive fissures on Mount Etna (Sicily, Italy). *Bulletin of Volcanology*, **60**, 252–259.

GIGGENBACH, W. F. 1976. Geothermal ice caves on Mt Erebus, Ross Island, Antarctica. *New Zealand Journal of Geology and Geophysics*, **19**, 365–372.

HERNANDEZ, P. A., NOTSU, K. *ET AL.* 2001. Carbon dioxide degassing by advective flow from Usu volcano, Japan. *Science*, **292**, 83–86.

HEILIGMANN, M., STIX, J., WILLIAMS-JONES, G., LOLLAR, B. S. & GARZON, V. G. 1997. Distal degassing of radon and carbon dioxide on Galeras volcano, Columbia. *Journal of Volcanology and Geothermal Research*, **77**, 267–283.

HOLDSWORTH, G. & UGOLINI, F. C. 1965. Fumarolic ice towers on Mount Erebus, Ross Island, Antarctica. *Journal of Glaciology*, **5**, 878–879.

KEYS, J. R., MCINTOSH, W. C. & KYLE, P. R. 1983. Volcanic activity of Mount Melbourne, northern Victoria Land. *Antarctic Journal of the United States*, **18**, 10–11.

KOEPENICK, K., BRANTLEY, S., THOMPSON, J., ROWE, G., NYBLADE, A. & MOSHY, C. 1996. Volatile emissions from the crater and flank of Oldoinyo Lengai volcano, Tanzania. *Journal of Geophysical Research*, **10**, 13 819–13 830.

KYLE, P. R., DIBBLE, R. R., GIGGENBACH, W. F. & KEYS, J. 1982. Volcanic activity associated with the anorthoclase phonolite lava lake, Mt. Erebus, Antarctica. *In:* CRADDOCK, C. (ed.) *Antarctic Geosciences*, University of Wisconsin Press, 735–745.

KYLE, P. R. (ed.) 1994. *Volcanological and Environmental Studies of Mount Erebus*. Antarctic Research Series, **66**, American Geophysical Union, Washington D.C.

KYLE, P. R., SYBELDON, L. M., MCINTOSH, W. C., MEEKER, K., & SYMONDS, R. 1994. Sulfur dioxide emission rates from Mount Erebus, Antarctica. *In:* Kyle, P. (ed.) *Volcanological and Environmental Studies of Mount Erebus, Antarctica*. Washington, D.C., American Geophysical Union. Antarctic Research Series, **66**, 69–82.

LONGINELLI, A., COLOMBO, T., GIOVANELLI, G., LENAZ, R., ORI, C. & SELMO, E. 2001. Atmospheric CO₂ concentrations and δ¹³C measurements along a hemispheric course (1998/99, Italy to Antarctica). *Earth and Planetary Science Letters*, **191**, 167–172.

LYON, G. L. & GIGGENBACH, W. F. 1974. Geothermal activity in Victoria Land, Antarctica. *New Zealand Journal of Geology and Geophysics*, **17(3)**, 511–521.

MARTY, B. & GIGGENBACH, W. F. 1990. Major and rare gases at White Island volcano, New Zealand: origin and flux of volatiles. *Geophysical Research Letters*, **17**, 247–250.

MCGEE, K. A. & GERLACH, T.M. 1998. Annual cycle of magmatic CO₂ in a tree-kill soil at Mammoth Mountain; California: implications for soil acidification. *Geology*, **26**, 463–466.

MCGEE, K. A., GERLACH, T. M., KESSLER, R. & DOUKAS, M. P. 2000. Geochemical evidence for a magmatic CO₂ degassing event at Mammoth Mountain, California, September–December 1997. *Journal of Geophysical Research*, **105**, 8447–8456.

MCINTOSH, W. C. & DUNBAR, N. 1999 New Mexico Bureau of Geology and Mineral Resources, pers. comm.

MORI, T., HERNANDEZ, P., SALAZAR, J. M., PEREZ, N. M. & NOTSU, K. 2001. An in-situ method for measuring CO₂ flux from volcanic-hydrothermal fumaroles. *Chemical Geology*, **177**, 85–99.

NORMAN, J., GARCIA, R. & VERMA, S. 1992. Soil surface CO₂ fluxes and the carbon budget of a grassland. *Journal of Geophysical Research*, **97**, 18 845–18 853.

NSF 1995. *Antarctic Conservation Act of 1978. Public Law 95-541*. National Science Foundation, Arlington, VA.

PINEAU, F. & JAVOY, M. 1983. Carbon isotopes and concentrations in mid-ocean ridge basalts. *Earth and Planetary Science Letters*, **62**, 413–421.

RAHN, T. A., FESSENDEN, J. E. & WAHLEN, M. (1996). Flux chamber measurements of anomalous CO₂ emission from the flanks of Mammoth Mountain, California. *Geophysical Research Letters*, **23**, 1861–1864.

ROGIE, J. D., CHIODINI, G., GALLOWAY, D. L., KERRICK, D. M. & SOREY, M. L. 2001. Dynamics of carbon dioxide emissions at Mammoth Mountain, California. *Earth and Planetary Science Letters*, **188**, 535–541.

ROSS, J. C. 1847. *Voyage to the Southern Seas*. Murray, London.

SAKAI, H., DES MARAIS, D. J., UEDA, A. & MOORE, J. G. 1984. Concentrations and isotope ratios.of carbon, nitrogen and sulfur in ocean-floor basalts. *Geochimica et Cosmochimica Acta* **48**, 2433–2441.

SANO, Y., GAMO, T., NOTSU, K. & WAKITA, H. 1995. Secular variations of carbon and helium isotopes at Izu-Oshima Volcano, Japan. *Journal of Volcanology and Geothermal Research*, **64**, 83–94.

SHEPPARD, D. S., LE GUERN, F. & CHRISTENSON, B. W. 1994. Composition and mass fluxes of the Mount Erebus volcanic plume. *In:* P. KYLE (ed). *Volcanological and Environmental Studies of Mount Erebus*, Antarctica. Antarctic Research Series, **66**, 83–96, Washington D.C., American Geophysical Union.

SOREY, M. L., EVANS, W. C., KENNEDY, B.M., FARRAR, C. D., HAINSWORTH, L. J. & HAUSBACK, B. 1998. Carbon dioxide and helium emissions from a reservoir of magmatic gas beneath Mammoth Mountain, California. *Journal of Geophysical Research*, **10**, 15 303–15 323.

SPARKS, R. S. J. 2003. Dynamics of magma degassing. *In*: OPPENHEIMER, C., PYLE, D. M. & BARCLAY, J. (eds) *Volcanic Degassing*. Geological Society, London, Special Publications, **213**, 5–22.

SUGISAKI, R., IDO, M. *ET AL.* 1983. Origin of hydrogen and carbon dioxide in fault gases and its relation to fault activity. *Journal of Geology*, **91**, 239–258.

TAYLOR, B. E. 1986. Magmatic volatiles: Isotopic variation of C, H, and S. *In*: VALLEY, J.W., TAYLOR, H. P. & O'NEIL, J. R. (eds), *Stable Isotopes in High Temperature Geological Processes*. Reviews in Mineralogy, Mineralogical Society of America, Chelsea, MI, 185–226.

TEDESCO, D. 1997. Systematic variations in the ³He/⁴He ratio and carbon of fumarolic fluids from active volcanic areas in Italy: evidence for radiogenic ⁴He and crustal carbon addition by the subducting African plate? *Earth and Planetary Science Letters*, **151**, 255–269.

VARLEY, N. R. & ARMIENTA, M. A. 2001. The absence of diffuse degassing at Popocatepetl volcano, Mexico. *Chemical Geology*, **177**, 157–174.

WADA, H. & OKADA, H. 1990. Isotopic studies of carbonates from CIROS-1 drillhole, western McMurdo Sound, Antarctica. *Proceedings from the NIPR Symposium on Antarctic Geoscience*, **4**, 149–164.

WARDELL, L. J. & KYLE, P. R. 1998. Volcanic carbon dioxide emission rates; White Island, New Zealand and Mt. Erebus Antarctica. *EOS, Transactions of* the *American Geophysical Union, 1998 Fall Meeting*, **79**, V71C–09.

WARDELL, L. J. & KYLE, P. R. 2003. Carbon dioxide flux measurements from Mt. Erebus, Antarctica and the contribution to the global atmosphere. *Journal of Volcanology and Geothermal Research*, submitted.

ZIMBELMAN, D. R., RYE, R. O. & LANDIS, G. P. 2000. Fumaroles in ice caves on the summit of Mount Rainier – preliminary stable isotope, gas, and geochemical studies. *Journal of Volcanology and Geothermal Research*, **97**, 457–473.

ZREDA-GOSTYNSKA, G., KYLE, P. & FINNEGAN, D. 1993. Chlorine, fluorine, and sulfur emissions from Mount Erebus, Antarctica and estimated contributions to the Antarctic atmosphere. *Geophysical Research Letters*, **20**, 1959–1962.

ZREDA-GOSTYNSKA, G., KYLE, P. R., FINNEGAN, D. & PRESTBO, K. 1997. Volcanic gas emissions from Mount Erebus and their impact on the Antarctic environment. *Journal of Geophysical Research* **102**, 15 039–15 055.

Fumarole migration and fluid geochemistry at Poás Volcano (Costa Rica) from 1998 to 2001

O. VASELLI[1,2], F. TASSI[1], A. MINISSALE[2], G. MONTEGROSSI[2], E. DUARTE[3], E. FERNÁNDEZ[3] & F. BERGAMASCHI[1]

[1]Department of Earth Sciences, Via G. La Pira, 4-50121 Florence, Italy.
(e-mail: orlando@steno.geo.unifi.it)
[2]CNR-Geosciences and Earth Resources, Via G. La Pira, 4-50121 Florence, Italy.
[3]Volcanological and Seismological Observatory, Universidad Nacional, Heredia, Costa Rica.

Abstract: We report the results of a geochemical survey of fumaroles, thermal springs, and gas discharges from areas in and around the active crater lake of Poás volcano (Costa Rica) from February 1998 to February 2001. The springs are highly acidic-sulphate waters with temperatures approaching boiling point, whereas gas chemistry is characterized by typical magmatic species, such as SO_2, HF, HCl, H_2, and CO. From February 1998 new fumarolic fields formed inside the southern part of the crater. They moved anticlockwise from the S to the NE inner walls of the crater, while those located in the southern part of the crater and close to the pyroclastic cone south of the crater lake diminished or disappeared altogether, during 1999 and 2000. This shift was also characterized by chemical variation of the magmatic gas species. In spite of the chemical changes of fumaroles, the composition of the lake changed little during this time. This fact, together with the chemical profile with depth of the lake, suggests that the lake is a very efficient condenser of magmatic fluids. An apparent chemical stratification of the lake suggests that dilution with meteoric water is not complete, due to the presence of liquid sulphur at the lake bottom and/or due to the continuous influx of new magmatic components.

Introduction

Active volcanic systems characterized by fumarolic or solfataric activity, summit crater lakes, and thermal waters are of special interest for geochemical surveillance. Continuous long-term geochemical monitoring is still hard to achieve at most volcanoes, due to difficult environmental conditions, uncertainties in the data gathered, paucity of the analysed gaseous and aqueous species, and expense of the equipment in terms of both purchasing and maintenance. Thus, periodic gas and water collection remain the most reliable means to carry out accurate and precise chemical analyses for many volcanoes (Giggenbach 1987).

Crater lake volcanoes, such as Poás in Costa Rica, represent an important case where the lake waters may act as magmatic heat and fluid collectors. Geochemical surveillance of such systems, which are generally characterized by highly acidic and saline waters (e.g. Varekamp et al., 2000), may shed light on the mechanisms and processes that lead to chemical variability in both the lake waters and fluid emissions in the surrounding areas (e.g. Christenson, 2000).

Recent episodes of volcanism at Poás in 1953-1954, 1964, 1972–1974, 1976-1979 (Casertano et al. 1983), 1980, 1987–1991 have been mainly characterized by phreato-magmatic (1953–1954) and phreatic events. Detailed studies of the origin of fluid discharges at Poás have been carried out by Brantley et al. (1987), Rowe et al. (1992a, b), successively supported and refined by stable isotopic (Rowe 1994), and chemical and hydrogeological (Rowe et al. 1995) investigations. On the basis of temperature, seismic, and geochemical observations, Rowe et al. (1992a) suggested that hydrofracturing episodes, triggered by the rupture of the chilled margin of shallow intrusions, may explain the increases in heat and volatile fluxes to the crater and adjacent sub-aerial fumaroles. This would cause the release of volatiles at magmatic temperature and magmatic intrusion, as may have occurred in 1986. Such shallow degassing would feed into complex, high-level aquifers. Meteoric ground-

From: OPPENHEIMER, C., PYLE, D.M. & BARCLAY, J. (eds) *Volcanic Degassing*. Geological Society, London, Special Publications, **213**, 247–262. 0305–8719/03/$15.00

waters at Poás play an important role in feeding the crater basin and lake, and summit rainfall may strongly affect the presence and the variations in level of the crater lake (Rowe *et al.* 1992*a*; Sanford *et al.* 1995).

The relationships between the chemical evolution of the crater lake (Laguna Caliente) and volcanic activity during 1993–1997 were investigated by Mártinez *et al.* (2000). They suggested that enhanced seismic activity (type A and B events and volcanic tremor) and the formation of new fumaroles from 1994 indicated 'renewed magma ascent beneath the active crater'. Since 1998, the Volcanological and Seismological Observatory of Heredia and the Department of Earth Sciences of Florence (Italy) have carried out a joint geochemical project on Poás volcano. These groups have sampled the volcanic fluids (crater lake, fumaroles, and thermal springs) once or twice per year, in order to assess the status of the volcanic system and to understand the links between geochemistry, seismicity, and other parameters as recognized by Mártinez *et al.* (2000).

Here we present the results of four years of discontinuous observation (1998–2001) of fluid discharges at Poás volcano, and measurements of the chemical composition of waters collected at different depths in the crater lake. The physical and chemical variations of fumarolic activity, including fumarole migration, that we document for this period, may reflect changes in the hydrothermal system, and we propose a possible model for the evolution of the volcanic system.

Geological and volcanological background

Poás is a composite volcano in the Cordillera Central of Costa Rica. Two other historically-active volcanoes are located nearby: Irazu and Turrialba. This volcanic range is the result of the subduction of the Cocos plate beneath the Caribbean plate (e.g. Johnston & Thorkelson 1997 and references therein). The volcanic products of Poás mainly consist of calc-alkaline basalts and andesites (Prosser & Carr 1987).

Poás was most recently active during the 1988–1991 crisis (Mártinez *et al.* 2000). The recorded historical activity of Poás dates back to 1828 (e.g. Krushensky & Escalante 1967; Malavassi *et al.* 1993, 1994, Castillo 1994; Mártinez *et al.*. 2000), and is mainly characterized by small phreatic, phreato-magmatic and Strombolian eruptions. In 1952, the style of eruption changed from mainly phreatic to phreato-magmatic, with the opening of two vents, one of which developed into a pyroclastic cone

that still stands today (hereafter referred to as the Dome, Fig. 1), while the other collapsed and formed Laguna Caliente. The presence of a crater lake is a typical feature of Poás, although at times it has become partially or completely emptied. For example, during 1988–1991, the lake dried out, revealing sulphur volcanoes (Oppenheimer & Stevenson 1989; Oppenheimer 1992).

Presently, Laguna Caliente is a highly acidic (pH ≈ 0), above-ambient temperature (30–40°C), sulphate-chloride lake, that has changed its shape in the last few decades (Brown *et al.* 1989, 1991; Rowe *et al.* 1992*a, b*). Two strong but poorly accessible fumarolic fields, with outlet temperatures of 95–100°C, are presently located at the interface between the Dome and the E and NE flanks of the crater walls. These were not present when gas sampling commenced in 1998. At that time, the main active fumaroles lay close to the S part of the crater and S region of the Dome.

Laguna Caliente overlies sulphur-rich sediments and altered and relatively porous volcanic rocks. Gravity studies of the crater suggest that the top of the magma body is located at a depth of about 500 m (Thorpe *et al.* 1981; Rymer & Brown 1987, 1989; Rymer *et al.*. 2000). The fumarolic system in the crater is probably governed by a shallow 'weak' hydrothermal system, able to reduce the temperature of the magmatic fluid to the boiling point of water, but not sufficient to completely condense magmatic components such as SO_2 and HCl. Magmatic components do condense in the crater lake (Rowe *et al.* 1992*a*) and reach the different fumarolic fields, which in turn may be locally affected by lake fluids (Rowe *et al.* 1992*b*).

Sampling and analytical methods

The sampling of gas and thermal water discharges (Fig. 1) has been affected by migration of the fumarole fields from February 1998 to February 2001. As already mentioned, the fumarolic field at the southern crater wall (Sur in Fig. 1), which was vigorously active in February 1998, no longer exists. The fumarole fields moved towards the eastern flank and eventually, a new field in the NE flank developed. Similar considerations apply to the Dome fumaroles. The south-central part of the Dome was affected by intense fumarolic activity up to November 1999. Presently, only diffuse and weak emissions prevail. The fumaroles located in the northern part of the Dome are located on the very steep flank where it meets the crater lake, and could not be accessed. Figure 1 summarizes these changes as reported by the OVSICORI personnel, and the sampling points discussed here.

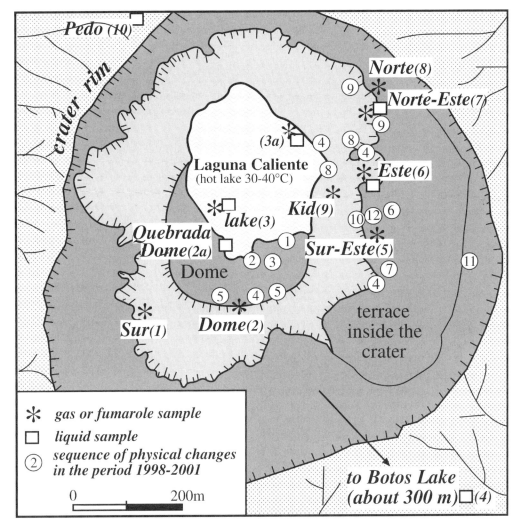

Fig. 1. Map of Poás summit crater with sampling locations marked. Numbers between brackets refer to liquid and gas samples. Sequence of physical changes in the period 1998–2001.

1. February 1999. Fumaroles appear in the NE wall of the pyroclastic cone.
2. March 1999. Fumaroles appear in the NW wall of the pyroclastic cone.
3. 3 April 1999. Fumaroles appear above the pyroclastic cone.
4. August 1999. Fumaroles appear S of the pyroclastic cone, thermal springs occur in the SE wall, in the eastern part of the inner crater and in the NW of terrace inside the crater.
5. October 1999. Fumaroles appears in the SE and SW part of the pyroclastic cone.
6. July 1999. Cracks appear in the upper area of the inner crater terrace.
7. February 2000. Fumaroles appear in the eastern part of the inner crater. Fumaroles from the southern part of the inner crater and from S, SW and SE of the pyroclastic cone disappear.
8. April 2000. Gas bubbling appears in the NE part of the Laguna Caliente. New fumaroles occur in the north-eastern part of the crater.
9. June–July 2000. New fumaroles appear in the northern part of the inner crater. The gas plume from the pyroclastic cone decreases.
10. August 2000. New fumaroles appear in the eastern part of the eastern wall.
11. September 2000. New fumaroles appear in the north-eastern part of the inner crater terrace.
12. December 2000 – February 2001. New fumaroles and thermal springs appear in the eastern flank of the inner crater.

Gas samples were collected by inserting a titanium tube into the fumarole (Piccardi 1982) and passing gases into pre-evacuated and weighed thorion-tapped 50 cc vials ('Giggenbach' bottles; Giggenbach 1975) filled with 20 ml of degassed 4N NaOH and 0.15 N $Cd(OH)_2$ until the headspace pressure reached that of the vent. Uncondensable gases (N_2, O_2, H_2, CO, Ar, He, Ne, CH_4 and light hydrocarbons) were analysed by gas chromatography. The CO_2 and HCl were determined by titration and ion chromatography, respectively, in the alkaline solution. Sulphur species (SO_2, H_2S and S^0) were analysed as SO_4^{2-} by ion chromatography as discussed by Montegrossi *et al.* (2001). Condensate samples were analysed for SO_4^{2-} (after complete chemical oxidation of the sulphur species), Cl^-, F^-, Br^- and NO_3^- by ion chromatography and B^{3+} by colorimetry (Bencini 1985).

Spring samples were collected in plastic bottles. No filtering was carried out for the lake samples. Temperature, pH, electrical conductivity, HCO_3^- (titration with HCl) and NH_4^+ and SiO_2 concentrations were determined in the field using standard spectrophotometric methods. Atomic absorption spectrophotometry (AAS), ion-chromatography and spectrophotometric analyses were used to determine cations (except for Al^{3+}, which was analysed by colorimetry), anions, and boron, respectively.

Sampling in the Laguna Caliente.

Summit crater lakes at active volcanoes represent a significant hazard because of the larger amounts of perched water that can potentially be displaced (e,g. during an eruption), and the quantities of dissolved gases (e.g. Kusakabe 1996; Mastin & Witter 2000). Landslides, earthquakes, etc., can disturb lake stratification, leading to overturn and release of dissolved gases (e.g. Freeth & Kay 1987; Barberi *et al.* 1989; Kusakabe *et al.* 1989; Christenson 1994). Lake chemical composition may reflect the interactions between the magma body and hydrothermal system, since crater lakes can act as condensers of the discharged volcanic fluids. Furthermore, sampling of deep waters in a crater lake can supply important information on the chemo-stratigraphy of the lake.

In February 2001, we crossed the Laguna Caliente in a small boat to sample the lake water (see: http://www.una.ac.cr/ovsi/lagos_eng_archivos/lagos_eng.htm). The exterior of the boat was covered with two folded plastic sheets to protect the boat surface. Several traverses of the lake were completed, and bathymetry was crudely measured every 5 m using a weighted

rope. At the deepest part of the lake (–41 m), we immersed a 0.5 mm diameter Rilsan tube (impermeable to both water and gas; Martini *et al.* 1994) and started pumping with a three vial-equipped syringe. After removing the water from the tube until we were sure that the water from the bottom of the lake was being extracted, we began sampling. We collected dissolved gas by means of the syringe and transferred it into a two-vial gas tube. Water was collected at different depths, i.e. –41 m, –30 m, –20 m, –10 m and 0.3 m, while gases were taken at –41 m, –20 m and -0.3 m. Temperature and pH were measured during sampling. We approached areas where lake temperature was up to 70°C. We also sampled a geyser that erupted every three to five minutes to about 2–3 m in height, located on the Dome near the water's edge (Quebrada Dome, Fig. 1), as well as a relatively cold gas bubbling through the lake, close to the Dome by using an inverted funnel attached to a gas vial using silicon tubes. Although temperature and density profiles of the lake have been measured in the past (Brantley *et al.* 1987; Neshyba *et al.* 1988), to the best of our knowledge this is the first vertical chemical profile through Poás crater lake.

Results

Chemistry of the crater lake and spring water discharges

Chemical analyses of the active crater lake (Laguna Caliente), thermal waters discharging inside the crater, and Botos lake and Pedo mineral spring, the latter two located outside the crater (Fig. 1), are shown in Table 1. All of the water emissions (into) inside the crater (Quebrada Dome spring, Este spring, Quebrada Este, Quebrada Roja, Quebrada de Hierro, Norte-Este spring) have a low pH (often <3), while those of Botos and Pedo are slightly higher (up to 5). Laguna Caliente has the lowest pH values (always <1).

Temperatures of Laguna Caliente varied from 25°C (#3, Poás Lake) at -0.3 m in November 1999 to 46°C at –0.3 m in February 2000. The temperatures found while crossing the lake, up to 70°C in February 2001, indicate the presence of fumaroles and condensation of steam within the lake. Spring temperatures varied between 15 (#7, Norte-Este Spring, Feb. 1999) and 94.8°C (#6d, Quebrada de Hierro, Feb. 2001), the latter suggestive of boiling pools due to condensation of fumarolic steam near the surface, rather than real springs.

Table 1. Chemical composition (in mg/l) of liquid phases sampled in and around the Laguna Caliente lake. Left-hand side numbers refer to the sampling location reported in Fig. 1.

n.	Sample	Date	pH	T(°C)	Na^+	K^+	Ca^{2+}	Mg^{2+}	NH_4^+	CO_3^-	SO_4^{2-}	Cl^-	F^-	Br^-	NO_3^-	B^{3+}	Fe_{tot}	Mn_{tot}	Al^{3+}
2a	Quebrada Dome	Feb. 2001	3.85	78	439	80	494	26	39	9250	9250	11 500	790	26		7.0	808	26	1100
3	Laguna Caliente (−0.3m)	Feb. 2001	0.80	30.8	438	78	495	461	48	10 500	10 900	730	22			830	26.4	1020	
3	Laguna Caliente (−10 m)	Feb. 2001	0.83	32	452	80	518	485	45	11 000	11 600	680	27		7.2	845	27	970	
3	Laguna Caliente (−20 m)	Feb. 2001	0.83	32	466	83	520	501	64	11 000	11 900	720	28		8.9	857	26	920	
3	Laguna Caliente (−30 m)	Feb. 2001	0.83	32	470	82	524	504	51	9750	11 300	740	23.5		7.1	883	28	860	
3	Laguna Caliente (−41 m)	Feb. 2001	0.83	32.5	452	83	508	493	41	9750	11 400	890	26		6.6	865	28	1190	
3a	Laguna Caliente (−0.3 m)	Feb. 1998	0.89	37	498	69	1130	534	62	8250	8000	480	22	5.0	6.8				
3a	Laguna Caliente (−1 m)	Feb. 1998			492	78	1250	540	76	8000	7500	300	19	4.0	7.6				
3a	Laguna Caliente (−2 m)	Feb. 1998			453	79	1094	530	64	8100	8000	490	17	4.0	8.5				
3a	Laguna Caliente (−3 m)	Feb. 1998			438	80	896	546	83	7900	7500	460	20	6.0	8.1				
3a	Laguna Caliente (−0.3m)	Mar. 1999	0.38	31.3	508	90	1040	483	138	9750	12 800	700	27	25	<0.03	1008	28		
3a	Laguna Caliente (−0.3m)	Nov. 1999	0.75	25	600	59	745	285	24	5500	4750	325	20	19	2.1	457	13	450	
3a	Laguna Caliente (−0.3m)	Feb. 2000	1.06	46	417	102	1110	490	53	9200	9400	700	30	5.2	6.2	875	23	390	
4	Botos Lake (surface)	Feb. 1998	4.73	19	0.8	0.9	5.7	0.8	15	9	11	1.5	0.12	0.02	0.0	0.02			
4	Botos Lake (−0.3 m)	Feb. 2001	5.03	16.8	0.59	0.16	3.0	0.6	0.08	6.1	12	0.7	0.09	<0.01	0.05	0.2	0.12	<0.01	0.1
6	Este spring	Nov. 1999	1.20	42	26	3.2	340	10	4		1725	16	7	<0.01	<0.01	<0.03	128	0.6	0.6
6b	Quebrada Este	Feb. 2000	0.12	89	178	13	547	352	32		12 200	25	16	0.35	2.2	1.5	1000	13	520
6c	Quebrada Roja	Feb. 2000	2.02	84	245	33	291	165	8		4100	26	1.4	0.25	12	2.6	575	9	26
6d	Quebrada de Hierro	Feb. 2001	2.77	94.8	131	19	193	81	58		3500	6.2	6.4	0.05	0.15	4.3	909	5.4	11
6c	Quebrada Roja	Nov. 1999	0.96	87	188	6.3	355	215	32		4650	29	5.4	<0.01	<0.01	<0.03	785	12	
6c	Quebrada Roja	Feb. 2001	2.41	85	73	2.3	597	29	13		2900	16	7.5	0.05	0.21	2.0	127	1.9	40
7	Norte-Este spring	Mar. 1999	3.51	15	22	2	516	36	15		2150	15.8	2.25	0.1	0.5	0.13	39	0.4	131
10	Pedo spring	Feb. 1998	4.51	20	6.7	3.6	20	5.7	0.1	3.5	87	5	0.7	<0.01	<0.01	0.04	5.4	0.1	
10	Pedo spring	Feb. 2000	5.06	19	20	4.7	20	6.5	1.2	7.3	107	6.5	0.6	0.01	0.25	<0.03	0.35	0.17	

Apart from H^+, sulphate and chloride ions are the main dissolved species in the lake. Their contents ranged between 5,500 (–0.3 m, Nov. 1999) and 11 000 (–20 m, Feb. 2001) mg/l and 4750 (–0.3 m, Nov. 1999) and 12 800 (–0.3 m, March 1999) mg/l, respectively. The thermal spring discharges in the crater showed a more variable composition, with SO_4^{2-} always the main anion (up to 12 200 mg/l, #6b Quedraba Este, Feb. 2000) while Cl^- is subordinate (<30 mg/l). One exception is the Quebrada Dome (# 2a which has SO_4^{2-} and Cl^- contents similar to those of the crater lake, 9250 and 11 500 mg/l, respectively). Botos Lake (#4) and Pedo (#10) mineral springs are characterized by much lower salinity than the crater samples, with values of SO_4^{2-} and Cl^- never exceeding 12 and 1.5 mg/kg (Botos) and 107 and 6.5 m/kg Pedo), respectively (Table 1).

Apart from H^+, the main cations in Laguna Caliente are, in order of abundance, Ca^{2+} (max: 1250 mg/l at –1 m, March 1998), Al^{3+} (max: 1190 mg/l at –40 m, Feb. 2001), $Fe_{(tot)}$ (max: 1008 mg/l at –0.3 m, March 1999), Na^+ (max: 600 mg/l at –0.3 m, Nov. 1999), Mg^{2+} (max: 546 mg/l at –3.0 m, March 2001), K^+ (max: 102 mg/l at –0.3 m, Feb. 2000) (Table 1).

The crater discharges have slightly lower concentrations of the same cations. The cation concentrations in Botos Lake and Pedo spring are up to 4 orders of magnitude less than those of the crater lake (Table 1). Among the 'trace' species, we find remarkable contents of F^- (up to 890 mg/l at –40 m, Feb. 2001), Br^- (up to 26 mg/l at –40 m, Feb. 2001), NO_3^- (up to 19 mg/l at –0.3 m, Nov. 1999), B^{3+} (up to 8.9 mg/l at –20 m, Feb. 2001) and NH_4^+ (up to 138 mg/l at –0.3, March 1999) in the Laguna Caliente samples.

Thermal seeps in the crater (fumarole condensates and springs) can easily be distinguished chemically from Laguna Calient, Botos and Pedo samples. In Figure 2, the F^-–Cl^-–SO_4^{2-} ternary diagram shows that the crater lake acts as a condenser, as suggested elsewhere (e.g. Rowe *et al.* 1992*b*, 1995). HCl, HF and sulphur-rich gases (mainly SO_2 and H_2S) dissolve in the lake water, so that the gases that escape from the lake are enriched in CO_2 and other insoluble gases. However, a different mechanism must apply to the thermal discharges that are enriched in SO_4^{2-} and depleted in both F^- and Cl^-, suggesting that the different solubilities of these components are important. The composition of these fluids may indicate the presence of a shallow aquifer that

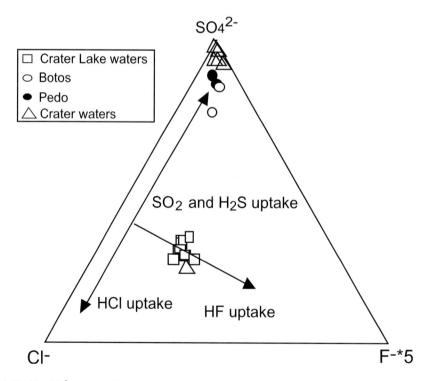

Fig. 2. $5*F^-$–Cl^-–SO_4^{2-} ternary diagram for thermal and mineral waters from Poás crater summit, using meq/l.

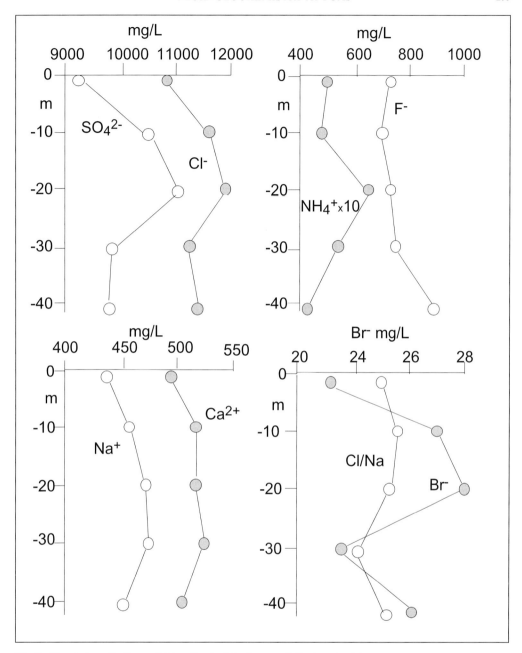

Fig. 3. Chemical profile (from –0.3 to –41 m) of the Laguna Caliente crater lake.

scrubs F⁻ and Cl⁻ with respect to sulphur species. It is noteworthy that the Quebrada Dome sample chemically resembles the Laguna Caliente samples. Its geyser-like nature suggests uptake of water from the lake through a gas lift mechanism. Botos and Pedo waters, characterized by

a lower salinity than the crater samples, lie slightly below the SO_4^{2-} apex in Figure 2.

The chemical profile of Poás crater lake is shown in Figure 3. Sulphate, chloride, bromide, and ammonia show peak concentrations between –10 and –20 m. At the surface and in the deepest

Table 2. *Chemical composition of gas samples (in μmol/mol) sampled in the Laguna Caliente area. Left-hand side numbers refer to the sampling location in Fig.1.*

n.	Sample	Date	Type	T(°C)	H_2O	CO_2	SO_2	H_2S	S^0	S_{TOT}	HCl	HF	He	Ar	H_2
1	Sur	Feb. 1998	Fumarole	98	987 322	9900		838.9			432.1		1.71	11.41	279.27
1	Sur	Feb. 1999	Fumarole	98	978 257	18407	2.3	1880.9	0.09	1883.2			2.26	7.36	94.07
2	Dome	Feb. 1999	Fumarole	92	936 387	30066	29 347.8		3.36	29 351.1	1732.7	4.04	1.49	7.92	454.16
2	Dome	Nov. 1999	Fumarole	92	945 681	24108	26 349.6	573.5	37.20	26 960.3	1563.2	5.48	4.46	32.67	51.84
2	Dome	Feb. 2000	Fumarole	93.6	992 026	739	2951.0	859.9	16.46	3827.3	1429.5	6.78	0.02	6.80	1912.90
3	Lake	Feb. 2001	Gas bubbling	78	282 028	667998							0.01	55.47	31585.53
5	Sur-Este	Feb. 2000	Fumarole	92	995 455	2124	1500.1	149.2	39.62	1688.9			0.22	2.50	18.06
6	Este	Feb. 2000	Fumarole	89	955 610	7566	34 459.9	1573.6	39.63	36 073.1	266.4	59.83	0.17	7.19	20.18
6	Este	Feb. 2001	Fumarole	97.2	923 176	74215	1143.8	262.0	14.14	1420.0	473.0		0.05	6.27	0.55
6c	Quebrada Roja	Feb. 2000	Boiling pool	87	970 590	24918		3252.2	11.09	3263.3			0.12	9.21	245.87
7	Norte-Este	Feb. 2001	Boiling pool	101	497 794	245 575	247 043.8	6440.9	57.63	253 542.3	2294.1	0.23	0.89	10.58	25.17
8	Norte	Feb. 2001	Fumarole	101	894 659	63321	40 635.0	742.1	3.03	41 380.1	419.8	0.21	0.66	1.00	20.91
9	The Kid	Feb. 2001	Fumarole	94.5	929 493	64698		5385.4	2.87	5388.3			0.15	4.19	0.55

n.	Sample	Date	Type	N_2	O_2	Ne	CH_4	CO	H_2O/CO_2	S_{tot}/CO_2	S_{tot}/HCl	SO_2/H_2S	HCl/HF	S_{tot}/HCl
1	Sur	Feb. 1998	Fumarole	1197.9	14.3	1197.8724	2.274	0.016	99.73					
1	Sur	Feb. 1999	Fumarole	1345.0	2.0	1344.9517	1.163	0.440	53.15	0.10		0.001		
2	Dome	Feb. 1999	Fumarole	1956.2		1956.2403	0.226	38.912	31.14	0.98	16.94		428.8	16.9
2	Dome	Nov. 1999	Fumarole	1583.1		1583.0859	0.106	9.533	39.23	1.12	17.25	45.946	285.0	17.2
2	Dome	Feb. 2000	Fumarole	46.9		46.9005	0.075	4.954	1342.81	5.18	2.68	3.432	210.9	2.7
3	Lake	Feb. 2001	Gas bubbling	15899.5	2410.9	0.0320	0.312	21.990	0.42					
5	Sur-Este	Feb. 2000	Fumarole	704.3	6.1	0.0023	0.588	0.251	468.61	0.80		10.056		
6	Este	Feb. 2000	Fumarole	384.1	12.2	0.0054	0.002	0.674	126.31	4.77	135.43	21.899	4.5	135.4
6	Este	Feb. 2001	Fumarole	573.0	135.9	0.0036	0.001	1.200	12.44	0.02	3.00	4.365		3.0
6c	Quebrada Roja	Feb. 2000	Boiling pool	793.4	178.5	0.0062	0.005		38.95	0.13				
7	Norte-Este	Feb. 2001	Boiling pool	757.9		0.0063	0.026	0.407	2.03	1.03	110.52	38.355	9844.4	110.5
8	Norte	Feb. 2001	Fumarole	196.5	0.2	0.0004	0.003	0.208	14.13	0.65	98.57	54.756	2008.6	98.6
9	The Kid	Feb. 2001	Fumarole	408.9	6.6	0.0028	0.004	0.046	14.37	0.08				

Table 3. *Chemical composition of fumarole condensates (in mg/l). Left-hand side numbers refer to the sampling location reported in Fig. 1.*

n.	Sample	Date	Cl⁻	SO₄²⁻	Br⁻	F⁻	NO₃⁻	B³⁺	NH₄⁺
1	Fumarole Sur	Feb. 1998	26	4	<0.01	0.1	<0.01	2.1	1.8
1	Fumarole Sur	Feb. 1999	<0.01	11	nd	0.07	0.02	0.24	0.39
2	Fumarole Dome	Feb. 1999	14	612	0.02	0.75	0.12	0.19	
2	Fumarole Dome	Nov. 1999	1.2	582	nd	0.06	nd	<0.03	0.5
2	Fumarole Dome	Feb. 2000	470	96	nd	135	nd	<0.03	0.05
5	Fumarole Sur-Este	Feb. 2000	0.2	67	nd	0.48	0.03	<0.03	0.85
7	Fumarole Norte-Este	Feb. 2001	637	4125	2.4	0.50	1.6		
8	Fumarole Norte	Feb. 2001	32	501	3.9	0.40	1.6		
9	The Kid	Feb. 2001	26	385	2.6	0.40	15		

part of the lake, i.e. −30 and −41 m, the abundances are relatively uniform (Table 1). Fluoride tends to increase slightly from the surface to the bottom and behaves differently from the other main anions. The main cations have a more uniform trend with depth as shown by Na^+ and Ca^{2+} in Figure 3. In general, the main dissolved cation and anion contents show a convex trend from the surface to −41 m, suggesting that different surficial (meteoric and channel flow) and deep (magmatic fluids, lateral fumaroles) inputs inhibit complete mixing of the lake waters. Although the temperature along the sampled lake profile is rather uniform (from 30.8 to 32.5°C), localized increases in temperature (up to 70°C) have been recorded, especially close to the Dome.

Gas and condensate samples

The compositions of gas and fumarolic condensate samples are reported in Tables 2 and 3, respectively. Poás fumaroles are characterized by H_2O ranging between 28.2×10^4 (Dome Lake, Feb. 2001) and 99.6×10^4 (Fumarole Sur-Este, Feb. 2000) μmol mol^{-1} with relatively high contents of SO_2, H_2, HCl, HF and CO (Table 2).

During the period of observation, no significant variations of fumarolic temperatures were observed: most are at the boiling temperature appropriate for about 2400 m. Only fumaroles Norte-Este and Norte have a higher temperature (of 101°C; Table 2). Setting aside boiling and bubbling gases (Quebrada Roja, Feb. 2000 and Dome Lake, Feb. 2001, respectively), H_2O contents are from 49.8×10^4 (Fumarole Norte-Este, Feb. 2001) to 99.5×10^4 (Fumarole Sur-Este, Feb. 2000) μmol. mol.$^{-1}$. Sulphur species vary from 2.29 (Fumarole Sur, Feb. 1999) to 24.7×10^4 (Fumarole Norte-Este, Feb. 2001) μmol mol^{-1}, 149 (Fumarole Sur-Este, Feb. 2000) to 6441 (Fumarole Norte-Este, Feb. 2001) μmol mol^{-1} and 0.09 (Fumarole Sur, Feb. 1999) to 57.6

(Fumarole Norte-Este, Feb. 2001) μmol. mol.$^{-1}$ for SO_2, H_2S, and S^0, respectively. The CO_2 contents range between 739 (Fumarole Dome, Feb. 2000) and 66.8×10^4 (Fumarole Dome Lake, Feb. 2001) μmol mol^{-1}.

The highest value of HCl was measured at Fumarole Norte-Este (Feb. 2001): 2294 μmol. mol.$^{-1}$, whereas HF had the highest content at Fumarole Este (Feb. 2000): 59.8 μmol. mol.$^{-1}$. The highest abundances of H_2 and CO pertain to the fumaroles of the Dome Lake (Feb. 2001) and Dome (Feb. 1999), respectively. N_2 contents were generally below 46 μmol. mol.$^{-1}$, the lowest values being found at Fumarole Dome (Feb. 2000); Ar, He, and Ne contents are <55, 4.5, and 0.028 μmol. mol.$^{-1}$ (Table 2). The fumarole collected next to the dome (Dome Lake, Feb. 2001) had a peculiar composition, being characterized by relatively high CO_2 and H_2 content (67×10^4 and 3.2×10^4 μmol. mol.$^{-1}$, respectively), whereas acidic gases such as SO_2, H_2S, HCl, and HF were below the instrumental detection limit.

During the period of observation, no individual fumarole was analysed more than three times apart from Fumarole Dome, because of changes in the disposition of fumaroles between February 1998 and February 2001. This is reflected in the large variations observed in ratios of chemical species, which in turn may provide useful information on the evolution of the fluids discharging at Poás volcano. For instance, H_2O/CO_2, S_{tot}/CO_2, SO_2/H_2S, HCl/HF and S_{tot}/HCl ratios (Table 2) show quite large variations: 0.4–1343, 0.01–5.2, 0.001–54.8, 4.5–9844 and 2.7–135, respectively. The highest ratios were generally observed for the fumaroles Dome and Norte-Este, suggesting that the fluids feeding these gas discharges either take a more direct pathway from depth to the surface or experience less interaction with the shallow aquifer.

Chemical analyses of selected condensate samples are reported in Table 3. The results refer

Table 4. *Chemical composition of stripped gas (in μmol/mol) from the Laguna Caliente and Botos Lakes at increasing depth and Pedo spring. Left-hand side numbers refer to the sampling location reported in Fig. 1.*

n.		Sample	Date	*T*°C	CO_2	N_2	O_2	Ar	H_2	He	Ne	CH_4	CO
2	3	Laguna Caliente (–3 m)	Feb. 1998	31.5	235 600	616 600	120 900	8200	10520	6.0		24.0	
3	3a	Laguna Caliente (–0.3 m)	Feb. 2001	32	26 200	767 200	186 700	9940	9190	<1	5.5	1.8	35
4	3a	Laguna Caliente (–20 m)	Feb. 2001	32	136 100	679 100	165 100	9540	11810	<1	5.5	1.4	75
5	3a	Laguna Caliente (–41 m)	Feb. 2001	32.5	181 100	645 400	157 800	9450	10070	<1	5.0	2.6	150
6	4	Botos Lake (–8 m)	Feb. 2001	12.5	160	735 600	250 200	14 200				9.0	25.0
1	10	Pedo spring	Feb 1998	20	382 300	589 900	15 800	11 900			21.0		207.0

only to the fumarolic discharges while the 'natural' condensates ('boiling pool' such as Quebrada Roja, Quebrada Este, etc.) are included in Table 1. Sulphates and Cl⁻ are the main dissolved species, although concentrations vary widely from 11-4125 and 0.2-637 mg/l, respectively. The same is true for Br⁻ and NO_3^-, which range between 0.02–3.9 and 0.02–15 mg/l, respectively. F⁻ contents are slightly less variable (0.05–1.4 mg/l) with the exception of the Fumarole Dome, Feb. 2000, which had a F⁻ content of 135 mg/l.

Dissolved gas analyses were performed on Pedo spring and Botos and Poás lakes, and the results are presented in Table 4. Nitrogen, O_2 and Ar are generally the main species, although CO_2 contents are high in the Pedo mineral spring discharge (38.2 vol.%) and at Poás Lake (2.62–23.56 vol.%, Table 4). Gas samples from Botos have a composition similar to air saturated water. Laguna Caliente's dissolved gases show a notable increasing content of CO_2 with depth, and high content of H_2 (up to 1.2 vol.%).

Discussion

Many variables might influence the gas compositions observed at the summit crater of Poás, e.g. rock permeability, thickness of the water table, gas–gas, rock–fluid and water–gas reactions, etc. (e.g. Casertano *et al.* 1987; Rowe *et al.* 1992a, b; 1995). During the period of study (February 1998–February 2001), the fumarolic manifestations showed variations of chemical composition, flow discharge and location. The latter has prevented use of a single fumarole vent as a reference point. For instance, the Fumarole Sur (Fig. 1), located about 300 m from the Dome, had virtually disappeared by February 2000. At the same time, newly formed fumaroles and boiling pools appeared at the ESE crater wall some 150 m from the lake (Fumarole Sur-Este, Fumarole Este, Quebrada Roja, Fumarole Norte-Este, Fumarole Norte, 'The Kid', Fig. 1). Similarly, the Fumarole Dome was sampled in

two different places due to flux variation in time, until both fumaroles disappeared by February 2001. Although we are not aware of any flux measurements having been made in this period, Fernandez *et al.* (2000a, b) and Mártinez *et al.* (2000) have reported apparent variations in the plume emission. From early 1999, the gas plume reached a height of 0.7–1.0 km above the crater (it was <0.5 km in 1998), and coffee crops on the WNW flanks of the volcano were damaged by acid rain (Fernandez *et al.* 2000b). In 2000 and early 2001, the plume seemed to have decrease in flux.

Figure 4 summarizes the chemical data from the gas and water discharges and condensates at Poás from 1998 to 2001 on a Cl⁻ v. SO_4^{2-} diagram. The cold, mineral (Pedo and Botos Lake) and meteoric (Brantley *et al.* 1987) water samples, and the majority of the boiling pools and condensates from the eastern, NE and northern fumarolic fields, lie on a straight line, suggesting the dilution of deep fluids with meteoric waters. Despite the fact that the crater lake samples were obtained at different depths, they also lie close to the same line. Shallow (<–10 m) lake waters are relatively less saline than the >20 m samples, suggesting a slight dilution by meteoric waters (Fig. 3). This would also explain the relatively higher concentrations of the main cations and anions between –10 and –20 m. The decreasing pattern of most dissolved species from –20 to –41 m remains unclear. Meteoric inputs, thermal discharges into the lake, and lake-bed vents may account for the convex pattern observed for most cation and anion contents along the studied profile (Fig. 3). Microbacterial activity may be important, as suggested by the highly negative $\delta^{13}C$–CO_2 values (–34‰ PDB) at –41 m, compared with the values of –2 to –3‰ PDB measured in the fumarolic discharges (Vaselli & Tassi, unpublished data). However, further investigation needs to be carried out to confirm this.

Among the fumaroles and boiling pools, only the Fumarole Norte-Este (Feb. 2001) and the

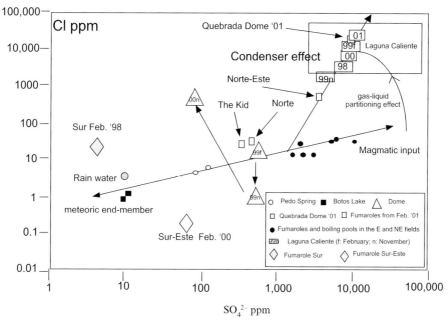

Fig. 4. The Cl^- v. SO_4^{2-} binary diagram for fumarolic condensates and thermal and mineral waters from Poás summit crater. Numbers inside the different symbols indicate the year of sampling. Rainwater from Brantley *et al.* (1987); the rectangle represents SO_4^{2-} and Cl^- concentrations in Laguna Caliente from January 1993 to November 1997 (Mártinez *et al.* 2000).

small geyser close to the lake shore on the Dome (Quebrada Dome) lie on the dilution line (Fig. 4). The abrupt change in slope of the line shows the condensation of volcanic fluids in Laguna Caliente, as already observed by Rowe et al. (1992*a*, 1995). Laguna Caliente scrubs acid gases such as SO_2, HCl, and HF, enriching them in the liquid phase with respect to the gas phase. This can be seen from both the high Cl^- and SO_4^{2-} contents, and the gas composition, mainly CO_2 and atmospheric gases, at different water depths (Table 4), and from the gas bubbling into the lake, where significant enrichments in CO_2 and H_2 are recorded (Fumarole Lake in Table 2). Furthermore, the SO_4 and Cl contents in the Fumarole Norte-Este (Table 3) suggest that the lake brine may locally interact with the fumarolic discharges.

The data for Fumarole Dome (Nov. 1999 and Feb. 2000), 'The Kid' and Norte (Feb. 2001) diverge from these two trends. The same is true for the Fumaroles Sur (Feb. 1998) and the Sur-Este (Feb. 1999). It is worth pointing out that the fumaroles from the dome (from Feb. 1999 to Feb. 2000) follow a decreasing trend with respect to Cl^- from February 1999 to Nov. 1999. A sharp increase of Cl^- and a minor decrease in the contents of SO_4^{2-} and F^- in Feb. 2000 were observed.

Binary diagrams of redox and HCl/HF and H_2/Ar pairs from the different fumarolic fields are reported as a function of time in Figure 5a to 5d. Here, we report chemical data for fumaroles for which there are at least two consecutive samplings, (Fumarole Sur, Fumarole Dome, and Fumarole Este). We suggest that Fumarole 'The Kid' and Fumarole Norte may reflect the gas composition of the Fumarole Dome after this switched off (February 2000, Table 2 and Fig. 9), on the basis of Figure 8. These two fumaroles were indeed approaching the composition of Fumarole Dome in February 1999. Fumarole Dome provides useful information, since this was sampled three times in a relatively short period of time, while Fumarole Sur and Fumarole Este look like the pre-February 1999 and the post-February 2000 prolongation of Fumarole Dome (Fig. 5), when the redox pairs (e.g. CO/CO_2, CH_4/CO_2, H_2/CH_4, H_2S/SO_2 and CH_4/CO) and H_2/Ar and HCl/HF are considered.

The CO/CO_2 and CH_4/CO_2 log ratios (Fig. 5a) show relatively high values from February 1998 to February 1999, followed by a slight increase in November 1999. There is a new increase in February 2000 and, eventually, an abrupt decrease in February 2001. The H_2/Ar and H_2/CH_4 log ratios (Figs 5b and c) tend to

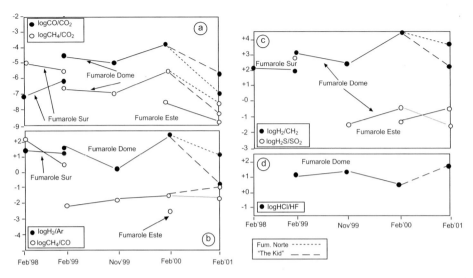

Fig. 5. Variation with time of: (a) CO/CO_2 and CH_4/CO_2, (b) H_2/Ar and CH_4/CO, (c) H_2/CH_4 and H_2S/SO_2 and (d) HCl/F log ratios for the fumarolic gas discharges at Poás crater.

decrease in November 1999; then increase and, finally, in February 2001 they abruptly decrease. From this general trend, the CH_4/CO log ratio (Fig. 5b) shows a slight but fairly stable increase, whereas the HCl/HF log ratio (Fig. 5d) has an opposite trend with respect to the previously considered redox pairs, showing a slight increase in November 1999 followed by a decrease in February 2000 and, recently, a clear increase in February 2001, when the Fumarole Norte is considered.

On the basis of these chemical variations and field observations, we reconstruct the evolution of the fluids at Poás volcano from February 1998 to February 2001 in a conceptual model as follows (Fig. 6).

1. In February 1998, Fumarole Sur (Fig. 1, Table 1) had a typical high-temperature composition, and a gas plume that reached 0.5 km above the vent (Fernandez *et al.* 1998). Between February and November 1999, the emission rate appeared visually to have increased (e.g. Fernandez *et al.* 2000a, b), consistent with observed agricultural damage due to acid rain. However, no chemical changes were observed in the Fumarole Sur. Contemporaneously, fumarolic activity started moving ENE. The decrease in H_2/Ar, CO/CO_2, and CH_4/CO_2 ratios suggests that surficial water was penetrating the hydrothermal system, and the deep environment became slightly more oxidizing

(Fig. 5a). Further, the slight decrease in the Cl^- content in the condensate, and the increase in HCl/HF in the gas phase (Dome Feb. 1999 and Nov. 1999, Fig. 4 & Fig. 5d, respectively), is consistent with dilution and oxidation of the Poás fluids as a shallow aquifer interacted with a deeper portion of the ascending magmatic fluids. The enhanced plume emission may have resulted from hydrofracturing, as occurred between 1978 and 1990 (Rowe et al. 1992a,b), when a surficial aquifer, mainly fed from Botos Lake (Rowe *et al.* 1995), entered the hydrothermal system (Brown *et al.* 1989).

2. After November 1999, the fumarole chemistry continued to change, and new fumarolic fields developed in the NE part of the crater. In February 2000, the Cl^- content in the condensate increased sharply (Dome: Feb. 2000, Fig. 4), suggesting an enhanced release of fluids from the hydrothermal system. At the same time, the plume flux apparently decreased. The increases in H_2, CO, and H_2S, recorded in February 2000, may relate to variations of both temperature and redox conditions of the magmatic-hydrothermal system. This is also supported by increases of the CO/CO_2, CH_4/CO_2, H_2/Ar, H_2/CH_4, and H_2S/SO_2 ratios (Figs 5a to c) indicative of more reducing conditions, related to a more efficient dissociation of the surficial water entering the system at depth.

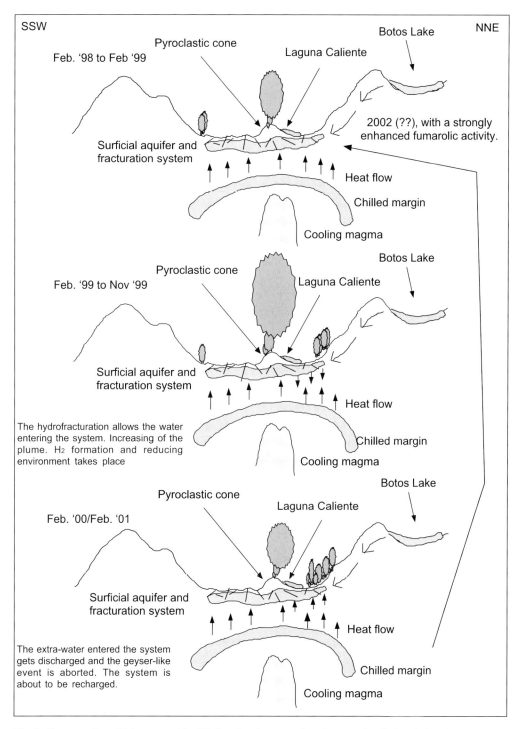

Fig. 6. Conceptual model (not to scale) of Poás volcanic system, based on geochemical variations in gas emissions from February 1998 to February 2001, and field observations. The orientation of the cross-section is roughly SSW–NNE.

3. After February 2001, the situation seems to have reset, since all the parameters considered decreased quite dramatically (Tables 2 and 3). However, the fumarolic activity remains strong, and the fumarolic fields are now mostly located in the northern and NE parts of the crater.

Rainfall may play an important role in gas chemistry. Seasonal precipitation can be variable, and the wet and dry seasons are not well defined at Poás. Rainfall data from a gauge located at about 2 km south of Poás summit indicate that from 1981 to 1983 the annual precipitation was 3.8 m/yr, varying between 420 mm month^{-1} for May–November and 120 mm month^{-1} for January-April (Rowe *et al.* 1992*a*). However, the Poás summit has a particular micro-climate, and rainfall measurements should be performed at the top of the summit itself. For example, in November 2001 (during the rainy season), the level of Laguna Caliente dropped by 2 m (OVSICORI, pers. comm.).

The shallow depth of the magma chamber and the presence of the surficial aquifer seem to regulate volcanic activity at Poás Volcano. Permeability changes due to hydrofracturing favour the vaporisation of water, which results in a change in the *P–T* redox conditions of the deep hydrothermal system. As a consequence, eruptive events may vary from geyser-like to minor phreato-magmatic activity according to the magma/water ratio. In this scenario, gas chemical variations can indicate modification of the system, even in the absence of seismic phenomena. The situation in February 2001 is similar to that in February 1998, except for the increased fumarolic activity in the NE and northern parts of the crater, and newly formed fumarolic fields.

Conclusions

Geochemical surveys carried out on both crater fumaroles and thermal waters discharging inside Poás crater indicate considerable temporal variability in the gas chemical composition. In addition we observed a migration of fumaroles from 1998 to 2001, which continued through November 2001. We recommend a sustained programme of regular (bi-weekly to monthly) geochemical surveys of the fumarolic discharges, although short-term events, due to the strong hydrothermal activity in the eastern and northern flanks of the crater, landslide and/or flank failure, can be expected. These could lead to instantaneous release of the fluids hosted in the hydrothermal system, causing phreatic- to weak phreato-magmatic eruptive events. Even

without flank failures, phreatic activity is possible, as witnessed during the 1987–1990 crisis.

We thank the OVSICORI staff, and C. Giolito and A. Nencetti, for their help during the February and November 2000 field seasons, respectively. This work was supported financially by A.S.I. (Italian Space Agency, Resp. OV) projects. We are grateful to D. M. Pyle, P. Delmelle, and M. Todesco for helpful comments on the manuscript.

References

ARMIENTA, M. A., DE LA CRUZ-REYNA, S. & MACIAS, J. L., 2000. Chemical characteristics of the crater lakes of Popocatepetl, El Chichon and Nevado de Toluca, Mexico. *Journal of Volcanology and Geothermal Research*, **97**, 105–126.

BARBERI, F., CHELINI, W., MARINELLI, G. & MARTINI, M. 1989. The gas cloud of the Lake Nyos (Cameroon 1986): results of the Italian technical mission. *Journal of Volcanology and Geothermal Research*, **39**, 125–134.

BENCINI, A. 1985. Applicabilità del metodo dell'azometina-H alla determinazione del Boro nelle acque naturali. *Rend. Soc. It. Mineral. Petrol.*, **40**, 311–316 [in Italian].

BRANTLEY, S. L., BORGIA, A., ROWE, G., FERNANDEZ, J. F. & REYNOLDS, J. R. 1987. Poas volcano crater lake acts as a condenser for acid metal-rich brine. *Nature*, **330**, 470–472.

BROWN, G., RYMER, H., DOWDEN, J., KAPADIA, PH., STEVENSON, D., BARQUERO, J. & MORALES, L.D. 1989. Energy budget analysis for Poás crater lake: implications for predicting volcanic activity. *Nature*, **339**, 370–373.

BROWN, G., RYMER, H. & STEVENSON, D. 1991. Volcano monitoring by microgravity and energy budget analysis. *Journal of the Geological Society of London*, **148**, 585–593.

CASERTANO, L., BORGIA, A.& CIGOLINI 1983. El Volcan Poás, Costa Rica: cronologia y caracteristicas de actividad. *Geofisica Internacional*, **22**, 215–236 [in Spanish].

CASERTANO, L., BORGIA, A., CIGOLINI, C., MORALES, L. D., MONTERO, W., GOMEZ, M. & FERNANDEZ, J. F. 1987. An integrated dynamic model for the volcanic activity at Poás volcano, Costa Rica. *Bulletin of Volcanology*, **49**, 588–598.

CASTILLO, R.M. 1984. *Geológia de Costa Rica*. Editorial de la Universidad de Costa Rica, San José, Costa Rica, 188 pp.

CHRISTENSON, B.W. 1994. Convection and stratification in Ruapehu Crater Lake, New Zealand: implications for Lake Nyos-type gas release eruptions. *Geochemical Journal*, **28**, 185–197.

CHRISTENSON, B.W. 2000. Geochemistry of fluids associated with the 1996-1996 eruption of Mt. Ruapehu, New Zealand: signatures and processes in the magmatic–hydrothermal reservoir. *Journal of Volcanology and Geothermal Research*, **97**, 1–30.

DELMELLE, P. BERNARD, A., KUSAKABE, M., FISCHER,

T. P. & TAKANO, B. 2000. Geochemistry of the magmatic–hydrothermal system of Kawah Ijen volcano, East Java, Indonesia. *Journal of Volcanology and Geothermal Research*, **97**, 31–54.

FERNANDEZ, E., BARBOSA,V., DUARTE, E., SAENZ, R., MALAVASSI, E., MARTINEZ, M. & VAN DER LAAT, R. 1998. Gas plumes to 500 m high; modest seismicity during March–May. BGVN, **6/98**.

FERNANDEZ, E., DUARTE, E., MARTINEZ, M., VASELLI, O., TASSI, F., VALDES, J., MALAVASSI, E., BARBOZA, V. & SAENZ, W., 2000a. Fumarole and crater lake monitoring at Poás Volcano, Costa Rica. 7th Field Workshop on Volcanic Gases, 17–25 October, 2000 Satsuma–Iwojima and Kuiju (Japan), 39–42.

FERNANDEZ, F., DUARTE, E., BARBOSA,V., SAENZ, R., MALAVASSI, E., VAN DER LAAT, R., MARINO,. J., BARQUERO, J. & HERNANDEZ, E., 2000b. Conspicuous plumes and abundant low-frequency earthquakes in late 1999. BGVN, 3/00.

FREETH, S.J. & KAY, R.L.F. 1987. The Lake Nyos disaster. *Nature*, **325**, 104–105.

GIGGENBACH, W.F. 1975. A simple method for the collection and analysis of volcanic gas samples. *Bulletin of Volcanology*, **39**, 132–145.

GIGGENBACH, W. F. 1987. Redox processes governing the chemistry of fumarolic gas discharges from White Island, New Zealand. *Applied Geochemistry*, **2**, 143–161.

JOHNSTON, S. T. & THORKELSON, D. J. 1997. Cocos–Nazca slab window beneath Central America. *Earth and Planetary Science Letters*, **146**, 465–474.

KEMPTER, K. A. & ROWE, G. L. 2000. Leakage of Active Crater lake brine through the north flank at Rincon de La Vieja volcano, northwest Costa Rica, and implications for crater collapse. *Journal of Volcanology and Geothermal Research*, **97**, 143–160.

KRUSHENSKY, R. D. & ESCALANTE, G. 1967. Activity of Irazù and Poás volcanoes, Costa Rica, November 1964–July 1965. *Bulletin of Volcanology*, **31**, 75–84.

KUSAKABE, M. 1996. Hazardous crater lakes. *In:* SCARPA, R. & TILLING, R. I. (eds) *Monitoring and Mitigation of Volcano Hazards*, Springer-Verlag, 573–598.

KUSAKABE, M., OHSUMI, T. & ARAMAKI, S. 1989. The Lake Nyos disaster: chemical and isotopic evidence in water and dissolved gases from three Cameroonian crater lakes, Nyos, Monoun and Wum. *Journal of Volcanological Research*, **39**, 167–185.

MALAVASSI, E., BARQUERO, J., FERNANDEZ, E., BARBOZA, V., VAN DER LAAT, R., MARINO, T. & DE OBALDIA, F. 1993. Excursion al Volcán Poás. *Proceedings of the 1st US–Costa Rica Joint Seminar in Volcanology.* Bol. Volcanol., OVSICORI–UNA, **14**, 119–131.

MALAVASSI, E., BARQUERO, J., FERNANDEZ, E., BARBOZA, V., VAN DER LAAT, R., MARINO, T., DE OBALDIA, F. & RODRIGUEZ, H. 1994. Field trip to Poás Volcano. Obs. Vulcanologia y Seismologia de Costa Rica, Universidad Nacional.

MARTINEZ, M., FERNANDEZ, E., VALDEZ, J., BARBOZA, V., VAN DER LAAT, R., DUARTE, E., MALAVASSI, E., SANDOVAL, L., BARQUERO, J. & MARINO, T. 2000.

Chemical evolution and volcanic activity of the active crater lake of Poás volcano, Costa Rica 1993–1997. *Journal of Volcanology and Geothermal Research*, **97**, 127–141.

MARTINI, M., GIANNINI, L., PRATI, F., TASSI, F., CAPACCIONI, B. & IOZZELLI, P. 1994. Chemical characters of crater lakes in the Azores and Italy: the anomaly of the Lake Albano. *Geochemical Journal*, **28**, 173–184.

MASTIN, L. G. & WITTER, J. B. 2000. The hazards of eruptions through lakes and seawater. *Journal of Volcanology and Geothermal Research*, **97**, 195–214.

MONTEGROSSI, G., TASSI, F., VASELLI, O., BUCCIANTI, A. & GAROFALO, K, 2001. Analysis of sulphur species in volcanic gases. *Analytical Chemistry*, **73**, 3709–3715.

NESHYBA, S., FERNANDEZ, W. & DIAZ-ANDRADE, J. 1988. Temperature profiles from Poás crater lake. *EOS, Transactions of the American Geophysical Union*, **69**, 588–589.

OPPENHEIMER, C. 1992. Sulphur eruptions at Volcán Poás, Costa Rica. *Journal of Volcanology and Geothermal Research*, **49**, 1–21.

OPPENHEIMER, C. & STEVENSON, D. 1989. Liquid sulphur lakes at Poás Volcano. *Nature*, **342**, 790–793.

PICCARDI, G. 1982. Fumaroles: gas collection and analysis. *Bulletin of Volcanology*, **45**, 257–260.

PROSSER, J. T. & CARR, M. J. 1987. Poás volcano, Costa Rica: geology of the summit region and spatial and temporal variations among the most recent lavas. *Journal of Volcanology and Geothermal Research*, **33**, 131–146.

ROWE, G. L., BRANTLEY, S. L., FERNANDEZ, M., FERNANDEZ, J. F., BORGIA, A. & BARQUERO, J. 1992a. Fluid interaction in an active stratovolcano: the crater lake system of Poás volcano, Costa Rica. *Journal of Volcanology and Geothermal Research*, **49**, 23–51.

ROWE, G. L., OHSAWA, S., TAKANO, B., BRANTLEY, S. L., FERNANDEZ, J. F. & BARQUERO, J. 1992b. Using crater lake chemistry to predict volcanic activity at Poás volcano, Costa Rica. *Bulletin of Volcanology*, **54**, 494–503.

ROWE, G. L. 1994. Oxygen, hydrogen, and sulfur isotope systematics of the Crater Lake system of Poas volcano, Costa Rica. *Geochemical Journal*, **28**, 264–275.

ROWE, G.L., BRANTLEY, S.L., FERNANDEZ, J.F. & BORGIA, A. 1995. The chemical and hydrologic structure of Poás Volcano, Costa Rica. *Journal of Volcanology and Geothermal Research,* **64**, 233–267.

RYMER, H. & BROWN, G. C. 1987. Causes of microgravity changes at Poás volcano, Costa Rica. *Bulletin of Volcanology*, **49**, 389–398.

RYMER, H. & BROWN, G. C. 1989. Gravity changes as precursors to volcanic eruption at Poás volcano, Costa Rica. *Nature*, **342**, 902–905.

RYMER, H., CASSIDY, J., LOCKE, C. A., BARBOZA, M. V., BARQUERO, J., BRENES, J. & VAN DER LAAT, R., 2000. Geophysical studies of the recent 15-eruptive cycle at Poás Volcano, Costa Rica. *Journal of Volcanology and Geothermal Research*, **97**, 425–442.

SANFORD, W. E., KONIKOW, L. F., ROWE JR, G. L. & BRANTLEY, S. L. 1995. Groundwater transport of crater lake brine at Poás volcano. *Journal of Volcanology and Geothermal Research*, **64**, 269–293.

THORPE, R. S., LOCKE, C. A., BROWN, G. C., FRANCIS, P. W. & RANDAL, M. 1981. Magma chamber below Poás Vocano, Costa Rica. *Journal of the Geological Society of London*, **138**, 367–373.

VAREKAMP, J. C., PASTERNAK, G. B. & ROWE JR, J. L., 2000. Volcanic lake systematics II. Chemical constraints. *Journal of Volcanology and Geothermal Research*, **97**, 161–179.

Degassing processes of Popocatépetl and Volcán de Colima, Mexico

N. R. VARLEY[1] & Y. TARAN[2]

[1]*Facultad de Ciencias, Universidad de Colima, Av. 25 de Julio #965, Col. San Sebastián Apdo. Postal 25, Colima, Col. CP 28045, Mexico.*
(e-mail: nick@cgic.ucol.mx)
[2]*Instituto de Geofísica, Ciudad Universitaria, Coyoacán, Mexico.*

Abstract: To understand the behaviour of a volcano and try to predict future eruptive activity, it is imperative to investigate its degassing processes. Areas of study include direct degassing of the magma through the conduit, the interaction between the hydrothermal system and volcanic gases and fluids, and diffuse degassing through the volcanic edifice. Various aspects of the degassing processes of Popocatépetl and Volcán de Colima in Mexico have been studied. The results are summarized in this chapter, and new data on diffuse degassing at both volcanoes and analyses of fumarolic gases from Volcán de Colima are presented.
Variations in the flux of SO_2 at both volcanoes have led to models of the degassing processes. At Colima, isotopic analyses of condensates suggest a shallow degassing magma body. Volcán de Colima showed geochemical precursors prior to its 1998/9 eruption and variations in certain parameters continue to relate to the behaviour of the volcano during its on-going eruption. Both volcanoes yield interesting data on their diffuse degassing of CO_2 and radon: at Popocatépetl, the large plume degassing contrasts with a small diffuse contribution. Volcán de Colima has anomalous concentrations of diffuse CO_2 associated with faults. The challenge is how to interpret the geochemical data to provide a fresh insight into the mechanics of the volcanic system.

The two active Mexican volcanoes, Popocatépetl and Volcán de Colima, present interesting case studies for the investigation of degassing processes. They are quite different in terms of eruptive style and history, and have produced contrasting surface manifestations of their gases and fluids. During its current active period (1994–present), Popocatépetl has released large volumes of both SO_2 and CO_2 in its plume. However, it shows little diffuse degassing, with low concentrations of both carbon dioxide and radon measured over the majority of the volcano, including the several major faults that dissect it. This contrasts with other active volcanoes which have been shown to release significant volumes of gas through their edifices (e.g. Mount Etna, Giammanco *et al.* 1998; Vulcano, Chiodini *et al.* 1996). Popocatépetl also does not show any surface evidence of a hydrothermal system. A model is presented here that relates these two characteristics.

Volcán de Colima has more frequent eruptions than Popocatépetl, but is smaller both in terms of edifice size and magmatic system. Several geochemical precursors were identified prior to the 1998/9 eruption, and correlations between further geochemical changes and its current state of activity are being sought. Over 500 measurements of CO_2 concentration have been measured across its flank. Concentrations of CO_2 up to 37% (by volume) have been recorded, and a preliminary map shows the presence of linear structures, probably regional faults. One particular area has also yielded high levels of CH_4 (up to 51%).

Currently the fumaroles of Popocatépetl are inaccessible, so studies at this volcano are limited to plume measurements, analyses of spring waters and studies of diffuse degassing. Limited access to the fumaroles of Volcán de Colima has been possible, so for this volcano data from direct measurements have also been available.

Geological background

Popocatépetl

Popocatépetl is a large andesitic volcano located in the central part of the Trans-Mexican Volcanic Belt (TMVB, Fig. 1) with an altitude of 5452 m. Its most recent major eruption occurred around 822 AD. Prior to this, eruptions occurred around 800–215 BC and 3195–2830 BC. (Siebe *et al.* 1996). These eruptions produced extensive

From: OPPENHEIMER, C., PYLE, D.M. & BARCLAY, J. (eds) *Volcanic Degassing.* Geological Society, London, Special Publications, **213**, 263–280. 0305-8719/03/$15.00

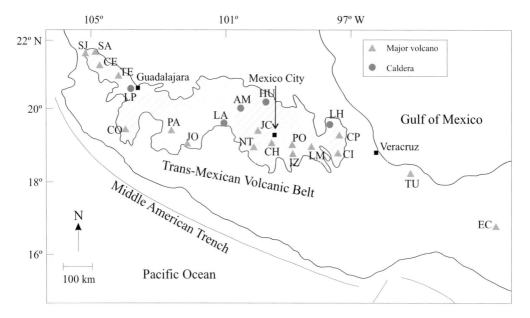

Fig. 1. Trans-Mexican Volcano Belt with the major volcanoes and calderas. AM, Amealco; CE, Ceboruco; CH, Chinchinautzin; CI, Citlaltépetl; CO, Colima Volcanic Complex; CP, Cofre de Perote; EC, El Chichonal; HU, Huichapan; JC, Jocotitlán; JO, Jorullo; IZ, Iztaccíhuatl; LA, Los Azufres; LH, Los Humeros; LM, La Malinche; LP, La Primavera; NT, Nevado de Toluca; PA, Paricutín; PO, Popocatépetl; SA, Sangangüey; SJ, San Juan; TE, Tequila; TU, Tuxtla Volcanic Field.

pumice fall, hot ash flow, and mudflow deposits. At least four prehistoric debris avalanches occurred from the Popocatépetl–Iztaccíhuatl complex (Siebe *et al.* 1995). The largest avalanche produced a deposit that extends 70 km south from the volcano and has a volume of at least 9 km³. Due to the large population living close to this volcano, the potential for an enormous catastrophe exists; over one million people live on its flanks, and the large cities of Puebla and Mexico City are only 50 and 65 km from the crater, respectively.

The most recent eruptive phase started in December 1994 with a swarm of volcanotectonic earthquakes, followed by sustained tremor and an explosion that produced a large ash plume (Arciniega-Ceballos *et al.* 1999). Since this date, the volcano has seen repeated periods of dome growth within its crater, followed by explosions and their subsequent destruction.

Volcán de Colima

Volcán de Colima has an altitude of 3860 m and is located in the western part of the TMVB (Fig. 1). It is the youngest cone of a larger complex, which includes Nevado de Colima. The younger volcanic cone is growing on the south side of an

older caldera. The first dated activity from this volcano was 8100 years BP (Robin *et al.* 1990); however, the charcoal used for ¹⁴C dating was obtained from a palaeosol overlying an older pyroclastic flow and debris avalanche deposit. The eruptive history was documented by Luhr and Carmichael (1990), and the last major Plinian eruption occurred in 1913. Various ideas have been postulated regarding the cyclicity of eruption styles (Luhr & Carmichael 1990; Robin *et al.* 1991) in a debate that continues.

Many debris avalanches have been associated with this complex, the most recent about 4300 years ago (Stoopes & Sheridan 1992). A previous avalanche (18 500 years BP) from Nevado de Colima reached over 120 km from the summit. The rocks associated with the complex are varied and fall into three groups: alkaline, calc-alkaline and high-potassium calc-alkaline (Macías *et al.* 1993).

The 1913 eruption created a summit crater 350 m deep and 400 m in diameter. Further lava extrusion filled this crater, and by 1962 a dome protruded above the former crater rim (Espíndola 2000). In recent history, the volcano has produced many small blocky lava flows (Luhr & Carmichael 1990; Komorowski *et al.* 1991). Lava flows from effusive eruptions occurred in

1961–1962, 1975–1976, 1981–1982 and 1991. Explosive eruptions occurred in 1987 and 1994. The most recent eruptive episode of the volcano started in November 1998 with an effusive phase. Lava flows reached a distance of 3.5 km from the crater and small pyroclastic flows were associated with repeated collapse of the edge of the dome and lava flows. The effusive episode ceased in early February 1999 and the first major explosion occurred on 10 February 1999. This was followed by further explosions in May and July 1999 and, most recently, in February 2001. A new dome started to grow in May 2001 (Varley & Gavilanes 2001) and its growth continued until the crater was filled. New lava flows from the crater commenced in February 2002.

The region is tectonically complex, with the Colima Volcanic Complex located at the junction of two structures: the Colima Graben and the Tamazula Fault (Garduño-Monroy et al. 1998). A recent He-isotopic study of many of the hot springs of the Jalisco Block region supported an earlier suggestion that the Colima Rift extends to the south of the volcano (Taran et al. 2002b). Some geomagnetic investigations have been carried out (Lopez & Urrutia-Fucugauchi 1999), however, the regional fault systems still require further clarification.

Geochemical studies of active volcanoes

Geochemical studies here concentrate on surface releases of gases or fluids that have a variable magmatic component. It is necessary to study the interaction with meteoric waters and/or the atmosphere when constructing models to try and better understand a volcano's behaviour. Although much progress has been made, a lot more work is required before the degassing processes of volcanoes are fully understood.

Today the value of remote-sensing techniques such as the correlation spectrometer (COSPEC) or Fourier Transform Infrared Spectroscopy (FTIR) is being realized (Francis et al. 2000). The interpretation of changes in the relative concentrations of different volcanic gases remains a significant goal. It also remains unclear why certain silicic magmas erupt effusively at some volcanoes, but explosively at others. Remote-sensing data can be used to postulate the mode of degassing of the magma bodies. For certain areas of geochemical study, it is still necessary to access the fumaroles directly to obtain gas samples. Isotopic and trace-element analysis remain important aspects of volcanic gas studies.

The principal gas measured in studies of diffuse degassing at volcanoes has been CO_2 (Bruno et al. 2001; Williams-Jones et al. 2000;

Giammanco et al. 1998; Chiodini et al. 1996). Carbon dioxide is relatively inert, and is exsolved early from a degassing magma body. It has been measured either as a concentration by volume in soil gas or as a flux at the surface. Both methods have their advantages and disadvantages. The isotopic composition of C in CO_2 may indicate the origin of the gas (Taylor 1986); however, fractionation effects can influence the data. Isotopic analysis of He associated with the CO_2 may give a more reliable indication of the gas origin (Poreda & Craig 1989). Spatial variations can give important structural information, such as the location of faults, while temporal variations might indicate changes in the magmatic system (Farrar et al. 1995; Connor et al. 1996; Bruno et al. 2001).

Of the world's volcanoes, the degassing processes at Mount Etna in Italy have been the most extensively studied. Here, anomalous CO_2 concentrations have been detected at certain locations on its flanks (Allard et al. 1997; Giammanco et al. 1998). At Etna, diffuse degassing almost always occurs near faults or active vents. Several other volcanoes have demonstrated high soil gas levels of CO_2 and/or radon close to faults outside the crater region: Vulcano, Italy (Chiodini et al. 1996); Galeras, Columbia, (Heiligmann et al. 1997; Williams-Jones et al. 2000); Poás, Costa Rica (Williams-Jones et al. 2000) and Oldoinyo Lengai, Tanzania (Koepenick et al. 1996).

Various geochemical studies at active volcanoes have revealed precursors to eruptive activity. For example at Etna, changes in CO_2 soil gas concentrations have been interpreted as an indication of magma migration which, when combined with SO_2 flux data, has allowed modelling of magma movement in the weeks and months prior to summit activity (Bruno et al. 2001).

Climatic influence

It is important to consider the variation and influence of the climate in the measurement of soil gases. Studies have shown that Rn concentrations can vary by up to a factor of four with increasing soil moisture (Toutain & Baubron 1999). Washington and Rose (1990) showed that the phase partitioning of Rn is controlled by soil moisture and temperature, and can have a major effect on measured concentrations. These authors discuss the various other processes associated with soil moisture that influence both its transport and production.

For CO_2, soil temperature controls the rate of biogenic production (Amundson & Davidson

1990; Terhune & Harden 1991) for both root respiration and microbial production. Increases in CO_2 concentration of more than a factor of three may occur as temperature changes from 10 to 30°C (Crill 1991; Terhune & Harden 1991).

After rainfall, an impermeable moisture layer near the surface can have a 'capping' effect and thus decrease flux measurements while increasing soil gas levels beneath this level. This effect has been observed for both Rn (Asher Bolinder et al. 1991) and CO_2 (Solomon & Cerling 1987; Hinkle 1991). Depending upon the depth of the sampling probe, the measured concentration may be reduced or increased, which can result in complex depth profiles (Varley & Flowers 1992).

The regional climate at both volcanoes is characterized by wet and warm summer months (May to October) and dry and cooler winters. The size and altitude of Popocatépetl results in several climatic zones around its edifice. Both volcanoes are subject to intense rainfall during the summer, which can produce lahars.

Previous geochemical studies

Popocatépetl

Remote sensing at Popocatépetl has recorded some of the highest sustained gas fluxes of any volcano (Delgado-Granados et al. 2001). Sulphur dioxide fluxes of up to 60 000 metric tonnes per day (t d^{-1}) have been measured (Love et al. 1998), along with intermittent values of CO_2/SO_2 of up to 140 (Goff et al. 2001). While other gas ratios were unremarkable, the large and variable CO_2/SO_2 ratios suggested a non-magmatic source for CO_2. Goff et al. (2001) suggested that occasional fluxes of CO_2 exceeded 100 000 t d^{-1}, with an average level estimated at 38 000 t d^{-1}, and proposed that assimilation of the carbonate-bearing strata that underlie the volcano into the magma might explain the pulses in CO_2 flux.

The total volume of SO_2 released during the latest period of activity at Popocatépetl (9 Mt to 1 January 1998) is of the same order as that produced by short-lived but large-magnitude explosive eruptions, such as Pinatubo (Delgado-Granados et al. 2001). Emission rates exceeded 2000 t d^{-1} for more than four years prior to January 1998 and have since continued at that level. At Popocatépetl, more SO_2 has been emitted than can be accounted for by degassing of the volume of magma erupted. This scenario is now commonly recognized, and the most easily acceptable explanation is that a gas-rich region exists at the top of a magma body which will supply most of the gas in an explosive or effusive eruption, while not reflecting the gas contents of the magma as a whole (Wallace 2001).

In the case of Popocatépetl, Delgado-Granados et al. (2001) concluded that the excess SO_2 is most probably due to new injections of more mafic volatile-rich magma into a silicic magma chamber. It is suggested that the large fluctuations in emission rate may result from convection and crystallization in the magma chamber or conduit, opening and sealing of the conduit system, and perhaps scrubbing by the hydrothermal system.

Werner et al. (1997) analysed the major- and trace-element chemistry of several springs located on the lower flanks of Popocatépetl, and concluded that they were not directly influenced by magmatic activity. The springs are between six and 60 km from the volcano, with the more distant thermal waters thought to be related to a separate fault system. A more recent study of the $\delta^{13}C$ values of dissolved CO_2 and of $^3He/^4He$ in free gas, however, has led to the suggestion that a relationship does exist (Inguaggiato et al. 2001). It remains unclear whether Popocatépetl has a significant hydrothermal system, since there is no clear surface manifestation.

A study of Rn in soil gas at three locations on the flanks of Popocatépetl has been carried out on a continuous basis, using track-etch and solid-state detectors (Segovia et al. 1997). It was suggested that the data showed correlations with eruptive activity, since peaks in Rn concentration were recorded between January and May 1995, which coincided with an active phase of the volcano. During this period, the volcanic system was described as being 'semi-closed' with greater migration of volcanic gas through the edifice. Contrastingly, no Rn peak was detected for the effusive stage that started in March 1996. The authors described the system as being open for this stage of the eruption, with a greater gas flow through the conduit.

Volcán de Colima

Fewer geochemical studies have been carried out at Volcán de Colima than Popocatépetl. Here is a summary of the work undertaken, excluding that of the University of Colima and Institute of Geophysics, UNAM, since 1995, which is discussed in greater detail below.

The volcano has various fumaroles located in the summit region. The rate of SO_2 emission has been studied sporadically over the past twenty years by different researchers, starting with the effusive 1981–1982 eruption (Casadevall et al. 1984) with a measurement of 320 t d^{-1}. During the effusive 1991 eruption a value of 600 t d^{-1}

was reported (S. Williams, unpublished data). Connor *et al.* (1993) studied the variation in the temperatures of five fumaroles by measuring them at twenty-minute intervals with a remote system during one year. Average fumarole temperatures changed by less than 100 °C during the period, with a decrease following the effusive activity of 1991. An inverse correlation was found between the temperature variation and barometric pressure.

Methods

Fumarole sampling and analyses

Since 1996, samples of fumarolic gas have been collected and analysed from Volcán de Colima. The fumaroles were earlier divided into three major fields, each with a characteristic temperature (Connor *et al.* 1993). These fields were studied until the explosive activity of 1999, which changed the morphology of the summit zone and forced an interruption in the gas sampling. The gases proved to be very diluted by atmospheric air, due to the highly permeable dome and no undiluted gas jets were present – unusual for high temperature gases (Taran *et al.* 2001). Sampling recommenced in March 2001 and, prior to the filling of the summit crater by the new dome, concentrated samples of the gas discharges were taken from a new fumarole field that appeared between May and August 2001. The field was located within the crater at the northern edge of the dome. It had many incandescent discharges within cracks in the crater floor and under large blocks, with temperatures of 800–900 °C, although pressurized gas jets were still absent (Varley *et al.* 2001). Continued dome growth and collapse caused this field to be covered in talus, and by November 2001 was inaccessible.

The fumaroles of Volcán de Colima were sampled using the methods of Giggenbach (1975) and Trujillo *et al.* (1987): quartz tubes were used with evacuated flasks containing 4 N NaOH to absorb acid gases, and gas flasks to sample dry gas. Pre-1999 samples were collected by passing the gas through two or three consecutive traps containing NaOH, since the high air contamination did not allow the use of evacuated flasks. The fumarolic gas was also condensed using ice and taken for later analysis. Gas chromatography was used to analyse the non-condensable gases and wet chemical techniques for the acid gases. Condensates were analysed for major ions (Cl, F, SO_4, Na, K, Ca, Mg, and B) by ion chromatography and atomic absorption spectroscopy. Trace elements were measured by ICP–MS, and oxygen and hydrogen isotope ratios were determined by mass spectrometry.

Plume measurements

The SO_2 flux has been measured periodically since 1995 by the University of Colima using a COSPEC. Airborne and ground-based measurements (both stationary and by car) have been performed using conventional methods (Stoiber *et al.* 1983; Casadevall *et al.* 1984; Williams-Jones & Stix 2002). Various factors, both meteorological and physical, have reduced the number of days when measurement is possible. During the summer months, the plume is often totally obscured by cloud cover. Although there are predominant seasonal wind directions, its day-to-day variability also creates difficulties. The lack of good road access to all sides of the volcano has limited the number of vehicle-based measurements. Airborne measurements are difficult when the wind is directed towards the north, due to the close proximity of Nevado de Colima, which is the older edifice and most massive part of the Colima Volcanic Complex, located only 5 km to the north of Volcán de Colima.

Diffuse gas measurements

Diffuse gas measurements have been made for CO_2, Rn, CH_4, and O_2. Field data have been obtained with a portable infrared spectrometer (for CO_2 and CH_4) with an integral cell for oxygen (Gas Data LMSx). Radon was measured using an alpha scintillometer (Pylon AB-5) using Morse's (1976) method to separate the two principal isotopes (^{222}Rn and ^{220}Rn). The short-term counts were calibrated with samples which were left to reach equilibrium. Two calibration curves were fitted to the data, one for low concentrations (<7 kBq/m^3), the other for higher concentrations. Probes with an internal diameter of 1 cm and length of up to 1 m were used to sample the soil gas. The integral pump of each instrument was used to extract the gas sample. Sampling was carried out at a depth of 50–90 cm in order to limit the environmental effects mentioned above.

Some samples of CO_2 have been analysed for stable carbon isotopes ($^{13}C/^{12}C$) using an isotope ratio mass spectrometer (IRMS: Finnigan MAT 250). At Popocatépetl, low levels of CO_2 were concentrated by pumping a large volume of soil gas through liquid nitrogen. The precision of the isotopic analysis was 0.1%.

Maps have been created of Rn and CO_2 concentrations in the soil gas over a semi-circular area with a radius of 15 and 60 km for Volcán de Colima and Popocatépetl, respectively. Geostatistical methods are being used to analyse the data. Sampling points have been selected to try and achieve a good coverage of the region, but this is obviously dictated to an extent by accessibility. At several locations on both volcanoes, measurements were made periodically to observe the temporal variation of the soil gases. Two criteria were considered when choosing these locations: good accessibility and high soil gas concentrations.

Results and discussion

Volcán de Colima

FUMAROLE ANALYSES
Taran *et al.* (2001) published chemical and isotopic analyses of gas and condensate samples

collected from 1996–1998. Carbon isotopic analyses of CO_2 and of total sulphur isotopes gave results typical for subduction-type volcanoes: mean $\delta^{13}C=-6.6‰$ and $\delta^{34}S=3.5‰$. Before 2001, all fumarolic samples had been highly air diluted. However, the high-temperature fumaroles associated with the new dome emplacement permitted samples of relatively undiluted gas to be taken in August 2001. Figure 2 shows the location of the principal fumarole fields at this time. Table 1 shows the analysis of these samples for major gases with some of the previous results from the high temperature fumarole zone previously designated Z3 (Taran *et al.* 2001). Table 2 presents the results of isotopic analyses.

The August 2001 samples represented the first samples of fumarolic gas from this volcano without a heavy dilution by atmospheric air. This was demonstrated by the high He/Ne ratio of 44,

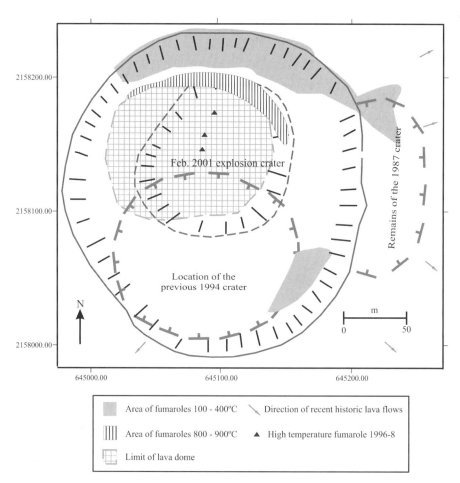

Fig. 2. Summit region of Volcán de Colima, as mapped on 19 August 2001.

Table 1. *Analyses of samples of high-temperature fumarolic gas from Volcán de Colima (mol.%).*

Date	T(°C)	H_2O	CO_2	CO	S_{tot}	HCl	HF	H_2	He	N_2	O_2
19/8/01	820	95.22	0.99	0.006	2.04	0.42	0.010	0.75	0.0001	0.39	
15/5/98	789	97.9	0.97		0.80	0.31	0.021				
10/3/98	763	98.48	1.54		0.79	0.52	0.052				
24/11/97	782	97.56	0.82		1.4	0.21	0.013				
10/8/97	n.d.	96.58	1.18		2.0	0.23	0.015				
10/8/97*	n.d.		3.56					0.24		79.4	16.8
28/6/97	747	95.56	2.24		1.81	0.37	0.023				
28/6/97*	747		4.52					0.55		75.4	19.5
18/3/97	791	98.12	0.94		0.36	0.53	0.048				
12/12/96	742	97.23	2.04		0.41	0.30	0.022				
7/10/96	802	89.15	9.23		1.08	0.49	0.046				
21/9/96	801	97.36	1.54		0.62	0.46	0.041				
14/8/96	820	97.67	1.36		0.56	0.38	0.034				
2/5/96	752	97.23	1.85		0.53	0.36	0.029				
20/1/96	740	95.77	2.62		1.11	0.46	0.043				

*dry gas sample.
n.d. – not determined.
Blank spaces indicate where the concentrations were too low to be detected.

Table 2. *Isotopic analysis of fumarolic gas from Volcán de Colima ($\delta^{13}C$‰ relative to PDB and $\delta^{34}S$‰ relative to CDT).*

Date	R/R_A	He/Ne	$\delta^{13}C$ CO_2	$\delta^{34}S$
19/8/01	6.2	44		
10/8/97			–5.9 to –6.8	+3.8

Table 3. *Isotopic analysis of fumarolic gas and condensates from Volcán de Colima (δD and $\delta^{18}O$‰ relative to SMOW)*

Date	δD	$\delta^{18}O$
19/8/01	–17	+8.4
8/7/98	–27	+6.8
15/5/98	–38	+8.9
10/3/98	–30	+6.2
24/11/97	–26	+6.9
23/8/97	–36	+7.9
28/6/97	–50	+5.8
18/3/97	–36	+5.4
7/10/96	–57	+7.5
21/9/96	–46	+7.3
2/5/96	–43	+8.1
20/1/96	–50	+7.0

since the Ne is entirely atmospheric (Craig *et al.* 1978). Isotopic analysis of He gave a value for R/R_A of 6.2, where R_A is the atmospheric $^3He/^4He$ ratio. This represents a typical value for an arc volcano, which usually fall in the range six to nine (Poreda & Craig 1989). Values close to 7.4 have been reported for volcanoes and geothermal regions of North and Central America (Poreda & Craig 1989). The results of H- and O-isotopic analysis of water samples from 1996 to 2001 are presented in Table 3 and Figs 3 & 4. The local meteoric values are based on analyses of water from the springs on the SW flank of the volcano, at an elevation of 1500 to 1800 m. Their depletion in D and $\delta^{18}O$ is a reflection of their altitude (Clark & Fritz 1997).

The δD value of the water discharge varied from –26 ‰ (typical value for an andesitic volcano) to –57‰ for both the high temperature (Z3) and mid-temperature fields (400° Z2). Taran *et al.* (2001) offered three possible explanations: the samples with depleted δD were from more degassed batches of magma; mixing with meteoric water, but with heavy oxygen enrichment from rapid high-temperature isotopic exchange within the dome interior; or finally, loss of vapour during sampling which would enrich the condensate in Cl and D by different amounts.

To investigate this relationship further, Cl was studied. A more degassed magma would be expected to yield greater concentrations of Cl, due to its high solubility. When Cl was plotted against δD, it was found that the two fields gave different trends. Z2 data indicated mixing between Cl-free meteoric water and Cl-rich magmatic gas; but Z3 showed a negative correlation perhaps related to more degassed magma (Taran *et al.* 2001). Taran *et al.* (2002a) further developed the model by suggesting that this negative correlation may reflect the mixing of two magmas: andesite with δD close to –20‰

and lower Cl, and basalt with δD of –60‰ and a higher Cl content. However, this is not supported by rock analyses (Luhr 1992) and therefore Taran *et al.* (2002*a*) conclude that shallow degassing is the more likely explanation.

Prior to the 1998/9 eruption, isotopic analyses showed an increase in the magmatic water component (Fig. 3, Taran *et al.* 2002a). The trend has continued after this eruptive period with a high value for δD of –17 ‰ in August 2001. This may suggest that a new batch of less degassed magma had entered the system. However, this sample coincided with the early stages of dome growth, which progressed at a relatively slow effusion rate (0.04 m³s⁻¹). Shortly afterwards, in October, a spine formed on the dome, which is typical for slow dome growth with shallow degassed magma as has been seen at Montserrat (Watts *et al.* 2002). Therefore the style of dome growth would suggest the magma was degassed.

Ratios between a number of volatile species also showed long-term changes prior to the 1998/99 eruption (Taran *et al.* 2002*a*). The S/Cl ratio of Z2 increased in the middle of 1997, 14, to 15 months prior to the onset. The Cl/F ratio

also showed an early anomaly. The model presented by Taran *et al.* (2002*a*) suggests two sources of gases in the 1996–1998 period: one from a deeper source containing less water, Cl and F, but higher CO_2 and S gases, than the second, a shallow, partially degassed, and highly crystallized magma source. The proportions of the two varied in time as the contribution from the deeper source changed.

Major and trace elements were analysed within the condensates. Enrichment factors were similar to analyses of samples from Kudryavy (and other) volcanoes (Taran *et al.* 1995; Taran *et al.* 2001), with a few exceptions (Ba, Au, V, Cr, Co, Cd, and Zn), which may reflect variation in the magma oxidation state or the high temperature mixing of volcanic gas and air at Colima (Taran *et al.* 2001).

Taran *et al.* (2000) used silica tubes to collect mineral precipitates from the high-temperature fumarolic gases. Their analyses showed significant differences compared to other volcanoes; for example, native gold was detected for the first time directly in a fumarolic gas. A lack of NaCl and KCl has been explained by the oxidizing conditions of the highly air contaminated gas

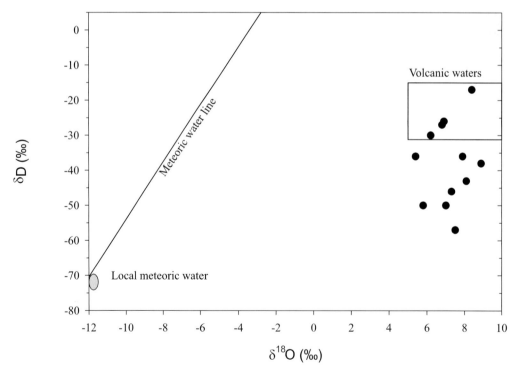

Fig. 3. Isotopic composition of H and O in water in samples of condensates from Volcán de Colima fumaroles. Box represents typical values for subduction volcanoes (Giggenbach 1992).

(Taran *et al.* 2001). Thermodynamic modelling was carried out to also investigate the lack of Mo and Cd minerals and enrichment in V minerals. The differences were explained by the high oxygen fugacity of the Colima gases, which is a result of the mixing of magmatic gas with atmospheric air and high temperatures.

Sulphur dioxide flux

Sulphur dioxide levels in the plume varied from below detection limits to >16 000 t d^{-1} during the effusive eruption of 1998/9 (Fig. 5, Taran *et al.* 2002*a*). From 1995 until October 1998 the flux did not exceed 100 t d^{-1}, except during two seismic swarms when it increased, but did not exceed, 500 t d^{-1}. Several seismic swarms were measured in the period 1997–1998 (Dominguez *et al.* 2001). An increase in flux was recorded one month before the onset of the 1998/9 eruption. In addition, a good correlation was observed between SO_2 flux and seismic activity measured in terms of events/day (Taran *et al.* 2002*a*). From the first measurements made in 1983 until the anomalous level in November 1998, the mean flux was 198 t d^{-1}. The eruption precursor gave a flux of 1600 t d^{-1}.

Dome emplacement obstructs the conduit and may have a dramatic effect on the degassing of a volcano. The summit region was highly fractured before and during the first stages of the effusive eruption, thereby allowing degassing and producing little overpressurization. The SO_2 flux was highly variable at Galeras prior to the 1992/3 eruptions (Zapata *et al.* 1997), and it was suggested that this was due to progressive sealing and opening of fractures. High fluxes and associated long-period seismicity were seen after various eruptions in 1993, thought to represent periods of rapid degassing of newly mobilized magma. It is notable that the flux decreased at Volcán de Colima in the two weeks following the major explosion of 10 February 1999. Prior to the explosion the flux was highly variable, so a situation similar to that at Galeras may have existed, with the progressive sealing and opening of fractures, culminating in a larger overpressurization of the degassing magma prior to the February explosion. Juvenile material was erupted during the February explosion, leaving a smaller degassing volume in the upper part of the conduit afterwards. However, a similar pattern was not seen for the 10 May 1999 explosion since much a lower flux was observed both before and after. There are insufficient data relating to the two later explosions in July 1999 and February 2001.

From June 1999 until June 2000 and August 2000 until March 2001, there are no COSPEC data, due to logistical problems. Subsequent measurements carried out during 2001 yield a mean SO_2 flux of 350 t d^{-1} with a maximum of 900 t d^{-1}, seen in November (Fig. 5). This represents a greater than average level of degassing for this volcano, but much lower than the levels recorded during the 1998/9 effusive period. The absence of seismicity shown throughout this period (Reyes-Dávila *et al.* 2001) suggests no overpressurization of the magma body, which may have led to explosions like those that occurred in 1999. Instead, it would appear that only small volumes of magma are degassing, and both the material filling the conduit and the new dome are sufficiently fractured to allow the degassing of these rising volumes. Although the data were sparse, a clear increase in degassing was observed visually during June and July 2001. The degassing was particularly strong during an aerial reconnaissance flight in mid-July. A small explosion occurred sometime between the summit observations of May and August, which formed a new crater (about 15 m diameter) within the main crater. It is possible that the conduit was partially sealed and there was some pressurization of the degassing magma for a period, which was ended by the explosion, and followed by more intense degassing before a new equilibrium state was reached.

Diffuse degassing

Mapping of the concentrations of diffuse CO_2 and Rn on the edifice of Volcán de Colima was started in November 2000. At the end of 2001, measurements had been made at over 500 locations around the volcano. As shown in Figure 6, low concentrations of the gases have been detected on the flanks. Many measurements have been carried out in the relatively flat area known as El Playón, located 1–2 km to the N and NW of the volcano within the caldera. Only one small anomaly was found for CO_2 within this region.

Table 4 summarizes the data for CO_2 and CH_4. The geometric mean is more representative for CO_2, since soil gas measurements typically give a log-normal distribution (e.g. Varley & Flowers 1998). In the case of Volcán de Colima, a more complex distribution is shown in Figure 7, with two populations of concentrations. The higher CO_2 population is dominated by measurements from anomalous regions, where there is a significant contribution of gas of a magmatic origin. The lower population is largely pure biogenic gas. In the case of CH_4, the geometric mean is not representative since the large number of zero values (94% of the total) is excluded

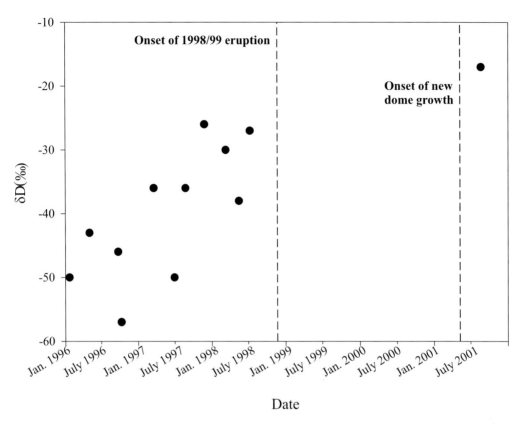

Fig. 4. Variation in δD in samples of condensates from Volcán de Colima fumaroles. Onset of 1998/9 eruption was 20 November 1998.

when calculating the geometric mean. Furthermore, all the non-zero values are located in just one zone which therefore must be treated separately from the volcano as a whole. The geometric mean can be considered as valid for the zone of high CH_4 degassing (discussed below).

A preliminary map of the CO_2 concentrations in presented in Figure 6. A linear structure can be seen to the SW of the volcano passing through the crater. This is likely to be a fault, possibly a continuation of the Tamazula Fault mapped to the NE (Garduño-Monroy et al. 1998). A second linear structure has possibly been located that lies in a NW–SE direction, or the anomalies could lie above parallel faults to the main structure.

While Rn concentrations are very low over the majority of the edifice, mapping has highlighted an area to the SE with significantly higher concentrations. Debris-avalanche deposits cover the whole southern side of Volcán de Colima. The area covered by these deposits is far more extensive than the high Rn zone, which does not cover a specific geological unit. Another explanation for the high Rn anomaly could be a zone of large regional faulting, however the zone does not have a linear form and has a clear termination to the NW and SE. Further investigation is needed to explain this anomaly.

One area with particularly high CO_2 concentrations has been discovered in the vicinity of one of the springs. Here concentrations up to 37% (by volume) have been measured along the ravine. In addition, very high CH_4 concentrations have been measured, with a maximum of 51%. Figure 8 is a contour plot of the CO_2 concentrations within this zone. The high anomalous concentrations of CH_4 are indicated. A linear structure is clearly visible.

It is unclear whether the CH_4 is purely a result of fermentation processes that are common in fresh sediments and swamplands (Schoell 1988) or the result of the transport of hydrothermal gases through a fault system. A large proportion of the anomalous zone is covered by water for

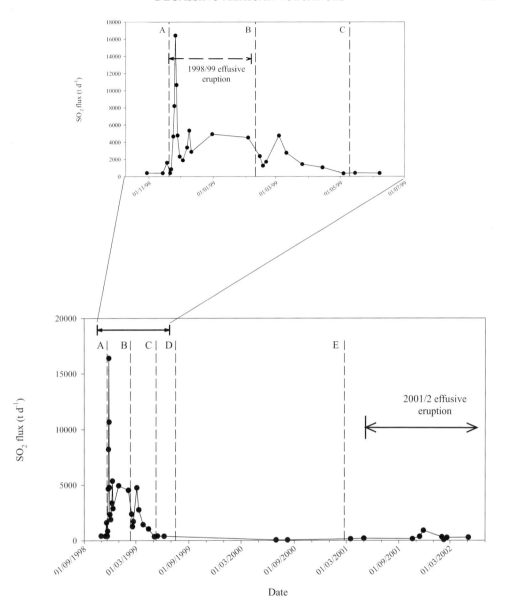

Fig. 5. Measured SO$_2$ fluxes from Volcán de Colima. Data from 1995 to 1999 (Taran *et al.* 2002*a*). A: onset of 1998/9 effusive eruption; B: explosion, 10 February 1999; C: explosion, 10 May 1999; D: explosion, 17 July 1999; E: explosion, 22 February 2001.

Table 4. *Summary of diffuse gas measurements at Volcán de Colima (composition in volume %). Standard deviation of arithmetic mean given.*

	No.	Median	Arithmetic mean	Geometric mean	Standard deviation	Min.	Max.
CO$_2$	552	0.6	2.26	0.92	4.11	0	37
CH$_4$	534	0	0.75	6.57	4.31	0	52

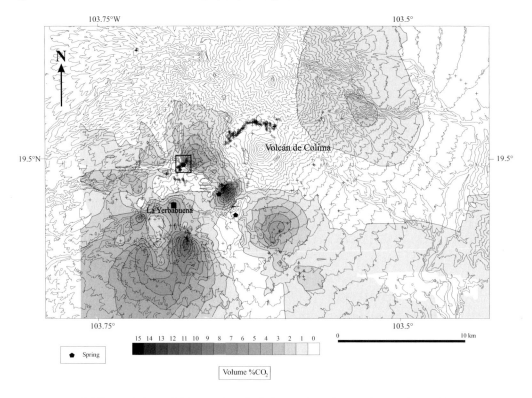

Fig. 6. Map of diffuse emissions of CO_2 at Volcán de Colima (vol.%). Contour interval is 1% (kriging performed in Surfer v7). Box represents area shown in Figure 8.

some of the year and could be the site for anaerobic microbial activity. However, high CH_4 values have been measured in dry locations and the anomalies persist even when the saturated areas have dried out in the dry season.

A few measurements have been made of the C-isotopic composition of CO_2 in soil gas, which produced a range of values of $\delta^{13}C$ from –17 to –23‰. This suggests a largely biogenic origin, but with some possible magmatic contribution. Further measurements need to be carried out to clarify the origin. Isotopic fractionation, such as that due to phase partitioning, could explain the low value for the ratios. Severinghaus *et al.* (1996) showed experimentally that isotopic fractionation can occur in soil gases as water vapour diffuses from a moist environment to dry air. Additionally, gravitational settling and thermal diffusion have an effect. A methane $\delta^{13}C$ value of –45‰ is within the region of overlap between thermogenic and biogenic methane (Schoell 1988). Again, further isotopic analyses are required to explain the high methane concentrations.

Popocatépetl

Low concentrations of both radon and CO_2 were measured over the edifice as a whole. This included some of the major faults that bisect the volcano. Unlike other active volcanoes that have been studied, Popocatépetl does not exhibit significant degassing through its edifice. Table 5 presents a summary of data. Varley & Armienta (2001) previously discussed some of the implications.

Figure 9 shows the variation in CO_2 across the study area. The three highest anomalous points, which were located close to thermal springs, have been excluded since they dominate the distribution and hide any underlying trend. The anomaly to the SW is close to the thermal spring at Atotonilco. No pattern can be seen related to anomalous values; however, locations with an altitude greater than 3000 m produced lower concentrations of CO_2. Often high concentrations were recorded at the bottom of ravines, but this could be explained by deposition of human-produced waste or lahar deposits rich in vegetation. In both cases there would be a greater

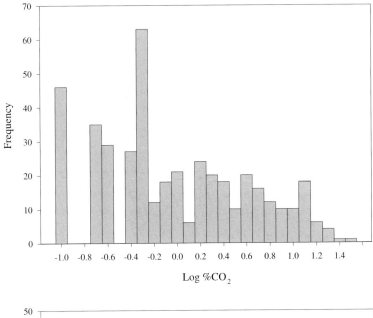

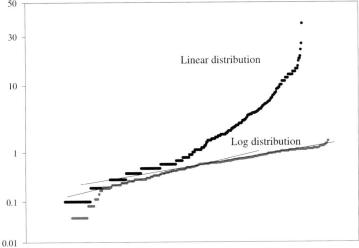

Fig. 7. Distribution of log CO_2 data from Volcán de Colima. Plotted as a frequency histogram (top) and cumulative frequency graph (below). Cumulative frequency graph shows two populations on the logarithmic plot represented by the two gradients.

Table 5. *Summary of diffuse gas measurements at Popocatépetl. Standard deviation of arithmetic mean given.*

	No.	Median	Arithmetic mean	Geometric mean	Standard deviation	Min.	Max.
^{222}Rn (kBq/m^3)	667	3.58	4.65	3.03	5.06	0	35.9
CO_2 (vol.%)	564	0.22	0.66	0.32	1.25	0.04	15
$\delta^{13}C - CO_2$ (‰)	16		−20.9	−20.8	2.0	−24.7	−17.5
^{3}He/^{4}He R/R$_A$	9		0.63	0.49	0.34	0.13	0.99

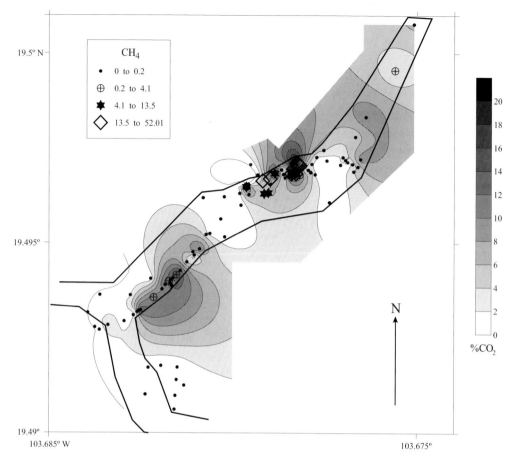

Fig. 8. Map of diffuse emissions of CO_2 and CH_4 at La Lumbre (vol.%). Contour interval is 2% (kriging performed in Surfer v7).

production of biogenic CO_2. The $\delta^{13}C$ analyses yielded values just above the usual range for biogenic origin. Signatures closer to volcanic (−14.7‰ and −7.12‰) were presented by samples from two anomalous locations close to the Atotonilco thermal spring. The spring is located almost 50 km from the crater and is either associated with the geothermal system, or related to the fault which is thought to bisect this region (Varley & Armienta 2001). Again, C-isotopic fractionation may have occurred.

Helium-isotopic analysis yielded no magmatic values (Table 5). Large concentrations were measured (up to 61 ppm), indicating that the gas had come from a deep source, which confirms that the low concentrations of CO_2 and Rn were not merely due to atmospheric infiltration. This was reinforced by the high He/Ne ratio.

Large seasonal variations were recorded for the CO_2 data, with differences up to approxi-

mately a factor of eight recorded (Varley & Armienta 2001). The highest levels were measured during the summer wet season and the early part of the dry season. As mentioned, this was a result of seasonal variation in the biogenic production of CO_2 and possible capping effects.

Conclusions

Geochemical studies of the two Mexican volcanoes Popocatépetl and Volcán de Colima have produced interesting results that reflect their degassing processes. Both have recently been active, characterized by effusive dome building or lava flows, interspersed with explosive events and periods of quiescence. The studies that have been carried out have helped to explain these processes. Measurements of the plume discharge of SO_2 have proven to be a valuable tool in the case of Volcán de Colima for predicting future

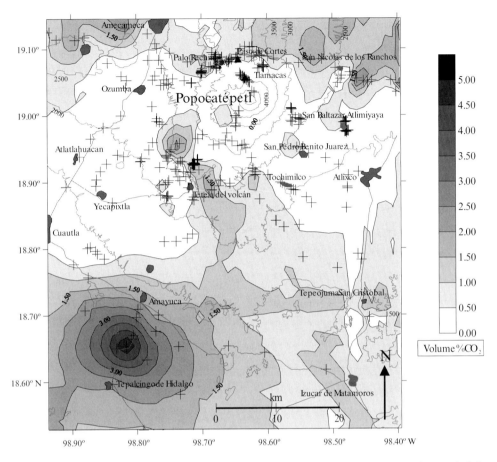

Fig. 9. Map of diffuse CO_2 at Popocatépetl (vol. %). The three highest anomalous points have been excluded (14, 10, and 7%).

explosive or effusive events. For Popocatépetl, the very large and frequently varying concentrations of both SO_2 and CO_2 may be indicative of the variable nature of its conduit system and the dynamics of the magma reservoir. Direct fumarole measurements at Volcán de Colima have highlighted precursors to eruptive activity in their geochemistry. The evolution of the summit region and magmatic system is reflected by changes in the distribution, temperatures, and chemistry of the fumaroles.

Neither volcano releases significant volumes of gas through the edifice, contrary to the case at various other volcanoes. Maps of diffuse CO_2 concentrations at Popocatépetl show no regional pattern, although some relatively high concentrations were measured. This is surprising considering the large summit output of volcanic gas. Low permeability of young volcanic rocks could be a factor, as was thought to be the case

at Galeras, Poás, and Arenal (Heiligmann *et al.* 1997; Williams-Jones *et al.* 2000), but unlike these Central American volcanoes, even the major fault systems were found not to offer a pathway for the gases produced at depth. The volcano morphology and the location of the magma chamber could both be factors. In addition, the lack of a surface manifestation of a hydrothermal system may be significant. Subsurface hydrothermal alteration may have produced a layer of low permeability above the system, which prevents significant mass transport of gases to the surface. A similar model was suggested for Nevado del Ruiz (Giggenbach *et al.* 1990).

Further work is needed to clarify the role of isotopic analysis in identifying the source of CO_2 in soil gases, since the results at both volcanoes have so far been inconclusive, and the role of isotopic fractionation needs to be clarified. At

Volcán de Colima the location of one or more
fault systems is revealed in the map of diffuse
CO_2. One area containing some significantly
large anomalies of both CO_2 and CH_4 has been
discovered, indicating perhaps an important
pathway for the products of the degassing
magma. At Popocatépetl the He data were rather
ambiguous: large concentrations were measured
in the soil gas; however, isotopic analyses did not
reveal a magmatic signature.

Funding for investigations at Colima has come from
grants to Dr Taran from CONACYT #27862-T and
DGAPA #IN104197 and the University of Colima. At
Popocatépetl funding was provided by the Instituto de
Geofísica, UNAM. Appreciation goes to the various
students of the University of Colima, who have
assisted in the fieldwork of Dr Varley. Thanks to Juan
Carlos Gavilanes for his collection of fumarole samples
and other assistance. The manuscript was greatly
improved by the reviews of G. Williams-Jones, D. Pyle,
and C.-J. de Hoog.

References

ALLARD, P., JEAN-BAPTISTE, P., D'ALESSANDRO, W.,
PARELLO, F., PARISI, B. & FLEHOC, C. 1997. Mantle-
derived helium and carbon in groundwaters and
gases of Mount Etna, Italy. *Earth and Planetary
Science Letters*, **148**, 501–516.

AMUNDSON, R. G. & DAVIDSON, E. A. 1990. Carbon
dioxide and nitrogenous gases in the soil
atmosphere. *Journal of Geochemical Exploration*,
38, 13–41.

ARCINIEGA-CEBALLOS, A., CHOUET, B. A. & DAWSON, P.
1999. Very long-period signals associated with vulcanian explosions at Popocatépetl volcano, Mexico.
Geophysical Research Letters, **26**, 3013–3016.

ASHER BOLINDER, S., OWEN, D. E. & SCHUMANN, R.
R. 1991. A preliminary evaluation of environmental
factors influencing day-to-day and seasonal soil-gas
radon concentrations. *In:* GUNDERSEN, L. C. S. &
WANTY, R. B. (eds) *Field Studies of Radon in Rocks,
Soils, and Water*, US Geological Survey Bulletin
1971, 23–31.

BRUNO, N., CALTABIANO, T., GIAMMANCO, S. AND
ROMANO, R. 2001. Degassing of SO_2 and CO_2 at
Mount Etna (Sicily) as an indicator of pre-eruptive
ascent and shallow emplacement of magma.
Journal of Volcanology and Geothermal Research,
110, 137–153.

CASADEVALL, T. J., ROSE, W. I., JR *ET AL.* 1984. Sulfur
dioxide and particles in quiescent volcanic plumes
from Poas, Arenal, and Colima volcanos, Costa
Rica and Mexico. *Journal of Geophysical Research –
Atmospheres*, **89**, 9633–9641.

CHIODINI, G., FRONDINI, F. & RACO, B., 1996. Diffuse
emission of CO_2 from the Fossa crater, Vulcano
Island (Italy). *Bulletin of Volcanology*, **58**, 41–50.

CLARK, I. D. & FRITZ, P. 1997. *Environmental Isotopes
in Hydrogeology*. Lewis Publishers, New York.

CONNOR, C. B., CLEMENT, B. M., SONG, X., LANE, S. B.
& WEST-THOMAS, J. 1993. Continuous monitoring

of high-temperature fumaroles on active lava dome,
Volcan Colima, Mexico: evidence of mass flow
variation in response to atmospheric forcing.
Journal of Geophysical Research, **98**, 19 713–19 722.

CONNOR, C., HILL, B., LAFEMINA, P., NAVARRO, M. &
CONWAY, M. 1996. Soil ^{222}Radon pulse during the
initial phase of the June August 1995 eruption of
Cerro Negro, Nicaragua. *Journal of Volcanology
and Geothermal Research*, **73**, 119–127.

CRAIG, H., LUPTON, J. E. & HORIBE, Y. 1978. A mantle
helium component in Circum-Pacific volcanic
gases: Hakone, the Marianas, and Mt. Lassen. *In:*
ALEXANDER JR, E. C. & OZIMA, M. (eds) *Terrestrial
Rare Gases: Proceedings of the U.S.–Japan Seminar
on Rare Gas Abundance and Isotopic Constraints on
the Origin and Evolution of the Earth's Atmosphere.*
Center for Academic Publications, Tokyo, Japan,
3–16.

CRILL, P. M. 1991. Seasonal patterns of methane
uptake and carbon dioxide release by a temperate
woodland soil. *Global Biogeochemical Cycles*, **5**,
319–334.

DELGADO-GRANADOS, H., CÁRDENAS GONZÁLEZ, L. &
PIEDAD SÁNCHEZ, N., 2001. Sulfur dioxide
emissions from Popocatépetl volcano (Mexico):
case study of a high-emission rate, passively
degassing erupting volcano. *Journal of Volcanology
and Geothermal Research*, **108**, 107–120.

DOMINGUEZ, T., ZOBIN, V. M. & REYES-DAVILA, G. A.
2001. The fracturing in volcanic edifice before an
eruption: the June–July 1998 high-frequency earthquake swarm at Volcán de Colima, Mexico. *Journal
of Volcanology and Geothermal Research*, **105**,
65–75.

ESPÍNDOLA, J. M. 2000. *Recent Magma Discharge Rate
at Colima Volcano, Mexico, IAVCEI General
Assembly.* Volcanological Survey of Indonesia, Bali,
Indonesia.

FARRAR, C. D., SOREY, M. L., EVANS, W. C., HOWLE, J.
F., KERR, B. D., KENNEDY, B. M., KING, C. Y. &
SOUTHON, J. R. 1995. Forest killing diffuse CO_2
emission at Mammoth Mountain as a sign of
magmatic unrest. *Nature*, **376**, 675–678.

FRANCIS, P., HORROCKS, L. & OPPENHEIMER, C., 2000.
Monitoring gases from andesite volcanoes.
*Philosophical Transactions of the Royal Society
London*, **A358**, 1567–1584.

GARDUÑO-MONROY, V. H., SAUCEDO-GIRÓN, R. Z. J.,
GAVILANES, J.-C., CORTÉS, A. & URIBE, R. M. 1998.
La falla Tamazula, límite suroriental de Bloque
Jalisco, y sus relaciones con el complejo volcánico
de Colima, México. *Revista Mexicana de Ciencias
Geológicas*, **15**, 132–144.

GIAMMANCO, S., GURRIERI, S. & VALENZA, M., 1998.
Anomalous soil CO_2 degassing in relation to faults
and eruptive fissures on Mount Etna (Sicily, Italy).
Bulletin of Volcanology, **60**, 252–259.

GIGGENBACH, W. F. 1975. A simple method for the
collection and analysis of volcanic gas samples.
Bulletin of Volcanology, **39**, 132–145.

GIGGENBACH, W. F., GARCÍA, N., LONDOÑO, A.,
RODRÍGUEZ, L., ROJAS, N. & CALVACHE, M. L.
1990. The chemistry of fumarolic vapor and
thermal-spring discharges from the Nevado del

Ruiz volcanic–magmatic–hydrothermal system, Columbia. *Journal of Volcanology and Geothermal Research*, **42**, 13–39.

GIGGENBACH, W. F. 1992. Isotopic shift in waters from geothermal and volcanic systems along convergent plate boundaries and their origin. *Earth and Planetary Science Letters*, **113**, 495–510.

GOFF, F., LOVE, S. P., WARREN, R. G., COUNCE, D., OBENHOLZNER, J., SIEBE, C. & SCHMIDT, S. C., 2001. Passive infrared remote sensing evidence for large, intermittent CO_2 emissions at Popocatépetl volcano, Mexico. *Chemical Geology*, **177**, 133–156.

HEILIGMANN, M., STIX, J., WILLIAMS JONES, G., SHERWOOD LOLLAR, B. & GARZON, G., 1997. Distal degassing of radon and carbon dioxide on Galeras volcano, Columbia. *Journal of Volcanology and Geothermal Research*, **77**, 267–283.

HINKLE, M. E., 1991. Seasonal and geothermal production variations in concentrations of He and CO_2 in soil gases, Roosevelt Hot Springs Known Geothermal Resource Area, Utah, USA. *Applied Geochemistry*, **6**, 35–47.

INGUAGGIATO, S., CAPASSO, G., FAVARA, R., MARTIN DEL POZZO, A. L. & AGUAYO, A. 2001. Water–rock interaction processes at Popocatépetl volcano, Mexico. *In:* Cidu, R. (ed.), *Proceedings of the Tenth International Symposium on 'Water–Rock Interaction', WRI-10 Villasimius, Italy 10–15 July 2001, Vol. 2*, A. A. Balkema, 859–862.

KOEPENICK, K. W., BRANTLEY, S. L., THOMPSON, J. M., ROWE, G. L., NYBLADE, A. A. & MOSHY, C. 1996. Volatile emissions from the crater and flank of Oldoinyo Lengai volcano, Tanzania. *Journal of Geophysical Research*, **101**, 13 819–13 830.

KOMOROWSKI, J. C., SIEBE, C., RODRÍGUEZ-ELIZARRARAS, S., ESPÍNDOLA, J. M. & SAUCEDO, R. 1991. Pyroclastic and effusive activity of April 16–17, 1991 at Volcán de Colima, Mexico: field characteristics, sedimentology, chemistry and petrology of the products. *Geological Society of America – Abstracts with Programs*, **23**, 451–452.

LOPEZ LOERA, H. & URRUTIA-FUCUGAUCHI, J. 1999. Spatial and temporal magnetic anomalies of Colima Volcano, western Mexico. *Geofisica Internacional*, **38(1)**, 3–16.

LOVE, S. P., GOFF, F., COUNCE, D., SIEBE, C. & DELGADO GRANADOS, H., 1998. Passive infrared spectroscopy of the eruption plume at Popocatépetl volcano, Mexico. *Nature*, **396**, 563–567.

LUHR, J. F. 1992. Slab-derived fluids and partial melting in subduction zones: insights from tow contrasting volcanoes (Colima and Ceboruco). *Journal of Volcanology and Goethermal Research*, **54**, 1–8.

LUHR, J. F. & CARMICHAEL, I. S. E. 1990. Petrological monitoring of cyclic eruptive activity at Volcán Colima, México. *Journal of Volcanology and Geothermal Research*, **42**, 235–260.

MACÍAS, J. L., CAPACCIONI, B., CONTICELLI, S., GIANNINI, L., MARTINI, M. & RODRÍGUEZ, S., 1993. Volatile elements in alkaline and calc-alkaline rocks from the Colima graben, Mexico: constraints on their genesis and evolution. *Geofisica Internacional*, **32**, 575–589.

MORSE, R. H. 1976. *Radon Counters in Uranium Exploration, Exploration for Uranium Ore Deposits,* Vienna, 229–239.

POREDA, R. & CRAIG, H., 1989. Helium isotope ratios in circum-Pacific volcanic arcs. *Nature*, **338**, 473-478.

REYES-DÁVILA, G. A., NUÑEZ-CORNÚ, F. & RAMÍREZ VÁZQUEZ, C. A. 2001. Actividad sísmica del Volcán de Colima. *GEOS – Unión Geofísica Mexicana; Resúmenes y Programa*, **21**, 313.

ROBIN, C., KOMOROWSKI, J., BOUDAL, C. & MOSSAND, P. 1990. Mixed-magma pyroclastic surge deposits associated with debris avalanche deposits at Colima volcanoes, Mexico. *Bulletin of Volcanology*, **52**, 391–403.

ROBIN, C., CAMUS, G. & GOURGAUD, A., 1991. Eruptive and magmatic cycles at Fuego de Colima volcano (Mexico). *Journal of Volcanology and Geothermal Research*, **45**, 209–225.

SCHOELL, M. 1988. Multiple origins of methane in the Earth. *Chemical Geology*, **71**, 1–10.

SEVERINGHAUS, J. P., BENDER, M. L., KEELING, R. F. & BROECKER, W. S. 1996. Fractionation of soil gases by diffusion of water-vapor, gravitational settling, and thermal diffusion. *Geochimica et Cosmochimica Acta*, **60**, 1005–1018.

SEGOVIA, N., MENA, M., MONNIN, M., PENA, P., SEIDEL, J. L. & TAMEZ, E. 1997. Radon in soil variations related to volcanic activity. *Radiation Measurements*, **28**, 745–750.

SIEBE, C., ABRAMS, M. & MACIAS, J. L. 1995. Derrumbes gigantes depósitos de avalancha de escombros y edad del actual cono del volcán Popocatépetl. *Volcán Popocatépetl Estudios Realizados Durante la Crisis de 1994–1995.* CENAPRED, Mexico City, 195–220.

SIEBE, C., ABRAMS, M., MACIAS, J. L. & OBENHOLZNER, J. 1996. Repeated volcanic disasters in Prehispanic time at Popocatépetl, central Mexico: past key to the future? *Geology*, **24**, 399–402.

SOLOMON, D. K. & CERLING, T.E. 1987. The annual carbon dioxide cycle in a montane soil: observations, modeling, and implications for weathering. *Water Resource Research*, **23**, 2257–2265.

STOIBER, R. E., MALINCONICO, L. L. & WILLIAMS, S. N. 1983. Use of the correlation spectrometer at active volcanoes. *In:* TAZIEFF, H. & SABROUX, J.C. (eds) *Forecasting Volcanic Events.* Elsevier, New York, 425–444.

STOOPES, G. R. & SHERIDAN, M. F. 1992. Giant debris avalanches from the Colima Volcanic Complex, Mexico: implications for long-runout landslides (>100 km) and hazard assessment. *Geology*, **20**, 299–302.

TARAN, Y. A., HEDENQUIST, J. W., KORZHINSKY, M. A., TKACHENKO, S. I., SHMULOVICH, K. I. 1995. Geochemistry of magmatic gases from Kudryavy volcano, Iturup, Kurile Islands. *Geochimica et Cosmochimica Acta*, **59**, 1749–1761.

TARAN, Y. A., BERNARD, A., GAVILANES, J.-C. & AFRICANO, F., 2000. Native gold in mineral precipitates from high-temperature volcanic gases of Colima volcano, Mexico. *Applied Geochemistry*, **15**, 337–346.

TARAN, Y. A., BERNARD, A., GAVILANES, J.-C., LUNEZHEVA, E., CORTES, A. & ARMIENTA, M. A. 2001. Chemistry and mineralogy of high temperature gas discharges from Colima volcano, Mexico. Implications for magmatic gas atmosphere interaction. *Journal of Volcanology and Geothermal Research*, **108**, 245–264.

TARAN, Y. A., GAVILANES, J. C. & CORTÉS, A. 2002a. Chemical and isotopic composition of fumarolic gases and the SO_2 flux from Volcán de Colima, Mexico, between the 1994 and 1998 eruptions. *Journal of Volcanology and Geothermal Research*, **117(1–2)**, 105–119.

TARAN, Y. A., INGUAGGIATO, S., VARLEY, N, CAPASSO, G. & FAVARA, R. 2002b. Helium and carbon isotopes in thermal waters of the Jalisco Block, Mexico. *Geofísica Internacional*, **41(4)**, 459–466.

TAYLOR, B.E. 1986. Magmatic volatiles: isotopic variation of C, H, and S. Chapter 7, *In:* TAYLOR, H. P., O'NEIL, J. R., AND VALLEY, J. W. (eds). Stable isotopes in high temperature processes. *Mineralogical Society of America Reviews in Mineralogy*, **16**, 185–225.

TERHUNE, C. L. & HARDEN, J. W., 1991. Seasonal variations of carbon dioxide concentrations in stony, coarse textured desert soils of southern Nevada, USA. *Soil Science*, **151**, 417–429.

TOUTAIN, J.-P. & BAUBRON, J.-C. 1999. Gas geochemistry and seismotectonics; a review. *Tectonophysics*, **304**, 1–27.

TRUJILLO, P. E., COUNCE, D., GRIGSBY, C. O., GOFF, F. & SHEVENELL, L. 1987. Chemical analysis and sampling techniques for geothermal fluids and gases at the Fenton Hill Laboratory. LA-11006-MS, Los Alamos National Laboratory.

VARLEY, N. R. & FLOWERS, A. G. 1992. Radon and its correlation with some geological features of the south-west of England. *Radiation Protection Dosimetry*, **45**, 245–248.

VARLEY, N. R. & FLOWERS, A. G. 1998. The influence of geology on radon levels in S.W. England. *Radiation Protection Dosimetry*, **77**, 171–176.

VARLEY, N. R. & ARMIENTA, M. A. 2001. The absence of diffuse degassing at Popocatépetl volcano, Mexico. *Chemical Geology*, **177**, 157–173.

VARLEY, N. R. & GAVILANES, J. C. 2001. The explosive activity of Volcán de Colima 1999–2001. *GEOS – Unión Geofísica Mexicana; Resúmenes y Programa*, **21**, 315.

VARLEY, N. R., TARAN, Y. A. AND GAVILANES, J. C. 2001. Degassing processes of Volcán de Colima. *GEOS – Unión Geofísica Mexicana; Resúmenes y Programa*, **21**, 312.

WALLACE, P. J. 2001. Volcanic SO_2 emissions and the abundance and distribution of exsolved gas in magma bodies. *Journal of Volcanology and Geothermal Research*, **108**, 85–106.

WASHINGTON, J. W. & ROSE, A. W. 1990. Regional and temporal relations of radon in soil gas to soil temperature and moisture. *Geophysical Research Letters*, **17**, 829–832.

WATTS, R. B., HERD, R. A., SPARKS, R. S. J. & YOUNG, S. R. 2002. Growth patterns and emplacement of the andesitic lava dome at Soufrière Hills, Montserrat. *In:* DRUITT, T. H. & KOKELAAR, B. P. (eds) The eruption of Soufrière Hills Volcano, Montserrat, from 1995 to 1999. *The Geological Society, London, Memoirs*, **21**, 115–152.

WERNER, C., JANIK, C. J. *ET AL.* 1997. *Geochemistry of Summit Fumarole Vapors and Flanking thermal/mineral waters at Popocatépetl volcano, Mexico.* LA-13289-MS, Los Alamos National Laboratory.

WILLIAMS-JONES, G., STIX, J., HEILIGMANN, M., CHARLAND, A., SHERWOOD LOLLAR, B., ARNER, N., GARZON, G. V., BARQUERO, J. & FERNÁNDEZ, E. 2000. A model of diffuse degassing at three subduction-related volcanoes. *Bulletin of Volcanology*, **62**, 130–142.

WILLIAMS-JONES, G. & STIX, J. 2002. Using the COSPEC in the field. *In:* STIX J. & HICKSON, C. J. (eds) *Theory, Use, and Application of the COSPEC Correlation Spectrometer at Active Volcanoes.* Geological Society of Canada Bulletin.

ZAPATA, J. A., CALVACHE, M. L. *ET AL.* 1997. SO_2 fluxes from Galeras Volcano, Colombia, 1989–1995: Progressive degassing and conduit obstruction of a Decade Volcano. *Journal of Volcanology and Geothermal Research*, **77**, 195–208.

FTIR remote sensing of fractional magma degassing at Mount Etna, Sicily

M. BURTON[1], P. ALLARD[1,2], F. MURÈ[1] & C. OPPENHEIMER[3]

[1]*Istituto Nazionale di Geofisica e Vulcanologia, Sezione di Catania, Catania, Italy.*
[2]*Laboratoire Pierre Süe, CNRS-CEA, Gif-sur-Yvette, France.*
[3]*Department of Geography, University of Cambridge, Downing Place, Cambridge, CB2 3EN, UK.*

Abstract: The chemical composition of volcanic gas emissions from each of the four summit craters of Mount Etna was measured remotely in May 2001, using a Fourier transform infrared (FTIR) spectrometer operated on the upper flanks of the volcano. The results reveal constant HCl/HF ratio but distinct SO_2/HCl and SO_2/HF ratios in the emitted gases, which, in the light of melt inclusion data for Etna basalts, can be interpreted in terms of escape of gases from partially, and variably, degassed magma at different depths beneath the summit. Gases released from the three main summit craters (Bocca Nuova, Voragine, and Northeast) had an identical composition, controlled by bulk degassing of a single magma body that had previously lost $c.25\%$ of its original sulphur. The similar gas composition at all three main craters suggests that these are connected to a central conduit system that branches at relatively shallow depth. Measurements of the bulk volcanic plume on the same day, $c.7$ km downwind, show that degassing from these craters dominated the total gas output of the volcano, and that no significant chemical evolution occurred within the plume over a time-scale of $c.12$ min. Weaker gas emissions from the Southeast crater were comparatively depleted in SO_2 (SO_2/HCl and SO_2/HF ratios a factor of two lower), implying that this crater is fed either by a separate conduit or by a branch of the central conduit whose geometry favours solubility-controlled volatile fractionation. Still lower SO_2/HCl and SO_2/HF ratios measured for residual degassing of a lava flow erupted from the Southeast crater verify the lower solubility and earlier escape of sulphur compared to halogens at Etna. Fractional magma degassing is also implied by strong chemical contrasts between the bulk volcanic plume and fissure gas emissions measured during the July–August 2001 flank eruption. These results highlight the ability of FTIR spectrometry to detect fine spatial and temporal variations in magma degassing processes, and thereby constrain models of shallow plumbing systems.

Introduction

Magmas contain dissolved volatiles (H_2O, CO_2, S, Cl, F, etc.) with differing solubility behaviour, which gradually reach a saturation pressure and exsolve into a separate gas phase (bubbles) during magma ascent and crystallization. This volatile phase plays a central role in magmatic and volcanic processes (e.g. Anderson 1975), and its chemical composition changes from depth to the surface according to the pressure-controlled solubility behaviour of each volatile species, but also as a function of the dynamics of magma supply and ascent (Sparks, 2003, this volume). In fact, gas bubbles may rise with either the same velocity as surrounding magma, allowing continuous gas–melt equilibration and single-step 'bulk' gas emission at the surface, or with a higher velocity, thereby reaching the surface independently of the parental magma batch (e.g. Sparks 1978; Vergniolle & Jaupart 1986). In the latter case, chemical equilibrium between gas and magma may be inhibited. Sustained high gas fluxes in excess of lava production on basaltic volcanoes, such as Etna and Stromboli, typically require a separated bubble flow and, in the long term, convective renewal of volatile-rich magma from depth (Francis *et al* 1993; Allard *et al.* 1994; Kazahaya *et al.* 1994; Allard 1997; Stevenson & Blake 1998). Both the rate and depth of convection, and the amount and volatile content of supplied magma, will eventually determine the chemical composition of the gases emitted by the volcano. Therefore, geochemical monitoring of volcanic gas emissions can provide valuable information on the dynamics and evolution of the magmatic system, with obvious implications for eruption forecasting.

In the simplest volcanic system, gas bubbles generated within a central feeding conduit escape from a single point source at the surface, which may be monitored. Bulk equilibrium degassing of a magma body in this way can be termed

From: OPPENHEIMER, C., PYLE, D.M. & BARCLAY, J. (eds) *Volcanic Degassing.* Geological Society, London, Special Publications, **213**, 281–293. 0305-8719/03/$15.00

'primary' degassing (see Fig. 1a). If a branch leading from the central conduit exists, then gases and lavas may be emitted at more than one point at the surface. This occurs at several volcanoes with separate summit craters and/or lateral vents (e.g. Kilaeua, Dixon *et al.* 1991). In situations where gas bubbles ascend faster than magma, the geometry of the branch will influence the route to the surface taken by the bubbles. Moreover, the initial depth of the branch will determine the composition of the bubbles that enter it, as this depends on the exsolution depth of each volatile component. Thus the composition of volcanic gases emitted from lateral vents may either resemble, or strongly differ from, that observed at central conduits. In the case of a branching system that allows bubbles to freely enter a lateral branch, the gas composition will be controlled mainly by the depth of the branch; if this is below the depth of initial exsolution of measured gases or is shallow enough that magma is completely degassed, then primary magma degassing could occur at a lateral vent as well (see Fig. 1b). In contrast, in the case of a branch for which bubbles preferentially rise through the central conduit, only the magma contained within the branched conduit will degas, leading to what we term fractional magma degassing, as the magma in the branch has already lost some volatiles via degassing from the central conduit (see Fig, 1c).

Fractional (also termed secondary or type II in the literature) degassing has been observed and well documented on Kilauea volcano, Hawaii (Gerlach & Graeber 1985). In this system basaltic magma rises vertically beneath the central summit caldera before intruding laterally into a rift zone with horizontal magma transport to one or more surface vents. Pu'u 'O'o crater is currently the most active eruption site on Kilaeua's Eastern rift. Kilauea magmas are saturated in CO_2 beneath Halemaumau caldera, and large quantities of CO_2 are released through the caldera. In contrast, SO_2 is apparently not saturated before horizontal transport takes place and, therefore, much greater fluxes of SO_2 are observed at Pu'u 'O'o volcano than at Halemaumau. Measurements have been made of submarine lavas on the Puna ridge that is also fed via rifting zones from Kilauea (Dixon *et al.* 1991). Their analyses suggested that CO_2 and H_2O degassing had already occurred, pointing to shallow, possibly sub-aerial degassing of the magma prior to it sinking into the subvolcanic plumbing system.

Mount Etna is another active mafic volcano where fractional magma degassing has been detected (Allard 1986; Lambert *et al.* 1985/1986; Gauthier & Le Cloarec 1998). Etna has four active summit craters (Fig. 2), several of which may exhibit strong degassing and Strombolian activity at any one time. These four craters can erupt synchronously or separately, with widely varying magma levels despite their proximity. These observations suggest a complex subsurface plumbing system. In addition to this summit activity, Etna periodically delivers flank lavas through fractures and lateral vents. Compared with central conduit degassing, lateral gas venting at Etna is characterized by lowered CO_2/SO_2 ratios (Allard 1986) and a depletion in the most volatile radioactive isotopes and trace metals (Lambert *et al.* 1985/1986; Gauthier and Le Cloarec 1998). However, fractional degassing has also been detected amongst the summit craters themselves. Gauthier and Le Cloarec (1998)

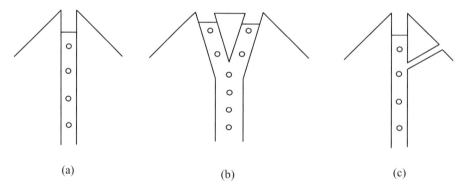

(a)   (b)   (c)

Fig. 1. Schematic models of conduit branching and degassing: (**a**) Bubbles (indicated by circles) rise with magma in a single central conduit (primary degassing); (**b**) Bubbles rise within a branched conduit, maintaining the same composition in both branches; (**c**) Gas/magma separation at a branch, leading to fractional degassing from the branched conduit if the magma has already lost volatiles via the central conduit.

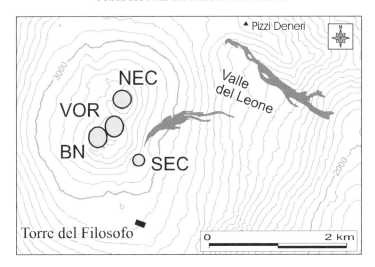

Fig. 2. Map of the summit craters of Mount Etna. Contour lines have 50 m spacing. Easterly winds on 2 May 2001 permitted the plumes from the Northeast Crater (NEC), Central Craters (Voragine, VOR and Bocca Nuova, BN) and Southeast Crater (SEC) to be measured separately by measuring at different points west of the summit craters. Lava flows from the SEC (May 2001) and Valle del Leone (July 2001) were measured from north of the Valle del Leone. Piano Provenzana is located 7 km northeast of the summit craters.

showed that during the period 1991–1995, which included a major effusive flank eruption in 1991–1993, the Voragine and Bocca Nuova central summit craters were the main sites of primary magma degassing, whereas the Southeast crater displayed transitions from primary to fractional degassing depending on the magma level and the intensity of volcanic activity.

Here we present new evidence for fractional magma degassing at Mount Etna, based on remote-sensing observations collected in 2001 using an open-path Fourier transform infrared (FTIR) spectrometer. This technique allowed us to measure, simultaneously and accurately, the relative abundances of SO_2, HCl, and HF within the bulk volcanic plume and also, on one occasion (2 May 2001), in gases emitted by the separate summit craters of Etna. Measurements were also made of gases released from lava flows and fissure vents. Here we examine and discuss these results in light of the concepts of primary and fractional degassing described above, and of constraints provided by crystal melt inclusion data for volatiles dissolved in Etna basalt (Métrich & Clocchiatti 1989; Métrich et al. 1993; Allard & Métrich 1999; Métrich et al. 2002). We also examine the implications of our results for the geometry of the summit crater conduit system. Our measurements constitute the first real-time detection of fractional basalt degassing during both non-eruptive and eruptive volcanic activity at Etna.

Measurements and data reduction

All data were collected with a Bruker OPAG-22 FTIR spectrometer with ZnSe beam-splitter, at 0.5 cm^{-1} resolution, using medium Norton-Beer apodization. The detector was a liquid nitrogen-cooled In–Sb photovoltaic semi-conductor with sensitivity between 1500 and 10000 cm^{-1} (limited to 7899 cm^{-1} by memory constraints). Spectra were collected in both passive (hot rock or lava radiation source) and solar occultation modes (Francis et al. 1998). Measured spectra were analysed using a non-linear, least-squares-fitting program based on the Rodgers (Rodgers 1976) optimal estimation algorithm, and the Oxford RFM radiative transfer model (http://www-atm.atm.ox.ac.uk/RFM/), using spectral line data from the HITRAN 96 database (Rothman et al. 1998). Solar spectra were analysed by simulating the complete atmospheric transmittance, based on a 50-layer FASCODE standard atmosphere, together with an idealized single volcanic plume layer with fixed pressure and temperature. Passive spectra were simulated by assuming a single-layer atmosphere containing both atmospheric and volcanic constituents. An example of a passive spectrum collected on 1 May 2001 is shown, together with a fit and residual, in Figure 3.

Each spectrum was analysed to produce a path amount of SO_2, HCl, and HF, three gases which have negligible concentrations in the free troposphere but which are abundant within

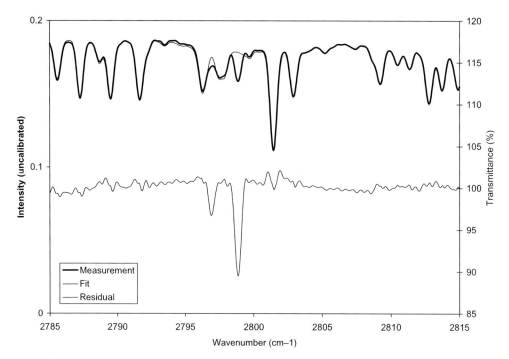

Fig. 3. Example of a spectrum collected on 1 May 2001, using radiation emitted from a lava flow on the NNE flank of the Southeast Crater (thick black line). The result of an attempted fit is also shown (thin black line), that had H_2O, N_2O, and CH_4 path amounts as free parameters. The ratio of the fit and spectrum is also shown, and this demonstrates the presence of HCl within the measurement path. The absorption is the P(4) ro-vibrational transition of HCl. The doublet is due to the presence of $H^{37}Cl$ as well as $H^{35}Cl$, with natural proportion of 1:3. The retrieved amount of HCl for this spectrum was 2.3×10^{17} molecules cm^{-2}.

volcanic emissions. The nature of FTIR spectrometry is such that all detectable wavelengths are measured simultaneously. This means that, despite the swiftly changing concentrations of gas in the line of measurement between the spectrometer and the Sun, each spectrum records the instantaneous composition of the volcanic gas and air mixture. By examining the ratio of one volcanic gas to another we can identify any systematic variations between different source compositions. Ratios are determined by measuring 50 or more spectra of a particular gas plume, and then plotting retrieved amounts of SO_2 against HCl and HF. The analytical error on concentrations ranges from 4 to 10%. The gradients of path amount plots are the ratios of SO_2/HCl and SO_2/HF.

Results

Etna summit, 1 and 2 May 2001

On 1 and 2 May 2001, volcanic activity on Etna was characterized by quiescent vapour-rich (white) fuming at three of the four summit craters, namely the northeast crater (NEC), Voragine and Southeast crater (SEC); plume emissions intermittently loaded with brown ash from the Bocca Nuova, resulting from both sporadic explosions deep in the conduit and conduit wall collapses; and a declining flow of lava from a NNE-trending flank fissure of the SEC that had continued since 20 January 2001. One week later, on 9 May, lava-fountaining episodes resumed at the SEC. On 1 May, we collected passive FTIR spectroscopic measurements of gas emissions from the lava flow issuing from the flank of SEC (3100 m a.s.l.), by operating the spectrometer at high elevation (2900 m) and close distance (*c.*2 km) on the volcano. Measurements on 2 May were also made close to the summit, but using the solar occultation mode (Francis *et al.* 1998), to analyse the crater plume emissions (distance range of 1–3 km). Favourable meteorological conditions on this day allowed the plumes from the four summit craters to be distinguished and measured separately. The bulk plume was subsequently measured downwind from Piano Provenzana (7 km northeast of the summit), using the same method.

The retrieved SO_2, HCl and HF amounts are plotted in Figures 4a and 4b, and the ratios of SO_2/HCl, SO_2/HF and HCl/HF are summarized in Table 1. These three ratios have almost iden- tical values for the separate plumes from both Northeast and central craters (Voragine and Bocca Nuova) and in the bulk volcanic plume. In contrast, the gases from the SEC and its lava flow show lower SO_2/HCl and SO_2/HF ratios (by a factor of 2 and 3, respectively), but a comparable HCl/HF ratio.

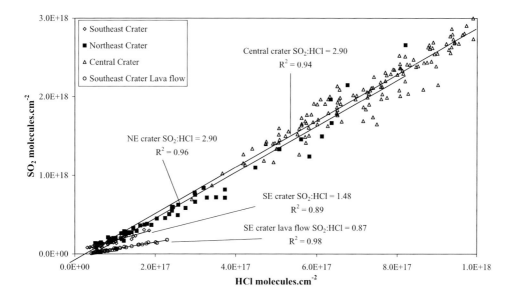

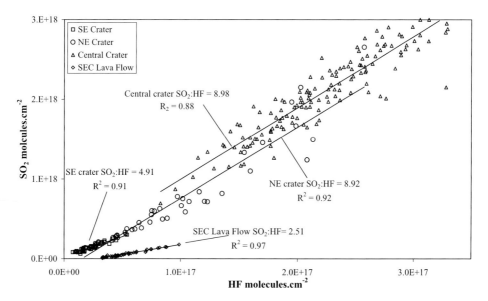

Fig. 4. (a) SO_2/HCl ratios measured in gas emissions from separate summit craters and SEC lava flow on 1–2 May 2001; (b) SO_2/HF ratios measured in gas emissions from separate summit craters and SEC lava flow on 1–2 May 2001.

Table 1. *Chemical composition (molar ratios) of gases emitted from the summit craters of Mount Etna and a lava flow on 1–2 May 2001.*

Gas source	SO$_2$/HCl ($\pm 5\%$ 1σ)	SO$_2$/HF ($\pm 8\%$ 1σ)	HCl/HF ($\pm 8\%$ 1σ)
Central crater	2.90	8.98	3.10
Northeast crater (NEC)	2.90	8.92	3.08
Bulk plume	2.91	9.12	3.13
Southeast crater (SEC)	1.48	4.91	3.31
Southeast crater lava flow	0.87	2.51	2.89

Valle del Leone, 25 July 2001

On 17 July 2001, an eruptive fissure opened on the south flank of Etna immediately below the SEC. This heralded the first major flank effusion on Etna since the 1991–1993 eruption (Research Staff INGV, 2001). On 20 July 2001, an eruptive fissure opened northeast of the SEC, within the Valle del Leone. This fissure was active until 30 July, and produced a flow approximately 2 km long. Gas emitted from a 'hornito' (steep spatter cone) at the lava flow source was measured on 25 July in passive FTIR spectroscopic mode, using active lava as the radiation source (Figs 5a &, 5b). Solar measurements of the bulk plume from the summit craters could not be made on the same day but were performed on 28 July (Figs 5a & 5b).

The chemical ratios from both sets of measurements are summarized in Table 2. Again strong differences between the fissure gas venting and the bulk summit crater plume are evident. The former displays SO$_2$/HCl and SO$_2$/HF ratios that are about three times lower than those in the bulk plume, and very similar to those measured from the SEC lava flow on 1 May 2001.

Interpretation

The two data-sets presented above reveal marked contrasts in the chemical proportions of SO$_2$, HCl, and HF simultaneously emitted from the summit craters and from fissure vents or lava flows on Etna in 2001. Compared with summit crater emissions, the gas mixtures from lateral vents and flows display a similar decrease of SO$_2$/HCl and SO$_2$/HF ratios, while steady or weakly modified HCl/HF ratio. This implies their relative depletion in SO$_2$ with respect to halogens. The data for the SEC, however, show that a similar, though more subtle, trend can occur among the summit craters themselves.

Below we briefly review the different factors that may account for such variations.

Potential factors controlling SO$_2$, HCl, and HF in Etna volcanic gases

The main processes and parameters that can determine the proportions of SO$_2$, HCl, and HF in volcanic gases are:

1. their original content and solubility behaviour in the magma;
2. the degree of chemical equilibrium between gas bubbles and surrounding melt, which depends on the dynamics of magma rise and supply, itself depending on parameters such as the conduit geometry;
3. their possible partitioning into minerals or some immiscible (e.g. sulphide) phases; and
4. chemical reactions within hydrothermal systems and on conduit walls; and
5. chemical reactions in the atmosphere. It is clear that magma degassing is a complex process, and unambiguous interpretation of volcanic gas data is challenging. However, Etna is a well-studied volcano, and reasonable inferences may be made about the respective influence of the different factors listed above.

1. The abundance and solubility behaviour of S, Cl, and F in magmas can be determined from laboratory experiments (e.g. Carroll and Holloway 1994) and from the analysis of dissolved volatiles in crystal melt inclusions (e.g. Anderson 1975). Both approaches are complementary and present advantages and drawbacks. One major advantage in studying crystal melt inclusions is that these provide data for a specific magma composition, which strongly influences the solubility behaviour of volatiles, and for degassing processes occurring under natural (real) conditions. On the other hand, this approach requires very careful investigations of the samples and interpretation of the data by experienced petro-geochemists. The behaviour of sulphur, chlorine, and fluorine in Etna magma has been studied through detailed analysis of volatiles dissolved in melt inclusions trapped in olivine crystals of both historical and present-day Etnean basalts (Métrich & Clocchiatti 1989; Clocchiatti *et al.* 1988; Métrich *et al.* 1993; Allard & Métrich 1999; Métrich *et al.*).

Melt inclusions trapped in the most primitive (most Mg-rich) olivines of present-day Etna basalts indicate contents of 0.34 wt% S, 0.18 wt % Cl and *c.*0.085 wt% F in the feeding magma. Fluid inclusions trapped in clinopyroxenes (Frezzotti *et al.* 1991) and olivines (Clocchiatti *et*

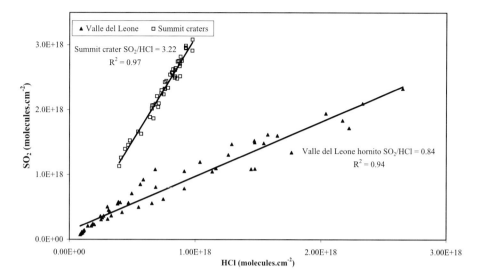

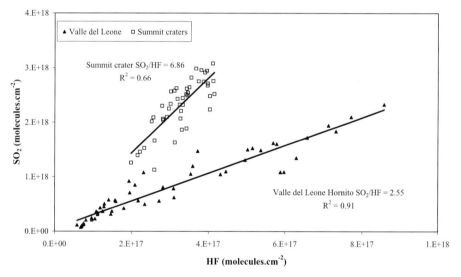

Fig. 5 (a) SO_2/HCl ratios measured in gas emissions from a hornito in Valle del Leone and bulk summit crater plume in July 2001. (b) SO_2/HF ratios measured in gas emissions from a hornito in Valle del Leone and bulk summit crater plume in July 2001.

Table 2. *Molar gas compositions for emissions from a hornito in the Valle del Leone, and for the bulk summit crater plume, 25–28 July 2001.*

Gas source and date	SO_2/HCl ($\pm 5\%$ 1σ)	SO_2/HF ($\pm 8\%$ 1σ)	HCl/HF ($\pm 8\%$ 1σ)
Hornito, Valle del Leone 25/7/01	0.84	2.55	3.04
Etna summit craters 28/7/01	3.22	6.86	2.13

al. 1992) found in ancient alkali basalts of Etna indicate that the gas phase exsolved at pressures greater than 2 kbar is pure CO_2, suggesting negligible exsolution of other species (H_2O, S, Cl, F) up to at least that pressure. This is a strong indication that the abundances of S, Cl, and F given above are representative of the original (pre-degassing) contents in magma. More evolved melt inclusions in less Mg-rich olivines formed during magma ascent show that about two thirds of sulphur and water exsolve into the gas phase between about 2 kbar and 0.5 kbar pressure (e.g. Métrich *et al.* 1993), that is between *c.*6 and 1.5 km depth below the volcano summit. The exsolution of chlorine is minor within this depth interval, and becomes efficient only at lower pressure. The behaviour of fluorine is less well constrained, but this element appears to degas in smaller proportion and to be more soluble than chlorine. Examination of residual volatile contents in the most chemically evolved melt inclusions and in matrix glasses of pyro-clasts and lavas demonstrates that, upon erup-tion, Etna basalts have lost *c.*97 % of their original S content, 40– 50 % of their Cl and only about 20% of their F (Métrich & Clocchiatti 1989; Métrich 1990; Métrich *et al.* 1993; Métrich *et al.* 2002).

Based on these data, single-step bulk equili-brium magma degassing is expected to produce a volcanic gas phase with SO_2/HCl, HCl/HF and SO_2/HF molar ratios averaging 4.0, 3.0, and 12, respectively, compared with 2.0, 1.2, and 2.4 in the undegassed magma and 0.08, 0.6, and 0.05 in degassed lava (Fig. 6). The SO_2/HCl bulk degas-sing ratio is well constrained, whereas the HCl/HF and SO_2/HF bulk values may be considered upper limits. Comparison with the original ratios in the feeding magma highlights the greater bulk volatility and earlier degassing

of S than Cl and of Cl than F. Accordingly, any volcanic gas produced through partial (fractional) magma degassing will have variable SO_2/HCl, HCl/HF and SO_2/HF ratios, whose values will depend on the depth of volatile exsolution, bubble-melt separation, bubble-melt equilibrium and the extent of previous volatile loss from the melt.

2. The degree of chemical equilibrium between the melt and gas bubbles is dependent on the diffusion coefficients of the dissolved volatiles, the relative velocity of bubble rise (a function of bubble size), and the mean free path between bubbles. If the bubbles rise at the same speed as the magma (homogeneous flow) there will be greater opportunity for them to maintain chemical equilibrium with the melt and thereby achieve bulk equilibrium degassing conditions at the surface. This is the case when magma rise is quite fast, typically *c.*1.0 m/s for Kilauea basalt (Parfitt and Wilson 1995). A lower magma rise speed (<0.1 m/s) will favour a separated flow of gas bubbles and their tendency to coalesce (e.g. Sparks 1978; Vergniolle & Jaupart 1986; Parfitt & Wilson 1995), thus leading to separated gas release at the surface. Magma convection, that is constrained by conduit geometry, is another important factor in determining bubble– melt equilibrium over the long term. Bulk degassing

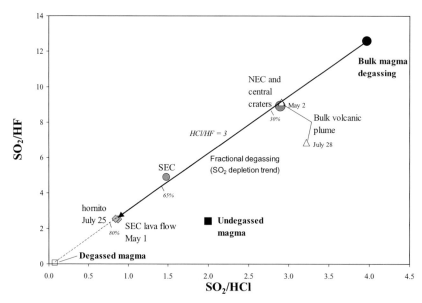

Fig. 6. FTIR-measured SO_2/HF versus SO_2/HCl ratios in gases from summit craters, lateral vents and lava flow in May–July 2001, compared with the bulk degassing ratios inferred from crystal melt inclusion data for S, Cl, and F contents in undegassed and degassed Etna basalt (Métrich & Clocchiatti 1989; Clocchiatti *et al.* 1988; Métrich *et al.* 1993; Allard & Métrich 1999).

can only persist if effective convection of magma constantly replenishes the upper conduit system; this mechanism is typically required to account for the time-averaged excess gas discharge of Mount Etna (Allard 1997), implying that the volcano has a wide enough central conduit system (see below) to allow efficient convection.

3. Volatile components usually have a negligible affinity for the minerals in basaltic rocks. Apatite and amphibole, which can fix Cl and F, are usually lacking or are only present as tiny inclusions in other phenocrysts in present-day Etna basalts (Métrich & Clocchiatti 1989; Métrich 1990) and, therefore, their potential influence on Cl and F behaviour is minimal. A different situation exists for sulphur, which, upon reaching saturation, may be affected by the formation of immiscible sulphide globules. Sulphide globules do occur in evolved Etnean melt inclusions trapped at relatively shallow depth in olivine and pyroxene crystals (Métrich & Clocchiatti et al. 1988; Clocchiatti 1989; Métrich et al. 1993). However, sulphide globules have never been observed in the primary melt inclusions trapped at greater depth, or in the extruded lavas. This strongly suggests that sulphide globules present in melt inclusions trapped at shallow depth are transient phases which decompose during final magma ascent and which, accordingly, have minor bearing upon the final composition and budget of gas emitted from Etna.

4. Magmatic gases can be strongly fractionated upon interacting with aquifers and hydrothermal systems. At Etna, groundwaters formed by rapid infiltration of meteoric water into the permeable volcanic rocks flow downslope along the interface with the impermeable sedimentary basement, and are generally non-thermal at their exit (Anzà et al. 1989). There is little evidence for a significant hydrothermal system existing in the upper part of the volcanic pile that could strongly interact with the conduit system. In particular, geochemical budgets show that the release of magmatic volatiles through the summit craters vastly exceeds the amount of magma-derived volatiles transported by groundwaters (Allard et al. 1997; Aiuppa et al. 2000). Reactions on conduit walls certainly take place, as indicated by the altered state of the conduit walls observable from the surface and in ash particles generated during wall erosion and/or collapse. However, it seems likely that, given the voluminous degassing, these reactions are rapidly saturated and have a minor effect on final observed compositions.

5. Finally, dissolution of HCl and HF into condensed water droplets within the volcanic plume (Burton et al. 2001), as well as oxidation of SO_2 (Oppenheimer et al. 1998), have been suggested as potentially significant processes in changing the chemical composition of volcanic gases once in the atmosphere. Although the bearing of these processes is not easy to quantify, here we note that, on 2 May 2001, no significant difference in composition was detected between our measurements made immediately after emission from the summit and at a point approximately 12 min downwind. This implies that HCl dissolution and SO_2 oxidation were insignificant, at least during that measurement period.

Fractional magma degassing and implications for the conduit system

We therefore conclude that the dominant factors controlling the chemical compositions observed in May and July 2001 on Etna were most likely the original volatile content of the melt, solubilities of volatiles, and conduit geometry. We now examine in further detail this interpretation and the implications of our results:

1. The identical plume composition at the NEC and central summit craters on 2 May indicates that a single magma body was degassing through these craters, via a branched conduit system. The depth and geometry of this branched system must have been such as to preserve the same final gas composition at individual craters, as discussed in more detail below.

2. The remarkable similarity of SO_2/HCl, HCl/HF and SO_2/HF ratios at NEC and central craters (2.9, 3.1, and 8.9, respectively) to those measured in the bulk volcanic plume, indicates that magma degassing through these craters was responsible for the total gas discharge of Etna on that day. This is consistent with visual observations of much weaker gas release from SEC and with the different chemical ratios found at that crater (see below). Note that the individual crater plumes were measured when they were approximately 1 km away from their source, whereas the bulk plume was measured when it was about 7 km away from Etna's summit (based on the geometry at the time of the solar measurement). Wind-speed at 5000 m altitude on 2 May was 35 km hr^{-1}, so the plume travel time between these two distances was approximately 12 min. The similar

Table 3. *Calculation of volatile loss during Mount Etna summit crater degassing on 2 May 2001 (see text).*

Species	Dissolved in undegassed melt (Mg)	Emission rate (Mg day^{-1})	Percentage degassed
SO$_2$	2000	1500*	75% (25% previously)
HCl	560	290	52%
HF	260	52	20%

*COSPEC measurement (Caltabiano *et al.* pers. comm., 2001).

chemical ratios measured with FTIR spectrometry (one spectrum collected every *c.* 6 s) over that interval of plume transport, and at different times in the day, lead us to consider that the chemical composition of the summit crater gas emissions was broadly stable over these time-scales.

3. The NEC and central crater plume emissions on May 2, however, differed from the bulk equilibrium magma degassing composition constrained by melt inclusion data (Fig. 6). While their HCl/HF ratio is compatible with bulk degassing, their lower SO$_2$/HCl and SO$_2$/HF ratios indicate a *c.* 25% relative depletion of SO$_2$ that suggests a preferential loss of less-soluble sulphur from the magma during previous degassing. This interpretation is consistent with the low bulk SO$_2$ plume flux measured with COSPEC on that day (1500 Mg d^{-1}) and during early May 2001 (between 1100 and 2400 Mg d^{-1} from 2 May to 11 May; Caltabiano *et al.* pers. comm., 2001), compared to the average output of *c.* 5000 Mg d^{-1} typical for time-averaged Etnean activity (Allard *et al.* 1991; Caltabiano *et al.* 1994; Bruno *et al.* 1999, 2001; Allard 1997). It is also consistent with observations of descent of the top of the lava column and of collapses in the conduit of Bocca Nuova central crater at that time.

4. Taking account of this 25% depletion in sulphur, the amount of degassing *melt* required to produce 1500 Mg of SO$_2$ on 2 May was *c.* 0.29 Tg or 1.1×10^5 m^3 (density = 2650 kg/m^3). Combining the SO$_2$ flux with our bulk plume spectroscopic measurements indicates corresponding HCl and HF fluxes of 290 Mg d^{-1} and 52 Mg d^{-1}, respectively. Scaling these fluxes to the above quantity of S-degassing melt suggests Cl and F degassed mass

fractions of 50% and 20%, respectively, of the original Cl and F concentrations in undegassed Etna basalt (0.185 and 0.085 wt%). These mass proportions of HCl and HF lost from the melt are similar to those for bulk degassing indicated by melt inclusion studies. Hence, we conclude that gas emissions at NEC and central summit craters on 2 May were being sustained by bulk equilibrium degassing of a body of magma that had previously lost 25% of its original sulphur but little of its Cl and F content.

5. The quite similar HCl/HF ratio (3.3) but lower SO$_2$/HCl (1.5) and SO$_2$/HF (4.9) ratios measured in the gas plume from the SEC imply a *c.* 50% reduction in SO$_2$ with respect to central crater emissions and a *c.* 65% SO$_2$ loss with respect to the bulk magma degassing composition (Fig. 6). Such a trend is compatible with fractional degassing of the same magma feeding the central craters. Lava flows from SEC in this period contained significantly more thorium (8 ppm) than recent lava from Bocca Nuova (7.5 ppm; J.-L Joron, unpublished data, 2002), suggesting about 5% more crystal fractionation of the melt filling the SEC conduit. This suggests that emissions from the SEC were sustained by restricted degassing of a slightly more evolved melt that had previously lost about two-thirds of its original sulphur via the central conduit.

6. The still lower SO$_2$/HCl (0.87) and SO$_2$/HF (2.51) ratios measured in gases emitted by the lava flow outpouring from the flank of the SEC demonstrate a further 50% reduction of SO$_2$ during late stage (residual) melt degassing at the surface (Fig. 6). This means that SO$_2$ was still more extensively released from the melt than both HCl and HF within the uppermost part (≤150 m) of the SEC conduit, in agreement with its much lower solubility also at low pressure (e.g. Métrich *et al.* 1993). The remarkably stable HCl/HF ratio (3.1 ± 0.12) for the central summit craters, SEC, and the SEC lava flow suggests that HCl and HF solubility and diffusion behaviour are invariant with respect to pressure in conditions of quiescent volcanic activity (slow magma rise). This suggests that this ratio may be a good indicator for non-equilibrium degassing (faster bubble rise). The similarity of this ratio to the bulk magma degassing ratio derived from melt inclusions indicates an equilibrium bulk release of Cl and F, with Cl being two to three times more volatile (or insoluble) than F.

7. Our results for the bulk plume on 28 July 2001, during a major flank eruption, show a slightly higher SO$_2$/HCl ratio (3.2) but lower

SO_2/HF (6.9) and HCl/HF (2.1) ratios, compared with those on 2 May. The bulk SO_2 plume flux on that day (7245 Mg d^{-1}) was also much higher than on 2 May, and even than the typical mean emission rate for Etna. Although the plumes from individual craters could not be distinguished, we interpret these slightly different values as reflecting (i) a more dynamic, closer-to-bulk degassing stage at the summit craters and (ii) an important contribution to the plume of gas emissions with SO_2/HCl ratio of 3.5 that were occurring from a new eruptive vent at 2550 m elevation (Allard *et al.* 2001*a*, *b*). In contrast, our measurements for the hornito within Valle del Leone on 25 July show a remarkable similarity with those made on the lava flow from SEC on 2 May. They demonstrate, again, a residual degassing stage of the lava that was issuing through this lateral vent.

The above observations provide insights into the upper conduit system of Etna. There is compelling evidence that Mount Etna has a main central conduit extending over the whole thickness of the volcanic pile (*c.*2–2.5 km above the crustal basement), whose branching at different depths feeds the separate summit craters (e.g. Chester *et al.* 1985). The Voragine and Bocca Nuova craters stand directly on top of this central conduit. The Voragine is a 250-m wide cylindrical pit whose depth varies widely over time, from a few tens of m up to as much as 1 km (Tazieff 1973). It can thus store abundant magma at high level (Wadge 1977). Both the Voragine and Bocca Nuova are the main sources of the high sulphur discharge of Mount Etna. The average 'excess' rate of this discharge with respect to the amount of erupted lava requires that bubble–melt separation and also convective magma overturn must occur within the central conduit (Allard 1997), whose diameter may be on the order of 50 m (Rymer *et al.* 1995). The NEC, which began forming in 1911 on the NE slope of Etna's summit cone, probably has a shorter and narrower conduit, but can also release abundant gas and sometimes contains magma well above the magma level in the Voragine. Finally, the SEC, which formed in 1968 at 2950 m elevation on the SE flank of the summit cone, has long behaved as a secondary vent of the Bocca Nuova, and may have a still shorter and narrower conduit whose branching is poorly known and may have changed over time.

The identical plume composition at NEC and the two central craters on 2 May 2001 implies that the NEC branching had no impact on the final composition of gas emissions. There are three possible explanations for this observation:

1. the branching was above the magma column head;
2. magma filled both the main conduit and the NEC branch, but the branching occurred above the level of final chemical equilibrium of the bubbles, in particular, well above the initial saturation depth of both HCl and HF in order to maintain a constant HCl/HF ratio; or
3. the branched conduit of NEC is deep and wide enough to permit gas bubble flow and magma convection in conditions comparable to those in the central conduit. The first two cases would imply a shallow (<1 km) to very shallow (only a few hundred metres) branching for the NEC, whereas the third hypothesis implies a depth probably greater than about 2 km below the summit of Etna. We do not presently have sufficient information to distinguish between these possibilities but note that a shallow rather than deep branch for NEC (at that time at least) provides a simpler explanation.

Both the low SO_2/HCl ratio measured in the gases from the SEC, and the slightly higher thorium content of the lava flows, indicate that the magma rising through the conduit of this crater was slightly more evolved but 50% poorer in sulphur than the magma filling the central conduit. This observation implies a branching from the central conduit at a depth where 50% of sulphur had already exsolved (*c.*2 km depth below the summit), but whose geometry inhibits gas bubble flow and/or convective magma replenishment. The long-lasting (3 months) but declining lava flow effused from the SEC at the time of measurement is compatible with gradual volatile depletion and crystallization of a magma batch of limited volume, relatively (or temporarily) isolated from the central conduit system. A depth of about 2 km for this magma batch is also consistent with inferences from seismic tremor and volcanological data registered during lava-fountaining activity at the SEC in 2000.

Finally, measurements on the hornito within the Valle del Leone on 25 July 2001 are consistent with branching at very shallow depth and a geometry that favours separation of deep gas bubbles. The altitude of the hornito, 2650 m, suggests that this flow may have been gravity-driven by a downward-angled branch from either the central conduit system or, more likely, the SEC feeding conduit.

Conclusions

The combination of FTIR spectroscopic measurements of gas emissions from various active vents on Mount Etna with knowledge of the solubility behaviour of SO_2 and halogen species in Etna magma provides important insights into the dynamics of magma degassing within the feeding system of this volcano. We have found that, during the measurement period, the Northeast and Central Craters of Mount Etna were supplied by a central conduit branched at a depth that was either sufficiently deep (>2 km) or, more likely, sufficiently shallow (<<1 km) to feed each crater with gas of identical composition. The Southeast Crater emissions demonstrate that SO_2 had been lost from a slightly more evolved melt rising through a branch from the central conduit that may extend down to approximately 2 km depth but prevents continuous magma replenishment and gas bubbles entering. The lava flow from the Southeast Crater in May 2001, and the gases from the Valle del Leone hornito in July 2001, had lost most of their SO_2, and provide an excellent demonstration of the fractionation effect due to the lower solubility of sulphur than halogens in the melt. On the contrary, the remarkably similar HCl/HF ratios observed at lava flows and all summit craters show that HCl and HF maintain a parallel solubility behaviour during low-pressure, bulk equilibrium degassing. Therefore, changes in HCl/HF ratio may be a sensitive indicator of disequilibrium degassing.

The approach presented here could be applied to other volcanoes that have more than one active vent. Further constraints could be placed on the depth and geometry of branching within the feeding system of Mount Etna if both the flux of gas from each crater could be routinely measured, and with an improved understanding of the solubility-pressure profiles of SO_2, HCl, and HF. Laboratory simulations of gas/magma separation and convection in branching conduits could also prove instructive.

We thank our colleagues in INGV-Catania for assistance in the field and logistical support, as well as useful discussions. We also thank N. Métrich and her colleagues in the Laboratoire Pierre Süe for providing melt inclusion data. We are grateful to D. Pyle, H. Keppler, and S. Sparks, whose reviews of the original manuscript helped to improve the paper. M. Neri kindly provided a map of the summit craters and flows. Finally, we wish to dedicate this paper to the memory of Peter Francis, an inspirational volcanologist, teacher, and friend.

References

AIUPPA, A., ALLARD, P., D'ALESSANDRO, W., MICHEL, A., PARELLO, F., TREUIL, M. & VALENZA, M. 2000. Mobility and fluxes of major, minor and trace metals during basalt weathering and groundwater transport at Mt. Etna volcano (Sicily). *Geochimica et Cosmochimica Acta*, **64**, 1827–1841

ALLARD, P. 1986.*Géochimie isotopique et origine de l'eau, du carbone et du soufre dans les gaz volcaniques: zones de rift, marges continentales et arcs insulaires*, State Thesis, Paris 7 University.

ALLARD, P. 1997. Endogenous magma degassing and storage at Mount Etna. *Geophysical Research Letters*, **24(17)**, 2219–2222.

ALLARD, P. & MÉTRICH, N. 1999. Dégazages magmatiques et flux volcaniques. Rôle de l'eau. *In: CNFGG Report to IUGG, XXII General Assembly, Birmingham, July 18 to 30*, 103–109.

ALLARD, P., CARBONNELLE, J. *ET AL.* 1991. Eruptive and diffuse emissions of CO_2 from Mount Etna. *Nature*, **351**, 387–391.

ALLARD, P. J., CARBONNELLE, N., MÉTRICH, H., LOYER, P. & ZETTWOOG, P. 1994.Sulphur output and magma degassing budget of Stromboli volcano, *Nature*, **368**, 326–330

ALLARD, P., JEAN-BAPTISTE P., D'ALESSANDRO, W., PARELLO F., PARISI, B. & FLEHOC C., 1997. Mantle-derived helium and carbon in groundwaters and gases of Mount Etna, Italy. *Earth and Planetary Science Letters*, **148**, 501–516.

ALLARD, P., ALPARONE, S. *ET AL.* 2001*a*. Short-term variations in magma dynamics at Mount Etna detected by combined geochemical and geophysical monitoring (August–November 2000). *European Geophysical Society Meeting*, Nice, 25–30 March 2001 (abstract).

ALLARD, P., BRUNO, N. *ET AL.* 2001*b*. Geochemistry of volcanic plume emisions during the July-August 2001 eruption of Mt Etna. *GNV (Gruppo Nazionale di Vulcanologia) Annual Meeting, Roma, Italy, October 8–11* (abstract).

ANDERSON, A. T. 1975. Some basaltic and andesitic gases. *Reviews in Geophysics and Space Physics*, **13**, 37–55.

ANZÀ, S., DONGARRÀ, G., GIAMMANCO, S., GOTTINI, V., HAUSER, S. & VALENZA, M. 1989. Geochimica dei fluidi dell'Etna. Le acque sotterranee. *Mineralogica e Petrographica Acta*, **23**, 231–251.

BRUNO, N., CALTABIANO, T. & ROMANO, T. 1999. SO_2 emissions at Mount Etna with particular reference to the period 1993–1995. *Bulletin of Volcanology*, **60**, 405–411.

BRUNO, N., CALTABIANO, T., GIAMMANCO, S & ROMANO, R. 2001. Degassing of SO_2 and CO_2 at Mount Etna (Sicily) as an indicator of pre-eruptive ascent and shallow emplacement of magma. *Journal of Volcanology and Geothermal Research*, **110**, 137–153.

BURTON, M. R., OPPENHEIMER, C., HORROCKS, L. A. & FRANCIS, P. W. 2001. Diurnal changes in volcanic plume chemistry observed by lunar and solar occultation spectroscopy. *Geophysical Research Letters*, **28**, 843–846.

CALTABIANO, T., ROMANO, R. & BUDETTA, G. 1994. SO₂ flux measurements at Mount Etna, Sicily. *Journal of Geophysical Research*, **99(D6)**, 12 809–12 819.

CARROLL, M. R. & HOLLOWAY, J. R. (eds) 1994. Volatiles in magmas. *Reviews in Mineralogy*, Mineralogical Society of America, **30**.

CHESTER, D. K., DUNCAN, A. M., GUEST, J. E. & KILBURN, C. R. J. 1985. *Mount Etna: the Anatomy of a Volcano.* Chapman and Hall, London, 404 pp.

CLOCCHIATTI, R., JORON, J. L. & TREUIL, M. 1988. The role of selective alkali contamination in the evolution of recent historic lavas of Mt. Etna. *Journal of Volcanology and Geothermal Research*, **34**, 241–249.

CLOCCHIATTI, R., WEISZ, J., MOSBAH, M. & TANGUY, J. C. 1992. Coexistence de 'verres' alcalins et tholèiitiques saturès en CO₂ dans les olivines des hyaloclastities d'Aci Castello (Etna, Sicilie, Italie). Arguments en faveur d'un manteau anormal et d'un reservoir profond. *Acta Vulcanologia*, **2**, 161–173.

DIXON, J. E., CLAGUE, D. A. & STOLPER, E. 1991. Degassing history of water, sulfur, and carbon in submarine lavas from Kilauea Volcano, Hawaii. *Journal of Geology*, **99**, 371–394.

FRANCIS, P. W., OPPENHEIMER, C. & STEVENSON, D. 1993. Endogenous growth of persistently active volcanoes. *Nature*, **366**, 554–557.

FRANCIS, P, BURTON, M. & OPPENHEIMER, C. 1998. Remote measurements of volcanic gas compositions by solar FTIR spectroscopy. *Nature*, **396**, 567–570.

FREZZOTTI, M. L., DEVIVO, B. & CLOCCHIATTI, R.1991. Melt mineral–fluid interactions in ultramafic nodules from alkaline lavas of mount Etna (Sicily, Italy) – melt and fluid inclusion evidence, *Journal of Volcanology and Geothermal Research*, **47**, 209–219.

GAUTHIER, P.-J. & LE CLOAREC, M.-F. 1998.Variability of alkali and heavy metal fluxes released by Mt. Etna volcano, Sicily, between 1991 and 1995. *Earth and Planetary Science Letters*, **81**, 311–326.

GERLACH, T. M. & GRAEBER, E. J. 1985. Volatile budget of Kilauea Volcano. *Nature*, **313**, 273–277.

KAZAHAYA, K., SHINOHARA, H. & SAITO, G. 1994. Excessive degassing at Izu–Oshima volcano: magma convection in a conduit. *Bulletin of Volcanology*, **56**, 207–216.

LAMBERT, G. M., LE CLOAREC, F., ARDOUIN, B. & LE ROULLEY, J. C. 1985/86. Volcanic emissions of radionuclides and magma dynamics, *Earth and Planetary Science Letters*, **76**, 185–192.

MÉTRICH, N. 1990. Chlorine and fluorine in tholeiitic and alkaline lavas of Etna. *Journal of Volcanology and Geothermal Research*, **40**, 133–148.

MÉTRICH, N. & CLOCCHIATTI, R. 1989. Melt inclusion investigation of the volatile behaviour in historic alkaline magmas of Etna, *Bulletin of Volcanology*, **51**, 185–198.

MÉTRICH, N., CLOCCHIATTI, R., MOSBAH, M. & CHAUSSIDON, M. 1993. The 1989–1990 activity of Etna magma mingling and ascent of H₂O–Cl–S-rich basaltic magma. Evidence from melt inclusions. *Journal of Volcanology and Geothermal Research*, **59**, 131–144.

MÉTRICH, N., ALLARD, P. & ANDRONICO, D. 2002. Preliminary constraints on volatile abundances in basalts erupted during the 2001 flank eruptions of Mount Etna. *XVII Assembly European Geophysical Society, Nice, 22–25 April 2002.*

OPPENHEIMER, C., FRANCIS, P. & STIX, J., 1998. Depletion rates of SO₂ in tropospheric volcanic plumes. *Geophysical Research Letters*, **25**, 2671–2674,

PARFITT, E. A. & WILSON, L., 1995.The 1983-86 Pu'u'O'o eruption of Kilauea Volcano, Hawaii: a study of dike geometry and eruption mechanism for a long-lived eruption. *Journal of Volcanology and Geothermal Research*, **59**, 179–205.

RESEARCH STAFF OF INGV CATANIA 2001. Multi-disciplinary approach yields insight into Mt. Etna eruption. *EOS,Transactions of the American Geophysical Union*, **82(52)**, 653–656.

RODGERS, C. D. 1976. Retrieval of atmospheric temperature and composition from remote measurements of thermal radiation, *Reviews in Geophysics and Space Physics*, **14(4)**, 609–624.

ROTHMAN, L. S., RINSLAND, C. P. ET AL. 1998.The HITRAN Molecular Spectroscopic Database and HAWKS (HITRAN Atmospheric Workstation): 1996 Edition, *Journal of Quantitative Spectroscopy and Radiative Transfer*, **60**, 665–710.

RYMER, H., CASSIDY, J., LOCKE, C. A. & MURRAY, J. B. 1995. Magma movement in Etna volcano associated with the major 1991–1993 lava eruption eruption: evidence from gravity and deformation. *Bulletin of Volcanology*, **57**, 451–461.

SPARKS, R. S. J., 1978. The dynamics of bubble formation and growth in magmas, *Journal of Volcanology and Geothermal Research*, **3**, 1–37,

SPARKS, R. S. J. 2003. Dynamics of magma degassing. *In*: OPPENHEIMER, C., PYLE, D. M. & BARCLAY, J. (eds) *Volcanic Degassing.* Geological society, London, Special Publications, **213**, 5–22.

STEVENSON, D. S. & BLAKE, S., 1998. Modelling the dynamics and thermodynamics of volcanic degassing, *Bulletin of Volcanology*, **60**, 307–317.

TAZIEFF, H. 1973. Structural implications of the 1971 Mt. Etna eruption. *Philosophical Transactions of the Royal Society of London, Series A*, **274**, 79–82.

VERGNIOLLE, S. & JAUPART, C., 1986. Separated two-phase flow and basaltic eruptions, *Journal of Geophysical Research*, **91**, 12 842–12 860.

WADGE, G., The storage and release of magma at Mount Etna, 1977. *Journal of Volcanology and Geothermal Research*, **2**, 361–384.

The tropospheric sulphur cycle and the role of volcanic SO$_2$

D. S. STEVENSON[1], C. E. JOHNSON[2], W. J. COLLINS[2],
AND R. G. DERWENT[2]

[1]*Institute for Meteorology, University of Edinburgh, King's Buildings,
Edinburgh, EH9 3JZ, UK.*
[2]*Climate Research, Meteorological Office, London Road,
Bracknell, RG12, 2SZ, UK.*

Abstract: A global three-dimensional chemistry–transport model has been applied to study the tropospheric sulphur cycle, and in particular the volcanic component. The model is in general agreement with previous studies of the global S budget. We find that volcanic emissions constitute 10% of the present-day global SO$_2$ source to the atmosphere, but form 26% of the SO$_2$ burden, and 14% of the sulphate aerosol burden. Two previous modelling studies suggested that the volcanic fraction of sulphate was 18% and 35%, from sources representing 7% and 14%, respectively, of the global total SO$_2$ emission. The results are dependent upon various assumptions about volcanic emissions (magnitude, geographical location, altitude), the global distribution of oxidants, and the physical processes of dry and wet deposition. Because of this dependence upon poorly constrained parameters, it is unclear which modelling study is closest to the truth.

Introduction

Sulphur occurs in Earth's atmosphere as a variety of compounds, in both gaseous and aerosol forms, and has a range of natural and anthropogenic sources. The life-cycles and atmospheric burdens of these compounds are determined by a combination of physical, chemical, and biological processes. Understanding the global S-cycle is important for many reasons. Most sulphur enters the atmosphere as gaseous sulphur dioxide (SO$_2$), a dangerous air pollutant. Sulphur dioxide has a lifetime in the atmosphere of about a day, before being deposited to the surface or oxidized to sulphate (SO$_4$) aerosol. In the gas phase, SO$_2$ oxidation occurs by reaction with hydroxyl radicals (OH), to form sulphuric acid (H$_2$SO$_4$). Sulphuric acid is hygroscopic, and rapidly condenses, either forming new aerosols, or adding to existing ones. Sulphur dioxide gas also partitions into the aqueous phase (in cloud droplets or pre-existing aerosols), where it reacts with dissolved hydrogen peroxide (H$_2$O$_2$) or ozone (O$_3$) to form SO$_4$. Sulphate is a major component of fine aerosol particles (PM$_{10}$ and PM$_{2.5}$: particulate matter less than 10 μm or 2.5 μm in diameter), which can penetrate deep into the lungs, and are harmful to health. Sulphate in precipitation is an important determinant of its acidity; at high levels it causes 'acid rain', which can have devastating effects on sensitive ecosystems. Sulphate aerosols also affect Earth's radiation balance (and hence climate) through the direct scattering of sunlight (Charlson *et al.* 1992), and also indirectly via modification of cloud albedoes (Twomey 1977) and lifetimes (Jones *et al.* 2001), influencing both radiation and the hydrological cycle (Penner *et al.* 2001). These links between atmospheric sulphur, climate, and the environment assume an even greater relevance since global anthropogenic emissions (60–100 Mt(S) year^{-1}) currently account for about 70% of all sulphur emissions, the remainder emanating from oceanic plankton (13–36 Mt(S) year^{-1}), volcanoes (6–20 Mt(S) year^{-1}), biomass burning (1–6 Mt(S) year^{-1}), and land biota and soils (0.4–5.6 Mt(S) year^{-1}) (Penner *et al.* 2001). On a regional scale, and in particular over NE America, Europe, and SE Asia, the anthropogenic fraction is much higher.

Spatial and temporal variations in the local lifetimes of sulphur compounds in the atmosphere mean that atmospheric concentrations do not necessarily linearly relate to emissions. To link concentrations to emissions, complex atmospheric models are required; the first such modelling study was carried out by Langner and Rodhe (1991). These models allow simulation of the global S-cycle through the synthesis of emissions, transport, chemistry, and deposition

From: OPPENHEIMER, C., PYLE, D.M. & BARCLAY, J. (eds) *Volcanic Degassing.* Geological Society, London, Special Publications, **213**, 295–305. 0305-8719/03/$15.00

processes (see Rodhe (1999) for a historical review).

This chapter briefly reviews global model estimates of the major components in the tropospheric S-cycle. New model results are then presented, with a particular focus on the volcanic fraction of the S-cycle. Results are compared with similar studies carried out by Chin and Jacob (1996) and Graf *et al.* (1997), which indicated that volcanic sulphur formed sulphate at a much higher efficiency as compared with other sources, because the emissions are at a higher altitude, where lifetimes are longer. Clearly, it is important to understand the behaviour of natural sulphur compounds so that we can assess the anthropogenic impact on the atmospheric S-cycle.

Recent model estimates of the atmospheric S-cycle

There have been several recent detailed reviews of the global sulphur cycle (Rodhe 1999; Penner *et al.* 2001), compiling results from a series of

studies over the last decade (Langner & Rodhe 1991; Pham *et al.* 1995; Chin *et al.* 1996; Chin & Jacob 1996; Feichter *et al.* 1996; Chuang *et al.* 1997; Graf *et al.* 1997; Restad *et al.* 1998; Roelofs *et al.* 1998; Kjellström 1998; Adams *et al.* 1999; Koch *et al.* 1999; Lohmann *et al.* 1999; Barth *et al.* 2000; Chin *et al.* 2000; Rasch *et al.* 2000). Figure 1 illustrates the main features of the tropospheric sulphur cycle, and indicates fluxes, burdens, and lifetimes, for both this study, and the average results of 11 models, as reported by the Intergovernmental Panel on Climate Change (IPCC) in their latest report (Penner *et al.* 2001).

Anthropogenic sulphur is almost exclusively emitted as SO_2 and is associated with fossil-fuel use and industry (Benkovitz *et al.* 1996). Over the last decade or so, SO_2 emissions have fallen in Europe (NEGTAP 2001), and to a lesser extent in North America (EPA 2001), through efforts to reduce acid rain, but have increased in parts of the developing world (e.g. SE Asia). These recent changes partially explain the spread in global totals of anthropogenic emissions used in global models. Similar emissions trends are expected

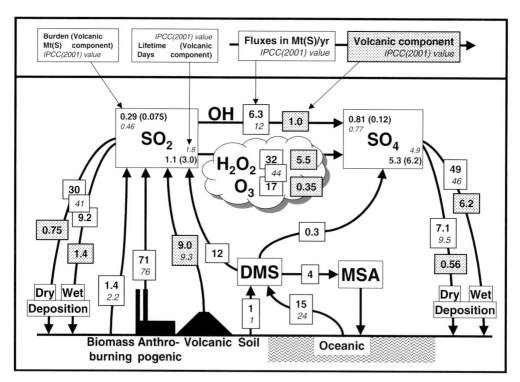

Fig. 1. The global atmospheric sulphur budget, for 1990 emissions. The numbers in bold refer to results from the STOCHEM-Ed model used in this study. Numbers in the shaded boxes refer to the volcanic component. Numbers in italics are from the IPCC Third Assessment Report (Penner *et al.* 2001). Fluxes are in Mt (S) year^{-1}, burdens in Mt (S), and lifetimes in days. Sulphate in sea-salt aerosol, and fluxes from minor sulphur compounds (e.g. OCS, CS_2), are not considered in this study.

over the first part of this century, but by 2100, global anthropogenic S emissions are predicted to be 20–60 Mt(S) year[-1], below present-day levels (Nakićenović *et al.* 2000). Biomass burning emissions of SO_2 (Spiro *et al.* 1992) are partly natural and partly anthropogenic, but are relatively small compared with the other sources of sulphur.

Lovelock *et al.* (1972) discovered that oceanic phytoplankton were a major source of dimethyl sulphide (DMS: $(CH_3)_2S$), and Charlson *et al.* (1987) suggested a possible biosphere–climate feedback, via the influence of sulphate on clouds, the Earth's radiation budget, ocean temperatures, and plankton productivity. In the context of current global-warming predictions for the next 100 years, oceanic DMS emission projections show relatively minor changes (Kettle *et al.* 1999; Penner *et al.* 2001). DMS is oxidized in the atmosphere by OH and nitrate (NO_3) radicals, mainly to SO_2, but with a significant fraction (*c.* 25% in the model used in this study) forming methane–sulphonic acid (MSA), and a small fraction (<2%) forming SO_4 directly.

The main other sources of S are volcanoes, which emit both SO_2 and hydrogen sulphide (H_2S), which rapidly oxidizes to SO_2 in the atmosphere. Andres and Kasgnoc (1998) estimated, based on volcanic gas measurements over the last 30 years, a global mean S flux of 9.3 Mt(S) year[-1] for these two gases. This flux varies in time and space, and is made up of contributions from continuously degassing volcanoes (e.g. Etna, Italy), sporadically erupting volcanoes (e.g. Popocatépetl, Mexico), and major individual explosive events (e.g. Pinatubo, Philippines). Large explosive events, like the Mount Pinatubo eruption in 1991, will add most S directly to the stratosphere, where it will oxidize to sulphuric acid aerosol, and then slowly settle into the troposphere over the years following the eruption. These large individual events cannot sensibly be studied in a time-averaged sense, but require case-study investigations. This study focuses instead on the 'background' volcanic component, introduced by continuously and sporadically active volcanoes, which generally emit their S into the free troposphere (i.e. above the boundary layer), and sometimes explosively lofting S to levels throughout the troposphere (i.e. altitudes up to *c.* 10–15 km). Estimates of the volcanic S source strength vary widely, and modellers have used values as low as 2.9 Mt(S) year[-1] (Pham *et al.* 1995) to as high as 14 Mt(S) year[-1] (Graf *et al.* 1997). The source strength, geographical location, and vertical spread of emissions will all influence their fate and overall contribution to the global S-cycle.

Two other sources of sulphur are carbonyl sulphide (OCS) and carbon disulphide (CS_2), both with minor oceanic and biomass burning sources (Andreae & Crutzen 1997; Kjellström 1998), and possibly volcanic sources of similar magnitude (Andres and Kasgnoc 1998). Carbon disulphide has a lifetime of about a week, oxidizing to OCS and SO_2. Carbonyl sulphide has a relatively long lifetime (nine years), and is consequently well mixed throughout the atmosphere. In the absence of large explosive volcanic eruptions, OCS is the main source of stratospheric sulphate aerosol, where its slow oxidation generates a constant small flux (*c.* 0.1 Mt(S) year[-1]) of SO_2 and H_2SO_4. Sea-spray is also a major source (40–320 Mt(S) year[-1]) of sulphate aerosol to the marine boundary layer (Berresheim *et al.* 1995). This study, in common with most others, neglects the contributions of OCS and CS_2, and only considers the non-sea-salt sulphate (nss-SO_4) part of the S-cycle.

Figure 1 indicates that about 60% of SO_2 is oxidized to SO_4 rather than being deposited to the surface as SO_2. Most oxidation occurs in the aqueous-phase, and the main oxidant is H_2O_2. Sulphate aerosol has a typical atmospheric lifetime of around five days before it is deposited to the surface, mainly through wet deposition.

STOCHEM-Ed model

STOCHEM-Ed is a global three-dimensional Lagrangian chemistry–transport model (CTM), developed initially at the UK Meteorological Office (Collins *et al.* 1997, 1999, 2000), and latterly at the University of Edinburgh. The main difference between the model version used here and those previously described is an increased vertical resolution in both the driving GCM (General Circulation Model), and the CTM, particularly at tropopause levels. The meteorological input to this version of the model is generated on-line by HadAM3, an atmosphere-only version of the Unified Model GCM (Johns *et al.* 1997). The GCM has a resolution of 3.75° longitude by 2.5° latitude, with 58 vertical levels, and supplies fields every three hours to STOCHEM-Ed (Johnson *et al.* 2001). The CTM atmosphere is divided into 50 000 equal-mass air parcels, which are advected using a fourth-order Runge–Kutta scheme, with interpolated winds, and an hourly time-step. For the purposes of mixing and model output, the Lagrangian air parcels are mapped to a grid of resolution 5° by 5°, with 22 vertical levels; this grid is also used for adding emissions to the model. Boundary-layer and convection parameterizations are included, and these have been tuned using [222]Rn observations (Stevenson *et al.* 1998). Winds used by the CTM are interpolated from the GCM grid to each air parcel location, using linear interpolation in the horizontal and cubic in the vertical. Other meteorological variables (e.g. cloud distributions) are kept fixed over the three-hour chemistry model time-step. The transport scheme is fully mass conservative, and has been compared with observations of both long-lived and short-lived tracers (Collins *et al.* 1998; Stevenson et al. 1998). Within each air parcel, the chemistry of 70 compounds is simulated, including the oxidation of methane (CH_4), carbon monoxide (CO), several non-methane hydrocarbons, and the fast photochemistry of the nitrogen oxides (NO_x: the sum of NO and NO_2), O_3, and several related oxidants and free radical species. Several previous model validation studies and model intercomparisons have assessed the model's performance for species such as NO_x, OH, HO_2, CO, and O_3 (Collins *et al.* 1999; Kanakidou *et al.* 1999a, b). The chemical mechanism also has a detailed description of several sulphur compounds, including DMS oxidation (Jenkin *et al.* 1996), and aqueous-phase chemistry. The reactions involving sulphur compounds (excluding DMS) are given in Table 1. Further details of the secondary aerosol (including sulphate) simulated by the model are presented by Derwent *et al.* (2003).

In the boundary layer, several species, including SO_2 and sulphate, are dry deposited. The model discriminates between land, ocean, and ice, and uses deposition velocities for SO_2 of 6, 8, and 0.5 mm/s over these surfaces, and values of 2, 1, and 0.05 mm/s for sulphate aerosol. The model calculates deposition rates using these velocities, together with the boundary layer height, and an effective vertical eddy diffusion coefficient derived from the surface stresses, heat flux and temperature.

Soluble species (including SO_2, sulphate, NH_3, and H_2O_2) are subject to wet removal through precipitation scavenging. Species-dependent scavenging rates are taken from Penner *et al.* (1994), and vary between large-scale and convective precipitation. Wet removal from large-scale precipitation only occurs below *c.*400 hPa (*c.*6 km), whereas it initiates in convective clouds when the precipitation rate exceeds 10^{-8} kg/m² s⁻¹. A simple scavenging profile in convective clouds is used, with a constant rate from the surface to *c.*850 hPa (*c.*1.5 km), and then a linear decrease to zero at the cloud top. Because most convection of large vertical extent occurs in the tropics, very little wet removal occurs above 400 hPa in the extra-tropics.

Table 1. *Main sulphur chemistry included in the model (excluding DMS reactions). T is temperature (K); $T^* = (1/T) - (1/298)$; [M] is the molecular density of air (molecules cm⁻³); [H⁺] is the hydrogen ion concentration (mol l⁻¹).*

Gas-phase reactions	Rate constant[1]
$SO_2 + OH + M \rightarrow$ $H_2SO_4 + HO_2$	Complex[5]: A6(A3)$^{(1/A7)}$

Species	Henry's Law Coefficients[2]
SO_2	1.23×10^0 exp(3120 T^*)
O_3	1.1×10^{-2} exp(2300 T^*)
HNO_3	3.3×10^6 exp(8700 T^*)
H_2O_2	7.36×10^4 exp(6621 T^*)
NH_3	7.5×10^1 exp(3400 T^*)
CO_2	3.4×10^{-2} exp(2420 T^*)

Aqueous-phase equilibria	Equilibrium constants[3]
$SO_2 + H_2O \rightleftharpoons H^+ + HSO_3^-$	1.7×10^{-2} exp(2090 T^*)
$HSO_3^- \rightleftharpoons H^+ + SO_3^{2-}$	6.0×10^{-8} exp(1120 T^*)
$HNO_3 \rightleftharpoons H^+ + NO_3^-$	1.8×10^{-5} exp(−450 T^*)
$NH_3 + H_2O \rightleftharpoons NH_4^+ + OH^-$	1.8×10^{-5} exp(−450 T^*)
$CO_2 + H_2O \rightleftharpoons H^+ + HCO_3^-$	4.3×10^{-7} exp(−913 T^*)
$H_2O \rightleftharpoons H^+ + OH^-$	1.0×10^{-14} exp(−6716 T^*)

Aqueous-phase reactions	Rate constants[4]
$HSO_3^- + H_2O_2 \rightarrow$ $H^+ + SO_4^{2-} + H_2O$	$([H^+]/([H^+]+0.1))$ 5.2 × 10^6 exp(−3650 T^*)
$HSO_3^- + O_3 \rightarrow$ $H^+ + SO_4^{2-} + O_2$	4.2×10^5 exp(−4131 T^*)
$SO_3^{2-} + O_3 \rightarrow SO_4^{2-} + O_2$	1.5×10^9 exp(−996 T^*)

[1]Units: (cm³ molecule⁻¹)$^{(\text{no. of reactants} -1)}$ s⁻¹
[2]Units: mol l⁻¹ atm⁻¹
[3]Units: (mol l⁻¹)$^{(\text{no. of products} - \text{no. of reactants})}$
[4]Units: mol l⁻¹ s⁻¹
[5]A1 = $[M]3.0 \times 10^{-31}(T/300)^{-3.3}$; A2 = 1.5×10^{-12}; A3 = 0.6; A4 = $0.75 - 1.27 \times \log_{10}A3$; A5 = A1/A2; A6 = A1/(1+A5); A7 = $1 + (\log_{10}A5/A4)^2$

The S emissions used are similar to those listed in Penner *et al.* (2001). Anthropogenic (71 Mt(S) year⁻¹) and biomass burning (1.4 Mt(S) year⁻¹) emissions of SO_2 are taken from the EDGAR v2.0 database (Olivier *et al.* 1996), representative of the year 1990. Biomass burning emissions are then distributed using the monthly maps of Cooke and Wilson (1996). Monthly varying emissions of DMS from oceans (15 Mt(S) year⁻¹) and soils (1 Mt(S) year⁻¹) are also included (Bates *et al.* 1992). Volcanic emissions of SO_2 total 9.0 Mt(S) year⁻¹, based upon emissions magnitudes and distribution estimated for 1980 by Spiro *et al.* (1992). These data show peaks associated with the Mount St. Helens (USA) eruption of 1980, and the continuously high SO_2 output of Mount Etna (Sicily). More recent estimates of volcanic emissions (Andres & Kasgnoc 1998) are of similar total magnitude, but vary somewhat in spatial distribution, due to the considerable fluctuations in gas output of specific volcanoes, depending on their state of activity. To simulate the vertical spread of volcanic emissions in the model, they are distributed evenly from the surface up to $c.300$ hPa ($c.8$ km). Note that 'the surface' does not equate with sea-level, as the GCM has orography, albeit at a resolution that will tend to flatten most volcanic peaks. This assumption of an even vertical distribution of volcanic emissions represents a 'best guess' of where volcanic emissions effectively enter the atmosphere. Most previous estimates of the global magnitude and geographic distributions of volcanic emissions (e.g. Andres & Kasgnoc 1998; Graf *et al.* 1997) have not suggested vertical profiles. One exception is Chin *et al.* (2000), who use a more sophisticated methodology for incorporating volcanic emissions. These authors emit volcanic SO_2 from continuously active volcanoes (Andres & Kasgnoc 1998) at altitudes within 1 km above the crater altitude. For sporadically active volcanoes they use the actual eruption dates and duration of individual eruptions, and the volcanic explosivity index (VEI) to estimate the volcanic cloud height (Simkin & Siebert 1994). They estimate the amount of SO_2 emitted by an individual eruption, using a relationship between VEI and SO_2 flux (Schnetzler *et al.* 1997), or satellite measurements of SO_2 amount from the Total Ozone Mapping Spectrometer (TOMS: Bluth *et al.* 1997). Finally, the SO_2 is released from the top one-third of the volcanic cloud.

Many volcanoes passively degas SO_2 from their summits and flanks. Others emit most SO_2 during sporadic explosive eruptions of varying magnitude that will loft the gas to various heights. The inherent variability in the magnitude and location of volcanic emissions means that calculations of the 'volcanic component' of the S-cycle inevitably have a high uncertainty. Further research is required to better characterize the vertical profiles of volcanic emissions to the atmosphere, and it should be noted that this represents perhaps the largest uncertainty in modelling the fate of volcanic SO_2.

Results and discussion

Two simulations have been carried using the model: one for present-day conditions, including volcanic emissions, and a second with volcanic emissions switched off. Each simulation was 16 months in length, starting in September, with the first four months considered as spin-up and not used in the analysis. All other factors (meteorology, non-volcanic emissions) were kept fixed between the two runs. The only differences between the two runs relate to the difference in volcanic SO_2, and any effects that this has on the chemistry. The simulation with no volcanic SO_2 will have slightly different oxidant (OH and H_2O_2) concentrations; however, these species are mainly determined by the background photochemistry, and sulphur has a minor impact upon them. Even very large volcanic perturbations, such as the 1783 Laki eruption, have been shown to have relatively small effects on oxidants (Stevenson *et al.* 2003).

Monthly mean concentrations and integrated reaction and deposition fluxes were calculated on the model's three-dimensional output grid. Annual and global average fluxes, burdens, and lifetimes of the main components of the S-cycle are shown in Figure 1, and annual and zonal (longitudinal) average concentrations and lifetimes for SO_2 and sulphate are shown in Figures 2 and 3. Lifetimes are defined as the burden divided by the total loss rate, either globally integrated (Fig. 1), or locally (Figs 2 & 3).

It is beyond the scope of this paper to present a comparison of modelled and observed SO_2 and sulphate concentrations. Stevenson *et al.* (2003) presented a limited comparison for the model at a few sites, and concluded that the model simulated the correct magnitudes for SO_2 and sulphate, and successfully captured the seasonal cycles of these species in Europe. Derwent *et al.* (2003) present a more comprehensive validation of the model's sulphate aerosol fields with global observations, and conclude that the model is performing well.

In general, the model's S-cycle is quite similar to the IPCC average values, and is within the range of all other models for each category. The flux of SO_2 gas-phase oxidation is a little on the low side, and this version of the model is known to have slightly low OH concentrations, so the ratio of gas-phase to aqueous-phase oxidation may be underestimated. The DMS source is also lower than the IPCC average (but well within the range of uncertainty associated with this source), and the detailed DMS oxidation scheme employed also results in less of the DMS ending up as SO_2 (several models assume that all DMS is oxidized to SO_2). The volcanic source is close to the IPCC average, although less than the study of Graf *et al.* (1997), who used a value 56% higher. The burden of SO_2 (0.29 Mt(S)) is 37% lower than the IPCC average, and the SO_2 lifetime (1.1 days) is similarly 39% lower, despite the similar magnitude of total S sources, indicating that the SO_2 sink processes must operate

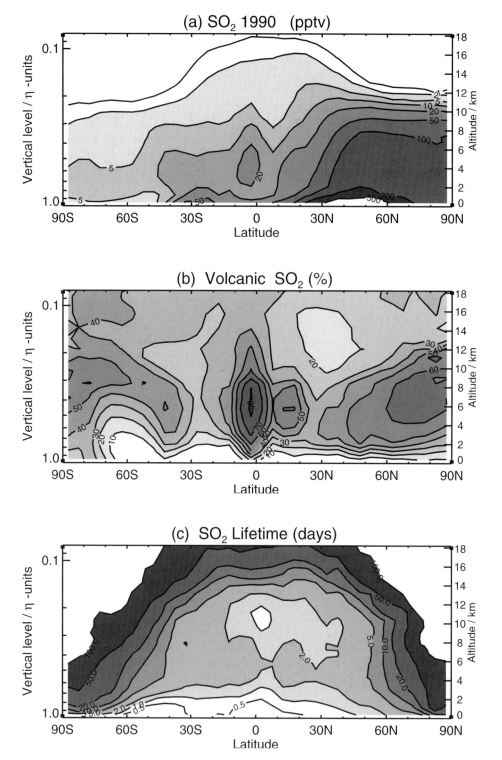

Fig. 2. Zonal annual mean (latitude against altitude) results from the model: (**a**) 1990 SO$_2$ (pptv); (**b**) volcanic fraction (%); (**c**) SO$_2$ lifetime (days).

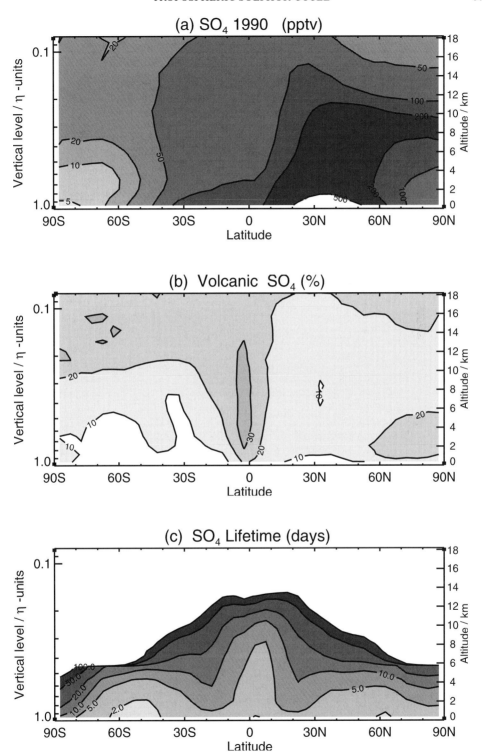

Fig. 3. Zonal annual mean (latitude against altitude) results from the model: (**a**) 1990 SO₄ (pptv); (**b**) volcanic fraction (%); (**c**) SO₄ lifetime (days).

more efficiently in the STOCHEM-Ed model. The SO_4 burden (0.81 Mt(S)) is 5% higher than the IPCC average, and the lifetime (5.3 days) is 8% longer, indicating that SO_4 removal is slightly less efficient than the average of other models.

Figure 2a shows the zonal (averaged around all longitudes) annual mean distribution of SO_2 simulated by the model, clearly showing highest concentrations in the polluted Northern Hemisphere (NH), particularly in mid-latitudes near the surface, close to the main industrial source regions. Due to the short lifetime of SO_2 (Fig. 2c), the remote troposphere has relatively low concentrations, except for regions with significant natural sources. Very little SO_2 reaches the stratosphere, but note that the model lacks sources from OCS or large explosive volcanic eruptions. Figure 3a shows the corresponding SO_4 distribution. Sulphate has a longer lifetime, particularly in the upper atmosphere (Fig. 3c), where the lack of clouds means that the only removal mechanism is transport to the lower atmosphere.

A further simulation of the present-day atmosphere, where volcanic emissions are switched off, allows the volcanic component to be isolated. The annual global fluxes, burdens, and lifetimes of the volcanic component are also shown in Figure 1. The volcanic component of the SO_2 distribution (Fig. 2b) shows that volcanic SO_2 dominates large regions of the free troposphere, particularly in the tropics (Indonesia and Central America), but also in the Northern Hemisphere (NH) (North America, Japan, Kamchatka) and Antarctica (Erebus). Clearly, it is the NH volcanic emissions, into a region with relatively long lifetime (Figs 2b, c) that result in the long lifetime of the volcanic component. These results are highly dependent upon the geographical distribution of volcanic emissions. Because volcanic emissions are added to the atmosphere at higher altitudes than other S sources, they are less likely to be deposited to the surface as SO_2, and more likely to be oxidized to SO_4. Oxidant concentrations generally decrease with increasing height (and latitude) through the troposphere, largely because their main precursor is H_2O, which rapidly decreases in concentration as temperatures fall. This results in longer SO_2 lifetimes at higher altitudes and latitudes (Fig. 2c), and hence the volcanic fraction of the SO_2 budget has a much longer lifetime (3.0 days), and makes a contribution to the total SO_2 burden of 26%, despite only making up 10% of the source. These results are similar to those of Graf *et al.* (1997), who found that volcanic S accounted for 35% of the SO_2 burden, from 14% of the total source.

Graf *et al.* (1997) found a similar contribution (36%) of volcanic S to the global SO_4 burden, but we find the fraction to be only 14% (Figure 3b shows the distribution), only slightly higher than the emission component. Chin and Jacob (1996) found a global volcanic sulphate burden fraction of 18%, from a source of only 7%. The results presented here can be understood if we examine the fluxes in some detail (Fig. 1). Despite making up 26% of the SO_2 burden, volcanic S only makes up 12% of the total SO_2 to SO_4 flux. This is largely due to the fact that the volcanic SO_2 has a longer lifetime, and oxidizes more slowly than SO_2 at lower altitudes. The other controls on the volcanic fraction of the SO_4 burden are the SO_4 loss mechanisms, the main one being wet deposition. Modelled local SO_4 lifetimes lengthen with increasing altitude, and are essentially infinite above cloud top heights, but also show distinct maxima at latitudes of 15–20°, in the relatively cloud-free descending limbs of the Hadley Cells (Fig. 3c). Hence both the latitude and altitude of volcanic emissions are important. We find that volcanic SO_4 has a lifetime of 6.2 days, slightly (17%) longer than average SO_4 (5.3 days). Wet deposition schemes in global models are quite poorly constrained and variable (e.g. Roelofs *et al.* 2001; Penner *et al.* 2001), and this is a major source of uncertainty in modelling S budgets.

Graf *et al.* (1997) defined the 'efficiency' of a S source as the fractional contribution to the SO_4 burden divided by the fractional source strength, and found a value of 2.6 for volcanic S, compared with 0.74 for non-volcanic sources. Chin and Jacob (1996) found similar values of 2.6 and 0.85, respectively. In this study we find a less marked difference: 1.4 for volcanic S, and 0.96 for non-volcanic sources.

Conclusions

We have simulated the tropospheric S-cycle, and isolated the volcanic component, using a three-dimensional global chemistry–transport model. Modelled global S budgets are broadly in line with those reported by the IPCC (Penner *et al.* 2001). Results indicate that despite making up only 10% of the SO_2 source in the model, volcanic S makes up 26% of the SO_2 burden, and 14% of the SO_4 burden. The relatively large contribution of volcanic S to the SO_2 burden is due to the longer SO_2 lifetime at higher altitudes and latitudes, through reduced losses from deposition and oxidation. The lower contribution of volcanic S to the SO_4 burden (compared with the SO_2 burden) stems from the slower oxidation rates of SO_2 that limit the source of

SO₄, and also the less variable lifetime of SO_4 with latitude (Fig. 3c). The results for SO_2 are similar to those found by Graf *et al.* (1997), but these authors, together with Chin and Jacob (1996), also found that the large volcanic contribution was carried forward to SO_4, in contrast to the results presented here. The volcanic contribution to the global budget is clearly influenced by several factors, including: (1) the magnitude and location of volcanic emissions; (2) the assumed altitude profile of the emissions; (3) the distributions of oxidants; and (4) the deposition schemes employed by models. All of these require careful consideration if we are to further constrain the global S budget and its volcanic component.

References

ADAMS, P. J., SEINFELD, J. H. & KOCH, D. M. 1999. Global concentrations of tropospheric sulfate, nitrate, and ammonium aerosol simulated in a general circulation model. *Journal of Geophysical Research*, **104(D11)**, 13 791–13 823.

ANDREAE, M. O. & CRUTZEN, P. J. 1997. Atmospheric aerosols: biogeochemical sources and role in atmospheric chemistry. *Science*, **276**, 1052–1058.

ANDRES, R. J. & KASGNOC, A. D. 1998. A time-averaged inventory of sub-aerial volcanic sulphur emissions. *Journal of Geophysical Research*, **103**, 25 251–25 261.

BARTH, M. C., RASCH, P. J., KIEHL, J. T., BENKOWITZ, C. M. & SCHWARTZ, S. E. 2000. Sulfur chemistry in the National Center for Atmospheric Research Community Climate Model: description, evaluation, features, and sensitivity to aqueous chemistry. *Journal of Geophysical Research*, **105(D1)**, 1387–1415.

BATES, T. S., LAMB, B. K. GUENTHER, A., DIGNON, J. & STOIBER, R. E. 1992. Sulfur emissions to the atmosphere from natural sources. *Journal of Atmospheric Chemistry*, **14**, 315–337.

BENKOWITZ, C. M., SCHOLTZ, M. T. ET AL. 1996. Global gridded inventories of anthropogenic emissions of sulfur and nitrogen. *Journal of Geophysical Research*, **101**, 29 239–29 253.

BERRESHEIM, H., WINE, P. H. & DAVIS, D.D. 1995. Sulfur in the atmosphere. In: SINGH, H. B. (ed.). *Composition, Chemistry, and Climate of the Atmosphere*, Van Nostrand Reinhold, New York, 251–307.

BLUTH, G. J. S., ROSE, W. I., SPROD, I. E. & KRUEGER, A. J. 1997. Stratospheric loading of sulfur from explosive volcanic eruptions. *Journal of Geology*, **105**, 671–683.

CHARLSON, R. J., LOVELOCK, J. E., ANDREAE, M.O. & WARREN, S. G. 1987. Oceanic phytoplankton, atmospheric sulphur, cloud albedo and climate. *Nature*, **326**, 655–661.

CHARLSON, R. J., SCHWARTZ, S. E., HALES, J. M., CESS, R. D., COAKLEY, J.A., HANSEN, J. E. & HOFFMAN, D. J. 1992. Climate forcing by anthropogenic aerosols. *Science*, **255**, 422–430.

CHIN, M. & JACOB, D. J. 1996. Anthropogenic and natural contributions to tropospheric sulfate: A global model analysis. *Journal of Geophysical Research*, **101**, 18 691–18 699.

CHIN, M., JACOB, D. J., GARDNER, G. M., FOREMAN-FOWLER, M. S., SPIRO, P. A. & SAVOIE, D. L. 1996. A global three-dimensional model of tropospheric sulfate. *Journal of Geophysical Research*, **101**, 18 667–18 690.

CHIN, M., ROOD, R. B., LIN, S.-J., MÜLLER, J.-F. & THOMPSON, A. M., 2000. Atmospheric sulfur cycle simulated in the global model GOCART: model description and global properties. *Journal of Geophysical Research*, **105**, 24 671–24 687.

CHUANG, C. C., PENNER, J. E., TAYLOR, K. E., GROSSMAN, A. S. & WALTON, J. J. 1997. An assessment of the radiative effects of anthropogenic sulfate. *Journal of Geophysical Research*, **102**, 3761–3778.

COLLINS, W. J., STEVENSON, D. S., JOHNSON, C. E. & DERWENT, R. G. 1997. Tropospheric ozone in a global-scale 3-D Lagrangian model and its response to NOₓ emission controls. *Journal of Atmospheric Chemistry*, **86**, 223–274.

COLLINS, W. J., STEVENSON, D. S., JOHNSON, C. E. & DERWENT, R. G. 1998. A simulation of long-range transport of CFCs in the troposphere using a 3-D global Lagrangian model with 6-hourly meteorological fields. *Air Pollution Modelling and Its Application*, **XII**, 227–235.

COLLINS, W. J., STEVENSON, D. S., JOHNSON, C. E. & DERWENT, R. G. 1999. Role of convection in determining the budget of odd hydrogen in the upper troposphere. *Journal of Geophysical Research*, **104**, 26 927–26 941.

COLLINS, W. J., DERWENT, R. G., JOHNSON, C. E. & STEVENSON, D. S. 2000. The impact of human activities upon the photochemical production and destruction of tropospheric ozone. *Quarterly Journal of the Royal Meteorological Society*, **126**, 1925–1952.

COOKE, W. F. & WILSON, J. J. N. 1996. A global black carbon aerosol model. *Journal of Geophysical Research*, **101**, 19 395–19 409.

DERWENT, R. G., COLLINS, W. J., JENKIN, M. E., JOHNSON, C. E. & STEVENSON, D. S. 2003. The global distribution of secondary particulate matter in a 3-D Lagrangian Chemistry Transport Model. *Journal of Atmospheric Chemistry*, **44**, 57–95.

EPA 2001. Latest Findings on National Air Quality: 2000 Status and Trends. (http://www.epa.gov/airtrends) *US EPA Report*, **EPA 454/K-01-002**, Research Triangle Park, NC, USA.

FEICHTER, J., KJELLSTRÖM, E., RODHE, H., DENTENER, F., LELIEVELD, J. & ROELOFS, G.-J. 1996. Simulation of the tropospheric sulfur cycle in a global climate model. *Atmosphere and Environment*, **30**, 1693–1707.

GRAF, H.-F., FEICHTER, J. & LANGMANN, B. 1997. Volcanic sulfur emissions: estimates of source strength and its contribution to the global sulfate burden. *Journal of Geophysical Research*, **102(D9)**, 10 727–10 738.

JENKIN, M. E., CLEMENT, C. F. & FORD, I. J. 1996. Gas-to-particle conversion pathways. *AEA Technology Report*, **AEA/RAMP/20010010/001/Issue 1**, Culham Laboratory, Oxfordshire, UK.

JOHNS, T.C. *ET AL.* 1997. The second Hadley Centre Coupled Ocean–Atmosphere GCM: model description, spin-up and validation. *Climate Dynamics*, **13**, 103–134.

JOHNSON, C. E., STEVENSON, D. S., COLLINS, W. J. & DERWENT, R. G. 2001. Role of climate feedback on methane and ozone studied with a coupled Ocean–Atmosphere–Chemistry model. *Geophysical Research Letters*, **28**, 1723–1726.

JONES, A., ROBERTS, D. L., WOODAGE, M. J. & JOHNSON, C. E. 2001. Indirect sulphate aerosol forcing in a climate model with an interactive sulphur cycle. *Journal of Geophysical Research*, **106**, 20 293–20 310.

KANAKIDOU, M., DENTENER, F. J. *ET AL.* 1999*a*. 3-D global simulations of tropospheric CO distributions – results of the GIM/IGAC intercomparison 1997 exercise. *Chemosphere: Global Change Science*, **1**, 263–282.

KANAKIDOU, M., DENTENER, F. J. *ET AL.* 1999*b*. 3-D global simulations of tropospheric chemistry with focus on ozone distributions. *Eur. Comm. Rep.* **EUR18842**.

KETTLE, A. J., ANDREAE, M. O. *ET AL.* 1999. A global database of sea surface dimethylsulfide (DMS) measurements and a procedure to predict sea surface DMS as a function of latitude, longitude and month. *Global Biogeochemical Cycles*, **13**, 399–444.

KJELLSTRÖM, E. 1998. A three-dimensional global model study of carbonyl sulphide in the troposphere and the lower stratosphere. *Journal of Atmospheric Chemistry*, **29**, 151–177.

KOCH, D. M., JACOB, D., TEGEN, I., RIND, D. & CHIN, M. 1999. Tropospheric sulfur simulation and sulfate direct radiative forcing in the Goddard Institute for Space Studies general circulation model. *Journal of Geophysical Research*, **104(D19)**, 23 799–23 822.

LANGNER, J. & RODHE, H. 1991. A global three-dimensional model of the tropospheric sulfur cycle. *Journal of Atmospheric Chemistry*, **13**, 225–263.

LOHMANN, U., VON SALZEN, K., MCFARLANE, N., LEIGHTON, H. G. & FEICHTER, J. 1999. The tropospheric sulphur cycle in the Canadian general circulation model. *Journal of Geophysical Research*, **104**, 26 833–26 858.

LOVELOCK, J. E., MAGGS, R. J. & RASMUSSEN, R. A. 1972. Atmospheric dimethyl sulphide and the natural sulphur cycle. *Nature*, **237**, 462–463.

NAKIĆENOVIĆ, N., ALCAMO, J. *ET AL.* 2000. *IPCC Special Report on Emissions Scenarios.* Cambridge University Press, Cambridge, United Kingdom and New York, NY, USA, 599 pp.

NEGTAP 2001. *Transboundary Air Pollution: Acidification, Eutrophication and Ground-level Ozone in the UK.* (http://www.nbu.ac.uk/negtap) DEFRA Report, London, UK

OLIVIER, J. G. J., BOUWMAN, A. F. *ET AL.* 1996. Description of EDGAR Version 2.0: A set of global emission inventories of greenhouse gases and ozone-depleting substances for all anthropogenic and most natural sources on a per country basis and on a 1°×1° grid. (http://www.rivm.nl/env/int/coredata/edgar) *National Institute of Public Health and the Environment (RIVM) Report*, **771060 002/TNO report no. R96/119**

PENNER, J. E., ATHERTON, C. S., DIGNON, J., GHAN, S. J., WALTON, J. J. & HAMEED, S. 1994. *Global Emissions and Models of Photochemically Active Compounds. In:* PRINN, R. G. (ed.) *Global Atmospheric Biospheric Chemistry* Plenum, New York, 223–247.

PENNER, J. E., ANDREAE, M. *ET AL.* 2001. Aerosols, their direct and indirect effects. *In:* HOUGHTON, J. T., DING, Y. *ET AL.* (eds) *Climate Change 2001: the Scientific Basis. Contribution of Working Group I to the Third Assessment Report of the Intergovernmental Panel on Climate Change*, Cambridge University Press, Cambridge and New York.

PHAM, M., MÜLLER, J.-F., BRASSEUR, G. P., GRANIER, C. & MEGIE, G. 1995. A three-dimensional study of the tropospheric sulfur cycle. *Journal of Geophysical Research*, **100**, 26 061–26 092.

RASCH, P. J., BARTH, M. C., KIEHL, J. T., SCHWARTZ, S. E. & BENKOWITZ, C. E. 2000. A description of the global sulfur cycle and its controlling processes in the National Center for Atmospheric Research Community Climate Model, Version 3. *Journal of Geophysical Research*, **105**, 1367–1385.

RESTAD, K., ISAKSEN, I. S. A. & BERNTSEN, T. K. 1998. Global distribution of sulphate in the troposphere. A three-dimensional model study. *Atmosphere and Environment*, **32**, 3593–3609.

RODHE, H. 1999. Human impact on the atmospheric sulfur balance. *Tellus*, **51A-B**, 110–122.

ROELOFS, G.-J., LELIEVELD, J. & GANZEVELD, L. 1998. Simulation of global sulphate distribution and the influence on effective cloud drop radii with a photochemistry sulphur cycle model. *Tellus*, **50B**, 224–242.

ROELOFS, G.-J., KASIBAHTLA, P. *ET AL.* 2001. Analysis of regional budgets of sulfur species modeled for the COSAM exercise. *Tellus*, **53B**, 673–694.

SCHNETZLER, C. C., BLUTH, G. J. S., KRUEGER, A. J. & WALTER, L. S. 1997. A proposed volcanic sulfur dioxide index (VSI). *Journal of Geophysical Research*, **102**, 20 087–20 091.

SIMKIN, T. & SIEBERT, L. 1994. *Volcanoes of the World: a Regional Directory, Gazetteer, and Chronology of Volcanism during the last 10000 years.* Geoscience Press, Tucson, Arizona.

SPIRO, P. A., JACOB, D. J. & LOGAN, J. A. 1992. Global inventory of sulfur emissions with 1°×1° resolution. *Journal of Geophysical Research*, **97**, 6023–6036.

STEVENSON, D. S., JOHNSON, C. E., COLLINS, W. J. & DERWENT, R. G. 1998. Intercomparison and evaluation of atmospheric transport in a Lagrangian model (STOCHEM) and an Eulerian model (UM) using ^{222}Rn as a short-lived tracer. *Quarterly Journal of the Royal Meteorological Society*, **124**, 2477–2491.

STEVENSON, D. S., JOHNSON, C. E., HIGHWOOD, E. J., GAUCI, V., COLLINS, W. J. & DERWENT, R. G. (2003). Atmospheric impact of the 1783–1784 Laki eruption: Part I Chemistry modelling. *Atmospheric*

Chemistry and Physics Discussions, **3**, 551–596.
TWOMEY, S. 1977. Influence of pollution on the short-wave albedo of clouds. *Journal of Atmospheric Science,* **34**, 1149–1152.

The 12 900 years BP Laacher See eruption: estimation of volatile yields and simulation of their fate in the plume

C. TEXTOR[1], P. M. SACHS[2], H.-F. GRAF[3] & T. H. HANSTEEN[2]

[1]Max-Planck Institute for Meteorology, Bundestraße 55, D-20146 Hamburg,
Germany.
(e-mail: textor@dkrz.de)
[2]Forschungszentrum GEOMAR, Vulkanologie und Petrologie,
Wischhofstraße 1–3, D-24148, Kiel, Germany.
[3]Max-Planck Institute for Meteorology, Bundestraße 55, D-20146 Hamburg,
Germany.

Abstract: We estimated the volatile emissions of the 12 900 years BP eruption of Laacher See volcano (Germany), using a modified petrological method. Glass inclusions in phenocrysts and matrix glasses sampled over the Laacher See tephra profile were analysed by synchrotron X-ray fluorescence microprobe and electron microprobe to obtain the emitted masses of halogens, sulphur, and water. These data were used to initialize the numerical plume model ATHAM in order to investigate the fate of volcanic gases in the plume, and to estimate volatile masses injected into the stratosphere. The scavenging efficiency of each volatile component depends on its interactions with both liquid water and ice. We found a scavenging efficiency of c. 5% for the sulphur species, and of only c. 30% for hydrogen halides, despite their high water solubility. Our simulations showed that the greatest fraction of hydrometeors freeze to ice, due to the fast plume rise and great height of the eruption column. For the dry atmospheric conditions of the Laacher See eruption, the amount of liquid water was not sufficient to completely scavenge HCl and HBr, so that a large proportion could reach the stratosphere.

Volcanic eruptions reach the stratosphere, on average, at least once every two years (Simkin 1993). Plinian eruptions contribute to the stratospheric sulphate aerosol via injection of sulphur gases that are subsequently oxidized to form sulphate aerosol. Volcanic sulphur is emitted primarily as sulphur dioxide (SO_2) and hydrogen sulphide (H_2S). The H_2S is oxidized within days to SO_2 (e.g. McKeen 1984), which, in turn, is oxidized to sulphate, with a lifetime of approximately 35 days in the dry stratosphere (Bluth *et al.* 1992). The stratospheric aerosol burden can be significantly enhanced in the years following major volcanic eruptions. Sulphate aerosols in the stratosphere have radiative effects, altering the Earth's radiation balance (e.g. Charlson *et al.* 1991, 1992; Stenchikov *et al.* 1998), and hence can influence the global climate. A reduction of stratospheric ozone after large volcanic eruptions has also been observed. The column ozone reduction after the 1991 Mount Pinatubo eruption, which could be attributed to the volcanic effect, ranged from about 2% in the tropics, to about 7% at mid latitudes (Angell 1997; Solomon *et al.* 1998). The observed ozone changes are a combined effect of perturbations in heating and photolysis rates, and in stratospheric chemistry. Volcanic hydrated sulphate aerosols can serve as sites for heterogeneous reactions, which destroy ozone in the presence of halogens by converting passive halogen compounds into active ones (e.g. Hofmann & Solomon 1989; Granier & Brasseur 1992; Solomon *et al.* 1996). Hence, the increase in stratospheric halogens caused by anthropogenic activities has caused the observed decrease in stratospheric ozone after major volcanic eruptions. Since the human-induced increase of chlorine concentration in the stratosphere has peaked, the effect of ozone destruction by volcanic aerosol will probably decrease in the next few decades (Brasseur *et al.* 1990; Tie & Brasseur 1995).

From: OPPENHEIMER, C., PYLE, D.M. & BARCLAY, J. (eds) *Volcanic Degassing*. Geological Society, London, Special Publications, **213**, 307–328. 0305–8719/03/$15.00

The amount of volcanic sulphur injected into the stratosphere during a Plinian eruption is difficult to determine exactly with the methods available (e.g. Rose *et al.* 2000). The quantification of gas and particle concentrations in a volcanic plume is challenging, because of the cloud's opacity and the inherent risks of direct observation and sampling. Volcanic emissions can be studied remotely by airborne and ground-based instruments, and by satellite observations. The significant differences in the observational data are due to uncertainties in each individual measuring technique, but they also result from the fact that the plume is investigated at different distances from the crater and during different states of volcanic activity. Changes in the emissions at (and between) single sources over orders of magnitude can take place depending on levels of activity (and magma type).

A post-eruptive increase in the amount of stratospheric SO_2 on the second day after the eruption has been observed by the TOMS instrument (see Carn *et al.*, 2003, Chapter 11, this volume) after several explosive volcanic eruptions (Bluth *et al.* 1995). The reason for this post-eruptive increase is not yet clear. The favoured explanation is that the additional SO_2 stems from the oxidation of co-emitted H_2S, which cannot be detected by the TOMS instrument (Rose *et al.* 2000). The magmatic H_2S fraction increases with increasing pressure (i.e. depth of the magma chamber) and with decreasing temperature and oxygen activity of the magma (Gerlach *et al.* 1986). Another reason could be the release of SO_2, which had been incorporated into frozen hydrometeors during the plume rise, when these hydrometeors sublimate in the dry stratosphere (Rose *et al.* 2001). Indications of ice in volcanic plumes were found in the eruption columns of Redoubt in 1989–1990 (Schneider *et al.* 1994), Rabaul in 1994 (Rose *et al.* 1995), Soufrière Hills Volcano, Montserrat in 1998–1999 (Mayberry *et al.* 2001), Hekla in February 2000 (Rose *et al.* 2000; Krotkov & Krueger 2000), and in the 1992 Mount Spurr eruption cloud (Rose *et al.* 2001). Unusually low concentrations of SO_2, together with high ice concentration, are suggestive of gas scavenging by ice (Rose *et al.* 1995, 2001). The stability of ice in the stratosphere, which could subsequently release SO_2, is dependent on the amount of water in the plume, which is in turn dependent on the volcanic and environmental conditions. An increased concentration of H_2O could accelerate SO_2 or H_2S oxidation in the stratosphere. In addition, it would influence the composition of sulphate aerosol, and hence the radiative effects of the eruption. The amount of

H_2O (vapour and ice) injected into the stratosphere during a volcanic eruption has not yet been quantified, but can be substantial because of the tropospheric water entrained into the rising plume, which is generally considered to far exceed the amount of magmatic water. Numerical simulations with a 'top-hat' model indicated that large volcanic eruptions could deposit a mass of water in the stratosphere equivalent to up to 7% of the total stratospheric water burden (Glaze *et al.* 1997).

Direct injection of halogens into the stratosphere during a Plinian eruption could enhance ozone destruction. The volcanic emission of halogens can be significant (e.g. Varekamp *et al.* 1984; Westrich *et al.* 1992), but after the eruption of Mount Pinatubo the concentration of HCl in the stratosphere was not significantly enhanced (e.g. Mankin *et al.* 1992; Wallace & Livingston 1992). On the other hand, a clear increase in chlorine concentration was detected after the eruption of El Chichón in 1982, (Mankin & Coffey 1984; Woods *et al.* 1985). Until now, little attention has been paid to the potential stratospheric effects of heavy halogens released from volcanoes, such as bromine and iodine (Sachs & Harms 1998, 2000; Bureau *et al.* 2000). Bromine atoms are about 60 times more effective in destroying ozone than chlorine atoms (Daniel *et al.* 1995; Montzka *et al.* 1996).

The proportion of volcanic volatiles injected into the stratosphere by a Plinian eruption in relation to those erupted at the vent is governed by the scavenging efficiency of the individual species. Tabazadeh and Turco (1993) investigated the scavenging of HCl and SO_2 in an explosive volcanic plume using a one-dimensional, steady-state 'top-hat' model (Wilson 1976; Woods 1988; Woods 1993). The temperature distribution in the plume was obtained from this model. It was assumed that the existence of supercooled droplets was favoured as compared with ice formation. The authors argued that ice nucleation requires cooling below –20 °C, as in typical meteorological convective clouds. The scavenging of chemical species in the eruption column was parameterized by assuming solubility equilibrium in these supercooled droplets. The concentration of volatiles remaining in the gas phase was derived from sophisticated thermodynamic theory.

Tabazadeh and Turco (1993) concluded that HCl was almost completely transferred into supercooled droplets, resulting in an HCl vapour pressure reduction of up to four orders of magnitude. On the other hand, it was found that the scavenging of SO_2 in the eruption column was insignificant: due to its low solubility in liquid water it reaches the stratosphere almost unaffected by any scavenging in the plume. Although the study of Tabazadeh and Turco (1993) stands as an important first attempt to simulate the chemistry in a Plinian plume and considers a complex thermodynamic theory for phase equilibrium, it was based on a relatively simple treatment of the dynamics, and it did not consider cloud microphysical processes. In their simulations, all hydrometeors were liquid, and incorporation of gases in ice particles was not considered. The parameters that determine the scavenging efficiency need to be further investigated for different volcanic and environmental conditions.

In this chapter we describe the experimental set-up to estimate the amount of volatiles released by the 12 900 years BP Laacher See eruption. We then explain the processes occurring in the eruption column, which determine the scavenging efficiency of these volatiles during plume rise. In the last part, we present numerical simulations with the non-hydrostatic plume model ATHAM (Active Tracer High Resolution Atmospheric Model) for conditions similar to the Laacher See eruption, including scavenging processes in the eruption column. These simulations provide an estimate of the potential injection of sulphur and halogen gases into the stratosphere.

Laacher See volcano

Volcanological and petrological background

The magnitude of the 12 900 years BP Laacher See eruption has been estimated at between 5.1 and 6.3 km^3 DRE (dense rock equivalent) (Bogaard & Schmincke 1985; Schmincke et al. 1999; Harms & Schmincke 2000). In the following we will use an average value of 5.6 km^3. The proximal tephra sequence is subdivided into three major units: Lower Laacher See Tephra (LLST, first Plinian stage, dominantly fallout except for the most proximal facies), Middle Laacher See Tephra (MLST A, B, C; second Plinian stage, dominantly pyroclastic flows in the lower, and alternating fallout and flow in the upper part) and Upper Laacher See Tephra (ULST, phreatomagmatic stage with dominantly surge breccias, dunes and flows). The distribution of Laacher See tephra fallout is shown in Figure 1.

The Laacher See phonolite tephra sequence represents an inverted, chemically zoned magma reservoir. Miaskitic (Na+K/Al<1) and peralkaline phonolites (Na+K/Al>1), represent the lowermost mafic and the uppermost differ-

iated erupted portion of the Laacher See magma chamber, respectively. Fractionation calculations indicate that the erupted phonolitic magma could be derived from 56 km^3 of parental basanite magma (Wörner & Schmincke 1984a, b). The pressure was between 100 and 200 MPa (Wörner et al. 1985). The temperature in the upper part of the magma reservoir was <760 °C (probably down to 720 °C in the most differentiated levels). Temperatures >840–860 °C prevailed in the lower part, as indicated by experimental determination of the phase relationships (Harms 1998; Berndt et al. 2001).

The earliest erupted phonolites are almost aphyric, while those erupted near the end contain up to 40 vol.% crystals (mainly plagioclase, sanidine, clinopyroxene, amphibole, phlogopite, hauyne, titanite, magnetite, apatite, olivine). Amphibole/clinopyroxene phenocryst ratios show a roof-ward increase in the magma chamber (Tait et al. 1989). Crystal cumulates are common in the upper part of the tephra deposit; they range from syenites to clinopyroxenites and hornblendites (Tait 1988; Tait et al. 1989). Xenoliths comprise fragments of quartz–feldspar gneisses, mica schists, Devonian slates and greywacke.

Analytical methods

We estimated masses emitted of S, F, Cl, Br, I, and H$_2$O over the entire Laacher See tephra profile. Glass inclusions in phenocrysts and matrix glasses were analysed by synchrotron X-ray fluorescence microprobe (SYXRF) and electron microprobe (EMP).

Major elements, iron, magnesium, fluorine, chlorine, and sulphur were analysed with a CAMECA SX-50 wavelength-dispersive electron microprobe. Analytical conditions were 15 kV accelerating voltage and a beam current of 6 nA. A rastering electron beam (15 μm in diameter) was used for glass analyses in order to minimize Cl, S, and F migration, these being among the first elements measured during an analysis. Major elements were measured for 20 s, F and Cl for 30 s, and S for 300 s to raise the detection limit (145 ppm) for the analytical conditions used.

Trace-element analyses were performed with the SYXRF set-up at beamline L of HASYLAB (Hamburger Synchrotronstrahlungs-Labor) located at DESY (Deutsches Elektronen-Synchrotron) in Hamburg, Germany (Lechtenberg et al. 1996; Hansteen et al. 2000). Due to the limited interaction between the sample material and the X-ray photons, SYXRF is a completely non-destructive method for volatile analysis. A fundamental parameter approach was used to compute element concentrations (Vincze *et al.* 1993; Hansteen *et al.* 2000). The sample-specific thickness, density, and Fe concentration, measured by electron microprobe, were used as input variables for the simulation procedure. Detection limits for an acquisition time of 3600 s were between 0.1 and 0.3 µg/g (Z=55; Br) and 7–10 µg/g (Z=64; Gd).

Compositional parameters of halogens and sulphur in the Laacher See magma

The Laacher See matrix glasses show a distinct compositional change throughout the entire tephra sequence, indicating that a chemically zoned magma reservoir was tapped during the eruption. Concentrations of MgO, FeO* (=all Fe recalculated as FeO), CaO, and Sr are highest in ULST matrix glasses (corresponding with the lower parts of the magma reservoir) and decrease towards LLST (upper parts of magma chamber). Concentrations of Nb, Zr, Th, Y, and rare-earth elements (REE) increase from ULST to LLST. Apparently, the concentrations represent a particular position in the magma reservoir. We can therefore relate matrix glasses (MG) and glass inclusions (GI) to specific positions in the magma chamber, using chemical variation diagrams. Concentrations of volatile elements in the glass inclusions correlate positively with high-field-strength (HFS) elements, and reflect the zonation of the magma chamber prior to MG melt formation. Examples are Mo v. Nb, Br v. Nb or Mo v. Br, having low concentrations in

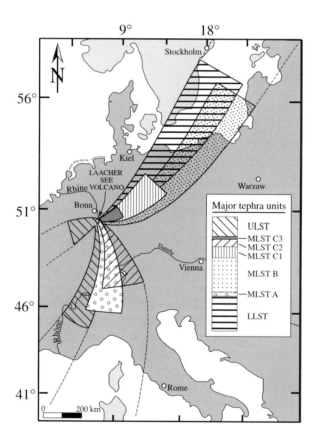

Fig. 1. Areal distribution of Laacher See tephra fallout (after van den Bogaard & Schmincke 1985). The volume of erupted melt has been estimated to be between 5.1 and 6.3 km³ DRE (dense rock equivalent) (van den Bogaard & Schmincke 1985; Harms & Schmincke 2000). The proximal tephra sequence is subdivided into three major units: Lower Laacher See Tephra (LLST, first Plinian stage, dominantly fallout except for the most proximal facies), Middle Laacher See Tephra (MLST A, B, C; second Plinian stage, dominantly pyroclastic flows in the lower and alternating fallout and flow in the upper part) and Upper Laacher See Tephra (ULST, phreatomagmatic stage with dominantly surge breccias, dunes and flows).

deep parts of the magma chamber and high concentrations in the upper parts.

By comparing matrix glasses with glass inclusions, we can thus distinguish between those compositional patterns indicating late-magmatic volatile depletion and those representing late-magmatic enrichment. The covariation of the volatile elements Br and S (e.g. the representations of Br v. Nb or S v. MgO) indicate a depletion of both Br and S in MG chlorine concentrations (e.g. Cl v. MgO), and are significantly higher in GI as compared with MG fluorine correlations (e.g. F v. MgO), indicating a significant enrichment during formation of MG. Bromine provides the clearest evidence for the action of a fluid phase within the Laacher See magma chamber during formation of the MG melts. The matrix glasses are characterized by a plateau-like concentration of Br, which ranges between 3 and 7 µg/g, over the entire stratigraphic sequence. The plateau provides evidence that a simple mechanism, and therefore a single process, controlled the concentration levels. Most likely, this was the release of a fluid phase limited by the quenching rate of the melt during the eruption.

The ratios Cl/Br, F/Br and SO_2^*/Br v. Br (SO_2^*=all S recalculated as SO_2) increase strongly with decreasing Br concentration, i.e.

with increasing depth within the magma chamber, as shown in Figures 2 and 3.

This indicates selective enrichment of S, F, and Cl relative to Br. Breakdown of mafic phenocrysts in the lower parts of the magma chamber must be taken into account as a source of fluorine and chlorine. This is supported by the roof-ward increase in the amphibole/clinopyroxene phenocryst ratio of the magma chamber (Tait *et al.* 1989). The ratios F/Br and Cl/Br of amphibole, phlogopite and biotite (occurring as phenocrysts and corroded crystals) are possible end-members of the related paths, and provide evidence for contamination by these phases. Amphibole, phlogopite/biotite and apatite appear to be incompatible for bromine (bromine concentrations <0.5 µg/g). This indicates that contamination through assimilation cannot provide enrichment of bromine over F and Cl, and will increase F/Br and Cl/Br ratios. The breakdown of hauyne has no significant influence (<2 vol. %), because the apparent partition coefficient of Br in hauyne and coexisting glass inclusions (concentration in hauyne/concentration in melt) is close to unity ($KBr^{Hau/liq} \approx 1$). This is also indicated by the plot of SO_2^*/Br v. Br (Fig. 3).

The absence of pyrrhotite in the upper parts of the Laacher See magma chamber supports the

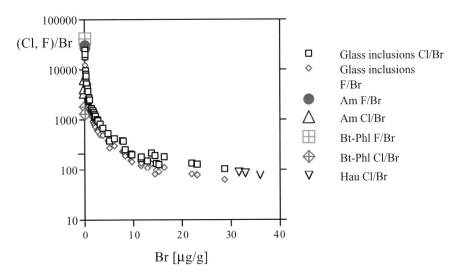

Fig. 2. Representation of F/Br and Cl/Br v. Br. Low Br concentrations in the glass inclusions are representative of the deep regions of the chamber, while high concentrations occur in the upper part. The relative enrichment of Cl and F at low Br concentrations appears to be related to the breakdown of amphibole and/or biotite and phlogopite, which define possible end-members at low bromine concentrations. Element ratios were estimated through a best fit by F/Br=1586.162*$Br^{-0.989}$ (r^2=0.996); and Cl/Br=2379.676*$Br^{-0.981}$ (r^2=0.991). The Cl/Br ratio of the average continental crust is from Bureau *et al.* (2000). The Cl/Br and F/Br ratios of amphibole and phlogopite/biotite represent a minimum value (Br was below the detection limit of about 0.1 µg/g). Am=amphibole, Bt–Phl=biotite/phlogopite, Hau=hauyne.

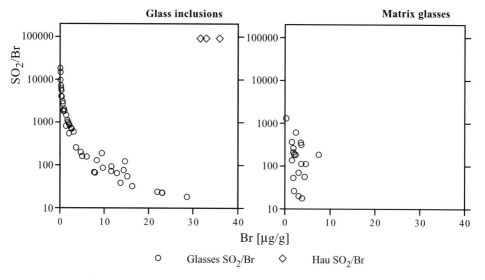

Fig. 3. Sulphur/bromine ratios v. bromine contents of glass inclusions and matrix glasses. Glass inclusions with low Br concentrations are representative of the deep regions of the chamber, and high concentrations of the upper part. The concentrations in matrix glasses show the plateau concentration of bromine over the entire tephra profile. The strong hyperbolic increase of the ratio SO_2*/Br for the glass inclusions, with decreasing Br concentrations, indicates that sulphur has been added to the Laacher See magma and cannot be explained by the breakdown of hauyne. The decrease of SO_2*/Br with decreasing Br concentrations during formation of the matrix glass melts is probably controlled by the release of a fluid phase. Element ratios were estimated through a best fit by $SO_2*/Br = 1467.334*Br^{-1.200}$ ($r^2 = 0.966$).

hypothesis of sulphur enrichment of the phonolite melt through sulphide breakdown. Pyrrhotite globules ($Fe_{1-x}S$, ≤ 10 μm in diameter) are trapped in mafic phonolite glass inclusions and in amphibole, clinopyroxene, plagioclase, and titanite crystals in the lowermost parts of the magma chamber (ULST to MLSTB). This demonstrates that the Laacher See melt was FeS-saturated in the deep chamber, and provides evidence that sulphide has been resorbed in shallower parts of the magma chamber, probably due to an increase in oxygen fugacity.

Estimate of the volatile release

Estimation of volatiles released during an eruption by subtraction of concentrations in matrix glasses from concentrations in the glass inclusions (the so-called 'petrological method') can lead to severe underestimation of the atmospheric input (see Scaillet & Pichavant, 2003, Chapter 3, this volume). For SO₂, data obtained with the petrological method can yield an apparent release one to two orders of magnitude less than those obtained by other methods such as satellite data (e.g. Andres *et al.* 1991). Due to late-stage volatile enrichment of the Laacher See MG melts, involving breakdown of

amphibole (±phlogopite, biotite) and of sulphide-bearing phases (most likely FeS, CuFeS₂), the eruptive release of most of the volatiles cannot be estimated by the petrological method. Unrealistically low or even negative masses of volatiles (fluorine) released into the atmosphere would be obtained. We therefore determined the bromine release using a combination of the petrological method and known fluid/melt partition coefficients (Bureau *et al.* 2000).

We calculated the emissions from the Br release as follows. The definitions of the concentrations of the masses m_i of a component I (index: i) in the melt (index: liq) and in the fluid (index: f) with masses m_{liq} and m_f are:

$$C_i^{liq} = m_i/m_{liq} \text{ and } C_i^f = m_i/m_f \qquad (1)$$

The partition coefficient of component i distributed between fluid and melt is:

$$D_i^{f/liq} = C_i^f/C_i^{liq} \qquad (2)$$

The concentrations of components i and Br in the fluid are given by:

$$C_i^f = D_i^{f/liq}C_i^{liq} \text{ and } C_{Br}^f = D_{Br}^{f/liq}C_{Br}^{liq} \qquad (3)$$

Combining equations 1 and 3 yields:

$$m_i^f = m_{Br}^f (D_i^{f/liq}/D_{Br}^{f/liq})(C_i^{liq}/C_{Br}^{liq}) \qquad (4)$$

The masses m_i^f and m_{Br}^f are released from the melt into the fluid. In order to determine the atmospheric release of component i we assume that the fluid is completely released to the atmosphere, $m_i^{atm} \approx m_i^f$. The release of Br, m_{Br}^f, must be estimated independently. The apparent saturation concentration of a Br-bearing fluid is reflected in the MG plateau concentrations for Br of approximately 3–7 µg/g. We estimate the ratio C_i^{liq}/C_{Br}^{liq} from a representation of C_{Br}^{liq} through a best fit with a function of the type $C_i^{liq}/C_{Br}^{liq} = A(C_{Br}^{liq})^B$, where A and B are constants. The ratio C_i^{liq}/C_{Br}^{liq} reflects degassing at best through its minimum ratio, whereas higher values are progressively controlled through contamination.

One has to take into account that a considerable fraction of the fluid possibly consisted of H_2S. The partition coefficient for sulphur is strongly dependent on the oxygen fugacity fO_2, varying from $D_S^{f/liq} = 47$ (high fO_2; fluid consists predominantly of SO_2) up to $D_S^{f/liq} = 468 \pm 32$ (predominantly H_2S; Keppler 1999). A $D_{H_2O}^{f/liq} = 100/6.55 = 15.27$ is taken as an approximation for the concentration of H_2O in glasses quenched from experimentally melted phonolite glass coexisting with aqueous fluid (Carroll & Blank 1997). As an extrapolation to multi-component fluids, we use $D_{H_2O}^{f/liq} = 95/6.55 = 14.5$. We determined the Br release to the atmosphere using the formula (GI: glass inclusions; MG: matrix glasses):

$$m_{Br} = (C_{Br}^{GI} - C_{Br}^{MG})\rho_{liq}\Phi_{liq}V_{liq} \qquad (5)$$

through the difference $C_{Br}^{GI} - C_{Br}^{MG}$ between Br concentrations in glass inclusions of phenocrysts (clinopyroxene, hauyne, titanite, amphibole) and in MG, where $_{liq}$ is the density of the melt, and $\Phi_{liq} = 0.97$ the mass fraction of melt relative to other phases. V_{liq} is the volume of magma from which the fluid component i was released. We assume that the melt density was 2300 kg/m³ over the entire magma volume. The Br saturation concentration in melt was $C_{Br}^{MG} \approx 3$–7 µg/g. Lower Br concentrations do not contribute to degassing. Only magma batches corresponding with LLST and MLST stratigraphic positions contribute to Br degassing (estimated volume $V_{liq} = 4$ km³ DRE). Deeper stratigraphic levels did not contribute to Br degassing, because the pre-eruptive concentration was below the MG concentration. The difference of volatile concentrations caused by fluid release is $C_{Br}^{GI} - C_{Br}^{MG} = 17$–13 µg/g.

We determined therefore the mass M of released fluid components using the difference of bromine concentrations in glass inclusions and matrix glasses, with $M = M_{Br}(D/D_{Br})(C_m/C_{m,Br})$, whereby M = mass of released volatile, M_{Br} = bromine mass; $D = C_{fluid}/C_{melt}$: partition coefficients; and C_m = volatile concentration at maximum Br concentration. The resulting mass of released bromine is $M_{Br} = 0.19$–0.29 Tg. Using equation 4, we obtain the following mass releases M in Tg: F = 0.214, Cl = 11.5, I = <0.03, S = 3.38 (assuming pure SO_2) or S = 52.4 (assuming pure H_2S), and $H_2O = 698$. The resulting estimates for volatile release during the Laacher See eruption, and the parameters involved, are summarized in Table 1.

For comparison, the SO_2 emission can be crudely estimated from the relationship between the volcanic explosivity index VEI (Newhall & Self 1982) and typical SO_2 emissions for non-arc volcanoes (Schnetzler et al. 1997). The VEI for the Laacher See eruption is VEI = 4–5 (column height 18 km, volume of erupted tephra 10^9–10^{10} m³). This yields an average SO_2 release of about $mSO_2 = 10 \pm 5$ Tg. This suggests that at least part of the sulphur was released in the form of H_2S.

Processes in the eruption column

Radical chemistry in a volcanic plume

During the rise of volcanic emissions from the crater to the stratosphere, i.e. within the volcanic plume, radical chemistry is negligible. This has been shown by sensitivity studies with a chemistry box module under volcanic conditions. The rise time of volcanic gases from the crater to the stratosphere is of the order of 10 minutes. This is shorter than the characteristic time of chemical transformations under normal atmospheric conditions. In addition, the optical depth of the eruption column is so high (due to the presence of ash) that photochemistry is strongly suppressed. Thus, the volcanic gas injection into the stratosphere is controlled by the plume height and by scavenging through hydrometeors, which might remove the gases from the atmosphere when they precipitate.

Scavenging by liquid droplets

The physical solubility of an arbitrary gas, HA, in water is described by the Henry coefficient He. Within the context of this work, all concentrations are given in units of mol. kg^{-1} $_{tot.mass}$. In these units, He increases with increasing liquid water content:

$$He = \frac{[HA]aq}{[HA]g} \qquad (6)$$

Table 1. *Estimation of volatile release and related parameters for the 12 900 year BP Laacher See eruption.*

Component	Plateau concentration in matrix glass (µg/g)	Concentration in melt C_i (µg/g)	Partition coefficient $D_i^{f/liq}$	Erupted mass m_i (Tg)
F	1617	231	0.18	0.214
Cl	1932	276	8.1	11.5
Br	7	1	17.5	0.19–0.29
I	<0.5	<0.07	104	<0.03
SO_2*				
(pure SO_2 or H_2S)	SO_2*=68 ± 17; Br=3.8	14	SO_2: 47–137	Pure SO_2: 3.38
			H_2S: 468	Pure H_2S: 52.4
H_2O	65 500	9357	14.5	698

The partition coefficient is $D_i^{f/liq}=C_i^f/C_i^{liq}$. m_i is the mass in the fluid phase, which is assumed to be completely released to the atmosphere: $m_i^f=m_{Br}^f (D_i^{f/liq}/D_{Br}^{f/liq})(C_i^{liq}/C_{Br}^{liq})$.

where the parentheses indicate the species concentration in the gas and water phase, *g* and *aq*, respectively. *He* refers to the pure physical solubility equilibrium of a gas in water, regardless of its subsequent fate in the droplet. However, acidic gases undergo acid–base reactions like $HA \leftrightarrow A^- + H^+$, described by the dissociation constant K_s:

$$Ks = \frac{[A^-]_{aq}\,[H^+]_{aq}}{[HA]_{aq}} \qquad (7)$$

The dissociation reaction in the liquid phase enhances the uptake of gases in droplets. The total solubility, given by the effective Henry coefficient *He**, is then also a function of the pH value:

$$He^* = \frac{[HA]_{aq} + [A^-]_{aq}}{[HA]_g} = He(1+\frac{K_s}{[H^+]}) \qquad (8)$$

Corresponding expressions are valid for two-protonic acids like H_2S and SO_2. All equilibrium constants are temperature dependent according to the van't Hoff equation:

$$K = K_0 \exp\left(\frac{\Delta H}{R}(\frac{1}{T} - \frac{1}{T_0})\right) \qquad (9)$$

The Henry coefficients generally increase as the temperature decreases, reflecting a greater solubility at lower temperatures. The reaction enthalpy, ΔH, is the energy change involved with dissolution of gases in water, and T_0=289 K is the reference temperature for the values of the Henry coefficients and the acidity constants, K_0, which are taken from Sander and Crutzen (1996). The solubility of HCl in water is about four orders of magnitude greater than that of the sulphur containing gases. Hence, HCl is likely to be completely scavenged by water drops, and its revolatilization would require a drastic decrease of the system's liquid water content. The time-scales to adjust to phase equilibrium are of the order of a fraction of a second for the dissolution of slightly soluble gases; however, highly soluble gases need much longer times (e.g. Seinfeld & Pandis 1997). The time to establish phase equilibrium increases with droplet radius and liquid water content. The characteristic times needed to achieve the Henry's law equilibrium (including subsequent dissociation reaction inside the droplets) are long when compared with the model time step, of about 0.5 s simulation time in ATHAM, especially for HCl. Hence, we have to consider the time dependency of phase transfer.

We assume that the characteristic phase transfer time of gases into the liquid phase, and vice versa, is dominated by gas phase diffusion and interfacial mass transfer. For simplicity we suppose that the droplets are internally well mixed and that rapid dissociation equilibria in the aqueous phase are instantaneously reached. We neglect any other liquid phase reactions. A further simplification is achieved by applying the steady-state approximation: species concentrations, fluxes, and reaction rates are no longer a function of time during one model time step (Schwartz 1986). The phase transfer rate of volatiles into liquid droplets with subsequent dissociation reactions of acidic gases in the liquid phase is then proportional to the deviation from the solubility equilibrium:

$$\frac{\partial}{\partial t}c_{aq} = -\frac{1}{L}\frac{\partial}{\partial t}c_g = k_t(c_{g,\infty} - c_{g,eq}) \qquad (10)$$

where $c_{aq}=[HA]_{aq}+[A^-]_{aq}$ is the total concentration in the aqueous phase and $c_{g,eq}=[HA]_g$ denotes the concentration in the gas phase at the droplet surface, given by He^* in equation 8. $c_{g,\infty}$ is the gas concentration in the undisturbed environment, and L, in $kg_{aq}\,kg^{-1}_{tot.mass}$, the liquid water content. The phase transfer constant k_t, in s^{-1}, is defined as the inverse sum of the characteristic times of mass transport of a gas to the drop surface τ_{dg} and that across the air–water interface, including the possible establishment of solubility equilibrium locally at the interface τ_i (Schwartz 1986).

$$k_t = (\tau_{dg}+\tau_i)^{-1} = (\frac{r^2}{3D_g}+\frac{4r}{3\bar{v}\alpha})^{-1} \quad (11)$$

where

$$D_g = 2\lambda\bar{v}(1+0.22\mathrm{Re}^{0.5}) \quad (12)$$

and

$$\bar{v} = \sqrt{\frac{8RT}{M\pi}} \quad (13)$$

r is the volume mean radius of the particle, in m, D_g the gas phase diffusion coefficient in m^2/s, including the effects of turbulence caused by circulation around a falling drop, Re is the Reynolds number. $\bar{v}$ denotes the mean speed of gas molecules from the kinetic gas theory in m/s, $R=8.3143$ mol/kJ is the general gas constant, M, in kg/mol., is the molecular weight, and λ, in m, the mean free path in air. The sticking coefficients $\alpha(HCl)=0.2$ and $\alpha(SO_2)=0.11$ are taken from DeMore et al. (1997). The value for H_2S used, $\alpha(H_2S)=0.1$, was chosen to be in the range of the other values, because no observational data were available.

The resulting equations are linearized by using a Taylor expansion, with truncation after the first term, as in Newton's method (Press et al. 1992); the Jacobian is iteratively solved with an efficient realization of a Gauss elimination (J. M. Oberhuber, pers. comm. 1996). We use an implicit time stepping procedure to solve the set of stiff non-linear equations.

Scavenging by ice particles

Field studies and a number of laboratory experiments have indicated that ice crystals are able to scavenge gaseous species from the surrounding air (for references, see Diehl et al. 1998). The solubility of gases in ice is much lower

than in liquid water, since ions are rejected by the ice matrix. The gas uptake is dependent on the type of gas, temperature, and crystalline structure of the ice. In addition, gas uptake is different for growing and non-growing ice (Pruppacher & Klett 1997). It has been observed that the contamination of ice does not correspond with the thermodynamic equilibrium solubility of chemical species in ice. Among others, Valdez & Dawson (1984), Mitra et al. (1992), Diehl et al. (1995), and Thibert & Dominé (1997) performed laboratory experiments to investigate the uptake of gases by ice crystals. The experiments indicated that the diffusivities of electrolytes in ice are very low compared with liquid water values. Species, once incorporated in ice, will not be able to considerably change their position within the crystal. Thus the phase equilibrium cannot be established after the initial gas incorporation within the time of a volcanic eruption simulated with ATHAM.

It has been observed that the contamination of ice does not correspond with the thermodynamic equilibrium solubility of chemical species in ice, but is ruled by condensation kinetics (e.g. Dominé et al. 1995; Diehl et al. 1995). Gaseous species are incorporated during diffusional ice particle growth, due to the deposition of water vapour. Gas scavenging is proportional to the mass of water vapour converted to ice. This process is parameterized in ATHAM, according to the ideas of Dominé et al. (1995), and Dominé and Thibert (1996):

$$x_i = \frac{n_c\alpha_c}{n_{H_2O}\alpha_{H_2O}}\frac{\bar{v}_c}{\bar{v}_{H_2O}} \quad (14)$$

where α denotes the sticking coefficient and $\bar{v}$ the mean speed of gas molecules from the kinetic gas theory given in equation 13. The low diffusion constant of electrolytes in ice prevents volcanic volatiles, once incorporated into ice crystals, from re-evaporating. Using the expressions for the mean gas speed $\bar{v}$ given in equation 13 we obtain for the time-dependent change of a chemical species due to incorporation into ice crystals:

$$\frac{\partial}{\partial t}c_i = -\frac{\partial}{\partial t}c_g =$$
$$\frac{\partial}{\partial t}q_i\frac{c_g}{q_v}\frac{\alpha_c}{\alpha_{H_2O}}\sqrt{\frac{M_{H_2O}}{M_c}} \quad (15)$$

where c_i and c_g are the contents of chemicals in ice and in the gas phase in mol $kg^{-1}_{tot.mass}$, respectively. q_i and q_v denote the specific contents of ice and water vapour in kg kg^{-1}$_{tot.mass}$. The sticking coefficient α(HCl)=0.3 is taken from DeMore *et al.* (1997). For SO_2 and H_2S we assume the same values as for liquid water, $\alpha(SO_2)$=0.11 and $\alpha(H_2S)$=0.1, because no observational data were available. We apply for water vapour $\alpha(HO_2)$=1. In the context of this work, we neglect the temperature dependence of α. Considering the limited data available, the sticking coefficients applied in our simulations may hold for a first investigation of the significance of gas incorporation into ice particles. The efficiency factor $f_{inc,c}$

$$f_{inc,c} = \frac{\alpha_c}{\alpha_{H_2O}}\sqrt{\frac{M_{H_2O}}{M_c}} \qquad (16)$$

is for HCl $f_{inc,HCl}$=0.21, for SO_2 f_{inc,SO_2}=0.06 and for H_2S f_{inc,H_2S}=0.07, respectively. Hence, HCl will be most effectively incorporated into ice particles.

Release of gases from ice

Diehl *et al.* (1995) observed in laboratory experiments during the sublimation of polluted ice, that pure water vapour is transferred to the gas phase at first, leading to increased concentrations of dissolved species in the remaining hydrometeor. After reaching a critical contamination, simultaneous sublimation of water vapour and dissolved chemicals occurs. However, no quantitative information of this process is available. Probably, the release of solutes depends on the rate of water vapour transfer. There might be no time to build up an accumulation zone during fast sublimation, and instead, solutes and water vapour leave the ice crystal simultaneously. In this study, we assume that the fraction of chemicals released to the gas phase is proportional to that of sublimating water vapour. For consistency, the amount of released gases is weighted by the inverse of the factor applied in the gas incorporation equation (equation 15). The behaviour of the species concentration caused by release of gases from ice particles is given by:

$$\frac{\partial}{\partial t}c_g = -\frac{\partial}{\partial t}c_i =$$
$$\frac{\partial}{\partial t}q_v \frac{c_i}{q_i}\frac{\alpha_{H_2O}}{\alpha_c}\sqrt{\frac{M_c}{M_{H_2O}}} \qquad (17)$$

Transfer of solutes during microphysical processes

Coagulation of different hydrometeor classes leads to a mixture of the original solutions, thus producing new droplets or ice particles with average species concentrations. The retention coefficients for gases in water during freezing of the solution seem to be dependent on the species' nature. Iribarne & Pyshnov (1990) demonstrated experimentally that, during freezing of liquid droplets, some highly soluble chemical species, among them HCl, are totally retained in the ice phase. Iribarne (1990) found that S(IV) dissolved in droplets is partially evolved as SO_2 during freezing; the retention of S(IV) increases with increasing growth rate of the ice particles. In a volcanic eruption column, liquid droplets experience a strong temperature decrease because of the quick ascent (about 100 m/s) leading to rapid freezing. Here, we assume that the total amount of the chemicals contained in the liquid phase is shifted into the ice phase during droplet freezing. Correspondingly, the species previously contained in the ice phase are completely transferred into the liquid phase during ice melting. The time-dependent change of the specific content c_x, in mol kg^{-1}$_{tot.mass}$, of a chemical species contained in a hydrometeor q_x, in kg kg^{-1}$_{tot.mass}$, is assumed to be proportional to that of the hydrometeor. It is calculated from the sum over the microphysical processes involved with the particular type of hydrometeor, x, under consideration:

$$\frac{\partial}{\partial t}c_x = \sum_{procs} \frac{c_x}{q_x}(\frac{\partial}{\partial t}q_x). \qquad (18)$$

Condensation of water vapour on liquid hydrometeors leads to dilution of the solutions; evaporation of water drops causes an increase of the concentration. At the same time, the phase transfer kinetics of chemical species work towards a phase equilibrium. Total evaporation releases the species back into the gas phase, neglecting a possible aerosol formation due to the crystallisation of salt particles. The treatment of incorporation and resublimation of chemicals into ice particles during their growth has been shown above. The processes included in the scavenging module guarantee that volcanic species, initially erupted at the vent as gases, can be contained in each class of hydrometeors. Once scavenged, they experience all microphysical processes, as shown in Figure 4.

Numerical simulations with the plume model ATHAM

The ATHAM model is described in detail by Oberhuber *et al.* (1998) and Herzog (1998). This model is capable of dealing with the development of the dynamics in space and time, and it

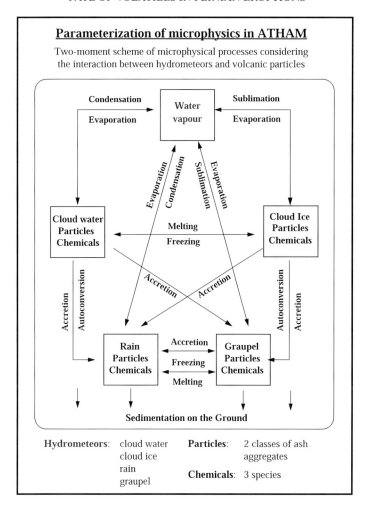

Fig. 4. Scheme of the processes included in the scavenging module.

considers the microphysics and physicochemical processes taking place in volcanic clouds (Textor 1999; Textor *et al.* 2003*a, b*). It has been tested for different applications (Graf *et al.* 1999, Trentmann *et al.* 2002). Here, we use the ATHAM model to simulate the development of a Plinian eruption cloud in the atmosphere, focusing on the fate of sulphur and halogen species.

In the ATHAM model, the full set of Navier–Stokes equations is solved using a finite difference method with an implicit time step scheme on a regular grid. For a complete description of the model equations, see Herzog (1998) and Oberhuber *et al.* (1998). In this study we use five modules:

- The dynamic part solves the Navier–Stokes equation for the gas–particle mixture, and includes the transport of active tracers (Herzog 1998; Oberhuber *et al.* 1998).
- The turbulence closure scheme delivers the turbulent exchange coefficients for each dynamic quantity, thereby describing the entrainment of ambient air into the plume (Herzog 1998, Oberhuber *et al.* 1998).
- The cloud microphysics describes condensation of water vapour and formation of precipitation. All phases of water are included: vapour, liquid, and solid. The feedback of thermal energy changes on the dynamics is considered (Herzog *et al.* 1998; Graf *et al.* 1999; Textor 1999, 2003*a*).
- The ash module describes particle growth and aggregation based on microphysical interactions between hydrometeors and ash (Textor 1999; Textor *et al.* 2003*a*).

• The scavenging module calculates dissolution of volcanic gases into droplets, including the dissociating reactions of the acidic gases, and the incorporation of volatiles into ice particles. The redistribution of species contained in hydrometeors due to micro-physical processes is considered (Textor 1999; Textor *et al.* 2003*b*).

The numerical experiments using the ATHAM model refer to processes close to the volcano. We focus on the exploration of the fate of volcanic gases within the eruption column, which is relevant for the mesoscale effects of the eruption on time-scales of several hours. We are interested in the amount of material injected into the strato-sphere, and not in the distribution of volcanic emissions on the global scale.

Numerical experiment of an explosive volcanic eruption similar to the Laacher See eruption, 12 900 years BP

For this study we used the axi-symmetrical version of the plume model formulated in cylindrical coordinates, as it is more economical in terms of computer memory and time. Cross-wind cannot be considered in this scheme, but the dilution of the mixture by entrainment of surrounding air is captured well (Herzog 1998). The simulations are performed on a stretched lattice with 126×126 grid points. The model domain was 200 km in the horizontal and 50 km in the vertical direction. In the centre of the model domain we use a spatial resolution of 120 m, coarsening to about 5 km at the margins. This grid choice permits the simulation of the full plume development with restricted computer resources without disturbances from the model boundaries for a simulation time of 90 min. The numerical experiments begin just after the earliest mixing of the erupting gas–particle mixture with the atmosphere, after equilibration with atmospheric pressure. The volcanic forcing in the model refers to the situation just after the decompression phase; small-scale processes in the vicinity of the crater in the high-temperature regime are not resolved within the concept of ATHAM. We focus on processes occurring in the plume in the spatial scales of about 100 m to some tens of km. The input of volcanic material during the eruption is specified by defining the vertical velocity, the temperature, and the composition of the ejecta at five vent grid points.

The volcanic and environmental conditions are based on the phonolitic Plinian eruption of the Laacher See volcano. The chemical species are initialized in concentrations according to the conditions of the eruption, as given in the pre-vious section.

• Geometry of the volcano: height 400 m, crater diameter 600 m, the crater depth 200 m.
• Vent exit velocity 350m/s, vent temperature 1000 K.
• Mean volume radii of the two ash classes: 2.5 and 50 μm, with the larger class contributing 60 % of the total ash mass.
• Particle density $\delta = 1800$ kg/m^3.
• Gas mass fraction of the gas–particle-mixture: 6 wt%, where water vapour con-tributes a fraction of 72.5 %.
• Gases

Gases	total	6	wt%
	H_2O	4.35	wt%
	SO_2	0.154	wt%
	HCl	8.42×10^{-2}	wt%
	HBr	2.59×10^{-3}	wt%

• Density of the gas–particle mixture: 3.9 kg/m^3
• Ash mass eruption rate $\approx 4 \times 10^8$ kg/s.

For initializing the environmental profiles of temperature and humidity, we used typical data for mid-latitude summer (McClatchey *et al.* 1972). The tropopause is at 13 km, as shown in Figure 5.

The simulation time was 90 min, and the eruption lasted for 30 min. Within the first 10 s, the eruption velocity was increased to its maximum, followed by a phase of 27 min of continuous eruption. During the last 3 min of the eruption, the vent exit velocity was reduced to zero again. We continued the simulation for additional 60 min in order to investigate the post-eruptive development of the volcanic plume.

The dynamic and environmental conditions of the volcanic eruption are constant for all experiments. The dispersal of volcanic material in the atmosphere, especially the injection into the stratosphere, depends on the volcanic conditions (composition of the magma, strength of the eruption) and on the meteorological conditions (stability of the atmosphere, lateral wind) in the ambient atmosphere. The impact of the environmental conditions on the plume's shape and height has been investigated by Herzog (1998) and Graf *et al.* (1999) through numerical simulations with ATHAM, and is not the subject of this study.

Results

Volcanic particles

The plume that develops under the conditions employed in this study reaches the stratosphere;

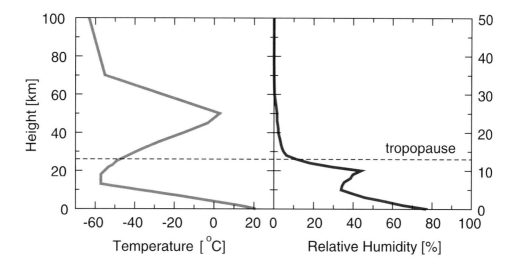

Fig. 5. Atmospheric background profiles for temperature and relative humidity.

the neutral buoyancy height is at 15 km. The time to rise from the crater to the tropopause at ~13 km is about 5 min; vertical velocities in the central rising zone are higher than 40 m/s on average. Smaller ash particles (radius 2.5 μm), cloud ice and volcanic gases form a layer in the stratosphere at the neutral buoyancy height, which spreads horizontally. Sedimentation removes larger particles from the stratosphere. ~10% by mass (in the following, all percentages refer to % by mass) of the particles are deposited 60 min after the eruption ends, indicating that gas particle separation is quite efficient in our simulation. The plume of volcanic particles after 30, 60 and 90 minutes of simulation are shown in Figure 6 a–c. The ash dispersal and the effect of aggregation on the plume height and shape are discussed elsewhere (Textor *et al.* 2003*a*).

Hydrometeors

Figure 7 a–b shows the plume of hydrometeors, and the vertical profiles at 30 min, and 60 min after the end of the eruption. The hydrometeors in our simulation contain volcanic ash (which is shown in Fig. 6), as determined by parameterisation of the microphysics in ATHAM (Textor *et al.* 2003*a*). Hence, water or ice is part of hydrometeor–ash-aggregates. As a result of the dry conditions of the surrounding atmosphere, the hydrometeor fraction in these aggregates is less than 20% at all grid points.

Condensation mainly occurs in the rising zone; the condensation level is at about 5 km height. Liquid water exists only in the central lower eruption column, and frozen hydrometeors predominate (>99% of the total hydrometeor mass). Most of the ice can be found in the umbrella region. A layer of cloud ice forms in the stratosphere, graupel (larger ice particles) slowly precipitates into the troposphere. At 90 min simulation time, i.e. 60 min after the end of the eruption, only ice exists in the plume. Before melting to rain, graupel evaporates, and precipitation cannot be detected at the ground.

Volcanic gases

The plume of total HCl at 30 min, and 60 min after the end of the eruption, is shown in Figure 8 a–b. Note that a large fraction of HCl reaches the stratosphere and, like the particles and hydrometeors, it spreads horizontally at the neutral buoyancy height. Some of this HCl, however, is scavenged by particles and transported back into the troposphere, as can be seen in Figure 8b.

The behaviour of volcanic gases in the eruption column is determined by the scavenging efficiency. The concentration of volcanic gases in different phases is dependent on the solubility of the individual species. The hydrogen halides HCl and HBr are highly soluble in liquid water, whereas the sulphur species SO_2 and H_2S are only slightly soluble. The vertical profiles of the

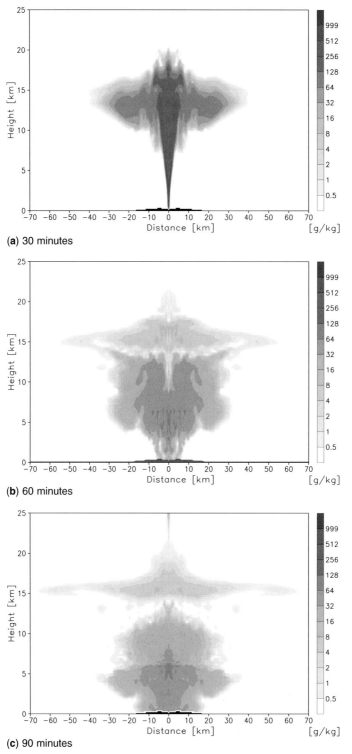

(a) 30 minutes

(b) 60 minutes

(c) 90 minutes

Fig. 6. The plume of volcanic particles after **(a)** 30, **(b)** 60 and **(c)** 90 minutes of simulation. The eruption starts at the beginning of the simulation and lasts 30 minutes. Ash mass mixing ratio is in g/kg total mass.

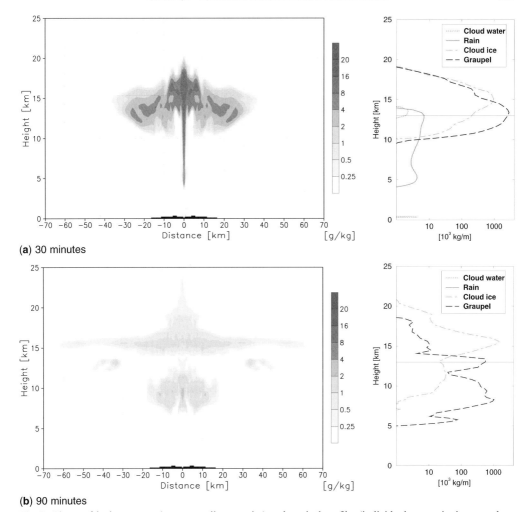

(a) 30 minutes

(b) 90 minutes

Fig. 7. Plume of hydrometeors (sum over all categories) and vertical profiles (individual categories integrated at each height level at (**a**) 30 min and (**b**) 90 min of the simulation.

species contained in all hydrometeor categories and in the gas phases are shown in Figure 9.

The halogens are contained in all phases of hydrometeors. These gases are scavenged by liquid water drops in the central rising zone of the plume. However, only ~1% by mass of the erupted amount is contained in liquid water, more then 70% by mass of the erupted halogens remain in the gas phase, because very little water is available. Droplet freezing and direct gas incorporation transfers halogens into cloud ice and graupel.

The sulphur gases, SO_2 and H_2S, are also contained in all phases of hydrometeors but about 95% of the erupted gases remain in the gas phase. Scavenging is mainly caused by direct gas incorporation. Due to their lower solubility, the scavenging by liquid water is insignificant (~0.005%).

Figure 10 shows the fractions of HCl and SO_2 erupted that reach the stratosphere. The species are shown in all phases. For comparison, the fraction of an inert gas in the stratosphere is included. This gas is not scavenged by hydrometeors, i.e. its stratospheric injection of ~85% is determined only by the plume height. More than 60% of the erupted halogens reach the stratosphere, and the scavenging efficiency is 30% when compared with the potential injection of the inert gas. Approximately 25% of the halogens in the stratosphere is contained in cloud ice. The growth of ice to graupel, and subsequent precipitation, would remove halogen species from the stratosphere.

More than 80% of the total erupted sulphur reaches the stratosphere. The scavenging effici-

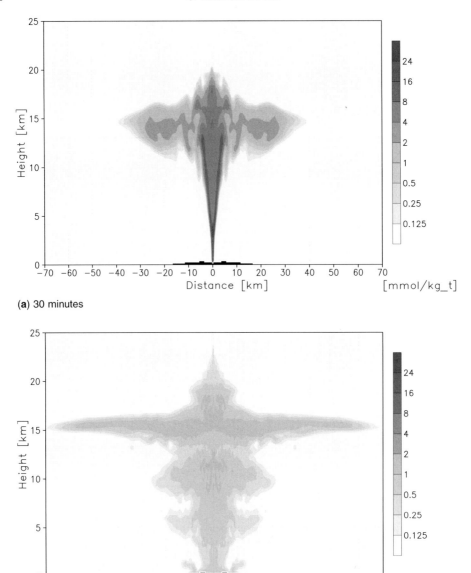

(a) 30 minutes

(b) 90 minutes

Fig. 8. The HCl eruption: plumes of total HCl (sum over HCl in all phases) (**a**) 30 min into the eruption, and (**b**) 60 min after the end of the eruption (90 min simulation time) in mmol/kg.

ency is 5% when compared with the potential injection of an inert gas; ~2% of the sulphur in the stratosphere is contained in ice.

Conclusions

We investigated zoned phonolitic Plinian eruption of Laacher See volcano, (12 900 years BP).

The ratios Cl/Br, F/Br, and SO_2*/Br v. Br increase strongly with decreasing Br concentration, i.e. with increasing depth of the magma chamber. Breakdown of mafic phenocrysts in the lower parts of the magma chamber must be taken into account as a source of fluorine and chlorine. Amphibole, phlogopite/biotite, and apatite appear to be incompatible for bromine

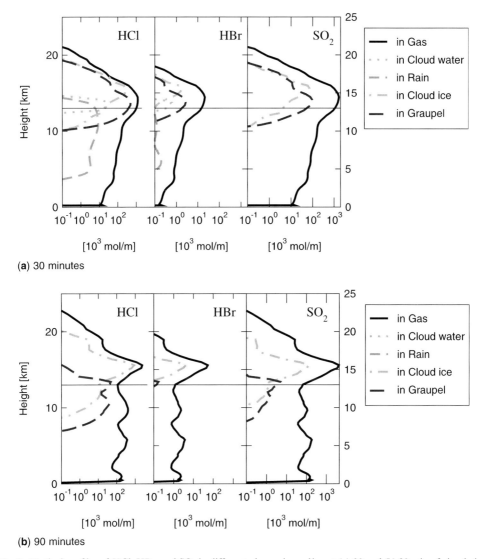

Fig. 9. Vertical profiles of HCl, HBr, and SO$_2$ in different phases, in mol/m, at (**a**) 30 and (**b**) 90 min of simulation.

(bromine concentrations <0.5 µg/g). In addition, the Laacher See melt was FeS-saturated in deep parts of the magma chamber, and provides evidence that sulphide has been resorbed in the shallower parts of the magma chamber, probably due to the increase of oxygen fugacity, fO_2. We therefore determined the masses of released fluid components, using the difference of bromine concentrations in glass inclusions and matrix glasses, and recalculating to volatile concentration at maximum Br concentration. The resulting masses M in Tg are: F=0.21, Cl=11.5, Br=0.19 −0.29, I:<0.03, S=3.38 (assuming pure SO$_2$) or S=52.4 (assuming pure H$_2$S), and H$_2$O=698.

We performed a numerical experiment with the plume model ATHAM for the conditions of the Laacher See eruption. The focus of this study was the investigation of the fate of volcanic gases in the plume and their injection into the stratosphere. The eruption column penetrated the tropopause, the neutral buoyancy height being reached about 2 km above it. The simulations showed that all volcanic gas species reach the neutral buoyancy height in the stratosphere. Without scavenging, about 85% of the gases erupted at the vent would reach the stratosphere. However, volcanic gases are partly scavenged by hydrometeors. The scavenging efficiency depends

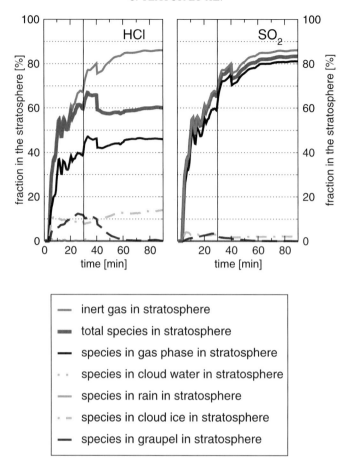

Fig. 10. Fraction of total erupted HCl (left plot) and SO₂ (right plot) that reached the stratosphere.

on the individual water solubility of the species, and on the incorporation in ice during diffusional growth. For the dry troposphere through which the Laacher See plume rose, we found a scavenging efficiency of only 30% for hydrogen halides, despite their high water solubility, and of 5% for the sulphur species.

The majority of the hydrometeors were frozen to ice, due to the fast plume rise and the great height of the eruption column. Hence, only a small amount of HCl and HBr was scavenged by liquid water in the rising plume. A small fraction of volcanic gases was incorporated into ice particles, but many of these were transported upwards and reached the neutral buoyancy height as well.

A large amount of SO₂ and H₂S stays in the gas phase at high levels in the umbrella region. The sulphur species are only slightly soluble in liquid water, and so they are not removed by

cloud and raindrops at lower heights. However, they might be scavenged by frozen hydrometeors via direct gas incorporation during diffusional growth. The proposed mechanism of gas trapping in ice within a volcanic plume is supported by observations of eruption clouds in which a lot of water was present in the plume due to interaction with sea-water: extremely high amounts of ice were accompanied by unusually low SO₂ concentrations. However, the exact value of the scavenging efficiency for the individual species is sensitive to the sticking probabilities of gas molecules at the ice particle's surface. These are based on limited data, which should be improved.

The scavenging efficiency depends on the availability of hydrometeors, and on the fraction of liquid water in the plume. The Laacher See eruption occurred in a dry environment. In a wet troposphere, the entrainment of humid ambient air increases the hydrometeor content. This might strongly enhance the scavenging of volcanic gases. A co-ignimbrite plume with a slower vertical velocity might also contain a much higher content of liquid water, which could efficiently remove HCl from the atmosphere.

The ATHAM simulations showed that the highest fraction of volcanic species that reached the umbrella region was still in the gas phase. Earlier numerical studies by Tabazadeh and Turco (1993) indicated that HCl was totally removed from the plume by scavenging in supercooled drops, while SO_2 was almost completely injected into the stratosphere. However, these authors did not consider freezing of hydrometeors, and probably overestimated the amount of liquid water in the plume. In addition, they did not consider scavenging by ice particles. Our numerical experiments show that, in a dry atmosphere, the amount of water condensing in a plume might not be sufficient to completely scavenge HCl, such that a large proportion can reach the stratosphere.

Volcanic species once scavenged by hydrometeors are not necessarily transferred to the troposphere and deposited at the ground via precipitation of contaminated rain. The ATHAM simulations show that precipitation evaporated in the dry atmosphere before reaching the ground, thus releasing the gases back to the troposphere. A large fraction of contaminated hydrometeors even reach the stratosphere. Gravitational settling would remove species from the stratosphere, and sublimation would release them in the gas phase. Our simulations suggest that the secondary increase of SO_2 during the first days after a stratospheric injection, which has been observed in some satellite data of eruption clouds, could be caused by SO_2 release from ice particles. The efficiency of gas scavenging by ice through co-condensation with water vapour depends on the growth mechanism of ice in the eruption column, and on the sticking coefficient of SO_2 on the ice particle. Further laboratory and field work are necessary to clarify this process.

The final amount of volcanic gases in the stratosphere depends on the fate of contaminated ice particles in the stratosphere. The effect of explosive volcanic eruptions on stratospheric chemistry and microphysics, and on the global climate, is determined by the specific volcanic and atmospheric conditions during and after the eruption.

Reviews by anonymous referees are greatly appreciated. This research was supported by the Volkswagen Foundation under the project EVA (emission of volcanic volatiles into the atmosphere).

References

ANDRES, R.J., ROSE, W. I., KYLE, P. R., DESILVA, S., FRANCIS, P., GARDEWEG, M. & ROA, H. M. 1991. Excessive sulfur dioxide emissions from Chilean volcanoes. *Journal of Volcanology and Geothermal Research*, **46**, 323–329.

ANGELL, J. K. 1997. Estimated impact of Agung, El Chichón and Pinatubo volcanic eruptions on global and regional total ozone after adjustment for the QBO. *Geophysical Research Letters*, **24(6)**, 647–650.

BERNDT, J., HOLTZ, F. & KOEPKE, J. 2001. Experimental constraints on storage conditions in the chemically zoned phonolitic magma chamber of the Laacher See volcano. *Contributions to Mineralogy and Petrology*, **140**, 469–486.

BLUTH, G. J. S, DOIRON, S. D., SCHNETZLER, C. C, KRUEGER, A. J., WALTER, L. S. 1992. Global tracking of the SO_2 clouds from the June, 1991 Mount Pinatubo eruptions. *Geophysical Research Letters*, **19**, 151–154.

BLUTH, G. J. S., SCOTT, C. J., SPROD, I. E., SCHNETZLER, C. C., KRUEGER, A. J. & WALTER, L. S. 1995. Explosive SO_2 emissions from the 1992 eruptions of Mount Spurr, Alaska. *US Geological Survey Bulletin*, **2139**, 37–45.

BRASSEUR, G. P., GRANIER, C. & WALTERS, S. 1990. Future changes in stratospheric ozone and the role of heterogeneous chemistry. *Nature*, **348**, 626–628.

BUREAU, H., KEPPLER, H. & MÉTRICH, N. 2000. Volcanic degassing of bromine and iodine: experimental fluid/melt partitioning data and applications to stratospheric chemistry. *Earth and Planetary Science Letters*, **183**, 51–60.

CARROLL, M. R. & BLANK, J. G. 1997. The solubility of H_2O in phonolitic melts. *American Mineralogist*, **82**, 549–556.

CHARLSON, R. J., LANGNER, J., RODHE, H., LEOVY, C. B. & WARREN, S. G. 1991. Perturbation of the Northern Hemisphere radiative balance by backscattering from anthropogenic sulfate aerosols. *Tellus*, **43A–B(4)**, 152–163

CHARLSON, R. J., SCHWARTZ, S. E., HALES, J. M., CESS, R. D., COAKLEY JR, J. A., HANSEN, J. E. & HOFFMAN, D. J. 1992. Climate forcing by anthropogenic aerosols. *Science*, **255**, 423–430.

DANIEL, J. S., SOLOMON, S. & ALBRITTON, D. L. 1995. On the evaluation of halocarbon radiative forcing and global warming potentials, *Journal of Geophysical Research*, **100**, 1271–1285.

DEMORE, W. B., SANDER, S. P. ET AL. 1997. *Chemical Kinetics and Photochemical Data for Use in Stratospheric Modeling.* Evaluation No. **12**; Jet Propulsion Laboratory: Pasadena, CA.

DIEHL, K., MITRA, S. K. & PRUPPACHER, H. R. 1995. A laboratory study of the uptake of HNO_3 and HCl vapor by snow crystals and ice spheres at temperatures between 0-degrees-C and –40-degrees-C. *Atmospheric Environment*, **29(9)**, 975–981

DIEHL, K., MITRA, S. K. & PRUPPACHER, H. R. 1998. A laboratory study on the uptake of HCl, HNO_3 and SO_2 gas by ice crystals and the effect of these gases on the evaporation rate of the crystals. *Atmospheric Research*, **48**, 235–244.

DOMINÉ, F. & THIBERT, E. 1996. Mechanism of incorporation of trace gases in ice grown from the gas phase. *Geophysical Research Letters*, **23(24)**, 3627–3630.

DOMINÉ, F., THIBERT, E. & SILVENTE, E. 1995. Determining past atmospheric HCl mixing ratios from ice core analyses. *Journal of Atmospheric Chemistry*, **21(2)**, 165–186.

GERLACH, T. M. & CASADEVALL, T. J. 1986. Fumarole emissions at Mount St. Helens Volcano, June 1980 to October 1981: degassing of a magma–hydrothermal system. *Journal of Volcanology and Geothermal Research*, **28**, 141–160.

GLAZE, L. S., BALOGA, S. M. & WILSON, L. 1997. Transport of atmospheric water vapor by volcanic eruption columns. *Journal of Geophysical Research*, **102(D5)**, 6099–6108.

GLEASON, J. F. *ET AL*. 1993. Record low global ozone in 1992. *Science*, **260**, 523–526.

GRAF, H.-F., HERZOG, M, OBERHUBER, J. M. & TEXTOR, C. 1999. The effect of environmental conditions on volcanic plume rise. *Journal of Geophysical Research*, **104**, 24 309–24 320.

GRANIER, C. & BRASSEUR, G. 1992. Impact of heterogeneous chemistry on model predictions of ozone changes. *Journal of Geophysical Research*, **97**, 18 015–18 033.

HANSTEEN, T. H., SACHS, P. M., LECHTENBERG, F. 2000. Synchrotron–XRF microprobe analysis of silicate reference standards using fundamental-parameter quantification. *European Journal of Mineralogy*, **12**, 25–31.

HARMS, E. 1998. Volatile composition and syn-eruptive degassing of the Laacher See phonolite magma (12,900 yr BP). *Reihe Geowissenschaften*, **39**.

HARMS, E., SCHMINCKE, H.-U. 2000. Volatile composition of the phonolitic Laacher See magma (12900. yr BP): implications for syn-eruptive degassing of S, F, Cl, and H₂O. *Contributions to Mineralogy and Petrology*, **138**, 84–98.

HERZOG, M. 1998. *Simulation der Dynamik eines Multikomponentensystems am Beispiel vulkanischer Eruptionswolken*. PhD Thesis, University of Hamburg.

HERZOG, M., GRAF, H.-F., TEXTOR, C. & OBERHUBER, J. M. 1998. The effect of phase changes of water on the development of volcanic plumes. *Journal of Volcanology and Geothermal Research*, **87**, 55–74.

HOFMANN, D. J. & SOLOMON, S. 1989. Ozone destruction through heterogeneous chemistry following the eruption of El Chichon. *Journal of Geophysical Research*, **94**, 5029–5041.

IRIBARNE, J. V. & PYSHNOV, T. 1990. The effect of freezing on the compositions of supercooled droplets – I. retention of HCl, NH₃ and H₂O₂. *Atmospheric Environment*, **24A(2)**, 383–387.

IRIBARNE, J. V., PYSHNOV, T. & NAIK, B. 1990. The effect of freezing on the compositions of supercooled droplets – II. Retention of S(IV). *Atmospheric Environment*, **24A(2)**, 389–398.

KEPPLER, H. 1999. Experimental evidence for the source of excess sulphur in explosive volcanic eruptions. *Science*, **284**, 1652–1654.

KROTKOV, N. A. & KRUEGER, A. J. 2000. Composition of the plume from the February 26, 2000 eruption of Mt. Hekla, Iceland: a combined satellite – model study. *EOS, Transactions of the American Geophysical Union*, **81(48)**, Fall Meeting Supplement, Abstract V61B–10.

LECHTENBERG, F., GARBE, S. *ET AL*. 1996. The x-ray fluorescence measurement place at beamline L of HASYLAB, *Journal of Trace and Microprobe Techniques*, **14(3)**, 561–587.

MCKEEN, S. A., LIU, S. C. & KIANG, C. S. 1984. On the chemistry of stratospheric SO₂ from volcanic eruptions. *Journal of Geophysical Research*, **89(D3)**, 4873–4881.

MCCLATCHEY, R. A., FENN, R. W., SELBY, J. E. A., VOLZ, F. E. & GARING, J. S. 1972. *Optical Properties of the Atmosphere*, 3rd edn, Environmental Research Papers, No. 411.

MANKIN, W. G. & COFFEY, M. T. 1984. Increased stratospheric hydrogen chloride in the El Chichon cloud. *Science*, **226(4671)**, 170–172.

MANKIN, W. G., COFFEY, M. T. & GOLDMAN, A. 1992. Airborne observations of SO₂, HCl, and O₃ in the stratospheric plume of the Pinatubo volcano in July 1991. *Geophysical Research Letters*, **19**, 179–182.

MAYBERRY, G. C., ROSE, W. I. & BLUTH, G. J. S. 2001. Dynamics of the volcanic and meteorological clouds produced by the December 26, 1997 eruption of Soufrière Hills volcano, Montserrat, W.I. *In:* DRUITT, T. & KOKELAAR, P. (eds) *The Eruption of Soufrière Hills Volcano, Montserrat, 1995–99*, Geological Society of London, Memoir, **21**, 539–555

MITRA, S. K., WALTROP, A., FLOSSMANN, A., PRUPPACHER, H. R. 1992. A windtunnel and theoretical investigation to test various theories for the absorption of SO₂ by drops of pure water and water drops containing H₂O₂ and (NH₄)₂SO₄. *In:* SCHWARTZ, S. E. & SLINN, W. G. N. (eds) *Precipitation Scavenging and Atmospheric–Surface Exchange*, Vol. I of The Georgii Volume: Precipitation Scavenging Processes, Hemispheric Publishing Corporation, Washington DC 123–141.

MONTZKA, S. A., BUTLER, J. H. *ET AL*. 1996. Decline in the tropospheric abundance of halogen from halocarbons: Implications for stratospheric ozone depletion. *Science*, **272(5266)**, 1318–1322.

NEWHALL, C. G. & SELF, S. 1982. The volcanic explosivity index (VEI): an estimate of explosivity magnitude for historic volcanism. *Journal of Geophysical Research*, **87**, 1231–1238.

OBERHUBER, J. M., HERZOG, M., GRAF, H.-F., SCHWANKE K 1998. Volcanic plume simulation on large scales. *Journal of Volcanology and Geothermal Research*, **87**, 29–53.

PRESS, W. H., TEUKOLSKY, S. A., VETTERLING, W. T., FLANNERY, B.P. 1992. *Numerical Recipes in FORTRAN, the Art of Scientific Computing*, Cambridge University Press, 2nd edition.

PRUPPACHER, H. R. & KLETT, J. D. 1997. *Microphysics of Cloud and Precipitation*, Kluwer Academic Publishers, The Hague, 2nd edition.

ROSE, W. I., DELENE, D. J., SCHNEIDER, D. J., BLUTH, G. J. S., KRUEGER, A. J., SPROD, I., MCKEE, C., DAVIES, H., ERNST, G. G. J. 1995. Ice in the 1994

Rabaul Eruption Cloud: implications for volcano hazard and atmospheric effects. *Nature*, **375**, 477–479.

ROSE, W. I., BLUTH, G. J. S. & ERNST, G. G. J. 2000. Integrating retrievals of volcanic cloud characteristics from satellite remote sensors: a summary. *Philosophical Transactions of the Royal Society of London Series A – Mathematical, Physical and Engineering Sciences*, **358(1770)**, 1585–1606.

ROSE, W. I., BLUTH, G. J. S., RILEY, C. M., WATSON, I. M, YU, T. & ERNST, G. G. J. 2000. Potential mitigation of volcanic cloud hazards using satellite data – a case study of the February 2000 Hekla Event and an unexpected NASA DC8 encounter. *EOS – Transactions of the American Geophysical Union*, **81(48)**, Fall Meeting Supplement, Abstract V61B-09.

ROSE, W. I., BLUTH, G. J. S., SCHNEIDER, D. J., ERNST, G. G. J., RILEY, C. M. & McGIMSEY, R. G. 2001. Observations of 1992 Crater Peak/Spurr volcanic clouds in their first few days of atmospheric residence. *Journal of Geology*, **109**, 677–694.

SACHS, P. M. & HARMS, E. 1998. The injection of bromine into the atmosphere by the Plinian Laacher See eruption (Germany), 12000 BP: relevance for the global stratospheric ozone layer. *EOS – Transactions of the American Geophysical Union*, **79**, 936 (abstract).

SACHS, P. M. & HARMS, E. 2000. Atmospheric release of Br, I, Cl, F and SO2 by the Laacher See volcanic eruption (Germany), 12900 BP. *Berichte der Deutschen Mineralogischen Gesellschaft, Beiheft zum European Journal of Mineralogy*, **12**, 174.

SANDER, R. & CRUTZEN, P. J. 1996. Model study indicating halogen activation and ozone destruction in polluted air masses transported to the sea. *Journal of Geophysical Research*, **101D**, 9121–9138.

SCAILLET, B. & PICHAVANT, M. 2003. Experimental constraints on volatile abundances in arc magmas and their implications for degassing processes. In: OPPENHEIMER, C., PYLE, D. M. & BARCLAY, J. *Volcanic Degassing*. Geological Society, London, Special Publications, **213**, 23–52.

SCHMINCKE, H. U., PARK, C. & HARMS, E. 1999. Evolution and environmental impacts of the eruption of Laacher See Volcano (Germany) 12,900 a BP. *Quaternary International*, **61**, 61–72.

SCHNEIDER, D. J. & ROSE, W. I. 1994. Observations of the 1989–90 Redoubt Volcano eruption clouds using AVHRR Satellite Imagery. In: T. CASADEVALL (ed.) Proceedings of International Symposium on Volcanic Ash and Aviation Safety. *US Geological Survey Bulletin* **2047**, 405–418.

SCHNETZLER, C. C., BLUTH, G. J. S., KRUEGER, A J. & WALTER, L. S. 1997. A proposed volcanic sulphur dioxide index (VSI). *Journal of Geophysical Research*, **102(B9)**, 20 087–20 091.

SCHWARTZ, S. E. 1986. Mass-transport considerations pertinent to aqueous phase reactions of gases in liquid-water clouds. In: *Chemistry of the Multiphase Atmosphere*. JAESCHKE, W. (ed.), Springer-Verlag, Berlin.

SEINFELD, J. H. & PANDIS, S. N. 1997. *Atmospheric Chemistry and Physics: from Air Pollution to Global Change*, John Wiley, New York.

SIMKIN, T. 1993. Terrestrial volcanism in space and time. *Annual Review of Earth and Planetary Sciences*, **21**, 427–452.

SOLOMON, S., PORTMANN, R. W., GARCIA, R. R., THOMASON, L.W., POOLE, L. R. & McCORMICK, M. P. 1996. The role of aerosol variations in anthropogenic ozone depletion at northern midlatitudes. *Journal of Geophysical Research*, **101**, 6713–6727.

SOLOMON, S., PORTMANN, R.W. ET AL. 1998. Ozone depletion at mid-latitudes: coupling of volcanic aerosols and temperature variability to anthropogenic chlorine. *Geophysical Research Letters*, **25(11)**, 1871–1874.

STENCHIKOV, G. L., KIRCHNER, I. ET AL. 1998. Radiative forcing from the 1991 Mount Pinatubo volcanic eruption. *Journal of Geophysical Research*, **103**, 13 837–13 857.

TABAZADEH, A & TURCO, R. P. 1993. Stratospheric chlorine injection by volcanic eruptions: HCl scavenging and implications for ozone. *Science*, **260**, 1082–1086.

TAIT, S. R. 1988. Samples from the crystallising boundary layer of a zoned magma chamber. *Contributions to Mineralogy and Petrology*, **100**, 470–483.

TAIT, S. R., WÖRNER, G. V. D., BOGAARD, P., SCHMINCKE, H.-U. 1989. Cumulate nodules as evidence for convective fractionation in a phonolite magma chamber. *Journal of Volcanology and Geothermal Research*, **37**, 21–37.

TEXTOR, C 1999. *Numerical simulation of scavenging processes in explosive volcanic eruption clouds.* Dissertation, Max-Planck-Institut für Meteorologie, Examensarbeit 65, Hamburg.

TEXTOR, C., GRAF, H.-F., HERZOG, M., OBERHUBER, J. M., ROSE, W. I. & ERNST, G. G. J. (2003a) Volcanic particles in explosive eruption columns, Part I and II: to be submitted to *Journal of Volcanology*.

TEXTOR C., GRAF H.-F., HERZOG, M. & OBERHUBER, J. M. (2003b) Injection of Gases into the Stratosphere by Explosive Volcanic Eruptions, *Journal Geophysical Research* (in press).

THIBERT, E. & DOMINÉ, F. 1997. Thermodynamics and kinetics of the solid solution of HCl in ice. *Journal of Physical Chemistry*, **101**, 3554–3565.

TRENTMANN, J., ANDREAE, M. O., GRAF, H.-F., HOBBS, P. V., OTTMAR, R. D. & TRAUTMANN, T. 2002. Simulation of a biomass burning plume: comparison of model results with observations, *Journal of Geophysical Research* **107 (D2)**, 10.1029–10.1043.

TIE, X. X. & BRASSEUR, G. 1995. The response of stratospheric ozone to volcanic eruptions – sensitivity to atmospheric chlorine loading. *Journal of Geophysical Research*, **22(22)**, 3035.

VALDEZ, M. P. & DAWSON, G. A. 1984. Sulfur dioxide incorporation into ice depositing from the vapour. *Journal of Geophysical Research*, **23**, 39–68.

VAN DEN BOGAARD, P., SCHMINCKE, H.-U. 1985. Laacher See tephra: a widespread isochronous late Quternary tephra layer in central and northern Europe. *Geological Society of America Bulletin*, **96**, 1554–1571.

VAREKAMP, J. C., LUHR, J. F. & PRESTEGAARD, K. I. 1984. The 1982 eruptions of El Chichón volcano

(Chiapas, Mexico): character of the eruptions, ash-fall deposits, and gas phase. *Journal of Volcanology and Geothermal Research*, **23**, 39–68.

VINCZE, L., JANSSENS, K. & ADAMS, F. 1993. A general Monte Carlo simulation of energy dispersive X-ray fluorescence spectra. *Spectrochimica Acta*, **48B**, 553.

WALLACE, L. & LIVINGSTON, W. 1992. The effect of the Pinatubo cloud on hydrogen chloride and hydrogen fluoride. *Geophysical Research Letters*, **19(12)**, 1209.

WESTRICH, H. R. & GERLACH, T. M. 1992. Magmatic gas source for the stratospheric SO_2 cloud from the June 15, 1991 eruption of Mount Pinatubo. *Geology*, **20**, 867–870.

WILSON, L. 1976. Explosive volcanic eruptions – III. Plinian eruption columns. *Geophysical Journal of the Royal Astronomical Society*, **45**, 543–556.

WOODS, A. W. 1988. The fluid dynamics and thermo-dynamics of eruption columns. *Bulletin of Volcanology*, **50**, 169–193.

WOODS, A W. 1993. Moist convection and the injection of volcanic ash into the atmosphere. *Journal of Geophysical Research*, **98**, 17 627–17 636.

WOODS, D. C., CHUAN, R. L. & ROSE, W. I. 1985. Halite particles injected into the stratosphere by the 1982 El Chichón eruption. *Science*, **230**, 170–172

WÖRNER, G , SCHMINCKE, H. U. 1984*a* Mineralogical and chemical zonation of the Laacher See sequence (East Eifel, Germany). *Journal of Petrology*, **25**, 805–835.

WÖRNER, G. & SCHMINCKE, H. U. 1984*b*. Petrogenesis of the zoned Laacher See tephra sequence. *Journal of Petrology*, **25**, 836–851.

WÖRNER, G., STAUDIGEL, H. & ZINDLER, A. 1985. Isotopic contraints on open system evolution of the Laacher See magma chamber (Eifel, West Germany). *Earth and Planetary Science Letters*, **75**, 37–49.

Changes in stratospheric composition, chemistry, radiation and climate caused by volcanic eruptions

R. G. GRAINGER[1] & E. J. HIGHWOOD[2]

[1]*Atmospheric, Oceanic & Planetary Physics, Clarendon Laboratory,*
Parks Road, Oxford OX1 3PU, UK.
(e-mail: r.grainger@physics.ox.ac.uk)
[2]*Department of Meteorology, University of Reading,*
Reading RG6 6BB, UK.

Abstract: The primary effect of a volcanic eruption is to alter the composition of the stratosphere by the direct injection of ash and gases. On average, there is a stratospherically significant volcanic eruption about every 5.5 years. The principal effect of such an eruption is the enhancement of stratospheric sulphuric acid aerosol through the oxidation and condensation of the oxidation product H_2SO_4. Following the formation of the enhanced aerosol layer, observations have shown a reduction in the amount of direct radiation reaching the ground and a concomitant increase in diffuse radiation. This is associated with an increase in stratospheric temperature and a decrease in global mean surface temperature (although the spatial pattern of temperature changes is complex). In addition, the enhanced aerosol layer increases heterogeneous processing, and this reduces the levels of active nitrogen in the lower stratosphere. This in turn gives rise to either a decrease or an increase in stratospheric ozone levels, depending on the level of chlorine loading.

Introduction

This paper addresses the composition, chemistry, radiation and climate effects caused by large amounts of material injected into the stratosphere by volcanic eruptions. The primary effect of a volcanic eruption is to alter the composition of the stratosphere by the direct injection of ash and gases. The ejecta themselves have a relatively small effect on the atmospheric state, but the secondary product, stratospheric sulphate aerosol, has a major effect on stratospheric radiation, chemistry and climate. The two most recent large eruptions were those of El Chichón, Mexico in April 1982 and of Mount Pinatubo, Philippines, in June 1991. Detailed reviews of these eruptions can be found in Hofmann (1987) and McCormick et al. (1995). For reviews of the atmospheric effects of stratospheric aerosols, see Lamb (1970) or Pueschel (1996). An extensive review of the impact of volcanic eruptions on climate is given by Robock (2000).

In general, only eruptions that penetrate into the stratosphere produce atmospheric effects on time-scales greater than a few days, as concentrations of volcanic ejecta in the troposphere are relatively quickly depleted through precipitation, diffusion and rainout. The significant exceptions are long-lived effusive eruptions which can create a tropospheric 'steady state' of enhanced levels of volcanic debris. The eruption of Laki in Iceland in 1783 is one such example.

Indirect effects of volcanic perturbations considered elsewhere include:

- cooling of the ocean surface (Robock & Mao 1995),
- changes in cirrus microphysical properties (Minnis et al. 1993),
- changes in polar stratospheric cloud properties (Deshler et al. 1994).

Volcanic episode

Eruption

A volcanic event occurs when there is a sudden or continuing release of energy caused by near-surface or surface magma movement, and can include explosions with an eruption plume. Eruption duration can range from a few minutes to thousands of years, with the median duration being seven weeks (Simkin & Siebert 1994). Volcanic ash clouds can be produced in extremely small eruptions of duration less than one minute. Violent eruptions often occur after

From: OPPENHEIMER, C., PYLE, D.M. & BARCLAY, J. (eds) *Volcanic Degassing.* Geological Society, London, Special Publications, **213**, 329–347. 0305-8719/03/$15.00

long periods of repose, so dangerous volcanoes may not currently be recognized as active. Of the 16 largest explosive eruptions in the last 200 years, 12 were the first historic eruption known from the volcano.

During a single eruption, styles of activity and types of products may change within minutes to hours, depending upon changes in magma composition, volatiles, or other magma chamber and vent conditions. The diversity of volcanoes and volcanic products is due to differences in the composition of the magma (molten or liquid rock), which control its viscosity and gas content. Gases become less soluble in magma as it approaches the surface and the pressure decreases. The greater the gas content of a magma, the more explosive the eruption. Additionally, magma water interaction can generate very explosive eruptions.

Eruptions with a Volcanic Explosivity Index (VEI) greater than 4 are likely to penetrate into the stratosphere (see Newhall & Self 1982, for definition of the VEI). Table 1, adapted from Bluth *et al.* (1997), lists such eruptions from 1979 to 1994. Although all penetrated into the stratosphere, most of these eruptions did not have a strong effect on the atmosphere. Figure 1 shows a measure of global stratospheric aerosol loading from 1850 to 2000. During this period there were 26 eruptions that produced a global stratospheric optical depth greater than 0.02. This suggests that, on average, there is a significant eruption into the stratosphere about every 5.5 years.

Volcanic plume

The most abundant gases typically released into the atmosphere from volcanic systems are water

Table 1. *Recent Eruptions with Volcanic Explosivity Index (VEI) ≥4 (from Bluth et al. 1997).*

Volcano	Latitude of volcano	Volcano height (km above sea-level)	Eruption date
St Helens	46. 2° N	3.1	18 May 1980
Pagan	18.1° N	0.6	15 May 1981
El Chichón	17.3° N	1.1	4 April 1982
Colo	0.2° S	0.5	23 July 1983
Augustine	59.4° N	1.2	27 March 1986
Kelut	7.8° S	1.7	11 February 1990
Pinatubo	15.1° N	1.7	15 June 1991
Hudson	45.9° S	2.5	12 August 1991
Rabaul	4.3° S	0.2	19 September 1994
Kliuchevskoi	56.1° N	4.8	1 October 1994

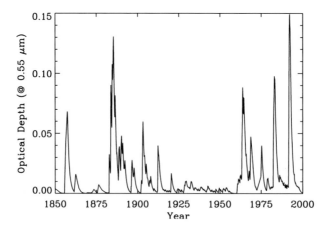

Fig. 1. Global stratospheric aerosol optical depth at 0.55 μm (from the data of Sato *et al.* 1993, including updates to 2000).

vapour (H_2O), followed by carbon dioxide (CO_2) and sulphur dioxide (SO_2). Volcanoes also release smaller amounts of other gases, including hydrogen sulphide (H_2S), hydrogen (H_2), helium (He), carbon monoxide (CO), hydrogen chloride (HCl), hydrogen fluoride (HF), nitrogen (N_2), and argon (Ar).

In addition to the release of a number of gases, an explosive eruption blasts molten and solid rock fragments (tephra) into the air. The largest fragments (bombs) fall back to the ground near the vent, usually within 3 km. The ash (rock fragments with diameter <2 mm), continues rising into the air, forming an eruption column.

Eruption columns can grow rapidly, reaching heights of more than 20 km above the volcano in less than 30 minutes. The upper surface of the eruption cloud may be tens of degrees cooler than the surrounding environment, owing to intertial overshoot of the erupted mixture above the neutral buoyancy height (Woods & Kienle 1994). This can complicate the estimation of cloud height from thermal satellite imagery.

Analysis of the Geostationary Meteorological Satellite (GMS) and Advanced Very High Resolution Radiometer (AVHRR) images of the Mount Pinatubo eruption plume by Holasek *et al.* (1996) gave the initial plume radius as 50 km; this increased to about 275 km after about 2 hours 45 minutes. Woods & Kienle (1994) state that the 18 May 1980 Mount St Helens ash plume increased in radius from 20 km to 50 km in about 10 minutes. It also took about 10 minutes for the 21 April 1990 Redoubt volcanic plume to increase in radius from about 6 km to over 15 km.

Volcanic cloud

After its initial expansion the ash cloud drifts following the local wind patterns, becoming separated from the volcanic source. The rates of drift of ash clouds are typically in the range of 20–100 km/h. Vertical wind shear may result in the cloud moving in different directions as a function of altitude. This happened following the 28 March 1982 eruption of El Chichón, when the tropospheric component of the ash cloud spread in a northeasterly direction, whereas the stratospheric component moved to the southwest (Matson 1984).

Sawada (1994) tabulates the dimensions of the highest ash clouds for 17 volcanic eruptions detected using the GMS from December 1977 to June 1991. These clouds had a typical area equivalent radius of about 110 km, with the largest being the 14–15 June 1991 Mount Pinatubo cloud, which had an area equivalent radius of about 1230 km.

For equatorial latitudes, the typical time for the cloud of volcanic debris to circle the globe was measured as 21 days (Matson & Robock 1984) and 22 days (Bluth *et al.* 1992) for the eruptions of El Chichón and Mount Pinatubo respectively. At higher latitudes, the time is less, e.g. Schoeberl *et al.* (1993a) show the SO_2 plume from the Cerro Hudson (45.9° S) eruption of August 1991 circled the globe in seven days.

Volcanic ash properties

COMPOSITION

The physical properties of volcanic ashes depend mostly on their relative proportions of glass, mineral fragments and rock fragments (Heiken 1994). Volcanic ash is abrasive, mildly corrosive, and conductive (especially when wet), and may also carry a high static charge. Bayhurst *et al.* (1994) give the density of ash from the 15 December eruption of Mount Redoubt as 2.42 ± 0.79 g/cm^3. In addition, they found the average aspect ratio and surface area of an ash particle to be 3.5 and 284 μm^2 respectively.

SIZE DISTRIBUTION

The initial particle-size distribution of volcanic ejecta is poorly understood, although Sparks *et al.* (1994) note that 70% of ejecta from explosive eruptions is less than 1 mm in radius. Hobbs *et al.* (1991) measured the *in situ* particle-size distributions of ash emissions from Mount Redoubt, Mount St Helens and Mount Augustine. The size distributions were approximately multimode log-normal distributions with a nucleation mode (r_{mode} <0.05 μm), an accumulation mode (r_{mode} 0.05–0.5 μm), and one or more giant modes (r_{mode} >0.5 μm). Hobbs *et al.* (1991) considered the nucleation mode to be composed of sulphuric acid–water drops, where the H_2SO_4 was produced either in the volcanic throat or by gas to particle conversion of the SO_2 in the eruption plume. The accumulation and giant modes were thought to be composed of silicate particles.

The evolution of the ash cloud was principally a decrease in the concentration at all particle sizes. This is not surprising as the residence time of a volcanic ash particle is strongly controlled by its mass (i.e. size) and non-spherical morphology (Mackinnon *et al.* 1984). Table 2 from Bursik *et al.* (1994) shows the estimated terminal velocity and typical residence times as a function of particle size for an ash cloud with a particle density of 2 g/cm^3 at 12.9 km. Some of the smaller particles aggregate into clusters due to electrostatic attraction, giving them settling

Table 2. *Estimated particle terminal velocities and residence times. Adapted from Bursik et al. (1994).*

Radius (μm)	Fall speed (m/s)	Residence time
700	9	9.3 min
355	6.4	13 min
173	3.2	26 min
85	1.9	43 min
45	0.64	2.2 h
22	0.15	9.3 h
11	0.05	1.1 days
5.5	0.012	4.8 days
2.75	0.0025	23 days

velocities higher than those shown, i.e. ≈0.3–1.0 m/s (Macedonio *et al.* 1994).

It is important to realize that most of the ash mass in the early lifetime of a cloud is contained in relatively large particles (i.e. 90% of the mass of the volcanic cloud is contained in particles bigger than 2 μm) which rapidly sediment out of the atmosphere. This is consistent with the conclusion of Knollenberg & Huffman (1983) that volcanic material injected into the stratosphere by large volcanic eruptions is typically less than 1 μm in radius. From the measurements of Gooding *et al.* (1983) for the El Chichón eruption, the *e*-folding time for volcanic ash is estimated to be about 40 days (the *e*-folding time is the time it takes for an amount to decay to $1/e$ of its initial value).

Although the amount of ash injected for recent eruptions is relatively well known, considerable research is still required to quantify the effect of ash on the stratosphere. The relatively minor role of the ash component in climate modification is largely due to its short residence in the atmosphere; rapid aggregation leads to the fallout of even the finest tephra within a few hundred to 1000 kilometres from the source (Sigurdsson & Laj 1992).

Development of the aerosol cloud

The flow of sulphur into the stratosphere is dominated by large explosive eruptions which account for about 60% of stratospheric sulphur

budget (Sedlacek *et al.* 1983). Pyle *et al.* (1996) estimate that on average about 0.06–0.15 Mt/y of stratospheric sulphur (as SO_2) is from non-volcanic sources, while about 1 Mt/y arises from volcanic injection. Individual eruptions such as those detailed in Table 3 may increase the SO_2 loading by more than an order of magnitude. Historic eruptions such as the 1815 Tambora and the 1783 Laki eruptions are thought to have injected about 50 Mt (SO_2 equivalent) into the stratosphere (Sigurdsson & Laj 1992).

Volcanic emissions also include sulphur in the form of H_2S. This reacts to form HS which in turn forms SO_2 though reaction mechanisms involving O_2, O_3, or NO (Sigurdsson & Laj 1992). As this process is very rapid H_2S can be thought of as an additional source of SO_2.

The enhancement in gas concentrations reduces the ability of solar and terrestrial radiation to penetrate the atmosphere in the gas absorption bands. For example, increased absorption by SO_2 in the wavelength intervals 180–235 nm, 260–340 nm and 340–390 nm reduces the transmission of solar flux and so reduces the photolysis rates of key species such as ozone (Bekki *et al.* 1993). Stratospheric ozone can also be directly influenced by SO_2. Bekki *et al.* (1993) suggest that ozone production is catalysed by SO_2 above about 25 km. Below this level the absorption of radiation by SO_2 dominates.

Once in the stratosphere, SO_2 is oxidized to H_2SO_4 through:

$$SO_2 + OH + M \rightarrow HSO_3 + M$$
$$HSO_3 + O_2 \rightarrow SO_3 + HO_2$$
$$SO_3 + H_2O \rightarrow H_2SO_4$$

where M is any third molecule (McKeen *et al.* 1984). The removal rate of SO_2 has an *e*-folding time of about 35 days for equatorial eruptions (Heath *et al.* 1983; Bluth *et al.* 1992; Read *et al.* 1993).

Properties of volcanically enhanced stratospheric aerosol

A volcanically enhanced stratospheric aerosol layer is formed as H_2SO_4 that has been produced

Table 3. *Estimates of the amount of SO_2 injected into the stratosphere from recent major eruptions.*

Volcano	Latitude	Eruption date	SO_2 emitted (Mt)	Reference
El Chichón	17.3°N	April 1982	7	Hofmann & Rosen (1983)
Mount Pinatubo	15.1°N	June 1991	12–15	McPeters (1993)
			20	McCormick *et al.* (1995)
Cerro Hudson	45.9°S	August 1991	1.5	Schoeberl *et al.* (1993a)

from the SO_2 condenses onto pre-existing condensation nuclei such as existing sulphuric acid particles, and perhaps ash particles, ion clusters, or trace meteoric material. It is this aerosol layer, whose mass is enhanced by several orders of magnitude following a large eruption, which gives rise to the strong perturbations to atmospheric chemistry and radiation discussed later.

There is no 'typical' volcanic aerosol during the decay of the cloud. The aerosol evolves with time through transport and through aerosol processes of evaporation, condensation, collision, coalescence, and sedimentation. As a result, estimates of the impact of such aerosol on the radiation budget of the Earth have appropriately large error estimates.

Morphology

The increase in temperature with height makes the stratosphere extremely stable, so that there is little vertical convection. The injected aerosol cloud tends to spread with the horizontal winds and to slowly descend through gravitational motion. The main removal mechanism for aerosols is gravitational settling into the troposphere, after which the particles are removed by deposition processes. Aerosols can remain in the stratosphere for up to a few years; during this time they can be transported a significant distance from the source.

The rate of descent of the core of the Mount Pinatubo volcanic cloud was about 17 m day^{-1} at 23 km (Lambert et al. 1993), which was consistent with particles with an aerodynamic radius of about 0.25 μm. The removal rate from the stratosphere is dependent on season and the size of the particles. Pinto et al. (1989) suggested that aerosol residence time in the stratosphere is self-limiting, as larger eruptions produce larger

particles that precipitate out more quickly. This is consistent with data from a number of eruptions shown in Table 4, where the estimates of the stratospheric aerosol e-folding loss rate do not increase linearly with injected SO_2 mass.

Eruptions at tropical latitudes are particularly effective at producing global-scale perturbations to the background stratospheric aerosol amounts, since the aerosol can be transported around the equator in about 20 days, and to the poles of both hemispheres on time-scales of a few weeks. Figure 2 shows the evolution of the Mount Pinatubo aerosol cloud observed by instruments on the Upper Atmosphere Research Satellite. Evident in the images is the slow descent of the aerosol and the containment of the cloud in a tropical reservoir which is slowly eroded through transport to higher latitudes (principally the winter hemisphere). Large amounts of sulphuric acid deposition in ice cores in both the Arctic (Zielinski 1995) and Antarctic (Delmas et al. 1992) in the years following major eruptions also testify to the global spread of aerosols.

Composition

Because of its low vapour pressure, almost all of the H_2SO_4 vapour condenses to form liquid H_2SO_4–H_2O particles. The larger sulphuric acid particles typically contain volcanic ash particles (Pueschel et al. 1994). However, it is not clear if this is an indication of heterogeneous nucleation or if these are particles that have undergone coagulation. The weight fraction of sulphuric acid in the particles is determined by the temperature and humidity (Steele & Hamill 1981): the higher the humidity the lower the sulphuric acid concentration. Lambert et al. (1997) used satellite temperature and water vapour measurements to calculate that the Mount Pinatubo aerosol cloud had compositions typically in the range

Table 4. Stratospheric aerosol e-folding time loss rates estimated from either point measurements or from near-global satellite data. The SO_2 amounts are taken from Bluth et al. (1997).

| Volcano | SO_2 (Mt) | Loss rate (months) | | Reference |
		Point	Near global	
St Helens	1.0	3.6		Jäger & Carnuth (1987)
Alaid	1.1	6.6		Jäger & Carnuth (1987)
El Chichón	7	10.4–12.3		Hofmann & Rosen (1984)
		11.5–14.3		Jäger & Carnuth (1987)
			14	Yue et al. (1991)
Mount Pinatubo	20	11.3		Rosen et al. (1994)
			8.3–10.9	Kent & Hansen (1998)
			11.3	Lambert et al. (1997)

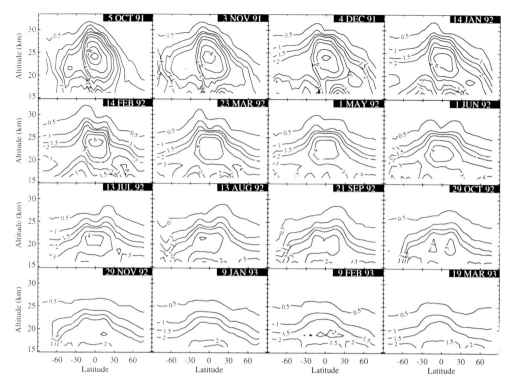

Fig. 2. Zonal mean distribution of the Pinatubo aerosol volume density. Contour levels are set at 0.5, 1, 1.5, 2, 3, 4, 6, 8, and 10 $\mu m^3/cm^3$ (from Lambert *et al.* 1997). Reproduced by permission of the American Geophysical Union.

55–80% sulphuric acid by weight. The core of the aerosol cloud had a composition of about 70% sulphuric acid by weight (Grainger *et al.* 1993; Rinsland *et al.* 1994*b*).

Size distribution

If the H_2SO_4 concentration is sufficiently high, homogeneous nucleation may occur. Aerosols grow rapidly through condensation to obtain a radius of about 0.01 μm (Hofmann 1987) and additionally through coagulation to about 0.1 μm.

The size distribution, $n(r)$, is usually expressed so that $n(r)dr$ is the number of drops per unit volume having a radius between r and $r+dr$. Several mathematical functions have been used to express $n(r)$, the commonest being the sum of log-normal distributions, i.e.

$$n(r) = \sum_{i=1}^{M} \frac{N_i}{\sigma_i\sqrt{2\pi}} \frac{1}{r} \exp\left[\frac{(\ln r - \ln r_i)^2}{2\sigma_i^2}\right]$$

where M is the number of modes and N_i, r_i, and σ_i are the particle number density, the mode

radius and the spread for the ith distribution. The particle-size distribution is a strong function of height, location, and time since eruption (Deshler *et al.* 1993; Lambert *et al.* 1997). In general the increase in aerosol density is associated with the size distribution having more than one mode (Thomason 1992; Pueschel 1996).

The size distribution is often characterized in terms of the effective radius, r_e, defined by

$$r_e \equiv \frac{\int_0^\infty r^3 n(r)dr}{\int_0^\infty r^2 n(r)dr}$$

Like the particle-size distribution, the effective radius varies strongly with altitude, location, and time (Grainger *et al.* 1995).

Figure 3 shows the particle-size distributions for measurements made at Laramie, Wyoming, before and after the arrival of the Mount Pinatubo aerosol cloud. Following the eruption, the number of particles was typically enhanced by two orders of magnitude (Deshler *et al.* 1993).

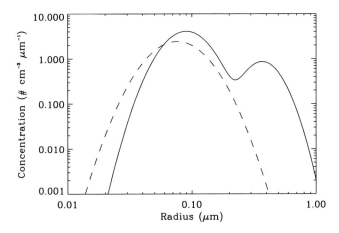

Fig. 3. Particle-size distributions measure at 41°N before (dashed line) and after (solid line) the eruption of Mount Pinatubo (Deshler *et al.* 1993).

These results are consistent with the impactor measurements of Pueschel (1996), who found the aerosol surface area and volume density increased from values of 0.48 ± 0.12 $\mu m^2/cm^3$ and 0.04 ± 0.02 $\mu m^3/cm^3$ in early 1989 to values of 20.4 $\mu m^2/cm^3$ and 11.5 $\mu m^3/cm^3$ about six months after the eruption.

Optical properties

The influence of stratospheric aerosol on the radiative field at a particular location can be assessed from three components:

- the volume extinction coefficient, β^{ext}, can be thought of as the cross-sectional area per unit volume that intercepts a beam of light
- the single scatter albedo, $\tilde{\omega}$, is the ratio of the scattered energy to the energy that is both scattered and absorbed, hence if $\tilde{\omega}=0$ all intercepted energy is absorbed while if $\tilde{\omega}=1$ all intercepted energy is scattered
- the asymmetry parameter, g, which indicates the distribution of directions of scattered light. A value of 1 indicates forward scattering, -1 backscattering and 0 isotropic scattering.

These parameters can be calculated using Mie theory given the composition of the aerosol and its particle size distribution. Figure 4 shows these parameters for a volcanically enhanced sulphuric acid cloud as a function of wavelength. The plots indicate two regimes; in the visible the extinction is about a factor of 10 higher than the infrared, the single scatter albedo is close to unity while

the asymmetry parameter is about 0.8, so that almost all the intercepted radiation is scattered mostly in the forward direction. In the infrared the asymmetry parameter approaches 0 so that single scattered radiation is approximately isotropic. However, in the infrared, single scatter albedo is generally much less than 1, so that most of the intercepted radiation is absorbed rather than scattered.

Radiative changes

Stratospheric aerosols scatter incoming solar radiation and absorb outgoing terrestrial radiation. At short wavelengths the pattern of scattered light is a function of the aerosol size distribution and the composition of the particles. Generally, there is an increase in the solar radiation that is reflected back into space; also the amount of diffuse radiation incident on the Earth's surface increases, while there is a concomitant decrease in the direct solar beam. The change in the direct and diffuse ratio was noted after the eruption of Agung (Dyer & Hicks 1965) when the solar flux was reduced by 24% from the mean unperturbed level. This was concurrent with a 100% increase in the diffuse flux (De Luisi & Herman 1977). The change in the radiative field caused by volcanic aerosols also has the potential to alter the photolysis rates of key species such as O_2 and O_3 that induce chemical changes in the stratosphere (Huang & Massie 1977; Michelangeli *et al.* 1992).

A measure of the radiative effects of stratospheric aerosols is given by the stratospheric optical depth, $\tau(\lambda)$, at wavelength λ, defined by

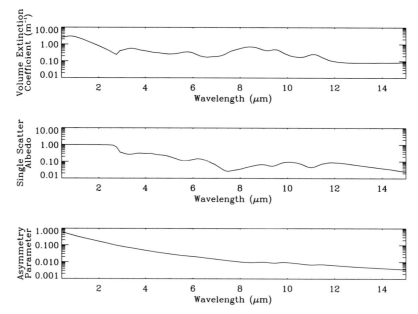

Fig. 4. Optical properties of a volcanically enhanced stratosphere aerosol for a composition of 75% H_2SO_4 by weight.

$$\tau(\lambda) = \int_{\text{tropopause}}^{\infty} \beta^{\text{ext}}(\lambda, z)dz,$$

where β^{ext}, the volume extinction coefficient, changes with height as a function of the particle composition and size distribution. The peak global loading following an eruption will occur at different times at different wavelengths as the aerosol size distribution evolves. Grant *et al* (1996) observed this effect when comparing measurements from a number of instruments following the eruption of Mount Pinatubo. Measurements made at longer wavelengths are more sensitive to larger particles (which precipitate out of the stratosphere more quickly) and so have an earlier peak aerosol loading and more rapid aerosol decay. For example, multi-wavelength LIDAR observation of the same aerosol volume gave aerosol decay rates following the Mount Pinatubo eruption of 10.9 months at 335 nm and 8.3 months at 1064 nm (Kent & Hansen 1998).

In addition to decay times changing with observing wavelength, Kent & Hansen (1998) show that the decay rate changed as a function of time since eruption, and as a function of location. Point measurements are unable to differentiate between the decay of the cloud through dilution and decay through precipitation.

Figure 5 shows the SAGE II optical depth at 1.02 μm from 1984 to 1998. The extreme left of the plot shows the decay of the El Chichón aerosol as a function of time. The increase in optical depth from about 0.002 to 0.04 following the Mount Pinatubo eruption is the most striking feature of the image. Also apparent is the dispersal of the cloud to high latitudes and its gradual decay with time.

Chemical and ozone changes

The odd-chlorine species (Cl, ClO, HCl, HOCl, and $ClONO_2$) are important to stratospheric chemistry because of the potential of Cl and ClO to catalyse the removal of O_3. Additionally the heavy halogens, bromine and iodine, are also efficient in destroying stratospheric ozone (Bureau *et al.* 2000). Up to a 40% enhancement in the abundance of HCl was observed after the El Chichón eruption by Mankin & Coffey (1984). Not all of this change was due to the volcanic injection of HCl gas, as halite particles were also observed in the stratosphere and these are thought to form HCl through the reaction (Woods *et al.* 1985):

$$2NaCl + H_2SO_4 \rightarrow Na_2SO_4 + 2HCl \qquad (1)$$

Following collision with an aerosol, a gas molecule may briefly stick to the aerosol surface or be

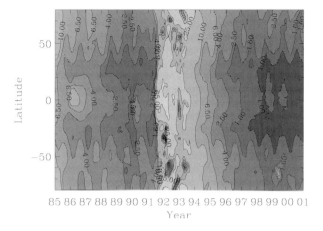

Fig. 5. SAGE II measurements of stratospheric optical depth (1000x) at 1.02 μm.

temporarily absorbed into the aerosol volume. In this way the aerosols can promote reactions between species whose reactions are much slower in the gas phase. The reactions between species that involve an aerosol particle in this way are called heterogeneous reactions.

Laboratory studies have shown that:

$$N_2O_5 + H_2O \rightarrow 2HNO_3 \qquad (2)$$

proceeds rapidly in the presence of H_2SO_4 aerosol (Mozurkewich & Calvert 1988). The background level of sulphuric acid aerosol in the high-latitude winter stratosphere is required to explain the low values of N_2O_5 and NO_2 (Evans et al. 1985) and the high values of HNO_3 (Austin et al. 1986).

If the reaction in solution is very fast, then the surface area of the drop is the rate-controlling aerosol parameter. If the reaction is slow compared with the rate at which the reactants diffuse into the aerosol, then the aerosol volume is the limiting parameter (Hanson et al. 1994). The heterogeneous reaction (2) is sufficiently fast that it effectively occurs on the surface of the aerosol and is limited by the amount of available aerosol surface area. The volcanically enhanced stratospheric aerosol perturbs stratospheric chemistry by providing additional surface area and volume for heterogeneous reaction to occur.

Reaction (2) can have a significant impact on the ratio of reactive nitrogen NO_x ($NO+NO_2+NO_3$) to its reservoir species, HNO_3, in the lower stratosphere. At low aerosol loadings an increase in aerosol surface area decreases NO_x. The

system can be summarized (Seinfeld & Pandis 1998) as

$$NO \underset{O}{\overset{O_3,ClO}{\rightleftharpoons}} NO_2 \underset{h\nu}{\overset{O_3}{\rightleftharpoons}} NO_3 \underset{h\nu}{\overset{NO_2,M}{\rightleftharpoons}} N_2O_5 \overset{heterogeneous}{\rightarrow} HNO_3$$

where the additional reactants are shown above or below the reaction symbol and $h\nu$ represents photolysis. As the aerosol area increases there is a point reached where the rate of removal of N_2O_5 exceeds the rate of formation, in which case the rate-limiting step for the $NO_x \rightarrow HNO_3$ conversion is the

$$NO_2 + O_3 \rightarrow NO_3 + O_2 \qquad (3)$$

reaction. This point occurs for surface area concentrations greater than 0.5 $\mu m^2/cm^3$ near altitudes of 20 km, and for concentrations greater than about 3 $\mu m^2/cm^3$ at about 30 km (Mills et al. 1993).

The removal of NO_2 reduces the active catalytic destruction of O_3 (see Dessler 2000). The reduction of NO_x levels additionally increases the amount of ClO as the scavenging of ClO through

$$ClO + NO_2 \rightarrow ClONO_2$$

is reduced. Hence increases in aerosol surface area increase the amount of reactive Cl.

Under colder conditions the heterogeneous reaction

$$ClONO_2 + H_2O \rightarrow HNO_3 + HOCl \qquad (4)$$

can become significant (Tie & Brasseur 1995). Importantly, Reaction (4) does not saturate as the aerosol loading increases.

Additional heterogeneous reactions that are included in modelling studies are (Hendricks *et al.* 1999).

$$ClONO_2 + HCl \rightarrow Cl_2 + HNO_3$$

$$BrONO_2 + H_2O \rightarrow HOBr + HNO_3$$

$$HOBr + HCl \rightarrow BrCl + H_2O$$

$$HOBr + HBr \rightarrow Br_2 + H_2O$$

These reactions effectively release chlorine or bromine from their relatively inactive state and in some cases move nitrogen from a more to a less reactive state.

Observational evidence consistent with heterogeneous processing on aerosols is very strong. Observed changes following the El Chichón and Mount Pinatubo eruptions include:

- decreases in stratospheric NO_2 (Johnson *et al.* 1993; Koike *et al.* 1993),
- enhanced levels of HNO_3 (Spreng & Arnold 1994; Rinsland *et al.* 1994*a*),
- enhanced levels of ClO (Avallone *et al.* 1993).

In addition, modelled mid-latitude and polar ozone values are in much better agreement if heterogeneous reactions on aerosols are included (Portman *et al.* 1996; Solomon *et al.* 1996).

In the absence of enhanced chlorine loading of the stratosphere, a Mount Pinatubo-like volcanic eruption would be expected to enhance ozone levels by about 3%, as the loss of ozone in the middle stratosphere is dominated by NO_x (Tie Brasseur 1995). However, the high levels of stratospheric chlorine from anthropogenic sources allow a decrease in ozone through the catalytic cycle

$$ClO + O \rightarrow Cl + O_2$$

$$Cl + O_3 \rightarrow ClO + O_2$$

$$\text{Net: } O_3 + O \rightarrow O_2 + O_2$$

Typically, reported ozone reductions of up to 15% were observed in the tropics following the Mount Pinatubo eruption (Schoeberl *et al.* 1993*b*; Weaver *et al.* 1993; Hofmann *et al.* 1994; McGee *et al.* 1994; Grant *et al.* 1994; Randel & Wu 1995). Figure 6 shows the ozone loss measured by the Total Ozone Mapping Spectrometer after the Mount Pinatubo eruption. The ozone changes observed at mid-latitudes after the Pinatubo eruption may not be entirely caused by heterogeneous chemistry, because some of the changes were due to changes in the stratospheric general circulation.

By about 2015 the Cl loading should have dropped so that the response of the stratosphere to an increase in aerosols will be ozone enhancement rather than depletion (Tie & Brasseur 1995).

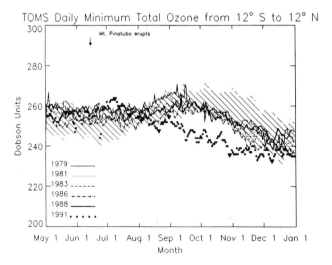

Fig. 6. Minimum total ozone amounts recorded by the Total Ozone Mapping Spectrometer in the region 12°S to 12°N. The dotted line shows the anomalously low ozone measurements made after the eruption of Mount Pinatubo (from Schoeberl *et al.* 1993*b*). Reproduced by permission of the American Geophysical Union.

Radiative forcing

Radiative forcing is a useful measure of the perturbation to the Earth's energy budget that occurs due to an external influence. It is easier to calculate than the full climate response (i.e. changes in temperature, precipitation, etc.), since knowledge of the complex feedbacks between different components of the climate system is not required. Radiative forcing is defined as the change in net irradiance at the tropopause as a result of, for example, changes in the atmospheric composition (after the stratosphere has been allowed to return to radiative equilibrium). A negative radiative forcing implies a net loss of energy to the coupled surface–troposphere system, while a positive radiative forcing implies a net gain of energy. Thus negative radiative forcing will tend to lead to a cooling of the surface, while a positive forcing leads to warming. Global and annual mean radiative forcing due to changes in external influences since 1750 have been used by Houghton et al. (2001) to compare the effect of different anthropogenic and natural influences. The spatial distribution is also crucial, especially for short-lived species such as aerosols or ozone.

In the case of volcanoes, the main source of radiative forcing is the large increase in stratospheric sulphuric acid aerosols. Such sulphate aerosols mainly scatter solar radiation back to space, with the immediate effect of reducing the solar irradiance at the ground and causing a negative radiative forcing. Additionally, the relatively large stratographic aerosol also interacts with absorbing long-wave radiation that would otherwise be emitted to space from the surface and lower atmosphere, and re-emits less radiation (since the stratosphere is at a lower temperature). Some of this radiation is re-emitted back towards the Earth's surface. Thus the system loses less long-wave radiation to space and this results in a small positive radiative forcing. Since the aerosol tends to be largest immediately following the eruption (Lacis et al. 1998), this 'greenhouse effect' will be largest then. Generally, however, this effect is overwhelmed by the negative radiative forcing (Stenchikov et al. 1998). The global mean radiative forcing due to Mount Pinatubo peaked at -3 W/m^2 and persisted for approximately two years (Stenchikov et al. 1998).

A small amount of absorption of solar and terrestrial radiation occurs in the aerosol layer, and this, accompanied by an increase in absorption of the reflected short-wave radiation above the aerosol layer by ozone and SO$_2$, tends to lead to heating in the stratosphere, in turn leading to an increase in long-wave radiation emitted downwards to the troposphere. Again, this contribution to radiative forcing is generally small (although the effect of the heating of this layer is an important part of the climate response to volcanic aerosol, as will be discussed in the next section).

As discussed earlier, the other particulate material ejected by the eruption includes dust and volcanic ash. These larger, heavier particles tend to have an impact on the radiation budget on smaller spatial and temporal scales than the stratospheric sulphate aerosol, as they are much more quickly removed from the atmosphere. However, locally these effects can be very large. There are large uncertainties in some of the critical properties of volcanic ash, in particular the refractive index, meaning that reliable modelling of these effects is still some way in the future.

Sulphur dioxide gas itself is a greenhouse gas. Bekki et al. (1996) showed that the lifetime of SO$_2$ was considerably extended after the large Toba eruption. Stevenson et al. (2003) also simulated an increase in the lifetime of tropospheric SO$_2$ following the effusive eruption of Laki in 1783. Such changes in SO$_2$ can affect the concentration of OH in the atmosphere (Bekki 1995). In addition, ozone depletion occurs in the stratosphere when chlorine loading is high and ozone production when Cl loading is low (see previous section for more details of the chemistry involved). The former case (as in Pinatubo) would lead to an additional negative radiative forcing, while the latter (as in Toba) would lead to a small positive radiative forcing. However, even for the large Toba eruption, the positive radiative forcing due to these changes only slightly moderated the negative forcing due to the aerosols (Bekki et al. 1996). Dehydration of the stratosphere is thought to occur following eruptions, due to the conversion of SO$_2$ to sulphuric acid aerosol. This effect potentially results in a positive radiative forcing. The relative length of these effects compared with that of the direct forcing from stratospheric sulphate aerosol may have implications for the time-scale on which the atmosphere returns to radiative equilibrium following an eruption. Radiative forcing calculations (and climate simulations) including all these effects have yet to be investigated, although Zhong et al. (1996) demonstrated that the long-wave heating rates in the stratosphere due to volcanic sulphur dioxide can be comparable with those due to heating by the absorption of UV by SO$_2$. Kirchner et al. (1999) demonstrated that stratospheric heating in a GCM due to the Pinatubo eruption was reduced by including the radiative effect of decreasing ozone.

Eruptions that do not penetrate the stratosphere are usually regarded as being unimportant for longer-term or global climate impacts as the aerosol is removed quickly from the troposphere. However, if such an effusive eruption persists with any strength for an extended period of time, it can at least produce a large radiative forcing over local or regional scales. This would have a large impact on the surface fluxes of radiation, and therefore on evaporation, soil moisture, etc., as well as on surface temperature. The eruption of Laki in Iceland in 1783 is one such example. There is still much controversy over the extent to which material was injected into the stratosphere by this eruption. Although some sources suggest there is little evidence for stratospheric injection (e.g. Grattan & Pyatt 1999) and therefore we would not expect a prolonged climatic impact, Franklin (1785) suggested that subsequent cold winters in Europe were a direct result of aerosol from this eruption. Wood (1992) and Briffa *et al* (1998) found cold anomalies in the Northern Hemisphere mean temperature records, but the attribution of these anomalies to the Laki eruption is difficult. It is known that significant amounts of SO_2 gas were emitted to the troposphere on and off during the period June 1783 to February 1784 (Thordarson *et al*. 1996). A recent simulation of these injections and the resulting effect on atmospheric chemistry found that a tropospheric aerosol veil extended across much of the Northern Hemisphere (Stevenson *et al*. 2003). This is consistent with Europe-wide observations of a 'dry fog' (Stothers 1996). Subsequent simulations using the resulting sulphate aerosol distributions demonstrated that the negative radiative forcing caused by this aerosol reached – 4.5 W/m² over much of the Northern Hemisphere during the month following the start of the eruption, and peaked at –20 W/m² over small regions. A significant Northern Hemisphere mean forcing persisted until March 1784 (Figure 7 and Highwood & Stevenson 2003).

Time series of radiative forcing due to volcanic eruptions have been produced, relying on proxy data such as tree rings and ice cores, as well as on geological evidence of the type of eruption, to determine the likely impact (e.g. Sato *et al*. 1993). These can then be used in climate models. A recent attempt by Andronova *et al*. (1999) assumes that the radiative forcing generated by each eruption is similar to that of

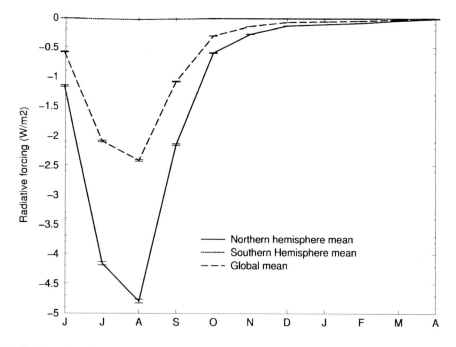

Fig. 7. Global and hemispheric mean radiative forcing due to sulphate aerosols from the eruption of Laki in 1783. The aerosol distribution has been simulated using the chemical transport model STOCHEM as in Stevenson *et al*. (2003), and the radiative forcing calculated using the Reading Intermediate General Circulation Model as in Highwood & Stevenson (2003).

Pinatubo, depending only on the distribution of the optical depth from each eruption. That study found that the radiative forcing can vary widely due to the atmospheric circulation and the geographical location and strength of the eruption. For eruptions more distant in time, and those in the data-sparse Southern Hemisphere, the estimates of radiative forcing become increasingly uncertain. It is difficult to compare volcanic radiative forcing with other forcings such as greenhouse gases, because they are discrete events. However, Shine & Forster (1999) include volcanic forcings by considering the difference between 'active' and 'quiescent' decades, considering a forcing of -0.8 W/m^2 to be appropriate when comparing the effect in an active decade to that in an inactive decade.

In summary, the main effect of volcanic eruptions is to produce a negative radiative forcing due to the reflection of solar radiation by extra stratospheric sulphate aerosol. The next part of the puzzle is to determine the effect on climate of this radiative forcing.

Climate response

Climate response to volcanic eruptions is much more complex than a negative radiative forcing leading to a surface cooling. In general this is true: a global mean temperature decrease of around 0.2 K was observed at the surface following the Pinatubo eruption, while the stratosphere warmed by 1 K (Houghton *et al.* 2001, and Figure 8). These temperature changes have been successfully simulated by a number of climate models (e.g. Kirchner *et al.* 1999). Angell & Korshover (1985) studied temperature records after six major eruptions and concluded that the average temperature at the surface was statistically significantly colder during the five years after each eruption than during the five years preceding the eruption.

Relatively simple energy-balance models can be of great use in understanding the influence of individual eruptions on the global mean climate. Lindzen & Ginnitsis (1998) modelled the impact of the 1883 Krakatau eruption in this way. The

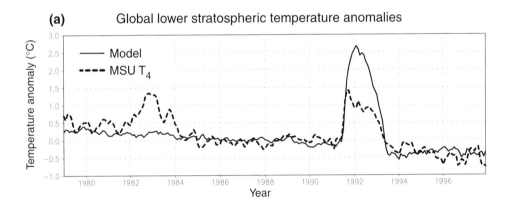

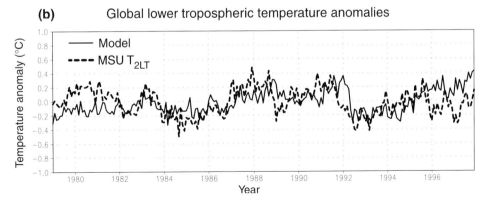

Fig. 8. Satellite observations and model predictions of lower-stratospheric and tropospheric temperature anomalies after the eruptions of El Chichón and Pinatubo (from Houghton *et al.* 2001).

importance of frequent volcanic eruptions for the global annual mean temperature over the past 150 years, using the time series of forcing of Sato *et al.* (1993) and the associated uncertainties, has been demonstrated in Shine & Highwood (2002). The importance of the cumulative effect of periods of several eruptions can clearly be seen in Figure 9. There is certainly justification for including volcanic forcings in climate simulations; however, the impact on climate in that model is necessarily simplified. The magnitude of the results is also sensitive to the value of 'climate sensitivity' that is used. Observations of lower-stratospheric temperature changes over the past 30 years have led to speculation that trends have not been linear, and there is an apparent step change to cooler temperatures after each large eruption; however, the shortest length of the data-set prevents any more concrete conclusions from being drawn.

As well as reducing the solar radiation reaching the ground, the after-effects of an eruption can alter the large-scale circulation of the atmosphere, producing complex spatial patterns of change. Robock (2000), and references therein, highlight the importance of dynamical changes brought about as a result of the changing aerosol. In particular, for a tropical eruption the heating of the tropical lower stratosphere by aerosol increases the meridional temperature gradient, which can affect the strength of the polar vortex and therefore the strength of the zonal flow in mid-latitudes. Dynamical coupling of the stratosphere and troposphere through the interaction of large-scale planetary waves with the mean flow modulates tropospheric temperatures. This type of

extended influence in the Northern Hemisphere has been used to explain the frequent observations of warm European temperatures following large tropical eruptions, despite a global mean surface cooling. Such a pattern was seen after Mount Pinatubo and has been successfully simulated using climate models (e.g. Kirchner *et al.* 1999; Graf *et al.* 1993). After other eruptions, including that of Laki in 1783 (Stothers 1999), a warm summer is experienced in Europe and it is suggested that this too is the result of complex dynamical changes brought about by the different distribution of heating, although the precise mechanism by which this occurs is still the subject of much research. In the study by Highwood & Stevenson (2003), the climate response to the radiative forcing due to sulphate aerosols alone produced a cold Northern Hemisphere mean temperature over the summer of the eruption, rather than a warming; however, the response had a complex spatial structure.

Further changes to the climate response could be due to the indirect effect of tropospheric aerosols, whereby they could act as cloud condensation nuclei and thus alter the microphysics of clouds (Jensen & Toon 1992). After eruptions such as Laki there could also be substantial modification of the vegetation as a result of the deposition of fluorinated gases and sulphuric acid. This might also introduce unexpected feedbacks to amplify or reduce the climatic impact of volcanic eruptions. To date there have been few attempts to quantify these effects.

It is worth remembering that even if an eruption does not penetrate the stratosphere directly, the impact on local climate can be large immediately following the eruption. This was

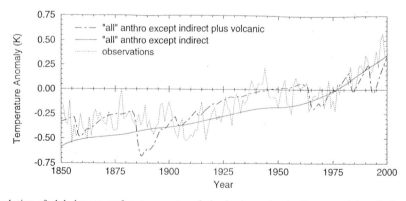

Fig. 9. Evolution of global mean surface temperature derived using a simple climate model, radiative forcings from Myhre *et al.* (2001), and a climate sensitivity of 0.67 K (W/m²)⁻¹ for all anthropogenic forcings except the indirect aerosol effect, with and without volcanic aerosol forcing. The observations are from Parker *et al.* (2000) and all temperatures are shown as anomalies from the 1960–1990 mean of each series. Adapted from Shine & Highwood (2002).

particularly apparent after the Mount St Helens eruption in 1980. This eruption did not produce much enhancement of stratospheric aerosol since it emitted mainly into the upper troposhere and lower stratosphere and did not release much sulphur. Hence no prolonged or global signal was observed in temperature records at this time. However, Mass & Robock (1982) demonstrated that local surface temperatures were up to 8 K cooler during the daytime immediately after the eruption. Night-time temperatures over a considerable region were up to 8 K warmer as a result of the greenhouse effect of the low-level volcanic dust.

There have been several very large volcanic eruptions during Earth's history (e.g. Toba, 71 000 years ago). There is great interest in these mega-eruptions, not least from the media and the general public; however, it is extremely difficult to extrapolate results on climate impact from known/observed eruptions. There is little evidence that aerosol production, and certainly not the climate response to those aerosols, would be at all linear with eruption strength. However, recent advances in observations (particularly the advent of satellite remote sensing of emissions and climate response) and modelling studies suggest that we are at a point where we can begin to gain a much improved understanding of climate response to volcanic eruptions.

Summary

On average there is a stratospherically significant volcanic eruption about every 5.5 years. The principal effects of large volcanic injection of material into the stratosphere are:

- the injection of a large amount of volcanic ash, which precipitates out with an e-folding time of about 40 days
- the injection of a large amount of sulphur, principally in the form of SO_2, which converts into H_2SO_4 and condenses, enhancing the stratospheric aerosol loading
- a reduction in the amount of direct radiation reaching the ground and a concomitant increase in diffuse radiation
- an increase in heterogeneous processing, mostly of active nitrogen into less reactive forms
- either a decrease or an increase in stratospheric ozone levels, depending on the level of chlorine loading
- an increase in stratospheric temperature
- a decrease in global mean surface temperature, although the spatial pattern of temperature changes is complex.

The authors wish to acknowledge the corrections and improvements in the manuscript suggested by Dr S. Bekki and an anonymous reviewer. Dr A. Lambert also made helpful suggestions.

References

ANDRONOVA, N., ROZANOV, E. V., YANG, F., SCHLESINGER, M. & STENCHIKOV, G. 1999. Radiative forcing by volcanic aerosols from 1850 to 1994. *Journal of Geophysical Research*, **104**, 16 807–16 926.

ANGELL, J. & KORSHOVER, J. 1985. Surface temperature changes following the six major volcanic episodes between 1780 and 1980. *Journal of Climate and Applied Meteorology*, **24**, 937–951.

AUSTIN, J., GARCIA, R. R., RUSSELL, J. M., SOLOMON, S. & TUCK, A. F. 1986. On the atmospheric photochemistry of nitric acid. *Journal of Geophysical Research*, **91**, 5477–5485.

AVALLONE, L. M., TOOHEY, D. W., PROFFITT, M. H., MARGITAN, J. J., CHAN, K. R. & ANDERSON, J. G. 1993. In situ measurements of ClO at mid-latitudes: is there an effect from Mt. Pinatubo? *Geophysical Research Letters*, **20**, 2519–2522.

BAYHURST, G. K., WOHLETZ, K. H. & MASON, A. S. 1994. A method for characterizing volcanic ash from the December 15, 1989 eruption of Redoubt volcano, Alaska. *In*: CASADEVALL, T. J. (ed.) *Volcanic Ash and Aviation Safety, Proceedings of the 1st International Symposium on Volcanic Ash and Aviation Safety*, USGS Bulletin **2047**, 13–17. Washington D.C.

BEKKI, S. 1995. Oxidation of volcanic SO_2 – a sink for stratospheric OH and H_2O. *Geophysical Research Letters*, **22**, 913–916.

BEKKI, S., TOUMI, R. & PYLE, J. 1993. Role of sulphur photochemistry in tropical ozone changes after the eruption of Mount Pinatubo. *Nature*, **362**, 331–333.

BEKKI, S., PYLE, J., ZHONG, W., TOUMI, R., HAIGH, J. & PYLE, D. 1996. The role of microphysical and chemical processes in prolonging the climate forcing of the Toba eruption. *Geophysical Research Letters*, **23**, 2669–2672.

BLUTH, G. J. S., DOIRON, S. D., SCHNETZLER, C. C., KRUEGER, A. J. & WALTER, L. S. 1992. Global tracking of the SO_2 clouds from the June, 1991, Mount Pinatubo eruptions. *Geophysical Research Letters*, **19**, 151–154.

BLUTH, G. J. S., ROSE, W. I., SPROD, I. E. & KRUEGER, A. J. 1997. Stratospheric loading of sulfur from explosive volcanic eruptions. *Journal of Geology*, **105**, 671–683.

BRIFFA, K., JONES, P., SCHWEINGRUBER, F. & OSBORN, T. 1998. Influence of volcanic eruptions on northern hemisphere summer temperature over the past 600 years. *Nature*, **393**, 450–454.

BUREAU, H., KEPPLER, H. & MÉTRICH, N. 2000. Volcanic degassing of bromine and iodine: experimental fluid/melt partitioning data and applications to stratospheric chemistry. *Earth and Planetary Science Letters*, **183**, 51–60.

BURSIK, M., SPARKS, R., CAREY, S. & GILBERT, J. 1994. The concentration of ash in volcanic plumes, inferred from dispersal data. *In*: CASADEVALL, T. J. (ed.) *Volcanic Ash and Aviation Safety, Proceedings 1st International Symposium on Volcanic Ash and Aviation Safety*, USGS Bulletin **2047**, 19–29. Washington D.C.

DELMAS, R., KIRCHNER, S., PALAIS, J. & PETIT, J.-R. 1992. 1000 years of explosive volcanism recorded at the South Pole. *Tellus*, **44**, 335–350.

DE LUISI, J. J. & HERMAN, B. M. 1977. Estimation of solar radiation absorption by volcanic stratospheric aerosols from Agung using surface-based observations. *Journal of Geophysical Research*, **82**, 3477–3480.

DESHLER, T., JOHNSON, B. J. & ROZIER, W. R. 1993. Ballonborne measurements of Pinatubo aerosol during 1991 and 1992 at 41 N – vertical profiles, size distribution, and volatility. *Geophysical Research Letters*, **20**, 1435–1438.

DESHLER, T., JOHNSON, B. J. & ROZIER, W. R. 1994. Changes in the character of polar stratospheric clouds over Antarctica in 1992 due to the Pinatubo volcanic aerosol. *Geophysical Research Letters*, **21**, 273–276.

DESSLER, A. 2000. *The Chemistry and Physics of Stratospheric Ozone*. Academic Press, London.

DYER, A. J. & HICKS, B. B. 1965. Stratospheric transport of volcanic dust inferred from solar radiation measurements. *Nature*, **208**, 131–133.

EVANS, W. F. J., MCELROY, C. T. & GALBALLY, I. E. 1985. The conversion of N_2O_5 to HNO_3 at high latitudes in winter. *Geophysical Research Letters*, **12**, 825–828.

FRANKLIN, B. 1785. Meteorological imaginations and conjectures. *Memoirs of the Literary and Philosophical Society of Manchester*, **2**, 357–361.

GOODING, J. L., CLANTON, U. S., GABEL, E. M. & WARREN, J. L. 1983. El Chichón volcanic ash in the stratosphere: particle abundances and size distributions after the 1982 eruption. *Geophysical Research Letters*, **10**, 1033–1036.

GRAF, H.-F., KIRCHNER, I., ROBOCK, A. & SCHULT, I. 1993. Pinatubo eruption winter climate effects: model versus observations. *Climate Dynamics*, **9**, 81–93.

GRAINGER, R. G., LAMBERT, A., TAYLOR, F. W., REMEDIOS, J. J., RODGERS, C. D., CORNEY, M. & KERRIDGE, B. J. 1993. Infrared absorption by volcanic stratospheric aerosols observed by ISAMS. *Geophysical Research Letters*, **20**, 1283–1286.

GRAINGER, R. G., LAMBERT, A., RODGERS, C. D. & TAYLOR, F. W. 1995. Stratospheric aerosol effective radius, surface area and volume estimated from infrared measurements. *Journal of Geophysical Research*, **100**, 16 507–16 518.

GRANT, W. B., BROWELL, E. V. *ET AL.* 1994. Aerosol-associated changes in tropical ozone following the eruption of Mount Pinatubo. *Journal of Geophysical Research*, **99**, 8197–8211.

GRANT, W. B., BROWELL, E. V., LONG, C. S., STOWE, L. L., GRAINGER, R. G. & LAMBERT, A. 1996. Use of volcanic aerosols to study the tropical stratospheric reservoir. *Journal of Geophysical Research*, **101**, 3973–3988.

GRATTAN, J. P. & PYATT, F. B. 1999. Volcanic eruptions, dry fogs and the European palaeoenvironmental record: localised phenomena or hemispheric impacts? *Global and Planetary Change*, **21**, 171–179.

HANSON, D. R., RAVISHANKARA, A. R. & SOLOMON, S. 1994. Heterogeneous reactions in sulfuric acid aerosols: a framework for model calculations. *Journal of Geophysical Research*, **99**, 3615–3629.

HEATH, D. F., SCHLESINGER, B. M. & PARK, H. 1983. Spectral change in the ultraviolet absorption and scattering properties of the atmosphere associated with the ruption of El Chichón: stratospheric SO_2 budget and decay. *EOS, Transactions of the American Geophysical Union*, **64**, 197.

HEIKEN, G. 1994. Volcanic ash: what it is and how it forms. *In*: CASADEVALL, T. J. (ed.) *Volcanic Ash and Aviation Safety, Proceedings of the 1st International Symposium on Volcanic Ash and Aviation Safety*, USGS Bulletin **2047**, 39–45. Washington D.C.

HENDRICKS, J., LIPPERT, E., PETRY, H. & EBEL, A. 1999. Heterogeneous reactions on and in sulfate aerosols: implications for the chemistry of the midlatitude tropopause region. *Journal of Geophysical Research*, **104**, 5531–5550.

HIGHWOOD, E. & STEVENSON, D. 2003. Atmospheric impact of the 1783–1784 Laki eruption: Part II climatic effect of sulphate aerosol. *Atmospheric Chemical Physics* (submitted).

HOBBS, P. V., RADKE, L. F., LYONS, J. H., FEREK, R. J., COFFMAN, D. J. & CASADEVALL, T. J. 1991. Airborne measurements of particle and gas emissions from the 1990 volcanic eruptions of Mt Redoubt. *Journal of Geophysical Research*, **96**, 18 735–18 752.

HOFMANN, D. J. 1987. Perturbations to the global atmosphere associated with the El Chichón volcanic eruption of 1982. *Reviews of Geophysics*, **25**, 743–759.

HOFMANN, D. J. & ROSEN, J. M. 1983. Stratospheric sulfuric acid fraction and mass estimate for the 1982 volcanic eruption of El Chichón. *Geophysical Research Letters*, **10**, 313–316.

HOFMANN, D. J. & ROSEN, J. M. 1984. On the prolonged lifetime of the El Chichón sulfuric acid cloud. *Journal of Geophysical Research*, **92**, 9825–9830.

HOFMANN, D. J., OLTMANS, S. J. *ET AL.* 1994. Ozone loss in the lower stratosphere over the United States in 1992–1993: evidence for heterogeneous chemistry on the Pinatubo aerosol. *Geophysical Research Letters*, **21**, 65–68.

HOLASEK, R. E., SELF, S. & WOODS, A. W. 1996. Satellite observations and interpretation of the 1991 Mount Pinatubo eruption plumes. *Journal of Geophysical Research*, **101**, 27 635–27 655.

HOUGHTON, J. T., DING, Y., GRIGGS, D., NOGUER, M., VAN DER LINDEN, P., DAI, X., K. M. & JOHNSON, C. (eds) 2001. *Climate Change 2001: the Scientific Basis*. Cambridge University Press, Cambridge.

HUANG, T. Y. W. & MASSIE, S. T. 1997 Effect of volcanic particles on the O_2 and O_3 photolysis rates and their impact on ozone in the tropical stratosphere. *Journal of Geophysical Research*, **102**, 1239–1249.

JÄGER, H. & CARNUTH, W. 1987. The decay of the El Chichón stratospheric perturbation, observed by lidar at northern midlatitudes. *Geophysical Research Letters*, **14**, 696–699.

JENSEN, E. J. & TOON, O. B. 1992. The potential effects of volcanic aerosols on cirrus cloud microphysics. *Geophysical Research Letters*, **19**, 1759–1762.

JOHNSTON, P. V., MCKENZIE, R. L., KEYS, J. G. & MATHEWS, W. A. 1993. Observations of depleted stratospheric NO_2 following the Pinatubo volcanic eruption. *Geophysical Research Letters*, **19**, 211–213.

KENT, G. S. & HANSEN, G. M. 1998. Multiwavelength observations of the decay phase of the stratospheric aerosol layer produced by the eruption of Mount Pinatubo in June 1991. *Applied Optics*, **37**, 3861–3872.

KIRCHNER, I., STENCHIKOV, G., GRAF, H.-F., ROBOCK, A. & ANTUNA, J. 1999. Climate model simulation of winter warming and summer cooling following the 1991 Mount Pinatubo volcanic eruption. *Journal of Geophysical Research*, **104**, 19 039–19 055.

KNOLLENBERG, R. & HUFFMAN, D. 1983. Measurements of the aerosol size distributions of the El Chichón cloud. *Geophysical Research Letters*, **10**, 1025–1028.

KOIKE, M., KONDO, Y., MATHEWS, W., JOHNSTON, P. & YAMAZAKI, K. 1993. Decrease of stratospheric NO_2 at 44°N caused by Pinatubo volcanic aerosols. *Geophysical Research Letters*, **20**, 1975–1978.

LACIS, A., HANSEN, J. & SATO, M. 1998. Climate forcing by stratospheric aerosols. *Geophysical Research Letters*, **19**, 1607–1610.

LAMB, H. 1970. Volcanic dust in the atmosphere: with a chronology and assessment of its meteorological significance. *Philosophical Transactions of the Royal Society of London*, **266**, 425–533.

LAMBERT, A., GRAINGER, R. G., REMEDIOS, J. J., RODGERS, C. D., CORNEY, M. & TAYLOR, F. W. 1993. Measurement of the evolution of the Mt. Pinatubo aerosol cloud by ISAMS. *Geophysical Research Letters*, **20**, 1287–1290.

LAMBERT, A., GRAINGER, R., RODGERS, C., TAYLOR, F., MERGENTHALER, J., KUMER, J. & MASSIE, S. 1997. Global evolution of the Mt. Pinatubo volcanic aerosols observed by the infrared limb-sounding instruments CLAES and ISAMS on the Upper Atmosphere Research Satellite. *Journal of Geophysical Research*, **102**, 1495–1512.

LINDZEN, R. & GINNITSIS, C. 1998. On the climatic implications of volcanic cooling. *Journal of Geophysical Research*, **103**, 5929–5941.

MACEDONIO, G., PAPALE, P., PARESCHI, M. T., ROSI, M. & SANTACROCE, R. 1994. A statistical approach to the assessment of volcanic hazard for air traffic: application to Vesuvius, Italy. *In*: CASADEVALL, T. J. (ed.) *Volcanic Ash and Aviation Safety, Proceedings of the 1st International Symposium on Volcanic Ash and Aviation Safety*, USGS Bulletin **2047**, 245–252, Washington, D.C.

MCCORMICK, M. P., THOMASON, L. W. & TREPTE, C. R. 1995. Atmospheric effects of the Mt. Pinatubo eruption. *Nature*, **373**, 399–404.

MCGEE, T. J., NEWMAN, P., GROSS, M., SINGH, U., GODIN, S., LACOSTE, A.-M. & MEGIE, G. 1994. Correlation of ozone loss with the presence of volcanic aerosols. *Geophysical Research Letters*, **21**, 2801–2804.

MCKEEN, S. A., LIU, S. C. & KIANG, C. S. 1984. On the chemistry of stratospheric SO_2 from volcanic eruptions. *Journal of Geophysical Research*, **89**, 4873–4881.

MCPETERS, R. D. 1993. The atmospheric SO_2 budget for Pinatubo derived from NOAA-11 SBUV/2 spectral data. *Geophysical Research Letters*, **20**, 1971–1974.

MACKINNON, I. D. R., GOODING, J. L., MCKAY, D. S. & CLANTON, U. S. 1984. The El Chichón stratospheric cloud, solid particulates and settling rates. *Journal of Volcanology and Geothermal Research*, **23**, 125–146.

MANKIN, W. & COFFEY, M. T. 1984. Increased stratospheric hydrogen chloride in the El Chichón cloud. *Science*, **226**, 170–172.

MASS, C. & ROBOCK, A. 1982. The short-term influence of the Mount St Helens volcanic eruption on surface temperature in the northwest United States. *Monthly Weather Review*, **110**, 614–622.

MATSON, M. 1984. The 1982 El Chichón volcano eruptions – a satellite perspective. *Journal of Volcanology and Geothermal Research*, **23**, 1–10.

MATSON, M. & ROBOCK, A. 1984. Satellite detection of the 1992 El Chichón eruptions and stratospheric dust cloud. *Geofisica Internacional*, **23**, 117–127.

MICHELANGELI, D. V., ALLEN, M., YUNG, Y. L., SHIA, R.-L., CRISP, D. & ELUSZKIEWICZ, J. 1992. Enhancement of atmospheric radiation by an aerosol layer. *Journal of Geophysical Research*, **97**, 865–874.

MILLS, M. J., LANGFORD, A. O. *ET AL.* 1993. On the relationship between stratospheric aerosols and nitrogen dioxide. *Geophysical Research Letters*, **20**, 1187–1190.

MINNIS, P., HARRISON, E. F., STOWE, L. L., GIBSON, G. G., DENN, F. M., DOELLING, D. R. & SMITH, W. L. 1993. Radiative climate forcing by the Mount Pinatubo eruption. *Science*, **259**, 1411–1415.

MOZURKEWICH, M. & CALVERT, J. 1988. Reaction probability of N_2O_5 on aqueous aerosols. *Journal of Geophysical Research*, **93**, 22 535–22 541.

MYHRE, G., MYHRE, A. & STORDAL, F. 2001. Historical evolution of total radiative forcing. *Atmospheric Environment*, **35**, 2361–2373.

NEWHALL, C. G. & SELF, S. 1982. The volcanic explosivity index (VEI): an estimate of explosive magnitude for historical volcanism. *Journal of Geophysical Research*, **87**, 1231–1238.

PARKER, D., HORTON, E. B. & ALEXANDER, L. 2000. Global and regional climate in 1999. *Weather*, **55**, 188–199.

PINTO, J. P., TURCO, R. P. & TOON, O. B. 1989. Self limiting physical and chemical effects in volcanic eruption clouds. *Journal of Geophysical Research*, **94**, 11 165–11 174.

PORTMAN, R. W., SOLOMON, S., GARCIA, R. R., THOMASON, L. W., POOLE, L. R. & MCCORMICK, M. P. 1996. Role of aerosol variations in anthropogenic ozone depletion in the polar regions. *Journal of Geophysical Research*, **101**, 22 991–23 006.

PUESCHEL, R. F. 1996. Stratospheric aerosols: formation, properties, effects. *Journal of Aerosol Science*, **27**, 383–402.

PUESCHEL, R. F., RUSSELL, P. B. *ET AL.* 1994. Physical

and optical properties of the Pinatubo volcanic aerosol: aircraft observations with impactors and a sun-tracking photometer. *Journal of Geophysical Research*, **99**, 12 915–12 922.

PYLE, D. M., BEATTIE, P. D. & BLUTH, G. J. S. 1996. Sulphur emissions to the stratosphere from volcanic eruptions. *Bulletin of Volcanology*, **57**, 663–671.

RANDEL, W. J. & WU, F. 1995. Ozone and temperature changes in the stratosphere following the eruption of Mt Pinatubo. *Journal of Geophysical Research*, **100**, 16 753–16 764.

READ, W., FROIDEVAUX, L. & WATERS, J. 1993. Microwave limb sounder measurements of stratospheric SO_2 from the Mt Pinatubo volcano. *Journal of Geophysical Research*, **20**, 1299–1302.

RINSLAND, C. P., GUNSON, M. R. *ET AL.* 1994a Heterogeneous conversion of N_2O_5 to HNO_3 in the post-Mount Pinatubo eruption stratosphere. *Journal of Geophysical Research*, **99**, 8213–8219.

RINSLAND, C. P., YUE, G. K., GUNSON, M. R., ZANDER, R. & ABRAMS, M. C. 1994b Midinfrared extinction by sulfate aerosols from the Mt Pinatubo eruption. *Journal of Quantitative Spectroscopy and Radiative Transfer*, **52**, 241–252.

ROBOCK, A. 2000. Volcanic eruptions and climate. *Reviews of Geophysics*, **38**, 191–219.

ROBOCK, A. & MAO, J. 1995. The volcanic signal in surface temperature observations. *Journal of Climate*, **8**, 1086–1103.

ROSEN, J. M., KJOME, N. T., MCKENZIE, R. L. & LILEY, J. B. 1994. Decay of Mount Pinatubo aerosol at midlatitudes in the northern and southern hemispheres. *Journal of Geophysical Research*, **99**, 25 733–25 739.

SATO, M., HANSEN, J. E., MCCORMICK, M. P. & POLLACK, J. B. 1993. Stratospheric aerosol optical depths, 1850–1990. *Journal of Geophysical Research*, **98**, 22 987–22 994.

SAWADA, Y. 1994. Tracking of regional volcanic ash clouds by geostationary meteorological satellite (GMS). *In*: CASADEVALL, T. J. (ed.) *Volcanic Ash and Aviation Safety, Proceedings of the 1st International Symposium on Volcanic Ash and Aviation Safety*, USGS Bulletin **2047**, 397–404, Washington, D.C.

SCHOEBERL, M. R., DOIRON, S. D., LAIT, L. R., NEWMAN, P. A. & KRUEGERR, A. J. 1993a A simulation of the Cerro Hudson SO_2 cloud. *Journal of Geophysical Research*, **98**, 2949–2955.

SCHOEBERL, M. R., DOIRON, P. K. B. & HILSENRATH, E. 1993b Tropical ozone loss following the eruption of Mt. Pinatubo. *Geophysical Research Letters*, **20**, 29–32.

SEDLACEK, W., MROZ, E., LAZRUS, A. & GANDRUD, B. 1983. A decade of stratospheric sulfate measurements compared with observations of volcanic eruptions. *Journal of Geophysical Research*, **88**, 3741–3776.

SEINFELD, J. H. & PANDIS, S. N. 1998. *Atmospheric Chemistry and Physics.* John Wiley, New York.

SHINE, K. & FORSTER, P. 1999. The effect of human activity on radiative forcing of climate change: a review of recent developments. *Global Planetary Change*, **20**, 205–225.

SHINE, K. & HIGHWOOD, E. 2002. Problems in quantifying natural and anthropogenic perturbations to the Earth's energy balance. *In*: PEARCE, R. P. (ed.) *Meteorology at the Millennium.* London, Academic Press, 123–132.

SIGURDSSON, H. & LAJ, P. 1992. Atmospheric effects of volcanic eruptions. *In*: *Encyclopedia of Earth System Science*, 183–199. Academic Press, London.

SIMKIN, T. & SIEBERT, L. 1994. *Volcanoes of the World.*. Geoscience Press, Tucson, 2nd edition.

SOLOMON, S., PORTMAN, R., GARCIA, R., THOMASON, L., POOLE, L. & MCCORMICK, M. 1996. The role of aerosol variations in anthropogenic ozone depletion at northern midlatitudes. *Journal of Geophysical Research*, **101**, 6713–6727.

SPARKS, R., BURSIK, M., CAREY, S., WOODS, A. & GILBERT, J. 1994. The controls of eruption-column dynamics on the injection and mass loading of ash into the atmosphere. *In*: CASADEVALL, T. J. (ed.) *Volcanic Ash and Aviation Safety, Proceedings of the 1st International Symposium on Volcanic Ash and Aviation Safety*, USGS Bulletin **2047**, 81–86. Washington, D.C.

SPRENG, S. & ARNOLD, F. 1994. Balloon-borne mass spectrometer measurements of HNO_3 and HCN in the winter Arctic stratosphere – evidence for HNO_3-processing by aerosols. *Geophysical Research Letters*, **21**, 1251–1254.

STEELE, H. M. & HAMILL, P. 1981. Effects of temperature and humidity on the growth and optical properties of sulphuric acid–water droplets in the stratosphere. *Journal of Aerosol Science*, **12**, 517–528.

STENCHIKOV, G., KIRCHNER, I. *ET AL.* 1998. Radiative forcing from the 1991 Mount Pinatubo volcanic eruption. *Journal of Geophysical Research*, **103**, 13 837–13 857.

STEVENSON, D., JOHNSON, C., HIGHWOOD, E., GAUCI, V., COLLINS, W. & DERWENT, R. 2003. Atmospheric impact of the 1783–1784 Laki eruption: Part 1 chemistry modelling. *Atmospheric Chemical Physics*, **3**, 551–596.

STOTHERS, R. 1996. *Laki.* The Great Dry Fog of 1783. *Climatic Change*, **32**, 79–89.

STOTHERS, R. 1999. Volcanic dry fogs, climate cooling and plague pandemics in Europe and the Middle East. *Climatic Change*, **42**, 713–723.

THOMASON, L. 1992. Observations of a new SAGE II aerosol extinction model following the eruption of Mt. Pinatubo. *Geophysical Research Letters*, **19**, 2179–2182.

THORDARSON, T., SELF, S., OSKARSSON, N. & HULSEBOSCH, T. 1996. Sulfur, chlorine and fluorine degassing and atmospheric loading by the 1783–1784 and Laki (Skafter fires) eruption in Iceland. *Bulletin of Volcanology*, **58**, 205–225.

TIE, X. & BRASSEUR, G. 1995. The response of stratospheric ozone to volcanic eruptions: sensitivity to atmospheric chlorine loading. *Geophysical Research Letters*, **22**, 3035–3038.

WEAVER, A., LOEWENSTEIN, M. *ET AL.* 1993. Effects of Pinatubo aerosol on stratospheric ozone at midlatitudes. *Geophysical Research Letters*, **20**, 2515–2518.

WOOD, C. 1992. Climatic effects of the 1783 Laki eruption. *In*: HARINGTON, C. (ed.) *The Year Without a Summer? World Climate in 1816*, 58–77. Canadian Museum of Nature.

WOODS, A. W. & KIENLE, J. 1994. The injection of volcanic ash into the atmosphere. *In*: CASADEVALL, T. J. (ed.) *Volcanic Ash and Aviation Safety, Proceedings of the 1st International Symposium on Volcanic Ash and Aviation Safety*, USGS Bulletin **2047**, 101–106. Washington, D.C.

WOODS, D., CHUAN, R. & ROSE, W. 1985. Halite particles injected into the stratosphere by the 1982 El Chichón eruption. *Science*, **230**, 170–172.

YUE, G. K., MCCORMICK, M. P. & CHIOU, E. W. 1991. Stratospheric aerosol optical depth observed by Stratospheric Aerosol and Gas Experiment II: decay of the El Chichón and Ruiz volcanic perturbations. *Journal of Geophysical Research*, **96**, 5209–5219.

ZHONG, W., HAIGH, J., TOUMI, R. & BEKKI, S. 1996. Infrared heating rates in the stratosphere due to volcanic sulphur dioxide. *Quarterly Journal of the Royal Meteorological Society* **122**, 1459–1466.

ZIELINSKI, G. 1995. Stratosphere loading and optical depth estimates of explosive volcanism over the last 2100 years derived from the Greenland Ice Sheet Project 2 ice core. *Journal of Geophysical Research*, **100**, 20 937–20 955.

Compositional variation in tropospheric volcanic gas plumes: evidence from ground-based remote sensing

L. A. HORROCKS[1], C. OPPENHEIMER[2], M. R. BURTON[3] & H. J. DUFFELL[4]

[1]Met Office, London Road, Bracknell, RG12 2SZ, UK.
(e-mail: lisa.horrocks@metoffice.com)
[2]Department of Geography, University of Cambridge, Cambridge, CB2 3EN, UK.
[3]Istituto Nazionale di Geofisica e Vulcanologia, Sezione di Catania,
Via Monte Rossi 12, Nicolosi, 95030 CT, Italy.
[4]Department of Earth Sciences, University of Cambridge, Cambridge,
CB2 3EQ, UK.

Abstract: Remotely sensed measurements of volcanic plumes have been undertaken for 30 years with instruments such as the correlation spectrometer, and more recently, open-path Fourier transform infrared (OP–FTIR) spectrometers. Observations are typically made several kilometres from the source, by which time chemical reactions may have occurred in the plume, overprinting the source composition and flux. Volcanological interpretations of such data therefore demand an understanding of the atmospheric processes initiated as gases leave the volcanic vent. Ground-based remote sensing techniques offer the temporal resolution, repeatability and quantitative analysis necessary for investigation of these processes. Here we report OP–FTIR spectroscopic measurements of gas emissions from Masaya Volcano, Nicaragua, between 1998 and 2001, and examine the influence of atmospheric processes on its tropospheric plume. Comparisons of observations made at the summit and down-wind, and in different measurement modes confirm that tropospheric processes and local meteorology have only minor impact on gas composition after the plume has left the crater. This study demonstrates that plume monitoring downwind provides a reliable proxy for at-crater sampling, and that volcanological information content is not obscured by the intervening transport. From February 1998 to May 2000, Masaya's plume composition was strikingly stable and characterized by SO_2/HCl and HCl/HF molar ratios of 1.6 and 5.0, respectively. Departures from this stable background composition are likely to signify changes in the volcanic system or degassing regime, as identified in April–May 2001.

Although less dramatic than the stratospheric injection of gases during explosive eruptions, the phenomenon of passive volcanic degassing is no less important. A number of volcanoes are renowned for extended periods of strong gas emission that are not associated with major eruptive events, and these form a significant proportion of the global volcanic gas contribution to the atmosphere. Moreover, most large explosive eruptions are followed or preceded by periods of more quiescent degassing. The question of which gas species carry the most useful information for volcano monitoring is important: this has been addressed recently by Symonds et al. (2001). Equally important, since measurements are increasingly made by remote sensing and sampling methods, is the issue of

how volcanic gas compositions are modified by interaction with the troposphere prior to or during sampling, and whether this obscures their volcanological information content. To progress in these areas requires targeted monitoring campaigns and the accumulation of high-quality data-sets, as well as developments in modelling and theoretical understanding.

Until around 30 years ago, volcanic gas monitoring relied on direct sampling techniques, which, although they provide detailed information on the sample collected, are restricted to safely accessible vents or fumaroles, and are susceptible to secondary contamination. These techniques are also limited in time and space, with analyses unlikely to be representative of the volcanic plume as a whole. The advent of remote-sensing

From: OPPENHEIMER, C., PYLE, D.M. & BARCLAY, J. (eds) *Volcanic Degassing*. Geological Society, London, Special Publications, **213**, 349–369. 0305-8719/03/$15.00

L. A. HORROCKS *ET AL.*

techniques has enabled the measurement of more representative integrated plume compositions, and significantly, the capability for high temporal resolutions. This kind of information is important in three respects. First, to provide insight into processes occurring at the volcano–atmosphere interface: the plume composition on fine temporal scales may be affected by the shallowest-level processes of gas storage and release. Second, to provide insight into the immediate interaction of volcanic gases with the troposphere, and the effects of local meteorology. Third, to indicate a range of 'natural' compositional variation given a particular state of activity at a volcano, so as to define a background level and identify departures from it, for purposes of eruption monitoring and risk mitigation.

As well as dispersal by wind, a plume is subject to modification by chemical reactions. The range of potential processes includes not only gas-phase reactions, but also reactions on, in, or with suspended solid and liquid particles. This is a burgeoning field of research in its own right, carrying with it implications for the climatic impact of particles released via anthropogenic pollution. Many of the reactions of interest are still only poorly understood. With regard to the fate of tropospheric volcanic plumes, information about the processes and rates of removal of species such as SO_2, HCl and HF from the gas phase is desirable.

Since there is little known about the tropospheric chemistry and physics of volcanic plumes, we have adopted an observational approach. Measurements made under a range of field situations have been used to delimit the range of processes that may affect tropospheric plumes. Such studies are feasible with ground-based remote sensing, and are desirable given the increasing use of these techniques in volcano-monitoring campaigns.

Here we investigate the influence of tropospheric processes on the composition of the volcanic plume from Masaya Volcano, Nicaragua. Masaya is an ideal location for these studies because the volcano is characterized by strong degassing that is not accompanied by significant effusive or explosive activity. We collected gas data using an open-path Fourier transform infrared (OP–FTIR) spectrometer during fieldwork in 1998 and 1999.

We have three questions in mind, and explore answers in the Masaya context. (1) If OP–FTIR measurements in different modes sample different paths through the plume, do they record the same composition, or is the plume modified locally by tropospheric processes? (2) Is the plume composition significantly altered during transport downwind? (3) How does local meteorological variability affect repeated measurements at the same location? Finally, we discuss the implications of this research for remote monitoring of volcanic plumes.

Masaya volcano

Masaya (600 m a.s.l.) is a persistently active basaltic volcano on the Central American Volcanic Front in Nicaragua (Fig. 1). The active crater complex is situated within a 6×11 km elongate caldera (Fig. 1(b)) formed by a Plinian eruption less than 6000 years BP (Williams 1983). Behaviour in the historic period has been predominantly passive, and dominated by gas emission rather than eruption.

There is currently one active pit crater, Santiago (Fig. 1(b)), which has been the centre of all activity for the last 150 years. At least 6 episodes of strong degassing, none associated with major eruptions, have occurred since 1850. During our field campaigns, the crater was *c.* 500 m in diameter, and *c.* 150 m deep; high temperature gases were emitted from a single *c.* 10-m diameter vent which was often incandescent. Considerable mixing between the 'cloudy' volcanic gas and ambient air was visible within the crater, with a reliable plume sustained from the top of the crater by prevailing north-easterly winds.

(a)

Fig. 1. (a) Map of Nicaragua showing Masaya Volcano (11.98° N, 86.16° W), approximately 20 km south-west of Managua. Other Nicaraguan volcanoes are indicated by black dots. North is up the page.

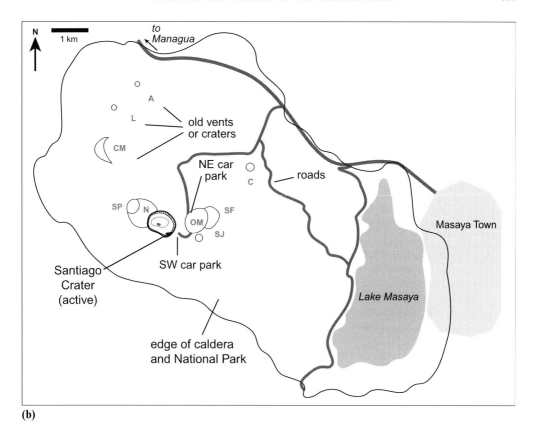

(b)

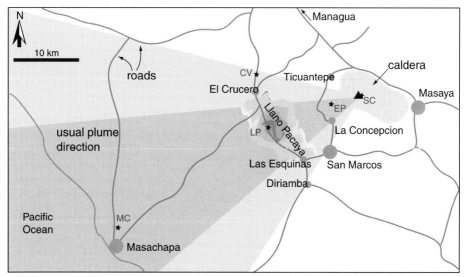

(c)

Fig. 1. (continued) (**b**) Map of Masaya caldera showing the currently active Santiago Crater and older cones and craters: A, Arenal; L, La Luna; CM, Cerro Montoso; SP, San Pedro; N, Nindiri; OM, Old Masaya; SJ, San Juan; SF, San Fernando; C, Comalito. (**c**) Map of the surrounding area. The central grey region marks out the usual plume swath. Llano Pacaya is a region of high land (*c.*900 m a.s.l.) downwind from the volcano (*c.*600 m a.s.l.). Stars mark locations where spectra were collected: SC, Santiago Crater; EP, El Panama; CV, Casa Vieja; LP, Llano Pacaya; MC, Masachapa.

There has been growing interest in Masaya's degassing behaviour, with most studies utilizing the good road network (Fig. 1(c)) for vehicle-borne COSPEC measurements of the SO_2 emission rate (e.g. Stoiber *et al.* 1986; Rymer *et al.* 1998; Delmelle *et al.* 1999*a*). Other gas measurement techniques have been employed both at the volcano's summit and downwind, including direct sampling with filter packs (Stoiber *et al.* 1986) and diffusion tubes (Delmelle *et al.* 2001), acid-rain sampling (Johnson & Parnell 1986), and ground-based remote sensing with OP–FTIR spectrometers (Horrocks *et al.* 1999; Burton *et al.* 2000; Duffell *et al.* 2001).

COSPEC measurements of the sulphur dioxide emission rate in 1998 and 1999 have been reported by Delmelle *et al.* (1999*a*). Results on different days fluctuated significantly, but the mean for the period February to April 1998 was 21.4 kg/s (with maximum and minimum values of 41.9 kg/s and 7.8 kg/s), and for February to March 1999 was 20.7 kg/s (with maximum and minimum values of 47.0 kg/s and 14.5 kg/s).

Johnson and Parnell (1986), studied some of the local effects of degassing from Masaya in 1980–1982. Their work demonstrated that rain falling through the gas plume was considerably acidified (pH as low as 2.47) from contributions of HCl and H_2SO_4. They attributed varying proportions of HCl and H_2SO_4 in the rain samples to the differing solubilities and scavenging mechanisms of HCl and SO_2 gas in the plume. Plume-polluted rainwater samples collected downwind from Masaya in March 1999 indicated similar high acidities of pH 3.5–4.0 (Delmelle *et al.* 1999*b*).

Volcanic plume monitoring

The composition of a volcanic plume measured at some distance away from the vent reflects both the composition of gas released from the magma, and subsequent modifications related to hydrothermal and atmospheric interactions. At Masaya, incandescence within the vent suggested gas release directly from a magma–air interface at shallow depth, and so gas interaction with a hydrothermal system is unlikely to have been significant.

Some studies have directly addressed atmospheric chemistry related to volcanic gases (e.g. Bekki & Pyle 1994; Oppenheimer *et al.* 1998*a*; Pinto *et al.* 1989; Tabazadeh & Turco 1993; Self *et al.* 1996). In general, these have focused on the global atmospheric impact of gases released during large explosive eruptions, rather than the tropospheric impact of continuous passively degassing volcanoes.

Although H_2O and CO_2 are volumetrically the most important constituents of volcanic plumes, and while CO_2 is potentially an important tracer of the magmatic contribution to volcanic gases, nevertheless the fate of these gases within the troposphere is of little interest because of their high ambient concentrations. However, the fact that large quantities of hot water vapour are present in tropospheric volcanic plumes is likely to be significant to the fate of other volcanic components. The local humidity within the gas plume may be significantly higher than ambient, and volcanic effluent contains a range of potential condensation nuclei. Gas emitted from volcanoes often looks 'cloudy', confirming condensation of liquid water droplets, with consequences for the fate of soluble species present in the plume.

Processes

The range of processes that may affect tropospheric volcanic plumes is summarized in Figure 2. The relative importance of individual reactions depends on the nature of both the emitted gases and the local troposphere (in turn controlled by local meteorology).

Recent research on chemistry in the troposphere was reviewed by Ravishankara (1997). Because the troposphere contains suspended solid and liquid particles, heterogeneous reactions (those occurring on the surface of a solid) and multiphase reactions (those occurring within an aqueous medium) are usually more important in controlling concentrations of soluble gases than slower homogeneous gas phase reactions. Although condensed water is likely to be an abundant form of suspended material, other substances (e.g. S-containing particles at various stages of evolution, sea-salt particles, soot, silicates, and organic aerosols) may also be important media for reactions. Apart from their direct involvement in reactions, suspended particles also control the available solar flux, affecting atmospheric heating rates and photochemical processes. Rates of tropospheric heterogeneous and multiphase reactions are poorly known, and reliant upon observation rather than prediction: better understanding of the microphysics of particle formation is needed for their constraint.

The tropospheric chemistry occurring within a volcanic plume will be complex. Rates of transformation and removal of gas species depend upon the availability of condensed water and solid particles in the plume, but also on the photochemical production of radicals (which in turn depends upon UV flux and the availability of

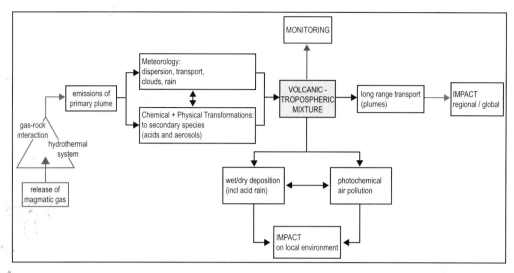

Fig. 2. Processes affecting volcanic gases after their release from magma. Emissions from the volcanic source are usually a mixture of acidic gases, trace metals, and solid particles (ash). Two sets of processes can be identified, those that modify the in-plume composition, and those leading to deposition. Atmospheric interaction begins immediately the gases enter free air, well before the plume leaves the crater (modified extensively from Finlayson-Pitts & Pitts 1986).

oxidants such as H_2O_2 and OH), and the changing pH within water droplets.

Meteorological effects A volcano's physical setting, such as the edifice height and local topography, and geographical situation, dictate patterns of local meteorology. Local weather conditions affect the fate of tropospheric plumes both directly, through dispersion and transport downwind, and indirectly, through factors such as temperature, humidity, fogs, precipitation, cloud cover, and the amount of sunlight reaching the plume. These factors constrain which chemical reactions are favoured: hydrolysis and photochemical processes in particular will be affected. Fog water droplets are a medium for liquid-phase SO_2 to sulphate conversion, and a cycle of condensation on aerosols at night followed by evaporation during the day can dramatically increase the concentrations of pollutants in the droplets.

Reactions occur over long distances as the gases are transported. At Masaya, a region of 1250 km^2 is affected by acid deposition, and time-averaged concentrations of SO_2 exceeding 30 ppb are commonly observed under the plume up to 30 km away from the active crater (P. Delmelle pers. comm.).

Wind speeds are important in plume transport, but if atmospheric inversion layers develop then these can control the further dispersion of

the plume. The development of temperature inversions overnight is not unusual at Masaya: these may trap the volcanic so that ground-level fumigation peaks during the night and early morning.

Chemical and physical reactions affecting SO_2 Sulphur gases are ultimately oxidized to sulphate aerosols, which are then rapidly rained out or deposited. There are a number of possible mechanisms. The most important gas phase process involves oxidation of SO_2 by OH radicals to SO_3 and then to H_2SO_4. However, it is widely accepted (e.g. Ravishankara 1997) that oxidation of SO_2 in the troposphere occurs predominantly as a multiphase reaction (i.e. in droplets) by attack from oxidants like H_2O_2 and O_3. One possible scheme for SO_2 oxidation in cloud droplets was investigated by Chandler *et al.* (1988). They found this process to be extremely rapid, and the rate constant estimated from their field measurements was almost an order of magnitude greater than similar estimates from laboratory studies. This scale of discrepancy serves to highlight the need for more detailed research in this area.

Photodissociation of SO_2 in the gas phase to SO and O, which may be important higher in the atmosphere, cannot occur in the troposphere because solar radiation at the necessary UV wavelengths does not penetrate this far. Other possible reaction routes for SO_2 oxidation are via transition metal catalysis, or via homogeneous aqueous phase reactions.

Because little is known in detail about the reactions that occur, SO_2 oxidation rates cannot be derived accurately from theory. Observations of power plant plumes provide some insight: oxidation rates could be up to 10% per hour, but higher in fog or cloud (Finlayson-Pitts & Pitts 1986). Rates also tend to be higher in summer than winter, suggesting the importance of photochemistry or temperature in the process. Rates increase when the gas is mixed with surrounding air containing photochemical oxidants. But significant SO_2 oxidation to sulphate still occurs at night, suggesting the importance of liquid phase reactions, and rates dramatically increase in the presence of liquid water or when humidities exceed c.75%.

Limited research at volcanoes does not contradict these observations. Martin *et al.* (1986) studied the plume chemistry of Mount Etna and observed a range of sulphur loss rates, and possibly very short residence times of aerosols, very likely influenced by variable weather and plume conditions. Deposition of SO_2 directly onto surfaces occurs in competition with SO_2 oxidation. Under conditions where rates of oxidation are slow (i.e. dry and cool) and there are a high concentration of dry particles in the plume or the plume is at ground level, dry adsorption of SO_2 may become an important process in its removal from the gas phase. At Masaya Volcano, Delmelle *et al.* (2001) showed that less than 10 % of the emitted SO_2 was dry deposited within 44 km of the source (i.e., *c.* 1 hour for average plume speeds).

Chemical and physical reactions affecting HCl
The most important property of HCl for tropospheric reactions is its solubility. The Henry's Law solubility constant for HCl is 2.53×10^5 mol. m^{-3} Pa^{-1} at 298 K, which is approximately three orders of magnitude larger than that for SO_2 (126 mol. m^{-3} Pa^{-1}, values quoted from Seinfeld, 1986). Because HCl is not a criterion air-quality pollutant like SO_2, its tropospheric chemistry has received less attention, despite the importance of chlorine in the stratosphere. However, because of its high solubility, its chemistry may be far simpler than that of SO_2.

Multiphase reactions are likely to be more important than surface reactions, and the rate of HCl removal will be even more strongly affected by the presence of liquid water than is the rate of SO_2 oxidation. Clouds, fog, or rain will significantly alter the composition of the remaining gas-phase plume due to HCl dissolution. In a limited study, Johnson & Parnell (1986) showed that the pH of acid rain-water at Masaya was controlled by the amount of dissolved HCl, and while SO_2 was still available for dissolution at long distances downwind, proximal rainfall removed almost all of the HCl from the plume.

Deposition processes Figure 2 indicates that deposition could occur by wet or dry processes. Dry deposition refers to the removal of particles or molecules at ground surfaces (e.g. soils, vegetation, water) via settling or sticking. Rates of dry deposition depend strongly on the nature of the surface: rates of acid deposition increase strongly if, for example, leaf surfaces are wet. Dry deposition velocities also depend on the reactivity of the species involved: experimental data indicate rates for HF (which has high absorptivity) of 1–4 cm/s and for SO_2 of 0.1–2 cm/s (Seinfeld 1986). The study by Delmelle *et al.* (2001) at Masaya showed that deposition rates for SO_2 and HCl onto PbO_2-coated sulphation plates were both around 1.6 cm/s.

Wet deposition refers primarily to precipitation events: particles or aerosols act as condensation nuclei and fall out with water droplets, while acids dissolve into water droplets in clouds and are subsequently removed during rainfall. Tabazadeh and Turco (1993) modelled the wet deposition of HCl from a stratosphere-bound eruption plume following the Mt Pinatubo eruption. Once water began to condense, HCl was readily dissolved to form solutions of 1–5 wt% HCl. This process was very rapid, with an equilibrium determined by Henry's Law. Large volcanic eruptions often induce rainfall, and the dissolved HCl is thereby efficiently removed.

Simplified models

OP–FTIR spectroscopy most readily yields information on the composition of the *gas* phase in the volcanic plume. Once a gaseous molecule has been converted to something else (e.g. aerosol or particle), it is effectively removed from the measurement, even if it has not yet been physically deposited from the plume. While rates of deposition are important for plume environmental impact, rates of heterogeneous and multiphase reactions are important in terms of changing plume composition. Of particular importance is the rapid rate of dissolution of HCl (and presumably HF) into water droplets. Water droplets may be present in the plume even if ambient humidities are low, due to the presence of condensation nuclei and variations in pressure and temperature as gas exits the volcanic vent. The presence of water droplets or aqueous films is also crucial for tropospheric SO_2 oxidation, so there is competition between a number of possible reactions. As reactions occur, aqueous aerosol becomes increasingly acidified, affecting the balance of subsequent reactions and dissolutions, and eventually saturated with respect to further scavenging of acid gas molecules. Figure 3 summarizes the factors involved in removal of acid gases by water droplets.

Consider, first, a volcanic plume emitted into an environment rich in condensed atmospheric water. Scavenging from the gas phase will be unlimited and controlled by the rates of reaction for different species. Scavenging rates for HCl and HF, which have higher solubilities, are likely to be faster than those for SO_2, which relies upon chemical reaction in preference to physical dissolution. The measured gas phase composition will reflect the relative rates of scavenging, so that SO_2/HCl or SO_2/HF ratios increase as the plume ages.

Alternatively, in a perfectly dry environment, no aqueous removal processes are possible. Reactions on the surfaces of solid particles might also be precluded as they are thought to involve thin aqueous or organic films. Dry deposition of HF is

relatively rapid, compared with SO_2, but otherwise, in this situation there may be only slow change in the gas phase composition as the plume ages.

For a situation in which limited condensed water is available for tropospheric reactions, the crucial factor is how rapidly the available water becomes saturated. There may be rapid removal of soluble species initially as plume water condenses on exit from the volcanic vent. Subsequently, the gas phase composition may change only through slower dry deposition processes or in short-lived precipitation events. The intermediate situation may be expected at Masaya, with rapid reaction and dissolution occurring as the plume convects within the crater until the aqueous aerosol is saturated, but with little subsequent gas phase compositional change as the plume ages and disperses downwind. A different set of reactions may become important as the plume disperses over the Pacific Ocean and mixes with the marine boundary layer.

Measurement technique

During field campaigns in February–March 1998 and March 1999 we used a MIDAC Corporation

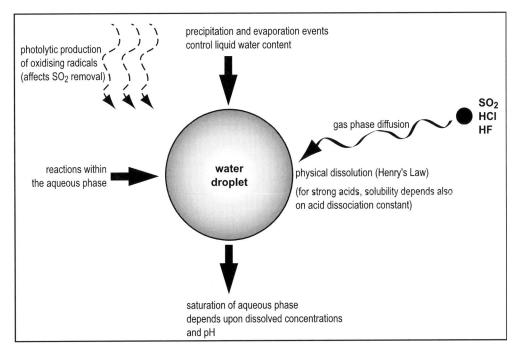

Fig. 3. Factors relevant to aqueous removal of acid species from a volcanic gas plume. Reaction rates depend upon diffusion, liquid phase reactions and solubilities. Local meteorology controls atmospheric water content, and affects gas-phase diffusion. A range of other possible catalysts and reaction pathways are available in the real troposphere.

spectrometer, fitted with an indium antimonide (InSb) detector, operating at 0.5 cm^{-1} resolution (Oppenheimer *et al.* 1998b). Gas absorption data can be collected under a range of field configurations. For this study, two modes were used, with the infrared energy source provided either by a portable lamp placed at some distance away from the spectrometer (active mode), or by the sun (solar mode). Typical field instrumentation is illustrated in Figure 4. Observations were made at Santiago Crater and at several locations downwind. Retrievals of active mode data away from the crater were challenging because of low volcanic gas concentrations, due to dilution and lifting of the plume away from ground level.

McGonigle *et al.* (2003, this volume) discuss the methodology for OP–FTIR measurement. In brief, a raw single beam measurement was analysed using a forward model and fitting routine, which mimics the transmittance through the atmosphere. This method can be applied equally well to both solar occultation data and short path active data. Infrared spectra were simulated, in specified frequency micro-windows, via a radiative transfer model (Reference Forward Model, version 4.0, available on the WWW at http://www.atm.ox.ac.uk/RFM), using line parameter data from the HITRAN96 molecular spectroscopic database (Rothman *et al.* 1998). The background response curve was fitted by a polynomial function. Simulated spectra were constrained by a priori values for

volcanic and atmospheric gas concentrations, then varied through a fitting procedure to generate the best fit to measured samples. The retrieval iteration was calculated following Rodgers (1976) with a Marquardt (1963) enhancement to allow variable step sizes. One benefit of this procedure was that a relative error for each of the fitted components was calculated with the retrieved quantities.

The SO_2, HCl, and HF were retrieved in spectral micro-windows at 2460–2520, 2690–2900 and 4020–4180 cm^{-1}, respectively. The H_2O, CH_4, N_2O and CO_2 were fitted simultaneously with the target gases, with quantitative estimates of H_2O retrieved in the same window as HCl. Molar ratios of SO_2/HCl and HCl/HF, derived either from each individual spectrum or by group regression of a set of spectra, were used to characterize the plume composition. Uncertainties associated with gas ratios were typically of the order of 10% (e.g. Horrocks *et al.* 2001).

Observations and discussion

Apparent variations in measured gas compositions could reflect:

1. Real, at-source variations in volcanic gas composition;
2. Variable rates of scavenging for different gas species due to tropospheric processes;
3. Spatial heterogeneities in the plume;

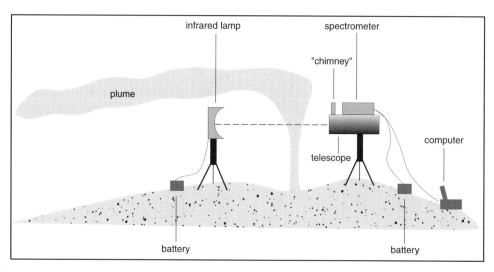

Fig. 4. Typical field configuration for active OP–FTIR measurements. The spectrometer and telescope are optically joined via the 'chimney', which houses a set of 45° mirrors. An artificial energy source is placed behind the plume. The spectrometer and telescope combination can be tilted so that measurements may be made in solar mode (with the Sun as the source).

4. Artefacts produced during data retrieval, arising from non-linear performance across the measured concentration range, especially associated with large errors for low concentrations.

Process (4) may have some impact at Masaya, but can be identified and discarded by careful examination of results. Here, we assess the evidence in Masaya field data for the contribution of processes (2) and (3) to measurements.

Summit measurements in active and solar mode

Spectra were collected at Santiago Crater in both active and solar modes. These measurements sampled different optical paths, and can be used to investigate spatial plume characteristics above the crater. If significant spatial heterogeneities exist within the plume (possibly resulting from rapid tropospheric chemistry as the gas exits the crater), then retrieved plume compositions from the two modes may be different. While active spectra represented a 500-m path between the NE and SW car parks (Figure 1(b)), solar measurements collected from the NE car park represented an inclined path as the Sun dropped behind the plume towards the end of the afternoon.

On 23 February 1998, 50 active spectra were collected across Santiago Crater at 13:00–13:30 h, followed by 50 solar spectra collected at 15:50–16:20 h. The active path mainly sampled the edge of the plume, while the solar path intersected the core of the plume. Figure 5 shows retrieved amounts of SO_2, HCl, and HF. Higher gas burdens were retrieved from solar spectra than from active spectra because the optical path encountered denser plume.

The SO_2/HCl ratios derived from the gradients of regression lines through the two data-sets in Figure 5(a) are the same, at 1.66. Regression lines trend through the origin, indicating sound retrieval of both SO_2 and HCl from both data-sets. The SO_2/HCl ratios calculated from individual spectra are also very consistent (Figure 5(c)). Figure 5(b) shows some discrepancy in retrieved HCl and HF between the active and solar data. While the regression line for the active data trends through the origin, that for the solar data has an intercept on the positive HCl axis. This offset arises from poorly constrained HF retrievals when the spectra are strongly contaminated by atmospheric H_2O, also indicated by the larger HF retrieved error bars. HF is underestimated by about 6% in the solar retrievals because of H_2O saturation in that spectral

region: the regression line intercepts the negative HF axis at approximately 3×10^{17} molecules cm^{-2}. The low HF retrieved from the solar spectra results in high HCl/HF ratios for individual spectra, compared with the active results (Fig. 5(c)). However, the gradients of regression lines on Figure 5(b), compensating for the underestimated solar HF, are the same within error, at 4.4 and 4.5 for the active and solar data, respectively.

These data from one afternoon at Santiago Crater show the importance of considering results in context and thereby identifying spurious retrievals. Ratios derived from individual spectra can be misleading if strong background contamination affects the accuracy of the retrieval. Within error, the gas compositions indicated by the two types of measurement are the same. There is no evidence from these data for spatial heterogeneities in the plume above the crater.

Consistent results from active and solar summit data were obtained throughout the field campaigns in 1998 and 1999. Figure 6 shows retrieved amounts of SO_2, HCl, and HF from active and solar data in 1998. The same problem with the solar HF retrieval is apparent, but ratios are comparable for the two sets of measurements.

For 1999 (not shown), correspondence between active and solar measurements was similar to that in 1998, with SO_2/HCl ratios of 1.6 and 1.8 for active and solar data, respectively, and HCl/HF ratios of 5.1 and 5.0. Given that these ratios represent data collected over a period of 5 weeks in 1998, and 2 weeks in 1999, the consistency in gas composition recorded in Figure 6 is striking. Weather systems in Nicaragua during the dry season are relatively stable, but ambient temperature, humidity and wind speed were not constant over the measurement period. Despite this, the plume composition above Santiago Crater was stable.

Summit measurements confirm two points. First, measurements collected in active and solar mode are directly comparable (over the same range of concentrations), and similar results are retrieved. The only discrepancy lies with the HF retrieval, since solar data are more affected by H_2O contamination in the relevant spectral region. If retrieved HF amounts are interpreted carefully, then mistaken conclusions can be avoided.

Second, the SO_2–HCl–HF gas compositions derived from both the solar and active data are very consistent. The plume appears to be compositionally well-mixed, and relatively unaffected by tropospheric processes above Santiago Crater. Stable gas concentrations have been established

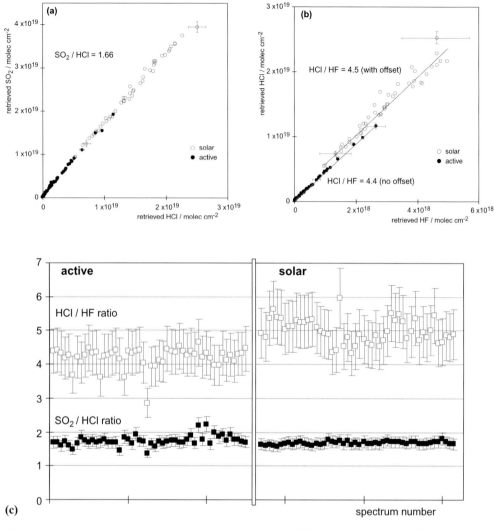

Fig. 5. Retrieved amounts from spectra collected on 23 February 1998 at Santiago Crater. (**a**) SO_2 plotted against HCl, (**b**) HCl plotted against HF. Typical error bars are indicated: retrieved errors were greater for the solar data than the active data. While in (a) the regression lines for solar and active data are indistinguishable and trend through the origin, in (b) the regression line through the retrieved solar data has an intercept to positive HCl. (**c**) SO_2/HCl (filled squares) and HCl/HF (open squares) ratios calculated from individual spectra, plotted against spectrum number. Error bars are ±15% on the HCl/HF ratios, and ±10 % on the SO_2/HCl ratios. The increased scatter in SO_2/HCl ratio for active data compared to solar data is due to lower gas concentrations. The HCl/HF ratios calculated from solar spectra are higher than those from the active data because HF is underestimated in strongly H_2O contaminated solar spectra.

by the time the plume exits at the top of the crater and is measured. Processes occurring as the volcanic gas enters the atmosphere may be confined to within the crater itself, aided by the strong convection and rapid mixing observed within the crater. Any further chemistry would require plume dispersion and ageing, and mixing with more tropospheric water.

Summit and downwind observations

Plume measurements both downwind and at the summit of the volcano were possible on several days during the field campaigns. The purpose of these measurements was to determine whether there was any change in gas composition as the plume was dispersed downwind. Because of plume dilution, maximum retrieved amounts

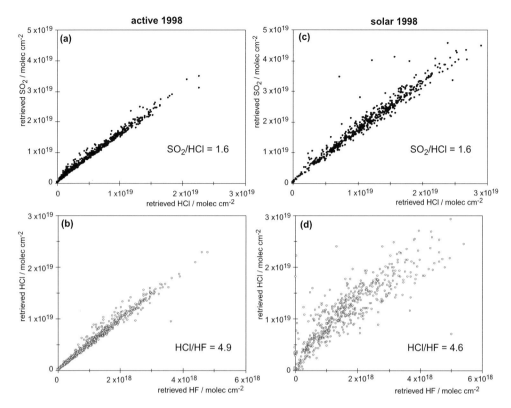

Fig. 6. Retrieved amounts from all summit data collected in February–March 1998, (**a**, **b**) active measurements, (**c**, **d**) solar measurements. (a) and (c) show retrieved SO_2 plotted against retrieved HCl; (b) and (d) show retrieved HCl and HF. Notice that in (d) a similar trend to that in Figure 5(b) due to underestimated solar HF is apparent. Gas ratios are calculated as the gradient of best regression lines.

downwind were typically an order of magnitude lower than maximum amounts at the crater. Only SO_2 and HCl are considered since HF was well below detection limit in the downwind data.

Figure 1(c) shows locations where spectra were collected. Unless measurements were made around noon, the composition represents an inclined path through the plume in the sun's direction. In general, spectra were collected in the afternoon, which meant that there was some contribution from plume further downwind (i.e. in a south or west direction).

Observations from El Panama Some 225 solar spectra were collected between 11:00 and 16:00 hours on 22 March 1998 from El Panama, a village on the caldera flank, approximately 5 km downwind from Santiago Crater. Retrieved errors were generally lower than those for summit measurements because the sun was at near-zenith, resulting in a shorter atmospheric path and less background contamination in the spectra.

Retrieved amounts of HCl and SO_2 from these downwind spectra are compared with retrieved amounts of similar concentrations and error selected from the entire set of summit solar measurements for 1998 in Figure 7(a).

Regression lines for both data sets have small positive offsets on the SO_2 axis: these offsets go unnoticed for data across a greater concentration range (e.g. Figure 6(c)). The SO_2/HCl ratios calculated by regression are 1.5 and 1.7 for the El Panama and Santiago data, respectively. Given a ± 10 % error boundary, the SO_2–HCl gas composition measured at El Panama was little different from that measured at Santiago Crater.

The plume gas above El Panama was approximately 10 min 'older' than that above Santiago Crater, for an average wind speed of 8.5 m/s. While rates for SO_2 oxidation to sulphate aerosol in water droplets are generally reported as 'extremely rapid' (e.g. Chandler *et al.* 1988), and dissolution of HCl should also be fast, the lifetime for *gas-phase* oxidation of SO_2 is only

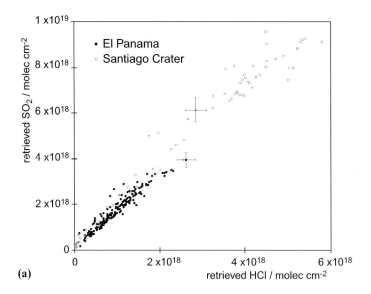

(a)

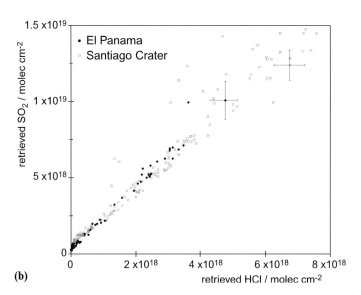

(b)

Fig. 7. Retrieved SO_2 and HCl from solar spectra collected at El Panama (black solid circles) compared with similar concentration data for spectra collected at Santiago Crater (grey open circles). (**a**) 22 March 1998. Retrieved error on the El Panama data was smaller because the atmospheric path length (and associated contamination) was smaller for these spectra. Best-fit regression lines yield SO_2/HCl ratios of 1.5 and 1.7 for the El Panama and Santiago data, respectively. (**b**) 12 March 1999. Best-fit regression lines yield SO_2/HCl ratios of 2.1 and 2.0 for the El Panama and Santiago data, respectively.

*c.*24 hours (Eatough *et al.* 1994). Multiphase processes might therefore have time to occur as the Masaya plume travels from Santiago to El Panama, but homogeneous gas-phase reactions would take much longer. Since there is no discernible compositional change, there are two possible explanations. First, rates of removal of gaseous SO_2 and HCl via multiphase processes may be similar, so that the SO_2/HCl ratio in the gas phase remains approximately constant. Second, there may be insufficient condensed water vapour within the dispersing plume to provide sites for downwind dissolution of HCl or multiphase oxidation of SO_2.

This second explanation is favoured for these day-time measurements. Within and above Santiago Crater, the plume often has a very 'cloudy' appearance, due to condensing water vapour, but as it disperses downwind, the plume becomes hazier, implying a decreasing amount of liquid water in plume particles. Mixing of the warmer volcanic gas with the ambient atmosphere is strong within Santiago Crater, but much less so as the plume moves downwind in temperature equilibrium with its surroundings. Thus, water droplets may quickly become saturated with dissolving gases within the crater, but as the plume moves downwind, the remaining gaseous SO_2 and HCl have little contact with fresh condensed water, and existing water droplets may evaporate.

On 12 March 1999, spectra were again collected from El Panama, but between 1600 and 1730 h, much later in the day than in 1998. The sun was lower in the sky (at elevation angles from 25° and 7° by the end of data collection), the atmospheric path was longer (so retrieved errors were higher), and the spectrometer was aligned in the direction of the Llano Pacaya. The gas composition recorded in the 1999 spectra therefore represents plume at greater distances from Santiago Crater than the 1998 measurements, approximately 9 to 18 km for an assumed plume altitude of 1.5 km. Figure 7(b) shows SO_2 and HCl retrieved from the 12 March 1999 data plotted with solar measurements at Santiago Crater for comparison.

The SO_2/HCl ratios derived from Figure 7(b) are 2.1 and 2.0, calculated by regression of the El Panama and Santiago data, respectively. As previously, these values are identical, within error. Despite the fact that the plume sampled by these measurements could have travelled for up to 45 minutes from Santiago Crater, mixing with the troposphere had little effect on the relative concentrations of SO_2 and HCl in the gas phase. Any changes in gas composition up to 15 km downwind are undetectable by this method.

Solar spectra from Casa Vieja and Masachapa
In order to compare gas compositions measured at two different distances downwind with the composition measured at Santiago Crater, we collected four sets of solar spectra over 17–18 March 1998. On 17 March, with an unusual southeasterly wind, 50 spectra were collected at Casa Vieja, approximately 15 km NW of Santiago Crater, between 1300 and 1415 h. Thirty-five spectra were then collected at Santiago Crater between 1655 and 1735 h. On 18 March, with the usual northeasterly wind, 80 spectra were collected between 12:35 and 15:00 h close to Masachapa, approximately 40 km SW of Santiago Crater. Thirty-five spectra were collected on return to Santiago, between 16:55 and 17:35 h. Retrieved amounts of SO_2 and HCl from these data are plotted in Figure 8. Approximate plume ages at Casa Vieja and Masachapa, given average wind speeds of 8.5 m/s, were 30 minutes and 1.5 hours, respectively.

Measurements at Santiago Crater on both days confirmed SO_2/HCl gas ratios of about 1.6. On both days, the downwind SO_2/HCl ratios were slightly higher than those derived from summit data, but the difference was insignificant. Within the bounds of error, all four datasets verify the same SO_2/HCl gas ratio, despite the fact that the retrieved amounts vary by almost two orders of magnitude. Although retrieved errors are substantial for the low concentration downwind measurements (Figs 8(c) and (d)), these data are still reliable, with R^2 correlation coefficients of 0.8.

In general, solar data collected even up to 40 km from the volcano (i.e. a plume age of approximately 1.5 hours) show little evidence for a differential influence of tropospheric processes on plume SO_2 and HCl. Downwind measurements have inherently low gas concentrations and high associated errors, and would be unsatisfactory as the *only* information on volcanic gas composition. Nevertheless, these data show that for the Masaya situation, spectra collected at some distance are a reliable proxy for at-crater sampling.

Active spectra on the Llano Pacaya Some 14 km southwest from Masaya volcano, the land rises steeply to form a broad ridge called the Llano Pacaya (900–1000 m a.s.l., see Fig. 1(c)). The volcanic plume leaves Santiago Crater at 600 m a.s.l., and is blown by northeasterly trade winds directly into, and over, the Llano Pacaya ridge. Active spectra were collected on the Llano Pacaya to investigate the near-ground level plume composition.

Thirty, 100, and 50 spectra were recorded on 3, 10, and 14 March 1998, respectively. Pathlengths between lamp and spectrometer were approximately 300 m. Retrieved amounts of SO_2 and HCl are plotted in Figure 9. Retrieved amounts at similar concentration levels from active spectra collected on 3 and 9 March 1998 at Santiago Crater are shown for comparison.

The SO_2/HCl ratios of 1.9 and 1.7 calculated by regression of the Llano Pacaya and Santiago Crater data, respectively, are the same within error. The relative proportions of SO_2 and HCl

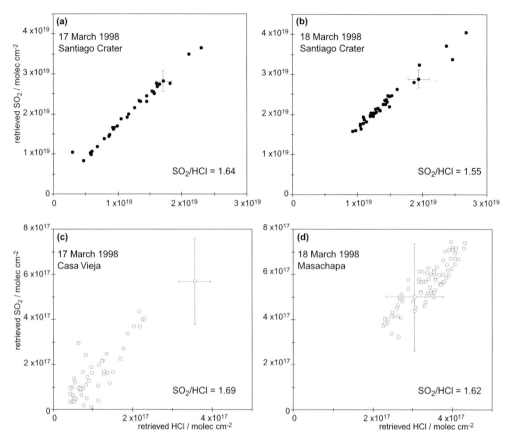

Fig. 8. Retrieved SO_2 and HCl amounts from solar spectra collected downwind (open circles) and at the crater (solid circles) in 1998: (**a**) 17 March at Santiago Crater, (**b**) 18 March at Santiago Crater, (**c**) 17 March at Casa Vieja, and (**d**) 18 March at Masachapa. Sample error bars calculated from retrieved errors are shown. The SO_2/HCl ratios were calculated as the gradient of regression lines fitted to the data. Note the different scales.

in the gas at ground level 14 km downwind were unchanged from the proportions measured above Santiago Crater. This result implies either that SO_2 and HCl are deposited from the plume at approximately equal rates, or that deposition as the plume gas comes into contact with vegetation is negligible. Delmelle *et al.* (2001) indicate that dry deposition onto the land is not negligible and may remove up to 10 % of the total emitted SO_2 and HCl from the plume within 44 km of the vent. These authors confirm that HCl and SO_2 dry deposition rates are similar at Masaya.

The maximum retrieved amounts of SO_2 and HCl from the Llano Pacaya active spectra are 4×10^{17} molecules cm^{-2} and 2×10^{17} molecules cm^{-2}, respectively (Figure 9). These values are equivalent to 0.6 and 0.3 ppm by volume for the 300 m pathlength. Time-averaged SO_2 concen-

trations over 4-week periods in 1998 and 1999 of greater than 0.09 ppm were derived by Delmelle *et al.* (1999a) for the core of Masaya's plume at the Llano Pacaya, using a network of diffusion tubes and PbO_2 sulphation plates. The values derived from the OP–FTIR measurements compare well, since these represent a temporary maximum. At night, ground-level concentrations are expected to be higher as a result of atmospheric inversions trapping the plume at low altitude.

Discussion Both active and solar mode data point to negligible changes in SO_2/HCl gas composition as Masaya's plume disperses. It seems that negligible oxidation of SO_2 and dissolution of HCl occur as the tropospheric plume travels downwind, under the daytime

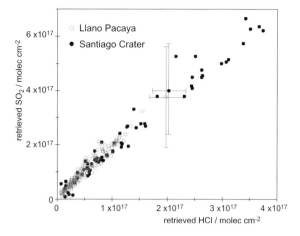

Fig. 9. Retrieved SO_2 and HCl from active spectra collected at Llano Pacaya on 3, 10, and 14 March 1998 (grey open circles) compared with similar concentration data for active spectra collected at Santiago Crater on 3 and 9 March 1998 (black solid circles). Sample error bars calculated from the retrieved error are shown. Regression lines yield SO_2/HCl ratios of 1.9 and 1.7 for the Llano Pacaya and Santiago data, respectively.

conditions in which measurements were made, and that dry deposition of these species occurs at similar rates. A greater concentration of available condensed atmospheric water, such as during the rainy season or periods of low altitude cloud, could provide the appropriate environment for further multiphase chemistry, and the measured plume gas composition might then be expected to change.

The absolute amounts retrieved from downwind solar spectra represent column amounts along an inclined path through the plume at that location. These values are controlled not only by source gas emission rate, but also by patterns of plume dispersion, in turn affected by wind speeds, turbulence and atmospheric stratification. Solar spectra collected at different points along a transect under the plume may be integrated to provide a plume concentration cross section (Duffell *et al.* 2001).

For active field spectra, SO_2 detection limits were estimated at 10^{17} molecules cm^{-2} (Horrocks *et al.* 2001): most of the data presented in Figures 7 to 9 represent concentrations above that limit. For the solar measurements, retrieved error also varied considerably with air mass factor and the amount of background contamination in the optical path. While the errors associated with the low concentration downwind measurements preclude them from providing satisfactory plume data alone, in conjunction with comparable data collected at the summit, these spectra are valuable.

Short time-scale variability in summit measurements

Variations in weather may contribute to the type and rate of tropospheric processes that affect the volcanic plume. Changes in atmospheric water content and state are likely to be most significant. Temperature is also a critical parameter as it controls the saturated vapour pressure of water in air and determines the proportion of liquid phase water available. Data collected over several hours at Santiago Crater enable investigation of the short timescale behaviour of the plume composition in response to these effects.

Observations Night-time temperatures were much lower than those during daytime, and the relative humidity consequently increased. Measurements collected during morning periods highlighted changes associated with the switch from nocturnal to diurnal regime. Some 320 spectra were collected on 16 March 1999 between 08:25 and 12:45 h. Figure 10 shows retrieved amounts and gas ratios through time.

Retrieved amounts of volcanic gases (SO_2, HCl, HF) covered a consistent range for the duration of the measurements. Gas ratios in Figure 10 were calculated from individual spectra and some variability is revealed in the time-series. While the SO_2/HCl ratio remained roughly constant, a gradual increase in the HCl/HF ratio from approximately 4.8 at 09:20 h to 5.5 at 12:45 h is apparent. Over the same period, the retrieved water vapour in the optical path increased from

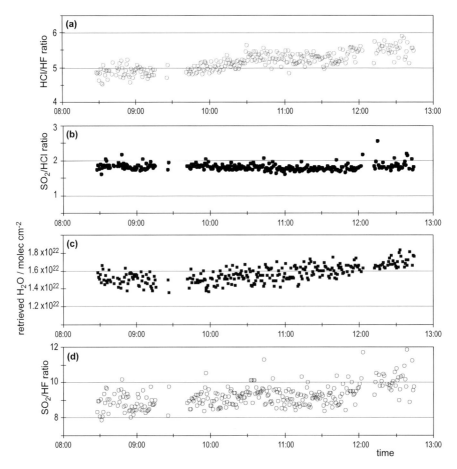

Fig. 10. Gas ratios and retrieved H$_2$O from active spectra collected at Santiago Crater on 16 March 1999. (**a**) HCl/HF, (**b**) SO$_2$/HCl, (**c**) retrieved H$_2$O, and (**d**) SO$_2$/HF through time. The data gap around 09:30 hours represents a period of instrument realignment and calibration.

approximately 1.4×10^{22} molecules cm^{-2} to 1.75×10^{22} molecules cm^{-2}. Retrieved amounts of the volcanic gases did not increase similarly: the change in H$_2$O concentration is attributed to a change in the background atmospheric water vapour content.

Contemporaneous meteorological data from a portable weather station confirmed a 20% increase in ambient water vapour associated with a temperature rise from 23 °C to 29 °C between 09:20 h and 12:45 h. The absolute values of ambient water vapour concentration are difficult to compare directly with the amounts retrieved from OP-FTIR spectra because of additional quantities of magmatic water present in the optical path.

The increase in HCl/HF ratio between the start and end of the measurement period accom-

panied the increase in ambient water vapour. While an increase in SO$_2$/HF ratio was also detectable, SO$_2$/HCl was roughly constant: the background water vapour concentration appears principally to have affected the proportions of HF in the plume relative to the other gases.

A similar effect was apparent in two sets of data collected on the afternoon of 24 February and the morning of 25 February 1998. Results are plotted in Figure 11. Different HCl/HF ratios of 4.7 and 5.3 were obtained from the 24 and 25 February data, respectively, while SO$_2$/HCl ratios were the same, at 1.6. The background atmospheric water vapour concentrations indicated by the intercept on Figure 11(c) were approximately 2.0×10^{22} molecules cm^{-2} and 2.3×10^{22} molecules cm^{-2} for 24 and 25 February respectively. As previously, the higher

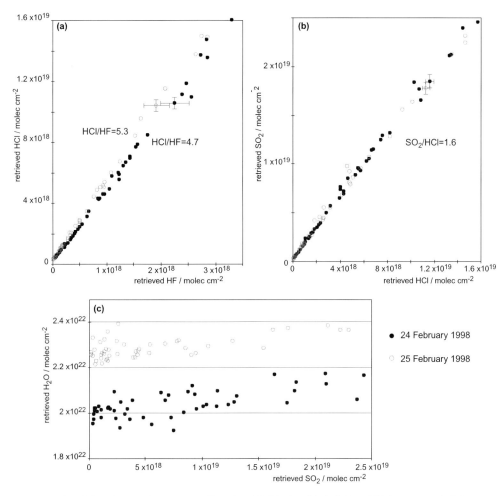

Fig. 11. Retrieved data from active spectra collected on 24 (black solid circles) and 25 (grey open circles) February 1998. (**a**) HCl against HF, with ratios given by the gradient of the regression lines, and sample error bars. (**b**) SO_2 against HCl, with a ratio of 1.6 for both data-sets, and sample error bars. (**c**) H_2O against SO_2, showing higher background atmospheric water vapour on 25 February.

HCl/HF ratio on 25 February was linked to a higher background water content. The change in HCl/HF ratio over the two days was associated with a change in the relative proportions of HF in the gas phase, confirmed by the constant SO_2/HCl ratios but an increase in SO_2/HF ratio (not shown).

Discussion Meteorological variability during the day appears to have only a limited effect on the plume gas composition measured at Santiago Crater. The controlling variable seems to be atmospheric water vapour content. While relative proportions of SO_2 and HCl in the gas phase are

consistent regardless of local weather conditions, the relative amounts of HF, and consequently HCl/HF and SO_2/HF ratios reflect changes in atmospheric water vapour.

There is little published information about important reactions of HF in the troposphere. Two important properties of this species are its high solubility (reactivity) in water, and its strong tendency for adsorption onto particles or other molecules via hydrogen bonds.

As shown earlier, the plume outside the crater, appeared compositionally well-mixed, and no longer susceptible to the influence of tropospheric reactions. In particular, water droplets were probably saturated with respect to SO_2 and HCl before the plume left the crater. Removal of HF by dissolution into water droplets is therefore also unlikely as the cause for the observed increasing HCl/HF ratios with atmospheric water content.

One suggestion for the link between HF removal from the gas phase and increased water vapour concentration is that HF undergoes H-bonded adsorption onto H_2O molecules and aqueous aerosol. However, the validity of this suggestion is unconfirmed.

Overall, meteorological effects on the measured gas composition are minor: those species important for downwind plume monitoring (SO_2, HCl) appear immune. However, more substantive changes in local weather are likely to induce larger-scale alterations in plume chemistry. We suggest, therefore, that remote measurements of volcanic plume composition should be examined for their dependence upon atmospheric variables before being used as conclusive indicators of the source composition.

Concluding remarks

Our work at Masaya Volcano has illustrated that a range of processes can modify volcanic plume compositions in the troposphere. Specific tropospheric heterogeneous and multiphase reactions of relevance are still relatively ill-defined, especially for HCl and HF. Local meteorology is effective via its control of atmospheric water content and plume dispersion. Sulphur dioxide oxidation to sulphate is faster via multiphase processes than via gas phase reactions in the troposphere, and where condensed water content is high, this process can be extremely rapid. Hydrogen chloride is expected to be removed predominantly by dissolution into water droplets. For situations comparable to Masaya, the balance and rates of processes may be controlled by the availability and size distribution of water droplets and particles in the plume: once saturation with respect to acid gases is reached then there is little scope for further compositional change.

We draw three conclusions from the data presented here. First, the gas above Santiago Crater was essentially well-mixed and its composition stable. Second, the composition measured downwind was indistinguishable from that measured at the summit; and third, over short time-scales, local atmospheric water content affected only the proportion of HF in the plume. These are summarized schematically in Figure 12, and discussed below.

Tropospheric processes

Rapid tropospheric chemistry within the crater is favoured by a number of factors. Temperature and compositional gradients, established as hot volcanic gases are injected into the base of the crater, induce strong convection, and are likely to result in condensation of at least some volcanogenic water vapour. Water droplets and other particles come into contact with large volumes of gas as mixing continues, providing opportunity for reactions. Local weather also influences the ambient water content. Rates and extent of heterogeneous and multiphase processes depend upon competition between several species able to dissolve in, or react with, water. Reactions continue until the water droplets are saturated, or too acidic for further reaction, or begin to evaporate as they move up through the crater and disperse. High gas emission rates ensure that water saturation occurs long before all of the volcanic gas has been scavenged.

Beyond the crater, evidence suggests that there is little modification of the plume composition. A regime of wind-blown dispersion operates, and since ambient humidity is low, water droplets tend to evaporate during the day. The ash burden in Masaya's plume was negligible, and so, once remnant water droplets have evaporated and the particle distribution is diluted, there is little scope for heterogeneous or multiphase chemistry as the plume travels downwind. Dry deposition as the plume reaches the Llano Pacaya is negligible by day, though deposition onto damp vegetation at night may be important.

Depletion rates of SO_2 from the plume were negligible over the range of field measurements. In contrast, Oppenheimer *et al.* (1998a) showed that at other volcanoes tropospheric SO_2 depletion rates may be fast, and variable. The significant downwind variation in SO_2 from Soufrière Hills Volcano (Montserrat) reported by these authors is likely related to the moist atmosphere (orographic clouds) and potentially high liquid water content of the plume, coupled with the effect of interaction with the marine boundary layer. For Masaya, SO_2 depletion rates may be high within the crater, but negligible downwind in the absence of liquid water in the atmosphere.

The scenario suggested in Figure 12 is relevant only for the conditions under which our field data were collected, and cannot be extended beyond these limits. During the night, there is potential for a different regime since lower temperatures and higher relative humidities favour formation of water droplets (Burton *et al.* 2001), and inversion layers may trap the plume at low levels. During periods of low cloud or in the

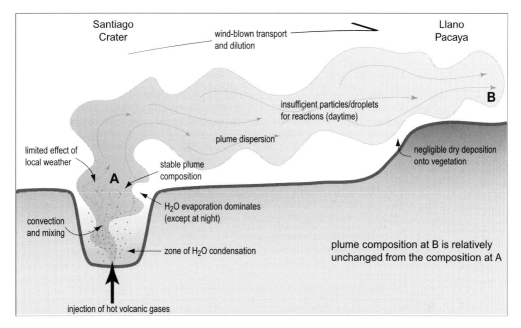

Fig. 12. Tropospheric processes affecting Masaya's plume. This description is valid only for the conditions experienced during the period of field work. Rapid tropospheric chemistry is likely to occur within the crater where water vapour is condensing but nowhere else, as evaporation becomes the dominant process. Cloud or rain interaction with the plume could have severe impact with significant wet deposition of components. As the plume continues downwind to the Pacific, interaction with the marine boundary layer may encourage different scavenging processes.

rainy season, acid dissolution into water droplets and wet deposition will increase dramatically. At such times, rain falling through the plume will become significantly acidified (Johnson & Parnell 1986; Delmelle *et al.* 1999*b*) and the composition of the gas plume is expected to change significantly downwind from Santiago Crater..

Implications for remote plume monitoring

Under the conditions for our field measurements, OP–FTIR spectra collected downwind from Masaya volcano were representative of the at-crater volcanic SO_2–HCl plume composition. At distances exceeding *c.*5 km from the vent, HF concentrations were below reliable detection. Measurement of the plume downwind would be a reliable volcano-monitoring tool, since significant changes in SO_2/HCl under these conditions are more likely to be volcanological than plume chemistry-related.

A strikingly consistent composition with SO_2/HCl and HCl/HF ratios of 1.6 and 5.0, respectively, characterized Masaya's plume in 1998 and 1999. The typical range of variation in

these ratios was less than 10–15 %, and similar results were obtained during a return trip in 2000 (Duffell *et al.* 2001). In April–May 2001, while gas emission rates were similar to previous measurements, gas ratios were different and more variable, at *c.*4.5 and *c.*7.6 for SO_2/HCl and HCl/HF, respectively, suggesting a significant shift in degassing regime prior to these observations. A minor explosion from Santiago Crater on 23 April 2001, resulted in the formation of a new vent, close to the location of the old one. These events point to a change in the shallow structure of the volcanic system, with gases sampled during the 2001 campaign likely to have followed a new route to the surface. The establishment of new pathways may explain the observed increase in gas ratios: interaction with rocks and moisture in newly exposed zones initiates increased scavenging of the more reactive species (HF > HCl > SO_2) until these zones dry out and stabilize. Further work will be needed to develop a conclusive explanation.

At other volcanoes, or during different times of year at Masaya, it is essential that near-vent and downwind variability is thoroughly investigated. Downwind plume monitoring can only be used to assess volcanological changes if variations arising from plume chemistry are minimal, or at least well-understood.

While plume compositions may appear stable and consistent over time-scales of weeks or months, small-scale short-term variability can arise as a result of local weather changes. Relationships between measured gas compositions and meteorological variables must be defined before short-term patterns can be confidently linked to the behaviour of the volcano.

This work was supported by NERC studentships GT4/97/212 to LAH and GT4/99/ES/43 to HJD, by NERC grants GR9/4655 and GR9/03608 to CO, by the National Institute of Geophysics and Volcanology (INGV), Italy, and by the European 5th Framework project 'MULTIMO'. We are grateful to the British Embassy in Managua and to INETER for logistical support in Nicaragua, and to the friendly staff of the Masaya Volcano National Park for their kindness and cooperation in hosting us during many fruitful weeks of gas surveillance. Comments from three referees improved the clarity of the manuscript. Peter Francis was an inspirational PhD supervisor for LAH in 1997–1999; as colleague and senior scientist in this work he is sorely missed.

References

BEKKI, S. & PYLE, J. A. 1994. A 2-dimensional modeling study of the volcanic eruption of Mount Pinatubo. *Journal of Geophysical Research*, **99(D9)**, 18 861–18 869.

BURTON, M. R., OPPENHEIMER, C., HORROCKS, L. A. & FRANCIS, P. W. 2000. Remote sensing of CO_2 and H_2O emission rates from Masaya Volcano, Nicaragua. *Geology*, **28(10)**, 915–918.

BURTON, M. R., OPPENHEIMER, C., HORROCKS, L. A. & FRANCIS, P. W. 2001. Diurnal changes in volcanic plume chemistry observed by lunar and solar occultation spectroscopy. *Geophysical Research Letters*, **28(5)**, 843–846.

CHANDLER, A. S., CHOULARTON, T. W. *ET AL.* 1988. Measurements of H_2O_2 and SO_2 in clouds and estimates of their reaction rate. *Nature*, **336**, 562–565.

DELMELLE, P., BAXTER, P. *ET AL.* 1999a. Origin, effects of Masaya's volcano continued unrest probed in Nicaragua. *EOS, Transactions of the American Geophysical Union*, **80(48)**, 575, 579, 581.

DELMELLE, P., STIX, J. *ET AL.* 1999b. Global volcanism network report. *Bulletin of the Global Volcanism Network*, **24(4)**.

DELMELLE, P., STIX, J., BOURQUE, C. P. A., BAZTER, P. J., GARCIA-ALVAREZ, J. & BARQUERO, J. 2001. Dry deposition and heavy acid loading in the vicinity of Masaya Volcano, a major sulphur and chlorine source in Nicaragua. *Environmental Science and Technology*, **35**, 1289–1293.

DUFFELL, H., OPPENHEIMER, C. & BURTON, M. 2001. Volcanic gas emission rates measured by solar occultation spectroscopy. *Geophysical Research Letters*, **28(16)**, 3131–3134.

EATOUGH, D. J., CAKA, F. M. & FARBER, R. J. 1994. The conversion of SO_2 to sulfate in the atmosphere. *Israel Journal of Chemistry* **34**, 301–314.

FINLAYSON-PITTS, B. J. & PITTS, J. N. 1986. *Atmospheric Chemistry: Fundamentals and Experimental Eechniques*. Wiley-Interscience, New York.

HORROCKS, L., BURTON, M., FRANCIS, P. & OPPENHEIMER, C. 1999. Stable gas plume composition measured by OP–FTIR spectroscopy at Masaya Volcano, Nicaragua, 1998–1999. *Geophysical Research Letters*, **26(23)**, 3497–3500.

HORROCKS, L. A., OPPENHEIMER, C., BURTON, M. R., DUFFELL, H. J., DAVIES, N. M., MARTIN, N. A. & BELL, W. 2001. Open-path Fourier transform infrared spectroscopy of SO_2: an empirical error budget analysis, with implications for volcano monitoring. *Journal of Geophysical Research – Atmospheres*, **106**, 27 647–27 659.

JOHNSON, N. & PARNELL, R. A. 1986. Composition, distribution and neutralization of 'acid rain' derived from Masaya volcano, Nicaragua. *Tellus*, **38**, 106–117.

MARQUARDT, D. W. 1963. An algorithm for least squares estimation of nonlinear parameters. *Journal of the Society of Industrial and Applied Mathematics (SIAM)*, **11**, 431–441.

MARTIN, D., ARDOUIN, B. *ET AL.* 1986. Geochemistry of sulfur in Mount Etna plume. *Journal of Geophysical Research*, **91(B12)**, 12 249–12 254.

McGONIGLE A. J. S. & OPPENHEIMER, C. 2003. Optical sensing of volcanic gas and aerosol emmissions. *In*: OPPENHEIMER, C., PYLE, D. M. & BARCLAY J. (eds) *Volcanic Degassing*. Geological Society, London, Special Publications, **213**, 149–168.

OPPENHEIMER, C., FRANCIS, P. & STIX, J. 1998a. Depletion rates of sulfur dioxide in tropospheric volcanic plumes. *Geophysical Research Letters*, **25(14)**, 2671–2674.

OPPENHEIMER, C., FRANCIS, P., BURTON, M., MACIEJEWSKI, A. J. H. & BOARDMAN, L. 1998b. Remote measurement of volcanic gases by Fourier transform infrared spectroscopy. *Applied Physics B*, **67**, 505–515.

PINTO, J. P., TURCO, R. P. & TOON, O. B. 1989. Self-limiting physical and chemical effects in volcanic eruption clouds. *Journal of Geophysical Research*, **94(D8)**, 11 165–11 174.

RAVISHANKARA, A. R. 1997. Heterogeneous and multiphase chemistry in the troposphere. *Science*, **276**, 1058–1065.

RODGERS, C. D. 1976. Retrieval of atmospheric temperature and composition from remote measurements of thermal radiation. *Reviews of Geophysics and Space Physics*, **14(4)**, 609–624.

ROTHMAN, L. S., RINSLAND, C. P. *ET AL.* 1998. The HITRAN molecular spectroscopic database and HAWKS (HITRAN Atmospheric WorKStation): 1996 edition. *Journal of Quantitative Spectroscopy and Radiative Transfer*, **60(5)**, 665–710.

RYMER, H., VAN WYK DE VRIES, B., STIX, J. & WILLIAMS-JONES, G. 1998. Pit crater structure and processes governing persistent activity at Masaya

Volcano, Nicaragua. *Bulletin of Volcanology*, **59**, 345–355.

SEINFELD, J. H. 1986. *Atmospheric chemistry and physics of air pollution*. John Wiley, New York.

SELF, S., ZHAO, J.-X., HOLASEK, R. E., TORRES, R. C. & KING, A. J. 1996. The atmospheric impact of the 1991 Mount Pinatubo eruption. *In:* NEWHALL, C. G. & PUNONGBAYAN, R. S. (eds) *Fire and Mud: the Eruptions and Lahars of Mount Pinatubo, Philippines*. University of Washington Press, Seattle, 1089–1115.

STOIBER, R. E., WILLIAMS, S., N. & HUEBERT, B., J. 1986. Sulfur and halogen gases at Masaya Caldera Complex, Nicaragua: total flux and variations with time. *Journal of Geophysical Research*, **91(B12)**, 12 215–12 231.

SYMONDS, R. B., GERLACH, T. M. & REED, M. H. 2001. Magmatic gas scrubbing: implications for volcano monitoring. *Journal of Volcanology and Geothermal Research*, **108**, 303–341.

TABAZADEH, A. & TURCO, R. P. 1993. Stratospheric chlorine injection by volcanic eruptions: HCl scavenging and implications for ozone. *Science*, **260**, 1082–1086.

WILLIAMS, S. N. 1983. Plinian airfall deposits of basaltic composition. *Geology*, **11**, 211–214.

Correlations between eruption magnitude, SO$_2$ yield, and surface cooling

S. BLAKE

Department of Earth Sciences, The Open University, Walton Hall,
Milton Keynes, MK7 6AA, UK.
(e-mail: s.blake@open.ac.uk)

Abstract: Sulphurous gases from explosive eruptions have the potential to form stratospheric aerosols and so produce surface cooling on a hemispheric to global scale. However, testing for any correlation between SO$_2$ yield and surface cooling is hampered by instrumental SO$_2$ and temperature measurements being available for time periods that include only a few large eruptions. To overcome this, published dendroclimatological data, satellite (Total Ozone Mapping Spectrometer) data on SO$_2$ emissions, stratospheric optical depth data, and volcanological observations are integrated, revealing several relevant new correlations. First, the efficient conversion of SO$_2$ into stratospheric aerosols occurs when the ratio of plume height to tropopause height is greater than about 1.5. Second, the mass of emitted SO$_2$ correlates well with the mass of erupted magma. The SO$_2$ yield is 0.1 to 1% by mass of magma, irrespective of composition. The best-fit power law (r^2=0.67) is mass of SO$_2$ in Mt=1.77(mass of magma in Gt)$^{0.64}$. Third, of the eruption clouds that are believed to have entered the stratosphere in the period 1400–1994, those with masses <5 Gt magma (DRE <2 km^3) appear to have had insignificant effects on Northern Hemisphere summer temperature. The scattered data for eruptions of >10 Gt (>4 km^3) magma suggest a mean cooling effect of about 0.35 °C.

Volcanic gases can influence the Earth's surface environment in many ways. One of these is the surface cooling in the one or two years following large volcanic eruptions. Notable examples of this effect are the unusually cold weather conditions reported after the 1815 eruption of Tambora (Stommel & Stommel 1983; Stothers 1984) and the instrumental record of a decreased global mean surface temperature after the 1991 eruption of Pinatubo (McCormick *et al.* 1995; Self *et al.* 1996). The cooling mechanism has been described lucidly by Peter Francis (Francis 1993; Colling *et al.* 1997) and reviewed most recently by Robock (2000). For sufficiently high eruption rates, tephra and gas are lofted into the stratosphere, where volcanic SO$_2$ gas is converted to H$_2$SO$_4$ aerosol droplets and dispersed. The aerosol layer increases the optical depth of the stratosphere and reflects some solar radiation, leading to cooling of the troposphere. The increase in optical depth is predicted to increase with the mass of SO$_2$ (Stothers 1984; Pinto *et al.* 1989) and the radiative forcing is predicted to be proportional to the increase in optical depth (Pollack *et al.* 1976; Lacis *et al.* 1992; Andronova *et al.* 1999; Grieser & Schönwiese, 1999). Therefore, for those eruptions that penetrate the stratosphere, surface cooling should correlate with the mass of SO$_2$ released. Understanding this correlation is important for estimating the likely effects of poorly documented historic eruptions, assessing the environmental impacts of extremely large prehistoric eruptions, and for predicting climatic and therefore agricultural responses to any future eruptions that are larger than those experienced in historic times. The purpose of this chapter is to investigate this proposed correlation, using data from historical eruptions.

Devine *et al.* (1984), Rampino and Self (1984) and Palais and Sigurdsson (1989) gave evidence that sulphur-rich eruptions caused decreases in global mean surface temperature of 0.1 to 0.5 °C. However, they estimated the SO$_2$ by using a petrological method that, as will be discussed below, is now known to underestimate the sulphur yield by up to two orders of magnitude in some cases (e.g. Westrich & Gerlach 1992). In addition, instrumental data on global and hemispheric mean surface temperature are reliable only after the 1850s, so that important eruptions such as Tambora 1815 pre-date the period of good temperature data. The correlation between SO$_2$ and cooling proposed by Devine *et al.* (1984) and Palais and Sigurdsson (1989) was partly based on eruptions that apparently caused cooling of about 0.1 °C, but this is similar to the uncertainty in mean surface

From: OPPENHEIMER, C., PYLE, D.M. & BARCLAY, J. (eds) *Volcanic Degassing*. Geological Society, London, Special Publications, **213**, 371–380. 0305-8719/03/$15.00

temperature estimates (Hansen & Lebedeff 1987). It is therefore appropriate to re-evaluate the link between volcanic SO_2 emissions and surface cooling.

Data selection

Seeking to define the nature of any correlation between SO_2 yield and surface cooling presents a number of challenges. These include the estimation of the mass of SO_2 gas released by an eruption and the change (if any) in mean surface temperature following an eruption. Allied to the latter point is the question of isolating a volcanic signal from all the other random and non-random controls on temperature (e.g. Kelly & Sear 1984; Mass & Portmann 1989; Robock & Mao 1995; Sadler & Grattan 1999). Furthermore, temperature and SO_2 data must be available for as many eruptions as possible.

Briffa *et al.* (1998) showed that the density of late growth tree rings is a good proxy for mean summer land temperature, and they presented a tree ring record of Northern Hemisphere summer temperature for the period 1400 to 1994. They give values of the difference between annual tree ring density and the mean 1881–1960 tree ring density, normalized by the standard deviation (s.d.) of the 1881–1960 data. 1 s.d. is equivalent to a temperature difference from the mean of 0.117 °C. Most of the tree ring data lies within ±2 s.d. of the mean; few values are greater than +2 standard deviations, but several are less than

–2 s.d. (Fig. 1). Briffa *et al.* (1998) showed that many of the extreme negative temperature anomalies are associated with large volcanic eruptions (see also Jones *et al.* 1995; Pyle 1998). The NHD1 series of Briffa *et al.* (1998) (http://www.ngdc.noaa.gov/paleo.html) is therefore a useful data-set with which to further investigate volcano–climate linkages. One reason for this is that it covers a time-span that is much longer than the instrumental hemispheric or global mean surface temperature record (1860 onwards). This allows the effects of many eruptions to be investigated with a common climate indicator. In addition, because the potential climatic effects of volcanic eruptions may damage crop production, it is useful to measure climate impact using an index that is directly relevant to crop growth. The NHD1 record of mean summer surface land temperature satisfies this requirement more than, say, annual or global temperature data.

The mass of SO_2 released by volcanic eruptions is often estimated by a petrological method, based on the mass of magma erupted and the difference in S content of melt inclusions that were trapped in phenocrysts prior to eruption, and degassed matrix glass (Devine *et al.* 1984). However, independent estimates of the amount of SO_2 released in several recent eruptions are now available from Total Ozone Mapping Spectrometer (TOMS) instruments with detection limits ranging from 5 to 20 kt and an uncertainty of ±30% (Bluth *et al.* 1997; Schnetzler *et*

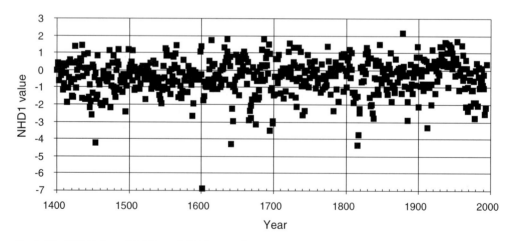

Fig. 1. The NHD1 data of Briffa *et al.* (1998) (http://www.ngdc.noaa.gov/paleo.html) showing Northern Hemisphere summer temperature anomalies, with respect to the 1881–1960 mean, in standard deviation units for the period 1400 to 1994. 1 s.d. unit represents 0.117 °C. Note the lack of extreme positive values. Extreme negative values coincide with known eruptions, in particular those of Kuwae 1452, Huaynaputina 1600, Mount Parker 1641, Tambora 1815, Krakatau 1883, and Novarupta 1912.

al. 1997; Krueger *et al.* 2000). In cases where the two methods can be compared, the petrological method has so far been found to underestimate the SO_2 yield substantially (Fig. 2). The reason for the discrepancy is probably related to the assumption in the petrologic method that syn-eruptive melt-degassing is the only source of erupted SO_2. The most likely source of the 'excess' sulphur is a S-bearing vapour in the pre-eruptive magma (Westrich & Gerlach 1992; Scaillet *et al.* 1998; Wallace 2001), with possible additional contributions from un-erupted magma (Andres *et al.* 1991) and hydrothermal sources (Oppenheimer 1996). So, although the petrological method is relatively easy to apply, its results give only a minimum estimate of SO_2 yield, and must be treated with caution. The most robust estimate of SO_2 yield is therefore thought to be TOMS measurements of SO_2 present in the atmosphere. Values have been compiled for eruptions in the period 1979 to 1994 by Bluth *et al.* (1993), Symonds *et al.* (1994) and Bluth *et al.* (1997). Data from TOMS and NHD1 are therefore used to underpin the investigation reported in this chapter.

Correlation between mass of SO_2 and optical depth of the stratosphere

Stothers (1984) derived a relationship between the mass of stratospheric aerosol, M_D, in grams, and the resultant increase in optical depth, $\Delta\tau$

$$\Delta\tau = 6.5 \times 10^{-15} M_D \qquad (1)$$

The aerosol particles are assumed to have a chemical composition of 75% H_2SO_4 and 25% H_2O by mass (Toon & Pollack 1973), so equation 1 can be rewritten in terms of the mass of SO_2 responsible for the aerosols, M_{D,SO_2}:

$$\Delta\tau = 0.013 M_{D,SO_2} \qquad (2)$$

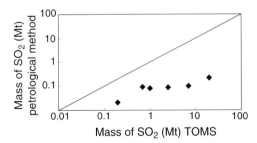

Fig. 2. Comparison of petrological and TOMS estimates of volcanic SO_2 yields. Data and data sources in Table 1.

where M_{D,SO_2} is expressed in megatonnes (1 $Mt = 10^{12}$ g).

Of the total mass of SO_2 released by an eruption, M_{SO_2}, only some fraction will end up in the stratosphere and be available to form aerosol particles. Plumes that rise only into the lower troposphere should have a negligible effect on stratospheric aerosols ($M_{D,SO_2}/M_{SO_2} \approx 0$), whereas plumes that rise far into the stratosphere will transfer most of the SO_2, such that $M_{D,SO_2} \approx M_{SO_2}$. The ratio $\Delta\tau/M_{SO_2}$ should approach 0.013 as the ratio of plume height to tropopause height increases above 1. Data with which to test this are available for nine plumes and bear out the prediction (Table 1 & Fig. 3). Plumes that reach heights of more than about 1.5 times the tropopause height transport essentially all of their SO_2 to the stratosphere. Lower eruption clouds that still breach the tropopause will have a lesser effect on aerosol production (all else being equal) than predicted by equation 1.

Correlation between mass of SO_2 and mass of magma

As already discussed, the petrological method of estimating M_{SO_2} does not always give results that are consistent with TOMS data. Using the petrological method is unlikely, therefore, to provide adequate values of M_{SO_2} with which to compare the summer cooling signal in the 1400 to 1994 NHD1 record. An alternative means of estimating M_{SO_2} is required. In Figure 4, M_{SO_2} from TOMS data is plotted against the mass of magma erupted, and shows that the SO_2 released is usually between 0.1 and 1% by mass of the magma erupted (equivalent to 500 to 5000 ppm S). The good correlation is similar to those given by Oppenheimer (1996) and Wallace (2001), although these authors included a mixture of petrological, COSPEC, and selected TOMS estimates on their diagrams. Using exclusively TOMS data, Pyle *et al.* (1996) and Schnetzler *et al.* (1997) found good correlations between M_{SO_2} and volcanic explosivity index (VEI). VEI is a compound measure of an eruption's characteristics (Newhall and Self 1982), with the result that some eruptions may be difficult to classify uniquely. Carey and Sigurdsson (1989) found that several Plinian eruptions would be classified differently on the basis of column height or mass erupted. So, using VEI as a predictor of an individual eruption's SO_2 yield carries a potentially large uncertainty. Eruption mass (or volume) is a more precise measure of eruption size, so Figure 4 should present the best chance of assessing any correlation between eruption size and M_{SO_2}.

Table 1. *Data for selected eruptions detected by TOMS.*

Volcano	Date	Mass of magma (Gt)	Plume height above sea-level (km)	Tropopause height (km)	Mass of SO₂ (Mt), TOMS	Mass of SO₂ (Mt), petrological estimate	Increase in stratospheric optical depth
Sierra Negra	13/11/79	2.43[1]	14	16	1.2		0.0005
Nyamuragira	30/1/80	0.23[2]		16	0.2		
Mount St Helens	18/5/80	0.71[3]	16[18]	11.5[18]	1	0.08[22]	0.0023
Hekla	17/8/80	0.034[4]	15	8	0.5		
Ulawun	6/10/80	0.044[5]	20	16	0.2		0.0002
Alaid	27/4/81		15	12	1.1		0.0012
Pagan	15/5/81	0.5[6]	16	16	0.3		
Nyamuragira	25/12/81	0.32[2]	8	16	4		
El Chichón	4/4/82	2.3[3]	25	16	7	0.1[23]	0.0856
Galunggung	4/82 to 1/83	0.55[7]	16	16	2.5[19]	0.09[7]	
Pavlof	14/11/83	0.03[8]	10	10	0.05		
Mauna Loa	3–4/84	0.55[9]			2[20]		
Krafla	9/84	0.28[10]			0.4[20]		
Ruiz	13/11/85	0.07[11]	31	16	0.7	0.092[11]	0.0061
Nyamuragira	16/7/86	0.19[2]		16	0.8		
Banda Api	9/5/88	0.025[12]	16	16	0.2		
Redoubt	14/12/89	0.0375[13]	13	9	0.2	0.021[13]	0.0021
Pinatubo	15/6/91	10[14]	30	16	20	0.22[14]	0.1439
Hudson	12–15/8/91	6.85[15]	18	15	3.3[21]		0.009[22]
Spurr	27/6/92	0.031[16]	14.5	8	0.2		
Spurr	18/8/92	0.036[16]	13.7	8	0.4		
Spurr	17/9/92	0.039[16]	13.9	8	0.23		
Láscar	21/4/93	0.25[17]	23	16	0.4		

Tropopause height estimated from Jakosky (1986), other data from Bluth *et al.* (1997) except for:
[1]Reynolds *et al.* (1995); [2]Burt *et al.* (1994); [3]Carey and Sigurdsson (1989); [4]Plinian phase only, from data in Gronvold *et al.* (1983) recalculated according to Pyle (1989);[5]McLelland *et al.* (1989); [6]Banks *et al.* (1984); [7]de Hoog *et al.* (2001); [8]McNutt (1999); [9]Lipman and Banks (1987); [10]Rossi (1997); [11]Sigurdsson *et al.* (1990); [12]Smithsonian Institution (1988); [13]Gerlach *et al.* (1994), [14]Westrich and Gerlach (1992); [15]Scasso *et al.* (1994), [16]Neal *et al.* (1995); [17]Matthews *et al.* (1997); [18]Holasek and Self (1995); [19]Bluth *et al.* (1994) includes TOMS data for explosive degassing and COSPEC data for non-explosive degassing throughout the eruption; [20]Bluth *et al.* (1993); [21]Constantine *et al.* (2000); [22]Gerlach and McGee (1994); [23]Luhr *et al.* (1984), [22]estimated value above the large Pinatubo signal.

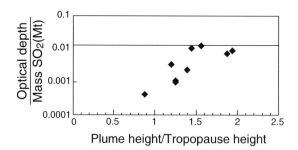

Fig. 3. Ratio of maximum increase in global stratospheric optical depth to mass of SO₂, M_{SO_2}, detected by TOMS, plotted against maximum plume height divided by tropopause height. Data and data sources from Table 1, apart for the 1991 eruption of Hudson, for which only the 15 August plume, with 2.75 Mt SO₂, is considered because its plume was higher (18 km) than that of the tropospheric 12 August plume (Constantine *et al.* 2000). The horizontal line gives the value expected from Stothers' (1984) model, assuming that all SO₂ enters the stratosphere and that there is 100% conversion to aerosol.

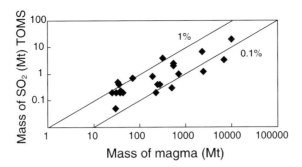

Fig. 4. TOMS data versus mass of magma erupted (data and data sources in Table 1).

The correlation in the 22 data plotted in Figure 4 can be represented by the power law

$$M_{SO_2} \text{ (in Mt)} = 1.77 \ (M_{magma} \text{ (in Gt)})^{0.64} \quad (3)$$

with $r^2 = 0.67$. This power law is similar to the proportionality between M_{SO_2} and $VEI^{0.75}$ given by Pyle *et al.* (1996) for eruptions with $4 \leq VEI \leq 6$. At a first-order level, magma mass can be used as a proxy for the mass of SO$_2$ released.

Correlation between mass of magma and summer cooling

Eruptions that reach well into the stratosphere should cause an increase in stratospheric optical depth that is proportional to M_{SO_2} (Fig. 3 and equation 2). The resultant surface cooling should therefore scale with M_{SO_2}, which is in turn correlated with the mass of magma, M_{magma} (Fig. 4). Taking all eruptions of known mass that are believed to have entered the stratosphere in the period 1400–1994, is there a correlation between the mass of magma and amount of NH summer cooling?

The amount of summer cooling in any year is taken as that year's NHD1 anomaly minus the mean of the previous four years' anomalies. This definition allows an eruption that caused the temperature to fall to be distinguished from a benign eruption that just happened to have occurred in a generally cold period. The time series of this cooling signal derived from the data of Briffa *et al.* (1998) (http://www.ngdc.noaa.gov/paleo.html) is shown in Figure 5, and again reveals the volcanic signals of 1453, 1601, 1641, 1816, and 1912. The same conclusion emerges if the change in NHD1 anomaly from the previous year is plotted.

Figure 6 plots the summer cooling signal against magma mass, taken as a proxy for mass of SO$_2$, for eruptions that reached the stratosphere (Table 2). Note that the Mount Parker eruption of 1641 is excluded from the plot, because there is no measurement of the mass of magma erupted. For NH eruptions occurring at high latitude in January to June, the cooling signal for the summer in the eruption year is plotted. For all other eruptions, the signal in the year following the eruption is plotted to take account of the slow northward transport of stratospheric aerosols.

Figure 6 shows that eruptions with masses <5 to 10 Gt magma (DRE <2 to 4 km^3) are associated with signals within ±2 s.d. of the mean (i.e. $\Delta T < \pm 0.23$ °C), and are therefore regarded as having had insignificant effects on NH summer temperature. In contrast, of the eight larger eruptions, all but Santa Maria 1902 and Quizapu 1932 are associated with detectable summer cooling. The large cooling signal of –4.476 associated with the Mount Parker 1641 eruption, which had a VEI of 5 (Simkin & Siebert 2000b) and therefore a likely mass of order 10 Gt, is consistent with this trend. The eight plotted eruptions larger than 10 Gt (>4 km^3 dense magma or >10 km^3 tephra deposit; VEI ≥5) have a mean cooling effect of about 0.35 °C, but the data are scattered. In other words, there is a threshold eruption magnitude of 10 Mt magma, or 5 to 10 Mt SO$_2$ (equation (3) predicts that 10 Gt magma will release about 8 Mt SO$_2$) required to cause detectable NH summer cooling. Eruptions above this threshold occur on average once in a century (Simkin & Siebert 2000a).

Conclusions and discussion

For eruptions that penetrate well into the stratosphere, the mass of SO$_2$ measured by TOMS, and the increase in mean global stratospheric optical depth, are correlated by the model of Stothers

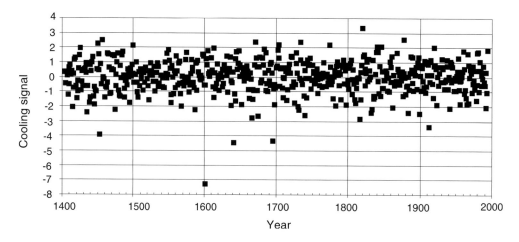

Fig. 5. The dendroclimatological record of Northern Hemisphere summer cooling in standard deviation units for each year from 1405 to 1994, calculated from the NHD1 data of Briffa *et al.* (1998) (http://www.ngdc.noaa.gov/paleo.html) using cooling signal=NHD1 value minus mean of previous four years' values. One s.d. unit represents 0.117 °C.

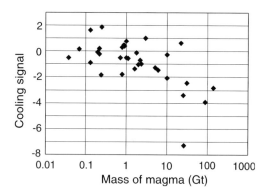

Fig. 6. Variation in cooling signal (NHD1 value minus mean of previous for years' values) with mass of erupted magma for eruptions that reached the stratosphere (data and data sources in Table 2). One s.d. unit represents 0.117 °C.

(1984). This result (Fig. 3) strengthens the argument that TOMS estimates of SO_2 released during eruptions are realistic and therefore that the petrological method frequently underestimates the S yield (Fig. 2 and Wallace 2001). The correlation between the masses of SO_2 and magma for eruptions recorded by TOMS (Fig. 2) indicates a typical yield of 0.1 to 1% SO_2 (500 to 5000 ppm S). The mass of magma erupted is therefore a guide to the mass of SO_2 released, to within half an order of magnitude.

In contrast to previous attempts to correlate SO_2 with hemispheric or global surface cooling (summarized by Sigurdsson 1990), this study does not find a simple correlation between SO_2 (or magma mass) and cooling. Instead, a threshold eruption magnitude of 10 Gt magma or equivalently 5 to 10 Mt SO_2 must be exceeded for a detectable summer cooling signal to appear. One explanation for these different conclusions is that the types of data used were different. The earlier studies used mainly the petrological method to estimate SO_2 loading and instrumental data on mean annual surface temperature. The petrological method is now recognized to sometimes be flawed, and the quality and coverage of instrumental temperature data are only sufficient for detecting significant cooling

Table 2. *Magma masses and subsequent NHD1 values (in units of standard deviation) for eruptions reaching the stratosphere.*

Eruption year	Month	Volcano	Year of NHD1 signal	Mass of magma (Gt)	NHD1 value	Change in NHD1 from from previous year	Change in NHD1 from mean of previous four years
1452		Kuwae	1453	88[1]	−4.24	−3.827	−3.914
1471	11	Sakurajima	1472	0.875[2]	−0.253	−0.471	0.468
1477	3	Veidivötn	1477	3[3]	0.403	0.814	0.998
1480		Mount St Helens	1480	5[4]	−1.299	−0.344	−1.271
1482		Mount St Helens	1482	1[4]	0.017	1.615	0.767
1510	7	Hekla	1511	0.22[5]	−0.298	−0.278	0.220
1563	6	Fogo	1563	1.1[6]	−0.585	−0.898	0.556
1597	1	Hekla	1597	0.2[5]	−0.561	0.023	−0.092
1600	2	Huaynaputina	1601	26[7]	−6.903	−6.641	−7.308
1641		Mount Parker	1641	Unknown	−4.312	−5.084	−4.476
1663	8	Usu	1664	0.8[8]	0.483	1.262	0.298
1707	12	Fuji	1708	2.2[9]	−0.349	−1.263	−0.713
1800		Mount St Helens	1800	1[4]	−0.321	−0.335	−0.505
1815	4	Tambora	1816	140[10]	−4.326	−2.798	−2.819
1835	1	Cosiguina	1835	6[11]	−2.021	−2.732	−1.469
1875	3	Askja	1875	0.89[6]	0.167	0.529	0.381
1883	8	Krakatau	1884	31[12]	−2.887	−2.585	−2.447
1886	6	Tarawera	1887	1.8[6]	−0.109	0.931	−0.111
1902	10	Santa Maria	1903	22[6]	0.037	0.98	0.626
1907	3	Ksudach	1907	2[13]	−1.143	−1.797	−1.050
1912	6	Novarupta	1912	25[6]	−3.328	−3.873	−3.409
1932	4	Quizapu	1933	10[14]	0.565	−0.786	−0.294
1947	3	Hekla	1947	0.13[5]	0.122	−0.88	−0.905
1956	3	Bezymianny	1956	0.78[15]	−1.175	−1.548	−1.798
1963	3	Agung	1964	1.6[16]	−1.031	−0.659	−1.371
1964	11	Sheveluch	1965	0.24[17]	−2.101	−1.07	−1.824
1974	10	Fuego	1975	0.22[18]	−1.177	−0.042	−0.208
1979	4	Soufriere	1979	0.13[19]	0.01	2.814	1.641
1980	5	Mount St. Helens	1980	0.71[6]	−1.851	−1.861	−0.516
1982	4	El Chichon	1982	2.3[6]	−2.071	−2.452	−1.005
1985	11	Ruiz	1986	0.07[20]	−0.655	0.376	0.176
1989	12	Redoubt	1990	0.0375[21]	−1.027	−0.149	−0.532
1991	6	Pinatubo	1992	10[22]	−2.562	−2.338	−2.055
1993	4	Láscar	1994	0.25[23]	0.339	2.533	1.841

Data sources: NHD1 values from Briffa *et al.* (1998) (http://www.ngdc.noaa.gov/paleo.html), magma masses as follows: [1]Robin *et al.* (1994); [2]Yanagi *et al.* (1991); [3]Larsen (1984); [4]Carey *et al.* (1995); [5]Larsen *et al.* (1999); [6]Carey and Sigurdsson (1989); [7]Adams *et al.* (2001); [8]Tomiya and Takahashi (1995); [9]Miyaji *et al.* (1992); [10]Sigurdsson and Carey (1989); [11]Self *et al.* (1989); [12]Mandeville *et al.* (1996); [13]Volynets *et al.* (1999), [14]Hildreth and Drake (1992); [15]Belousov (1996); [16]Self and King (1996); [17]Belousov (1995); [18]Rose *et al.* (1978); [19]Sparks and Wilson (1982); [20]Sigurdsson *et al.* (1990); [21]Gerlach *et al.* (1994); [22]Westrich and Gerlach (1992); [23]Matthews *et al.* (1997).

signals after *c.*1860. These problems have been alleviated in the present study by using magma mass as a first-order proxy for SO₂ (as justified by the correlation shown in Fig. 4) and the long, internally consistent tree-ring series of Briffa *et al.* (1998) as a proxy for temperature. Furthermore, analyses that use the annual mean temperature combine the summer cooling and winter warming signals that can be produced by the atmospheric effects of volcanic eruptions

(Robock 2000). A clearer climate signal should therefore come from treatments that consider summer cooling (or winter warming) alone. The results shown in Figure 6 indicate that a direct link between eruption magnitude and summer cooling in the Northern Hemisphere only becomes apparent for eruptions larger than 10 Gt magma that reach the stratosphere. Variation in the size of the mean cooling signal associated with eruptions above this threshold magnitude is likely to be due to uncertainties in the calibration of the tree-ring record and the variation in factors such as eruption latitude and date, aerosol production and destruction rates, and atmospheric dispersal patterns.

I sincerely acknowledge the influence of Peter Francis, whose knowledge, ideas, and dry wit are greatly missed. S. Carn, D. M Pyle, and S. Self are thanked for useful comments on this chapter.

References

ADAMS, N. K., DE SILVA, S. L., SELF, S., SALAS, G., SCHUBRING, S., PERMENTER, J. L. & ARBESMAN, K. 2001. The physical volcanology of the 1600 eruption of Huaynaputina, southern Peru. *Bulletin of Volcanology*, **62**, 493–518.

ANDRES, R. J., ROSE, W. I., KYLE, P. R., DE SILVA, S., FRANCIS, P., GARDEWEG, M. & MORENO ROA, H. 1991. Excessive sulfur dioxide emissions from Chilean volcanoes. *Journal of Volcanology and Geothermal Research*, **46**, 323–329.

ANDRONOVA, N. G., ROZANOV, E. V., YANG, F., SCHLESINGER, M. E. & STENCHIKOV, G. L. 1999. Radiative forcing by volcanic aerosols from 1850 to 1994. *Journal of Geophysical Research*, **104**, 16 807–16 826.

BANKS, N. G., KOYANAGI, R. Y., SINTON, J. M. & HONMA, K. T. 1984. The eruption of Mount Pagan Volcano, Mariana Islands, 15 May 1981. *Journal of Volcanology and Geothermal Research*, **22**, 225–269.

BELOUSOV, A. 1995. The Shiveluch volcanic eruption of 12 November 1964 – explosive eruption provoked by failure of the edifice. *Journal of Volcanology and Geothermal Research*, **66**, 357–365.

BELOUSOV, A. 1996. Deposits of the 30 March 1956 directed blast at Bezymianny volcano, Kamchatka, Russia. *Bulletin of Volcanology*, **57**, 649–662.

BLUTH, G. J. S., SCHNETZLER, C. C., KRUEGER, A. J. & WALTER, L. S. 1993. The contribution of explosive volcanism to global atmospheric sulphur dioxide concentrations. *Nature*, **366**, 327–329.

BLUTH, G. J. S., CASADEVALL, T. J., SCHNETZLER, C. C., DOIRON, S. D., WALTER, L. S., KRUEGER, A. J. & BADRUDDIN, M. 1994. Evaluation of sulfur dioxide emissions from explosive volcanism: the 1982–1983 eruptions of Galunggung, Java, Indonesia. *Journal of Volcanology and Geothermal Research*, **63**, 243–256.

BLUTH, G. J. S., ROSE, W. I., SPROD, I. E. & KRUEGER, A. J. 1997. Stratospheric loading of sulfur from explosive volcanic eruptions. *Journal of Geology*, **105**, 671–683.

BRIFFA, K. R., JONES, P. D., SCHWEINGRUBER, F. H. & OSBORN, T. J. 1998. Influence of volcanic eruptions on Northern Hemisphere summer temperature over the past 600 years. *Nature*, **393**, 450–455 (and http://www.ngdc.noaa.gov/paleo.html).

BURT, M. L., WADGE, G. & SCOTT, W. A. 1994. Simple stochastic modelling of the eruption history of a basaltic volcano: Nyamuragira, Zaire. *Bulletin of Volcanology*, **56**, 87–97.

CAREY, S. & SIGURDSSON, H. 1989. The intensity of plinian eruptions. *Bulletin of Volcanology*, **51**, 28–40.

CAREY, S., GARDNER, J. & SIGURDSSON, H. 1995. The intensity and magnitude of Holocene plinian eruptions from Mount St. Helens volcano. *Journal of Volcanology and Geothermal Research*, **66**, 185–202.

COLLING, A., DISE, N., FRANCIS, P., HARRIS, N. & WILSON, C. 1997. *The Dynamic Earth. S269 Earth and Life*. The Open University, Milton Keynes, UK.

CONSTANTINE, E. K., BLUTH, G. J. S. & ROSE, W. I. 2000. TOMS and AVHRR observations of drifting volcanic clouds from the August 1991 eruptions of Cerro Hudson. *In:* MOUGINIS-MARK, P. J., CRISP, J. A. & FINK, J. H. (eds) *Remote Sensing of Active Volcanism*. American Geophysical Union, Geophysical Monograph, **116**, 45–64.

DE HOOG, J. C. M., KOETSIER, G. W., BRONTO, S., SRIWANA, T. & VAN BERGEN, M. J. 2001. Sulfur and chlorine degassing from primitive arc magmas: temporal changes during the 1982–1983 eruptions of Galunggung (West Java, Indonesia). *Journal of Volcanology and Geothermal Research*, **108**, 55–83.

DEVINE, J. D., SIGURDSSON, H., DAVIS, A. N. & SELF, S. 1984. Estimates of sulfur and chlorine yield to the atmosphere from volcanic eruptions and potential climatic effects. *Journal of Geophysical Research*, **89**, 6309–6325.

FRANCIS, P. 1993. *Volcanoes: a Planetary Perspective*. Clarendon Press, Oxford, UK.

GERLACH, T. M. & MCGEE, K. A. 1994. Total sulfur dioxide emissions and pre-eruption vapor-saturated magma at Mount St Helens. *Geophysical Research Letters*, **21**, 2833–2836.

GERLACH, T. M., WESTRICH, H. R., CASADEVALL, T. J. & FINNEGAN, D. L. 1994. Vapor saturation and accumulation in magmas of the 1989–1990 eruption of Redoubt Volcano, Alaska. *Journal of Volcanology and Geothermal Research*, **62**, 317–337.

GRIESER, J. & SCHÖNWIESE, C.-D. 1999. Parameterization of spatio-temporal patterns of volcanic aerosol induced stratospheric optical depth and its climate radiative forcing. *Atmósfera*, **12**, 111–133.

GRONVOLD, K., LARSEN, G., EINARSSON, P., THORARINSSON, S. & SAEMUNDSSON, K. 1983. The Hekla eruption 1980–1981. *Bulletin Volcanologique*, **46**, 349–363.

HANSEN, J. & LEBEDEFF, S. 1987. Global trends of measured surface air temperature. *Journal of Geophysical Research*, **92**, 13 345–13 372.

HILDRETH, W. & DRAKE, R. E. 1992. Volcan Quizapu, Chilean Andes. *Bulletin of Volcanology*, **54**, 93–125.

HOLASEK, R. E. & SELF, S. 1995. GOES weather satellite observations and measurements of the May 18, 1980, Mount St. Helens eruption. *Journal of Geophysical Research*, **100**, 8469–8487.

JAKOSKY, B. M. 1986. Volcanoes, the stratosphere, and climate. *Journal of Volcanology and Geothermal Research*, **28**, 247–255.

JONES, P. D., BRIFFA, K. R. & SCHWEINGRUBER, F. H. 1995. Tree-ring evidence of the widespread effects of explosive volcanic eruptions. *Geophysical Research Letters*, **22**, 1333–1336.

KELLY, P. M. & SEAR, C. B. 1984. Climatic impact of explosive volcanic eruptions. *Nature*, **311**, 740–743.

KRUEGER, A. J., SCHAEFER, S. J., KROTKOV, N., BLUTH, G. & BARKER, S. 2000. Ultraviolet remote sensing of volcanic emissions. *In:* MOUGINIS-MARK, P. J., CRISP, J. A. & FINK, J. H. (eds) *Remote Sensing of Active Volcanism*. American Geophysical Union. Geophysical Monograph, **116**, 25–43.

LACIS, A., HANSEN, J. & SATO, M. 1992. Climate forcing by stratospheric aerosols. *Geophysical Research Letters*, **19**, 1607–1610.

LARSEN, G. 1984. Recent volcanic history of the Veidivötn fissure swarm, southern Iceland. *Journal of Volcanology and Geothermal Research*, **22**, 33–58.

LARSEN, G., DUGMORE, A. & NEWTON, A. 1999. Geochemistry of historical-age silicic tephras in Iceland. *The Holocene*, **9**, 463–471.

LIPMAN, P. W. & BANKS, N. G. 1987. Aa flow dynamics, Mauna Loa 1984. *United States Geological Survey Professional Paper*, **1350**, 1527–1567.

LUHR, J. F., CARMICHAEL, I. S. E. & VAREKAMP, J. C. 1984. The 1982 eruptions of El Chichon, Chiapas, Mexico: mineralogy and petrology of the anhydrite-bearing pumices. *Journal of Volcanology and Geothermal Research*, **23**, 69–108.

MCCORMICK, M. P., THOMASON, L. W. & TREPTE, C. R. 1995, Atmospheric effects of the Mt Pinatubo eruption. *Nature*, **373**, 399–404.

MCLELLAND, L., SIMKIN, T., SUMMERS, M., NIELSEN, E. & STEIN, T. C. 1989. *Global Volcanism 1975–1985*. American Geophysical Union, Washington D.C.

MCNUTT, S. 1999. Eruptions of Pavlof volcano, Alaska, and their possible modulation by ocean load and tectonic stresses: re-evaluation of the hypothesis based on new data from 1984–1998. *Pure and Applied Geophysics*, **155**, 701–712.

MANDEVILLE, C. W., CAREY, S. & SIGURDSSON, H. 1996. Magma mixing, fractional crystallization and volatile degassing during the 1883 eruption of Krakatau volcano, Indonesia. *Journal of Volcanology and Geothermal Research*, **74**, 243–274.

MASS, C. F. & PORTMANN, D. A. 1989. Major volcanic eruptions and climate: a critical evaluation. *Journal of Climate*, **2**, 566–593.

MATTHEWS, S. J., GARDEWEG, M. C. & SPARKS, R. S. J. 1997. The 1984 to 1996 cyclic activity of Lascar Volcano, northern Chile: cycles of dome growth, dome subsidence, degassing and explosive eruptions. *Bulletin of Volcanology*, **59**, 72–82.

MIYAJI, N, ENDO, K., TOGASHI, S. & UESUGI, Y. 1992. *Tephrochronological history of Mt. Fuji.* 29th IGC Field trip Guidebook Volume 4: Volcanoes and Geothermal Fields of Japan, Geological Survey of Japan, 75–109.

NEAL, C. A., MCGIMSEY, R. G., GARDNER, C. A., HARBIN, M. L. & NYE, C.J. 1995. Tephra-fall deposits from the 1992 eruptions of Crater Peak, Mount Spurr volcano, Alaska: a preliminary report on distribution, stratigraphy, and composition. *United States Geological Survey Bulletin*, **2139**, 65–79.

NEWHALL, C. G. & SELF, S. 1982. The volcanic explosivity index (VEI): an estimate of explosive magnitude for historical volcanism. *Journal of Geophysical Research*, **87**, 1231–1238.

OPPENHEIMER, C. 1996. On the role of hydrothermal systems in the transfer of volcanic sulfur to the atmosphere. *Geophysical Research Letters*, **23**, 2057–2060.

PALAIS, J. M. & SIGURDSSON, H. 1989. Petrologic evidence of volatile emissions from major historic and pre-historic volcanic eruptions. *In:* BERGER, A., DICKINSON, R. E. & KIDSON, J. W. (eds) *Understanding Climate Change*, American Geophysical Union Geophysical Monograph, **52**, IUGG Volume 7, 31–53.

PINTO, J. P., TURCO, R. P. & TOON, O. B. 1989. Self-limiting physical and chemical effects in volcanic eruption clouds. *Journal of Geophysical Research*, **94**, 11 165–11 174.

POLLACK, J. B., TOON, O. B., SAGAN, C., SUMMERS, A., BALDWIN, B. & VAN CAMP, W. 1976. Volcanic explosions and climate change: a theoretical assessment. *Journal of Geophysical Research*, **81**, 1071–1083.

PYLE, D. M. 1989. The thickness, volume and grainsize of tephra fall deposits. *Bulletin of Volcanology*, **51**, 1–15.

PYLE, D. M. 1998. How did the summer go? *Nature*, **393**, 415–416.

PYLE, D. M., BEATTIE, P. D. & BLUTH, G. J. S. 1996. Sulphur emissions to the stratosphere from explosive volcanic eruptions. *Bulletin of Volcanology*, **57**, 663–671.

RAMPINO, M. R. & SELF, S. 1984. Sulphur-rich volcanic eruptions and stratospheric aerosols. *Nature*, **310**, 677–679.

REYNOLDS, R. W., GEIST, D. & KURZ, M.D. 1995. Physical volcanology and structural development of Sierra Negra volcano, Isabela Island, Galápagos archipelago. *Geological Society of America Bulletin*, **107**, 1398–1410.

ROBIN, C., MONZIER, M. & EISSEN, J.-P. 1994. Formation of the mid-fifteenth century Kuwae caldera (Vanuatu) by an initial hydroclastic and subsequent ignimbritic eruption. *Bulletin of Volcanology*, **56**, 170–183.

ROBOCK, A. 2000. Volcanic eruptions and climate. *Reviews of Geophysics*, **38**, 191–219.

ROBOCK, A. & MAO, J. 1995. The volcanic signal in surface temperature observations. *Journal of Climate*, **8**, 1086–1103.

ROSE JR., W. I., ANDERSON, A. T., WOODRUFF, L. G. & BONIS, S. 1978. The October 1974 basaltic tephra from Fuego Volcano: description and history of the magma body. *Journal of Volcanology and Geothermal Research*, **4**, 3–53.

ROSSI, M. J. 1997. Morphology of the 1984 open-channel lava flow at Krafla volcano, northern Iceland. *Geomorphology*, **20**, 95–112.

SADLER, J. P. & GRATTAN, J. P. 1999. Volcanoes as agents of past environmental change. *Global and Planetary Change*, **21**, 181–196.

SCAILLET, B., CLEMENTE, B., EVANS, B. & PICHAVANT, M. 1998. Redox control of sulfur degassing in silicic magmas. *Journal of Geophysical Research*, **103**, 23 937–23 949.

SCASSO, R. A., CORBELLA, H. & TIBERI, P. 1994. Sedimentological analysis of the tephra from the 12–15 August 1991 eruption of Hudson volcano. *Bulletin of Volcanology*, **56**, 121–132.

SCHNETZLER, C. C., BLUTH, G. J. S., KRUEGER, A. J. & WALTER, L. S. 1997. A proposed volcanic sulfur dioxide index (VSI). *Journal of Geophysical Research*, **102**, 20 087–20 091.

SELF, S. & KING, A. J. 1996. Petrology and sulfur and chlorine emissions of the 1963 eruption of Gunung Agung, Bali, Indonesia. *Bulletin of Volcanology*, **58**, 263–285.

SELF, S., RAMPINO, M. R. & CARR, M. J. 1989. A reappraisal of the 1835 eruption of Cosigüina and its atmospheric impact. *Bulletin of Volcanology*, **52**, 57–65.

SELF, S., ZHAO, J–X., HOLASEK, R.E., TORRES, R. C. & KING, A. J. 1996. The atmospheric impact of the 1991 Mount Pinatubo eruption. *In*: NEWHALL, C. G. & PUNONGBAYAN, R. S. (eds) *Fire and Mud: Eruptions and Lavas of Mount Pinatubo, Philippines*. University of Washington, Seattle, 1089–1115.

SIGURDSSON, H. 1990. Evidence of volcanic loading of the atmosphere and climate response. *Palaeogeography, Palaeoclimatology, Palaeoecology (Global and Planetary Change Section)*, **89**, 277–289.

SIGURDSSON, H. & CAREY, S. 1989. Plinian and co-ignimbrite tephra fall from the 1815 eruption of Tambora volcano. *Bulletin of Volcanology*, **51**, 243–270.

SIGURDSSON, H., CAREY, S., PALAIS, J. M. & DEVINE, J. 1990. Pre-eruption compositional gradients and mixing of andesite and dacite magma erupted from Nevado del Ruiz Volcano, Colombia in 1985. *Journal of Volcanology and Geothermal Research*, **41**, 127–151.

SIMKIN, T. & SIEBERT, L. 2000a. Earth's volcanoes and eruptions: an overview. *In*: SIGURDSSON, H., HOUGHTON, B. F., MCNUTT, S. R., RYMER, H. & STIX, J. (eds) *Encyclopedia of Volcanoes*. Academic Press, London, 249–261.

SIMKIN, T. & SIEBERT, L. 2000b. Appendix 2: Catalog of historically active volcanoes on Earth. *In*: SIGURDSSON, H., HOUGHTON, B. F., MCNUTT, S. R.,

RYMER, H. & STIX, J. (eds) *Encyclopedia of Volcanoes*. Academic Press, London, 1365–1383.

SMITHSONIAN INSTITUTION, 1988. *Banda Api, Scientific Event Alert Network Bulletin*, **13:06**.

SPARKS, R. S. J. & WILSON, L. 1982. Explosive volcanic eruptions – V. Observations of plume dynamics during the 1979 Soufrière eruption, St Vincent. *Geophysical Journal of the Royal Astronomical Society*, **69**, 551–570.

STOMMEL, H. & STOMMEL, E. 1983. *Volcano Weather: the Story of 1816, the Year Without a Summer*. Seven Seas Press, Newport, Rhode Island.

STOTHERS, R. B. 1984. The great Tambora eruption in 1815 and its aftermath. *Science*, **224**, 1191–1198.

SYMONDS, R. B., ROSE, W. I., BLUTH, G. J. S. & GERLACH, T. M. 1994. Volcanic-gas studies: methods, results, and applications. *In*: CARROLL, M. R. & HOLLOWAY, J. R. (eds) *Volatiles in Magmas*. Mineralogical Society of America, Reviews in Mineralogy, **30**, 1–66.

TOMIYA, A. & TAKAHASHI, E. 1995. Reconstruction of an evolving magma chamber beneath Usu Volcano since the 1663 eruption. *Journal of Petrology*, **36**, 617–636.

TOON, O. B. & POLLACK, J. B. 1973. Physical properties of the stratospheric aerosols. *Journal of Geophysical Research*, **78**, 7051–7056.

VOLYNETS, O. N., PONOMAREVA, V. V., BRAITSEVA, O. A., MELEKESTEV, I. V. & CHEN, CH. H. 1999. Holocene eruptive history of Ksudach volcanic massif, South Kamchatka: evolution of a large magmatic chamber. *Journal of Volcanology and Geothermal Research*, **91**, 23–42.

WALLACE, P. J. 2001. Volcanic SO_2 emissions and the abundance and distribution of exsolved gas in magma bodies. *Journal of Volcanology and Geothermal Research*, **108**, 85–106.

WESTRICH, H. R. & GERLACH, T. M. 1992. Magmatic gas source for the stratospheric SO_2 cloud from the June 15, 1991, eruption of Mount Pinatubo. *Geology*, **20**, 867–870.

YANAGI, T., ICHIMARU, Y. & HIRAHARA, S. 1991. Petrochemical evidence for coupled magma chambers beneath the Sakurajima volcano, Kyushu, Japan. *Geochemical Journal*, **25**, 17–30.

Environmental impacts of tropospheric volcanic gas plumes

P. DELMELLE

*Department of Environmental Sciences & Land Use Planning, Soil Sciences Unit,
Université Catholique de Louvain, B-1348 Louvain-la-Neuve, Belgium.
(e-mail: delmelle@sols.ucl.ac.be)
Present address: Geochemistry CP 160/02, Université Libre de Bruxelles,
Av. F. Roosevelt, 50, B-1050 Brussels, Belgium
(e-mail: pdelmell@ulb.ac.be)*

Abstract: Recent studies suggest that the environmental effects of volcanic gas emissions in the lower troposphere have been underestimated. This chapter first briefly summarizes the techniques available for characterizing tropospheric volcanic gas plumes, including the composition and fluxes of emitted gases and aerosols, as well as their atmospheric dispersion. The second part documents the contribution of gas emissions from degassing craters to the composition of the atmosphere, including effects from dry and wet deposition chemistry. The third section deals with the detrimental impacts on vegetation, soils, and groundwater in relation to passive degassing activity. Improved understanding of the impacts of volcanic degassing on the atmospheric and terrestrial environment will require: (1) systematic two-dimensional and three-dimensional measurements of tropospheric volcanic plumes, (2) development of general physical and chemical models to describe the fate of volcanic gases and aerosols during transport in the troposphere, and (3) investigation of the response of diverse ecosystems to volcanogenic air pollution.

Gases released non-eruptively into the troposphere by degassing volcanoes have been the subject of numerous investigations, since volcanic emissions may convey valuable information about subsurface magma activity and magma–hydrothermal interactions, which can be used in conjunction with other geophysical techniques for eruption monitoring (Symonds *et al.* 1994). Such volcanic plumes are important because the release of gases and aerosols may significantly influence the chemistry of the troposphere at the local, regional, and global scales (e.g. Graf *et al.* 1998; Thornton *et al.* 1999; Delmelle *et al.* 2001). Because the physico-chemical environment of tropospheric volcanic plumes can be quite different from anthropogenic emissions, distinct chemical transformation pathways in the atmosphere may result. In a similar manner, volcanogenic air contaminants may affect exposed ecosystems through distinct reactions. However, with a few notable exceptions, the potential roles of tropospheric volcanic gas effluents have not been quantitatively examined. Understanding the interaction of volcanic gases with the troposphere is also essential to interpret remote-sensing observations of emitted plumes correctly (Horrocks *et al.* 2003).

The goal of this chapter is to provide a survey of what is currently known about volcanic gas plumes in the troposphere, especially in terms of their monitoring, composition, emission rates, dispersion, and influence on the atmosphere and ecosystems (i.e. vegetation, soils, and groundwater). Although volcanic gases and related aerosols may have effects that are harmful to human health, this aspect is not considered here. As this review will show, much more work is required to describe and model the short- and long-term atmospheric and environmental impacts of tropospheric volcanic gas plumes.

Monitoring of tropospheric volcanic gas plumes

Plume monitoring techniques

Monitoring the composition of tropospheric volcanic gas plume is difficult. Conventional measurements of crater emissions involving direct sampling of fumarole effluents (Symonds *et al.* 1994) cannot account for the various reactions which affect the hot gas emissions as they enter – and are diluted and oxidized by – the comparatively cool atmosphere. Therefore, these data are unlikely to be representative of the

From: OPPENHEIMER, C., PYLE, D.M. & BARCLAY, J. (eds) *Volcanic Degassing*. Geological Society, London, Special Publications, **213**, 381–399. 0305–8719/03/$15.00

integrated composition of volcanic plumes, and cannot be used as such to evaluate their atmospheric and environmental impacts.

Direct sampling of tropospheric volcanic plumes has been conducted by flying filter packs, gas sensors, and cascade impactors through the wind-dispersed emissions (e.g. Hobbs et al. 1982; Phelan et al. 1982; Casadevall et al. 1984; Martin et al. 1986; Varekamp et al. 1986; Zreda-Gostynska et al. 1997). These techniques can also be operated from the ground when access to crater rims is possible, or when the plume is transported at low altitude in the atmospheric boundary layer (e.g. Stoiber et al. 1986; Gauthier & Le Cloarec 1998; Allen et al. 2000). While the method is subject to practical difficulties and to the effects of spatial and temporal plume heterogeneities, it has provided a basis for describing the compositions of airborne volcanic effluents.

Passive monitoring of volcanic SO_2 emissions across a large area downwind from the gas vent can be carried out using a network of diffusion tubes, especially at sites where there is a stable prevailing wind direction (Downing 1996; Delmelle et al. 2002). The sampling yields time-averaged atmospheric SO_2 concentrations, and is based on the principle that the gases of interest are taken up at a rate controlled by a physical process, such as diffusion through a static air layer or permeation through a membrane (Brown & Wright 1994). Lead dioxide-treated plastic surfaces (or sulphation plates, Huey 1968) can be exposed under similar conditions to obtain an estimate of the plume's SO_2/HCl ratio. The method relies on the observation that SO_2 and HCl appear to collect on such surfaces with roughly similar dry deposition velocities (Delmelle et al. 2001).

An attractive alternative to direct sampling is the use of optical remote-sensing technologies, which can probe regions inaccessible or otherwise difficult to sample, such as plumes from volcanoes. The range of optical sensing techniques which has been applied to measurements of the composition and emission of volcanic emissions is reviewed by McGonigle & Oppenheimer (2003).

Plume composition and emission rate

More than 60% of the total molar gas content in crater fumaroles consists of H_2O. The next most abundant species is CO_2, with typical molar contents between c. 10 and c. 40%. The gas species SO_2, H_2S, HCl, and HF, which are potentially harmful to the environment, typically occur in lower concentrations. The amount of total sulphur ($S_{tot} = SO_2 + H_2S$) is lower than that of CO_2, but usually higher than that of HCl, although the relative abundances of S_{total} and HCl in volcanic gases can vary greatly (Symonds et al. 1994). Chlorofluorocarbon compounds have been shown to be negligible in volcanic emissions (Jordan et al. 2000).

Compared with these compositions measured at the source, tropospheric volcanic plumes may be diluted by factors of c. 10^2 to 10^5, due to ingestion of large amounts of air during the first seconds or minutes of transport (e.g. Casadevall et al. 1984; McGee 1992). It follows that only volcanic species such as SO_2, H_2S, HCl, and HF, which have very low atmospheric background concentrations, can be detected downwind from a degassing vent. For example, a maximum SO_2 concentration of c. 2.6 mg/m³ was measured in the plume of White Island, New Zealand, at 5 km from the active crater (Rose et al. 1986). Open-path Fourier transform infrared (OP–FTIR) spectroscopic measurements performed downwind of the summit of Soufrière Hills, Montserrat, indicated HCl concentrations averaging about 150 μg/m³ and 44 μg/m³ at distances of c. 2 and 3.4–4.9 km, respectively (Oppenheimer et al. 1998a). The same method deployed 15 km downwind from Masaya volcano, Nicaragua, showed concentrations of SO_2 and HCl of c. 1.6 mg/m³ and c. 440 μg/m³, respectively (Horrocks et al. 2003). For context, the background concentrations of tropospheric SO_2 and HCl over land areas typically range from c. 0.05 to 3 μg/m³ and from <0.01 to 5 μg/m³, respectively (Berresheim et al. 1995; Graedel & Keene 1995).

Despite relatively low concentrations in volcanic plumes, the amounts of SO_2 injected into the atmosphere by passively degassing volcanoes are significant (Berresheim & Jaeschke 1983; Graf et al. 1997; Andres & Kasgnoc 1998; Halmer et al., 2002) (Table 1). According to Andres and Kasgnoc (1998), at least 49 volcanoes emitted SO_2 continuously or semi-continuously at rates ranging from <0.1 to 50 kg/s over the period 1972–1997. This is equivalent to a total yearly flux to the troposphere of c. 9.66 Tg SO_2, which corresponds with about 6% of the global anthropogenic sulphur flux. Non-eruptive volcanic plumes also constitute a significant source of tropospheric HCl and HF. Measurements made at a limited number of volcanoes suggest HCl and HF emission rates of c. <0.5–10 kg/s and c. <0.05–1.5 kg/s, respectively (Symonds et al. 1988; Table 1). Other trace volatile substances detected in volcanic effluents include Hg, As, and Se. Mercury emissions from Vulcano, Stromboli, and Mount Etna, Italy, were recently estimated to be in the range 1.3–5.5,

7.3–77, and 62–537 kg/year [1], respectively (Ferrara *et al.* 2000).

Besides the gas species, airborne volcanic emissions contain a variety of particles enriched in S, Cl, F, Br, and trace metals, such as Cr, Cu, Zn, As, Se, Cd, Sn, Hg, Pb, and Bi (e.g. Phelan *et al.* 1982; Vié Le Sage 1983; Varekamp *et al.* 1986; Zreda-Gostynska *et al.* 1997; Hinkley *et al.* 1999; Allard *et al.* 2000; Obenholzner *et al.* 2003). Particulate sulphur is present as H_2SO_4, sulphate compounds, and sometimes native sulphur. Chlorine and fluorine may occur in acids and in various salts, while the metals are associated with halide, sulphide, and sulphate particulate forms.

The total concentration of particles measured in non-eruptive plumes (from above the crater to 5–6 km distance) ranges widely from <20 to several thousand $\mu g/m^3$ (e.g. Vié Le Sage 1983; Casadevall *et al.* 1984; Chuan *et al.* 1986; Rose *et al.* 1986; Zreda-Gostynska *et al.* 1997; Allard *et al.* 2000; Allen *et al.* 2000). In addition to plume dilution, particle ageing also affects the total concentration. Reported total aerosol mass fluxes are in the range of *c.* <0.01–0.6 kg/s (Casadevall *et al.* 1984; Rose *et al.* 1986; Watson & Oppenheimer 2000; Porter *et al.* 2002; Allen *et al.* 2002). As indicated in Table 1, atmospheric injection of some trace metals during quiescent degassing is significant. The most abundant elements are generally Cu, Zn, and Pb. At Mount Etna, non-eruptive emissions of these metals averaged *c.*6.5, 5.1, and 1.9 kg/s, respectively, for the period 1991–1995 (Gauthier & Le Cloarec 1998).

Plume aerosol particle sizes range from <0.01 to >25 μm (Hobbs *et al.* 1982; Vié Le Sage 1983; Allard *et al.* 2000; Watson & Oppenheimer 2000, 2001, and references therein). Particles in the fine (<0.1 μm) mode may result essentially from a process of gas-particle conversion (Hobbs *et al.* 1982; Vié Le Sage 1983). Aggregation and growth of these fine aerosols are responsible for the existence of accumulation mode particles (0.1–2 μm), while larger particles (>2 μm) generally consist of silicate and salt fragments eroded from the gas vent(s). The size distribution of tropospheric plume aerosols remains poorly quantified and varies from site to site, probably due to source characteristics, rapid sedimentation of coarse particles, and gas-particle conversion and particle aggregation processes (Vié Le Sage 1983). At Mount Erebus, Antarctica, Chuan *et al.* (1986) measured most of the plume aerosol mass in the coarse particle mode (>10 μm). In contrast, small particles constituted the major portion (>95%) of the total mass of particles in the plume from White

Table 1. *Average emission rates ($Gg\,year^{-1}$) of acidic gases and some metals at selected passively degassing volcanoes.*

Volcanoes	Period	SO_2	HCl	HF	Br	Cu	Zn	As	Se	Cd	Pb	References
Mount Erebus	1986–1991	15.6	10.8	5.3	0.021	0.043	0.13	0.011	0.002	0.004		Zreda-Gostynska *et al.* (1997)
Mount Etna	1975–1996	1700±400	365–1460	37–180	5.6[†]	0.204	0.16			0.007	0.058	Aiuppa (2001) Gauthier and Le Cloarec (1998)
Kilauea	1984–1996	730	229	27		0.037	0.08	0.011	0.02	0.033	0.012	Hinkley *et al.* (1999)
Masaya	1998–1999	664					0.37					Horrocks *et al.* (1999)
Mount St Helens	09/1980	365	1.28						0.04	0.002		Phelan *et al.* (1982)
Stromboli	1993–1997	110	37*	1.8*	0.098	0.075	0.13	0.022	0.055	0.006	0.035	Allard *et al.* (2000)
White Island	1984–1985	123	29	0.6		0.11				0.003	0.046	Rose *et al.* (1986) Le Cloarec *et al.* (1992)

*Expressed as total Cl or F.
[†]Expressed as HBr.

Island, New Zealand (Rose *et al.* 1986). Sun-photometer observations of Mount Etna's aerosol plume indicated a trimodal distribution with particles of radius <0.1 μm contributing 6–18% of the total aerosol mass flux (Watson & Oppenheimer 2000). At Stromboli, 66% of the plume aerosol load corresponded with particles in the fine and accumulation modes (Allard *et al.* 2000).

An important issue directly related to injection of volcanic SO_2 into the troposphere is the conversion of SO_2 to sulphate particles. Sulphur dioxide can be involved in three types of reactions which ultimately lead to the formation of particulate sulphate: (1) gas-phase homogeneous reactions, (2) aqueous-phase reactions and (3) heterogeneous reactions on the surface of solids (Eatough *et al.* 1994). Gas-phase homogeneous reactions are driven by oxidation of gaseous SO_2 by hydroxyl radicals, with typical first-order reaction rates ranging from $c. 8.3 \times 10^{-7}$ to $c. 2.8 \times 10^{-5}$ s^{-1}. Aqueous-phase reactions involving ozone and hydrogen peroxide as the dominant oxidants lead to much faster oxidation rates ($c. 5.6 \times 10^{-5}–2.8 \times 10^{-4}$ s^{-1}). The third route for oxidation of SO_2 is generally considered to be minor compared with hydroxyl radical and aqueous hydrogen peroxide oxidation, but it may become important in volcanic plumes where high particle densities (>100 μg/m³) often prevail.

Only a few attempts have been made to estimate the conversion rate of SO_2 in tropospheric volcanic plumes. Gas-to-particle conversion rates in the post-eruptive effluents from Mount St Helens, USA, were in the range $1.9 \times 10^{-7}–1.6 \times 10^{-6}$ s^{-1} (Hobbs *et al.* 1982). Martin *et al.* (1986) studied the plume of Mount Etna and inferred rates between 2.2×10^{-6} and 4.0×10^{-5} s^{-1}. Recent measurements of the Hawaii Kilauea volcano plume suggest SO_2 oxidation rates ranging from $c. 2.0–5.5 \times 10^{-5}$ s^{-1} (Porter *et al.* 2002). Despite a large range, these values are in reasonable agreement with those deduced for power plant and smelter plumes (Newman 1981). However, considerably higher SO_2 loss rates reaching $c. 10^{-3}$ s^{-1} have also been measured in tropospheric volcanic plumes (Martin *et al.* 1986; Oppenheimer *et al.* 1998*b*). It is unclear whether this fast sulphur chemistry reflects enhanced aqueous phase and/or heterogeneous phase reactions. Moreover, conversion rate estimates which are based on SO_2 flux observations made at different distances downwind from the vent by UV correlation spectroscopy (or COSPEC, see McGonigle & Oppenheimer 2003) are subject to errors linked to instrumental drifts, uncertainties in wind-speed measurements and

rough estimates of the plume dimensions (Hamilton *et al.* 1978). In addition, observed SO_2 loss rates cannot simply be ascribed to oxidation/conversion processes, since dry deposition can also scavenge significant SO_2 from the plume.

Plume dispersion

Very few reports deal with the dispersion of non-eruptive plumes in the troposphere, although such data are essential to describe and predict the range and magnitude of environmental effects in relation to distance from the source. Different approaches have been applied, including (1) determinations of SO_2 plume cross-sections at different altitudes and distances from source, (2) measurements of near-ground ambient SO_2 levels across a given area downwind of the crater, (3) plume observations using photography, video, and satellite images, and (4) numerical modelling.

In principle, the COSPEC instrument can be used to study the horizontal dispersion of plumes, since it measures a vertically integrated SO_2 burden (Hamilton *et al.* 1978). The drawback is that the method neglects SO_2 loss via oxidation and dry deposition. The reported widths for typical non-eruptive plumes measured at distances of $c. 1$ to 20 km from the volcano are in the range $c. 2–20$ km (e.g. Hoff & Gallant 1980; Casadevall *et al.* 1984; McGee 1992; Oppenheimer *et al.* 1998*b*; Williams-Jones 2001). Zettwog & Haulet (1978) estimated that the width of the plume released by Mount Etna in May 1977 was 20 km at 100 km from the crater. McGee (1992) examined a large number of COSPEC transects collected at Mount St Helens in 1980–1988. McGee noticed that plume width tended to be inversely proportional to wind velocity. Additionally, puffs produced by irregular degassing conditions at the source caused the plume to contract significantly for a short time, resulting in a temporarily denser plume at short distances from the volcano. The width-to-thickness ratio of the Mount St Helens' plume varied from $c. 3$ to 30.

Under favourable circumstances, the average dispersion of tropospheric volcanic plumes may be deduced from simultaneous determinations of near-ground levels of SO_2 at multiple sites. The method has been successfully applied to Masaya volcano, a low-elevation ($c. 560$ m above sea-level) basaltic complex, which emits a strong plume into the boundary layer (Delmelle *et al.* 2002). In this study, SO_2 concentrations in ambient air were monitored downwind from the vent, using a large network of diffusion tubes. As shown in Figure 1, isopleths of constant SO_2 concentration give a

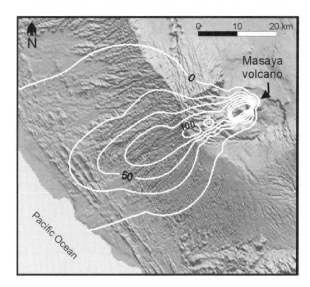

Fig. 1. Map showing the average dispersion of the SO$_2$-bearing plume discharged into the atmospheric boundary layer by Masaya volcano, Nicaragua. The contour lines correspond to iso-concentration (ppbv) of atmospheric SO$_2$ based on measurements made during February–March 1999 (Delmelle *et al.* 2000). 1 ppbv = 2.6 µg/m^3 at $P = 1000$ mbar.

time-averaged picture of the horizontal plume dispersion. During the period of study (February–March 1999), the volcanic emissions were dispersed by the northeasterly trade winds over an 80–85° sector, which is equivalent to average plume widths of about 9 and 29 km at distances of 5.5 and 15 km from the active crater, respectively. The SO$_2$ survey also highlighted a remarkable dispersion feature, that is, plume grounding downwind. This seems to relate to a rise in terrain associated with a prominent topographic feature, located approximately 15 km to the west of the volcano. Plume grounding is probably favoured by the existence of a low-level capping temperature inversion, and results in land fumigation and elevated SO$_2$ concentrations several kilometres from Masaya (Fig. 1).

The rising behaviour of volcanic plumes emitted into the troposphere can be observed and photographed from the ground, while aircraft and satellites provide a means to view the characteristics of horizontal dispersion and plume meandering. Like the smoke plumes from industrial stacks, the observed plume shapes include fanning, fumigation, looping, coning, and lofting. Some of these plume patterns are illustrated in Figure 2. Fanning is generally associated with weak and variable winds in a stable atmosphere. The plume forms a fan when viewed from above, due to a large horizontal spread and very little, if any vertical spread (Fig. 2a). This type of plume may be the precursor to

fumigation (Fig. 2a) if there is a strong temperature inversion which limits mixing above. Typically, fumigation (Fig. 2b) will result from downward mixing of the plume material when the temperature inversion is being dissipated from below due to surface heating. This phenomenon may lead to high concentration of volcanic gases at the surface over a wide area. Emissions from a low-elevation crater into a well-mixed boundary layer may also result in extremely high levels of air pollutants in the vicinity of the source. This occurs when large and intense turbulent eddies advect the whole plume down to the ground. In contrast, the plume will form a cone downstream if the turbulent eddies are smaller than the plume (Fig. 2c). In some cases, the plume may be forced to flow downslope if the atmosphere is extremely stable and strong winds in the lee of the volcano topography prevail (Fig. 2d). A lofting plume is formed when a strong surface inversion develops up to the plume level. This prevents the material from diffusing downward, while vertical motion may persist above the plume (Fig. 2e).

Numerical simulations of the dispersion of gas plumes have only recently been applied to volcanoes. The most comprehensive studies of Graziani *et al.* (1997) and Pareschi *et al.* (1999) have generated various computational scenarios to evaluate the atmospheric diffusion and near-ground concentrations of volcanic CO$_2$ and SO$_2$ over Vulcano Island, Italy, for a number of

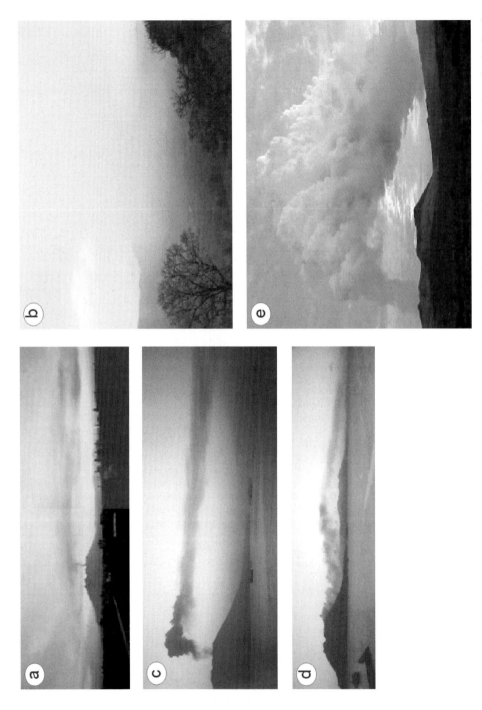

Fig. 2. Selected photographs of instantaneous patterns of tropospheric volcanic plumes: (**a**) plume fanning, Mount Sakurajima, Japan; (**b**) plume fumigation downwind from Masaya volcano; (**c**) plume coning, Mount Sakurajima; (**d**) plume is forced to flow downslope by strong winds in a very stable atmosphere, Mount Sakurajima; and (**e**) plume lofting, Masaya volcano. Photographs of Mount Sakurajima's plume used with permission from K. Kinoshita. See also Kinoshita (1996).

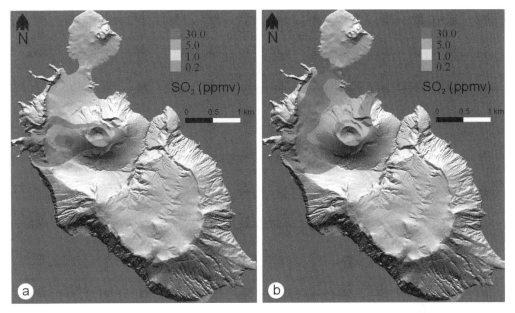

Fig. 3. Maximum SO$_2$ concentration distributions at Vulcano Island during: (**a**) daytime (10:00–17:00 LST) and (**b**) at dawn (05:00–08:00 LST), in the absence of synoptic wind, computed at 1 m a.s.l. The sources considered are the crater fumaroles, emitting about 0.12–1 kg SO$_2$/s. 1 ppbv=2.6 μg/m^3. Modified from Pareschi et al. (1998). Used by permission of the American Geophysical Union.

meteorological conditions and gas emission rates. To do so, they combined a three-dimensional mesoscale meteorological flow model simulating the wind field over a complex volcanic terrain with a Lagrangian particle model. The calculation produced maps such as those shown in Figure 3. They indicate that dispersion of the main gas plume is favoured by the highly convective regime prevailing during the daytime at Vulcano. The presence of a thermal anomaly below the volcano, which prevents stable stratification, also results in dispersion of the gas plume during the night. The only period during which the inhabited area of Vulcano may be subject to a gas hazard corresponds with the transition hours between nocturnal and daytime circulation. However, this requires a set of particular meteorological conditions, which were successfully identified by the model.

Passive volatile release from volcanoes into the troposphere typically occurs at higher altitudes than anthropogenic emissions, thus resulting in a longer atmospheric residence time mainly due to a lower dry deposition rate (Graf et al. 1997). Coherent tropospheric gas plumes have been detected at considerable distances from the source for a number of volcanoes (Fig. 4), suggesting that volcano-derived emissions may affect the environment not only locally but

also regionally. Using a COSPEC, Zettwog and Haulet (1978) measured the plume from Mount Etna at about 250 km from its point of emission. Anfossi and Sacchetti (1994) studied the long-range transport of Mount Etna's plume at an altitude of c.3800 m by applying a cluster analysis to trajectory model results. They identified a series of typical pathways for the plume, and suggested that the volcano contributed about 1% of the total sulphur deposition in the northern Italian Alps, several hundreds of kilometres from the volcano. Similarly, Graf et al. (1998) showed that long-range transport of Mount Etna's emissions in the free troposphere reach southern Europe and probably extend to the west of Scotland.

Atmospheric impacts of tropospheric volcanic gas plumes

Air pollution and tropospheric sulphur burden

The occurrence of short-term (hours to days) or prolonged (months to years) local air pollution events in relation to renewed or sustained gas emissions has been observed at a number of volcanoes. Justifiably, much attention has been focused on ambient levels of SO$_2$ – the primary

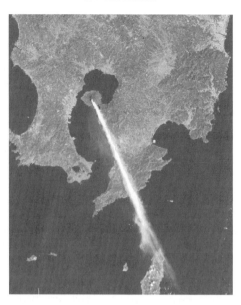

Fig. 4. Satellite image (Landsat-5/MSS) showing a volcanic gas plume transported coherently in the troposphere, Mount Sakurajima, Japan. Photograph used with permission from K. Kinoshita.

volcanogenic air contaminant. For example, the effluents from the ongoing activity of Kilauea crater and Pu'o O'o vent, Hawaii, are responsible for short episodes (two to 24 hours) of elevated atmospheric SO_2 concentration (up to 130 $\mu g/m^3$) measured several tens of kilometres downwind (Luria *et al.* 1992). In southern Japan, persistent degassing at Mount Sakurajima volcano generates monthly average SO_2 concentrations at the foot of the mountain in the range of 40 to 360 $\mu g/m^3$ (Kawaratani & Fujita 1990). During 1986–1995, the plume of Poàs volcano, Costa Rica, created high ambient SO_2 conditions (up to 400 $\mu g/m^3$) over the southwestern flanks (Downing 1996; Nicholson *et al.* 1996). At Montserrat, Allen *et al.* (2000) reported mean SO_2 concentrations in the range *c.*1.2–29 $\mu g/m^3$ within 1.4–6.7 km of the Soufrière Hills' crater. In the same area, ambient HCl and HF levels ranged from *c.*0.7 to *c.*290 $\mu g/m^3$ and from *c.*0.016 to *c.*2.5 $\mu g/m^3$, respectively.

A well-known case of recurrent volcanogenic air pollution events is Masaya volcano, currently one of the world's strongest sources of SO_2 in the troposphere, with emissions in the range *c.*9 to 21 kg/s. Delmelle *et al.* (2002) have investigated the average level and distribution of SO_2 pollution downwind from the source using a network of diffusion tubes. Their results indicate that plume emissions influence ambient SO_2 concentrations across an estimated *c.*1250 km^2 area southwest of

the gas vent. In this sector, concentrations ranged from <5 to *c.*240 $\mu g/m^3$ (<2 to *c.*91 ppbv) in March–April 1998, and from <5 to *c.*610 $\mu g/m^3$ (<2 to *c.*230 ppbv) in February–March 1999 (Fig. 1). The distribution of near-ground SO_2 levels mainly reflects dilution of the plume by air, although surface deposition and gas-to-particle conversion may also decrease SO_2 concentrations in the plume. Noticeably, grounding of the plume several kilometres from the volcano results in intense fumigation events, which create zones of secondary SO_2 maxima (Fig. 1). While the source strength did not vary significantly between 1998 and 1999, ambient SO_2 levels tended to be higher in 1999 than in 1998. This was tentatively attributed to variable atmospheric conditions, which led to more frequent concentrated plumes and fumigation episodes over the 1999 study period.

The existence of high tropospheric SO_2 levels from dispersion of volcanic emissions also raises the possibility of enhanced concentrations of sulphate aerosols (H_2SO_4 and SO_4^{2-}) in the vicinity of the volcano, or even far away from it. For example, the Big Island of Hawaii is regularly affected by a volcanic smog (vog) during normal easterly trade-wind conditions (Sutton & Elias 1993). The vog was shown to consist of a relatively concentrated suspension of fine H_2SO_4 aerosol produced by oxidation of SO_2 during transport of Kilauea's plume (Porter & Clarke 1997). As discussed below, the presence of sulphate aerosols in the air is a source of environmental (and health) concern.

Tropospheric volcanic plumes have also been shown to affect the composition of the atmosphere at distances far from the vent. For example, enhanced airborne sulphate aerosol concentrations over a wide area of the Kanto plain have been correlated with gas emissions from Mount Sakurajima (Mizuno et al. 1996). Similarly, the ongoing massive gas release at Mount Oyama (Miyake-jima) on Mihara Island, Japan, has resulted in rising atmospheric SO_2 levels to values of c.1050 $\mu g/m^3$ at sites located more than 100 km from the source (Katou & Umeda 2001). In Europe, Mount Etna contributes to the tropospheric sulphate burden at remote locations (Anfossi & Sacchetti 1994; Graf et al. 1998), and Camuffo and Enzi (1995) have related recurrent episodes of abnormal atmospheric acidification in northern Italy between 1374 and 1819 to degassing crises at Mount Etna, Vesuvius, Vulcano, and Stromboli. These events were characterized by the appearance of so called 'dry fogs' (fogs with low relative humidity), which consist of a dense suspension of acidic gases and aerosol particles. Finally, the dramatic air pollution event which occurred in Europe during the summer of 1783 was also attributed to volcanic gas emissions. At this time, the Laki fissure in Iceland was injecting exceptionally large quantities of sulphur-, chlorine- and fluorine-rich gases and aerosols into the upper troposphere (Thordarson et al. 1996). Owing to peculiar meteorological conditions, the dense acidic cloud was transported over a large area of western and central Europe and strongly enhanced the atmospheric acidity, perhaps for several months (Grattan & Pyatt 1994; Stothers 1996).

In addition to generating air pollution, the continuous injection of volcanic sulphur (mainly SO_2) effluents into the troposphere may influence the Earth's radiation balance, because they constitute a long-term source of secondary sulphate aerosols. Sulphate aerosols act as cloud condensation nuclei, possibly affecting cloud albedo and cloud lifetime (an indirect effect) and also scatter and absorb radiation (a direct effect) (Charlson et al. 1992). The significance of passive degassing and small eruptive sources on amounts of SO_2 in the mid and upper troposphere of the northern and southern hemispheres was recently highlighted by Thornton et al. (1999). Based on an experiment with a global atmospheric circulation model which included sulphur chemistry, Graf et al. (1997, 1998) suggested that the radiative negative forcing of volcanic sulphate aerosols (–0.15 W/m^{-2}) is at least as important as that of anthropogenic emissions (–0.17 W/m^{-2}), despite the stronger input of the latter. This is principally attributed to the fact that volcanic plumes are usually emitted into the free troposphere, while anthropogenic emissions are confined within the planetary boundary layer and thus are subject to efficient removal processes.

Dry and wet deposition

The dispersion of tropospheric volcanic plumes containing acidic gases and aerosols obviously affects the compositions and amounts of dry and wet deposition. Direct measurements of dry deposition are difficult because the process depends on various factors such as the reactivity of the substance of interest (gaseous or particulate form), the nature of the surface on to which deposition occurs, wind speed, atmospheric stability, and possibly other factors (e.g. Wesely & Hicks 2000). Efforts have been made to estimate the percentage of SO_2 and HCl emissions dry-deposited downwind of Masaya volcano (Delmelle et al. 2001). Measurements were made by exposing a network of sulphation plates (Huey 1968) within 44 km of the source for three to four weeks. Although the method cannot adequately describe the complexity of natural surfaces, it may account for the combined effects of soil and vegetation on SO_2 deposition (Bourque & Arp 1996; Delmelle et al. 2001).

Analysis of the data collected over a 1250 km^2 area southwest of Masaya volcano in the dry season (February–March 1999) suggests that SO_2 dry deposition on to the land ranged from background values of c. <2 to 790 mg/m^2/day. For comparison, maximum sulphation rates measured by the same method close to industrial stacks are in the range of 10–100 mg SO_2/m^2/ day. Despite these relatively large deposition fluxes, the total daily amounts of SO_2 deposited dry on to the land within the area surveyed (i.e. c.0.15 Gg) corresponded with less than 10% of the total daily volcanic emission of SO_2 (c.1.8 Gg). The sulphation plates also detected the dry deposition of HCl gas at rates ranging from c. <1 to 300 mg/m^{-2}/day. The total dry deposition of HCl was inferred to be c.0.06 Gg, which is also 10% of the total daily HCl emission of c.0.6 Gg.

Wet deposition is another pathway through which volcanic contaminants suspended in the atmosphere are returned to the ground. Here wet deposition refers to acidic rain and fog. Rainwater with pH values less than 4, and containing elevated anion contents, is not unusual in areas exposed to volcanic gas emissions (Table 2). Note that the reported compositional data usually

Table 2. *Chemical compositions of volcanic and anthropogenic acid rainwater samples.*

Location	Date	Distance from source (km)	pH	F⁻ mg/L	Cl⁻ mg/L	SO₄²⁻ mg/L	NO₃⁻ mg/L	References
Volcanic acid rain								
Mount Etna	29/06/98	*c.*2.5 km		25.4	83.2	115		Aiuppa *et al.* (2001)
Kilauea		*c.*0.8 km	3.86	0.48	0.88	6.91	0.08	Harding and Miller (1982)
Masaya	24/10/81	*c.*5 km	2.90		30.0	9.1		Johnson and Parnell (1986)
Masaya	15/03/99	*c.*5 km		7.60	41.3	29.5		Delmelle (unpublished data)
Nevado del Ruiz	27/01/87	*c.*6 km	3.58		11.20	2.97		Parnell and Burke (1990)
Poàs	1988–1990	West Crater rim	1±0.8	39±40	8240± 7540	251±201		Rowe *et al.* (1995)
Poàs	05–12/94	*c.*10–15 km	3.5–4.5		0.2–1.7	1.7–3.7		Downing (1996)
Mount Sakurajima*		6.6 km		1.82	13.09	7.39	0.56	Kawaratani and Fujita (1990)
Anthropogenic acid rain								
Sudbury smelter area	1978–1979	<20 km	4.11	0.04	0.45	5.04	0.64	Chan *et al.* (1984)
Pennsylvania, USA	07/79		c.4.1		0.20	36.00	3.46	Hales (1995)

*Non-maritime excess concentration.

refer to the sum of wet and dry deposition in the rainwater sample. The ultimate sources of protons and anions are the acidic gases and related aerosols present in the volcanic emissions, which are dissolved by raindrops falling through the airborne plume. In addition, sulphate aerosol particles are effective cloud condensation nuclei, and this property renders them more susceptible to impactive scavenging by falling hydrometeors. In contrast to the acidity of rain in industrialized regions, which is primarily controlled by H_2SO_4 and HNO_3, the chemistry of precipitation affected by the sub-aerial degassing of a volcano is dominated by H_2SO_4, HCl, and to a lesser degree HF. In a few cases, Br has also been detected in significant concentrations in rainwater collected in the immediate vicinity of a volcanic vent (e.g. Mount Etna, Aiuppa *et al.* 2001).

The amount of chloride reported in acid rainfall close to gas vents is often higher than that of sulphate (Table 2), although volcanic emissions of SO_2 are normally higher than those of HCl. However, an increase in the sulphate-to-chloride ratio of the rainwater is generally observed with increasing distance from source (Johnson & Parnell 1986; Kawaratani & Fujita 1990; Parnell & Burke 1990; Aiuppa *et al.* 2001). This essentially reflects the characteristic time of oxidation of SO_2 to sulphate in the plume. Since the solubility of gaseous HCl in water is greater than that of SO_2, it is rapidly incorporated by hydrometeors. In addition, the acidity produced from HCl dissolution suppresses the solubility of SO_2, thereby impeding further the aqueous phase oxidation of SO_2 (which is more effective than the gaseous phase reaction). Thus, wet chloride deposition in the vicinity of the degassing volcano is relatively larger than that of sulphate. In fact, the sulphate content in wet precipitation from volcanic sources may result mainly from the uptake of primary sulphate emissions (Kawaratani & Fujita 1990). The reported dominance of sulphate over chloride in rainwater sampled within 12 km of Kilauea (table 2 in Harding & Miller 1982) hence may reflect a particularly high abundance of sulphate aerosols in the plume. Recently, Porter *et al.* (2002) calculated a flux of *c.*0.6 kg/s of sulphate from the Pu'u O'o vent.

Since volcano-derived gas emissions can modify the SO$_2$ and sulphate burden of the mid- and upper troposphere, it is not surprising to observe a substantial volcanic effect on the composition of regional dry and wet deposition. For example, Ichikawa and Fujita (1995) estimated that passively degassing volcanoes account for *c.*20% of the total wet-deposited sulphate in Japan. Arndt *et al.* (1997) also calculated that sulphur deposition from volcanoes accounts for *c.*30% of the total deposition in Japan, *c.*50% in Indonesia, and *c.*20% in the Philippines.

Volcanic gas plumes may also increase the amounts of trace contaminants in terrestrial ecosystems through dry and wet deposition processes. Compelling evidence for the contribution of tropospheric volcanic emissions to total trace-element deposition has been obtained from lichen studies. Lichens are known to accumulate a variety of xenobiotic substances in gaseous, liquid, or particulate form from the atmosphere over periods of tens to hundreds of years (e.g. Nieboer *et al.* 1972). Davies and Notcutt (1988) and Notcutt and Davies (1989) showed that the F contents in lichen thalli collected near Mount Etna and Kilauea were positively correlated with the dispersion of the volcanic emissions. The measured levels (from 3 to 300 µg F/g of dry material) were found to be similar to those in lichens contaminated by fluoride-rich effluents from aluminium smelters.

The concentrations and distribution of some metals in lichens from Mount Etna and Vulcano have been studied recently (Dongarrà & Varrica 1998; Grasso *et al.* 1999; Monna *et al.* 1999; Varrica *et al.* 2000). Selective metal enrichments indicate significant fallout of Cu, Au, Zn, Sb, and Pb from the emitted plumes. Bromide was also found to be systematically enriched in lichens. The enrichment trend was more pronounced in specimens exposed to the prevailing direction of plume transport. According to Pb isotopic analyses, volcanic Pb addition contributes 10 to 30% and 10 to 80% of the total Pb content in lichens from Mount Etna and Vulcano, respectively (Monna *et al.* 1999). Evidence that significant amounts of metals can be added to the environment during volcanic degassing has been obtained in Antartica, where Mount Erebus constitutes a significant source of Cu, Cd, V, and As in snow deposited over a wide area of the continent (Zreda-Gostynska *et al.* 1997).

Impacts of tropospheric volcanic gas plumes on terrestrial ecosystems

Impacts on vegetation

Temporary or continuous detrimental effects on natural and cultivated vegetation have been observed in relation to passive volcanic degassing (Kratky *et al.* 1974; Winner & Mooney 1980; Parnell & Burke 1990; Kempter *et al.* 1996; Sandoval *et al.* 1996, Martínez *et al.* 2000). The desert conditions of the Ka'u desert, Big Island, Hawaii, which extends about 30 km southwest from the summit caldera of Kilauea, may be the result of continuous acidic wet deposition, which forms in this area as the volcanic plume mixes with air (Harding & Miller 1982; Sutton & Elias 1993). The damage to crops and trees in many parts of Europe during the summer of 1783 was also attributed to acidic clouds generated by the Laki fissure eruption (Grattan & Pyatt 1994). Similar effects were observed in areas of northern Italy that have experienced episodes of elevated atmospheric acidity associated with strong gas emissions from the volcanoes of southern Italy (Camuffo & Enzi 1995).

A well-documented case of vegetative deterioration is found at Masaya, where a 140-year history of volcanic gas release episodes has created strong perturbations in the ecosystems downwind (McBirney 1956; Johnson & Parnell 1986; Stoiber *et al.* 1986; Delmelle *et al.* 2002). Within 15 km of the active crater, there is a tongue-like enclave of 22 km^2 in area where the original cloud forest has been totally destroyed by the low-altitude volcanic emissions (Fig. 5). Cultivation here is rendered difficult or impossible. An intermediate stage of vegetative impacts consisting of chlorotic and necrotic leaf symptoms and fruit injuries is also visible in a transition zone surrounding the devastated area. The general shape of the deforested enclave and the boundaries of the less impacted zone clearly relate to the average plume dispersion, strongly suggesting the noxious impact of the volcanic gases and aerosols (Delmelle *et al.* 2002).

The airborne volcanic compounds most likely to induce direct damage to vegetation are SO$_2$, HCl, and HF gases. The few available data on HCl downwind of degassing volcanoes suggest atmospheric levels that are too low to affect vegetation directly (Smith 1990). In contrast, SO$_2$ and HF may well be present at phytotoxic concentrations, even though HF is generally present at much lower concentrations than SO$_2$ in the plume. Direct damage to plants includes absorption of these compounds through stomatal pores of leaves and subsequent dissolution in free

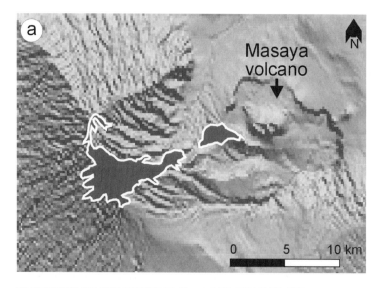

Fig. 5. (a) Map showing the approximate boundaries of the 22 km² area (dark grey) most affected by Masaya's gas plume; **(b)** photograph of the deforested valleys located in the immediate zone of plume impaction. Masaya volcano appears in the background at a distance of c.6 km.

space moisture in leaf interiors. The dissolved sulphur and fluorine induce biochemical interferences at the physiological level (e.g. Smith 1990 and references therein), which, in turn, produce foliar symptoms such as chlorotic and necrotic leaf injury, eventually leading to plant death. In this process, HF is regarded as considerably more toxic than SO_2, since susceptible plants may be injured at ambient concentrations that are 10–1000 times lower than SO_2. For a large number of trees, the fluoride dose for symptomatic injury ranges from approximately 0.75 to 50 µg/m³ for several hours to 10 or more

days. Comprehensive lists of relative sensitivity of plants to acute damage by SO_2 or HF are quoted in Smith (1990).

It is difficult, and probably misleading, to assign a single threshold SO_2 or HF dose above which damage to plant foliage occurs, because exposure conditions (concentration of pollutant, duration and frequency of exposure), environmental factors (weather conditions, light, soil moisture, etc.), the age of plant, stage of development, and species or variety influence the direct response of plant to pollutant exposure (e.g. Linzon et al. 1979; Weinstein & McCune

1979). Additionally, the simultaneous presence of SO_2 and HF may reduce SO_2 thresholds for vegetation injury or, on the contrary, may lessen the intensity of the impacts (Mandl *et al.* 1975; Smith 1990). Also, some plants may develop a form of resistance to long-term exposure to airborne pollutants. In this respect, it is interesting to note that abnormal concentrations of F (up to *c.*600 µg/g of dry matter) in plant leaves from the Masaya and Mount Etna areas do not necessarily coincide with visible foliar damage (Garrec *et al.* 1984).

In addition to the direct vegetative impacts of elevated atmospheric SO_2 and HF levels, volcano-derived acidic wet deposition may have a detrimental influence on plant health. This can occur through abnormally high losses of nutrient cations (Ca^{2+}, K^+, and Mg^{2+}) from foliage, due to enhanced ion exchange at the leaf surfaces. Such phenomena have been observed at several sites affected by volcanic gas emissions (Kratky *et al.* 1974; Johnson & Parnell 1986; Parnell & Burke 1990). In general, acidified fog and cloud, which may contain solute concentrations up to 10 times those found in rain, have a greater capacity for direct impact on vegetation (Cape 1993). Thus, vegetation vulnerable to the direct effects from dissolved ions will be found in hilly areas exposed to orographic clouds or advected coastal fog for prolonged periods.

Impacts on soil and groundwater

As is the case in areas affected by industrial emissions of sulphur and nitrogen oxides, atmospheric deposition of volcanogenic acid gases and aerosols downwind from degassing craters may interfere with soil constituents (organic matter and minerals). Sustained additions of acidic compounds to the soil may modify its physicochemical properties, eventually leading to soil acidification. A direct consequence of this process is the loss of exchangeable base cations (Mg^{2+}, Ca^{2+}, Na^+, and K^+) from the soil, with an associated decrease in soil fertility and/or consumption of the soil acid-neutralizing capacity. This in turn may result in a decline in pH and increase in concentrations of inorganic Al in drainage waters, with the latter element eventually reaching ecologically significant quantities (van Breemen *et al.* 1984). Importantly, the capacity of a soil to retain anions can potentially reduce or delay acidification reactions, i.e. the transport of hydrogen, aluminium and basic cations to surface waters is decreased. This results from the fact that sulphate and fluoride anion retention can involve release of hydroxyl anions to the bulk solution, as well as lead to increased soil cation-exchange capacity. Thus, in the case of volcanogenic acid inputs, the fate of the added sulphur, chlorine, and fluorine in soils is also of environmental importance.

Areas near active volcanoes are usually endowed with soils derived from volcanic tephra. Depending on age and climate, these soils exhibit various weathering stages and weatherable silicate mineral contents. They also often exhibit high contents of non-crystalline aluminium and iron minerals, including oxyhydroxides and short-range ordered silicates such as allophanes, which give them a variable electrical charge (Shoji *et al.* 1993). As such, they generally belong to the Andosol soil group, and can be distinguished by a large hydrogen ion adsorptive capacity and a strong affinity for some anions, including fluoride, phosphate, and, to a lesser extent, sulphate. Andosols are normally classified as soils with a high capacity to neutralize inputs of acidic or potentially acidic compounds, and thus may not be particularly sensitive to acidification processes.

The effects on Andosols of intermittent or prolonged exposure to volcanogenically derived acid loading remain poorly known. Parnell (1986) analysed some Andosol profiles at sites directly exposed to the gas emissions from Masaya volcano in 1979–1984. The study revealed that these soils were significantly depleted in exchangeable base cations relative to unaffected sites. The Masaya Andosols also showed a dramatic response to acidified rainfall events, consisting of a soil pH decrease accompanied by an increase in sulphate retention. The latter process is explained in terms of the dependence of the anion adsorption capacity on the soil constituent electrical charge, which for Andosols is strongly modulated by the soil pH (Shoji *et al.* 1983). Similar effects were observed for alpine Andosols of Nevado del Ruiz volcano, which received volcanic acid rainfall after the 13 November 1985 eruption (Parnell & Burke 1990).

In addition to supporting the previous results of Parnell (1986), new investigations on soils in the Masaya area demonstrate that enhanced retention of sulphur and fluorine by the soil horizons occurs in response to dry and wet deposition of volcanic SO_2 and HF emissions (Delmelle *et al.* 2002). In the soils directly exposed to the gas plume, extractable sulphur and fluorine in surface horizons reached concentrations in excess of 3000 mg/kg^{-1} (*c.*32 mmol./kg) and 2800 mg/kg (*c.*150 mmol./kg). In contrast, little or no chlorine accumulates in the Andosols, in accordance with the comparatively low affinity of chloride anions for the soil constituents (Gebhardt & Coleman 1974). Moreover, the young Andosols located close to the volcano tend to exhibit a significantly lower ability to retain sulphur and fluorine scavenged from the gas plume than the old, more weathered soils found further downwind, although the relative contents of extractable sulphur, chlorine and fluorine in the two soil types did not differ significantly (Fig. 6). This is a consequence of the higher content of allophanic minerals and greater surface area of the more evolved profiles. Comparison of the relative concentrations of sulphur, chlorine, and fluorine extracted from the soils and in the gas emissions also suggests that fluorine, and to a lesser degree sulphur, are strongly partitioned in the soil (Fig. 6). These results raise important questions concerning the spatial and temporal mobility of sulphur and fluorine added to ecosystems during passive degassing activity, and its relationships to soil acidification. Clearly, there is a need to consider the physicochemical properties of the receptor, because these dictate the sensitivity to the volcanogenic inputs of pollutants.

The chemical compounds released to the atmosphere by persistently degassing volcanoes, which are returned to the Earth's surface via dry and wet deposition processes, may ultimately enter the hydrological cycle and contaminate aquifers. At Etna, the ratio of chloride to total dissolved solids content (TDS) of groundwaters was consistently low during the inter-eruptive period 1993–1995, but rose by up to 20% during 1996–1998 when Strombolian activity resumed and gas emission rates increased at the summit craters. Since Etnean groundwaters are derived mainly from meteoric water, these changes were attributed to changes in the chemistry of the rainwater in response to intense plume degassing (Aiuppa *et al.* 2001).

Challenges and prospects

Detailed knowledge of tropospheric volcanic gas plume chemistry and emission rates is a prerequisite for investigations of the impacts of passively degassing volcanoes upon the local, regional, and global environment. At present, such data are insufficient due to intrinsic difficulties of monitoring airborne volcanic emissions with conventional direct sampling methods. Additionally, the influence of volcanic passive degassing on the chemistry of the atmosphere (e.g. oxidant capacity, aerosol load) and ecosystems may not be fully appreciated. This situation may be changing as new spectroscopic techniques are beginning to be applied on volcanoes. In particular, OP–FTIR can provide insights into plume reaction and removal processes involving sulphur, chlorine and fluorine species. This can already be gauged from the OP–FTIR data obtained at Masaya by Duffell *et al.* (2001) and Horrocks *et al.* (2003).

A poorly understood aspect of volcanic plume chemistry is that of aerosol phase

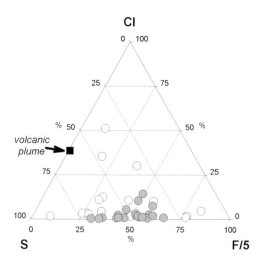

Fig. 6. Relative molal concentrations of extractable fluorine, chlorine, and sulphur in young (white circles) and old, more weathered (shaded circles) Andosols sampled within 15 km of Masaya volcano (Delmelle unpublished data.). The composition of the emitted gas plume is also shown (black square). The diagram indicates that preferential retention of volcanic F and S in the soils leads to marked enrichments in the soils relative to the airborne emissions.

characteristics (mode of formation and growth, distribution size, and scavenging pathways, Allen *et al.* 2002). New insights may be gained from carefully designed field and laboratory experiments. Further deployment of the Sunphotometer technique on volcanoes should also be encouraged. In addition, observations from space-borne multispectral infrared sensors such as MODIS (Moderate Resolution Imaging Spectroradiometer) should facilitate measurements of SO_2 and sulphate aerosols in relatively small volcanic plumes.

Quantification of tropospheric volcanic plume dispersion patterns as a function of source strength and local meteorology and topography, is essential to obtain reliable data on volatile emissions. Often, the concentrations of gases and aerosols in volcanic plumes are derived from vertical cross-sections, but with poor constraints on plume dimensions and plume dilution. Such data would benefit the overall effort of better scaling the contribution of volcanic degassing to the global atmospheric burden of sulphur and halogens. Detailed plume dispersion studies are also warranted to allow predictions of the type and extent of gas hazard downwind from a volcano. Models such as those developed by Graziani *et al.* (1997) and Pareschi *et al.* (1999) could be applied to various volcanic situations. The overall goal is to couple these numerical simulations with reliable plume chemistry models. The latter may originate from work on industrial point source emissions, but should progressively integrate the results of detailed studies on the composition, emission, and differential removal processes of airborne volcanic effluents. Further ahead, an integrated model accurately describing the fate of emitted sulphur and halogen gases during the first minutes to hours of plume transport in the troposphere will provide a better framework to evaluate the contribution and impacts of volcanic emissions on the regional and global atmosphere.

There is evidence that ecosystems around degassing volcanoes may be temporarily or continuously disrupted by plume gases, sometimes leading to extensive agricultural loss and social distress. Such damage is typically evaluated from visual observations, and few efforts have been made to map its extent in relation to plume dispersion. Similarly, no information is available on the temporal evolution and recovery of zones regularly exposed to volcanic gas emissions. The advent of imaging spectrometry, which allows the identification and quantitative assessment of several environmental characteristics, could change this situation. The Airborne Visible/InfraRed Imaging Spectrometer (AVIRIS) has recently been used by de Jong (1998) to monitor vegetation damage in Long Valley caldera in the Sierra Nevada, California, where diffuse degassing of volcanic CO_2 through the soil has generated areas of dying forest. The first results are promising, as dead and stressed trees areas were successfully recognized from the AVIRIS scenes.

The causative agents of direct vegetation damage downwind from volcanic gas sources probably relate to elevated concentrations of SO_2, HF, and acidic sulphate aerosols in ambient air. However, more extensive field and laboratory work is needed for detailed analysis of the combined effects of these pollutants on natural and cultivated vegetation. The respective impacts of wet and dry deposition of acidic compounds should also be addressed. Criteria used in Europe and North America to assess and predict the response of soils to atmospheric acid loading appear inadequate for volcanic regions. These should be revised to account for (1) the dominant occurrence of Andosols with distinct physico-chemical properties, and (2) the contribution of halogen compounds to total (i.e. dry plus wet) acid deposition. Such studies should be viewed in the broad context of the rapid increase of anthropogenic acid emissions in East Asia (Arndt *et al.* 1997), where volcanic sources are more important, and Andosols more common, than in Europe or North America. Finally, a sound understanding of ecosystem sensitivity to volcanogenic air pollution is necessary to evaluate the possibility of widespread environmental forcing caused by massive injection of volatiles into the troposphere during fissure eruptions such as the 1783 Laki event.

The support of the Fonds National de la Recherche Scientifique of Belgium is gratefully acknowledged. I thank colleagues from the Open University, University of Cambridge, McGill University, and the Université catholique de Louvain, who have worked with me in the field or in the laboratory over the last three years. Constructive comments by L. Horrocks, an anonymous reviewer, and J. Stix are greatly appreciated.

References

AIUPPA, A., BONFANTI, P., BRUSCA, L., D'ALESSANDRO, W., FEDERICO, C. & PARELLO, F. 2001. Evaluation of the environmental impact of volcanic emissions from the chemistry of rainwater: Mount Etna area (Sicily). *Applied Geochemistry*, **16**, 985–1000.

ALLARD, P., AIUPPA, A. ET AL. 2000. Acid gas and metal emission rates during long-lived basalt degassing at Stromboli volcano. *Geophysical Research Letters*, **7**, 1207–1210.

ALLEN, A. G., BAXTER, P. J. & OTTLEY, C. J. 2000. Gas

and particle emissions from Soufrière Hills Volcano, Montserrat, West Indies: characterization and health hazard assessment. *Bulletin of Volcanology*, **62**, 8–19.

ALLEN, A. G., OPPENHEIMER, C. *ET AL.* 2002. Primary sulphate aerosol and associated emissions from Masaya volcano, Nicaragua, *Journal of Geophysical Research – Atmospheres*, doi: 10.1029/2002JD 002120.

ANDRES, R. J. & KASGNOC, A. D. 1998. A time-averaged inventory of subaerial volcanic sulfur emissions. *Journal of Geophysical Research*, **103**, 25 251–25 261.

ANFOSSI, D. & SACCHETTI, D. 1994. Transport of volcano Etna emissions towards the Alpine region using ECMWF data. *Il Nuovo Cimento*, **17**, 473–484.

ARNDT, R. L., CARMICHAEL, G. R., STREETS, D. G. & BHATTI, N. 1997. Sulfur dioxide emissions and sectorial contributions to sulfur deposition in Asia. *Atmospheric Environment*, **31**, 1553–1572.

BERRESHEIM, H. & JAESCHKE, W. 1983. The contributions of volcanoes to the global atmospheric sulfur budget. *Journal of Geophysical Research*, **88**, 3732–3740.

BERRESHEIM, H., WINE, P. H. & DAVIS, D. D. 1995. Sulfur in the atmosphere. *In:* SINGH, H. B. (ed.) *Composition Chemistry and Climate of the Atmosphere*, VNR Publishers, New York, 251–307.

BOURQUE, C. & ARP, P. 1996. Simulating sulfur dioxide plume dispersion and subsequent deposition downwind from a stationary point source: a model. *Environmental Pollution*, **91**, 363–380.

BROWN, R. H. & WRIGHT, M. D. 1994. Diffusive sampling using tube-type samplers. *Analyst*, **119**, 75–77.

CAMUFFO, D. & ENZI, S. 1995. Impact of clouds of volcanic aerosols in Italy during the last 7 centuries. *Natural Hazards*, **11**, 135–161.

CAPE, J. N. 1993. Direct damage to vegetation caused by acid rain and polluted cloud: definition of critical levels for forest trees. *Environmental Pollution*, **82**, 167–180.

CASADEVALL, T. J., ROSE, W. I. *ET AL.* 1984. Sulfur dioxide and particles in quiescent plumes volcanic plumes from Poàs, Arenal, and Colima volcanoes, Costa Rica and Mexico. *Journal of Geophysical Research*, **89**, 9633–9641.

CHAN, W. H., VET, R. J., RO, C-U., TANG, J. S. & LUSIS, M. A. 1984. Impact of Inco smelter emissions on wet and dry deposition in the Sudbury area. *Atmospheric Environment*, **18**, 1001–1008.

CHARLSON, R. J. S., SCHWARTZ, S. E., HALES, J. M. CESS, R. D., COAKLEY, J. A., HANSEN, J. & HOFMANN, D. J. 1992. Climate forcing by anthropogenic aerosols. *Science*, **255**, 423–430.

CHUAN, R. L., PALAIS, J., ROSE, W. I. & KYLE, P. R. 1986. Fluxes, sizes, morphology and compositions of particles in the Mt. Erebus volcanic plume, December 1983. *Journal of Atmospheric Chemistry*, **4**, 467–477.

DAVIES, F. & NOTCUTT, G. 1989. Accumulation of fluoride by lichens in the vicinity of Etna volcano. *Water, Air and Soil Pollution*, **42**, 365–371.

DE JONG, S. 1998. Imaging spectrometry for monitoring tree damage caused by volcanic activity in the Long Valley caldera, California. *ITC Journal*, **1**, 1–10.

DELMELLE, P., STIX, J., BOURQUE, C. P. A., BAXTER, P., GARCIA-ALVAREZ, J. & BARQUERO, J. 2001. Dry deposition and heavy acid loading in the vicinity of Masaya volcano, a major sulfur and chlorine source in Nicaragua. *Environmental Science & Technology*, **7**, 1289–1293.

DELMELLE, P., STIX, J., BAXTER, P., GARCIA-ALVAREZ, J. & BARQUERO, J. 2002. Atmospheric dispersion, environmental effects and potential health hazard associated with the low-altitude gas plume of Masaya volcano, Nicaragua. *Bulletin of Volcanology*, **64**, 423–434.

DONGARRÀ, G. & VARRICA, D. 1998. The presence of heavy metals in air particulate at Vulcano island (Italy). *The Science of the Total Environment*, **212**, 1–9.

DOWNING, C. E. H. 1996. *Air and Precipitation Monitoring Around Pòas Volcano: Costa Rica*. Report RAMP/20106001/01Abingdon, AEA Technology.

DUFFELL, H., OPPENHEIMER, C. & BURTON, M. 2001. Volcanic gas emission rates measured by solar occultation spectroscopy. *Geophysical Research Letters*, **28**, 3131–3134.

EATOUGH, D. J., CAKA, F. M. & FARBER, R. J. 1994. The conversion of SO_2 to sulfate in the atmosphere. *Israel Journal of Chemistry*, **34**, 301–314.

FERRARA, R., MAZZOLAI, B., LANZILLOTTA, E., NUCARO, E. & PIRRONE, N. 2000. Volcanoes as emission sources of atmospheric mercury in the Mediterranean basin. *The Science of the Total Environment*, **259**, 115–121.

GARREC, J. P., PLEBIN, R. & FAIVRE-PIERRET, R. X. 1984. Impact of volcanic fluoride and SO_2 emissions from moderated activity volcanoes on the surrounding vegetation. *Bulletin of Volcanology*, **47**, 491–496.

GAUTHIER, P.-J. & LE CLOAREC, M.-F. 1998. Variability of alkali and heavy metal fluxes released by Mt. Etna volcano, Sicily, between 1991 and 1995. *Journal of Volcanology and Geothermal Research*, **81**, 311–326.

GEBHARDT, H. & COLEMAN, T. 1974. Anion adsorption by allophanic tropical soils: I. Chloride adsorption. *Soil Science Society of America Proceedings*, **38**, 255–258.

GRAEDEL, T. H. & KEENE, W. C. 1995. Tropospheric budget of reactive chlorine. *Global Biogeochemical Cycles,* **9**, 47–77.

GRAF, H-F., FEICHTER, J. & LANGMANN, B. 1997. Volcanic sulfur emissions: estimates of source strength and its contribution to the global sulfate distribution. *Journal of Geophysical Research*, **102**, 10 727–10 738.

GRAF, H.-F., LANGMANN, B. & FEICHTER, J. 1998. The contribution of Earth degassing to the atmospheric sulfur budget. *Chemical Geology*, **147**, 131–145.

GRASSO, M. F., CLOCCHIATTI, R., CARROT, F., DESCHAMPS, C. & VURRO, F. 1999. Lichens as bioindicators in volcanic areas: Mt. Etna and Vulcano island (Italy). *Environmental Geology*, **37**, 207–217.

GRATTAN, J. P. & PYATT, F. B. 1994. Acid damage in Europe caused by the Laki fissure eruption – an historical review. *The Science of the Total Environment*, **151**, 241–247.

GRAZIANI, G., MARTILLI, A., PARESCHI, M. T. & VALENZA, M. 1997. Atmospheric dispertion of natural gases at Vulcano island. *Journal of Volcanology and Geothermal Research*, **75**, 283–308.

HALES, J. M. 1995. Acidic precipitation. *In:* SINGH, B. H. (ed.) *Composition, Chemistry, and Climate of the Atmosphere*. Van Nostrand Reinhold, **7**, 443–479.

HALMER, M. M., SCHMINCKE, H.-U. & GRAF, H.-F. 2002. The annual volcanic gas input into the atmosphere, in particular into the stratosphere: a global data set for the past 100 years. *Journal of Volcanology and Geothermal Research*, **115**, 511–528.

HAMILTON, P. M., VAREY, R. H. & MILLÁN, M. M. 1978. Remote sensing of sulphur dioxide. *Atmospheric Environment*, **12**, 127–133.

HARDING, D. & MILLER, J. M. 1982. The influence on rain chemistry of the Hawaiian volcano Kilauea. *Journal of Geophysical Research*, **87**, 1225–1230.

HINKLEY, T. K., LAMOTHE, P. J., WILSON, S. A., FINNEGAN, D. L. & GERLACH, T. M. 1999. Metal emissions from Kilauea, and a suggested revision of the estimated worldwide metal output by quiescent degassing of volcanoes. *Earth and Planetary Science Letters*, **170**, 315–325.

HOBBS, P. V., TUELL, J. P., HEGG, D. A., RADKE, L. F. & ELTGROTH, M. W. 1982. Particles and gases in the emissions from the 1980–1981 volcanic eruptions of Mt. St. Helens. *Journal of Geophysical Research*, **87**, 11 062–11 086.

HOFF, R. M. & GALLANT, A. J. 1980. Sulfur dioxide emissions from La Soufrière volcano, St. Vincent, West Indies. *Science*, **209**, 923–924.

HORROCKS, L. A., BURTON, L., FRANCIS, P. W. & OPPENHEIMER, C. 1999. Stable gas plume composition measured by OP–FTIR spectroscopy at Masaya volcano, Nicaragua, 1998–1999. *Geophysical Research Letters*, **26**, 3497–3500.

HORROCKS, L. A., OPPENHEIMER, C., BURTON, M. R. & DUFFELL, H. J. 2003. Compositional variation in tropospheric volcanic gas plumes: evidence from ground-based remote sensing. *In:* OPPENHEIMER, C., PYLE, D. M. & BARCLAY, J. (eds) *Volcanic Degassing*. Geological Society, London, Special Publications **213**, 349–369.

HUEY, N. A. 1968. The lead dioxide estimation of sulfur dioxide pollution. *Journal of the Air Pollution Control Association*, **18**, 610–611.

ICHIKAWA, Y. & FUJITA, S. 1995. An analysis of wet deposition of sulfate using a trajectory model for East Asia. *Water, Air, and Soil Pollution*, **85**, 1927–1932.

JOHNSON, N. & PARNELL, R. A. 1986. Composition, distribution and neutralization of 'acid rain' derived from Masaya volcano, Nicaragua. *Tellus*, **38B**, 106–117.

JORDAN, A., HARNISCH, J., BORCHERS, R., LE GUERN, F. & SHINOHARA, H. 2000. Volcanogenic halocarbons. *Environmental Science & Technology*, **34**, 1122–1124.

KATOU, Y. & UMEDA, T. 2001. Acid rain by volcanic gases from Miyakejima (Japan). *Yokohama-shi Kankyo Kagaku Kenkyushoho*, **25**, 38–46, in Japanese.

KAWARATANI, R. K. & FUJITA, S.-I. 1990. Wet deposition of volcanic gases and ash in the vicinity of Mount Sakurajima. *Atmospheric Environment*, **24A**, 1487–1492.

KEMPTER, K. A., BENNER, S. & WILLIAMS, S. N. 1996. Rincòn de la Vieja volcano, Guanacaste province, Costa Rica: geology of the southwestern flank and hazards implications. *Journal of Volcanology and Geothermal Research*, **71**, 109–127.

KINOSHITA, K. 1996. Observation of flow and dispersion of volcanic clouds from Mt. Sakurajima. *Atmospheric Environment*, **30**, 2831–2837.

KRATKY, B. A., FUKUNAGA, E. T., HYLIN, J. W. & NAKANO, R. T. 1974. Volcanic air pollution: deleterious effects on tomatoes. *Journal of Environmental Quality*, **3**, 138–140.

LE CLOAREC, M. F., ALLARD, P., ARDOUIN, B., GIGGENBACH, W. F. & SHEPPARD, D. S. 1992. Radioactive isotopes and trace elements in gaseous emissions from White Island, New Zealand. *Earth and Planetary Science Letters*, **108**, 19–28.

LINZON, S. N., TEMPLE, P. J. & PEARSON, R. G. 1979. Sulfur concentrations in plant foliage and related effects. *Journal of the Air Pollution Control Association*, **29**, 520–525.

LURIA, M., BOATMAN, J. F. ET AL. 1992. Atmospheric sulfur dioxide at Mauna Loa, Hawaii. *Journal of Geophysical Research*, **97**, 6011–6022.

MCBIRNEY, A. R. 1956. The Nicaraguan volcano Masaya and its caldera. *Eos, Transactions of the American Geophysical Union*, **37**, 83–96.

MCGEE, K. 1992. The structure, dynamics and chemical composition of non-eruptive plumes from Mount St. Helens. *Journal of Volcanology and Geothermal Research*, **51**, 269–282.

MCGONIGLE, A. J. S. & OPPENHEIMER, C. 2003. Optical sensing of volcanic gas and aerosol emissions. *In:* OPPENHEIMER, C., PYLE, D. M. & BARCLAY, J. (eds). *Volcanic Degassing*. Geological Society, London, Special Publications **213**, 149–168.

MANDL, R. H., WEINSTEIN, L. H. & KEVENY, M. 1975. Effects of hydrogen fluoride and sulphur dioxide alone and in combination on several species of plants. *Environmental Pollution*, **9**, 133–143.

MARTIN, D., ARDOUIN, B. ET AL. 1986. Geochemistry of sulfur in Mount Etna plume. *Journal of Geophysical Research*, **91**, 12 249–12 254.

MARTÍNEZ, M., FERNÁNDEZ, E. ET AL. 2000. Chemical evolution and volcanic activity of the active crater lake of Poás volcano, Costa Rica, 1993–1997. *Journal of Volcanology and Geothermal Research*, **97**, 127–141.

MIZUNO, T., TANAKA, C. & FUJIMURA, M. 1996. A case study of particulate sulfur concentration over the Kanto plain (Japan). *Taiki Kankyo Gakkaishi*, **31**, 20–29 [in Japanese].

MONNA, F. AIUPPA, A., VARRICA, D. & DONGARRÀ, G. 1999. Pb isotope composition in lichens and aerosols from eastern Sicily: insights into the regional impact of volcanoes on the environment. *Environmental Science & Technology*, **33**, 2517–2523.

NEWMAN, L. 1981. Atmospheric oxidation of sulfur dioxide: a review as viewed from power plant and smelter plume studies. *Atmospheric Environment*, **15**, 2231–2239.

NICHOLSON, R. A., ROBERTS, P. D. & BAXTER, P. J. 1996. Preliminary studies of acid and gas contamination at Poas volcano, Costa Rica. *In:* APPLETON, J. D., FUGE, R. & McCALL, G. J. H. (eds) *Environmental Geochemistry and Health*. Geological Society, London, Special Publications, **113**, 239–244.

NIEBOER, E., AMHED, H. M., PUCKETT, K. J. & RICHARDSON, D. H. S. 1972. Heavy metal content of lichens in relation to distance from a nickel smelter in Sudbury, Ontario. *Lichenologist*, **5**, 292–304.

NOTCUTT, G. & DAVIES, F. 1989. Dispersion of gaseous volcanogenic fluoride, island of Hawaii. *Journal of Volcanology and Geothermal Research*, **56**, 125–131.

OBENHOLZNER, J. H., SCHROETTNER, H., GOLOB, P. & DELGADO, H., 2003. Particles from Popocateptl volcano, Mexico. In: OPPENHEIMER, C., PYLE, D. & BARCLAY, J. *Volcanic Degassing*, Geological Society, London. Special Publications **213**, 123–148.

OPPENHEIMER, C., FRANCIS, P. & MACIEJEWSKI, A. J. H. 1998a. Spectroscopic observation of HCl degassing from Soufrière Hills volcano, Montserrat. *Geophysical Research Letters*, **25**, 3689–3692.

OPPENHEIMER, C., FRANCIS, P. & STIX, J. 1998b. Depletion rates of sulfur dioxide in tropospheric volcanic plumes. *Geophysical Research Letters*, **25**, 2671–2674.

PARESCHI, M. T., RANCI, M., VALENZA, M. & GRAZIANI, G. 1999. The assessment of volcanic gas hazard by means of numerical models: an example from Vulcano Island (Sicily). *Geophysical Research Letters*, **26**, 1405–1408.

PARNELL, R. A. 1986. Processes of soil acidification in tropical durandepts, Nicaragua. *Soil Science*, **42**, 43–55.

PARNELL, R. A. & BURKE, K. J. 1990. Impacts of acid emissions from Nevado del Ruiz volcano, Colombia, on selected terrestrial and aquatic ecosystems. *Journal of Volcanology and Geothermal Research*, **42**, 69–88.

PHELAN, J. M., FINNEGAN, D. L., BALLANTINE, D. S., ZOLLER, W. H., HART, M. A. & MOYERS, J. L. 1982. Airborne aerosol measurements in the quiescent plume of Mount St. Helens: September 1980. *Geophysical Research Letters*, **9**, 1093–1095.

PORTER, J. N. & CLARKE, A. 1997. An aerosol size distribution model based on in-situ measurements. *Journal of Geophysical Research*, **102**, 6035–6045.

PORTER, J. N., HORTON, K. ET AL. 2002. Sun photometer and lidar measurements of the plume from the Hawaii Kilauea volcano Pu'u O'o vent: aerosol flux and SO₂ lifetime. *Geophysical Research Letters*, **28**, 10.1029/2002GL014744.

ROSE, W. I., CHUAN, R. L., GIGGENBACH, W. F., KYLE, P. R. & SYMONDS, R. B. 1986. Rates of sulfur dioxide and particle emissions from White Island volcano, New Zealand, and an estimate of the total flux of major gaseous species. *Bulletin of Volcanology*, **48**, 181–188.

ROWE, G. L., BRANTLEY, S. L., FERNANDEZ, J. F. & BORGIA, A. 1995. The chemical and hydrological structure of Poàs volcano, Costa Rica. *Journal of Volcanology and Geothermal Research*, **64**, 233–267.

SANDOVAL, L., VALDES, J., MARTINEZ, M., BARQUERO, J. & FERNANDEZ, E. 1996. Effect of emissions from Poàs volcano on vegetation in Costa Rica. *Ing Ciencas Quimica*, **16**, 62–64.

SHOJI, S., NANZYO, M. & DAHLGREN, R. 1993. Volcanic ash soils. *Developments in Soil Science*, **21**, Elsevier, Amsterdam, 288 pp.

SMITH, W. H. 1990. Air Pollution and Forests: Interaction Between Air Contaminants and Forest Ecosystems. Springer-Verlag, New York, 618 pp.

STOIBER, R. E., WILLIAMS, S. N. & HUEBERT, B. J. 1986. Sulfur and halogen gases at Masaya caldera complex, Nicaragua: total flux and variations with time. *Journal of Geophysical Research*, **91**, 12 215–1231.

STOTHERS, R. B. 1996. The great dry fog of 1783. *Climatic Change*, **32**, 79–89.

SUTTON, A. J. & ELIAS, T. 1993. Volcanic gases create air pollution in the island of Hawai'i. *Earthquakes and Volcanoes*, **24**, 178–196.

SYMONDS, R. B., ROSE, W. I. & REED, M. H. 1988. Contribution of Cl- and F-bearing gases to the atmosphere by volcanoes. *Nature*, **334**, 415–418.

SYMONDS, R. B., ROSE, W. I., BLUTH, G. J. & GERLACH, T. M. 1994. Volcanic-gas studies: methods, results, and applications. *In:* CARROLL, M. R. & HOLLOWAY, J. R. (eds) *Volatiles in Magmas*. Reviews in Mineralogy, **30**, 1–66. Mineralogical Society of America, Washington D.C.

THORDARSON, T., SELF, S., OSKARSSON, N. & HULSEBOSCH, T. 1996. Sulfur, chlorine and fluorine degassing and atmospheric loading by the 1783–1784 AD Laki (Skaftàr Fires) eruption in Iceland. *Bulletin of Volcanology*, **58**, 205–255.

THORNTON, D. C., BANDY, A. R., BLOMQUIST, B. W., DRIEDGER, A. R. & WADE, T. P. 1999. Sulfur dioxide distribution over the Pacific Ocean 1991–1996. *Journal of Geophysical Research*, **105**, 5845–5854.

VAN BREEMEN, N., DRISCOLL, C. T. & MULDER, J. 1984. Acidic deposition and internal proton sources in acidification of soils and waters. *Nature*, **307**, 599–604.

VAREKAMP, J. C., THOMAS, E., GERMANI, M. & BUSECK, P. R. 1986. Particle geochemistry of volcanic plumes of Etna and Mount St. Helens. *Journal of Geophysical Research*, **91**, 12 233–12 248.

VARRICA, D., AIUPPA, A. & DONGARRÀ, G. 2000. Volcanic and anthropogenic contribution to heavy metal content in lichens from Mt. Etna and Vulcano island (Sicily). *Environmental Pollution*, **108**, 153–162.

VIÉ LE SAGE, R. 1983. Chemistry of the volcanic aerosol. *In:* TAZIEFF, H. & SABROUX, J.-C. (eds) *Forecasting Volcanic Events*, Elsevier, Amsterdam, 445–474.

WATSON, I. M. & OPPENHEIMER, C. 2000. Particle size distributions of Mt. Etna's aerosol plume constrained by sun photometry. *Journal of Geophysical Research*, **105**, 9823–9829.

WATSON, I. M. & OPPENHEIMER, C. 2001. Photometric observations of Mt. Etna's different aerosol plumes. *Atmospheric Environment*, **35**, 3561–3572.

WEINSTEIN, L. H. & MCCUNE, D. C. 1979. Air pollution stress. *In:* MUSSEL, H. & STAPLES, R. (eds) *Stress Physiology in Crop Plants*, Wiley, New York, 328–341.

WESELY, M. L. & HICKS, B. B. 2000. A review of the current status of knowledge on dry deposition. *Atmospheric Environment*, **34**, 2261–2282.

WILLIAMS-JONES, G. 2001. *Integrated Geophysical Studies at Masaya volcano, Nicaragua*. PhD Thesis, Open University.

WINNER, W. E. & MOONEY, H. A. 1980. Responses of Hawaiian plants to volcanic sulfur dioxide: stomatal behavior and foliar injury. *Science*, **210**, 789–791.

ZETTWOG, P. & HAULET, R. 1978. Experimental results on the SO_2 transfer in the Mediterranean obtained with remote sensing devices. *Atmospheric Environment*, **12**, 795–796.

ZREDA-GOSTYNSKA G., KYLE, P. R., FINNEGAN, D. & MEEKER PRESTBO, K. 1997. Volcanic gas emissions from Mount Erebus and their impact on the Antarctic environment. *Journal of Geophysical Research*, **102**, 15 039–15 055.

Illness and elevated human mortality in Europe coincident with the Laki Fissure eruption

J. GRATTAN[1], M. DURAND[2] & S. TAYLOR[1]

[1]Institute of Geography and Earth Sciences, University of Wales Aberystwyth, Ceredigion SY23 3DB, UK.
[2]Natural Hazards Research Centre, Department of Geological Sciences, University of Canterbury, Private Bag 4800, Christchurch, New Zealand.

Abstract: Volcanic eruptions represent a significant source of volatile gases that are harmful to human health. This chapter reviews and develops current understanding of the human health response to volcanogenic pollution and dry fog events; in particular it explores the health impact of the gases from the Laki fissure eruption, and presents data that point to a significant increase in the national death rate in England coincident with the early phases of the eruption. It is noted that many common symptoms of severe exposure to air pollution can be linked to the dry fog of 1783; these included difficulty in breathing, eye and skin irritation, headaches, loss of appetite and tiredness.

Such multitudes are indisposed by fevers in this country, that farmers have with difficulty gathered in their harvest, the labourers having been almost every day carried out of the field incapable of work and many die.

(Cowper Letters, 1783)

Introduction

The Laki fissure eruption is notorious for its devastating impact upon the ecology of Iceland and the death of c.25% of the island's human population in the eruption's aftermath, the result of induced illness, subsequent environmental stress and famine (Thórarinsson 1979, 1981; Steingrimsson, 1998). The eruption has been the subject of extensive research, not only for its atmospheric effects but also because investigations of 18th-century written sources now confirm that profound health and environmental impacts occurred throughout Europe and beyond (Grattan & Charman 1994; Grattan & Pyatt 1994, 1999; Grattan & Brayshay 1995; Stothers 1996; Demarée et al. 1998; Jacoby et al. 1999; Durand & Grattan 1999; Grattan 1998; Grattan et al. 1998; Brayshay & Grattan 1999; Dodgshon et al. 2000; Durand 2000; Thordarson & Self 2001).

As a recent historical event it is possible to study the impact of the eruption across a wide range of human activity by tracing the written records left by contemporary observers during the eruption period and through detailed summaries written in the years immediately following. Other documentary sources, such as parish burial records, where available, may also yield valuable information. This chapter explores the material evidence for the impact of the 1783 dry fog upon human health and mortality, and suggests that certain features of English death rates during the year point to an episode of crisis mortality, where mortality was greater than 10% in excess of the moving 51-year mean (Wrigley & Schofield 1989). This chapter discusses the intriguing possibility that in England the environmental forcing associated with the eruption may have lead to a marked increase in the death rate in the summer of 1783.

Air pollution and volcanic eruptions

The scale of the air pollution generated by the Laki fissure eruption in terms of geographical extent and duration dwarfs any reported natural or anthropogenic event, including the recent smogs generated by the burning of the Indonesian rainforests and peats (Khandekar et al. 2000). It is now widely accepted that volcanic eruptions may affect distant environments via a number of mechanisms. In addition to climate cooling, which has been the focus of much research, recent work has investigated the association of volcanic gases with high surface air temperatures (Wood 1984, 1992; Grattan & Sadler 1999, 2001)

From: OPPENHEIMER, C., PYLE, D.M. & BARCLAY, J. (eds) Volcanic Degassing. Geological Society, London, Special Publications, 213, 401–414. 0305–8719/03/$15.00

and large-scale air-pollution events or dry fogs (Grattan & Charman 1994; Grattan & Brayshay 1995; Jacoby *et al.* 1999; Thordarson 1995; Demarée *et al.* 1998; Grattan 1998; Grattan *et al.* 1998). Many of the gases emitted by volcanoes are similar to those emitted from anthropogenic sources, and the toxicological and epidemiological properties of the latter have been widely studied (Wellburn 1994; Pope *et al.* 1995). Physiological and chemical evidence substantiates the importance of SO_2, H_2SO_4, H_2S, HCl, HF, NH_3 and sub-PM_{10} particles as toxic air pollutants, most of which are commonly emitted during volcanic activity.

Research into the impacts of volcanic gas upon human health and the environment has typically focused upon populations and environments relatively close to the volcano. Symptoms of moderate exposure of this type include skin, eye, and digestive irritation and respiratory problems, while fluorosis, bone damage, coma and even death are among the more severe problems that may be encountered in relative proximity to the volcanic vent (Thórarinsson 1979; Baxter *et al.* 1982, 1990; Hickling *et al.* 1999; Allen *et al.* 2000; Delmelle *et al.* 2001). High gas concentrations and pollution-related illnesses and fatalities have been noted at considerable distances downwind from active volcanoes following atmospheric transport of a volcanic plume. In many of the known cases of volcanogenic air-pollution, damage to vegetation and human physiological responses to the pollution have occurred (Thórarinsson 1979, 1981; Baxter *et al.* 1982). A notable modern example of this is in the region of Masaya volcano, Nicaragua. During the peak in its *c.*25-year activity cycle, Masaya emits up to 1300 t/day SO_2, 400 t/day HCl and 5 t/day HF (Baxter *et al.* 1982). Baxter *et al.* (1982) suggested that people exposed to the plume downwind from the volcano could regularly be exposed to SO_2 at concentrations above 1 ppm, or 20 times the World Health Organisation 24-h exposure limit of 100–150 µg/m³. Durand (2000) modelled the trajectory of the Stromboli volcanic plume around the Mediterranean and demonstrated that it may maintain its integrity over trajectories of considerable distances, to cities in Italy, Greece and North Africa, where it may contribute to ongoing anthropogenic air-pollution problems.

Air pollution and mortality

The concept that severe anthropogenic air pollution may cause respiratory illness and/or the death of vulnerable sections of the population is familiar in modern societies. Studies which have analysed mortality data from famous air-pollution events, such as that in London in 1952 (Wilkins 1954), the Meuse Valley in Belgium in 1930 (Firket 1936) and Donora, Pennsylvania, USA, in 1948 (Shrenk *et al.* 1949), have suggested that concentrations of SO_2 and levels of acidity were the primary cause of excess mortality. Subsequently, a large number of studies have reported statistical associations between air pollution and excess mortality (Mazumdar *et al.* 1982; Ostro 1984, 1993; Lippmann 1989; Fairly 1990; Schwartz & Marcus 1990; Ostro *et al.* 1991, 1993; Schwartz 1991; Dockery *et al.* 1992; Pope *et al.* 1992, 1995; Ito *et al.* 1993, Pope & Kanner 1993). There are no compelling reasons to propose that volcanogenic air pollution, of sufficient concentration, may not have a similar impact on human health to anthropogenic air pollution, and Stothers (1999, 2000) has already pointed to a clear relationship between significant volcanic eruptions, dry fogs and pandemics of considerable magnitude.

The pollution impacts of the Laki fissure eruption

Stothers (1996) suggested the total mass of aerosols produced by the erupted gases may have approached 200 Mt, while Thordarson and Self (2001) estimated that during June–July 1783 up to 6 Mt of acid aerosol was added to the European air mass each day, and that the concentration of the sulphuric acid aerosol in the boundary layer of the atmosphere may have exceeded several tens of mg/L; concentrations which are easily capable of causing a severe physiological reaction.

Eruption dynamics

The dynamics of the Laki fissure eruption are covered in great detail in a series of research papers (cf. Thordarson & Self 1993; Thordarson *et al.* 1995) and are only covered very generally here. In brief, the fissure eruption took place between June 1783 and February 1784 and emitted approximately 120 Mt SO_2, 6.8 Mt HCl and 15.1 Mt HF plus H_2S and NH_3, with peak emissions during June and July 1783, with the majority of emissions confined to the troposphere (Thordarson & Self 1993, 2001; Thordarson *et al.* 1996; Sparks *et al.* 1997).

Meteorology

A series of high-pressure air masses were positioned over northwest Europe throughout the summer of 1783 (Kington 1988). Several researchers (Grattan & Brayshay 1995; Thordarson & Self 2001) have proposed simple atmospheric circulation models which could account for the transport of significant quantities of volcanogenic volatiles from Iceland to the boundary layer of the atmosphere over the British Isles and Europe. This meteorological situation resulted in the concentration of eruptive gases, which were manifested as a persistent, foul-smelling dry fog, which was reported across Europe (Grattan & Pyatt 1994; Stothers 1996).

The presence of stable air masses in the European summer is usually associated with fine weather and high surface temperatures, and the summer of 1783 was no exception. What was exceptional about the summer of 1783 were the temperatures reached. The July of 1783 was one of the hottest ever recorded in Europe; while in England, with a mean daily temperature of

18.8°C, it was the hottest month recorded in Manley's (1974) 'Central England Temperature Record'. It has been suggested that these high temperatures were caused by the adsorption and retention of thermal energy by the dry fog (Grattan & Sadler 1999, 2001), which is in striking contrast to the emphasis given to climatic cooling in much other research.

Pollution damage to vegetation

Irrefutable evidence of the toxic nature of the dry fog beyond Iceland may be drawn from the numerous descriptions of acid damage to crops, trees and other plants which may be found in Britain, Norway, Sweden, The Netherlands, France, Germany and Italy (Table 1). Collectively, the available data suggest that on occasions the pH of the dry fog frequently fell below pH 2, and that as well as sulphur it contained

Table 1. *Summary of documentary accounts of acid damage to vegetation in 1783.*

Location	Observed weather	Summary of symptoms of damage	Source
England	'Uncommon gloom', smoky fog	Cereal crops: yellowed Barley: withered awns Oats: withered Rye: mildewed in appearance Beans: whitened & dying Pasture: dried Trees: shedding leaves and appear scorched as if by fire	Cullum (Grattan & Charman 1994) *Ipswich Journal*, 12 July 1783 *Cambridge Chronicle and Journal*, 5 July 1783 *Sherbourne Mercury*, 14 July 1783
France	Sulphurous dry fog	Vine flowers: burned Olives: fruit burned and falling Peas: badly damaged Marrows: badly damaged Melons: badly damaged Tree leaves: damaged Damaged the corn, which yielded hardly any crop	Rabartin & Rocher (1993)
Italy	Dry fog	Damaged wheat, empty ears, dried ears.	Camuffo & Enzi (1995)
Netherlands	Persistent 'strong' fog with a sulphurous smell.	Leaves of bean and pear trees 'affected' 'Changes to plants' Bleached leaves. Leaf and fruit fall Drying and bleaching of leaves, some developing spots Leaf fall	Swinden (1786, 2001) Brugmans (1787)
Norway	Smoky fog, 'Acrid rain'	Withered vegetation. Tree leaves 'partly burnt' Grass blackened	Thórarinsson (1981)
Sweden	Smoky fog	Crops destroyed; very poor harvest	Thórarinsson (1981)

fluorine, of which 8 Mt are thought to have been released to the atmosphere during the eruption (Thordarson *et al.* 1996).

Human illness in the summer of 1783

Accounts from England, France, Italy and Scandinavia confidently associate the dry fog, associated meteorology and other environmental changes with a variety of illnesses and even death. Contemporary descriptions of human ill-health in 1783 are remarkably consistent, and link the dry fog, or a strong sulphurous stench, with headaches, eye irritation, decreased lung function, and asthma, which are consistent with the expected health impacts of the suite of gases emitted. The health symptoms described point to considerable concentrations of volcanic gases and derived aerosols (Table 2). Modern research outlined above suggests that the health risk presented by volcanic air pollutants and sustained dry fogs may be significant.

The currently available literature describing the human health impacts of the 1783 dry fog have been reviewed in comprehensive detail elsewhere (cf. Durand & Grattan 1999; Thordarson & Self 2001, and references therein) and are summarized in Table 2. For an accessible translation of one of the most detailed eyewitness accounts of the impact of the dry fog in The Netherlands, the reader is referred to a recently published translation (Swinden 2001). However, a flavour of the times can be gained from the following passage, also written in The Netherlands:

After the 24th (of June), many people in the open air experienced an uncomfortable pressure, headaches and experienced a difficulty breathing exactly like that encountered when the air is full of burning sulphur ... asthmatics suffered to an even greater degree. (Brugmans 1787)

Where the symptoms of illness described are clear rather than general, it is possible to propose air pollution as a potential cause (Table 2). In particular, within the available data it is clear that respiratory problems were commonly associated with the dry fog, a physiological response that is typical of modern air-pollution incidents, particularly where SO_2 is present at concentrations greater than 570 μgm^3 (Dassen *et al.* 1986; Brunekreef *et al.* 1991; Dockery *et al.* 1992; Wellburn 1994; Beverland 1998).

In addition to the respiratory and cardiovascular health impacts associated with the volcanic gases, which are reported in the summer of 1783, it is necessary to consider other potential sources of illness associated with another major environmental factor present in the summer of 1783, the record high daily temperatures. Commentaries frequently discuss the distress felt by many at the 'intolerable heat'. One might reasonably suppose that the heat could have had an effect on water quality and thus enteric sickness, but as yet the specific symptoms described point to illness induced by air pollution rather than illness caused by bacteria and viruses. General comments, however, do make reference to fevers, epidemics and mortality of

Table 2. *Summary of human symptoms and possible causes in 1783. Suggestions for possible gases and their ambient concentrations required to induce the symptoms, as inferred from the historical literature, are given.*

Condition reported in the original literature	Gas	Exposure required	Possible explanation
'Disagreeable' symptoms and 'sensations' in chests	SO_2 SO_2	>80 $\mu g/m^3$ >572 $\mu g/m^3$	Bronchitis worsened Asthma worsened
'Pestilence' and 'tingling' of the throat	SO_2		Bronchitis induced (especially in those predisposed to asthma)
Headache	H_2S F (p)	<10 ppm	Headaches induced
'Tingling' and 'tired' eyes	H_2S SO_2	14.2–28.4 $\mu g/m^3$ 28.4–70.9 $\mu g/m^3$ 70.9 $\mu g/m^3$ 800 $\mu g/m^3$	Eye irritation threshold Severe eye irritation and impairment Eye damage Eye irritation occurs (concentration required is lower if other irritants or particulates are involved)
Loss of appetite	H_2S	<10 ppm	

Dosimetry data are from Wellburn (1994) and Beverland (1998).

which the following, from England are typical:

Letters from various parts agree that the season is very unhealthy; the lower order of people in the country have felt its effects severely. A fever rages in many parts, which the people term the Black Fever.
(Gilpin 1763–1785).

The epidemic begins to be more mortal as the autumn comes on . . . and in Bedfordshire it is reported . . . to be nearly as fatal as the plague. . . . This light atmosphere and these unremitting storms are very unfriendly to an asthmatic habit.
(Cowper correspondence, 8 September 1783).

In addition to illnesses, contemporary observers were quick to associate the dry fog with unusual patterns of mortality, as noted below in France, Italy and England.

A phenomenon of prolonged and very dense fog, which completely hid the sun, and at night made the moon appear reddish and murky. This fog caused, moreover, many illnesses and putrid and acute fevers, so that many people died.
(Fajonio, cited in Camuffo & Enzi 1995)

The fogs have been followed by great storms and sicknesses which have driven a third of the men in many parishes to their tombs.
(The Curé of Landelles, cited in Rabartin & Rocher 1993)

While the sun was obscured there was a sickness, which caused innumerable deaths'.
(The Curé of Broué, cited in Rabartin & Rocher 1993)

Such multitudes are indisposed by fevers in this country, that farmers have with difficulty gathered in their harvest, the labourers having been almost every day carried out of the field incapable of work and many die.
(Cowper correspondence, 7 September 1783)

The available qualitative data all point to human illness and mortality in the summer of 1783, phenomena that were clearly associated in the minds of the observers with the state of the atmosphere; below some quantitative data for this period are explored.

English mortality trends in 1783–1784

Methodology

English mortality trends at the national level have been explored by consulting the data published in the 'Population History of England' (Wrigley & Schofield 1989). At the level of individual parishes the 'Population History of England Database' (Schofield 1998) has been used; the quality of these data has been comprehensively verified. Mortality indices have been calculated for these data, following the procedures laid down in Dobson (1987, 1997).

Annual trends

In studies of the population history of England (Dobson 1987, 1997; Wrigley & Schofield 1989) the period July 1783 – June 1784 is recognized as containing a one-star mortality crisis, indicating an annual mortality rate 10–20% above the 51-year moving mean; which qualitatively describes the state of the nation's health in the period as 'unhealthy'. In fact the national death rate for 1783–1784 has been calculated to have been 16.7% above the projected trend for this period. In a world where clean water, sanitation and food hygiene were rarely prioritized, and where epidemic disease was common and infectious disease rife, mortality crises were not unusual. Twenty-two three- and two-star mortality crises (mortality that was 20–30% greater than the National Crude Death Rate; cf. Dobson 1997, p. 383) are listed by Wrigley and Schofield (1989), for the period 1541–1870; all of these were nationally more severe than the mortality evident in the annual death rate for 1783–1784. This period, therefore, while an acknowledged mortality crisis, is only one of many apparent in the annual national statistics. However, considering these data at a national level and in annual trends obscures the severity of the mortality experienced in different parishes across the country at this time, and its unusual seasonal pattern.

Seasonality of mortality

Even death has its season – in historical times, in the absence of epidemics, burials normally fell into predictable patterns, which reflect the periods of maximum environmental stress in any region or country. In European historical datasets, in the absence of a forcing factor such as disease, peak mortality usually occurs in March–April, with a trough expected in the summer and early autumn, given better weather and an adequate harvest (Wrigley & Schofield 1989). The national crisis apparent in the annual burial rates for 1783–1784 in England, is largely generated by an unusually high number of burials in the summer (July–September) of 1783. Using the 'Population History of England Database' (Schofield 1998) the anomalous nature of the deaths in the summer of 1783 can be explored. Dobson (1987) proposed the calculation of mortality indices (recorded burials divided by the 51-year moving average and multiplied by 100). The resulting indices are then classified as follows: 200–140 = crisis mortality, 140–120 = high mortality, 120–110 = unhealthy, 110–90 = average, 90–80 = healthy. In Figure 2 these indices have been calculated for the last thirty years of the 18th century. The summer burial rate in 1783 was the highest recorded in the entire 18th century, slightly higher than the burial rate recorded in the summer of 1728, when there was a national epidemic of typhus and smallpox (Figure 1). In 1783 the July–September burials totalled 56 089, as against a truncated 51-year mean of 33 159, and the mortality index assigned to the summer of 1783 is 169 (Table 3), which is indicative of crisis mortality at this time. However, while the mortality crises of the late 1720s are associated with recorded epidemics, the crisis of 1783 remains unexplained in population histories. The burial rate recorded in the summer of 1783 is clearly defined as a crisis, and falls into the highest category of event.

Monthly mortality

Cowper (cited above) suggested that the 'epidemic' worsened as the summer progressed, and

this trend is indeed apparent in the national data (Table 3). July deaths were near normal, and mortality for the month can be classified as entirely average. The summer crisis is mainly the result of the burials that occurred in August and September, with the crisis clearly worsening into September, which is assigned a mortality index of 158, placing it in the highest category of event (Table 3). These monthly data confirm that a severe crisis did occur in the summer of 1783. The calculated means for the summer months are very similar, and death rates through this period were usually low and stable, but this is clearly not the case in 1783, when it is reasonable to assume that an environmental forcing mechanism or disease vector must have been present; the environmental stresses introduced by the Laki fissure may be considered to be a plausible candidate for this event, indeed this is currently the only identified extraneous feature of this period.

Local mortality crises

The data discussed above may be refined further. As discussed in Appendix 10 of 'The Population History of England' (Wrigley & Schofield 1989), the data which point to national trends may in fact be generated by modest increases across the entire country or by a severe fluctuation in a limited number of parishes, the latter being defined as a 'local mortality crisis'. Crisis mortality in just 13.1% of the parishes in the 'Population History of England Database' generated the national and seasonal increase noted

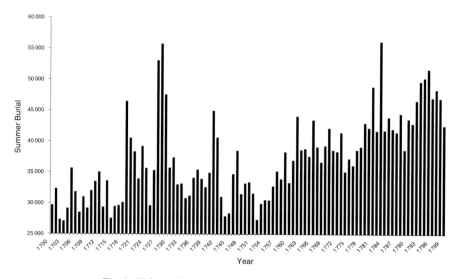

Fig. 1. Eighteenth century English summer burial record.

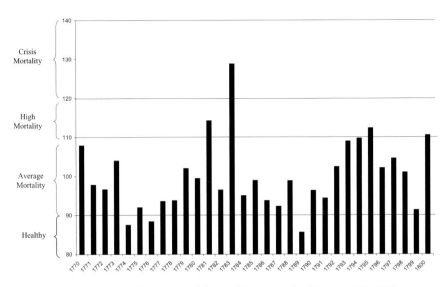

Fig. 2. Mortality indices calculated for English summer burial rates, 1770–1800.

Table 3. *Summary of national mortality statistics, 1783*

	July–Sept	July	August	September
Total deaths	56 089	15 000	18 338	22 751
Truncated 51-year mean	33 159	14 747	14 429	14 372
Mortality index	169	101	127	158
Mortality classification	Crisis	Average	Unhealthy	Crisis

above (Wrigley & Schofield 1989, pp. 645–694), and the pattern of mortality evident at this time typifies a local mortality crisis. How was this event manifested in the affected parishes? To interrogate the parish mortality data (Schofield 1998), seasonal totals have been calculated by summing the burial figures for each parish for the months July–September. As is typical of local mortality crises, the affected parishes are quite dispersed, with the clearest regional concentrations found in Bedfordshire and East Anglia, while parishes in Gloucestershire, Lincolnshire, and Leicestershire also feature prominently. Ten parishes have been chosen at random from those affected and are presented here (Figs 3a & b). All ten display the unusual mortality pattern typical of those affected in the summer of 1783: excess deaths in the summer months, which are commonly three or more standard deviations from the 1770–1795 mean. In each parish illustrated, it can be seen that the mortality figures for the summer of 1783 are anomalous when com-

pared with the trends over a twenty-five year period, but the data are nonetheless strikingly similar in respect of the deaths, which occurred in 1783.

In a letter written on 8 September 1783, in the midst of this crisis, Cowper specifically commented on the news of the mortality in Bedfordshire, where it was reported to be 'nearly as fatal as the plague'. The population history database (Schofield 1998), contains records for 28 Bedfordshire parishes; of these, thirteen experienced crisis mortality in the summer of 1783 (Table 4). The reality in people's lives behind the data presented in Table 4, and the anxiety that these unseasonable deaths must have generated, readily explains Cowper's comments.

Summary

Taken together, this consideration of mortality data at the national, annual, seasonal, monthly, regional, and parish levels all point to the

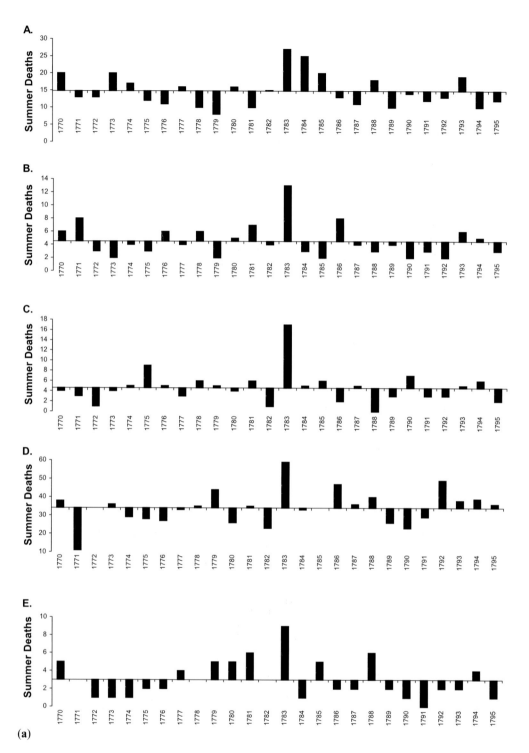

Fig. 3 (a) Summer mortality, 1770–1795. A, Minchinhampton, Gloucestershire; B, Wye, Kent; C, Great Grimsby, Lincolnshire; D, Edmonton, Middlesex.; E, Blunham, Bedfordshire.

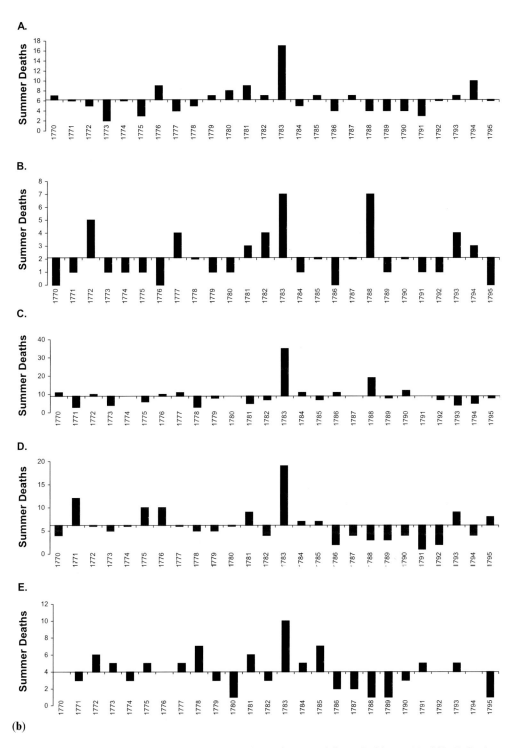

(b)

Fig. 3. (continued) (**b**) Summer mortality, 1770–1795. A, Banham, Norfolk; B, Sculthorpe, Norfolk; C, Castle Donington, Leicestershire; D, Cavendish, Suffolk, E, Fressingfield, Suffolk.

Table 4. *Summer 1783 mortality characteristics for twelve Bedfordshire parishes.*

	Ampthill	Blunham	Clophill	Cranfield	Flitwick	Kempston	Maulden
Total deaths	11	9	8	23	5	12	17
Truncated 51-year mean	5	3	3.6	6	1.5	5.4	5
Mortality Index	217	310	220	365	327	220	354
Mortality classification	Crisis	Crisis	Crisis	Crisis	Crisis	Crisis	Crisis

	Millbrook	Northill	Pavenham	Sandy	Studham	Wooton
Total deaths	8	6	10	15	6	6
Truncated 51-year mean	2	3	2	6.5	2	3
Mortality Index	400	190	467	228	286	190
Mortality classification	Crisis	Crisis	Crisis	Crisis	Crisis	Crisis

occurrence of a mortality crisis, which appears more acute as the focus of analysis is refined. Most other mortality events of this type in the population histories are associated with an environmental factor that may account for the anomalous burial rates. Current knowledge identifies the Laki fissure eruption as the major environmental forcing mechanism at this time. The association of these events will be discussed below.

Discussion

The events of the summer of 1783 appear to fall into a growing body of modern work which points to a clear link between air pollution, the ambient environment and mortality. Elsewhere in Europe, data-sets have not yet been collated so extensively. However, Wrigley and Schofield (1989) noted that while mortality crises in one European country were rarely shared by others, the period 1783–1784 is notable for mortality crises in northern Holland and Brabant. Sutherland (1981) has also noted a distinct mortality crisis in Brittany over the same period and Rabartin (pers. comm.) has suggested that the regions of Eure and Loire in central France appear to exhibit a similar pattern of crisis mortality.

Regardless of the cause of this phenomenon, the data presented above illustrate the serious nature of the mortality events occurring in widely separated areas of England, and perhaps elsewhere, in the summer of 1783, and deepen current understanding of a mortality event which has previously only been visible in annual data-sets and regional studies (Wrigley & Schofield 1989; Dobson 1997). The severity of the summer mortality, and the fact that anoma-

lous mortality in a relatively small number of parishes was large enough to influence the national trends, implicates an external forcing factor. The burial rate in the summer of 1783 was higher than the mortality reported during the typhoid and smallpox epidemics of the late 1720s, and it is reasonable to propose that the mechanism responsible for the death rates reported at this time must have been at least as severe. The Laki fissure eruption had a profound impact upon the English and European environment. It generated air pollution on a continental scale, of sufficient concentration to blight many areas of the countryside (Table 1), and induced a range of illnesses that we might expect to see during any modern air-pollution incident (Table 2). In addition to these direct impacts, the gases and aerosols quite probably are responsible for generating some of the hottest weather recorded in England (Manley 1974; Grattan & Sadler 1999), and this may have led to the contamination of vulnerable water supplies.

The degree of the physiological reaction to an environmental stress depends upon an individual's sensitivity and the prevalent micrometeorological conditions, in addition to the strength and duration of exposure. Sensitivity can also be affected by natural physiological differences, including age and sex, as well as socio-economic and life-style factors, in addition to the influence of pre-existing ailments (Goldberg, 1996). Modern studies of anthropogenic air-pollution incidents in and around major cities suggest that in addition to respiratory disorders, similar to those described above, death rates may rise as vulnerable groups are affected by severe air pollution. Elsom (1993) listed five features that are characteristic of a severe air-pollution incident: (1) damage to vegetation, (2) damage to animals, (3) damage to metals and painted surfaces, (4) damage to buildings, (5) weather changes, including reduced visibility and temperature increases. Observers of the dry fog and its impact noted all of these, on the European mainland and Britain in the summer of 1783. Where these factors are present, human illness is normally expected. The health effects of pollutants at the concentrations typical of severe air pollution are necessarily conditioned by the physiological conditions of individuals, but it is expected that a proportion of the individuals in an exposed population will be intolerant of the extra physiological stress and may die (Shy & Finklea 1979). In the context of the environmental variables which may have been present in 1783, high concentrations of sulphur dioxide and high surface air temperatures, it is interesting to note in particular the work of Katsouyanni et al. (1993). This study, based on deaths reported in Athens over seven years, noted that while any impact of air pollution alone was not statistically significant, high indices of air pollution in combination with high temperatures were associated with an extra 40 deaths a day in Athens, a relationship which was significant at the $p < 0.5$ significance level. A synergistic relationship between the two variables was proposed, in particular that the high temperatures induced physiological stress, which in turn lowered the thresholds at which the health impacts of air pollution became notable. Touloumi et al. (1994) also noted a clear relationship between air pollution and mortality in Athens. Lippmann and Thurston (1996) established positive regression coefficients for health and morbidity with sulphate, and fine suspended particulate material ($PM_{2.5}$–PM_{10}). These observations were broadly confirmed by Vigotti et al. (1996), who studied deaths and hospital admissions in conjunction with sulphur dioxide and total suspended particulates in Milan, Italy, in the period 1980 1989. Wichmann and Heinrich (1995) also reported increased mortality and the reported incidence of bronchial illness in association with high concentrations of sulphur dioxide in East Germany; again the similarity with the experience of Europe in 1783 is obvious. The critical factors reported in all these studies, several species of sulphur, suspended particulate material and high air temperatures are all present in the summer of 1783, and it is therefore reasonable to propose that the localized episodes of crisis mortality noted in this period may be also associated with these environmental factors.

It is clear therefore that in many respects the events of the summer of 1783 conform to the patterns established by the study of modern events of shorter duration. These are important factors to consider when the distribution of anomalous mortality in 18th-century England is considered. It is clear from the literature that the intensity of the aerosol impact varied considerably and was dependent on micro-meteorological and topographic features (Grattan & Charman 1994).

If it is accepted, as seems likely from modern air-pollution analogues, that all the anomalous environmental phenomena observed in the summer of 1783 are linked to the emission of gases from the Laki fissure eruption, then a plausible hypothesis can be constructed. Concentrations of SO_2 within the dry fog passed critical thresholds for human health on many occasions, and were clearly responsible for severe respiratory dysfunction in many people and concentrations of SO_2 may therefore have reached 1000 mg/m³ for long periods of time. However, pre-existing health conditions may be worsened at much lower gas concentrations. Although based on inferences drawn from qualitative data, it can be stated with some confidence that the 1783 dry fog, of several weeks' duration, approached the concentrations of the 1952 London smog (which killed 4000 people), and exceeded the concentrations reached in other notorious air-pollution events such as the Ruhr smog of 1987 (Elsom 1993). Gilpin and Cowper both commented on the distress of agricultural labourers working in the fields, and it has been noted that increased physical activity, which leads to a greater ventilation rate, may increase the exposure of individuals to pollutants in the air (Lawther et al. 1975). The high air temperatures may also have intensified the physiological impacts of the pollutants present in the dry fog (Matzarakis & Mayer 1991; Katsouyanni, et al. 1993; Mackenbach et al. 1993).

It is clear that in many respects the events of 1783 are typical of modern severe air-pollution events, and, in addition, all the contemporary accounts of illness reported in the summer months of 1783 point to air pollution. However, uncertainty does surround the time lag in the data. Modern events impact upon mortality very quickly, whereas in 1783 the excess deaths occurred over a much longer period. It may be that in modern events the precursor conditions are worse and human sensitivity greater than in 1783, but this will necessarily be the focus of further research. However, our current knowledge of the environmental processes active at this time and the abundant qualitative and quantitative data available suggest that acid volcanic gases were the key agent in the events of 1783.

Conclusion

A persistent and intense concentration of
volcanic gases from Laki in the atmosphere of
the British Isles and Europe during the summer
of 1783 has been demonstrated by considerable
scholarship, and is no longer in doubt. Direct
environmental forcing is clearly apparent in two
areas: firstly the numerous descriptions of acid
gases and aerosols and their impact upon plants
and upon human health, and secondly the
extremely high surface air temperatures recorded
(Thórarinsson 1979, 1981; Grattan & Charman,
1994; Camuffo & Enzi 1995; Thordarson *et al.*
1996; Stothers 1996; Grattan *et al.* 1998; Durand
& Grattan 1999; Durand 2000, Swinden 2001).
Contemporary writers were quite clear in their
association of all these factors: the sulphurous
dry fog, the high temperatures, the damaged
vegetation, human sickness and death. Many
writers also commented on the distress caused by
the extreme heat. All of these factors have been
observed to operate synergistically in modern
air-pollution events, and there are no compelling
reasons why this may not have happened during
the continental-scale events of 1783 (Mayer
1990; Matzarakis & Mayer 1991).

This chapter has demonstrated that a notable
mortality crisis had coincided with a major volcanic
eruption, and established that reasonable grounds
exist to associate the two events with some
confidence. In many areas of the world, air
pollution is a serious problem – one need only
consider the proximity of many rapidly growing
cities and volcanic centres to conclude that,
regardless of the events of 1783, volcanic gases
will inevitably wield a profound influence upon
human health in the future (Durand & Grattan,
2001).

References

ALLEN, A. G., BAXTER, P. J. & OTTLEY C. J. 2000. Gas and particle emissions from Soufriere Hills Volcano, Montserrat, West Indies: characterisation and health hazard assessment. *Bulletin of Volcanology*, **62**, 8–19

BAXTER, P. J., STOIBER, R. E. & WILLIAMS, S. N. 1982. Volcanic gases and health: Masaya volcano, Nicaragua. *The Lancet*, **July 17**, 150–151.

BAXTER, P. J.,& TEDESCO, D, MIELE, G., BOUBRON, J. C. & CLIFF, K. 1990. Health Hazards from volcanic gases. *The Lancet*, **July 21**, 176.

BEVERLAND, I. J. 1998. Urban air pollution and health. *In*: J. Rose (ed.) *Environmental Toxicology: Current Developments*. Gordon and Breach, London. 189–209.

BRAYSHAY, M. & GRATTAN. J. P. 1999. Environmental and social responses in Europe to the 1783 eruption of the Laki Fissure volcano in Iceland: a consideration of contemporary documentary evidence: *Geological Society, London, Special Publications*, **161**, 173–188.

BRUGMANS, S. J. 1787. *Naturkundige Verhandeling Over een Zwavelatigen, Nevel den 24 Juni 1783 Inde Provincie van Stad en Lande en Naburige Landen Waargenomen*. Isaac van Campen, Leyden.

BRUNEKREEF, B., KINNEY, P. L., WARE, J. H., DOCKERY, D., SPEIZER, F. E., SPENGLER, J. D. & FERRIS, B. G. 1991. Sensitive subgroups and normal variation in pulmonary function response to air pollution episodes. *Environmental Health Perspectives*, **90**, 189–193.

CAMUFFO, D. & ENZI, S. 1995. Impact of clouds of volcanic aerosols in Italy during the last seven centuries: *Natural Hazards*, **11(2)**, 135–161.

COWPER, W. 1981 (1783) *In:* King, J. & Ryskamp, C. (eds). 1981. *The letters and prose writings of William Cowper* (Vol. 2). Clarendon Press, Oxford.

DASSEN, W., BRUNKREEF, B. *ET AL.* 1986. Decline in children's pulmonary function during air pollution episodes. *Journal of the Air Pollution Control Association*, **36**, 1223–1227.

DELMELLE, P., STIX, J., BOURQUE, C. P.–A., BAXTER, P. J., GARCIA-ALVAREZ, J. & BARQUERO, J. 2001. Dry deposition and heavy acid loading in the vicinity of Masaya Volcano, a major sulphur and chlorine source in Nicaragua. *Environmental Science and Technology*, **35**, 1289–1293

DEMARÉE, G., OGILVIE, A. E. J. & ZHANG, D. 1998. Further documentary evidence of northern hemispheric coverage of the Great Dry Fog of 1783: *Climatic Change*, **39**, 727–730.

DOBSON, M. J. 1980. Marsh fever: the geography of malaria in England. *Journal of Historical Geography*, **6**, 357–89.

DOBSON, M. J. 1987. A chronology of epidemic disease and mortality in southeast England: 1601–1800. *Historical Geography Research Series*, **19**, 4–101.

DOBSON, M. J. 1997. *Contours of Death and Disease in Early Modern England*. Cambridge University Press, Cambridge.

DOCKERY, D., SCHWARTZ, J. & SPENGLER, J. D. 1992. Air pollution and daily mortality: associations with particulates and acid aerosols. *Environmental Research*, **59**, 362–373.

DOCKERY, D., POPE, C. A. *ET AL.* 1993. An association between air pollution and mortality in six US cities. *New England Journal of Medicine*, **329**, 1753–1759.

DODGSHON, R., GRATTAN, J. P. & GILBERTSON, D. D. 2000. Endemic stress, farming communities and the influence of volcanic eruptions in the Scottish Highlands. *Geological Society, London, Special Publications*, **171**, 267–280.

DURAND, M. 2000. *Impact of volcanic activity upon the air quality and environment of Europe,* Unpublished PhD Thesis, University of Wales, Aberystwyth.

DURAND, M. & GRATTAN, J. P. 1999. Extensive respiratory health impacts of volcanogenic dry fog in 1783 inferred from European documentary sources: *Environmental Geochemistry and Health*, **21**, 371–376.

DURAND, M. & GRATTAN 2001. Volcanoes, air pollution and health. *The Lancet*, **357**, 164.

ELSOM, D. M. 1993. *Atmospheric Pollution*. Blackwell, London.

FAIRLY, D. 1990. The relationship of daily mortality to suspended particulates in Santa Clara Country, 1980–1986. *Environmental Health Perspectives*, **89**, 159–168.

FIRKET, M. 1936. Fog along the Meuse Valley. *Transactions of the Faraday Society*, **32**, 1192–1197.

GILPIN, W. Undated. An historical account of the weather during twenty years from 1763–1785. Bodleian MS, Eng. Misc. d. 564.

GOLDBERG, M. 1996. Particulate air pollution and daily mortality: Who is at risk? *Journal of Aerosol Medicine*, **9**, 43–53.

GRATTAN, J. P. 1998. The distal impact of volcanic gases and aerosols in Europe: a review of the 1783 Laki fissure eruption and environmental vulnerability in the late 20th century. *In:* MAUND, J. G. & EDDLESTON, M. *Geohazards in Engineering Geology*. Geological Society, London, Engineering Geology Special Papers, **15**, 97–103.

GRATTAN, J. P. & BRAYSHAY, M.B. 1995. An amazing and portentous summer: environmental and social responses in Britain to the 1783 eruption of an Iceland Volcano. *The Geographical Journal*, **161(2)**, 125–134.

GRATTAN, J. P. & CHARMAN, D. J. 1994. Non–climatic factors and the environmental impact of volcanic volatiles: implications of the Laki Fissure eruption of AD 1783. *The Holocene*, **4(1)**, 101–106.

GRATTAN, J. P. & PYATT, F. B. 1994. Acid damage in Europe caused by the Laki Fissure eruption – an historical review. *Science of the Total Environment*, **151**, 241–247.

GRATTAN, J. P. & PYATT, F. B. 1999. Volcanic eruptions, dust veils, dry fogs and the European palaeoenvironmental record. *Global and Planetary Change*, **21**, 173–179.

GRATTAN, J. P. & SADLER, J. 1999. Regional warming of the lower atmosphere in the wake of volcanic eruptions: the role of the Laki fissure eruption in the hot summer of 1783. *Geological Society, London, Special Publications*, **161**, 161–172.

GRATTAN, J. P. & SADLER, J. 2001. An exploration of the contribution of the Laki Fissure gases to the high summer air temperatures in Western Europe in 1783. *In:* JUVIGNÉ, E. & RAYNAL, J. P. (eds) *Tephras: Chronology and Archaeology*, 137–144.

GRATTAN, J. P., BRAYSHAY, M. B. & SADLER, J. P. 1998. Modelling the impacts of past volcanic gas emissions: evidence of Europe-wide environmental impacts from gases emitted in Italian and Icelandic volcanoes in 1783. *Quaternaire*, **9(1)**, 25–35.

HICKLING, J., CLEMENTS, M., WEINSTEIN, P. & WOODWARD, A. 1999. Acute health effects of the Mount Ruapehu (New Zealand) volcanic eruption of June 1996. *International Journal of Environmental Health Research*, **9**, 97–107.

ITO, K., THURSTON, G. D., HAYES, C. & LIPPMANN, M. 1993. Associations of London, England, daily mortality with particulate matter sulphur dioxide and acidic aerosol pollution. *Archives of Environmental Health*, **48**, 213–220.

JACOBY, G. C., WORKMAN, K. W. & D'ARRIGO, R. D. 1999. Laki eruption of 1783, tree rings and disaster for the northwest Alaska Inuit. *Quaternary Science Reviews*, **18**, 1365–1371.

KATSOUYANNI, K., PANTAZOPOULOU, A. *ET AL*. 1993. Evidence for interaction between air pollution and high temperature in the causation of excess mortality. *Archives of Environmental Health*, **48**, 235–242.

KHANDEKAR, M. L., MURTY, T. S., SCOT, D. & BAIRD, W. 2000. The 1997 El Niño, Indonesian forest fires and the Malaysian smoke problem: a deadly combination of natural and man-made hazard. *Natural Hazards*, **21**, 131–144.

KINGTON, J. A. 1988. *The Weather for the 1780s over Europe*. Cambridge, Cambridge University Press.

LAWTHER, P. J., MACFARLANE, A. J., WALLER, R. W. & BROOKS, A. G. F. 1975. Pulmonary function and sulfur dioxide: some preliminary findings. *Environmental Research*, **10**, 355–369.

LIPPMANN, M. 1989. Background on health effects of acid aerosols. *Environmental Health Perspectives*, **79**, 3–6.

LIPPMANN, M. & THURSTON, G. D. 1996. Sulfate concentrations as an indicator of ambient particulate matter air pollution for health risk evaluations. *Journal of Exposure Analysis and Environmental Epidemiology*, **6(2)**, 123–146.

MACKENBACH, J. P., LOOMAN, C. W. N. & KUNST, A. E. 1993. Air pollution, lagged effects of temperature, and mortality: the Netherlands 1979–87. *Journal of Epidemiology and Community Health*, **47**, 121–126.

MANLEY, G. 1974. Central England temperatures: monthly means 1659 to 1973. *Quarterly Journal of the Royal Meteorological Society*, **100**, 389–405.

MATZARAKIS, A. & MAYER, H. 1991. The extreme heat wave in Athens in July 1987 from the point of view of human biometeorology. *Atmospheric Environment*. **25**, 203–211.

MAZUMDAR, S., SHIMMELL, H & HIGGINS, I. T. T. 1982. Relation of daily mortality to air pollution: an analysis of London winters, 1958/59–1971/71. *Archives of Environmental Health*, **37**, 213–220.

OSTRO, B. 1984. A search for a threshold in the relationship of air pollution to mortality: a reanalysis of data on London winters. *Environmental Health Perspectives*, **58**, 397–399.

OSTRO, B. 1993. The association of air pollution and mortality: examining the case for inference. *Archives of Environmental Health*. **48**, 336–342.

OSTRO, B. & LIPSETT, M. J., WIENER, M. B. AND SELNER, J.C. 1991. Asthmatic response to air-borne acid aerosols. *American Journal of Public Health*, **81**, 694–702.

OSTRO, B., LIPSETT, M. J. & MANN, J. K., KRUPNICK, A. & HARRINGTON, W. 1993. Air pollution and respiratory morbidity among adults in Southern California: *American Journal of Epidemiology*, **137**, 691–700.

POPE, C. A., & KANNER, R. E. 1993. Acute effects of PM–10 pollution on pulmonary function of smokers with mild to moderate chronic obstructive pulmonary disease. *American Review of Respiratory Disorders*, **147**, 1336–1340.

POPE, C. A. & SCHWARTZ, J. & RANSOM, J. R. 1992.

Daily mortality and PM10 air pollution in Utah Valley. *Archives of Environmental Health*, **47**, 211–217.

POPE, C. A., DOCKERY, D. W. & SCHWARTZ, J. 1995. Review of the epidemiological evidence of health effects of air pollution. *Annual Review of Public Health*, **15**, 107–132.

RABARTIN, R. & ROCHER, P. 1993. *Les Volcans et la Révolution Française Paris*. L'Association Volcanologique Européene.

SCHOFIELD, R. 1998. Parish register aggregate analyses: the 'Population History of England' database. *Local Population Studies Supplement*.

SCHRENK, H. H., HEINMANN, H., CLAYTON, G. D., GAFAFER, W. M. & WEXLER, H. 1949. *Air Pollution in Donora, Pa. Epidemiology of the Unusual Smog Episode of October 1948. Public Health Bulletin*, **306**, Washington, DC. Public Health Service.

SCHWARTZ, J. 1991. Particulate air pollution and daily mortality in Detroit. *Environmental Research*, **56**, 204–13.

SCHWARTZ, J. & MARCUS, A. 1990. Mortality and air pollution in London: a time series analysis. *American Journal of Epidemiology*, **131**, 185–194.

SHY, C. M. & FINKLEA, J. F. 1979. Air pollution affects community health. *Environmental Science and Technology*, **7**, 204–208.

SPARKS, R. S. J., BURSIK, M. I., CAREY, S. N., GILBERT, J. S., GLAZE, L. S., SIGURDSSON, H. & WOODS, A.W. 1997. *Volcanic Plumes*. Wiley, Chichester.

STEINGRIMSSON, J. 1998. *Fires of the Earth: the Laki eruption 1783–1784*. University of Iceland Press, Reykjavik.

STOTHERS, R. B. 1996, The Great Dry Fog of 1783: *Climatic Change*, **32**, 79–89.

STOTHERS, R. B. 1999. Volcanic dry fogs, climate cooling and plague pandemics in Europe and the Middle East. *Climatic Change* **42**, 713–723.

STOTHERS, R. B. 2000. Climate and demographic consequences of the massive volcanic eruption of 1258. *Climatic Change*, **45**, 361–374.

SUTHERLAND, D. 1981. Weather and the peasantry of upper Brittany 1780–1790. *In:* WIGLEY, T. M. L., INGRAM, M. J. & FARMER, G. (eds) *Climate and History: Studies in Past Climates and their Impact on Man*. Cambridge University Press, Cambridge, 434–449.

SWINDEN, S. P. 1786. Observations sur quelques particularités meteorologiques de l'année 1783. *Mémoires de l'Académie Royale du Sciences, Années 1784–1785*, 113–40.

SWINDEN, S. P. 2001. Observations on the cloud (dry fog) which appeared in June 1783. *Jökull, 50*, 73–80.

THÓRARINSSON, S. 1979. On the damage caused by volcanic eruptions, with special reference to tephra

and gases. *In:* SHEETS, P. D. & GRAYSON, D. K. (eds) *Volcanic Activity and Human Ecology*, Academic Press New York, 125–159.

THÓRARINSSON, S. 1981. Greetings from Iceland: ash falls and volcanic aerosols in Scandinavia: *Geografiska Annaler*, **63A**, 109–118.

THORDARSON, T. 1995. *Volatile release and atmospheric effects of basaltic fissure eruptions.* PhD Thesis,University of Hawaii at Manoa.

THORDARSON, T. & SELF, S. 1993. The Laki and Grímsvötn eruptions in 1783–85. *Bulletin Volcanologique*, **55**, 233–263.

THORDARSON, T, & SELF, S. 2001. Real-time observations of the Laki sulfuric acid aerosol cloud in Europe during 1783 as documented by Prof. S.P. van Swinden at Franeker, Holland. *Jökull*, **53**, 65–72.

THORDARSON, T. & SELF, S., OSKARSSON, N. & HULSEBOSCH, T. 1996. Sulfur, chlorine and fluorine degassing and atmospheric loading by the 1783–1784 AD Laki (Skaftár Fires) eruption in Iceland. *Bulletin of Volcanology*, **58**, 205–255

TOULOUMI, G., POCOCK, S. J., KATSOUYANNI, K. & TRICHOPOULOS, D. 1994. Short–term effects of air pollution on daily mortality in Athens: a time-series analysis. *International Journal of Epidemiology*, **23(5),** 957–967.

VIGOTTI, M. A., ROSSI, G., BISANTI, L., ZANOBETTI, A. & SCHWARTZ, J. 1996. Short-term effects of urban air pollution on respiratory health in Milan, Italy. *Journal of Epidemiology and Community Health*, **50**, 71–75

WELLBURN, A. 1994. *Air Pollution and Climate Change: the Biological Impact.* Second edition, Longman, Essex.

WICHMANN, H. E. & HEINRICH, J. 1995. Health effects of high level exposure to traditional pollutants in East Germany – a review and ongoing research. *Environmental Health Perspectives*, **103**, 29–35.

WILKINS, E. T. 1954. Air Pollution Aspects of the London Fog of December 1952. *Quarterly Journal of the Royal Meteorological Society*, **80**, 267–271.

WOOD, C. A. 1984. The amazing and portentous summer of 1783. *EOS, Transactions of the American Geophysical Union*, **65**, 410.

WOOD, C. A. 1992. The climatic effects of the 1783 Laki eruption. *In:* HARRINGTON, C. R. (ed.) *The Year Without a Summer?* Canadian Museum of Nature, Ottawa, 58–77.

WORLD HEALTH ORGANISATION 1979. *Environmental Health Criteria 8: Sulphur oxides and suspended particulate matter.* Geneva, WHO.

WRIGLEY, E. A. & SCHOFIELD, R. S. 1989. *The Population History of England 1541–1871.* London, Edward Arnold.

Index

Note: page numbers in *italics* refer to figures; those in **bold** refer to tables

ADEOS TOMS 178, 181, 189
Advanced Earth Observing Satellite (ADEOS)
    TOMS 178, 181, 189
Advanced Spaceborne Thermal Emission and
    Reflection Radiometer (ASTER) 150,
    198
Advanced Very High Resolution Radiometer
    (AVHRR) 331
aerosol cloud, development of 332
Agnano–Monte Spina (AMS) explosive
    eruption 53–61
Agung, Indonesia 335, **377**
air pollution
    mortality and 402
    tropospheric sulphur burden and 387–9
    volcanic eruptions and 401–2
Aleutians 186
andesitic compositions 26–7, *29*, *30*
Ardoukoba, Djibouti 243
Arenal, Costa Rica 206
Asama volcano, Japan 156
Aso, Japan 156
ASTER 150, 198
asymmetry parameter 335
ATHAM 309, 314, 315, 317–18, 319
    simulation 318, 323
atmospheric impacts of tropospheric gas plumes
    387–91
atomic force microscopy (AFM) 143
Augustine, Mount, Alaska 39, **182**, **184**, 188,
    330, 331
AVHRR 331
AVIRIS 395

Ballachulish, Scotland 134
Banda Api, Indonesia **182**, **184**, 188, **374**
basaltic compositions 27–32, *31*, **46**
basaltic eruption 6–9, *7*
basicity moderating parameter 97
Beer–Lambert law 56, 169, 175
Berlin, Mount, Antarctica 232
Bezymianny, Kamchatka **182**, 187, 188, **190**, **377**
Big Island, Hawai'i 388
Bishop Tuff 45, *45*, 139
Boltzmann–Matano analysis 57–8
buchites 127–9
Búrfell-Dreki lavas, Iceland **117**, 118

calc-silicates 125
Cameroon, Mount 9, **182**, **190**
carbon disulphide (CS_2) 297
carbonyl sulphide (OCS) 297
Cerro Azul, Galapagos **182**, 188, **190**
Cerro Hudson, Chile **182**, **184**, 188
Cerro Negro, Nicaragua 33, **182**
    volcanic fumarole 140
chemistry–transport model (CTM) 297–8
climate sensitivity 342
climatic influence 265–6
closed-path spectroscopy 150
C–O–H–S fluids, saturation 81–99
    rhyolitic composition 87–90
    tholeiitic composition 85–7
Colima Rift 265
Colima volcano, Mexico 39, 139, 169, 173
    diffuse degassing 271–4
    diffuse gas measurements 267–8
    fumarole sampling and analyses 267,
        268–71, **269**
    geological background 264–5
    plume measurements 267
    previous geochemical studies 266–7
    sulphur dioxide flux 271, *273*, **273**
Colo volcano, Indonesia **182**, **184**, 187, 188,
    330
Correlation Spectrometer (COSPEC) 134, 141,
    143, 150–4, *151*, 161, 162, **162**, **204**,
    219, 220, 265, **384**
    applications 171–3
    elevation effects in 169–75
    used at Masaya 352
    operation and accuracy 151–2
    pressure and temperature dependence
        169–71
        column abundances 169–70
        path-length concentration:column
            abundance relationship 171
        path-length concentrations 170–1
    SO_2 and mass of magma, correlation
        between 373
    volcanological interpretation of SO_2 fluxes
        152–3
COSPEC *see* Correlation Spectrometer
crystallization, degassing and, in ascending
    magma 13–16

DIAL 159
difference frequency generation (DFG) lasers 159, **163**
Differential Absorption LIDAR (DIAL) 159
differential optical absorption spectroscopy (DOAS) 150, 154–5, *154*, *155*, 161, 162, **163**
diffusion coefficients 57–8
dimethyl sulphide (DMS) 297
distributed feedback (DFB) lasers 159, **163**
DOAS 150, 154–5, *154*, *155*, 161, 162, **163**
dome-building eruptions 63–77
Doppler RADAR 162
dry deposition 389–91
dry fogs 340, 389, 401, 402, **403**, 404–06, 411
DUSTTRAK optical particle counter 160

Earth Probe (EP) satellite TOMS 178, 180, 181, 184, 189–93, 197
Eastern Volcanic Zone (EVZ), Iceland 104, *105*
El Chichón, Mexico 27, 33, 82, 142, **182**, **184**, 188, 308, **374**
    (1982 eruption) 178, 188, 329, **330**, 331, 332, 336, 338, **377**
    C/S ratio 45, *45*
Eldgjá (AD 934–940 eruption), Iceland 105, 106, 108, 114, *114*, 116, *116*, 118
electron microprobe (EMP) 309
environmental impacts of tropospheric volcanic gas plumes 381–95
Envisat-1 satellite 180
EOS/Aura satellite 180
Erebus, Mount, volcano, Antarctica 123, 157, 169, 173, 383
    Fumarolic Ice Towers 231–43
        carbon isotope samples 234–5, **236**
        ice cave observations 239
        flux from 233–4, 235–7
        monitoring inside ice towers and caves 237–9
        soil gas data 234, 239–41
        isotopes 241–2, 242–3
ERS-2 197
Erta 'Ale, Ethiopia 243
Etna, Italy 9, 123, 142, **182**, **190**, 231, 243, 265, 298, 387, 389
    (2001 eruption) 193, *194*, 284–5
    aerosol emissions 152, 155, 157, 158, 161
    ash leachates 205, 206
    FTIR 281–92
        factors controlling SO₂, HCl and HF 286–9
        fractional magma degassing 289–91
    mercury emissions 382
    TOMS observations of 196–7
excess sulphur 152

Fernandina, Galapagos Islands 178, **182**

FESEM/EDS 23–43
Fish Canyon Tuff, Colorado 27
Flood–Grjotheim treatment 95–6
Fourier Transform Infrared (FTIR)
    spectroscopy 150, 151, 153, 155–8, 161, **163**, 203–18, 220, 265, 349–69
    Mount Etna, Sicily 281–92
    measurements of water diffusivity 55–7
Fourier Transform Ultraviolet Spectroscopy (FTUV) **163**
Fuego volcano, Guatemala 123, **377**

Galeras volcano, Columbia 24, 70, 219, 243, 265
Galunggung volcano, Indonesia 181, **182**, **184**, 187, 188, 206, **374**
gas correlation filter spectrometry (GASCOFIL) 153, **162**
gas correlation imaging 154
gas segregation dynamics 6–13
    basaltic eruption 6–9, *7*
    silicic eruption 9–13
GASCOFIL 153, **162**
General Circulation Model (GCM) 297–8, 299
Geostationary Meterological Satellite (GMS) 331
glass inclusions 108–10
Global Ozone Monitoring Experiment (GOME) 197, **198**
GOES 196
Grímsvötn volcanic system, Iceland 103–19
    groundwater, impact of tropospheric gas plumes on 393–4

H₂O + CO₂ saturation model 94–5
Halema'uma'u, Hawai'i 282
halogens as tracers 63–77
Harry's Dream, Mt Erebus 237, *238*, 239, 242
Hawaiian fire-fountains 6
Heard Island, Southern Indian Ocean **182**, 186
Heimaey, Iceland (1973) 9
Hekla, Iceland (2000 eruption) **182**, **184**, **190**, 191, *193*, 308, **374**, **377**
Henry coefficient 313, 314
Henry's Law 354
hercynite 127, **132**
high-alumina basalts (HAB) 29–31
HITRAN database (High-resolution Transmission molecular absorption database) 156, 283, 356
Hólmsá fires, Katla, Iceland **117**, 118

ICP–MS 143
illness, human 401–12
instrumental neutron activation analysis (INAA) 143
Irazú volcano, Costa Rica 206, 248
Iztaccíhuatl volcano, Mexico 124
Izu–Oshima, Japan 243

Kalimantan 187
Kamchatka 186
Katla volanic system, Iceland 103–19
Katmai, Alaska 27
Kīlauea (Hawai'i) 2, 17, 123, 139, 231, 243, 384
    fractional degassing of 282
    Pu'u 'O'o vent 9, 161, 282
Krafla, Iceland **182**, 186, 188, **374**
    (1984 eruption) 193
Krakatau, Indonesia 27, 32, **377**
    (1883 eruption) 1
Kudryavy volcano, Kurile Islands, Russia 39,
    142
Kuriles 186

Laacher See volcano eruption, Germany
        (12 900 yr BP) 307–24
    compositional parameters of halogens and
        sulphur in 310–12
    estimate of volatile release 312–13
    HCl emission 319, *321*
    hydrometeors 319, *321*
    processes in the eruption column 313
    release of gases from ice 316–17
    scavenging by ice particles 315–17
    scavenging by liquid droplets 313–15
    transfer of solutes during microphysical
        processes 316
    volcanic gases 319–21
    volcanic particles 318–19, *320*
    volcanology and petrological background
        309
Laki, Iceland
    (1783–84 eruption) 2, 3, 103, 105, 106, 108,
        113–14, 114, 116, *116*, 118, 149, 329,
        332, 340, 342
    air pollution and volcanic eruptions 401–2
    air pollution and mortality 402
    English mortality trends (1783–84) 405–6, **410**
    eruption dynamics 402
    human illness after eruption 401–12, **404**
    local mortality crises 406–10
    meteorology during eruption 402–3
    pollution damage to vegetation 403–4, **403**
Langila, PNG **182**, 188
    (1997) 189
Láscar (Chile) 10, **182**, **184**, 188, **374**, **377**
Lau Basin, SW Pacific 83
Lesser Antilles arc 48
LI-COR spectrometer 134, 153, **162**
LIDAR 143, 155, 158–9, 161, 162, **163**, 336
LIDAR In-space Technology Experiment
        (LITE) 143
Lonquimay volcano, Chile (1989–90 eruption)
        9, **182**, 188
Lux–Flood acidity 96

mafic arc magmas 32

mafic melt compositions 38, 41, *43*, 48
magma chamber evolution, degassing and 16–18
magma volatile contents, degassing and 18–19
Makian, Indonesia **182**, **184**, 188
Mammoth Mountain, California 231
Manam volcano, PNG **182**, **190**, 193
Masaya volcano, Nicaragua 157, 158, 350–2,
        350
    environmental impacts 382, 385, *385*, *386*,
        388
    location of active craters *351*
        measurements FTIR 357–63
        short time-scale variability in FTIR
            measurements 363–6
    tropospheric processes 366–7
Mauna Loa, Hawai'i (1984 eruption) **182**, 193,
        374
Mayon, Mount, Philippines **182**, 188
Melbourne, Mount, Antarctica 232
melt inclusions 17, 26, 63, 103–21, 283, 307, 372
MELTS code 66, *67*, 68
Merapi, Mount, Java 39, 129, **182**, 188
Meteor-3 (MS) TOMS 178, 180
Michelson interferometer 156
mid-ocean ridge basalts (MORBs) 110
Mihara, Mount, Japan 150
Minoan eruption of Santorini 27
Miyake-jima volcano, Japan TOMS
        observations of SO_2 from **182**, **190**, 196
modelling degassing processes 64–5
    application to Mont Pelée and Santa Maria-
        Santiaguito 70–7
    closed- and open-system evolution 64
    correlation diagrams between residual
        volatile contents 68–9
    equations for open- and closed-system
        evolution 65–8
        closed-system evolution 66
        estimations of parameters 66
        open-system evolution 66
        partition coefficients 66–8
        vescularity 68
    erupted magmatic clasts 64–5
    halogens in glasses 65
Moderate Resolution Imaging
        Spectroradiometer (MODIS) 197, 395
MODIS 197, 395
Momotombo volcano, Nicaragua 39, 243
Montserrat 27, 33, 48, 203–18, 219–30, 308
Monzoni Complex, Italy 134
mortality, English trends during Laki eruption
        (1783–84) 405–6, **410**
moving-mirror interferometer 156
Mule Creek vent complex USA 10

National Polar-orbiting Operational
        Environmental Satellite System
        (NPOESS) 197

Nausea Knob, Mt Erebus 240
Navier–Stokes equations 317
Nevado de Colima volcano, Mexico 264, 267
Nevado del Ruíz volcano, Columbia 277, 393
Nimbus-7 (N7) satellite TOMS 177, 178, 179, *179, 180*, 191, 199
NPOESS 197
Nyamuragira, Congo **183**, **184**, 187, 188, **190**, 191, *192*, 193, 199, **374**
  (1978 eruption) 189
  (1996 eruption) 189
  TOMS observations of 194–5
Nyiragongo volcano, Congo (2002) 189, 197

Oldoinyo Lengai volcano, Tanzania 242, 265
OMI 180, 197, 199
OMPS 197
Open Path Fourier Transform Infrared Spectroscopy *see* Fourier Transform Infrared
optical basicity 97
optical particle counters 150, 160, **163**
optical sensing of gas and aerosol emissions 149–64
Oshima, Japan 9, **183**
oxygen fugacity (fO_2) 23–49, 83–99
Oyama, Mount, Japan 389
Ozone Mapping and Profiler Suite (OMPS) 197
Ozone Monitoring Instrument (OMI) 180, 197, 199

Pacaya volcano, Guatemala 123, **183**
Paricutín, Mexico (1949–56 eruption) 9
Parker, Mount, Philippines (1641 eruption) 375, **377**
particle-induced X-ray emission (PIXE) 143
Pelée, Mont (Martinique) 27, 33, 48
  modelling of degassing 64, 68, 70, 71, *71*, *72–3*, 75, 76
  (1902 eruption) 65
Phlegrean Fields, Italy (Campi Flegrei) **2**, 53–61
Pinatubo, Mount, Philippines 27, 33, 70, 118, 152, **183**, **184**, 219, 308, **330**, **374**, **377**
  (1991 eruption) 1, 13, 23, 26, 45, 90, 178, 188, 297, 371
  atmospheric effects of 329, 331, 333, 336, 338, 339–40, 341, 342
  partitioning of sulphur in 26
Pine Grove 26, 27
PIXE 143
Plinian eruptions 63–77
plume composition and emission rate 382–4
plume dispersion 384–7
plume monitoring techniques 381–2
Poás volcano, Costa Rica 39, 247–60, 265
  chemistry and spring water discharges 250–5, **251**, *252–3*, 257
  gas and condensate samples 255–6, **254–5**, 258
  geological and volcanological background 248
  map of crater *249*
  sampling and analytical methods 248–50
  sampling in Laguna Caliente 250
pollution
  air 401–2
  damage to vegetation 403–4, **403**
Popcatépetl volcano, Mexico 9, 124–5, 158, **183**, 187, 188, 189, **190**, 242
  aerosol particles from the 134–42
  contact-metamorphic particles 125–34
    calc-silicates 125
    wollastonite 125–7, *126–7*, 130, *130*, **131**
    spinel, buchites and indicators of contact metamorphism 127–9
    significance 129–34
  diffuse gas measurements 267–8, **275**
  fumarole sampling and analyses 267, 274–7
  geological background 263–4
  plume measurements 267
  previous geochemical studies 266
  TOMS observations of 195
pre-eruptive conditions 26–32
  basaltic compositions 27–32, *31*
  rhyolitic to andesitic compositions 26–7, *29*, *30*
pre-eruptive fluids, composition 32–3
  comparison with volcanic gases 38–9
Pu'u 'O'o (Hawai'i) 9, 161, 282

Q–Ab–Or diagram 66
quasi-chemical ionic species of sulphur and oxygen 95
QuikTOMS satellite 178, 197
Quizapu, Chile (1932 eruption) 375, **377**

Rabaul, PNG **183**, **184**, 308, **330**
Rainier, Mount, USA 232, 242
RSAM 220
Rayleigh distillation law 66
Real-time Seismic Amplitude Measurement (RSAM) 220, *222*, 223, 224, *225*, *227*
Redlich–Kwong equation of state, modified 32
Redoubt volcano, Alaska **183**, **184**, 186, 187, 188, 308, 331, **374**, **377**
remote-sensing, ground-based 349–68
rhyolitic composition 87–90
Rinjani volcano, Indonesia **183**, 187, 188
Ruapehu, NZ (1995 eruption) 188

S saturation model 95–9
Sakurajima, Mount, Japan 205, **377**, *386*, 388, 389
Santa Maria-Santiaguito, Guatemala 16, 27, 36, **377**
  modelling of degassing 64, 68, 70, *71*

(1902 eruption) 33, 375
(1922 eruption) 74–7
Sauna Cave, Mt. Erebus 239, *240*
Scanning Imaging Absorption Spectrometer for
Atmospheric Cartography
(SCIAMACHY) 143, 180, 198
SCIAMACHY 143, 144, 180, **198**
Sheveluch volcano, Kamchatka **183**, 188, **190**,
377
Shishaldin volcano, Alaska (1999 eruption) **183**,
190, 191
Showa-Shinzan volcano, Japan 39
Sierra Negra, Galapagos Islands **183**, **184**, 188,
374
(1979 eruption) 193
silicic eruption 9–13
silicic to andesitic melt compositions 33–8, **34**,
35, 36, 37, 39–41, *40, 41,* **46**
single scatter albedo 335
size distribution of volcanic particles 334, *335*
soil, impact of tropospheric gas plumes on 393–4
solar occultation geometry for FTIR
measurements 157
Soputan volcano, Indonesia **183**, **184**, 187, 188
Soufrière Hills volcano, Montserrat 10, 70, 76,
157, 158, **183**, 187, 188, **190**, 308, 366,
377, 382
(during 1997) *11, 12, 12,* 65
Chances Peak *12*
crystallization in magma 14, *14,* 15
rainwater and ash leachate analysis 203–16
ash leachate analysis 206, 208, **209**, 215
composition 204–6
geochemical and remote-sensing data
215–16
HCl/SO$_2$ in ash leachates 211–12
monitoring activity 204
rainwater analysis 206–8, **210–11**, 215
rainwater results for 1996–1997 212–15
magma extrusion dynamics 219–28
dome growth renewal 220–2
cyclic gas exhalations 226–7
gas measurement methods 222–3
magma flux and SO$_2$ flux 227–8
short-term variations in SO$_2$ flux 226
TOMS observations of 195–6
Soufriere St Vincent, West Indies **183**, 188
spinel 127–9
Spurr, Mount, Alaska **183**, **184**, 188, 308, 374
St Helens, Mount, USA 16, 27, 33, 39, 70, 82,
123, 142, **182**, **184**, **330**, **374**, **377**
(1980 eruption) 174, 178, 187, 188, 206, 298,
331, 343, 384
C/S atomic ratio 45, *45*
SO$_2$ flux 152, *153*
SO$_2$ mixing ratios 169, 173
Stokes' law 6
stratosphere 329–43

chemical and ozone changes 336–8
climate response 341–3
properties of volcanically enhanced
stratospheric aerosol 332–5
radiative changes 335–6
relative forcing 339–41, *340*
Stromboli, Italy 6, 9, 83, 155, 382, 389
sulphate capacity 98
sulphide capacity 97
sulphur cycle, tropospheric 295–303
recent model estimates 296–7
STOCHEM-Ed model 297–9, 302
sulphur dioxide yield
eruption magnitude and surface cooling
371–8
magma mass and 373–5
sulphur fugacity (fS$_2$) 23–49
sulphur partitioning 26
sulphur release 103–19
atmospheric venting, estimation 110–15
glass inclusions 108–10
two-stage degassing model 103, 105–6
sulphur solubility 24–6, *25*
summer cooling, erupted magma mass and 375
Sun photometry 150, 160–1, **163**, 395
SUPERFLUID code 84, 94
synchrotron X-ray fluorescence microprobe
(SYXRF) 309
SYXRF 309

Tamazula Fault, Colima volcano, Mexico 265,
272
Tambora, Indonesia (1815 eruption) 1, 332, 371,
377
Tar River valley, Montserrat 220
Taupo volcano, NZ 27, 33
Temkin model 83, 96
terrestrial ecosystems, impact of tropospheric
gas plumes on 391–3
theolite composition 85–7
Thermal Infrared Multispectral Scanner
(TIMS) 150
Thjórsá events (8600 BC), Iceland 105, 114, *114,*
116, *116,* 118
time-of-flight secondary mass spectrometry
(TOF SIMS) 143
Tláloc volcano, Mexico 124
Toba volcano, Indonesia 27, 343
TOF SIMS 143
Toop–Samis treatment of silicate melts 83, 95, 97
Total Ozone Mapping Spectrometer (TOMS)
150, 177–99, 299, 372–3
ADEOS TOMS 178, 181, 189
case studies 194–7
Etna 196–7
Miyake-jima 196
Nyamuragira 194–5
Popocatépetl 195

Soufrière Hills, Montserrat 195–6
Tungurahua, Ecuador 196
detection limits 181
Earth Probe (EP) satellite TOMS 178, 180,
181, 184, 189–93, 197
results (1996–2001) 189, **190**
Meteor-3 (MS) TOMS 178, 180
missions 1978–2001 **180**
after Mount Pinatubo eruption 338, *338*
Nimbus-7 (N7) satellite TOMS 177, 178, 179,
179, 180, 191, 199
QuikTOMS satellite 178, 197
regions with detected eruptions 188
tectonic settings with TOMS-detected
eruptions 189
TOMS Aerosol Index 178, 181, 184
UV remote sensing in the post-TOMS era
197–9, **198**
volcanic emissions database 180–9, **182–3, 184**
volcano types with detected eruptions 188
volcanoes with TOMS-detected eruptions
184–8, **185, 186**
Tramway Ridge, Mt Erebus 232, 234, 237, 241
Trans Mexican Volcanic Belt 124
transmission electron microscopy (TEM) 143
tropospheric volcanic gas plumes
atmospheric impacts 387–91
air pollution and tropospheric sulphur
burden 387–9
dry and wet deposition 389–91
challenges and prospects 394–5
environmental impacts 381–95
impact on soil and groundwater 393–4
impact on terrestrial ecosystems 391–3
impact on vegetation 391–3
plume composition and emission rate
382–4
plume dispersion 384–7
plume monitoring techniques 381–2
Tungurahua volcano, Ecuador, TOMS
observations of **183, 190**, 196
Turrialba volcano, Costa Rica 248

two-stage degassing model 103, 105–6

Unzen, Mount, Japan 27, 39, 156
Usu volcano, Japan 39, 142, 231, **377**

van't Hoff equation 314
vegetation, impact of tropospheric gas plumes
on 391–3
Veidivötn volcanic system, Iceland 103–19
Vesuvius, Italy 53, 129, 134, 140, 243, 389
Villarrica, Chile 9
Volcán de Colima, Mexico *see* Colima
volcanic ash properties 331–2
development of ash clouds 332
composition 331
size distribution 331–2
Volcanic Explosivity Index (VEI) 180, 299,
330, **330**, 373
volcanic plume monitoring 352–68
processes 352–4, *353*
chemical and physical reactions affecting
HCl 354
chemical and physical reactions affecting
SO_2 353–4
deposition processes 354
meteorological effects 353
simplified models 354–5
volume extinction coefficient 335
Vulcano, Italy 155, 156, 157, 231, 265, 382, 385,
387, 389

water diffusion experiments 53–61
calculation of water diffusivity 57–8
different melt compositions 59–61, *60*
diffusion-couple experiments 54–5
FTIR spectroscopy 55–7
temperature and water content dependence
58–9, *59*
wet deposition 389–91, 205
White Island, NZ 243, 382, 383–4
Wolf volcano, Galapagos **183**, 184
wollastonite 125–7, *126–7*, 130, *130*, **131**